# Urban Government

# URBAN

# GOVERNMENT

A READER IN POLITICS AND ADMINISTRATION

EDITED BY EDWARD C. BANFIELD

HARVARD UNIVERSITY

THE FREE PRESS OF GLENCOE, INC.

A DIVISION OF THE CROWELL-COLLIER PUBLISHING COMPANY

Library of Congress Catalog Card Number 61-9159

# PREFACE

This is a collection of the readings that I have found most valuable in teaching courses on urban government to both undergraduate and graduate students.

The readings come from so many places that even if each were readily available it would be a tedious task for a librarian to bring them all together on a reserve shelf. But many, like Henry Jones Ford's theory of corruption, would not be available at all in most libraries, and some, like Rexford G. Tugwell's evaluation of the career of Robert Moses, have never before appeared in print.

A book of this kind can be used in at least three ways: as a supplement to a textbook, in place of a textbook as an accompaniment to classroom lectures, or as a basis for a discussion series. It has been my experience that readings of this sort help give analytical depth to a course. The usual textbook provides a descriptive account of the more formal aspects of governmental structure and process, and then leaves it up to the instructor to show the student the larger meaning of what has been described. This book is designed to help him do this. Accordingly, I have selected the readings for the *ideas* that they contain.

Since some instructors will want to use the book without an accompanying text, the essential descriptive materials are supplied here in the form of a Glossary. Because the Glossary contains all of the background information necessary for understanding the readings, many students will find it useful to begin by reading the Glossary from start to finish.

The approach of this book differs from that of most texts in several respects. The most important difference, perhaps, is that this book tries to explain what really happens in urban government and to do so largely in terms of the concepts and theories of social scientists. Most textbooks on state and local government are preoccupied with what "experts" think *ought* to be the case; this one is occupied with what *really is* the case. While the views of reformers and experts are represented, they are not assumed to be authoritative, and they are placed in juxtaposition with those of social scientists. Thus, for example, the student is exposed not only to the usual criticisms of the big city machine but also to the views of the eminent sociologist, Robert K. Merton, on the machine's latent functions.

This emphasis on the social scientist's view of things as they are, as distinguished from what they ought to be, has inevitably led to a much heavier emphasis on politics than is common in most textbooks on urban government. Works on urban government all too often assume that the tasks of city government are almost entirely matters of administration— collecting garbage, repairing streets, putting out fires, and so on. Without belittling the importance of such activities, this book seeks to give politics—

» v «

the struggle for power and the management of conflict—the attention that it deserves.

Politics would be important even if it had no consequences extending beyond the boundaries of the city. But the fact is that American national politics is to a very large extent local politics, and no one can possibly understand the national political system without first understanding politics in the cities, especially the larger ones. This is another reason for the emphasis here on politics.

This book focuses on the processes rather than on the techniques of government. Most students, for example, do not need to know anything about the technique of designing and filling out the forms of a city budget. Not one in a thousand will ever have use for such information, and the rare one who will can certainly best get it on the job. On the other hand, all students should know the kinds of things that are explained by William H. Brown, Jr. and Charles E. Gilbert in their article on capital programming in Philadelphia: what capital programming is, why it is done, how it is organized, what its connection with city planning is, what its political setting is, and what are the practical and theoretical limitations upon its effectiveness.

Some of the readings provide models for students who would like to go into the local community and do research of their own. The selections from Mark K. Adams, James Q. Wilson, Robert A. Dahl, and Kenneth E. Gray and David Greenstone should all be suggestive to the student who wants to try his hand at this and to the class that is carrying on a joint research project. These examples show how much can be done without a computing machine, providing one has sound legs and a good mind.

Each Section of the book is preceded by an introductory note formulating the central questions around which it is organized, underlining the points that the editor believes are of the greatest analytical interest, and showing the relevance of each reading to the general themes of the book.

The bibliography lists items generally regarded as standard references on each topic. These are annotated for the benefit of the nonspecialist.

The author acknowledges with thanks the assistance of Martha Derthick, who prepared the Glossary and the Bibliography.

# CONTENTS
# AN OVERVIEW

# CONTENTS

## VII—PROBLEMS OF MANAGEMENT

## VIII—SOME QUESTIONS OF POLICY

# URBAN GOVERNMENT

# I

## URBAN GOVERNMENT AS
## A SUBJECT FOR STUDY

---

Government serves two very different functions. One is that of providing goods and services that cannot be, or at any rate are not, provided under other, private, auspices. With respect to this *service* function, government is in many ways like a private enterprise. Private enterprise provides certain kinds of goods and services to people called "customers"; public enterprise provides other kinds of goods and services to people called "taxpayers." Both types of enterprise are judged by how well and how cheaply they supply the goods and services that are wanted.

The other function of government is to deal with conflict. Wherever there are people, there are bound to be differences of opinion and of interest. Politics is any kind of activity—reasonable discussion, heated argument, bribery, fighting, balloting, and so on—by which conflict in matters of public importance is carried on. Government deals with this conflict by regulating the manner in which it is carried on, by arranging compromises and balancing interests, and by imposing settlements which the parties to the disputes have to accept.

Whereas the service function is of necessity performed consciously and deliberately, the political function is often, but not always, performed as a more or less accidental by-product of a politician's effort to get office or of a bureaucracy's effort to maintain and expand itself. Perhaps it is for this reason that many people regard "administration," or the carrying out of the service function, as the "real" justification for government, while they look on "politics," or the process by which conflict is handled, as a necessary evil, if not indeed as an irrational aberration.

Because the service function is so conspicuously important in the government of cities, many writers have treated it as if it were, or ought to be, the *only* function of city government. As Lawrence J. R. Herson points out, the usual textbook emphasis on the service role of city government relies implicitly, and often explicitly, upon a conceptual scheme appropriate to the normative study of administration. This perspective introduces a bias that hides other, perhaps more significant, dimensions of governmental activity.

In some places, city government is indeed much more a matter of administration than of politics. This is true in Great Britain, and also in many small, middle-class American cities. In these places, matters are usually decided on grounds that are (or at least seem to be) technical rather than political. In large, polyglot American cities, however, the case is different. In such cities, efficiency—the avoidance of waste—is of little or no interest to many voters, and conflict among groups and interests is pervasive and sharp. Despite the pleas of reformers, the people with something at stake have never agreed either to respect the neutrality of administration and to leave certain matters out of politics (although schools, perhaps, have come near to being an exception in some places) or to forego advantages that could be had by mixing local issues with state and national ones.

But the political character of government in all of our larger and many of our smaller cities need not necessarily be considered pathological. The successful management of conflict is a social function valuable enough in itself to justify, as a rule, whatever loss of efficiency in the performance of the service functions the injection of politics into administration may cause.

The effective management of conflict is valuable because it permits and encourages the expression of competing interests and opinions while at the same time preventing the eruption of violence and the eventual breakdown of social organization. But even more important, it is valuable as a way of discovering the concrete content of the common good. Political struggle is the means by which society develops the meaning of justice and of good. This is so even when the particular matter in question—say, the location of a housing project—is in itself trivial. Even though a concrete matter may be trivial to start with, it is often transformed and given great significance by ideological or symbolic elements that are introduced to serve someone's purpose. Thus the agitation over what is a trivial matter to begin with may prove useful in the elucidation of moral questions of the deepest interest to all mankind. For Aristotle, whose categories Professor Norton E. Long believes provide the most appropriate framework for the study of local government, the city is above all an ethical association. It comes into existence (to paraphrase Aristotle slightly) for the sake of its service functions, but it exists for the sake of the good life.

# THE LOST WORLD OF MUNICIPAL GOVERNMENT

## LAWRENCE J. R. HERSON

LIKE COLERIDGE'S ANCIENT MARINER, the study of American city government is faced with desiccation upon a sea of plenty. While the literature of municipal government continues to grow, fed by bureaus of government research and the teaching concerns of political scientists, there is very little in this literature that is of substance sufficient to rise above the level of specialized reporting and into the general stream of political science. Indeed, if the pages of this *Review* be taken as an index of the research concerns of our discipline, then *municipal government* would seem to be a stagnated area of political science, for not one article on this subject has appeared in this journal for over six years.[1]

It is not, however, the purpose of this essay to analyze the shortcomings of the literature of municipal government. These failings have been commented upon by several critics, and they can be simply summarized by noting that in conceptual construction and in execution, most of the research in this field falls short of the minimal requirements for a systematic political science: for the literature of municipal government is studded with an array of facts that have been gathered with little regard for the construction of general theories; and, at the same time, it is beset with theories that have been advanced without ever being checked against available empirical data.[2] That, in essence, is the case against the literature of municipal government; and it is the purpose of this essay, not to re-try the case, but to offer one explanation

---

Reprinted from *American Political Science Review*, 51, No. 2 (June, 1957), 330–345, by permission of the publisher.

1. One possible exception might be an article that dealt with the independent voter in a Massachusetts city. The reported research was not, however, upon the politics of that city *per se*: the city was merely a convenient focus for the study of a problem in national politics.

During the past decade, the *American Political Science Review* has carried seven other articles dealing with city government and politics. One of these clarified a legal term (the village in New Hampshire); a second set down the reminiscences of a candidate for town council. Two articles examined parties in New York City with special emphasis on PR. A fifth article was concerned with the impact of the urban electorate upon the allocation of votes in the Electoral College; another article had as its focus the voting behavior of nationality groups in four cities. The seventh article was concerned with gross changes in the voting behavior of a small town, from 1924 to 1948, as revealed by ballots cast in two elections.

2. See Allen Richards, "Local Government Research: A Partial Evaluation," *Public Administration Review*, Vol. 14, pp. 271–277 (Autumn, 1954).

for this alleged state of affairs by way of a close examination of the leading textbooks in the field.[3]

Briefly put, what is contended here is that the textbooks constitute the wellsprings of any stream of political science, for they serve not only to summarize the current state of the literature, but also to orient and guide the work of future contributors to it. A body of literature depends on its sources, and when these sources serve notice that basic problems have been solved, that principles of correct action have been discovered, then the need for further research seems to pass away, and the activities of students in the field are diverted into the making of plans and strategies for putting those "principles" into play. In short, it may be that the textbooks of municipal government constitute not so much wellsprings as barriers to the production of systematic research, and any reconstruction of this field must therefore begin with an examination of its basic texts.

# I

Perhaps the simplest approach to the textbooks in city government is by way of their component parts. With a regularity that makes the comparing reader seek the existence of some master-mold, the textbook organizes itself around the following concerns: first, detailed descriptions of legal relationships and organs of government; second, a description of urban political processes; third, a body of administrative theory; fourth, a series of recommendations for governmental reform; and fifth, a greater or lesser description of urban administrative processes. The relative number of pages devoted by each text to any of these components varies, of course, from text to text; but no matter what the length of treatment, the book's center of intellectual gravity is located within its treatment of administrative theory. That (to change the metaphor) is the linchpin for the wheel of endeavor; and, accordingly, it is worthy of first examination.

---

3. A note on method: The concern of this essay is with the "modal characteristics" of a body of literature; not with its specific contributors. Consequently, none of the generalizations affirmed here applies with equal force to any specific text; moreover, the multiplicity of texts within this field should make it apparent that texts vary in the degree to which they are vulnerable to the criticisms here advanced. Thus, a book such as Charles R. Adrian, *Governing Urban America* (New York, 1955) is highly conscious of the problems raised here and meets many of them with marked success. Again, a book such as Harold Zink, *Government of Cities in the United States* (New York, 1948) especially in its treatment of politics makes a significant departure from the general mode. In similar fashion, other books differ in one or more respects, both in the treatment given specific problems, and in the level of sophistication that attends this treatment. In general, however, the similarities of the texts are great enough to warrant a summary presentation that seeks (only) for central characteristics.

Given the concern of this essay for a *body* of literature, no attempt will be made to deal with the problem of "mean deviation," that is, the degree to which any single text approaches, or diverges from, the characterization made here. And, because this essay seeks only for modal characteristics, it is unnecessary to inject an *ad hominem* element into the discussion by identifying the sources of specific textbook quotations: Such quotations are offered only to illustrate; certainly not to indict.

But, before moving to this body of administrative theory, one further set of preliminary observations needs to be made; and they concern what, for want of a better term, might be described as the *vintage* qualities of the municipal government text. Where textbooks in other fields of political science have undergone marked changes in scope and content in the past thirty years, the texts in city government have displayed a remarkable constancy. So much so, that if earlier texts such as Goodnow and Maxey were to be dressed in new dustjackets they would be nearly indistinguishable from today's publications.[4]

Now, if the texts in city government were merely a descriptive endeavor, then this constancy would hardly be worth commenting upon, especially if the institutions being described had themselves undergone little change over recent decades. But, as has already been noted, the textbook in urban government is more than an enterprise in description. It is also a prescription, a proposal for reform that finds its justification, first, in a judgment pronounced upon the behavior of the urban electorate, and second, in a body of administrative theory that has been so elaborated that it has been made to yield up "principles" to guide the governmental operation. And it is here that vintage qualities shade into irony: for this view of the urban political process and this body of administrative theory are not indigenous to the textbook in city government. They were originally borrowed from other areas of political science, and while these other areas have put forth new views of politics and administration, the original views continue to live on, unchanged, in the textbooks of city government.

In short, what has happened here is that the urban political process being described in today's city government text is a picture seen through the eyes of Graham Wallas, Lincoln Steffens and James Bryce, rather than a view that might come from contemporaries such as Lubell, Riesman, Hunter, Key or Truman.[5] And as for the administrative theory, that too is a throwback to the 1910's (and earlier); for it represents an intellectual world that no longer

---

4. Frank J. Goodnow, *Municipal Government* (New York, 1909); Chester C. Maxey, *An Outline of Municipal Government* (New York, 1924).

5. Graham Wallas, *Human Nature in Politics* (London, 1908); Lincoln Steffens, *The Shame of the Cities* (New York, 1904); James Bryce, *The American Commonwealth* (London, 1888). Bryce's view that American cities were the "one conspicuous failure of the United States" seems to have had a chromosomatic impact upon subsequent texts in city government. *Cf.* Samuel Lubell, *The Future of American Politics* (New York, 1952); David Riesman, *The Lonely Crowd* (New Haven, 1950); Floyd Hunter, *Community Power Structure* (Chapel Hill, 1953); V. O. Key, Jr., *Politics, Parties and Pressure Groups*, 2d ed. (New York, 1947); and *American State Politics* (New York, 1956); David Truman, *The Governmental Process* (New York, 1951).

This second grouping is given merely to suggest the rich lode of constructs and conceptual schemes that more recent writings have opened up for the student of urban government: Lubell, the journalist, concerned with attitudinal sets carried through time; Riesman, the mass-observer, concerned with the socio-psychological matrix of urban life; Hunter, the sociologist, attempting to apply the inferences of sociometrics to urban power structures and elites; V. O. Key, Jr., the political scientist, concerned with the anatomy of power and the use of statistical inferences; and Truman, also a political scientist, concerned with the group basis of politics.

exists. It is an administrative theory that has been torn down by the writers on administration because (at least a decade ago) it was exposed as being incompatible with the realities of the administrative process. Thus, the textbooks in municipal government present a curious display. They have constructed an intellectual edifice that rests upon foundations that are long destroyed. But despite the friability of the foundations, the structure stands intact.

## II

Because the city government text is built upon a theory borrowed from the literature of public administration, any examination of this theory must be conducted within the margins of that latter body of writings. As a result, some fairly well marked trails must be crossed, including one that many regard as the staging ground for contemporary administrative thought: the once widely held view that the making of public policy, *i.e.*, politics, is a process separable and distinct—logically, chronologically and institutionally —from administration, *i.e.*, the carrying of this policy into effect.[6]

While this distinction between administration and politics can be traced at least as far back as 1900 and the writings of Frank Goodnow, there is reason to believe that Goodnow himself may have set it up solely for the purpose of creating an analytic construct, an intellectual tool for exploring two significant, interrelated aspects of the governmental process.[7] At the imitative hands of those who followed him, however, this construct was forced through a mill of reification, eventually to emerge as a view that administration *is* a process distinct from the making of public policy. And from here, construct passed over, first into normative theory and then into causal theory: for if these entities *were* distinct parts of the governmental process, then (it was argued) they *ought* to be institutionally isolated, one from the other; and *if* administration were separated out from politics, *then* there would follow felicitous consequences for government—a maximal return upon whatever resources were expended in making the wheels of government go 'round.

This idea of maximal return was, of course, administration's celebrated concept of efficiency which, as Robert Dahl notes, ran like a red thread through the writings on administration for at least four decades, until the mid 1940's.[8] This concept of efficiency, like the notion that administration is separable from politics, was based upon a premise extremely important to the

---

6. All who refer to the development of administrative theory must acknowledge their debt to Dwight Waldo, especially to his *Administrative State* (New York, 1948). See also his "Development of the Theory of Democratic Administration," this *Review*, Vol. 46, pp. 81–103 (March, 1952).

7. Frank J. Goodnow, *Politics and Administration* (New York, 1900). See also the comments of V. O. Key, Jr., "Politics and Administration," *The Future of Government in the United States*, ed. Leonard White (Chicago, 1942), pp. 145–163.

8. Robert A. Dahl, "The Science of Administration: Three Problems," *Public Administration Review*, Vol. 7, pp. 1–11 (Winter, 1947).

whole of administrative thought: namely, that values and normative judgments, while lying at the heart of policy-making, can be eliminated from the administrative act. That, in baldest form, was the basis for the distinction between administration and politics, and it was also the basis for a belief that efficiency could serve as the measuring stick for administrative action: for it was held that the products of administration could be reduced to quantifiable units, and upon the basis of these an objective (as distinguished from a valuational) measure of the administrative act could be devised.

So grounded, administrative writing produced a body of principles whose refinement into maxims ("Boards must give way to control by the single executive"; "No executive should attempt to supervise more than four or five persons") set in motion a critical examination that was eventually to overhaul the whole of administrative thought.[9] This attack upon the "principles" of administration came from several sources: from those who demanded to see tangible and visible results from governmental reforms made in accordance with these administrative maxims; from those who searched for quantifiable units upon which to develop a universal and objective measure for efficiency; and from those whose studies of decision-making led them to conclude that value judgments are a concomitant of every governmental act, including the administrative.[10]

By 1940 the earlier principles of administration (now regarded as dogma) were in full rout, and administrative theory (with a concern for things such as function and dysfunction, group analysis and influence) moved in new directions. It is not, however, the purpose of this essay to examine these directions, but rather to make a simple point: that the administrative theory that

---

9. One of the high-water marks in the development of this body of administrative principles was the publication of Luther Gulick and L. Urwick, eds., *Papers on the Science of Administration* (New York, 1937). In an essay titled "Organization as a Technical Problem," Urwick wrote (p. 49): ". . . there are principles . . . which should govern arrangements for human association of any kind. These principles can be studied . . . irrespective of the purpose of the enterprise . . . or any constitutional, political, or social theory underlying its creation." As an example of these principles, Urwick then went on to say (p. 52): "Students of administration have long recognized that, in practice, no human brain should attempt to supervise directly more than . . . six other individuals whose work is interrelated."

10. The most trenchant demand for evidence of results from reforms built upon these administrative principles came from Charles S. Hyneman, "Administrative Reorganization: An Adventure into Science and Theology," *Journal of Politics*, Vol. 1, pp. 62–75 (Feb. 1939). Other demands came from J. Mark Jacobson, "Evaluating State Administrative Structure," *American Political Science Review*, Vol. 22, pp. 928–935 (Nov. 1928); and William H. Edwards, "Has State Reorganization Succeeded?" *State Government*, Vol. 11, pp. 183–184 (Oct. 1938).

Among those who turned away from the idea of a value-free efficiency were several scholars who did so only after first attempting to search out this efficiency-in-itself. For a careful analysis of this concept and a defense of its utility for certain instrumental purposes, see Clarence E. Ridley and Herbert Simon, *Measuring Municipal Activities* (Chicago, 1938), and Herbert Simon, *Administrative Behavior* (New York, 1949).

On the relationship between the factual and valuational elements in the administrative act, see *ibid.*, ch. 3.

entered the city government text in 1920 did not adapt itself to subsequent changes in this theory, but persists unchanged. Administrative dogma, based upon the premise of a value-free administrative process, sank—in the literature of administration—beneath the waters of empirical investigation. But in the literature of city government, the dogma still exists, an ice-age inhabitant of a lost Atlantis.

Now, to understand the role played by administrative theory in the city government text, it is also necessary to understand something of the way in which it is brought into play, that is, the way in which it has come to serve as the focal point of the textual enterprise. Ironically enough, while the theory posits the idea of a value-free administrative process, the theory itself is made significant to the text only by a commitment to two important, but half-hidden, value judgments. One of these concerns the nature of the urban electorate; the other involves the function and purpose of municipal government.

Taking the latter first, it is no exaggeration to say that the text in municipal government has turned its back upon a great range of functions performed by the city in order to elevate the administrative function to a position of first importance. A city, after all, is a many-sided phenomenon. It is an institution that carries forward the cultural attainments of society. It is a matrix that throws its inhabitants into a series of significant social relationships. It is a frame of political reference that furnishes its citizens with first-hand experiences with the governmental process. It is an organization of power and influences felt within and outside its borders. And, it is also a machine that provides certain services for those within its boundaries.[11] The city government text, however, sees the city only in its service role, and in doing so implies: first, that providing services is *the* function of the city; second, that the administration of these services is, and should be, the major task of the city's government; and third, that the test for "good" government is the provision of these services at the least possible cost. This idea of least possible cost, of course, involves the concept of efficiency; and at this point we see value judgment *within* value judgment, for not only is it asserted that the furnishing of services should be the major task of city government, but also that, in testing the performance of that government upon a rack of "output over input," the sole criterion for input should be financial and not any of the other things that men also see as having utility and value. Thus, in the language of one textbook:

---

11. Representative of those who see the city in its many roles is Lewis Mumford. See his *Culture of Cities* (New York, 1938); *City Development* (New York, 1945); *From the Ground Up* (New York, 1956).

More significant, however, for systematic research are the writings of the urban sociologists, especially those of the "Chicago school." See for example the prospectus drawn up in 1925 by Robert E. Park, "Suggestions for the Investigation of Human Behavior in the Urban Environment," reprinted in Paul Hatt and Albert Reiss, *Reader in Urban Sociology* (Glencoe, 1951), pp. 2–32.

The city is an organization or institution devoted to service. It is created and maintained for the purpose of performing functions and delivering services which are essential to make living in the modern city more tolerable and more agreeable. If it does these things at a reasonable cost to the taxpayers it has served its purpose and fulfilled its mission. The goal is to deliver the essential or desired services at the minimum cost.[12]

The second of the value judgments that serve to bring administrative dogma into play also involves the presentation of a single facet of a many-sided phenomenon. Here the phenomenon is urban political behavior and the characterization made of this behavior is redolent of Hamilton's metaphor of the people as a great beast. What the city government text sees as most characteristic of the urban elector is that he is "befogged and confused" and incapable of rendering intelligent judgment upon important questions. ("The complexity of questions . . . is so great that it is asking too much to expect the citizen to vote intelligently.") He prefers the "appeals of emotions rather than issues" and sends into office "incompetents and numbskulls." He has a penchant for electing the dishonest politician instead of the "virtuous civic leader" and thus, if the text be read carefully, it will be seen to fly the gonfalons of some latter-day Federalist Party: the people are to reign but not to rule directly. For their own good, they are not to be entrusted with complete control over the instruments of government. Separation of powers and check and balance are once again the orders of the day; and they are to be achieved by separating the policy-making functions of government from the administrative. The former are to be restricted and placed with the representatives of the people and the latter are to be enlarged and lodged with the "policy-neutral administrative expert."[13]

That in blueprint is the grand design of the city government text; and once the case is made for separating policy-makers from administrators, the proposals for specific reforms now fall into place like a company of well-trained guardsmen.

First, to secure expertise in the ranks of the administrators, their offices must be made both appointive and permanent. They must be protected from the corrupting influence of office-seeking and placed, whenever possible, upon the civil service rolls. ("The ballot should be shortened until it includes only those officers who determine municipal policy. And the only persons on the municipal payroll whose primary duty is indisputably the formulation of policy are the members of the local legislative body. . . .")

Second, to promote efficiency in the governmental operation, boards must give way to the single-headed agency; and lines of authority must be clearly drawn. A scalar organization must be established with ultimate power coming to rest in as few hands as possible, ideally in the hands of a single

---

12. See note 3, above.
13. Separation of powers by means of an independently elected executive, however, is eschewed by the text in an effort to overturn ideological obstacles to the coming of the city manager.

administrator. ("Modern administration calls for the integration of control over administration in a single executive. . . .")

Third, and once again in the interest of efficiency, those who supervise administration must be given responsibility for preparing and supervising the city's budget; for only in this way can fiscal outlay be made to reflect the facts and needs of administrative life. ("Final responsibility for the accuracy, completeness, and wisdom of the budget plan should be centered in the chief executive.")

And finally, city government's basic forms must be altered to accord with the theories of proper administrative management. The city council is to be remade, both procedurally and substantively. Its enabling charter is to be rewritten so as to confine the council to policy activities, and to make impossible "council meddling" with administration. Moreover, to improve the quality of the council's policy functions, better men are to be brought into the council and its size is to be adjusted to the needs of proper debate and deliberation. To these ends, the textbooks generally agree that representation by wards must give way to city-wide elections. This, it is proclaimed, will reduce the influence of bossism and send a "higher type of man" to the council. (". . . election by wards is apt to produce an inferior type of councilman"; "election at large helps to attract better men to run for office. . . .") And in addition, it is agreed that small councils are preferable to larger ones, with at least one text claiming to have discovered fairly precisely the proper size for a city council: "Twenty or twenty-five councilmen may be more satisfactory for the largest communities."[14]

As to the office of mayor, there is complete agreement that the weak mayor who shares executive power with independently elected boards and administrators must give way to the strong mayor, a chief executive fashioned upon the templates of the national government's President. But weak or strong, the mayor is, after all, an *elected* administrator and having sprung from politics' dirty soil, he cannot be expected to be endowed with proper administrative qualities. As one text puts it: "Courage is not usually the stuff out of which mayors are made." And again: "Every mayor must decide whether to emphasize the technical or popular aspects of his office. He must be either a good administrator or a good fellow. He cannot be both." Thus, the textbooks prefer a form of government other than mayor-council, and they view the commission form of government with both regard and misgivings. The commission form has one great virtue. By offering an alternative to the mayor-council form of government, it has helped turn American cities away from that form. But in the last analysis, the commission form is a weak form, for "Commission government achieves merger of policy-formation and policy-execution in the same group of officers. This is wrong in principle, a fundamental error in design." And thus, the textbook comes at last to the form of government that epitomizes proper administrative theory, the

14. As will be discussed in the following section, the empirical evidence for these generalizations is nowhere laid out for inspection.

city manager form of government. In this form there is encapsulated all that is proper for city government, and in a representative outpouring of praise, one textbook writes: "The council-manager plan of municipal government is the best plan yet devised."

This, then, is the list of reforms being urged upon our cities, and in offering up this list, the city government text has come to serve as attending physician to the local bodies politic. The doctor's medicine is strong. But strong medicine is not necessarily good medicine; and it may be that the physician's formulary contains as yet no penicillin.

## III

Although administration is the pivot of the city government text, the faults that lie with these books are not confined to this pivot nor to its supposed dichotomy between policy and administration. From a critical point of view, the administrative phases of these books are no more than a surface manifestation of a deeper fault: the lack of concern for the standards of proof that comprise scientific analysis. Lacking a concern for this analysis, these texts therefore suffer from an inadequacy of presentation that embraces much that is touched upon, from the pivotal center out to the perimeter of the textual enterprise.

It is, of course, beyond the possibilities of this essay to examine all that is dealt with in these books; but it is possible to carry further the thrust of criticism by examining, under four headings, the most conspicuous of the textbooks' analytic failures: first, the failure of these texts to integrate their materials with the general body of political science literature. This is the shortcoming of *insularity*, and because of it these books offer up conclusions and remedies that are at variance with the general findings of political science. Second, the failure of these texts to weigh and evaluate (and even lay out openly) the evidence that is used to support their pronouncements and conclusions. This is the breakdown of *standards of proof* and because of it much that is contained in these texts is scientifically suspect. Third, the failure to pursue statements and commitments to logical ends. This is the breakdown of the *logical imperative* and because of it these texts are able to conceal, perhaps even from themselves, their elitist commitments within a democratic cloak. And finally, the failure of these books to appreciate the complexity of any important political activity. This is the shortcoming of *one-dimensional analysis*, and because of it these textbooks proceed to problem-examination by showing concern for only a single factor in a multi-factoral situation.

Under the heading of insularity, the most conspicuous case, of course, is the maintenance of the policy-administration dichotomy in the face of its abandonment by the rest of political science literature. Insularity does not stop here, however, but follows the development of the text's administrative line, shielding from refutation many of the key corollaries that flow from this basic dichotomy. Among those corollaries, protected from the leverage of the general writings of political science, are those that involve the pursuit of the merit system, proposals for budget management, and proposed reformation of the city's political process.

In one sense, all of these proposals stem from the fact that the city government text is still fighting the Tweed Ring of the 1870's. To secure government against patronage and pork-barreling, the merit system and the executive budget are urged, without reservation, upon the cities. This can be done, of course, since the textbooks view budget-making as no more than a mechanical process for relating income to outlay, while the civil servant is seen as being no more than a hollow vessel into whom the values of his masters can be poured. In the general stream of political science writing, of course, these views have been both challenged and rejected: for the budget stands revealed as government's most potent instrument of policy, while the civil servant's role in policy-making has led many to conclude that the lines of civil service reform have already been extended beyond the bounds of democratic responsibility.[15]

It is in the realm of political reform, however, that the text has its greatest say; and here, in an effort to smash bossism, the cities are to be thrust into the embrace of the direct primary and the independent (of national affiliation) local party. (". . . there is an evil effect in having municipal campaigns conducted along national party lines.") But while the city government text states its advocacy of the direct primary, political scientists in other fields question the efficacy of this reform, some going so far as to state that the primary may have an effect opposite to that proclaimed in the city government text. By robbing the parties of an opportunity for centralized "answerability" and by helping to send the minority (e.g. "watchdog") party into decline, the primary may actually work to increase the power of the political machine.[16] And, as regards the creation of local political parties, here the time schedule of the municipal government book is truly out of

---

15. On the relationship between budget-making and policy, see Herbert Simon, cited in note 10 above, ch. 9; V. O. Key, Jr., "The Lack of Budgetary Theory," *American Political Science Review*, Vol. 34, pp. 1137–1144 (Dec. 1940); Harvey C. Mansfield, "Fiscal Accountability," in Fritz Morstein Marx, ed., *Elements of Public Administration* (New York, 1946), ch. 25.

On the problem of the merit system and democratic responsibility, see Charles S. Hyneman, *Bureaucracy in a Democracy* (New York, 1950), especially, ch. 15; The American Assembly, *The Federal Government Service* (New York, 1954), especially the essays by Herbert Kaufman, Herman M. Somers, and Harvey C. Mansfield.

16. To state the textbooks' position within the context of this essay, they are still carrying forward the dictum of Frank Goodnow who wrote that the direct primary will deliver over to the people the "same control over nominations that they now have over elections." Goodnow, cited note 7 above, p. 248.

For some second thoughts on the primary, see V. O. Key, Jr., *American State Politics*, cited note 5 above, chs. 4, 5, 6; and Austin Ranney and Willmoore Kendall, *Democracy and the American Party System* (New York, 1956), pp. 281–286; V. O. Key, Jr., "The Direct Primary and Party Structure: A Study of State Legislative Nominations," *American Political Science Review*, Vol. 48, pp. 1–26 (March, 1954).

joint, for these books ignore what may be the central political phenomenon of our time: the growth of Presidential power and the intimate relation of urban political parties to that power.[17] To urge our cities to cut themselves off from the vital center of our political life is unrealistic, to say the least; but probably no more reflective of insularity than the proposal of one text which, after separating those officials who are to be elected from those who are to be appointed, says: "Members of the judiciary are not policy-determining officers and therefore they should not be elected"![18]

These proposals for reform, however, are made suspect by more than insularity. They can also be criticized by way of the evidence that supports them, and here (as might be expected in the seamlessness of systematic analysis) insularity shades over into the category of proper evidence and consequent standards of proof.

From one point of view, a proposal for political reform is more than a call to action; it is also the sounding of a body of causal theory that posits a series of relationships between political institutions and the general political process. To demonstrate these relationships (*e.g.*, to prove the theory) is at best an exceedingly difficult process; and, given the social scientist's inability to quantify certain data or subject them to reasonable control, there is a great range of causal theory that may lie forever out of the range of scientific demonstration. Even the simplest causal theory requires, for tentative demonstration, a wealth of carefully controlled observation; and unfortunately, the study of city government—lacking, for example, its first comparative study of the American city council—has yet to amass much of this necessary knowledge.[19] Thus, it is a fair question to ask whether the city government text has *any* causal theory that it may set before its readers as being "proven." But rather than hazard an answer here, it would be more useful to examine the evidentiary techniques that are used to create the keystone in the textual arch: the proposition that manager government is the best form of city government.

Bluntly put, this proposition in most of the textbooks is simply an *ipse dixit* proclamation. Those books, however, that seek to prove the validity of

---

17. On the relationship between presidential and urban politics, see Key, *American State Politics*, cited above, ch. 2; Samuel J. Eldersveld, "The Influence of Metropolitan Pluralities in Presidential Elections Since 1920," *American Political Science Review*, Vol. 43, pp. 1189–1206 (Dec. 1949); Samuel Lubell, *The Future of American Politics*, cited note 5 above, chs. 3, 4, 5.

18. The literature treating judicial activism is extensive. Two exceedingly useful items are Fred V. Cahill, *Judicial Legislation* (New York, 1952), and Jack W. Peltason, *Federal Courts in the Political Process* (New York, 1955).

19. It is somewhat presumptuous to offer bibliographic references for what is axiomatic to scientific investigation. The following, however, examine in detail the propositions that are merely encapsulated here. Hans Reichenbach, *The Rise of Scientific Philosophy* (Berkeley 1951); Ernest Greenwood, *Experimental Sociology* (New York, 1945); Morris Cohen and Ernest Nagel, *Logic and the Scientific Method* (New York, 1934), chs. 6–16; William Goode and Paul Hatt, *Methods in Social Research* (New York, 1952); V. O. Key, Jr., *A Primer of Statistics for Political Scientists* (New York, 1954).

the proposition rely chiefly upon two very shaky pieces of evidence. The first relates to the number of cities that have tried the manager plan and then abandoned it; and the second consists of citing Stone, Price and Stone, *City Manager Government in the United States.*[20] Now, whatever the real merits of this form of government, they can hardly be adduced from these pieces of evidence. The fact of abandonment is open to too many conflicting interpretations to be conclusive;[21] and the aforementioned book is hardly any more so. The Stone book, in fact, states in its introduction that its authors were unable to formulate any standards or tests of managerial achievement and therefore confines itself to a cataloging of the procedural and structural changes that accompanied the introduction of the manager form in each of the cities listed.[22] Reduced to its logical dimensions, this means simply that the manager form has introduced into certain cities the manager form of government. The textbooks in city government, however, have seized upon this catalogued tautology and offer it as evidence of the merits of the manager plan. In doing so, the bareness of the evidentiary cupboard stands revealed.

To turn now to the problem of logical consistency within these texts, it might be noted that they are very much of a logical whole, except at the juncture where democratic theory is to be spliced to the administrative line. Without exception, these books begin upon a note of devotion to the democratic ideal, and, going on to place city government within that ideal, most of them note that cities are vital to democracy; first because democracy can reach its fullest development within the relatively limited geographic confines of the city, and second, because the concrete experiences of city government constitute a training ground for a responsible citizenry.

But no sooner are these commitments to democracy launched, than they sink immediately from sight; and the text turns its attention to constructing a world of municipal government in which the expert is supreme. It may be that the city is the ideal area for democracy's fruition, but the text puts the ideal to rout by making much of "the shame of the cities" and their irrational inhabitants who are hardly fit for self rule. The training ground of democracy is rapidly surrounded by the barbed wire of expertise, and the citizen is kept from participating in the experiences of city government by being reminded that: "After all, there are only two ways of paving a street or enforcing quarantine regulations—a right and a wrong way . . . ," and the right way, of course, is known only to the expert. There is no suggestion here that the real issue may not be right *versus* wrong street paving, but rather the democratic issue of where the streets are to be paved; for the implication is

---

20. Harold Stone, Don K. Price and Kathryn Stone, *City Manager Government in the U.S.* (Chicago, 1940).

21. See Arthur Bromage, *Manager Plan Abandonments* (New York, 1940), revised, 1949.

22. *Op. cit.,* pp. vi–viii. For a prospectus for an empirical examination of city manager government, see Social Science Research Council, Inter-University Seminar, "Research in Political Behavior," *American Political Science Review,* Vol. 46, pp. 1003–1045 (Dec. 1952).

that the matter of *what* the city is to do has long ago been settled and that the real problem is simply the expert's problem of how. Legislative policy-making is to give way to a broad delegation of powers to an administrative, professional elite; and, even in those relatively few instances where training of citizens is to go forward through genuine policy debate, the textbook hardly rejoices over this debate but prefers to cluck sympathetically over the plight of the administrative expert "who finds his plans blocked by a stupid and obstinate majority in the [city] council."[23]

This concern for the stupidity of the majority, however, may be more revealing of the value-orientation of the text than of the actual state of city affairs; and it is at this juncture of value and "fact" that a final criticism can be made. A textbook, after all, is more than a purveyor of information. It is also an enterprise in analysis that is to serve its readers as a model for emulation in the setting out of data, in the weighing of evidence, in control over values, and in the total process of problem solving. The textual model is open to a degree of challenge in all of these areas, but especially in the area in which the texts attempt to grapple with any of the more complex problems that confront our cities.

Briefly put, what these texts do is solve a problem by building a maximizing model. In less charitable terms, they first seize upon the goal to be reached and then stake out the methods best calculated to reach that goal, without ever stopping to justify that goal, or to indicate to their readers what other goals will be stepped over in the process.

On the problems raised up, say, by suburban cities, the goal generally sought is a lowering of the total costs of government, and the technique most often recommended is that of annexation. No consideration is shown the cost-opportunities involved in seeking this goal and no attempt is made to justify this preference for lowered governmental costs as over and against other things that men might value, such as corporate identity or the greater opportunities for citizen training that might exist in small town affairs.

Thus, problem solving for these texts consists of seizing upon a single dimension of a complicated situation and then dealing only with that dimension. This, however, is not problem solving but shadow play. For in the

---

23. The textbooks offer little evidence that they have thought through the problem of the expert and his proper role in democratic government. Moreover, they appear to be unaffected by the attempts that others have made to deal with this problem. See, for example, John Dewey, *The Public and Its Problems* (New York, 1927); Robert A. Dahl, *Congress and Foreign Policy* (New York, 1950). See also the spate of administrative writings that treat this problem asymptotically in an attempt to clarify the problem of political controls over bureaucratic structures: Charles S. Hyneman, *Bureaucracy in a Democracy* (New York, 1950), especially chs. 2–4; Carl J. Friedrich, *Constitutional Government and Democracy* (Boston, 1946), ch. 19, and "Public Policy and the Nature of Administrative Responsibility," *Public Policy, 1940,* ed. Carl J. Friedrich and E. S. Mason (Cambridge, 1940), pp. 3–24; Herman Finer, "Administrative Responsibility in Democratic Government," *Public Administration Review,* Vol. 1 (Summer, 1941), pp. 335–350; Norton Long, "Power and Administration," *ibid.,* Vol. 9 (Autumn, 1949), pp. 257–264; Paul Appleby, *Morality and Administration* (Baton Rouge, 1949).

world of real politics, problems have many dimensions; and when confronted with decision-making in that world, most men do deal with these many dimensions: they consider cost opportunities and sacrifice of values; they eat their cake and keep at least a portion of it by compromising and by supporting half-way measures. As the economist would put it, they prefer to maximize at the margins, and in doing so, they preserve a sizable portion of what might be sacrificed if the reform were thoroughgoing and total.[24] Thus, the textbook offers little by way of guidance for problem solving in the world of real politics. But to say this, however, is not enough, for there is always the danger that students may take the books' analytic methods seriously and attempt to emulate them in the arena of practical politics. Disillusion is sure to dog the emulator, and that, in the last say, may be the real case against these texts.

# IV

To return to the theme upon which this essay opened, the question may now be fairly put: what kind of text will serve to correct the deficiencies of the present text, and, at the same time, will liberate scholarly energies for research in the field of city government? The answer is, perhaps, too simple to be of value, for the recast textbook must be one that weighs its evidence fairly, exposes the gaps in its own knowledge, and suggests areas in which fruitful research is to be done.

But, if present administrative theory is to be eliminated from the recast text, the problem arises as to what shall constitute the inner framework, the interlacing that holds the enterprise together and gives it form. Without this matrix, the text may be reduced to the description of legal relationships that for so many years characterized the textbooks on American national government; and here, the problem grows infinitely more difficult.

It may be, of course, that the conceptual framework that will mold the city government text cannot be determined in advance of a decision as to what shall be the field's developmental form. A continued concern for the city's administrative activities may utilize some such framework as *decision making,* while a concern for the city as a creator of public policy may involve a scaffolding such as the *group basis* of politics. Ideally, the conceptual framework should be an "open" one that permits development along several lines simultaneously; and it may be that the materials for this framework are already at hand.

In part, these materials would come from the literature of political science, and in part from the writings of the sociologists. And the justification for

---

24. See the discussion of marginal maximization and social reform in Robert A. Dahl and Charles E. Lindblom, *Politics, Economics and Social Welfare* (New York, 1953), ch. 3. See also the use of this principle of marginal maximization in the analyses of the Chicago Home Rule Commission as it dealt with questions of the size and method of election for the Chicago city council. Chicago Home Rule Commission, *Modernizing a City Government* (Chicago, 1954), pp. 31–75.

their use would lie in the fact that they are tied to two of the most significant elements in the study of city government. The first of these elements is the comparative, and it is grounded in the fact that the study of American city government (embracing some 16,000 separate governments) is in essence an exercise in comparative politics. The second of these elements is the socio-logical, and it is made important by the fact that the "irreducible, stable ele-ment" within each city and common to all cities, is its complex network of *interpersonal* relations. ("The city is people.")

To utilize these elements, there might be required a two-phase organiza-tion of the city government text. The first phase would borrow from the literature of comparative government, for it would be concerned with a central goal of that discipline: the forging of some dependable causal theory concerning the relationships between such variables as institutions, pro-cedures, forms of government, and patterns of political behavior.[25] In at-tempting to lay out this theory, the text could operate upon three levels of presentation. First, it could do a meticulous job of stating what is already known about these relationships as they apply to American cities. Second, it could join city government to the main streams of political science by acknowledging some of the more significant studies in politics and indicating their *inferential* importance for city government. And third, the text could open the way to future research by indicating the kinds of information that are still very much missing from the reservoir of knowledge in this area. Thus, to illustrate by example, as it dealt with legislative operations within the city, the text could examine some of the studies made of the legislative operation on the state and national levels and then attempt to draw inferences from these studies for city government. Equally important, the text could also indicate the importance and need for parallel and replicative studies of the city council.[26] Or, to take an example from the realm of politics, as the text dealt with patterns of political power within the city, it might lay out some of the elements that are generally said to constitute a political organiza-

---

25. For a statement of the concerns of comparative government see Roy C. Macridis, *The Study of Comparative Government* (New York, 1955); Social Science Research Coun-cil, Inter-University Research Seminar, "Research in Comparative Politics," *American Political Science Review*, Vol. 47, pp. 641–675 (Sept. 1953).

To suggest a comparative method for the study of city government is not to minimize the difficulties that abound in the use of this method. As V. O. Key notes, in speaking of the use of this method for the study of American states: "Even in the comparative analy-sis of American states, which should hold constant a great many factors that would com-plicate comparisons among nations, it is extraordinarily difficult to know when significant variables have been identified." "The Direct Primary and Party Structure," cited in note 16 above, pp. 21–22, footnote 21.

26. To take an example within the example, Stephen Bailey's studies of Congressional lawmaking seem rich in inference for the city council. See his *Congress Makes a Law* (New York, 1950), and Stephen Bailey and Howard Samuel, *Congress at Work* (New York, 1952). See also the role-perception framework as used by Ralph K. Huitt, "The Congressional Committee: A Case Study," *American Political Science Review*, Vol. 48, pp. 340–365 (June, 1954).

tion; and, going on to discuss the importance of the precinct worker, the text might then note that the four generally available studies of this "vital cog" the one study that is perhaps most informative was made some twenty-five years ago and dealt only with a non-random (*e.g.*, non-representative) sample of precinct workers in only one city.[27]

The second phase of textual organization, too, would involve the use of causal theory. Here, however, the emphasis would be upon an extended examination of patterns of political behavior. The relationship between these patterns and governmental forms might again be noted, but the central concern would be with *explanations* of urban political behavior. And to this purpose, the text would be able to draw upon an already developed body of literature, that of urban social-psychology.[28]

In attempting to categorize the effects of urban life upon the individual personality, this literature has created a body of concepts that are abstracted from a central feature of urban life: the aloneness, and lack of a sense of mastery over one's environment that spring from the routine and impersonalization of city life. These concepts (such as alienation, disorientation, group-dependence) have already done much to illuminate urban political behavior; and in the focus of a city government text, they are especially useful for their explanations of such vital aspects of urban politics as apathy toward the routine of government, the manipulative powers of the political machine, the urban dweller's willingness to experiment freely with the forms of his government, and his affinity for the colorful political leader.

Thus, if the textbook carefully explores the relationships between institutions and politics, it might be possible to employ these concepts so as to make all of urban government revolve around a single theorem: that urban politics is the product of the disorientation of urban man. This single proposition, if properly used, might serve as a substitute for the organizing framework provided by administrative theory in today's texts; and quite possibly, it will be with this substitution that a revitalized study of American city government can begin.

---

27. Sonya Forthal, *Cogwheels of Democracy* (New York, 1948), reissue. Other studies dealing with the precinct captain are: Harold F. Gosnell, *Machine Politics: Chicago Model* (Chicago, 1937), ch. 3; David Kurtzman, *Methods of Controlling Votes in Philadelphia* (Philadelphia, 1935); William Mosher, "Party Government Control at the Grass Roots," *National Municipal Review*, Vol. 24, pp. 15–18 (Jan. 1935).

28. Some items representative of this literature are: Erich Fromm, *Escape from Freedom* (New York, 1941); and *The Sane Society* (New York, 1955; Sebastian De Grazia, *The Political Community: A Study in Anomie* (Chicago, 1948); Robert C. Angell, *The Moral Integration of American Cities* (Chicago, 1951); William F. Whyte, *Street Corner Society* (Chicago, 1943); W. Lloyd Warner and Paul S. Lunt, *The Social Life of a Modern Community* (New Haven, 1941); Julie Meyer, "The Stranger and the City," *American Journal of Sociology*, Vol. 56, pp. 476–483 (March, 1951); Phillip Selznik, "Institutional Vulnerability in Mass Society," *ibid.*, Vol. 56, pp. 320–331 (Jan., 1951); Morris Axelrod, "Urban Structure and Social Participation," *American Sociological Review*, Vol. 21, pp. 13–18 (Feb., 1956); Scott Greer, "Urbanism Reconsidered," *ibid.*, pp. 19–25; and Paul Hatt and Albert Reiss, *Reader in Urban Sociology*, cited in note 11, above.

# ARISTOTLE AND THE STUDY
# OF LOCAL GOVERNMENT

## NORTON E. LONG

THE DISCIPLINE OF POLITICAL SCIENCE is characterized by compartmentalization into special fields of empirical research. These fields are most commonly treated as a species of contemporary institutional history, and scarcely more attempt is made to identify, test, and correlate key hypotheses and their logical consequences than is made by the historian. The preoccupation of political theorists with the monuments of the past, the history of ideas, and moral speculation has led to a neglect of the urgent task of providing theoretical unification for the discipline, a comprehensive theoretical description of our present body of empirical data, and an adequate directing framework for new research. Lack of such theory results in an anarchy of intellectual laissez faire, uncompensated for by any "unseen hand" producing an effective, productive cooperation among us. The net result is that research is not additive in its findings, and that each individual must in a sense go it alone.

The alternative to rugged intellectual individualism is not some theoretical five-year plan to regiment research. Rather it is to recognize the need, and get at the business of working up generalized empirical theory that can guide research in specific areas and meaningfully interrelate all areas. Hopefully there will be many such theories competing in the market place of ideas, subjecting themselves to the test of facts and guiding empirical research into theoretically significant channels. This neglected aspect of political science, so well appreciated by Aristotle, badly needs rehabilitation in the discipline. It does not mean a new plague of methodologists, with large foundation grants to work out schemes for working out schemes for manufacturing high-level theory. Methodology will most fruitfully develop out of serious work in important problems. The history of the discipline has pretty well indicated what a number of these are. It seems likely that the dearth of general empirical theory is due not to lack of methodology, but to lack of a sustained structured interest in the profession.

We have acted on a sort of hope that if enough facts are collected they will somehow sort and illuminate themselves. A becoming modesty and an overwhelming respect for the ancients have paralyzed our own originality and made historians of us all. It is high time we took courage and renewed the high enterprise that was carried forward not only by careful scientists

Reprinted from *Social Research*, 24, No. 3 (Autumn, 1957), 287–310, by permission of the publisher and of the author.

like Aristotle, but even by inspired dilettantes like Rousseau. We may well hope that if this enterprise is put on a continuing organized basis, empirical theory in political science can have an ongoing career in John Dewey's sense, rather than resembling as it now does the history of the great works of art, with no more interconnection and development than that between Rembrandt and Picasso.

Perhaps as promising a place as any to start the business of building an empirical theory is with the field of local government. The nearer we get to the ultimate face-to-face groups of the family, the clan, the tribe, the village, the town, the city, the county, the closer we come to dealing with phenomena that promise generality and provide useful points of departure for the investigation of the power and opinion structures that characterize differing political systems. The unity of politics for scientific inquiry, if unity there be, lies in the continuum of mutual influence and interaction that links the person, the family, the hamlet, the city, the region, the nation, and the world with one another as interrelated foci of interest and influence in a commonly shared dynamic field.

One of the major weapons of scientific inquiry is comparison, the notation of significant similarities and differences between the objects compared. Certainly the father of the profession, Aristotle, with his detailed comparison of constitutions, was a comparative-government man if ever there was one, and his conception of constitutions was broad and realistic enough to range from the ethos of the ruling class and the techniques of dictatorship and revolution to the statics and dynamics of prevailing economic systems. By itself, however, the commandment to compare is insufficient if we do not insist on the selection of the significant for comparison.

Here indeed is the rub for the crude empiricist: out of the multitude of things that might be compared, how to select the significant? Fortunately, this is no problem *ab ovo*. We are the heirs to a tradition that has wrestled for upwards of two thousand years with the question of what are the significant phenomena of politics; nor is our own contemporary culture barren of value systems to guide us in the selection of "interesting" hypotheses; and lastly, despite its lack of a satisfactory career, political science has empirical theories of politics sufficient to suggest "interesting topics" for comparative analysis. Indeed, were we to utilize some of our most promising empirical theory that has lain dormant in the clutches of metaphysicians, moral philosophers, and the historians of ideas, we might witness a renaissance in the discipline similar to that occasioned by the rediscovery of the classics in other ages.

But for such a rebirth, no servile and uncomprehending imitation will do. Only a creative use of the perennial sources of insight furnished by truly great minds deeply grounded in the realities of political behavior can give a Baconian direction to what in the past has lent itself to a priestly and snobbish ritual of the great books, where in all truth the wisdom of an Aristotle or a Plato is so securely embalmed that no dangerous breath of life can emerge to disturb the complacent and uncomprehending repetition of formulae grown meaningless and empty of contemporary significance.

It will be the contention of this paper that an application of the Aristotelian categories of analysis to the phenomena of local government will make for the development of theory capable of unifying the discipline.

## I

The key to Aristotle's political philosophy lies in his identification of politics with ethics—his conception of the state as being most significantly a medium for the realization of some conception of the good life, and indeed as being the master institution for this purpose, to which all others are teleologically subservient. Aristotle's exclusive preoccupation with the city-state as the chosen vehicle for man's ethical self-realization has given his work a deceptive appearance of irrelevance to later and widely different forms of political life. The ethical and sociological interest central to Greek political thought was replaced by Roman legalism, and the Christian separation of church and state undermined the primacy of the state's ethical role.

Rehabilitation of Greek political thought by theorists such as Rousseau and Hegel has seemed, on the one hand, to abandon empirical inquiry for metaphysical speculation and, on the other, to enthrone an ethical theory fraught with the menace of totalitarian absolutism. Empirical investigation into the ethical nature of political associations has by and large been treated either as identical with some variant of Hegelian metaphysics or as an attempt to resurrect the natural-law theory slain by Hume. But one may well reject Hegel, and Marx, and natural law, one may even be a good disciple of Hume, and still insist on the reality of ethics as an empirical datum of the first magnitude. Its neglect is little short of an evisceration of the subject matter of politics.

One may well go along with Aristotle in insisting on the prime significance of ethics as a "brute fact" of politics without accepting Aristotelian metaphysics. Aristotle the political scientist can be severed from Aristotle the metaphysician. The ethical structures of political societies are not merely oughts for the sermons of theologians and the homilies of moral philosophers, but in all scientific seriousness are most significant *is's* for empirical inquiry. Lest I be misunderstood on this point, I mean no disparagement of rational evaluation of ethical structures. There is no more important function than that of evaluation. It uses, but differs from, science. Value structures, however, are most significant empirical facts for scientific inquiry, if we would understand the groups and societies whose behavior is informed by them.

For Aristotle the structure of politics is a structure of institutions, running from the family through the village and the town to the state, each subordinate institution contributing its appropriate part to the final end embodied in the polis state. The state is characterized by its regime, which exemplifies a particular conception of the good life, be it the wealth of oligarchy, the freedom of democracy, or the martial spirit of a timocracy. The ethical principle embodied in the constitution sets the standard for distributive justice in the state; determines the nature and composition of the politeuma, the ruling class, whose members in one sense are or personify the constitution; and informs the subordinate institutions with their appropriate roles in each particular type of constitution.

The Aristotelian conception of autarchy or self-sufficiency sets the limit to the progression of social institutions. The final unit, the state, is self-sufficient and therefore inclusive of all the others. Self-sufficiency depends in part on military and economic considerations, but most significantly on ethical. It is for this reason that Aristotle, the tutor of Alexander and the friend of Antipater, could retain his allegiance to the city-state in the face of the bitter facts of Greek experience.

But again, Aristotle's predilection for the city-state form by no means limits to the city-state the applicability of the concept of ethical self-sufficiency. As a concept for analyzing the units of government, and the relations of individual and subordinate groups to them, ethical self-sufficiency can play a role similar to that of sovereignty, and more discriminating. The delimitation of ethical communities, and the description of their interrelationships and participants, may be sociologically and politically more meaningful than comparable legal analysis.

The nature of the state, as opposed to its lesser political subdivisions, is that it is ethically "sovereign." Its end is the highest, to which all other associations contribute or should contribute, and are subordinate. Aristotle was well aware that not all actual governments were of such a character. The governments of the barbarians, and indeed many of the Greek governments, exemplified no ethically satisfying end in which citizens as opposed to mere subjects could participate. An ethically satisfying state was for Aristotle a requirement for the fullest development of man. It is not merely a metaphysical requirement, but one that human nature will strive for, however imperfectly, in particular and adverse circumstances. It is thus an empirical fact of human behavior, not just a moral postulate.

The simple scheme of Book I of the *Politics* describes an ethically graded series of associations rising from the household to the polis, with each step in the ascent characterized by an ethically more inclusive and higher end. On the basis of this analysis, local government is differentiated from the higher levels of government as ethically insufficient to stand by itself and as merely ministerial to an end more adequately realized in a higher level. Thus for Aristotle and Plato the village is, if not a "city of pigs," still too uncivilized for the highest human self-realization. It is inadequate to provide the scope necessary to the fullest self-realization of man, and is therefore lacking in self-sufficiency.

If on one end of the ethical scale of associations, the village is inadequate and the household even more so, the polis itself is characterized by ethical self-sufficiency and a degree of economic and military competence. Aristotle is not talking about an isolated state in an international vacuum. There will be treaties and alliances, economic, military, and for other purposes; there may be Pan Hellenic Festivals and Olympic Games—and thus there are more broadly inclusive associations than the polis (the state). But these broader associations are characterized by partial and less inclusive purposes. They do not contemplate "the whole end of man."

If one puts the Aristotelian schema aside for the moment, and considers the ordering of associations and especially governmental associations in accordance with the value—and perhaps one should say the felt value—of their ethical ends, it is clear that the Aristotelian picture of a neatly ascending hierarchy, though logically attractive, may or may not be the case from one situation to another. Just as the Austinean schema would give us a neatly ascending order to the final sovereign, so the Aristotelian would give us a hierarchy mounting to the ethically sovereign association. The polemics on sovereignty have frequently led to metaphysical debates between monists and pluralists. A similar logomachy could develop from any conception of an ethically sovereign state. What is important is to investigate the ethical character of governmental associations as significant empirical data of political life.

As an empirical fact, any given state is a community of communities. Some of the most important of these communities are formally political in character. They serve ends that are variously interrelated, and these ends rate more or less highly as values to the participants in the communities. A well ordered state would be, for Aristotle, one in which the subordinate communities were articulated instrumentally and ethically with the final community, the state. This would mean that a democratic state would ideally call for democratic local government, or that an oligarchical state would call for oligarchical local government.

In practice, to be sure, the ideal may be far from realized. But this is more than a mere matter of the aesthetic disruption of a tidy-minded constitution-maker's organization chart. If Aristotle's theory of revolution is empirically warranted, this contradiction in the ethical constitution of the state is productive of stasis—is in fact a present indication of the disintegration of the ethical constitution of the state. In the more homely terms of Lincoln, "a house divided against itself cannot stand." For Lincoln as for Aristotle, ethical principles embodied in the values of living men struggle for institutional life, for survival and expansion. The very stuff of politics is made up of these conflicts, and the most significant meaning of institutions lies in the ethic that structures the variety of human attitudes toward them, ranging from ardent participation and advocacy through lukewarmness and apathy to violent protest and opposition.

A vast modern nation state, such as the United States, contrasts sharply in territory and population with the city-state of antiquity. It is not, however, the ethically formless mass that Aristotle so despised in Babylon, though Aristotle's strictures of Babylon are not without telling applicability to the megalopolis of our day and to the nation itself. The belief that a despotic rule over slaves is the only possible political organization for a large territory was not clearly Aristotle's final view, since his advice to Alexander urged the latter to rule the Greeks as a leader though the barbarian despotically, as a master. Be this as it may, the empirical fact is that however different the participation and the interaction, the modern nation-state can have citizens rather than subjects, and can and does have a constitution in the Aristotelian sense. This constitution is of great significance for the subordinate associations in the state.

Aristotle's analysis of constitutions is complex. It is nowhere systematically spelled out in the *Politics,* but in general I believe Sabine is right in contending that, for Aristotle, constitutional government ideally requires a government of law over willing subjects in the common interest. Any or all of these qualities might be lacking, however, and there would still be a kind of constitution—if, for Aristotle, a perverted one. Aristotle's empirical analysis led him to identify several interacting aspects of constitutions as going concerns. In one aspect they are a certain ordering of offices; this is the legal constitution, concerned with the formal division of power. In another there is the economic or, more broadly speaking, the sociological constitution, the actual economic and social structure of the society that underlies and informs the legal constitution. And there is finally the ethical constitution, the conception of the good life that rationalizes the whole social and legal structure and provides the principle of distributive justice in the state. These three aspects of the constitution are in dynamic interaction, though for Aristotle the ethical is clearly the most important. In shorthand, Aristotle describes the constitution as the ruling class and the ruling class as the constitution. The ruling class is the ethic of the constitution made flesh, embodying it. Because it does, it is the ruling class, and because this ethic is generally accepted it rules over willing subjects. How important the ethical constitution is, and how painful deviations from it may become, are illustrated by Gunnar Myrdal in *The American Dilemma.*

## II

Professor Louis Hartz has argued that American political life has been characterized by a massive acceptance of a Lockean ethic. Implicit in this ethic is a justification for a given "ordering of offices": a certain type of ruling class and its recruitment and a set of supporting economic and social institutions. The bearers of this ethic are driven to seek its institutionalization through society. The United States is certainly no tight little city-state, but a continent with wide variation in social and economic conditions. Local heresies from the central conception of the good life are inevitable. And yet, looking at the formal "ordering of the offices," the legal structure of the subpolities of the American polity, there is an apparent monotonous uniformity that makes most texts in state and local government arid in the extreme. Does this mean that the overriding ethic of the national polity has indeed informed the political subdivisions, as in Aristolelian theory it ideally should? Or does it mean that political scientists, despite Aristotle's example to the contrary, have confined themselves merely to the legal constitution, and have neglected the social-economic and the ethical?

In view of the continental sweep of American politics, we can expect state and local governments to show a wide deviation from the national norm, to have individual constitutions in the Aristotelian sense, with significant differences that cannot be adequately described in the strong-mayor, weak-mayor, city-manager, and commission legal typology that divides our municipal Gaul into four unequal parts. V. O. Key has urged, and in his *Southern Politics* has begun to make respectable, a recognition of the deviant that has hitherto been the province of the muckraker and the journalist rather than of the orthodox political scientist. A comparative approach would open a rich mine of local "constitutions," varying from the narrowest oligarchy to the freest democracy, and from the most brutal tyranny to a near philosopher-king. A recent *Saturday Evening Post* headlined a story, "Tyrant in Texas," the story of George Parr, so-called Duke of Duval County. This regime lasted for years, under the forms of law. Bell County, Kentucky, killed its opponents with impunity and dominated the courts, and its tyranny was finally overthrown only from without. The Imperial Valley in California exhibits a brutal oligarchy that tolerates no nonsense from its helots. The investigations of the La Follette Civil Liberties Committee documented the deviant local constitutions. The company towns of the nineteenth century not only illustrate the concentration of economic and political power in a ruling oligarchy or tyranny, but provide a classic example of the transition of oligarchy to a broader based polity.

Thus, under the deceptive uniformity of an apparently similar legal structure, a wide range of actual variance appears in the "constitutions" of our local governments. And it is under these "constitutions" that many, if not most, people have to live the most significant parts of their lives. We have no adequate information as to these "actual constitutions," the degree of their prevalence in their different forms, and the extent to which they cover, for practical purposes, the political life of those subject to them. We are even in the dark as to any cumulative trends.

It may be disquieting to realize that, in respects important for significant groups of the population, the American government that counts is oligarchical or tyrannical rather than democratic. The implications for the superior levels of government of variant constitutions below are serious. As Madison pointed out, an advantage that the expanse of the country gives to federalism is the possibility of restricting political contagion to the infected governmental cell, walling it off, and, after rallying the healthy corpuscles, restoring the normative order. Another advantage lies in the capacity to tolerate, under the cloak of lip service to the respectable national norm, wide deviations in practice dictated by differing social and economic situations.

Yet local government on the firing line must be a major determinant of the realities at the national level. Caciquism, the rule of local chieftains, made a mockery of parliamentary democracy in eastern Europe, parts of Italy, Spain, and South America. Perhaps the *tutelle administrative* of France may indicate the real possibility of centralized national democracy unsupported by extensive local foundations. Or one may see in France's apathetic masses a result that Burke foresaw in a metaphysical constitution that denies the necessity of mediating institutions between individual and nation. Surely the trends of our local constitutions, as they develop toward a more extensive prevalence of oligarchy, democracy, or ochlocracy, and their variants, are highly significant for the future of state and national government.

Each local jurisdiction, with important powers of police, justice, and taxation, can resemble a feudatory, with high, middle, and low justice; can constitute a little world for some, if not all, of its inhabitants; and can as truly represent a way of life as ancient Athens. The Aristotelian view sees the relationship between levels of government as most importantly a hierarchy of increasingly more self-sufficient ethical associations, until in the state self-sufficiency is attained. A part of the reason for the more primitive associations entering into the higher is military and economic, but by themselves these motives would not constitute a sufficient bond to produce a new political unity. Thus a NATO, or even an EDC, does not constitute a state, nor will a private or public international coal-and-steel cartel produce one. A community or friendship for business may produce a cartel or an International Rotary, a similar association for defense may produce a military alliance, but by themselves these purposes are insufficient to structure a political union. For this, according to Aristotle, a commonly shared and participated-in conception of a good life is essential.

The significance of this for local government, and its relation to the higher levels of government, lies in the widely felt differences regarding the importance of the various communities' purposes. The sense of the significance of the community's ethical value varies as between communities, and as between inhabitants of the same community. Thus a citizen of Quebec may find his provincial loyalty far more meaningful than his Canadian citizenship. Robert E. Lee, wending his way sadly back to his native Virginia, illustrates a type of conflict that reaches beyond the formal context of legal federalism. The scale of areal and governmental loyalties has a wide range of possibilities. While secession may not be a realistic possibility for Yorkville Nazis, a species of spiritual and even politically effective secession can occur. Nullification is not just a Southern states-rights phenomenon, and the non-enforcement of federal and state law is a significant aspect of political geography.

Not only may citizens of local governments limit or even cut their allegiance to state and national governments, by apathy and neglect, if not outright revolt; also at the local level they may exhibit little or no allegiance. Many an ardent young progressive is condemned to live in the Republican desert of an otherwise charming suburb. The split between the local citizens and the purely national citizens is a common problem of party politics. Thus the question of who are and who are not citizens is more than a mere legalism, although legal right is not without relevance. A most significant question of citizenship is that asking who participates in the ethical conception of the good life, embodied in the constitution of the community, and how the community's institutions, both formal and informal, are designed to effectuate participation.

If Aristotle, Plato, the Catholic church, the American Legion, the totalitarian states, and many others are right in the critical political importance they assign to education, then the educational systems, both formal and informal, that characterize our communities are of central significance. These institutions not only indoctrinate youth in the spirit of the polity; they also serve in part to separate the men of gold from the men of silver and the men of brass. The free and easy Periclean high school of the older small community mixed all social classes, nationalities, races, and religions in a school whose creed was likely to be Locke and Jefferson with a dash of the Napoleonic gospel that every private carries a marshal's baton in his knapsack.

A principal political effect of the motor car and the bedroom suburb has been the one-class school. For certain racial and national minorities, segregation and the peculiar operations of the real-estate trade had already, to some extent, produced this independently in the larger cities. The extent to which a counter-trend at institutions of higher learning may overcome the influence of early education is problematic. In so far as churches, boy scouts, other youth organizations are an important factor in the role training and indoctrination of youth, they well warrant study. Each community has a system of educational institutions to indoctrinate youth in the spirit of the polity and confirm them in the principle of distributive justice by which role allocation is justified.

The political effect of parochialization of the schools is widely recognized. Yet study of the school system as a "brute fact" of American politics, and as much so as the party system, is avoided—and at the cost of losing that refreshing and serene realism that characterizes Greek political thought. We may, and in fact as disciples of Locke we must, reject the Aristotelian identification of politics with pedagogy. The ideal of the state as a glorified Rugby is incompatible with a political philosophy that refuses to see the individual and society as reaching their fulfillment in the state. But while rejecting the metaphysical idea of the ethical ultimacy of the state, and its corollary that the state should be an all-inclusive educational institution, we must acknowledge the important political functions of education.

The struggle for the minds of men is a pervasive and never ending battle. Recently the newspapers of an Ohio city rebuked the local leaders of the AFL for seeking to organize the schoolteachers with the avowed intent of getting across to the students a point of view sympathetic to labor. The union leaders replied to the outraged rebuke that this was the only way they had to break the monopoly of their opponents on the formal educational system. The process of education is central to the indoctrination of the young and the recruitment of the governing class. It complements and sometimes competes with the family, the church, and other social organizations that perform similar functions.

## III

For Aristotle the key to the constitution is the governing class. Here is the human embodiment of the constitution. It spells out in clearly legible "big letters" what may be obscure or hidden in the legal constitution. The governing class represents or appears to represent the qualities that exemplify the conception of the good life that informs the constitution. Its members are looked up to and admired, since they most fully reflect the ideal. Their position is felt to be just, to be legitimate, because in terms of the particular constitution it is just that the richest, the most noble, the most learned, should rule.

The institutions of the society, if it is to be stable, must buttress and reinforce the principle of legitimacy. So viewed, ideally, all institutions are shaped to give effect to an ethical norm; viewed in another respect, all institutions are shaped to support the claims of a particular governing class. Thus the Federalist parson and pedagogue justified the government of the wise and the good, who turned out to be the rich and the well born. Art, literature, religion, and manners, and the social structures through which they operate, are pregnant with political consequences. They serve to support or undermine a given political order. As Irving Babbitt once remarked, all great revolutions are preceded by a revolution in the dictionary. The key value terms of a society undergo a change, sapping the symbols of legitimacy of a given order.

Governments, local and state, may range from a tight oligarchy of wealth to a demagogic mass dictatorship. For the most part, pure forms are rare. As Aristotle pointed out, there are many claims to political power: wealth, free birth, numbers, noble birth, military prowess, and the like. All of these have a real but limited justice. A stable constitution requires that no single claim prevail, and that at least wealth be tempered by numbers. In fact, this mixed government or polity is best achieved through the predominance of the middle class. Where the rich confront the poor with little or no middle class between them, the city is divided into irreconcilable armed camps. A sociological and economic substructure is necessary to support a given constitution, and that constitution will be radically altered by economic change, as from a peasant democracy to an urban proletariat. Thus Aristotle recognizes that ruling class, legal constitution, ethical order, and economy are interdependent. Changes in one aspect have significant consequences for all others in the dynamic equilibrium of the constitution.

When we apply Aristotle's conception of constitution to state and local governments, each unit of government may be conceived of as possessed of a ruling class. From the composition and character of this ruling class emerges the real nature of the local government's constitution, as opposed to the formal legal order. The holders of political office represent a small fraction of the ruling class; the offices of the formal political order may be among the less important in the community. The separation of church and state, of politics and economics, veils some of the jagged peaks of the pyramid of power. The princes of the church, the presidents of the banks, the editors of the newspapers, the manufacturers, the labor-union leaders, the leaders of society, of fraternal organizations, of nationality and racial groups are not, as such, officers of the formal government. But if government be regarded as a decision-making process, much of the action of the formal government is mere ratification of decisions made by these holders of social power. For this reason Marx and his followers have maintained that bourgeois democracy is a fraud, in which the pseudo-equality of the ballot box hides the realities of the unequal distribution of power. As John Adams wrote to Jefferson, there are nobles in Boston as well as in Madrid.

Conservatives in the early American state constitutional conventions protested again and again that abolition of the property qualification for office or suffrage would prove pernicious or nugatory. Property was an indestructible part of political power, and failure to recognize it in the constitution would lead either to a demagogic assault on wealth or to the devising of informal means whereby wealth would achieve its inevitable influence in the power structure of the community. To the realists of the eighteenth and early nineteenth centuries the struggle between the rich and the poor, the few and the many, seemed as invariant a problem of politics as it did to Plato and Aristotle. The opponents of the Daniel Shays, while doubtless seeking to provide in the constitution an instrumentality for the solution of common social problems, frequently argued in terms reminiscent of the pages of Thucydides. Their advocacy was couched in the language of frightened oligarchs seeking to band themselves together in a league to furnish mutual aid and comfort against one another's threatening democracies.

The wisdom of the fathers is full of reference to the bloody social politics of the republics of antiquity. In no respect does their political science seem more faulty than in its gloomy prophecies that political democracy means social democracy, and social democracy means class war. On the other hand, the twin inventions of representation and federalism—in which the authors of the *Federalist* set considerable stock as so extending the feasible territorial limits of free government as to diffuse and dilute interests, and so break the force of faction—have appeared to succeed beyond their fondest hopes. Given their dour view of the nature of man, the Federalists could scarcely have dreamed that our cities and local governments would be so free of the mischief of faction as would appear from contemporary textbooks. One would never gather from a text on local government that the prime fact of politics is the struggle of classes, or that the central question of government is the ruling class.

The gulf between Aristotle and the eighteenth-century realists, on the one hand, and contemporary political science on the other is vividly apparent in the preoccupation of the former with stasis and the problems of class rule, and our present attitude of avoidance or indifference toward these issues. In part, this difference of approach results from a belief that the phenomena of class struggle, which are fundamental in Aristotelian analysis, are simply not exemplified in the American scene. In part, it is due to a belief in a fundamental social-harmony theory, similar to that of classical economics. This view results in a conception of a system of political laissez faire in which, as in economic laissez faire, no one rules. Free political competition exists in much the same way as free economic competition.

A more realistic view would see our political organization as a system that, while differing in part, is nonetheless comparable to a system of Greek city-states or to the feudal lordships and free cities of the Middle Ages, clusters of power and local government under varying degrees of external control. In Aristotle's sense, each local government may, and often will, have a ruling class of its own, once independent and now subject to or participant in a ruling class of the new more comprehensive political unit. Looked at historically and analytically, there is a continuum between the independent small governments of one period and the local governments embraced in the empires and nation-states of succeeding epochs. The cycle of building larger aggregates may halt and reverse itself, bringing about the renewed independence of lesser communities; or both the process of aggregation and that of disintegration may go forward at the same time, interacting together. Thus the study of state formation and international relations joins hands with the study of local government.

Secession, separatism, colonial nationalism, revolution, and imperialism are pervasive categories of political analysis. The ethical self-sufficiency of the community and the supremacy and independence of its ruling class are two aspects of statehood that local governments approach as limits. If they are attained, local governments become independent states; if lost, they become incorporated in larger units.

Ethical self-sufficiency means in practice that a political community possesses ideal goals whose significance for the politically decisive part of the community transcends the goals of any more or less inclusive community. The supremacy of the ruling class is derived from its commonly accepted relation to those goals from which it derives its legitimatized power. In practice, the community may possess both ethical self-sufficiency and a ruling class of its own and still fail of political independence. The captivity of the Jews under Babylon and Rome is a case in point. Ireland and Poland in recent history were incorporated as foreign bodies into alien sovereignties. But in Hobbes' terms they indeed formed "worms in the body politic." In any event, the material conditions of independent statehood depend in part on the surrounding facts of other powers.

The ethical self-sufficiency or the ideal goals of communities can be regarded as technologies for permitting large-scale cooperation, both by giving a decisive number of inhabitants participating roles and by structuring and legitimatizing a ruling class and its roles—creating an area and a personnel with shared legitimate power. The possibility of creating such goals with an appropriate ruling group is decisive not only for the creation of larger state structures in the international sphere, but equally for the solution of metropolitan problems internally. Of course, in either the international or the domestic sphere, problems may be "solved" by the force of conquest or fiat. Even here, however, the transformation of might into an accepted and acceptable right remains.

# IV

The inappropriateness, for the solution of major current problems, of our existing structure of state and local governments is a common lament of citizen, scholar, and public official. The satellite suburb entrenched in its baneful legal autonomy, the rotten-borough state, the under-represented urban population, all exemplify the conflict between the dynamics of change and the statics of a vested interest in the institutional status quo, with its passing ideals and its challenged power structure. Just as internal local government structures are menaced by the sweep of change, so the international state structure itself, in its embodiment of a bygone distribution of power and purpose, is challenged by new and legally unrecognized facts and forces.

The process of adjustment of institutional structure to the emerging new facts of life may proceed more peacefully within states, where there exists a more or less accepted mechanism for the transfer of power, than between states, where commonly accepted instrumentalities for adjustment and the saving of face are lacking. In the extreme case, and always as a real alternative, there remains the possibility of revolution in the one case and war in the other. A major achievement of political institutions is to make possible the non-violent adaptation of the status quo to the necessities of change.

Edward Hallett Carr, in his *Twenty Years Crisis*, has well expressed the problem of politics as the institutionalization of peaceful change. In this sense war and revolution are extreme means necessitated by the failure of institutions to adapt to major new facts of power. One does not have to share in Carr's apparent worship of the "bitch goddess success" to appreciate the force of this position. From it, as from that of Marx and Aristotle, the assumption of the normality of "social harmony," that underlies much economic and political analysis, seems naive, hypocritical, or pollyanna. Thus a study of American politics that focuses on parties and elections is, while important, radically insufficient, open to the same criticism that Marx leveled at the economists. It assumes the permanence of the system and therefore neglects the dynamics of its structure. It neglects the dynamics of political structure. The evisceration of politics by abstracting from it vital Aristotelian elements, now isolated in sociology and economics, accounts in part for the emptiness and insufficiency of analysis.

For Aristotle the ruling class and revolution were two of the main concepts of political analysis. Investigation guided by these concepts inevitably leads to concern for the realities of social power, its acquisition, distribution, limits, transfer, and loss. Power capabilities, a term we glibly bandy about in the analysis of international relations, has equal meaning in terms of local, state, and national government. The process of political change can be fruitfully viewed from the standpoint of changes in the composition and techniques of the ruling class, its relation to the value symbols of the society, and the dynamics of economic and cultural change.

There is certainly room for the important study of the politics and technology of cooperation. In the larger sense, however, this is a subcategory of the greater process of the dynamics of group adjustment. And even in the study of supposedly instrumental politics—as for example the fringe problem of metropolitan cities—the structure of a local ruling class and the possibility of galvanizing it into effective action is a decisive element for success. The differing fortunes of urban redevelopment in Pittsburgh—where the Mellon family and its leading scion, Richard Mellon, exert an effective hegemony—and in those communities with a jealous group of contending notables bear witness to the very everyday and very practical consequences of the structure of the local ruling class.

The emergence of labor leaders as powerholders without social status constitutes a source of instability for local constitutions and local ruling classes. Whether they will be crushed or ignored, or admitted to the country clubs and the honor-laden posts of our society, is on the agenda of history. The nationality leaders, from the Boston Irish to the Slavonians, have fought a long-drawn battle for inclusion into the upper ranks of the status system. When Harvard College conferred an honorary degree on Cardinal O'Connell of Boston the reconciliation of State Street with Lake Street was finally ratified.

The basic adjustment of the ruling class to new facts of power, compelling the admission of new elements and signalizing the decline of old, is not always easy, and sometimes is violent. The La Follette Civil Liberties Committee records the violent objection to the emergence of union power.

Sometimes the problems of intergroup adjustment approximate those with which we are painfully familiar in international life. The Negro population strains at the dikes of segregation with all the pent-up energy of a nation seeking its place in the sun. Quite literally it seeks to conquer living space, space that cannot be purchased. Violence is a technique that lies ready at hand. Despite feelings of guilt, in terms of both the plutocratic principle of justice—they have the money—and the democratic principle—they are fellow citizens—those next to the problem, feeling menaced, deny Negroes membership in a community controlled by these principles. The prevention of warfare depends on the institutionalized technique of mobilizing the neutrals.

But the solution will require granting the same accolade to the Negro leaders that has been accorded other nationality groups by the ruling class. Failing that, the Negroes would remain a community within a community, struggling for a recognition that can finally be accorded only by the ruling class. In an important sense the Negroes as a group are excluded from becoming fully participating citizens, and thus are fair game for the revolutionary appeal of communists and alien agents. Symbolic participation in community acceptance, through the leaders' attainment of social-status positions, is a major attribute of citizenship in a mass state. Thus the ruling class becomes a medium for the representation of groups and the resolution of their conflicts. It may be a far more significant center of representation than city council or legislature.

The composition, interrelation, and changes of local ruling classes give significance to the local election returns. The president of the Central Labor Union Council and the archbishop do not change with the elections. What difference, then, do the elections make? How does the apparent change in formal political power relate to and affect the real distribution of social power? The political institutions are not only a device for doing the day-by-day work of meeting commonly accepted needs; they are also a mechanism for facilitating the peaceful readjustment of the balance of social power. The legal structure may obstruct or facilitate this. It may be more accessible to some groups, some levels of government, some agencies of government than to others, in their struggle for recognition and change. And the contest will be carried on in private organizations whose decisions may frequently outweigh the public in importance.

The concept of the ruling class provides a corrective for the superficialities of the formal legal order as a true description of the actualities of political power; and the Aristotelian analysis of revolutions provides a more searching analysis of political process than our preoccupation with formal elections. The seeming inapplicability of city-state experience to the macroscopic phenomena of the nation-state has served to limit Aristotelian analysis to the office of a profound but tenuous philosophic inspiration.

That this should have occurred despite the deep appreciation of early American theorists for the classic categories of analysis is in all probability due to the great appeal of both the facts and the myth of classless society. As Professor Hartz has pointed out, American experience has been peculiar in having a democratic revolution without the necessity of overthrowing a feudal order. The absence of class consciousness may well be due, as Professor Hartz contends, not only to the bounty of nature but even more to the fact that the middle class, never made class-conscious by struggle with a nobility, has failed to tutor the workers in their "historic" role.

Surely a part of the reason for the failure of political science to make use of the concept of the ruling class is the disrepute of Marxism and its works, and the crudity of much of vulgar Marxism. The Italian realists, such as Mosca, have remained curiosities from which to quote an occasional line with approval, but despite even the enormous vogue of Pareto they have failed to stimulate systematic study and reorientation. Elite studies there have been, but these have had the appearance of being esoteric when they have not been damned as antidemocratic.

The Aristotelian conceptions of citizen, constitution, and ruling class can be transferred from the city-state to an examination of the phenomena of government at local, state, and national levels, and even of politics, including the international. To raise the question of who are citizens, and in what sense, at each level of government, is to pin-point crucial political issues that legal categories neglect and obscure. A functional conception of citizenship is as fruitful as a functional conception of party membership.

That a city like New York may best be regarded as made up largely of resident alien merchants and mechanics, gathered for trade and pleasure, and therefore lacking in civic motivation may explain some of the necessities of its government. That the ruling class of town X are branch-plant managers taking their orders from Pittsburgh and hoping to be promoted elsewhere is a more vital political fact than the town's possession of a city-manager form of government, though the two may be related. The suburban residence of large elements of a metropolitan ruling class, and its ethos of irresponsibility, may be a more potent cause of central city disintegration than would be revealed by any analysis of the multiplicity of legal jurisdictions. Rural domination of state legislatures and the orientation of urban masses toward Washington and the presidency are deeply related to the current institutional technique for bolstering oligarchic power.

The interrelations between the geographically separated ruling classes, the difference in their composition, the formal legal constitutions through and alongside which they operate, the varying ethics that legitimatize their power, and the revolutionary movements for altering their composition, winning recognition for new elements, or overthrowing them—these are the vital stuff of politics. Their investigation can give real meaning to the shadowy phenomena of legal structures and elections, pointing to the large and cumulative phenomena and escaping the mere flux of the headlines.

# II

## URBAN GOVERNMENT IN
## THE FEDERAL SYSTEM

---

In a country as vast as the United States, a central government cannot very well carry on all public affairs. Some functions must be performed on a local basis and some on a more-than-local-but-less-than-national one. But although some such division of labor may be an evident necessity, the principles of it—and still less the concrete application of the principles—have never been easy to decide upon. Where the boundaries of the local and of the more-than-local-but-less-than-national jurisdictions should be drawn and what activities should be carried on within each of them are questions that have had to be agitated, discussed, and settled anew by each generation. The rate of social change, as well as the nature of the change, has made impossible any permanent or generally satisfactory answers.

Everyone agrees that local questions should be decided locally. And everyone agrees that when the two interests conflict, the interest of a local public should be subordinate to that of a larger one. But in their practical application these two principles have continually clashed, and efforts to formulate a workable compromise in abstract terms have again and again come to nothing. Part of the difficulty derives from one fact that it is impossible to define abstractly what is "local" and what is not. Moreover, the accidents of history—above all the great compromises by which the federal system was created in 1787—have had to be taken as fixed features of the situation. The problem has been further aggravated by the fact that party politicians have always been able to make political capital from mixing state and national politics with local ones.

The account of intergovernmental relations in New York City by Wallace S. Sayre and Herbert Kaufman shows how complicated the present division of labor among the levels of government may be in a single urban area. All three levels of government serve, regulate, and tax the people of New York, but, as Sayre and Kaufman explain, each is on a different basis both in constitutional theory and in actual fact. The historical developments that led to this complexity are described by Frank J. Goodnow in an excerpt taken from one of the first textbooks on local government. He shows how the centralization that characterized local government in Colonial times was replaced by extreme decentralization in the period of Jacksonian democracy; how the sphere of municipal activity grew and how local government changed from an organization for the satisfaction of local needs to one that was also, and primarily, an agent of state government; and how the legislatures interfered with cities for political reasons, thus engendering a long and largely unavailing struggle by the cities for "home rule." (For a definition of this term, see the Glossary.)

A recent evaluation of home rule by a committee of practical men looking for ways to improve the government of the nation's second largest city is reprinted from the report of the Chicago Home Rule Commission. Since the distribution of powers between cities and states must always be decided in the concrete rather than in the abstract, the committee concludes that the question of a proper distribution must always remain to some degree unsettled, and any decision—even one made by "experts"—must inevitably be essentially political in character.

The dependent position of the cities has been made worse by their underrepresentation in the state legislatures. (In 1960 there were only two states in which cities were fully represented, and none in which they were overrepresented.) Many writers have asserted that underrepresentation is the reason that city governments have not provided more and better services for their citizens, but this view is effectively challenged by Robert S. Friedman. The central cities, he says, are too much preoccupied with the problem of apportionment. Recent population changes mean that suburbia, not the central cities, is the chief victim of underrepresentation. Thus he concludes that the cities would still be frustrated even if representation were fair. Mark K. Adams shows how difficult it is to bring about a legislative reapportionment even under the most favorable circumstances: any concrete proposal is sure to contain bitter pills which legislators, even those whose party has most to gain from it, find very hard to swallow.

The rapid growth of urban populations has brought another question to the fore: how does one cope with metropolitan area problems? The census now identifies 212 metropolitan areas (see Glossary); in no case do their boundaries coincide with those of a general purpose government. Area-wide needs must therefore either go unmet or be served by cooperation among existing units of government or by the creation of new units.

The most common way of dealing with these metropolitan problems has been the creation of special districts. These, as John C. Bollens explains, usually deal with only one function of government—for example, water supply, sewage disposal, rapid transit, air pollution control, and so on. Since they serve only one function, special districts are unable to plan comprehensively for metropolitan area development. Edward T. Chase centers his criticism of the New York Port Authority, the biggest of the special districts in the United States, on precisely this ground.

Many proposals have been made for a multifunctional approach to metropolitan area government. But what problems are to be considered metropolitan? Edward C. Banfield and Morton Grodzins think that the number and importance of such problems has been somewhat exaggerated and that in any case sweeping reforms are politically out of the question. Their proposal for action—a realistic one, they say—assumes that the formal structure of government will remain fundamentally unchanged for a long time to come. Luther Gulick, a former city administrator of New York who is now the President of the Institute for Public Administration, believes that metropolitan reorganization is one of the urgent needs of the day. He finds more metropolitan problems than do Banfield and Grodzins, is more sanguine about the political possibility of bringing about change, and accordingly is led to propose the creation of an altogether new level of local government. Frank P. Zeidler, a former mayor of Milwaukee, believes that if the cold war continues, the federal government will gain ascendancy over the metropolitan areas while the states will lose their hold. Rexford G. Tugwell, who was once chairman of the New York City Planning Commission under Mayor La Guardia, thinks that metropolitan governments should have the status of states but sees no way to bring this about.

Sixty years ago, when Goodnow wrote his textbook on city government, he remarked that nothing need be said about the federal government since it had no connection with city affairs. How completely this has changed is shown by the first reading of this section. Clayton Knowles's account of the place of cities in the 1960 national party platforms and Robert H. Connery and Richard H. Leach's view of the proper role of the Federal government in metropolitan affairs give intimations of what is likely to be the trend of federal-local relations. In the last reading of the section, Morton Grodzins, a political scientist, explains why the efforts of the federal government to devolve certain of its functions to state and local governments have not worked and are not likely to work. The forces of history and politics, Grodzins shows, are strongly on the side of making our government one of shared functions, the symbol of which is the marble cake rather than the layer cake.

# INTERGOVERNMENTAL RELATIONS IN NEW YORK CITY

## WALLACE S. SAYRE AND HERBERT KAUFMAN

THE OFFICIALS of the governments of New York State, the United States, and of neighboring states and localities are deeply involved in the government and politics of New York City. This is due to the dependence of all the major components of a modern industrial society upon each other, an interdependence engendered by the economic, transportation, and communication systems. A more specific reason, however, is the division and sharing of powers, functions, and responsibilities among the city, the higher levels of government, and adjacent units of government. For both these reasons, officials and employees of other governments are constantly drawn, or inject themselves, into the contest for the stakes of politics in the city. By the same token, officials and employees of the city are constantly engaged in efforts to influence their counterparts in other governments.

## The City Is an Agent

All three levels of government operate within the City of New York, serving, regulating, and taxing the inhabitants. But there is an important difference between federal and state officials and employees as against city officials and employees. The personnel of the federal agencies (the largest in the area being the Post Office Department, the Department of Defense, the Treasury Department, and the State Department, but with many others also represented) are engaged exclusively in executing the provisions of federal law. Similarly, the personnel of the state agencies in the city (all 20 departments of the state government are represented here) are concerned primarily with the execution of state law. Most city officials and employees, however, are in both theory and practice agents of the state government (or, in a few instances, such as some phases of welfare, arterial highways, and urban renewal and slum clearance, also agents of the federal government).

Reprinted from *Governing New York City* (New York: The Russell Sage Foundation, 1960), pp. 558–62.

That is to say, the laws they administer are almost entirely laws enacted by the state government (or, in the cases noted, by the federal government), and their activities are supervised in varying measure by state (and/or federal) personnel.

This aspect of the situation of New York City is by no means unique to New York. In American constitutional theory, municipal corporations are traditionally regarded as creatures of the state governments. There is no inherent right of local self-government, and their existence and powers, as well as the designation and powers of their officials, are subject to state control except as the state constitution provides otherwise. They are held to function in a dual capacity, namely, as agents of the state and as organizations for the provision of local service. The attitude engendered by this tradition is particularly evident in the detail and specificity of the state laws administered by the New York City Board of Education, Department of Welfare, Department of Personnel, Board of Elections, finance agencies, as well as the Police, Fire, Buildings, and Correction Departments. (The first three of these are also tightly supervised by state administrative officers.) The Housing, Transit, and Triborough Bridge and Tunnel Authorities, creatures of the state like the city itself, are similarly circumscribed by state law. Indeed, while most of the remaining agencies and officers of the city carry out local law essentially, their programs planned and directed primarily at the municipal level, they, too, derive their authority from broad state legislative authorizations and are limited by a variety of broad statutory restrictions.

The influence of the federal government upon the city government springs not from constitutional theory but from fiscal pre-eminence. Federal financial assistance, it is true, has not only been warmly welcomed but actively sought by city officials. Nevertheless, the purposes for which federal money has been made available have been federal purposes, and the federal government has quite naturally exercised the prerogative of every donor to set conditions for every grant and to check up to make sure that the conditions are fulfilled.

Thus, constitutional theory and financial realities have combined to cast city officials and employees in the role of agents of the higher levels of government. The relationship is firmly established and widely accepted; many federal and state officials deem it their right and duty to influence decisions and actions of city officials and employees, and the latter have had little choice but to accept this as their lot.

## The City Is a Claimant

Federal and state officials are furnished with incentives to influence decisions and actions of city officials not only by the general view that the city is an agent of the higher units of government but also by the requests and demands of the city officials themselves. City officials exert these claims upon the other governmental levels for several reasons. First, they are not indifferent to the decisions and actions of federal and state personnel directly serving, regulating, and taxing the people of the city. Second, they are continually in need of financial assistance to maintain (let alone to expand) their own operations. Third, their powers are limited, and they are compelled constantly to seek new authority to meet new conditions.

Thus, for example, city leaders (as well as congressmen from the city and the United States Senators from New York) tend to seek increases in the New York harbor work of the United States Army Corps of Engineers. They labor to get for New York City a substantial share of the contracts for defense and other federal functions and to demand adequate federal services (which bring with them both jobs and payrolls) for this area. Mayor La Guardia used all the influence he could muster to try to persuade the Post Office Department to designate Floyd Bennett Field in Brooklyn instead of Newark Airport as the airmail terminus for the metropolitan region. Mayor Wagner urged the federal government to adjust its tax program so as to aid commuter railroad services. In much the same fashion, but on a smaller scale, city officials bring pressure to bear on the state government. If their demands are met, city leaders may regard as solved, at least temporarily, problems with which they would otherwise have to deal. If their requests are rejected, they may find themselves compelled to allocate their own time and energy and some of the fiscal resources of the city to solving or alleviating these problems. If the Corps of Engineers, for instance, were to reduce drastically its dredging of the harbor, it is not unlikely that the city government would have to assume all or part of this burden in order to protect the flow of commerce so important to the economy of the region. Curtailed defense contracts and federal expenditures in the city usually mean a heavier welfare load and perhaps a significant decline in tax revenues. One factor leading to the construction of La Guardia Airport was La Guardia's inability to persuade the Post Office Department to name Floyd Bennett Field as the regional airmail terminal; New York became the terminal when the new field was completed. It seems unlikely that federal and state tax policies will—or, for that matter, can—relieve fully the acute commuter railroad crisis in the metropolitan area, and this will continue to occupy the attention of city officials for a long time to come and probably to claim an increasing share of the finances of the municipality. In short, what state and federal officials do or fail to do in the way of direct service in the New York area will play an important part in the behavior and policies of city leaders. In this sense, then, the federal and state governments often influence the contest for the stakes of politics within the city, and the influence is frequently a response to a request of the city officials themselves.

City leaders also generate federal and state influence by their success in securing financial aid from those levels of government. State constitutional tax and debt limits circumscribe the ability of the city to raise and borrow money. Even if these were entirely removed, the city would still be restricted by economic considerations—specifically, the danger of driving business and residents out of New York, and of injuring the city government's credit standing in the bond market. Furthermore, many of the most productive forms of taxation—excise, liquor and tobacco and gasoline sales, and income—have been so extensively employed by the state and federal governments that any but the most modest additional city levies would make the totals prohibitive. This confines the city in effect to a relatively inelastic tax base (real property) supplemented by a variety of "nuisance" taxes and a general retail sales tax. To render even its traditional services, let alone the new ones for which a dynamic city constantly creates a demand, such as public health and social welfare, traffic management, air pollution control, and slum clearance, the city has been forced to seek fiscal help from the state legislature and Congress. Whenever such help is forthcoming, it usually brings with it some policy stipulations, some form of supervision and control, and occasionally some inquiry or investigation to assess the urgency of the alleged need. Indeed, Governor Dewey responded in 1953 to one of the city's repeated requests for funds by securing legislation creating a Temporary State Commission to study the government of the city to determine whether the needs could be met by increasing the efficiency of the city's governmental machinery. Governor Rockefeller in 1959 similarly obtained legislation establishing a temporary state-city commission (a "Little Hoover Commission") to examine the city government and propose improvements in its structure and functioning. The search for money often brings the city a measure of relief, but it also results in increased federal and state influence in the municipal governmental decision-making process.

The same is true of the city's quest for additional authority. Despite a home-rule amendment to the state constitution, and amplifying home-rule legislation, city leaders are not free to regulate or tax citizens within the city's borders in any way they like nor can they provide at will any services they want to. They must always find a constitutional or statutory base for the activities of the city government. In general, new enterprises, new programs and policies, and new forms of taxation cannot be fitted into existing provisions. The city is obliged to apply for grants of additional power. For some purposes—for example, to construct bridges over navigable waters—it needs the approval of federal officials. Consequently, city leaders themselves constantly involve state and federal officers in the local decision-making process. That is not to suggest that city officials are pleased with this state of affairs nor does it imply necessarily that the higher levels of government are displeased with it. On the contrary, it will shortly be seen that the state government in particular insists on preserving it. Nevertheless, things being as they are, the immediate cause of much of the participation of state and federal officials and employees in the government and politics of the city is the initiative taken by city leaders in quest of added powers.

In sum, not necessarily because city officials prefer it but because they often cannot help it, their role as claimants upon the higher levels of government for direct service, financial assistance, and additional authority has provided impetus and justification for the exercise of continual influence upon city decisions by the higher units of government.

# THE HISTORICAL DEVELOPMENT
# OF THE CITY'S POSITION

## FRANK J. GOODNOW

### English City Government in the Eighteenth Century

IN ORDER to understand the beginnings of city government in the United States it is necessary to consider briefly the system existing in England in the eighteenth century. For that was the model on which the American system was framed. The English system of city government existing at the time this country was settled was based on certain rather well-defined principles. In the first place, the cities, or boroughs, as they were commonly called, were incorporated through a grant by the crown to each locality of its own special charter. There was, therefore, no uniform system of city government in England, except in so far as all the special charters were governed by certain generally applied principles.

In the second place, what was incorporated by the English charter was not the district, nor the people living in the district, but only the municipal officers, or these officers and a narrow body of freemen or voters. The official name of an English municipal corporation was indicative of this condition of things, being, for example, "The Mayor, Aldermen, and Councillors of ———," or "The Mayor and Jurats of ———," or "The Mayor, Aldermen, and Commonalty of ———."

In the third place, and partly as a result of the character of the incorporation just described, the form of government provided by these charters was distinctly oligarchical in character. In most instances the council, which was the governing body of the corporation, was a self-perpetuating body, although in some cases its members were elected by the narrow body of freemen or voters already alluded to.

In the fourth place, the sphere of action of the English municipal corporation of the eighteenth century was a very narrow one. The corporation had control of its property and finances, and had the power to pass local ordi-

---

Reprinted from *City Government in the United States* (New York: Appleton-Century-Crofts, Inc., 1904), pp. 43–68; 73–75, and 77–79.

nances, mainly of a police character. Its officers, or certain of its officers, were further frequently intrusted by royal commission with important duties relative to the administration of civil and criminal justice, and the preservation of the peace.

During the latter part of the eighteenth century the population of cities had greatly increased. This increase of the population made necessary an enlargement of the sphere of municipal activity. The corporate organization of the cities was, however, bad. It was bad because the cities were prostituted in the interest of the national political parties. Under these conditions the city government could not with safety be intrusted with the discharge of the new functions of government. The result was the formation, by special acts of Parliament, of trusts or commissions, not connected with the borough council, for the discharge of these main functions, such as paving, lighting, and even watching the streets.

Such was the system of city government existing in England during the seventeenth and eighteenth centuries, and it is safe to say that whatever may have been the depths to which any American city has fallen, it is doubtful whether it ever sank so low as were English boroughs at the beginning of the nineteenth century.

## Early American City Government

But, with all its faults, the English system was made the model of the system which was established in the North American colonies.

The first municipal corporation of any importance to be established in this country was that of New York. New York received its first charter in 1665. This charter was unsatisfactory, and in 1683 a petition was made to Governor Dongan to give the city a more satisfactory frame of municipal government. Governor Dongan, in 1686, issued to the city of New York a charter which has been since that time the basis of its municipal government. It has, of course, been subjected to frequent amendment, but the history of New York, as a municipality, may be said to date from the time of its issue. In 1708 another charter, known as the Cornbury charter, was issued to the city, and in 1730 the most important provisions of the Dongan and Cornbury charters were incorporated into a new charter, known as the Montgomerie charter, which was issued to the city by Governor Montgomerie.

Soon after the issue of the charter of 1686 to the city of New York, the city of Philadelphia received a charter, namely, in 1701, from which year may be said to date the history of Philadelphia as a city. During the eighteenth century other charters were issued to various municipal corporations by the governors of the North American colonies. The municipal corporations which were thus established were in the main confined to the central colonies of New York, New Jersey, Pennsylvania, Maryland, and Virginia. We find almost no instances of the formation of municipal corporations in New England.[1]

By 1746 the colonial period of municipal incorporation seems to have closed. The advantages of the system were, however, apparent just as soon as population began to gather in the cities after the Revolutionary War. Beginning with the existence of the states as independent political communities there appeared a large number of new municipal charters; and by the beginning of the nineteenth century the only considerable urban community in the United States which was not incorporated was Boston, which, as late as 1820, continued to govern itself through the ordinary New England town organization.

While the charters that were issued after the Revolution were very similar to those which had been issued during the colonial period, there was this essential difference between them: the colonial charters had been granted by the governors of the colonies; the municipal charters that were issued after the Revolution were granted by the state legislatures. This difference in the incorporating authority was destined to have an important influence on the position of the community that was incorporated. For the charter that was granted by the governor was, like the municipal charter which was granted in England by the crown, regarded as something of the nature of a contract between the executive part of the colonial government and the community incorporated. The municipal charter, on that account, was not believed to be capable of amendment except as the result of an agreement between both parties to the contract. When, however, a charter was granted by the legislature, it was regarded not so much as of the nature of a contract, but as an ordinary act of legislation which, like all acts of legislation, was capable of amendment by the action of the legislature alone.

The municipal corporations which were established in this country during the colonial period departed in one respect from the English model. In very few instances was the council a self-perpetuating body. Indeed, Philadelphia may be said to have been the only important city in which the council was renewed by coöptation. As a general thing the people of the city were permitted by the colonial municipal charters to participate in the choice of local officers. . . . While the people were generally permitted to participate in the selection of municipal officers, no such principle as universal manhood suffrage was adopted. The power to vote for municipal officers was, as a general thing, confined to the well-to-do classes. The usual rule was to grant it to the freemen of the city, being freeholders. Thus in the Montgomerie charter of New York city the suffrage was granted to "the freemen of the

---

1. The probable reason why the idea of incorporating cities was not adopted in New England is to be found in the vitality of the New England town. The town system of government really gave to localities all the freedom of government that they desired, and was well adapted to the needs of the various districts which, until the beginning of the nineteenth century, did not contain any very large population.

said city, being inhabitants and the freeholders of each respective ward."[2]

The municipal organization provided by most of the colonial municipal charters followed very closely the English municipal organization of the eighteenth century. The governing body of the corporation was a council. This council, like the English council of the same period, consisted of a mayor, recorder, and a number of aldermen and councilmen, or assistants. The mayor, however, seems, even in the earliest charters, to have occupied a rather more important position than that which was accorded to the mayor by the English charters. In the first place, he was quite commonly the appointee of the governor of the colony.[3] In the second place, he seems to have had rather wider police powers than any other member of the council. For example, in New York and Albany he had full control of the licensing of the retail sale of liquors, and was the clerk of the markets. It may well be that the greater importance, which the mayor secured, as a result both of the peculiarity of his tenure and the rather wider powers that he possessed, was the cause of his development into the all-important mayor of the present day.

While the council thus composed was the only governing body in the city, certain of its members, namely, the mayor, recorder, and the aldermen were, after the English model, vested with important judicial powers not granted to the other members of the council. The mayor, recorder, and aldermen indeed were, by the charters of some of the cities, of which New York is an example, vested with almost all the judicial powers which were exercised within the limits of the city. The only important exception to this rule was to be found in the powers possessed by the court of the colony occupying a position similar to that of the state supreme court which was the only court of general common law jurisdiction to be found.[4]

The mayor, recorder, aldermen, and councilmen, or assistants, were then to constitute the common council of the colonial municipal corporation. As a general thing provision was made in the royal charters for district representation. For example, the Montgomerie charter of New York provided that one alderman and one assistant were to be elected in each of the wards into

---

2. A word of explanation is perhaps necessary with regard to the freemen of the city. Almost all the colonial charters contained provisions for bestowing the freedom of the city upon persons, either resident or non-resident. The advantages which the freemen of the city possessed in addition to that of voting was that they alone could practice any "art, trade, mystery, or manual occupation, or merchandising business" within the borough, except during the great fair. In some cases this monopoly of trade was a privilege of considerable value. For example, Albany had a monopoly of trade with the Indians, and New York at one time had a monopoly of bolting flour. In the later years of the colonial period, however, these advantages ceased to be of any particular importance, since trades were thrown open to all; and at the present time, while the freedom of the city is sometimes granted to distinguished visitors, it has come to be regarded as nothing but a compliment.

3. In some of the English cities, however, the titular officer corresponding to the early American mayor was appointed either by the crown or by some powerful nobleman.

4. It is perfectly easy to trace in the legislation of the state of New York the development, from these judicial powers of the mayor, recorder, and aldermen, of all of the courts within the city of New York which exercise civil and criminal jurisdiction, outside of the supreme court.

which the city was divided. Apart from the provisions of the charter, with regard to the members of the council, the royal charters did very little toward providing for the detailed organization of the city administration. This was left to the council to arrange by ordinance. . . .

## Original Sphere of Action of American Cities

The sphere of action of these early American municipal corporations was very much the same as that of the English municipal corporation of the same period. This sphere of action was quite narrow when compared with that possessed by the modern American municipal corporation. The functions possessed by the municipal authorities were more of a police and judicial than an administrative character. The judicial functions of certain members of the council have already been considered. The police functions of the council, using the word in its broad sense, were considerable. Thus the council had general authority to pass such ordinances as seemed "to be good, useful, or necessary for the good rule and government of the body corporate," subject merely to the limitation that these ordinances be "not contradictory or repugnant" to the laws of England.

The exercise of this police power, which was theoretically a very large one, was, however, very much limited by the fact that the financial resources of the corporations were very small. Some of the corporations, of which New York was a rather exceptional example, obtained by their charters large property rights, receiving among other things ferry, dock, and wharf rights. But in few instances was the income from the property, which a city possessed, supplemented by the right of local taxation. The result was that the income of these corporations was insufficient to defray the expenses of the very modest kind of municipal government which they carried on and resort had to be had to loans and to municipal lotteries, from whose income the debts which were incurred were discharged. At quite an early time in the history of the colonial corporations, however, the insufficiency of the revenues of the corporations resulted in an application by those bodies to the legislature for the power to levy taxes for specific purposes. The first instance of such an application is said to have been in 1676, when the corporation of New York, on its application, was authorized to levy a tax to pay off debts incurred in rebuilding one of its docks. By the middle of the eighteenth century, however, taxation became a regular source of a considerable part of the revenue of most all the colonial corporations. In some cases the power to tax was granted only for specific purposes; in other cases the power might be exercised for any of the purposes of municipal government, but limits were imposed upon the amount of money which could be raised.

The result of the narrow powers of the colonial municipal corporations was that little or no attention was paid to a long series of matters which we regard at the present time as essential parts of municipal administration. For example, little was done by the corporations to supply the cities with water. All that was usually done was for the council to pass regulations of a police character to prevent the fouling of the wells and pumps from which the people of the city obtained their water. In some cases the council appointed overseers of wells and pumps whose duty it was to keep the wells and pumps in good order. The first city in this country which attempted to establish a model waterworks plant was the city of Albany, which began its work in this direction in 1774. In the same way little or no attention was paid to charities or public schools. In Philadelphia alone was either of these matters under the control of officers provided by the city authorities. Elsewhere the poor officers were separately elected, as a general thing, in close connection with the ecclesiastical organizations, and schools were conducted by private persons or by the churches.

The position of the American municipalities at the end of the colonial period was, then, that of organizations which had been formed for the satisfaction of what were then regarded as the local needs of the district over which the corporation had jurisdiction. The conception of what were local needs was both broader and narrower than it is at the present time. It was broader in that judicial powers were regarded as sufficiently local to be delegated to the cities. During the nineteenth century these judicial powers have very largely been taken by the state into its own administration. The powers of municipal corporations were narrower than they are now, inasmuch as many, if not most, of the matters which receive attention by the municipal corporations of the present time not only did not receive attention but were not regarded as having been given into the charge of the municipal corporations by their charters. The narrowness of their powers and the rather local and *quasi*-private character of these powers were undoubtedly responsible in some degree for the conception which was held by the people of the day, that the municipal corporations were not liable to be controlled to any very great extent by the legislatures of the colonies.

## Change in the Position of American Cities

The nineteenth century brought about great changes, both in the position which the city occupied in the state government, and in the organization of the city for the purpose of discharging the functions which were intrusted to it.

The position of the city has been changed from that of an organization for the satisfaction of local needs to that of a well-recognized agent of state government. The state government of the present time makes use of the city or of its officers as agents for the purposes of general state administration.

In financial matters the city, when of large size, is often made the agent of the state for the assessment and collection of taxes. Indeed, the city itself is often the taxpayer of certain of the state taxes, as for example, the general property tax, and adds the amount, which it pays to the state, to the amount which it collects from the inhabitants for the purpose of paying the expenses of the city. In the colonial period, the state taxes were often collected by state officers acting within the city, but not a part of the general corporate organization. When the system of local taxation was developed, the beginning of which we have already noticed, it seemed advisable, for reasons of convenience and economy, to combine the collection of local and state taxes in the same officers. These officers were naturally the municipal officers, inasmuch as the general system of decentralized administration, which was adopted for the state as a whole, confided the care of such matters to officers chosen directly or indirectly by the localities in which the duties were performed.[5]

What has been said of the tax administration may be said also of other branches of administration, both those which were being attended to by governmental action at the beginning of the nineteenth century, and those which have been developed during the course of the nineteenth century. Thus in cities of large size, in accordance with the principles of decentralized administration, which have been spoken of, the care of the poor has often been vested in the local corporations or officers. The same may be said of education. The schools, which, at first, were really nothing more than private schools, have been made a part of the city administration. The result of this development has been to put the city in the position not merely of an organization for the satisfaction of local needs, but also in that of an agent for the purposes of general state administration.

But while the sphere of the state agency of cities has thus vastly increased, it must not be supposed that their functions as local organizations have not also increased in importance. In the early part of the nineteenth century the city of New York began the construction of the Croton aqueduct. Later on it established a professional police and fire force. About the middle of the century it began the laying out of a park system. The streets were very commonly sewered and paved, and, indeed, by 1850 the whole sphere of municipal activity had extended far beyond the dreams of the city inhabitants of 1800. What was done in New York was very soon copied in other cities, so that at the present time almost all cities of the country, while important agents of state government, have, as a result of the enormous extension of the sphere of distinctly municipal activity, become even more important as organs for the satisfaction of local needs. . . .

---

5. Within the last twenty-five years there has been somewhat of a change in this matter of taxation, and the modern tendency has been in the direction of providing separate taxes for the state, to be collected by its own officers,—taxes, for example, like the corporation tax, the succession tax, or the liquor tax, as in New York,—and a system of local taxation for the cities and other localities, which is put into the hands of local officers.

## Legislative Interference with Cities

This great development of the local side of municipal corporations has not, however, been accompanied by the application of the same principle that seems to have been applied to municipal corporations during the colonial period. It has been pointed out that during that period the corporations were regarded as in very large degree free from central control.[6] But about 1850 the legislatures of the states began to interfere in the government of cities. Undoubtedly one of the reasons for this interference is to be found in the more public character which had been assigned to municipal corporations. Legislative control over cities was the only state control possible under the general administrative system. Legislative control was necessary as to matters in which the cities acted as agents of the state government. Accustomed to interfere in matters which were of interest to the state government, the legislatures failed to distinguish between such matters and matters which were of main, if not of exclusive, interest to the cities themselves. The legislatures were able to carry this interference to the extent to which it was carried because of the adoption of the legal theory that the municipal corporation was a mere creature of the state. Legislative interference became so great, however, that a number of states inserted provisions into the state constitutions which were intended to prevent absolutely all interference with particular matters or to prevent the legislature from adopting certain methods of interference which had proved to be particularly bad. Some states, like the state of New York, inserted in their constitutions provisions securing to municipal corporations the local selection of their own officers. But the most common method which was adopted was to prohibit all special legislation with regard to cities.

## Change in the Organization of Cities

Not only has the position of the city been changed, but also its organization has been subjected to great modification. . . . Soon after the expiration of the first quarter of the nineteenth century, changes were introduced into the original municipal organization which had the result of making it conform to the system of government adopted for the state and the nation.

The result of the application to municipal organization of the principles at the bottom of the state and national governments was, in the first place, the according to the mayor a position similar to that of the governor in the state government, and the president in the national government. Thus the mayor was to be chosen by the people and not by the state governor or city

---

6. For example, Judge Spencer of the New York Supreme Court, said (Mayor *v.* Ordrenan, 12 Johns., 125) that it was the almost invariable course of procedure for the legislature not to interfere in the internal affairs of a corporation without its consent.

council. Popular election was provided in Boston and St. Louis in 1822 and in Detroit in 1824. In 1834 the mayor of New York became elective, and at the present time the principle of an elective mayor may be regarded as permanently adopted in the municipal system of the United States. In the second place, the council was treated as if it occupied a position in the city government similar to that of the legislature in the state and national governments. The council was quite frequently made to consist of two chambers. The only reason for the change that can be found is the desire to model the council upon the state legislature. . . .

By the first quarter of the nineteenth century, then, the municipal organization which had been developed was of a type modeled very closely upon the system of government in the state and the nation, and consisted of a mayor, who was elected by popular vote, and had very commonly a veto power over the resolutions of the council similar to that possessed by the president and state governor over the acts of Congress and the state legislature respectively, and a council, also elected by popular vote, which was frequently composed of two chambers.

This system of government was not, however, a satisfactory one. Prior to the making of these changes in the municipal organization, the complaints against the council were neither frequent nor severe. Very soon after the change was made they increased both in number and in vehemence. About this time the great national parties were developing throughout the country as a whole, and were reaching out in every direction for means by which to increase their power. There was no branch of the government whose possession could so much increase the power of political parties as the city governments. All the cities had, as compared with the other districts in the country, large numbers of officers and employees, and all were spending a large proportion of the money which was spent by the governmental authorities of the country. Either because of the inefficiency of the city governments, which certainly became quite marked soon after 1850, or because of the desire of the political parties to get control of the city governments in order to increase their power in the state and nation, changes were made in the system of city government as it existed in 1850, which resulted in the ushering in of a new period in the development of municipal organization in the United States. This new system we may speak of as the board system.

## Board System of City Government

As we originally find it, the board system was little more than a system of boards independent of the city council. The origin of the system is probably to be found in the New York charter of 1849. This made provision for independent executive departments and for taking from the council almost all administrative power. The reasons for the change were somewhat the same as those for the establishment of the mayor in a position of independence over against the council. That is, it was desired to model the city organization on that of the state and national government. The influence of the democratic spirit, so prevalent about the middle of the nineteenth century, is seen in the provision of the charter of 1849, that the heads of the new executive departments were to be elected by the people of the city. The election of the heads of these departments was seen at once to be unsatisfactory, and by the charter of 1853 the power was given to the mayor to appoint, subject to the approval of the city council, the heads of all departments except the comptroller, and the corporation counsel. The example set by New York was followed by other cities. Thus Cleveland provided for elective departments in 1852; Detroit, in 1857.

Soon after the adoption of this board system, however, the legislatures of the states began to provide for the state appointment of the members of city boards. This custom on the part of the legislature began just before 1860. The first point of attack was the police department. Later on the attempt was made to introduce this system into other branches of municipal administration.

By about 1860 it may be said that in all the important cities of the United States the most important parts of the city governments were in the hands of boards largely independent of the council, the members of which were in some instances appointed by the central state government, in some instances by the mayors of the cities, either acting alone or in conjunction with the city councils, and in some cases elected by the people of the city. At the time that this system was at its height, the members of these boards were not only independent of the council, but were also practically independent of the mayor. They were independent of the mayor even where he appointed them. For, as a general thing, they could not be removed from office by the mayor except for cause. This meant that they could be removed only as the result of charges and after a hearing, and the determination of the removing authority was subject to the review of the courts.

The result of the introduction of this system was completely to disorganize the municipal administration. Each important branch of city government was attended to by a board or officer practically independent of any other municipal authority. No one mayor, because of the shortness of his term as compared with that of these officers and the members of these boards, could appoint all the city officers or all the members of any one board. The result was that the municipal organization consisted of a collection of independent authorities, and that the mayor, where the right of local appointment was secured to him, was merely an officer who could fill vacancies in the various offices which happened to occur during his term.

Finally, it is to be noticed that frequently the acts of the legislature establishing these municipal boards or commissions, provided for what are sometimes called non-partisan, at other times bi-partisan, commissions. The provision for the bi-partisan or non-partisan board took one of two forms: It was enacted either that no more than a certain number, either half or a bare majority of the members, should belong to the same political party, or that half of the members of the board should belong to each of the two leading political parties. This common provision in the acts establishing the board system is an indication that one of the reasons for its establishment was the desire of the political parties to secure the influence which resulted from the possession of power in the city administration.[7]

We may say, then, that by the year 1860 the council had in most of the larger American cities ceased to be anything more than a legislative body in the city government. It had lost all its original administrative functions. These had been assumed, in the first place, by the mayor, and, in the second place, by the officers and boards, to which reference has just been made. The council had lost also important legislative powers. Among the important legislative powers which the council lost was the power it possessed, under the original charters, of organizing the details of the city administration. This power had been lost because of the fact that the new charters and acts of the legislature regulating the city government went into great detail. The assumption by the legislature of this former power of the city council had extremely bad effects. It resulted, in the first place, in the regulation of the details of city government by an authority which had little knowledge of the needs of the city. This authority was often governed in its action not by considerations which had anything to do with the welfare of the city, but by considerations of partisan politics. In the second place, the regulation of the details of municipal organization by the legislature offered a constant temptation and opportunity to interfere in matters which properly should have been left to the municipality to regulate. It cannot be doubted that the introduction of this board system, accompanied, as it was, by the assumption by the legislature of the power to regulate the details of city organization, was one of the chief causes for the great extension of the control of the legislature over municipal affairs generally.

## Mayor System of City Government

But about 1880 the people of the United States seem to have awakened to the fact that the board system did not work satisfactorily; that it diffused responsibility for municipal action; that it made it impossible for the people, at any given municipal election, to exercise any appreciable control over the municipal government, and that it offered a continual temptation to the legislature to interfere in the affairs of the city. The result was an attempt to change again the municipal organization. The changes that were introduced into the system, beginning with about the year 1880, may be said to have ushered in a new period of municipal development, which we may call the mayor period. The first modification of the board system which was

7. See Wilcox, "Party Government in Cities" in "Political Science Quarterly," XIV, p. 681.

made in any important city charter was made in the charter of the city of Brooklyn about the year 1882. By this charter, the mayor was given the right, within twenty days after assuming office, to appoint new heads of the executive departments. The example of Brooklyn was followed by the city of New York in the year 1895. As a result of the continued success of one political party at the city elections in the years preceding 1895, all of the boards and offices of the city were practically controlled by adherents of this organization. In 1894 this organization was defeated at the polls after a campaign of great interest and excitement. It was felt by the people of the city and by the legislature of the state that, under existing conditions, the new administration could not represent the wishes of the people who had put it into power, and therefore a law was passed in 1895 giving to the mayor the right, within six months after assuming his office, to remove the heads of departments from office arbitrarily and not subject to the review of the courts.

In the meantime the mayor had received an absolute power of appointment in a number of cities, among which was the city of New York, being relieved from the necessity of obtaining the consent of the council to his appointments. Later on a number of cities, to which the city of New York was added by its recent charter of 1901, adopted the principle of arbitrary removal by the mayor throughout his entire term. The change in the municipal organization which has just been outlined was accompanied in many instances by the substitution of single commissioners for boards as department heads. The single commissioner was regarded as a necessary part of the original Brooklyn plan.

This system of city government we may call the mayor system of government. It is characterized by the fact that the mayor is vested with the absolute power of appointing and removing most of the important municipal officers. The mayor system may possibly be regarded as the coming system in the United States. But it cannot be said that it has been generally adopted throughout the country. Indeed, it is difficult to say what at the present time is the American type of municipal government. Most of the charters of the cities of the United States show the influences of the different periods of municipal development which have been outlined. Thus we find in a number of cities that the council still has a great deal of power. We find again, in a number, independent departments, the heads of which in some cases are elected by the people of the city in accordance with the ideas of democratic government so prevalent about 1850, in other cases, appointed by the central government of the state, in other cases, but in the majority of cases, appointed by the mayor and confirmed by the council. . . .

## The City a Creature of the State Legislature

The character of our administrative system has several important effects on the position of the city. In the first place, the city is made by the system the creature of the state legislature. In the absence of a constitutional restriction the legislature of the state may do as it will with the cities within its jurisdiction. The charters of cities are at the present time regarded as mere statutes, which, in the absence of a constitutional limitation of the powers of the legislature, are subject to amendment by that body at any time.

The legislature then has, under our system of government, the absolute legal right to regulate municipal affairs as it sees fit. It has not only the legal right, it has also had in the past the moral right to interfere in city government. For the city became, during the course of the nineteenth century, an agent of the state government. The city has ceased to be what it once was, merely an organization for the satisfaction of local needs, and has become as well an important member of the general state governmental system. Our system of decentralized administration did not permit of the exercise by any state administrative authority of any control over the city, even where it was thus acting as an agent of the state. It was necessary, therefore, if any central control at all should be exercised, that it should be exercised by the legislature.

## The City an Authority of Enumerated Powers

In the second place, the city, in the absence of a constitutional provision, has no powers not granted to it by the legislature.[8]

It may be added that the legislatures of the states have not granted wide powers to the cities, but have generally enumerated in greater or less detail the powers which cities may exercise. Thus when the city of New York wished to build and lease a rapid-transit railway it had no power to do so, and had to apply to the legislature for the necessary authority. Thus again when it wished to establish a municipal electric-lighting plant, it had no power. When it applied to the legislature for authority in this instance its application was denied.

---

8. No better or more authoritative statement of the powers possessed by the municipal corporations in the United States can be found than that given by Judge Dillon in his great work on municipal corporations and approved by many of the later decisions of the courts themselves (Dillon, "Law of Municipal Corporations," 4th ed., p. 145). He says: "It is a general and undisputed proposition of law that a municipal corporation possesses and can exercise the following powers and no others: First, those granted in express words; second, those necessarily or fairly implied in or incident to the powers expressly granted; third, those essential to the declared objects and purposes of the corporation—not simply convenient but indispensable. Any fair reasonable doubt concerning the existence of power is resolved by the courts against the corporation and the power is denied. Of every municipal corporation the charter or statute by which it is created is its organic act. Neither the corporation nor its officers can do any act, or make any contract, or incur any liability not authorized thereby or by some legislative act applicable thereto. All acts beyond the scope of the powers granted are void." Judge Dillon adds that while the rule "of strict construction of corporate powers is not so directly applicable to the ordinary clauses in charters or incorporating acts of municipalities as it is to the charters of private corporations . . . it is equally applicable to grants of powers to municipal and public bodies which are out of the usual range or which may result in public burdens or which in their exercise touch the right of liberty or property or, as it may be compendiously expressed, any common law right of the citizen or inhabitant" (*ibid.*, p. 148).

In the third place, whatever may be the theoretical power of the city to enter upon any particular branch of governmental activity, the financial powers which it possesses are so limited that it is practically unable to exercise the powers of which it may be possessed without the grant to it by the legislature of the necessary financial power. That is, the American law recognizes the taxing power, from whose exercise most of the city's revenues must come, as a power of state government possessed alone by the state legislature. The city certainly does not possess it in the absence of legislative grant. The American law also does not accord to cities large powers of borrowing money in the absence of legislative authorization. In many cases the legislature has been as niggardly in its grants to cities of financial powers as it has been in the grants of other powers. . . .

## Cities Have Lost Their Autonomy

It has been said that the exercise of its powers by the legislature has deprived cities of their power of local government. The result has come about in the following way: No legislature is far-seeing enough to be able to determine for all time what powers it may be expedient for a city to exercise. No legislature, even under the régime of special city charters, can give a particular city powers which will be permanently satisfactory so long as these powers are enumerated in detail. The conditions, economic and otherwise, upon which city governments are based, are continually changing. As a result of these changing conditions American cities are forced to apply continually to the legislature for new and extended local powers. Such powers are often granted retrospectively through the exercise of the power the legislature possesses to ratify illegal action.

The necessity of changing and extending local powers has brought about an immense amount of special legislation, and the legislature, accustomed to regulate by special act municipal affairs on the proposition of the various cities, and obliged to exercise through special legislation the necessary central control over matters attended to by cities which are of vital interest to the state as a whole, has got into the habit of passing special legislation with regard to purely municipal matters of its own motion not only without the consent of the local people, but often against their will, and for reasons in many cases in no way connected with their local welfare. The condition of things which has resulted from this habit of the legislature is one about which there is no difference of opinion. In those states where such central interference has been most marked the people of the cities have very largely lost interest in the municipal government, and whenever they desire to see some concrete municipal policy adopted their point of attack is the state legislature rather than any local and municipal organ. In New York city, for example, the people have become so accustomed to this method of action that they regard it as perfectly natural and normal.

The loss of local government by the cities and the resulting lack of interest of municipal citizens in the conduct of city affairs are not, however, the worst results of the actual position which the city occupies in the American political system. More serious is the fact that owing to this position it is practically impossible to secure a solution of any one of our municipal problems uninfluenced by the consideration of the effect which the solution proposed may have on questions of state and national politics.

# A REAPPRAISAL OF CONSTITUTIONAL HOME RULE

## THE CHICAGO HOME RULE COMMISSION

CONSTITUTIONAL HOME RULE, as an abstract political concept, has an undeniably attractive appeal as a technique of establishing desirable state-city relationships. That cities should have the legal power of "self-government" or the power "to regulate their own affairs" or "to conduct local government in accordance with the wishes and demands of the governed" is a principle of broad content with which it is difficult to disagree. Limited as this abstract concept is to the legal power of cities to act with independence and initiative, with freedom from irksome legislative controls, in the area of municipal affairs only, and recognizing as it does the supremacy of the state in matters in which the state may have a paramount concern, the political concept of home rule may be said to reflect a meritorious and desirable policy of power allocation between the state and its municipalities.

When, however, the abstract political concept of constitutional home rule is weighed against the legal concepts of constitutional home rule, as these have been set out in state constitutions and court decisions, the disparities are strikingly evident. The diversity of constitutional home-rule provisions; the customary reservations of constitutional and legislative restraint upon the exercise of municipal power, particularly in the all-important area of revenue; and the futility, politically and judicially conceded, of attempting to draw a sharp division between municipal or local affairs or concerns and matters of state concern—all these factors which have been previously analyzed in detail—combine to effect a dilution of the political concept of constitutional home rule to an extent which renders it a symbol almost wholly devoid of substantive content and meaning. To heighten the paradox, sincere protagonists of constitutional home rule continue to view its political concept

Reprinted from *Modernizing a City Government* (Chicago: University of Chicago Press, 1954), pp. 309–314.

and legal expressions as identical, with mutually consistent objectives capable of attainment. This view is apparently the result of a failure to come to grips with the basic difficulties inherent in the reconciliation of both concepts.

Thus, in the 1948 National Municipal Policy Statement of the American Municipal Association, the declaration is made that cities "should have the right to decide for themselves what services they require, without asking for state permission for each new undertaking," and, further, "that cities should have the authority to raise revenues from any local sources, without being required to beg for funds to pay for the services they need."

This challenging doctrine is then followed by the statement that, "while no municipality can have complete autonomy, the cities should have the maximum local authority consistent with their positions as constituent elements in a sovereign state." The coalition of these statements—the first expressing the need for a maximization of municipal autonomy and the second, recognizing that complete autonomy is unattainable, is indicative of the lack of preciseness of definition which confounds the problem. Does the first statement imply that any new services which a city may desire to undertake must be within the exclusive power of local determination, without regard to the doctrines of state concern or state pre-emption or the question of conflict with state laws? More importantly, and conceding for the purpose of analysis that a new service may unquestionably fall within the area of municipal affairs and that there exists no question of conflict with a state law, does the statement respecting the power to finance the service imply complete autonomy in the revenue field? More specifically, does it argue against the propriety of property tax-rate limitations or indebtedness limitations, the application of which may prevent the undertaking of the new service? If so, there is no indication that such is the intent. If not, to what extent should the power of self-determination be subject to such restrictions? If the statement implies power to utilize non-property revenue sources, is this power to be exercised with regard to any subject or object of taxation permissible under constitutional principles, with complete municipal freedom in the establishment of tax rates? Does it deny the validity of any legislatively imposed restraints, either as to subjects or rates of taxation, or of any legislatively prescribed limitations on the appropriation or expenditure of tax funds so raised? If so, the intention is not clearly expressed in view of the concession that complete autonomy is unattainable. If not, to what extent are such limitations desirable?

The questions posed are not irrelevant. Nor are they intended to suggest either the desirability or the undesirability of legislative restrictions on municipal revenue powers. They do, however, point out the areas of uncertainty and ambiguity which surround the abstract concept of constitutional home rule. Until these questions are resolved and the ambiguities removed, generalizations concerning municipal autonomy are largely meaningless.

This conclusion applies with equal force to municipal powers other than revenue. Until recently, the consensus of constitutional home-rule theorists was that the grant of power should be couched in general terms for fear that a detailing of specific powers would be restrictively construed by the courts to deny local authority in areas not specified. With the unhappy experience resulting from that technique, a modification in viewpoint is now evident, as indicated by the following extract from the report of the Committee on State-Local Relations of the Council of State Governments:

> It is difficult . . . to separate state from local functions. A complete specific enumeration of powers to be exercised by home rule cities is therefore impossible. Nevertheless, it seems both possible and highly desirable that some specified powers be given to localities in addition to the general grant of authority over local affairs. Rather than leaving the entire field of home rule powers to the definition of the courts, there seems no valid reason why an enumeration of powers cannot be conferred upon cities in every home rule state. In the process of this enumeration, those powers which have been the cause of the greatest litigation in the past could be carefully considered. *As a matter of public policy, they can be granted or denied to home rule localities.*[1]

Note here, also, the fatal gap. The specific powers which have been the cause of the greatest litigation are those in respect to which there is the most controversy and the least measure of agreement. These include, among others, powers of taxation for local purposes, health, sanitation, regulation of private utilities, eminent domain, and the settlement of claims against a city. It is these powers which, after careful consideration *and as a matter of public policy,* are to be granted or denied.

The question arises immediately as to what agency or group is to make this crucial determination as a matter of public policy. Is it to be the legislature? A charter commission? A panel of governmental or public administration experts in state-local relations? What criteria are they to employ in making their determinations? Will there be any assurance that their determinations will be more valid than the conflicting determinations of the courts and that they will be any less the subject of controversy? These and many other relevant questions remain unanswered in the general statement respecting the proposed change in the method of specifying constitutional home-rule powers.

Again, the point is made that there is no quarrel with the general objectives of that report. It is in the translation of the general objectives into a definitive and meaningful constitutional concept that the difficulty lies. Until this is done, if it can be done, there is little hope that constitutional home rule will be any more effective an instrumentality in aid of municipal autonomy than it has been in the past.

The most recent attempt to redefine the constitutional home-rule concept is worthy of note as a further illustration of the extreme difficulty of investing it with any attributes of certainty. In a draft prepared by Professor Fordham for the Committee on Home Rule of the American Municipal

---

1. The Council of State Governments, *State-Local Relations* (1946), pp. 171, 172 (italics ours).

Association,[2] municipalities would have complete autonomy in respect to "executive, legislative and administrative structure, organization, personnel, and procedure" (the areas in which constitutional home rule provisions have been most effective in establishing the supremacy of municipal laws), subject only to the requirement that the members of the legislative body be chosen by popular vote and to a further exception respecting judicial review of administrative proceedings. In the area of substantive powers, the draft proposes the abandonment of the technique of granting general and specific powers and offers a "local federalism" formula which would authorize a city adopting a home rule charter under constitutional authority to "exercise any power or perform any function which the legislature has power to devolve upon a non-home rule charter municipal corporation and which is not denied to . . . [the home-rule city] by its . . . charter, *is not denied to all home rule charter [cities] by statute and is within such limitations as may be established by statute.*" (italics ours).

This proposal is designed to effect a shift in power distribution by placing the burden upon the legislature, by general laws applicable to all home-rule cities, to deny cities the authority to exercise any given power. Cities would no longer be dependent upon an express grant of power but could operate freely within the total area of municipal power, except as proscribed by the legislature. Whether such a proposal would effect its objective of expanded powers of local self-determination will depend entirely upon the legislature's desires. If, for example, the legislature enacts a general law prohibiting the exercise of any taxing power, excepting those expressly delegated by statute, a not inconceivable prospect in many states, municipal autonomy will be largely an illusion.

Other areas of uncertainty remain unresolved. Is it, for example, politically desirable as a concept of state-city relationships that the constitutional grant of home-rule powers be made subject to legislative implementation, definition, or restriction in the manner which prevails in West Virginia, Michigan, Pennsylvania, and Louisiana? Or should the grant be defined as "self-executing," emanating from the constitution and vesting in the people of the city directly, to be by them, rather than the legislature, translated into the definitive powers which their city government may exercise? This is the theory which sustains the extensive municipal autonomy of California cities in revenue matters and which supports the more limited autonomy in revenue matters enjoyed by cities in Ohio and Missouri.

A related, but highly significant, aspect of this inquiry concerns the legal character of the charter adopted by constitutional home-rule cities. Should the charter be viewed as a grant of powers by the people to their government, or should it be viewed as a limitation upon their government's powers? The legal consequences flowing from this distinction are of extreme importance in

2. Jefferson Fordham, *Model Constitutional Provisions for Municipal Home Rule* (Chicago: American Municipal Association, 1953).

respect to the measure of autonomy vested in the city government. Thus, as we have seen, California views the locally adopted charter, in revenue matters, as a limitation on power, and the crucial inquiry in respect to the exercise of a particular tax power is not whether the charter expressly permits such exercise but whether it proscribes it. On the other hand, in Texas and Missouri, among other states, the charter is viewed as a grant of powers, and the exercise of any specific tax power must be referable to an express grant. In the latter states, broadly defined grants of revenue powers have been held insufficient to sustain municipally imposed taxes, and city governments have found it necessary to seek authority from the legislature. This concept of constitutional home rule places municipalities in substantially the same legal position as municipalities in nonconstitutional home-rule states.

In respect to these issues, most of the political and legal literature on the subject of constitutional home rule is either silent or obscure—a further indication of the vagueness and uncertainty which underlies the concept. The failure to resolve these issues, in accordance with criteria and standards upon which a substantial political consensus may be reached, will continue to plague the development of constitutional home rule as a meaningful concept.

# THE REAPPORTIONMENT MYTH

### ROBERT S. FRIEDMAN

FOR A GREAT MANY YEARS those concerned with the problems of large cities have cited urban underrepresentation in state legislatures as a major stumbling block to the realization of the demands of city fathers. Preoccupation with this solution to the unrequited interests of city government has been almost paranoiac. In nearly every legislative session in states containing large cities, metropolitan representatives have introduced legislation to rectify the malapportionment.[1] Almost as frequently their efforts are thwarted.

As a result only four major cities in the United States—Chicago, Boston, Milwaukee and New Orleans—have obtained representation at all commensurate with their 1950 population. Nevertheless, rapid changes are

Reprinted from *National Civic Review*, April, 1960, pp. 184–188, by permission of the publisher.

1. Malapportionment is here defined as anything short of equal representation on the basis of population. There are, of course, many people who believe that area, political subdivision boundaries, citizens, voters and other criteria are more equitable. For a discussion of theories of representation see *Public and Republic* by Alfred de Grazia. Alfred E. Knopf, Inc., New York, 1951.

taking place in the distribution of our urban population. These should bring to a head what is really a long needed reappraisal by city governments of the value of expending a great deal of energy upon reapportionment as a solution to city problems with respect to intergovernmental affairs.

This is not to be misconstrued as a plea against reapportionment. Apportionment on the basis of population is defensible regardless of whether people live in cities, suburbs or farms. It is instead a plea for understanding of what are practicable techniques for the realization of city needs.

In spite of the tremendous proportional increase of urban population in the United States large cities with few exceptions have generally shown no increase and in fact have shown a percentage decline. As noted in Table I only two of the nation's fourteen largest cities (excluding Washington) displayed a percentage increase between 1950 and 1959. Even in one of these instances a large annexation program played a role in the change.

### Table I

#### Population Change in Fourteen Largest Cities In United States[a]

| City | Percentage of State Population 1950 Census | Percentage of State Population 1959 Estimate |
|------|-------------------------------------------|---------------------------------------------|
| New York | 53.2 | 46.6 |
| Chicago | 41.5 | 39.1 |
| Philadelphia | 19.7 | 19.4 |
| Los Angeles | 18.6 | 16.0 |
| Detroit | 29.0 | 24.7 |
| Baltimore | 40.5 | 32.4 |
| Cleveland | 11.5 | 10.0 |
| St. Louis | 21.7 | 20.2 |
| Boston | 17.1 | 14.9 |
| San Francisco | 7.3 | 5.4 |
| Pittsburgh | 6.4 | 6.1 |
| Milwaukee | 18.5 | 19.6 |
| Houston | 7.7 | 9.8 |
| Buffalo | 3.9 | 3.6 |
| Minneapolis | 17.5 | 16.6 |

a Source, *Sales Management,* Annual Survey of Buying Power.

In some cases declines have been substantial. New York City, for example, now has less than 50 per cent of the state population for the first time in many years, decreasing from approximately 53 per cent in 1950 to less than 47 per cent in 1959. Most dramatic decrease is unquestionably Baltimore which fell from 40.5 per cent to just over 32 per cent in the 1959 estimate. In both these cases as well as others city population has stabilized and adjacent urban counties have grown tremendously.

The net result is that it is no longer cities which are the chief victims of underrepresentation but suburbia. To illustrate this we need only examine four instances where city and suburbia are sharply declineated by county lines—see Table II.

## Table II
### City-Suburban Representation in Selected Metropolitan Areas[a]

| State and Subdivision | Percentage of State Population 1950 Census | Percentage of State Population 1959 Estimate | Percentage of State House of Representatives | Percentage of State Senate |
|---|---|---|---|---|
| **New York** | | | | |
| New York City | 53.2 | 46.6 | 43.3 | 43.1 |
| Nassau Co. | 4.5 | 7.8 | 4.0 | 5.2 |
| Suffolk Co. | 1.9 | 3.6 | 2.0 | 1.7 |
| Westchester Co. | 4.2 | 4.7 | 4.0 | 5.2 |
| **Maryland** | | | | |
| Baltimore City | 40.5 | 32.4 | 29.3 | 20.7 |
| Anne Arundel Co. | 5.0 | 6.1 | 4.9 | 3.4 |
| Baltimore Co. | 11.5 | 15.0 | 4.9 | 3.4 |
| Montgomery Co. | 7.0 | 10.2 | 4.9 | 3.4 |
| Prince George's Co. | 8.3 | 11.6 | 4.9 | 3.4 |
| **Missouri** | | | | |
| St. Louis City | 21.7 | 20.2 | 11.5 | 20.5 |
| St. Louis Co. | 10.3 | 14.3 | 5.7 | 8.8 |
| **Louisiana** | | | | |
| New Orleans | 21.3 | 21.1 | 19.8 | 20.5 |
| Jefferson Parish | 3.9 | 5.6 | 2.0 | 2.6[b] |

a Source, *Sales Management*, Annual Survey of Buying Power.
b Shared with two other parishes.

In all four instances the central city receives reasonable representation in at least one house if the 1959 estimate is used as a standard. In the case of New York, city representation is not out of line in either house. The picture is vastly different for the suburbs. Of the four metropolitan areas, only in New York did the suburbs obtain representation proportionate to 1950 population in both houses. When the 1959 estimates are used some of the distortions afford as great inequities as some of the more notorious injustices perpetrated on large cities in the past.

Oftentimes suburban inequities are accentuated by constitutional restriction. In Maryland, for example, representation has been frozen by a 1943 constitutional amendment. Despite the fact that Maryland amending procedure and political habit permit numerous constitutional changes there is no assurance that "overrepresented" areas will agree to an alteration of the status quo.

In Louisiana constitutional provisions limit the total number of members in each house in such a way as to make reapportionment favorable to Jefferson Parish extremely difficult.[2] This pattern has been repeated throughout the country. In some instances its ramifications are not as readily dis-

2. The constitution limits the House of Representatives to 101 members. Of these 80 are assigned one to each of the parishes and the seventeen wards of New Orleans. Only 21 are available for distribution by population. This leaves little maneuverability, especially since Baton Rouge and Shreveport are also experiencing growth.

cernible because a portion of the suburban area is within the same county as the central city although beyond city limits.

Regardless of what the future holds with respect to equitable apportionment the cities must now reexamine solutions to problem areas in their relations with states. No city has ever had a majority in either house of its state legislature despite the fact that several have at times had a majority of their state's population. New census figures will almost surely show that no central city is entitled to such representation on the basis of population even though some standard metropolitan areas are.

It is of course true that on many issues involving such matters as water supply, sewage disposal, public safety, highways, planning, etc., cities and suburbs have much in common and underrepresentation of suburbia is as detrimental to the central city as to the suburb. It is equally obvious, however, that there are interests of cities which are diametrically opposed to those of suburbia. As a result, reapportionment even if favorable to suburbia will not solve the problems of the central city in all respects. In fact in such matters as distribution of state funds to localities it might even hurt.

Old notions die hard, however. For example, the four large urban centers in Tennessee have complained of discrimination in the state's system of distributing funds for educational purposes. One of the proposals offered for compelling a reexamination of the formula is legislative reapportionment designed to remove inequities resulting from urban expansion. Because of unyielding opposition to reapportionment in the legislature a suit was brought to force action but was lost.[3]

Even if the cities had scored a victory in the courts they would not have been entitled to numerical control of either house of the legislature. The combined population of the four counties in which these cities are located was less than 40 per cent of the state total in 1950 and, despite proportionate increases in the population of the four big urban counties since 1950, any reapportionment agreed to by the legislature would leave the urban areas short of the magic 51 per cent of the total membership of the legislature.

The frustration of our cities is perhaps best exemplified by an illustration of the inability of a city administration to obtain accommodation of its interests in spite of reasonable representation and a long tradition of local legislation. (In the operation of the local legislation system the state legislature accedes to the wishes of the local delegates where the latter are in agreement.) The city administration which has governed New Orleans since 1946 long supported an urban renewal program. Despite this, state legislation has been enacted negating such a program by narrowing the meaning of public purpose under the power of eminent domain so as not to permit the city to dispose of expropriated property to private builders for redevelopment. The legislation was clearly designed to kill the mayor's program but it would

---

3. See the *National Civic Review*, February 1960, page 87.

be difficult to attribute this to urban-rural animosity or even antagonism to New Orleans as such. The opposition was led by a combination of forces which opposed the mayor and his program within the city and which opposed him on the state level as a result of his forays into gubernatorial politics.

The large cities are unquestionably the victims of a paradox. The United States is becoming an overwhelmingly urban nation, but an increasing number of urban dwellers seem to prefer not to live within large cities. Therefore, cities can no longer appeal to numerical strength alone to win struggles on the state level and failure to obtain reapportionment ceases to be a satisfactory smoke screen for legislative defeats.

It would seem that the decline in numerical strength of cities, which is taking place at an accelerated pace, ought to afford a splendid opportunity for those concerned with the welfare of cities to reappraise their problems vis-a-vis other governmental units and turn to more effective methods for achieving their solution. This is not to suggest the abandonment of support for reapportionment but a plea for the redirection of emphasis.

One of the most apparent solutions is municipal home rule. Meaningful home rule, however, must include more than the opportunity to determine government form. It must also carry with it power to effectuate substantive governmental programs unfettered by crippling restrictions. In this connection a central issue is control over finances. New York City, for example, has been granted home rule in a manner of speaking, but limitations on revenue sources are so restrictive as to place it at the mercy of state authorities.[4]

Similarly New Orleans has been the recipient of the benefits of a home rule provision but state constitutional limitations on its debt authority are so restrictive as to circumscribe seriously its capital improvement program. Alterations in restrictions such as these should be given priority in state legislative programs of city leaders. In states where traditions of local legislation persist, intelligent cultivation of legislative leaders can overcome rural numerical majorities. Additional efforts should be made to develop systems of distribution of state funds to localities which take into account mushrooming city needs in the face of a proportional decline in the property tax base of most cities.

Perhaps, because of the tremendous complexities of the problem, these efforts should be directed even to the creation of state administrative bodies for this purpose. With respect to metropolitan area problems, renewed efforts should be made to obtain permissive legislation affording solutions ranging from cooperation among all political subdivisions within given urban areas to unified metropolitan government.

To implement these solutions numerous techniques are available includ-

4. See, for example, "Notes on the Formation of State-Municipal Fiscal Policy: Chicago and New York," by Gilbert Y. Steiner. *Political Science Quarterly*, September 1955, page 387.

ing such familiar methods as the activity of state and national organizations to represent city interests, efforts by city administrators to cement cordial relations with the local delegation to the legislature, informal sessions with suburban leaders to deal with common problems, direct entreaties to the governor and his subordinates, etc.

These problem areas and techniques for solving them are, of course, suggestive rather than all encompassing. The important point for city fathers to recognize is that minority status within the state legislature is likely to remain permanent whether reapportionment takes place or not. And city interests can best be served by recognizing this and operating from this vantage point.

# A PAINFUL CASE OF REDISTRICTING

## MARK K. ADAMS

IN THE LANDSLIDE ELECTION of 1958 the Democrats gained complete control of Massachusetts for the first time in history. The Senate, a Republican bastion because of gerrymandered districts that combined halves and thirds of Democratic cities with enough surrounding GOP towns to offset the urban votes, went Democratic 24–16; the House and Governorship had been Democratic since 1954 and 1956.

The Democrats were gleeful. Now they could redraw the boundaries of Congressional and of state House and Senate districts without having to contend with a Republican-dominated Senate. If they were clever, they could assure themselves control of the state for many years to come. A Republican governor might be elected now and then, to be sure, but the Democrats could assure themselves of a two-thirds majority in the Senate, and this would be enough to override a governor's vetoes.

Late in the 1959 session of the General Court, a twelve-man Special Commission on Redistricting was formed of ten Democratic and two Republican legislators. It was to prepare reapportionment plans for the 1960 legislative session. Four of its Democratic members were from Boston.

Conflict between Boston and non-Boston Democrats developed almost immediately and this made it necessary to limit the scope of redistricting. Plans to reapportion state House districts were dropped when it became apparent that Boston would lose six or seven of its 41 seats. The four Boston Commission members, despite pressure from chairman Senator Maurice

Reprinted from *A Report on Politics in Boston* (Cambridge: Joint Center for Urban Studies of the Massachusetts Institute of Technology and Harvard University, 1960), by permission of the publishers and of the author.

Donahue, joined the Republicans to deadlock the Commission 6–6. This killed House redistricting.

Party factionalism also helped kill Congressional reapportionment plans. The Commission recommended a redistricting that would reduce the number of Congressional districts from 14 to 12, with two candidates running at large. The justification for that was that two seats would probably be lost because of the 1960 Census. The districts of Republicans Edith Nourse Rogers, a widow who had represented a Middlesex county district northwest of Boston for 35 years, and Laurence Curtis, who represented the Newton-Brookline-Boston district that had been created for Christian Herter, were the two chosen for extinction.

Although it pleased many metropolitan Democrats, especially those who hoped to benefit from the elmination of the Curtis district, the redistricting plan met substantial party opposition. Governor Furcolo, never on good terms with Boston Democrats and reluctant to see their strength increase, expressed a fear that the two at-large representatives "would both come from the same ward in South Boston." John W. McCormack of Boston, Democratic floor leader in the U.S. House, opposed the plan because he believed voters would resent the liquidation of Mrs. Rogers. Finally Congressional redistricting was postponed until after the 1960 Census.

Only the state Senate was left for redistricting. Senate redistricting plans, too, ran into strong Democratic opposition. Senate President Powers said the Democrats might better "leave well enough alone" and not tamper with districts they already held. Senator Michael LoPresti and others from impregnable Democratic districts in Boston feared that changes would make possible defeat in future primaries. Senator William C. Madden of Lexington charged that Commission members from Boston were trying to make certain non-Boston Democratic legislators dependent on votes from MTA communities in order to increase the power of the MTA bloc in the General Court. The pet plan of veteran Commission member Representative John J. Toomey of Cambridge to have his city represented by one senator (it was divided among four) was violently opposed by three Democratic Senators who depended on Cambridge wards in their primary fights.

The Commission's plan for Senate redistricting was killed when it became apparent that at least four Democratic Senators (LoPresti of East Boston, McCann of Cambridge, Corbett of Somerville, and Madden of Lexington) would join a united Republican minority to defeat it in the Senate.

Pressure for Senate redistricting remained strong, however, led by the six Democratic Senators (one among whom was Richard R. Caples, from Boston) who had won election in 1958 by less than 4,000 votes. Those who favored redistricting won an important ally when John Powers, who may have feared a primary challenge after his defeat in the Boston Mayoralty election, endorsed redistricting in order to add a "safe" ward to his district. A surprise victory by a Republican in a special election in a hitherto impregnable Democratic Senate district in New Bedford increased the pressure for redistricting among panicky Democrats who began to fear they might lose control of the Senate in the 1960 elections. At the request of alarmed Democrats, the Commission's redistricting plans were referred to the Senate Rules Committee for revisions that would obtain the united support of the Senate Democratic majority.

The Rules Committee first took care of its Democratic members by re-drawing district lines to give them safe constituencies. Then it re-divided Cambridge among four Senators to win their support. The Boston Democrats were not allowed to make non-Boston Senators dependent upon MTA district votes for election, but were satisfied by ward shuffling. Democratic Senator Caples was given Cambridge Ward 2 to make his Back Bay-Brighton district safe. Roxbury's Ward 9 was added to Powers' district to make him safe from primary challenges. James W. Hennigan, an opponent of Powers in the Mayoralty primary, benefited when in place of Ward 9 he was given suburban Ward 20, which had gone heavily for Collins in the Mayoralty election. LoPresti's East Boston-Charlestown-North End district was made more heavily Italian and "safer" by the deletion of Cambridge Ward 2. The Rules Committee attracted more Boston support for its bill by failing to reduce the city's representation in accordance with its population losses.

When at last there was unanimous Democratic support, the redistricting bill was introduced into the Senate (May 13, 1960) and at once passed 22–17 on a straight party vote.

When it reached the House the bill almost died. Democratic Representatives, led by Toomey of Cambridge, who was angry that his city had been parcelled out to satisfy incumbent Senators, joined with the united Republican minority to make the votes (May 23 and 24) close: 112–110, 114–108, and 103–100. As many as 23 Democrats voted with the Republicans; their reasons included friendship for Toomey, fear of voter reprisals, recognition that some district changes would hurt future political plans, and idealistic objection to gerrymandering. Of the 23 Representatives who bolted, six were from Boston, 12 from other metropolitan area communities, and only five from the rest of the state.

The Republicans played their last card on June 3 when a group of them led by state chairman Daniel McLean asked the state's Supreme Judicial Court for a writ of mandamus to set aside the redistricting bill. McLean's plea was based primarily on a constitutional provision that redistricting should be undertaken by the session of the General Court immediately following the decennial state census, which had last been held in 1955. Republican General Courts had violated this provision with redistricting laws in 1939 and 1947, however, and there is little chance that the Court will accommodate McLean.

# METROPOLITAN DISTRICTS

## JOHN C. BOLLENS

THE USE of metropolitan districts in the metropolitan areas of the United States is increasing. In operation in more than one-fourth of such areas, they are proportionately most prevalent in concentrations of 500,000 or more people. Approximately three-fourths of the thirty-three most populous areas have at least one metropolitan district, and it is not unusual for them to have more than one. Geographical location has constituted no barrier, for these districts are found in metropolitan areas in all sections of the United States. Although appearing in Philadelphia as early as 1790 and in such areas as Chicago and Portland, Oregon, in the latter part of the nineteenth century, metropolitan districts are largely a post–World War I development.[1] Once established, most of them have given indications of being permanent or long-lived. In contrast to many other types of districts, few of them have become inactive or been abolished or merged.

Collectively, metropolitan districts are concerned with a wide range of activities and have eliminated or mitigated some of the most important problems of specific metropolitan areas. Although their most frequent services have to do with port facilities, sewage disposal, water supply, and parks, they also own and operate bridges, tunnels, airports, housing, libraries, and mass transit facilities; furnish public health services, regional planning, power, ice, gas, and coke; regulate navigation channels; and control water to prevent disasters. They emphasize service rather than regulatory functions. Certain functions considered by many people to be metropolitan are not provided by any metropolitan district. The most notable omissions are fire protection and law enforcement.

## Mostly Single-Purpose

An overwhelming majority of these districts are legally limited to supplying a single service. Prominent examples among the relatively few districts

Reprinted from *Special District Governments in the United States* (Berkeley: University of California Press, 1957), pp. 67–71 and 87–92.

1. For details on early metropolitan districts, see Paul Studenski, *The Government of Metropolitan Areas in the United States* (New York: National Municipal League, 1930), pp. 256–265. Several districts discussed by Mr. Studenski are not independent or are less than metropolitan in jurisdiction.

that perform more than one function are the Port of New York Authority, the Hartford County (Connecticut) Metropolitan District, the Bi-State Development District (St. Louis metropolitan area), and the East Bay Municipal Utility District (San Francisco-Oakland metropolitan area). Although it has happened that one or more functions of these districts were authorized after their establishment, generally neither metropolitan districts nor their residents have shown much interest in assuming new obligations. Very few metropolitan districts have therefore increased functionally through subsequent authorization by the state legislature, or through the exercise of other powers originally granted them. The usual pattern has been to have one metropolitan district carry out one function, and to establish other metropolitan districts for additional single purposes if sufficient concern develops. As a result, no metropolitan district is presently serving as a comprehensive multifunctional metropolitan government. Instead, all of them are operating as limited governments of metropolitan jurisdiction.

## Large and Flexible Areas

Metropolitan districts have large areas, and on the average are larger than any other kind of special district. Some districts in rural sections, for example, are very extensive, but others contain only a fraction of a square mile or a few square miles. On the other hand, the territory of metropolitan districts is consistently measured in tens or hundreds of square miles and in some instances exceeds a thousand square miles. Then, too, since metropolitan districts have jurisdiction in densely settled areas, they usually encompass a large number of general and special district governments. Furthermore, the territory of some of them crosses state boundaries, a feature foreign to most special districts and to all general governments except the national government. Some metropolitan districts have grown substantially through annexation. An illustration is the Metropolitan Sanitary District of Greater Chicago which has almost tripled its original size of 185 square miles. Thousands, sometimes millions, of people reside within each metropolitan district and use or benefit from its service. In addition, many nondistrict residents benefit from the operations of certain functional kinds of metropolitan districts, such as those operating parks, mass transit, and ports.

## Sometimes Big Government

Although performing only one or a few functions, some metropolitan districts are very large governmental operations, and may even be larger than state governments in some respects. The Chicago Transit Authority, for example, outranked seventeen states in number of employees and twelve states in annual revenue in the fiscal year 1952. At the same time, the Port of New York Authority had more long-term outstanding debt than each of thirty-nine individual states.[2] Metropolitan districts with the most extensive operations also stand out in comparison with other districts. Of the twelve largest nonschool districts, eight are metropolitan and three others are located in metropolitan areas but are less than metropolitan territorially (see table).

### The Largest Nonschool Districts

| District | Number of employees, October, 1952 | Revenue for fiscal year 1952 ($ thousands) | Total long-term outstanding debt, 1952 ($ thousands) |
|---|---|---|---|
| **Metropolitan Districts** | | | |
| Chicago Transit Authority | 17,472 | 119,064 | 137,400 |
| Metropolitan Transit Authority (Boston) | 7,652 | 50,004 | 131,054 |
| Port of New York Authority | 3,745 | 57,097 | 241,688 |
| Metropolitan Sanitary District of Greater Chicago | 1,882 | 29,246 | 141,164 |
| Indianapolis Utilities District | 1,230 | 21,828 | 11,785 |
| East Bay Municipal Utility District (eastern section of San Francisco Bay area) | 1,208 | 17,708 | 69,530 |
| Omaha Public Power District | 1,116 | 17,942 | 71,528 |
| Omaha Metropolitan Utility District | 1,007 | 10,515 | . . . . . . |
| **Other Districts** | | | |
| Chicago Park District | 3,935 | 27,497 | 66,230 |
| Washington Suburban Sanitary District (Maryland) | 1,398 | 8,550 | 75,032 |
| Consumers Public Power District (Nebraska) | 1,193 | 13,775 | 40,698 |
| Imperial Irrigation District (California) | 1,040 | 10,946 | 62,412 |
| Totals | 42,878 | 384,172 | 1,048,521 |
| Per cent of nonschool district totals | 35 | 38 | 28 |

Source: *Special District Governments in the United States*, U.S. Bureau of the Census, Governments Division, State and Local Government Special Studies No. 33 (Washington: 1954), p. 3. The Chicago Park District is coterminous with the city limits of Chicago; the Washington Suburban District operates in part of the Washington Metropolitan area; and the Consumers Public Power District is state-wide. Of the twelve districts, only the Imperial Irrigation District operates entirely outside a metropolitan area.

These are the most important metropolitan districts in terms of operations, but in addition there are a number of others that are significant in one or more of the categories of personnel, revenue, and debt. These others similarly demonstrate the high relative operational importance of metropolitan districts, especially among nonschool special units. . . .

## Variations and Limitations

. . . [T]here is wide variation in the features of metropolitan districts despite their relatively limited number. This can be seen by recalling the

2. *Special District Governments in the United States*, U.S. Bureau of the Census, Governments Division, State and Local Government Special Studies No. 33 (Washington: 1954), p. 3.

formation, governing board composition, and financing characteristics of the districts presented as case studies. Even functionally similar districts operating in metropolitan areas in the same state may have marked differences. The Metropolitan Water District of Southern California and the East Bay Municipal Utility District supply water to residents of different California metropolitan areas. The former is largely financed by property taxation, the latter depends upon service charges. There are frequently great differences between two metropolitan districts in the same metropolitan area. For example, the formation procedure and the method of selecting the governing body of the Metropolitan Sanitary District of Greater Chicago and the Chicago Transit Authority contrast sharply.

Metropolitan districts differ appreciably in the proportion of the metropolitan area or population which they include, although all of them encompass at least a major part of one or the other. Beyond this, however, there is frequently little similarity. Some districts, such as the Huron-Clinton Metropolitan Authority, extend outside the metropolitan area into nonmetropolitan land, whereas the Metropolitan Water District of Southern California contains most of one metropolitan area and parts of two others. By contrast, the Metropolitan Sanitary District of Greater Chicago includes about one-half the territory and most of the population of only the core county of a metropolitan area. This district, as a result of territorial limitations, cannot prevent sewage dumping in the portion of the metropolitan area which is outside district boundaries. Its geographical limits lessen its functional effectiveness. Most metropolitan districts contain less than the entire metropolitan area.

Although metropolitan districts collectively engage in many functions, in no metropolitan area are all or even nearly all metropolitan functions handled by metropolitan districts. Such units are therefore solving only part of the over-all metropolitan problem. As noted previously, most metropolitan districts have not increased their functions since their establishment. Generally when they have grown in this manner they have taken on functions closely related to their initial functions. For example, the Port of New York Authority has enlarged its operations, but within the original field of transportation, and the East Bay Municipal Utility District, which started by supplying water, has added sewage disposal.

## Control and Complexity

One of the most striking features of metropolitan districts is the fact that metropolitan residents lack determination of and control over certain important aspects of the districts. This situation is not an isolated one, but appears with some frequency, especially in metropolitan districts containing territory in two states. Establishing a district by state legislative or judicial action, permitting the district directors to issue bonds on their own decision, effectuating annexations through state laws, and having members of the governing body chosen by a governor or a judge whose constituency is wider than that of the metropolitan area are important examples of the remoteness of some districts from the voters of metropolitan areas. A number of metropolitan districts utilize one or two of these procedures, but interstate metropolitan districts use all of them. Metropolitan districts with territory in two states are created by the adoption of similar laws by two state legislatures, approval by Congress, and the completion of an interstate compact. The members of the governing body are appointed by the respective governors and occasionally some of them are ex officio state officials. The governing body may issue bonds through its own unilateral action. The district area can be enlarged by amendment of the interstate compact. How can such districts, which operate in metropolitan areas and materially affect the local people, be held sufficiently accountable by the metropolitan population? The only possible regular channel of control is through the legislature or the governor, but such a route is often too circuitous to be effective.

With a substantial number of metropolitan areas already territorially interstate and more about to become so, district government is likely to be used more frequently. So far the uniform district pattern in interstate situations has been detachment from responsibility to the people most intimately affected by such governments. There is of course no logical reason why districts in these circumstances cannot be organized under a system calling for direct metropolitan determination and control. Such a procedure would, however, require a reshaping of the established mold.

These interstate metropolitan districts, and certain other metropolitan districts subject to repeated amendment by state law, seem to represent a hybrid level of government, neither truly local nor state. They are local governments principally in the sense that they function in a local area. At the same time they are operationally separated from the area they serve, or are affected by major changes initiated by the state legislature, which may or may not be directly responsive to the desires of the metropolitan people. These districts are very close to being adjuncts of the state government, a matter of concern to persons who want the approaches to metropolitan difficulties to be locally determined and locally accountable.

Another prominent feature of metropolitan districts is the complexity of their composition or functioning. This handicap, found in more than a few of these districts, renders metropolitan determination and control less effective. The Metropolitan Water District of Southern California is a prominent example, for the composition of its governing body, the distribution of voting power, the requirement of bloc voting, and the methods of annexing territory combine to make it an extremely complicated system. Furthermore, there is a stratification of governments within goverments as major parts and subordinate parts of this metropolitan operation. For example, in San Diego County the Crest Public Utility District and the cities of La Mesa and El Cajon are part of the La Mesa, Lemon Grove, and Spring Valley Irrigation

District, which in turn is a constituent member of the Metropolitan Water District of Southern California. A similar intricate pyramiding exists in Orange County, and numerous other areas within the metropolitan district are slightly less involved. There is no question that metropolitan determination and control were conceived as being part of the original arrangement, but the intricacies that have developed severely dilute the possibilities of their full and consistent attainment.

The complexity usually centers around the composition of the governing body. In the Chicago Transit Authority three of the seven members are appointed by the governor with the consent of the state senate and the approval of the mayor of Chicago. One of these three must reside outside the Chicago city limits. The remaining four are appointed by the mayor of Chicago with the consent of the city council and the sanction of the governor. The Milwaukee Metropolitan Sewerage District has two governing bodies, a city commission and a metropolitan commission. The city commission, consisting of five appointees of the mayor of Milwaukee, builds and operates intercepting sewers and the sewage plant inside Milwaukee and operates sewers outside the city in the district. The metropolitan commission, whose three members are selected by the governor, is responsible for the building of main sewers outside Milwaukee. Special districts should not be so complicated as to negate the worthy objectives of understanding and interest by metropolitan residents.

## Criticism and Potentialities

Strong objections to metropolitan districts are frequently raised, but some of them, of course, are based on specific situations and hence do not apply to all districts. Two of the most common criticisms are that districts are too remote from public influence and regulation, and that they have substituted control by a professional administrative guild of experts and an allied interest group for public control.[3] Also often stated are complaints about the limitations on types of district activities which result from mandatory reliance on nontax sources for financing, and about the lack of intergovernmental coöperation and coördinated planning. A more general objection to districts focuses on the effects of restricting their functional scope. It is argued that this type of functional consolidation, without any alteration of existing governmental areas, is simply a makeshift or expedient and lacks sufficient comprehensiveness to meet the many difficulties of the metropolitan problem. Putting the argument in the form of a medical analogy, a long-time analyst observed that "If a patient were suffering from cataracts, heart disease, dia-

3. The latter point is stressed by Victor Jones in his talk, "Methodology in the Study of Metropolitan Areas," which appears in *The Study of the Metropolitan Region of Chicago: Objectives and Methodology* (Evanston: Northwestern University Department of Political Science, 1952), p. 10.

betes and an infected toe, amputating the toe might enable him to walk around for awhile but it could not be considered a really important step toward restoring him to health. Just so with [metropolitan] districts and the metropolitan problem."⁴ The limited scope of each district therefore leads to further profusion of governmental units which increases the confusion of citizens. In addition, utilization of the metropolitan district device in a restricted manner takes the impetus and interest away from more thorough approaches by alleviating the most pressing difficulties.

In view of this general censure of metropolitan districts, it is significant that for a long time there have been expressions of interest in a remedial measure. This is the idea of broadening the range of functions so as to make metropolitan districts multipurpose operations. So far, however, districts of limited purpose have shown little inclination to seek authorization for additional services. Furthermore, in the relatively few district laws that allow the performance of several functions, most districts undertake only one. The same is true of the even rarer districts which may legally perform numerous diversified functions. Nevertheless, interest in creating new multipurpose metropolitan districts continues, as does optimism that some of the established districts will evolve into such governments.

The ease of establishing metropolitan districts, in contrast to the difficulty of achieving other types of metropolitan integration, makes this approach extremely inviting. In addition, public acceptance of the district idea does not seem to lessen with the granting of more than one function, probably because most metropolitan districts vested with multiple functions perform only one at the outset. This technique, unconsciously used for the most part, may well be a key strategy which advocates of multipurpose metropolitan districts should deliberately use. Will this transformation of the metropolitan district mechanism be attempted in efforts to accomplish metropolitan integration? An affirmative answer seemingly has broad implications for the future.

The apparent political feasibility of establishing multipurpose metropolitan districts, and the attractiveness of forming some type of metropolitan government, should not cause important parts of the plan to be overlooked. There should be metropolitan determination and control of metropolitan districts. There should also be an adequate and equitable financial base. Many metropolitan districts of limited functional scope do not adequately meet these standards. The question of success or failure in adoption of a plan should not overshadow the careful formulation of its proper elements, for governments tend to be permanent, and original provisions are sometimes difficult to change. Therefore, although the idea of multipurpose metropolitan districts may be very applicable in specific situations, the details of such proposals are highly important and should not be neglected in the early stages.

---

4. Thomas H. Reed, "The Metropolitan Problem—1941," *National Municipal Review*, 30 (July, 1941), 407.

# THE TROUBLE WITH THE NEW YORK PORT AUTHORITY

## EDWARD T. CHASE

WITH THE POSSIBLE EXCEPTION of the Yankees, New York's most splendidly successful institution has been the Port of New York Authority. The PA, as it's called, is the agency principally responsible for metropolitan New York's transportation well-being. The last thirty years of its thirty-nine-year life span have nearly all been vintage.

But, like the Yankees, it now seems to be heading for troubles. These are nowhere discernible in its annual reports, however. Last year it took in a record $105 million from its facilities and its net revenues were $60 million. Ninety-five million cars, trucks, and buses paid record tolls on its bridges and tunnels, a new high of 15 million passengers used its air terminals, over a million buses took off from its bus terminal. About $12.5 million of its income came from non-vehicular sources like its $5-million hotel at Idlewild International Airport. It relocated 1,800 families in upper Manhattan to make way for the cars that will converge on George Washington Bridge when its new $183-million lower level is finished in 1962. It even handled 50,000 animals at its Idlewild Animalport, which it proudly calls "the first shelter in the United States built exclusively for the care of animal air travelers."

Despite these awesome tidings the PA is uneasy. In recent months there have been demands that Congress investigate its powers, performance, and tax-free status; and mass protest meetings against its proposed jet airport. Important groups and planning organizations have called for a full-scale review of its responsibilities, and its wisdom has been questioned by the press. In sharp contrast to New York's prevailing aura of official dishonesty, there is no talk of corruption or incompetence. On the contrary, the PA's integrity and accomplishments are undisputed.[1]

Why all the fuss, then, and is it important? A long-time transportation buff and a native New Yorker, I recently set myself the task of answering these questions. What I have learned may shed light on the mess in most big cities.

First off, I found that on its own terms the PA is doing a grand job. But

---

Reprinted from *Harper's Magazine*, June, 1960, where it appeared under the title "How to Rescue New York from Its Port Authority," by permission of the author and the publisher. © 1960, by Harper & Brothers.
1. Legislative inquiries of the PA undertaken since this was written fortify my point: while there may be some evidence of petty dishonesty, it is irrelevant and worse to attack the PA on these grounds. The PA's great dereliction is its failure to see to New York's over-all transportation well-being. (ETC, February, 1961.)

those terms, today, are cockeyed. The world has changed but the PA stub-
bornly refuses to cope with the new problems.

It cheerfully reports one achievement after another. Yet at the same
time, mass transportation serving New York is faltering and the city is
foundering under the weight and pollution of traffic. The situation is a
matter of deep concern to nearly every adult New Yorker. There are a few
exceptions, of course. They include Austin Tobin, the PA's executive director, and his public relations chief, Mrs. Lee Jaffe. Talking with them and a
PA engineer not long ago I was offered a rather different picture.

Tobin is a well-groomed executive in his fifties, whose impressive head
of gray hair and forthright manner more than compensate for his rather
diminutive stature. He feels we should be grateful for heavy traffic. "If Thirty-
fourth Street weren't congested, we'd be in trouble," he told me. Mrs. Jaffe,
a lady now in her sixteenth year with the PA, reminded me that America's
economic destiny, and indeed the strength of the free world, depends on
moving cars. "Slow down Detroit, and the whole world's in trouble," she
observed. Similar views are held by the PA engineer charged with comprehensive planning, Frank Herring. A studious and charming man, his all-
absorbing concern with traffic flow resembles a plumber's concern for the
pipes in a house. But I searched in vain for the PA architect-planner concerned with the many other factors besides traffic flow that go into making a
city fit to live in.

## The First American "Authority"

The history of the PA casts some light on its current dilemma. A quasi-
public, tax-free organization, it was created in 1921 during the terms of two
far-sighted Governors, Al Smith of New York and Walter Edge of New
Jersey, to end the trouble caused by the artificial New York–New Jersey
boundary line which runs smack down the Hudson River's center, splitting
the natural unity of the port. An interstate Compact approved by Congress
gives the PA power to build, buy, lease, and operate any and all kinds of
transportation facilities within a "Port District" running in a twenty-five
mile radius from Manhattan's tip. It can function beyond these limits if both
Governors and their legislatures approve. The legislatures can also *order*
the PA to take over any transportation operation they deem necessary. Although this has never happened, it is not because the necessity has not arisen.
No one has been inclined to order the PA around because over the years
it has acquired a kind of power which was *not* conferred by the Compact,
namely, *political* power. In the past its influence over the state legislatures
has been used chiefly to stifle demands for lower tolls on its bridges and
tunnels. These are, of course, the agency's life blood, for it can't levy taxes.
It can, however, borrow money secured by tax-exempt bonds. Attracted by its

spectacularly profitable toll operations, the public, as of last year, had invested $920 million in PA facilities. The press calls this Tobin's billion-dollar empire.

The PA is guided by twelve Commissioners, half from each state. They are appointed by the Governors with Senate approval for overlapping six-year terms. Without exception leaders in business, finance, and the law have been chosen for these posts. The operating head is the executive director.

Since 1942 the executive director has been Mr. Tobin. A forceful, successful leader with a big say in policy, he is handsomely recompensed, his $60,000-a-year salary topping the New York Governor's by $10,000. And his is a very well paid staff. A half-dozen get $40,000 annually, a dozen others get between $27,000 and $33,000, including public relations director Mrs. Jaffe, who makes $30,000. Her department budget, incidentally, is a sizable $226,000 which, to some critics, seems excessive for a public-service organization with no need to drum up trade. The PA, however, conceives of itself as in a highly competitive situation vis-à-vis other revenue-raising institutions. Mrs. Jaffe's is thus a formidably high-pressure publicity operation, unceasingly aggressive in defending the PA and in bolstering its prestige. This market-place concept of its role may have a lot to do with the PA's shortcomings as a public institution serving all the people.

The PA's performance has significance far beyond the 1,500-square-mile Port District. New York's economic and social well-being are vital to the nation and its institutional arrangements are prototypes for other urban regions. Modeled after the granddaddy of all public authorities, the Port of London Authority, the PA has been a persuasive example. It has made the precedents and written most of the law for thousands of American regional authorities which have proliferated since World War II. Political scientists have called them the fastest-growing unit of local government in the United States. They have, on the one hand, been deplored as undemocratic repositories of public power unresponsive to the people, and on the other hand praised as an ingenious way to combine the best aspects of government and business. Rather than debate this point in the abstract, it is useful to consider closely what the PA is supposed to do and what in fact it is doing.

The founding Compact enjoins the PA to see to "the improvement of transportation and terminal facilities" in the District without limitation. It may operate any new kind of transport facility, even equipment unknown in the 'twenties. Its duty is to maintain the over-all transportation efficiency of metropolitan New York.

How has the PA chosen to interpret this mandate?

With his staff of 4,400 people, Tobin runs six bridges and tunnels for motor vehicles; five air terminals; six marine terminals; two terminals for over-the-road trucks, one for less-than-carload rail freight; and one for buses. Conspicuously absent from the list are bus lines, subways, commuter railroads, major highways, or, with minor exceptions, parking facilities. In short, the

PA has made an arbitrary selection of transportation facilities. This fractional approach is the basis of the PA's financial success and the key to its over-all failure.

Obviously the transportation systems the PA disclaims are no less important to the region's mobility than the enterprises it has favored. Indeed, a balance of diversified transportation systems is essential to the survival of a modern metropolis. (Two years back, for example, my fellow transportation buff, John Snyder, warned in a *Harper's* article that we'd better stop treating transportation as a "disconnected patchwork" or else.)

## The Sacred Bondholders

Even Mr. Tobin on occasion has conceded that New York needs mass transportation. Perhaps he has been moved by the vision of his bridges and tunnels swamped by the traffic that would descend on them should the commuter railroads and transit lines actually quit, as has been often threatened. At times he has even stressed the "interdependence of the port's transportation facilities." This was not, however, the official position a year or so ago when a bill before the New Jersey legislature proposed forcing the PA to run a suburban transit system. The lengthy PA brief said in part:

> The theory of transit "integration" seems to be based on the principle that by bringing about a complete integration of responsibilities of intra-metropolitan transportation in the New York–New Jersey metropolitan area, most of the serious transport problems can magically be solved. . . . Its devotees are imbued with something of the excitement of those who years ago became enamored with the mystic [sic] of "technocracy." And like "technocracy" the concept of "integration" of transit is based on a number of important assumptions that are wholly implicit and has [sic] not been objectively analyzed.

The illiteracies and irrelevances aside, the statement conflicts with every responsible analysis of the urban transportation plight. Like most PA literature, it is neither unbiased nor scholarly. Instead it is an ex parte argument by "realistic" business minds bent on upholding their anachronistic status quo. They are against an integrated system only because their toll revenues would be used to help support other necessary transport facilities, *not* because integration isn't desirable. Obviously it is.

Commenting on the PA's refusal to assume responsibility for any transport facilities except its own, the respected Regional Plan Association observed the other day: "The PA is like . . . a work horse that won't take its blinders off. Only the state can change this."

Despite survey after survey and impassioned recommendations, transportation in the metropolitan area is left to a *mélange* of conflicting authorities, state, city, county, and town departments, railroads, and transit companies. Long-time consultant to the PA, Wilfred Owen of Brookings Institution, is perhaps the nation's outstanding urban transportation expert. "Building a transportation system under these conditions," he says, "is like trying to build a house with the carpenters, bricklayers, electricians, and plumbers all working by separate plans."

What lies behind the PA's animus against a comprehensive approach to the transport problem? Tobin often refers to the PA's "very full powers" to take on any kind of transportation it chooses to. At the same time, he confides to his audiences, in a display of self-assurance that is not altogether endearing, that the PA, while matching the high level of private business management talent, must also be informed with a superior sense of responsibility to the public it serves, presumably beyond the reach of average politicians.

However, it turns out that this lofty ideal is secondary to something else, namely, an almost transcendental sense of obligation to the PA's bondholders. Accordingly, only such enterprises can be undertaken as will enrich it or, at the very least, not disturb its credit standing. Beyond all else, this is the number one guiding principle of every PA action. Tobin and his Commissioners are in full agreement with Robert Moses, chief of the Triborough Bridge and Tunnel Authority, which has no connection with the PA but shares its philosophy. "Financial folly," said Moses when questioned about using toll revenues to help New York's desperately-pressed rail system. "The funds of these authorities are not the treasure of the Count of Monte Cristo." He failed to add that they *are* the treasure of the general public within the Port District.

The practical effects of ranking bondholders first, public second, are these: The PA is indestructible so long as it can arrogate virtually all the area's money-making transportation facilities. Self-perpetuation of the organization is assured. As a result, unless the PA is forced to change its ways, or is superseded by a differently oriented body, New York is indefinitely committed to an un-unified transportation system. The whole metropolitan area thus remains in jeopardy of worse congestion and pollution and of mass-transportation bankruptcy.

There is, in other words, a basic conflict of interests between the Port Authority's narrow specialists and the people who live in the vast New York metropolitan region which today extends into three states—Connecticut as well as New York and New Jersey. Yet the PA is neither inept nor venal. It consists of skilled and honest if stubborn and unimaginative men. One villain has been identified by Mr. Tobin himself. Discussing Manhattan's traffic problem, he blamed "Detroit and the whole automobile economy."

What he failed to say was that the PA has neither volunteered nor been forced to adapt its role to ease the hardship wrought by this "automobile economy." The dereliction isn't the PA's alone. The Governors and legislatures of New York and New Jersey and even the national Congress have also shirked responsibility. They have awakened to it only as the commuter rail crisis has reached truly alarming proportions.

## The Brochure Approach

Until the present crisis few politicians have dared tangle with the PA. Its successes have been massive and public esteem has been assiduously cultivated through self-congratulatory brochures, slick reports, a high-powered community relations program, press conferences, news releases, and speeches. After witnessing the public relations director, Mrs. Jaffe, in action I rather sympathize with the timid politicos. When I visited her to ask a few questions she was in a state of high tension over an allegation by a New Jersey paper that the PA was living pretty high on the hog for a tax-free public agency. Such was her agitation that she could not concern herself with my pedestrian inquiries until she had delivered a ferocious and unsolicited defense of the PA and had led me to the pantry next to the board room to demonstrate that no booze or other goodies were stored there. I am not untutored in the aggressive ways of public relations. But her concentrated hard sell, unrelieved by the faintest hint of objectivity, has the effect, as one news reporter said to me, of making one distrust the whole PA operations. One discerns a similarly shrill defensiveness in the speeches in which Mr. Tobin seeks tirelessly to justify the PA's indifference to rail transit without, however, at any time, proposing remedies.

Over the years the state legislatures and the Governors have rubber-stamped practically all the PA's plans. The current outcry, paradoxically, has not been caused by the debacle in mass transportation but by the PA proposal to build a huge jet airport in New Jersey, about twenty-five miles west of New York City. It would eliminate a village and a number of large estates, and, spurred by popular protest, the New Jersey legislature overwhelmingly voted it down. Nonetheless, a PA official assured a New Jersey audience that the project was far from dead. Denouncing the Authority for arrogance, the Assembly then went on to order a full-scale investigation of it and Senate approval is awaited. Findings of the inquiry would go to the Governor by next January.

On top of this there have been demands for Congressional investigations of the PA. The most recent came from Senator Clifford P. Case, a New Jersey Republican. Earlier, the chairman of the House Judiciary Committee, Representative Emanuel Celler, Democrat of Brooklyn, introduced a bill calling for Congressional approval of future changes in the Port Compact and requiring the Authority to report regularly to Congress. On the day he took this action, Mr. Celler and other Congressmen had been guests of the Authority in a public relations-inspired "exchange of views" breakfast.

Celler sat through what he described as host Tobin's presentation of "brochures picturing the glories and grandeur of its operations and little more." Then he delivered a resounding attack and accused the Authority of "growing almost to a super-state."

Subsequently a legal expert of the House Judiciary Committee has begun a study of the Port Compact to discover what revisions, if any, may be in order. It has not been so scrutinized in nearly forty years and clearly the PA's performance is of more than local concern. In its quite legitimate effort to push the interests of New York to the competitive disadvantage of other American ports, it fought strenuously, for instance, against the St. Lawrence Seaway. It spends a million dollars a year on New York trade-promotion offices in cities here and abroad. It is appropriate that a *national* body determine whether the *national* interest is being best served by these assorted activities. For, unlike most regional authorities, the PA has grown so large and powerful that its program affects the whole nation.

In the past, its autonomy and freedom from politics have been virtues. But such privilege carries great responsibility. A dogmatic indifference to problems of commuter railroads and rapid transit pervades the pronouncements of Tobin and of Robert Moses (who is never loath to speak ex cathedra for Tobin's empire although it is separate from his own). There is good reason to wonder whether the Port Authority can, any longer, take the long, comprehensive view of its role.

The quarrel over the New Jersey jet airport, which has caused perhaps unwarranted irritation, is a case in point. Many aviation men question the validity of the PA's case but concede it is a difficult question calling for expert judgment. Yet, to the consternation of the industry, the PA presented its proposal before even consulting the airlines. This came about, to be sure, because the PA was forced to issue its report prematurely after reporters got wind of the proposal But the PA now refuses to admit this and declines to budge.

In view of this self-righteous rigidity, it is perhaps foolish to hope that the PA redefine its own role. It is, for one thing, a creature of the "automobile economy," which lifted it from obscurity to renown in the 1940s, as a torrent of cars poured through its toll booths. Sheer volume of traffic is its gauge of success. This is what pays the interest on bonds, builds up hefty reserve funds to ease the banker-commissioners' worries and pay handsome staff salaries.

To other planners, however, the experience of recent years has been sobering. Watching every new arterial highway become immediately overloaded, they now accept as axiomatic the fact that new roads, bridges, and tunnels stimulate new traffic. Without land-use planning the facilities rapidly become obsolete, precipitating an apparent need for more new highways—ad infinitum.

The fact that facilities beget the need for more facilities does not disturb the engineering mind. Lacking the planner's vision, it can conceive of nothing more important than traffic flow. Congestion is indeed a virtue to the traffic engineer or to a lawyer like Tobin who relies on engineering counsel. New York City's Traffic Commissioner, T. T. Wiley, is another fine example. He hopes to build fifteen parking garages costing $52.5 million strategically located to attract 10,000 more cars daily into the heart of Manhattan, already the most congested area in the world. But the clogged city and roadside blight that dismay residents and planners are reinterpreted in the engineering mind as "desirable concentration."

Most businessmen have yet to learn that traffic jams threaten their own economic interests. The engineers and financiers who dominate Port Authority thinking are technicians, absorbed with their bridges, tunnels, terminals. Perpetuation of the Port Authority is their prime goal. But this was not the intent of the Port Compact. It envisaged a very different kind of body dedicated to the Port District's over-all economic well-being, using transportation as a means not as an end.

# THE DESIRABLE AND THE POSSIBLE

## EDWARD C. BANFIELD AND

## MORTON GRODZINS

IN MANY DISCUSSIONS of metropolitan organization, there is a strong bias toward simplicity, uniformity, and symmetry of structure. It is often taken for granted that the presence of a large number of independent local governments in a single area means waste and duplication. That there may be even administrative advantages in decentralization is often overlooked entirely. Beyond problems of efficiency and economy, issues of community independence, sociability, and status are involved. Technical considerations concerning optimum areas for given services must compete for priority with political issues concerning the best organization for the public control of public officials. Issues of philosophy intrude: when does self-government in one locality impede self-government in another? Values of local control compete with values of area efficiency. A consideration of what is desirable in the way of organization ought to take into account the full range of problems. Intangibles—for example, the suburbanite's satisfaction in remaining apart from the central city—should be accorded some value. If a careful accounting is made with all relevant factors taken into consideration, the present "Balkanization" of government in the metropolitan areas may not be as undesirable as it is often made to appear. At any rate, arguments in favor of metropolitan integration on the grounds of administrative efficiency must compete with other arguments that favor independence and separateness.

Reprinted by permission from *Government and Housing in Metropolitan Areas,* by Edward C. Banfield and Morton Grodzins (New York: McGraw-Hill Book Company, Inc., 1958), pp. 155–166. Copyright, 1958, McGraw-Hill Book Company, Inc.

When the needed distinction is made between "problems which exist in metropolitan areas" and "problems which exist by virtue of the inadequacies of governmental structure in the metropolitan areas," the latter are relatively few. Transportation is probably the most common and the most pressing of the real metropolitan-area problems. Other common and important problems are air-pollution control and civil defense, and in some areas, water supply and waste disposal. Opinion, rather than technical considerations, may add other functions to this list. Even the few named do not require the same jurisdiction, a fact which makes it extremely difficult to say what the boundaries of an all-purpose general government should be. Moreover, there is no reason in technology why most of these functions cannot be carried on effectively by metropolitan governments which do not have general jurisdiction, or by several governments acting collaboratively.

Deep and persistent political conflicts divide the populations of most metropolitan areas. The conflict between the central city and the suburban ring—which also is a conflict between lower-classes and middle-classes and between Negroes and whites—in most places rules out any immediate possibility of "one local government for one local area." The sharpness of these conflicts makes it doubtful in some places whether metropolitan-area government would be immediately desirable even if it were possible. Though the argument for larger areas in the long run is a persuasive one, it is hard to say whether short-run conflicts are better managed if the parties to them are members of the same or of different political communities. But this question is not a practical one under present circumstances. The fact is that sweeping programs of governmental integration will be politically impossible in most metropolitan areas for a long time to come. Those who push for perfectionist schemes can do the cause of reform more harm than good. The very energy poured into allegedly "ideal" solutions diverts attention from less symmetrical but no less desirable steps. And in exciting opposition to grandiose schemes of complete integration, proponents of such schemes also stimulate opposition to the lesser alternatives.

Where strong political conflicts either do not exist or can be overcome, there may be progress toward genuine area-wide government. Large-scale annexations of territory to the central cities are least likely. Some form of urban federalism or some variant of city-county consolidation may be practicable. Of the latter, the "urban-county" idea is probably most feasible. The essence of this plan is the transfer of area-wide functions to the county and the transformation of the county into a government of general competence. State action to facilitate such transfers and to establish county structure as an effective organization for policymaking and administration is essential if the urban-county plan is to have a chance of substantial success.

If the twin questions of what is desirable and what is possible in metropolitan organization are considered in all their complexity, it will be apparent that no single scheme of reform will be applicable everywhere. Every metropolitan area presents a special case, and only detailed consideration of the intricacies and idiosyncrasies of a specific local situation can produce a "plan" that is both desirable and feasible. Recommendations found in reports like this one have their uses, but they are no substitute for the arduous process of local study, discussion, negotiation, and compromise.

## A "Model" for Action

The considerations outlined above lead to a "model" for action: a description in general terms of the means by which housing may be improved through changes in the structure of government in a "typical"—and therefore nonexistent—metropolitan area. The aim of the plan is to meet genuine area-wide housing needs with area-wide solutions while maintaining personal and community discretion. In the light of political and social obstacles to sweeping plans of governmental integration, the model places emphasis upon collaboration and the exchange of contractual services among independent governmental units. From the start, this creates a *de facto* local confederation; in the long run it looks forward to a scheme of local federalism.

The impulse for governmental reorganization affecting housing may come for reasons only indirectly related to housing: as a consequence of new transportation needs, or civil defense, or flood control, for example. Furthermore, the persons responsible for initiating structural change may be variously situated. They may be leaders of civic groups, powerful businessmen, members of a state commission, or state legislators. Whatever the immediate causes of reorganization and whoever the initiators, success of any plan will depend crucially upon the mayor of the central city. Even where others play the leading role, the mayor's acquiescence is mandatory. Where the central-city mayor opposes reorganization, it will fail. Where he supports it fully, chances for success are at their best. The central-city mayor is therefore the leading figure in the model.

What gives the central-city mayor his central role? The core city has more at stake in truly metropolitan matters than do the other governments. The biggest of the local governments, it is more likely to have the resources —financial, technical, and political—to initiate and carry on effective action. Moreover the mayor of the central city has a constituency large enough and diverse enough in its interests to permit him to view matters in metropolitan scale. A portion of this constituency, including heavy investors in downtown business districts, may demand rather than merely permit this course of action.

The mayor and his associates are therefore able to play the part of regional statesmen. That is to say, they can think in terms of the whole metropolitan area and when necessary can sacrifice the short-run special interests of the central city to its less immediate, but no less real, interest in the welfare of the area as a whole.

It is not unreasonable to expect statesmanship of this kind from the mayors of central cities. No doubt, in many cases nothing of the sort is to be expected. But in others—New York, Chicago, Philadelphia, Milwaukee, Denver, and St. Louis come to mind especially—action along these lines has already been taking place with encouraging results.

As the center and energizing force of metropolitan organization, the mayor of the central city will seek actively to bring the other units of government into the necessary cooperative relations. He will not do this merely by preaching or persuasion. The proposed model does not assume that the lesser officials of the metropolitan area will also be statesmen (though it does not rule out that possibility). In many cases the mayors of suburban towns or the county commissioners will be unwilling to cooperate in matters which offer no advantages to their jurisdictions. This unwillingness is not due solely to the lesser stature of the small-town official, although this may be a contributing factor. The decisive consideration is that the official elected by a relatively small and homogeneous constituency does not have the independence which would allow him to forego an immediate point for a more remote one, or to find support from one important constituency group when damned by another.

The mayor of the central city will not be without ability to impress others with the importance of cooperation. The merchants, bankers, real estate brokers, and other businessmen of the central cities suffer badly—in higher taxes, in lower income, and in difficulties of getting and keeping personnel— when property values decline in the core cities. Many of these leaders are influential residents of the suburbs, and often their interests, both economic and social, spill over the central-city boundary lines. Their civic groups are most often organized on a wider-than-single-city basis and have considerable influence in the affairs of many local governments. With the requisite leadership from the mayor, these citizens and their voluntary organizations may be mobilized to support area-wide collaborative activities. (An effort to enlist them in grandiose programs of governmental integration is far less likely to succeed; these are the very people to whom, in their role as family heads and homeowners, suburban independence is most important.) To utilize already existing voluntary groups is to maximize the effectiveness of such a citizen effort.

The governor's office can also be expected to help. Many governors in the past, in the words of Mayor Zeidler of Milwaukee, have been "not only indifferent to the problems of the central cities but also hostile to them." But, to a rapidly increasing extent, the populations of states are metropolitan-area populations. In almost every state, the governor has especially close ties to the rural areas—to "upstate" and "downstate"—but his electoral base is more and more bringing him into the orbit of metropolitan interests. And as those interests are mobilized and made effective by the central-city mayor, the governor's cooperation can be assured. Downstate opposition need not always be anticipated. The possible economies in state expenditures that may accompany collaborative action of local governments in metropolitan areas may, on the contrary, produce downstate support. A combination of rural and suburban opposition will be fatal to the governor's cooperation with the central-city mayor; but if suburban cooperation is achieved, the governor's will follow.

If he is to play his role on the metropolitan scene with full effect, the governor must have at his command more substantial staff aides than he has at present, and the state legislature must supply him with requisite programmatic tools. One important device available to him is the state grant-in-aid. State aid for such functions as sewage disposal, storm drainage, and water supply—and for housing and urban renewal as well—can be made contingent upon appropriate administrative collaboration at the metropolitan level. No such state requirements will appear spontaneously. They require political encouragement; and they have little chance of being passed without prior agreement of city and suburban leaders. The economies and program advances made possible by collaborative action are patent arguments for both the initial agreements and the state legislation itself. In short, with vigorous leadership from political leaders of the central cities, state aid can be used to promote an emerging federalism of the multiple governments in the metropolitan areas.

The mayor cannot hope for success in metropolitan arrangements by mobilizing citizen support or by lobbying at the state house. These are important adjuncts, not his principal weapons. In the main, he must rely upon direct negotiations with officials of other local governments. His bargaining position is good because he has power to give or withhold benefits which the smaller places want. Most of the local governments on the periphery of the central city need something from it. They want water and sewer lines extended. They want rapid transport to places of work. They want to use city parks and playgrounds. They want planning assistance.

If the mayor accommodates the suburbs overgenerously, he will not advance the cause of metropolitan collaboration. Once the petitioners get what they want, they are likely to be more indifferent to the needs of the central city than ever before The mayor will do most for metropolitan organization if he drives a hard bargain. The suburb may have water from the central city at a fair price—but only if it first agrees to subdivision regulations consistent with the requirements of metropolitan development. The suburb may have its policemen trained in the central city and it may use the central city's crime laboratory—but only after it agrees to a plan for exchanging information about fugitives. The central city will agree to help support a planning staff—but only on the understanding that some of the planners will work on a metropolitan highway system while others do zoning chores for the suburbs.

Here again there is nothing new. Many central cities have brought an element of order into metropolitan relations in just such ways. The compact between Denver and its suburbs is a case in point. Salt Lake City is in an excellent position to bring about the orderly development of the entire county through bargaining with the smaller communities, because it controls the water supply. Grand Rapids has established uniform subdivision regulations on its peripheries by negotiating an agreement with suburbs concerning water, sewer, and other services.

Specialists in public administration frequently object to the creation of special-function districts because they further complicate the already complicated structure of metropolitan government. This is not a weighty objection if such special governments are utilized only for genuine area-wide problems. As noted previously, there are not many functions that really require a metropolitan jurisdiction. A more relevant objection to special-district governments, as they are usually constituted, is that they remove needed bargaining power from the mayors of the central cities. And this, even if special districts are few in number, becomes a towering obstacle to general inter-community collaboration over a wide range of problems. A suburb that has its water supplied by an independent agency can cease to cooperate without penalty in other functions. The solution for this difficulty is apparent: when special-function governments are established, they should be governed not by separate, independent boards but by the regular political heads of the governments concerned. The mayor of the largest city on such a board will find his effectiveness augmented in fostering general area-wide collaboration; where independent boards are established, this effectiveness is diminished.

In the absence of metropolitan government, metropolitan planning has an important, but not decisive, role. In the proposed model, there is not a single plan for an entire metropolitan region; rather, there are several. The mayor's office must obviously contain a planning staff; so must the governor's. Other planning groups will exist in the special-function districts. The important point is not to leave planning in limbo. It must be attached to the arms of action—all of them. In the long run, this may mean that the most decisive planning comes from the largest general-purpose government. But it may also develop as an adjunct to a special-purpose government for handling water, sewers, or transportation. The latter development will produce unified planning over a broad range of problems if political control runs, as has been suggested, to the offices of general government in the area concerned.

The mayor's bargaining for specific area-wide programs should be geared to his larger purpose of achieving a more comprehensive regional organization. Where more than one local cooperative arrangement exists between two or more communities, efforts should be made to combine them into a single contract and to use common administrative machinery. As William Rafsky, Philadelphia Development Coordinator, has written, "Thus cumbersome and overlapping devices are avoided, and the concept of broad regional cooperation is advanced."[1] More than this, the steady accretion of cooperative programs, fitted together through the normal push and haul of political bargaining, provides an organic method of constructing, through time, a new form of metropolitan federalism. Special staffs from the core cities, augmented by representatives of other communities, should be assigned to cultivate this development, performing, at least initially, planning and professional services for suburban areas for which no return is expected. Simultaneously—or as a second step—central cities can make available on a cost basis to small municipalities and other local units such services as those governments cannot easily provide for themselves—for example, a comprehensive plan for a suburban village; central purchasing services for a school district; or an application for Federal aid on behalf of a county. Here, as elsewhere, the advantages of collaboration are best demonstrated by collaborative action, and the central city mayor must display initiative and resourcefulness in matters of small importance if he is to make progress toward his larger goals. It bears repeating that he will find substantial political support for such efforts.

These suggestions obviously do not add up to a "solution" to the metropolitan-organization problem. There is no solution in any absolute or final sense. There is, however, the possibility of moving step by step from where metropolitan organization now is to where it ought to be. The advantage of the proposed model is that it can accomplish some things immediately while simultaneously traveling toward a more comprehensive regional organization. In both the short and long run, the model takes account of the importance of community discretion and local freedoms. It recognizes that some joint programs will appear unpalatable at times to some communities, and that joint voluntary action adversely affecting the interests of any given community will not be achieved through simple exhortation or come about easily as one in a series of contractual relationships. It recommends that such difficulties be met through the usual political processes of bargaining and compromise within a large framework of intent: that of sharing joint functions through some sort of local federalism. The program can only succeed if it has energetic leadership from central-city mayors and other political leaders. With such leadership it can find support from the governor, from business and social groups, and from professional planners and administrators. The advances that are to be made through this scheme of development may be slow; but they have the positive virtue of respecting local options and the negative one of avoiding the complete failure that may follow insistence upon politically unattainable "ideal" programs.

---

1. Personal communication to the authors. They are indebted to Mr. Rafsky for several suggestions incorporated into this section. They have also profited from a memorandum by Luther Gulick. But neither Mr. Rafsky nor Mr. Gulick should be charged with responsibility for the "model" or any of its details.

# NEEDED: A NEW LAYER OF LOCAL SELF-GOVERNMENT

## LUTHER GULICK

A STRIKING CHARACTERISTIC of the new metropolitan pattern of settlement in the United States is its amorphous structure, dynamism and unprecedented scale. The metropolitanized sections of the country now contain well over 60 per cent of the total population, while single "clusters" have three million, five million, or as many as 23 million human beings. In geographic extent the individual complexes run to as much as 18 thousand square miles.

The scale of what exists and is coming on top is so colossal that we are carried into a new dimension, a new world.

There are three aspects of scale and growth which must concern us as we think about the organization of government in the metropolitan regions. These are the management problems, the cost problems, and the problems of democracy.

From the standpoint of *management,* scale and dynamism are extremely significant. With large scale we can no longer rest back on simple, inherited, amateur, informal, and voluntary approaches to government. As in other large-scale operations, we will be forced to define functions, divide the work, formalize structures and interrelations, professionalize the staffs, and institutionalize activities and communications. With growth also there will be more and more subdivision of work and in consequence a parallel development of integration through formalized co-ordination and control.

These shifts from the "beautiful simplicity of the past" to institutionalized management, forced on us by scale, are not all losses for the community. In most cases, there is at the same time a marked increase in the quality of service and the skill and competence of management.

There are those who think that our bigger cities are already "too big to govern effectively." A little analysis will show, however, that it is not the size that creates the "impossible" situation. The biggest cities are smaller than the states and nations of which they are a part, yet no one says the state or the nation is too big to govern effectively. The problem is not the size; the problem is adjustment of management devices to the size which is forced upon us by events. And when it comes to this, it will be recognized that we now know how to deal with size. We have the organizational and managerial knowledge and tools. There is no reason for running away from scale.

Reprinted from the *Annals of the American Academy of Political and Social Science,* 314 (November, 1957), 57–65, where it appeared under the title "Metropolitan Organization," by permission of the publisher.

As to the *costs of scale* it is generally believed that most per capita costs increase with size because people who live in big urban centers need more service and protection. Fortunately, there are also certain *economies of scale*. When quality and costs are compared, it is clear that costs of scale are partly neutralized by the economies of scale so that there appear to be no economic "laws" which will automatically limit the scale of metropolitan operations.

A great deal needs to be known also concerning the effect of scale on *democracy*. Particularly when we deal with local government it is fashionable to think and talk about little communities. Most of our "democratic dogmas," developed through our early history, sentimentalize over this kind of small-scale democracy. While everyone recognizes that with size we cannot have direct democracy but must move to representative institutions, they do so with nostalgic regret. However, no one has drawn up a clear statement of "the democracy of scale" nor given our people a dogma of big democracy by which they can authenticate their present-day institutions.[1] We still measure big democracies with the yardstick of the town meeting and test their democratic validity by the words of Jefferson and de Tocqueville. This is a philosophical blunder based on the scale fallacy.

Scale cannot be avoided now. Either we develop a clear philosophy and machinery for large-scale democracy or we inflict on our people and their leaders a painful sense of frustration and guilt. The truth is, the tests for ideal self-government in a large population which is widespread geographically, but knit together in a new structured web of economic, social, and communicational existence, must be radically different from the tests for small-scale democracy.

## Does the Metropolitan Area Need "a Government"?

Every metropolitan area in the United States has many governments and much governmental activity. Many of the activities are federal, still more are state, and both operate through their several independent departments. In addition there are the activities of the cities, counties, "authorities," villages, towns, school, and other districts.

Even with all these governments severally at work, with the added influence of countless voluntary agencies, and with many intergovernmental arrangements and contracts, there are a number of clearly unmet requirements in most areas.

The unmet needs give a clue to what is required. They differ from place to place. In some areas the work which falls between the many jurisdictions is water supply; in others it may be waste disposal, pollution control, education or housing, health, crime or flood and fire protection. Generally, there is an imbalance of local financial resources with resulting luxury for some

---

1. However, a good start has been made by Paul H. Appleby in his *Big Democracy* (New York: Alfred A. Knopf, 1945).

and tax deficiences for others. But everywhere there is chaos as to the major circulation system and pattern including highways, railroads, air facilities, mass transportation, and provision for traffic.

It is now evident that there are inherent reasons why such problems cannot be handled effectively by bits and pieces, each in the hands of independent jurisdictions.

And when it comes to zoning, land use regulation, and the system for circulation and traffic, the underlying problems become impossible of rational attack unless there is a single center for co-ordinated analysis, planning, and action. It is inherently impossible to "solve the traffic problem" within boundaries which are less than those of the normal area of circulation, that is, the entire metropolitan area; nor by separate and competing jurisdictions; nor by ignoring the fact that land uses and the transportation system and pattern are two sides of the same coin.

This statement does not prove that there must be "a single metropolitan government." It suggests, rather, that there must be several new area-wide governmental activities.

Some of these might be assigned to the federal government. The minimum civilized standards might be set and enforced by various federal and state departments. The states might be required to take over the broader metropolitan regional land use controls and to develop and enforce the general pattern of the highway system, controlling federal and state highway funds to this end. Tax difficulties and imbalances may be dealt with through state aid and various equalization formulas. And where some special service is required, like a single great sewage treatment plan or an interjurisdictional bridge or transit system, an "authority" may be set up with its own sources of support from charges or tolls.

Thus it may be possible to design governmental machinery to deal with each and every present need of the metropolitan regions without setting up any specific "metropolitan government." This *ad hoc* approach with a separate metropolitan agency of some sort for each metropolitan job is possible.

What does such an *ad hoc* approach lack? It lacks two very important elements:

First, the *ad hoc* approach lacks comprehensiveness. If we rely on existing state and federal departments each to take care of one or more of the area-wide needs of the metropolitan regions or set up special new agencies or authorities each to perform a specific service, it is evident that this arrangement cannot give a comprehensive or integrated treatment of the several metropolitan needs. Nor would fiscal resources be interrelated or pooled. There would be no possibility of over-all planning, integration, or mutual adjustment and compromise. Each activity would go it alone, and there would be nobody to hold things in balance or to tackle a new development not originally provided for.

Second, the *ad hoc* approach makes self-government by the people of the metropolitan area as concerns their own metropolitan problems impossible as a practical matter. The state and federal agencies are democratically but distantly responsible to their larger electorates, not specifically to the metropolitan area. In fact, metropolitan areas are markedly underrepresented in most state legislatures and in the national political structure. The *ad hoc* agencies and authorities are legally parts of the state government, though in fact floating around in a sort of irresponsible political limbo. Even if such *ad hoc* agencies were made responsible entirely to local electorates, they would confront the electorates competitively with unresolved problems of balance and priorities in a form with which large-scale constituencies cannot deal directly.

These two inescapable deficiencies of the *ad hoc* approach, both of which are greatly accentuated by scale, lead one to explore the possibility of designing one or more governmental "models" planned to give the metropolitan area a government which is comprehensive as to area-wide matters and gives the region at the same time a large measure of local democratic self-government.

## Structure of Required Metropolitan Government

The design of such a governmental structure for any metropolitan area must be settled after functions and locale are known. But we need to keep a few central desiderata clearly in mind. These may be noted as:

1. The need to put together within a single viable political boundary the people and the territories which have to be together to work out the local problems of the metropolitan area. By this engineered strategy we make it possible for the people to think, debate, act, and work together politically as a community; and we create the political habitat within which responsible political leadership will arise.

2. The need to achieve geographic, social, and economic comprehensiveness so that the metropolitan government may not be confronted by the impossible task of building half a bridge, regulating traffic on one part of a through highway, controlling land use for one side of a street, or fighting to hold down crime in half of a slum.

3. The need to create workable joint and balanced action between interrelated activities like water supply and waste disposal; crime control, traffic regulation, and recreation; building permits and fire prevention; housing, health, and welfare; and especially to tie together in one package the control over developing land use and density and the control over the major pattern of circulation.

4. The need to create a governmental representative body drawn from the metropolitan area as a whole to which may be given both the legal and the pragmatic power to consider each and every major metropolitan problem on an integrated basis, to devise remedial programs, to listen to all shades of opinion, to develop compromises and community agreements, and then to

take action to carry out the decisions made and to require compliance with these decisions not only from individuals and private groups but from subordinate municipal corporations concerning area-wide metropolitan matters.

5. The need to protect the local communities, natural neighborhood subdivisions, and incorporate units against being swallowed up and destroyed by the metropolis and its government in the performance of their separable local activities and in the maintenance of their desired above-standard services and environments.

6. The need to develop a fiscal system for the metropolitan government in its own right, so that (a) the wealth, power, and credit of the area as a whole may be mobilized for the solution of the over-all problems of the area; (b) the sudden new wealth created through the activities of the metropolitan government may make a fair contribution toward the costs; and (c) the fortuitous tax resources of one lucky subregion may contribute to support the basic community requirements of another small subunit which has no such metropolitan windfall.

7. The need to equip the metropolitan government with suitable arms for (a) analysis, comprehensive and balanced planning, and compromise development; (b) policy decision-making; and (c) execution, management, and enforcement. And finally,

8. The need to remember that we are not working with eternal and fixed boundaries, but with volatile, dynamic, and expanding settlements; that we are always striving in the United States to keep government and political decisions "close to the people."

There are situations in which these eight requirements may be met within reason without creating a new layer of metropolitan government. Where this is the case, it goes without saying that we should develop and adapt existing machinery to do the job, turning to new creations only where this is the best and only way out.

Approaching our problem from this point, it will be found that there are situations, as noted above, in which we can turn to the federal government, to the states, to the counties, and to existing *ad hoc* agencies or to interjurisdictional contracts to handle the activities now called for.

Where none of these devices is available or adequate to meet the requirements we have laid down above, we shall need entirely new political invention.

With this in mind, four such "inventions" are here sketched, with no claim that they are original with the author. These are:

1. The creation of a state department of local affairs with an independent bureau or "desk" for each major metropolitan area within the state.

2. The reconstruction of the county so that the county may become the metropolitan government of its region.

3. The creation of a new limited purpose metropolitan service agency with a built-in power to expand as to functions, finance, and representation.

4. The creation of a new layer of local government above the existing localities and below the state to be known as the metropolitan council of XYZ, having the authority and financial power to deal with broad but specified metropolitan activities.

These four inventions are not necessarily mutually exclusive, though 2 and 3 would not be needed where a metropolitan council is established. The four proposals are briefly discussed in the following paragraphs.

## A State Department of Local Affairs

The proposed state department of local affairs would take over responsibility for handling all general relations of the state with county, city, village, town, and special district governments, and with their officials. The new department would collect local statistics, especially financial statistics, make administrative surveys and financial audits, offer "efficiency" advice and assistance, and would carry on extensive officer training and in-service-training programs for local elective and appointed personnel. The department would work directly with existing associations of local officials, participate in conferences, and defend the interests of the local governments as a group before the legislature and with all administrative departments.

Such a state department would not take the place of the state department of education in dealing with the local schools nor of the health department, the welfare department, the highway department, the state planning department, the tax department, or any other functional department in its specialized and professional functions. But the state department of local affairs would be concerned with the general impact of these specialized departments on local governments as such.

Under this concept, it would be desirable to set up in the proposed department a separate "desk" for each major metropolitan area of the state and to appoint to this desk a man of broad experience and competence. He would not only "clear" all state activities concerning their combined impact on "his metropolitan area" but would work directly with the local governments of his area. On occasion he would call their officials together for conference in order to develop the maximum co-operation and participation in the local solution of metropolitan problems and the fullest possible reflection of local needs and desires in all state decisions.

Co-operation in planning, the establishment of standards, and the development of services and compacts across state lines concerning metropolitan problems would be a responsibility of the "desk" and the department.

Under this plan, it would be most helpful if the local governments would set up voluntary regional councils like that developed in the New York tri-state region some years ago under the chairmanship of Mayor Robert F. Wagner.

## The Metropolitan County

A second possible approach is the complete reconstruction of the county government in densely populated regions so that it may add to its existing functions and become "the metropolitan government" of its area. Where the county already has an adequate geographical extent and a reasonable level of political responsibility and administrative competence, this might well meet the eight requirements stated above.

The major disadvantage of using the county as the foundation for metropolitan government is that the county is generally imbedded constitutionally in the state administrative, representational, and political structure. Its boundaries are most inflexible and its operation can be raised in managerial competence only with the greatest effort.

Wherever the county is used as the metropolitan government, issues of political representation arise as in the case of the new Dade County charter (Miami, Florida). Such a county falls into the same category as the great metropolitan city, or the city-county, in terms of political representation. The governing body must, preferably, be so designed as to represent the voters directly either by election at large, by districts, or by some combination of these methods. The size of the county council must be articulated to the form of county government. If a county manager is used, the council would be small and representative. If the county mayor is elected and assisted by an appointive chief administrative officer, then the council can be designed more freely in regard to size and methods of election. However structured in detail, the design of such a federated county council should be based on the representative system already tested in our great cities and city-counties and tailored to the political needs of the specific area.

## The Open-Ended Metropolitan Commission

A third possible approach is the creation of a limited-purpose special "authority," service unit or commission designed to cover a large metropolitan area and to perform from the beginning some needed service, such as water supply or airport construction and operation, with the authority to add to its functions and powers by local action.

The recently enacted law in the State of Washington, the Metropolitan Council Act, is along this line although its possible added functions are rather narrowly limited. Presumably these could be extended by the state legislature in future years if occasion warrants.

Where this approach is adopted, it would seem important to establish something more than a small board of directors appointed by the governor, as is so often the case. If the board is to make extensive policy decisions as to planning, land use controls, and the general pattern of the transportation system, it is not likely that a small specifically chosen board can be effective.

## A New Metropolitan Council

A fourth approach is the creation of an entirely new layer of local self-government, what we may call a metropolitan council.

This would be, first of all, a legislative body. It would be designed to bring together officially and regularly all of the major local governmental interests and problems of the metropolitan area so that the regional governmental shortfalls may be fully considered; remedial and developmental programs may be evolved with adequate planning; compromises arrived at, and decisions made and carried out.

These are primarily "policy" assignments; they are the stuff of politics.

We know from much experience that such functions cannot appropriately be left to experts or bureaucrats working alone. This kind of work calls for politically sensitive and responsible "representatives."

We know also that the real essence of the problem is the laying of the political foundation for the development of the metropolitan community as a political reality with rising political leadership, political education, and political following. This alone will make possible effective and balanced political action and community commitment for the metropolitan area as a whole.

Because of scale, we must have representative institutions, and for these to work we must have political leadership and political action. It is to this end that we need a political entity coextensive with the area and consequently a metropolitan political constituency.

Furthermore, we know that it is generally safer to build political institutions on what we already have, rather than to wipe the slate clean and start all over again.

From these considerations it follows that the membership of the metropolitan council should be made up initially from the chief elected officials of the local governments of the region which is being brought together. This would include, in most situations, the mayors of the larger cities and incorporated units and the chief elected official of each county comprised in the "metropolitan area." It might be desirable to add to this group a number of specifically elected representatives and a president of the metropolitan council to be elected at large, although these developments might well be postponed until the region is ripe for this type of leadership and direct representation.

The metropolitan council would establish a strong and well-staffed program development and planning unit, placing this directly under its chairman or president. The council would set up several special working committees for which the program and planning unit would furnish an appropriate staff.

The metropolitan council would do its administrative work, such as building a bridge or a water works or running a sewage treatment plant or a transit system, by using existing regional and local operating agencies as far as possible. Where no agency exists which can handle the operation, the council would by ordinance create such an administration. This could be done by setting up "an authority" or by creating an operating department under a manager to be appointed by the council president. Where one or more authorities or special district bodies exist already within the boundaries of the metropolitan council, these could be continued as they are, bringing certain of their powers under the supervision of the council.

Especially important is the definition of the responsibility of the metropolitan council. The effort would be made to assign to the council the overall, interunit metropolitan matters and activities and to guarantee to the existing and underlying governmental units the responsibility to carry on their normal non-metropolitan local activities. This can only be approached through trial and error: With a general statement of this principle, the listing of the arrangements with reference to a number of the more obvious services where the division of work is required, and by authorizing the localities which so desire to protect their unique advantages and to have local services of a higher standard than those of their neighbors.

While many of the metropolitan services and facilities developed by the metropolitan council will be "self-supporting" on the basis of prices and tolls collected, the council should not be required to rely solely on such receipts.

As to metropolitan areas which extend across state lines, as is already true of more than a score of such metropolises, the metropolitan council would be set up by joint action of the states involved, presumably utilizing the interstate compact procedure. In such cases the original compact should provide for territorial extension and for functional and fiscal modifications without requiring congressional reconsideration. As to modifications which do not change the arrangement fundamentally, it would be desirable for the contracting states to leave these to the area concerned, rather than to require the state legislatures to review the arrangement again.

Each such interstate metropolitan compact will have to be tailormade, primarily because of the required fiscal provisions. The present local government provisions, court decisions, and tax and debt systems are so diverse among neighboring states, that a great deal of constitutional ingenuity will be required to develop workable arrangements in all cases. It may even be necessary to consider the in-state members of an inter-state metropolitan council as a separate "municipal corporation" with the right to act concerning matters within its state along lines agreed on jointly in the metropolitan council.

## Character of the Council

The metropolitan council as thus conceived is, first, an old-fashioned American "body of overseers" with authority limited to the over-all interests, concerns, and problems of the defined metropolitan region. It is democratically constituted from locally elected officials, with the eventual addition of directly elected members. As such it is also a federation of the existing local governments. The council is initially primarily a policy-developing and -adopting body; that is, a legislative agency. However, the council is given the authority, as are local legislatures generally, to develop such administrative units as may be required, using existing agencies as far as this is possible, or to create new units where necessary.

Under this proposal, the existing local governments—the cities, counties, towns, villages, and special districts—could be continued as they now are in relation to their local functions. Only the metropolitan aspects of functions would come under the oversight of the metropolitan council. At the same time, the existing local jurisdictions would be authorized to shift to the council by mutual consent any activities which they wish to handle in this way.

This proposal is not only elastic in its boundaries since it is not tied by definition to a specific set of existing city or county boundaries, but is extensible across state lines, following precedents already well established in many jurisdictions for more limited activities.

Under this proposal, finally, there is brought into legal and political existence what is now evolving naturally as a matter of social and economic life; namely, the metropolitan community. With a representative council, this emergent community is given political being. The metropolitan area becomes a single constituency for metropolitan representation, for metropolitan policy discussion, for metropolitan administration, and above all, for metropolitan political leadership and political action. While this in no way supersedes existing governmental organizations, it fills the vacuum and makes it possible for the rising metropolis to deal effectively and democratically with its now unmet metropolitan needs.

# THE METROPOLITAN AREA IN
# THE NUCLEAR AGE

FRANK P. ZEIDLER

IN A DISCUSSION of the impact of urbanism on government in the two decades from 1957 to 1977, the basic question of whether or not the United States will be at war or peace during that time must be answered. Two assumptions might be made—one, that there will be a war with the full

Reprinted from *Annuals of the American Academy of Political and Social Science,* 314 (November, 1957), 74–81, where it appeared under the title "Urbanism and Government, 1957–1977," by permission of the author and the publisher.

or partial use of atomic weapons, and the other, that there will be peace, but with the continual threat of war in the background. To tell which of these conditions will result is too difficult for me, so that I must give two answers, based on each assumption, of the impact of urbanism on federalism.

The first assumption that seems most probable to me, despite its inherent pessimism, is that the United States government and the government of the Soviet Union will be unable to come to a decision of permanent peace. The result will be the devastation by nuclear bombs of the principal cities of the United States and Russia. The main reason I have for believing this is the condition that seems to exist inside of the Soviet Union. The leaders of that nation are not similarly responsive to public pressures as are American leaders. They are caught in the cage of Leninist ideas and all that system for the seizure of power implies. Anyone in government who speaks softly toward the "enemies" of the Soviet system as conceived under Leninism cannot come to power. Anyone who ascends to power has reached it with the use of force and violence—a pattern of conduct which will not be shed upon arrival at the pinnacle of authority. It is not logical to assume that Soviet leaders will be any less given to using force and violence against other nations, particularly the United States which is the selected enemy, than they were against using such force and violence on their own people and comrades.

As a result, the public expressions of the leaders of the Soviet Union must of necessity be one of hostility toward the United States; or if the terms directed toward the United States are terms calling for co-existence, these terms must be so expressed that the party clique in Russia believes that their leaders are merely seeking to lull this country to a sense of security while they further improve the position of Russia to attack and destroy the United States.

The actions of the Russian leaders naturally bring a reaction in the United States; communism becomes the principal object of attack by many orators—political, religious, and economic. The resulting continual denunciations of the leaders of each nation by the other over a period of time, in my opinion, must inevitably lead to an international conflict. This may be a gloomy view, but many current developments seem to point to a renewed struggle even if there is an attempt at disarmament.

The targets of destruction in an atomic war are the places from which a counterattack may be launched, important military installations, and urban districts where concentrations of people and industry are to be found. If tensions were to grow more severe and if disappointments in the disarmament program turn to bitterness people who have sought a disarmament program, it is inevitable that friends and enemies alike will start to think of the fate of people and structures in the urban areas. These areas are the most vulnerable parts of the United States and its federal system. It seems quite probable that a form of blackmail can be directed against a government such as that of the United States by threatening the destruction of its principal cities. It seems to me that we are in this situation at the present time.

## Vulnerability of Urban Areas

The existence of this threat has caused some thought on the part of urban and federal officials concerning the method of reducing the vulnerability of the urban areas of the United States. State officials have not paid much attention to this problem at all. It is my fear that by the time an atomic war may come, nothing of any great significance to reduce this vulnerability will have occurred. Some cities may have developed evacuation plans without the proper reception areas in the rural districts for the evacuees. It is my fear also that the rural districts will be poorly equipped to deal with the masses of a fleeing urban population at the time of an atomic showdown.

I suspect, therefore, that for the next decade there will be a continued concentration of people in the metropolitan areas who are attracted by employment and high standards of living available in such areas. I suspect also that very little attention will be paid either by industry, the federal government, or state governments to the decentralization of industrial establishments or to the reduction of the increasing vulnerability which is occurring in the metropolitan areas of the United States.

The increasing vulnerability of the urban areas has the gravest consequences for the nation; it could mean the destruction of the country and the end of our federal system. Herein lies the greatest weakness of federalism at the present time.

The role of the state governments in the protection of the federal system in atomic defense is most important. At the present time these governments are almost completely inactive about, or unaware of, the atomic threat. Since most state governments are dominated by small-town people acting in the name of farmers and since the rural animosity of the urban dweller persists as a foundation fact of each legislature, the legislatures will not take the proper action to protect the urban areas; and they see little danger to rural areas.

The ignorance and indifference of governors and state legislatures on the question of the atomic home defense of the United States are colossal. The primary reason for this is that the state parties vying for control in each state find no political value in civil defense or protection of the vulnerable urban areas. They carry on politics as usual as if the great scientific achievements that have occurred in the past fifteen years have never existed. The indifference to, and the hostility toward, the urban areas by state governments can conceivably be fatal to the United States federal system. It may bring us to our first major military defeat and perhaps destruction of the nation in our 181 years of history. In view of the weakness and inefficiency of state governments, the impact of increased urban growth on the United States may cause a chain of events which will bring the federal system of the nation crashing down in an atomic war.

To reduce the vulnerability of the United States would require a decentralization of the urban population and of industry. Neither the states nor the federal government at this time is prepared to exercise the necessary power and authority to achieve this result; neither are the cities. One course of action requires an increase in federal and state taxation to provide the necessary shelters for people against intercontinental ballistic missiles. In another action, the state governments would necessarily have to re-create metropolitan regions, overriding both the central cities and competing suburbs in order to provide a master plan of development and growth which would reduce the vulnerability of the masses of population. In a third move, the state and federal governments would have to insist on the relocation of critical industry so that it is more evenly dispersed throughout the United States and so that a single massive blow directed at the country would not cause irreparable devastation and effect from which the nation could not recover.

## Lack of Protection Against Atomic Warfare

To achieve all of these results, in my opinion, is beyond the capacity of either the state or federal government and also beyond the desire of the urban residents. When this public incapacity to act in self-protection is matched against a hardened system such as that of the Soviet Union—which can order populations to move, force the relocation of industry, and reduce vulnerability—it becomes apparent that the American system of federalism has some weaknesses and maintains its position only because of its potential striking power. However, the lack of proper planning for the atomic age cannot be laid entirely upon the state governments nor upon the weakness of the leadership in the federal government. It is also due to the psychology of people who are weary of the sound of war, who desire luxurious suburban living, and who cannot as a group begin to exert themselves to perform the necessary but disagreeable tasks which would result from a proper plan for urban defense in the United States.

The major parties in power, reflecting the popular view, refuse to stare the prospect of atomic war in the face or to propose the necessary measures which would diminish the effects of an attack on this nation. Only in the urban communities do there seem to be pressures on the part of a few leaders to make the governments more effective in the defense of people. The action of urban leaders may bring some modification in the pattern of urban growth. It may result in a slightly increased urban pressure on the federal government to do something about urban problems as state governments fail to act. There will be, then, up until the time an atomic showdown occurs, some closer liaison between the urban centers and the federal government and some drawing away from the state governments by urban governments.

A condition of increased hostility between large cities and state governments may result. The voters in large cities, in the North particularly, may continue to follow the Democratic party while suburban and rural voters will continue to follow the Republican party. Since rural and suburban voters may likely total the largest bloc, such a division will also increase the chances of the taking away from the urban areas of their proper representation in state legislatures. Also there will develop permanently in state constitutions the system which in Wisconsin is called the "Areacrat" form of government—namely, that form in which area rather than people is represented in the state legislature.

## Suburban vs. Urban Interests

I also look in this decade for increased state concern for some suburban areas in opposition to the central cities. This will occur largely because suburbanites will have considered their status and life improved to the point that they will leave the Democratic party and vote for the party of conservatism and the status quo, the Republican party. Legislation directed against the development and improvement of the urban centers will often be sponsored by wealthy suburbanites who make their living in the central area.

I also look for a continued migration of southern Negroes and southern white workers to northern cities. The core is the only part of these cities where they can go to live, and because of their numbers and poverty, this core will continue to deteriorate faster than local authorities, state governments, or the federal government can rebuild it. For political reasons, the state governments in this situation may try to lend their weight to increasing the density of population and making the minority problem in the central areas greater. They may do so because of their dislike of the central cities, their fear of the political philosophy held by people in them, and their desire to maintain the economic and class differences between the people of the suburban communities and the lower economic groups that migrate into the cities seeking work.

Thus, because of these political divisions that exist between the people in the cities and the state governments there will be even less opportunity for the threatened peoples in the target areas to make their voices heard in the state and national governments.

In view of the struggle that is going on, therefore, between the United States and the Soviet Union—sometimes hot, sometimes cold—there is a likelihood that the disagreement may come to a head some time within the next decade. The result will be that both the Soviet Union and the United States will be devastated. I do not believe that the American people can live successfully under the tensions placed upon them by the Soviet Union. Neither do I believe that the Soviet leaders realize what they are doing to the people of the United States in keeping them at a boiling point with their intransigence and constant propaganda attacks which are reported in the United States' press.

Assuming that by 1977 an atomic attack will have occurred and a war concluded some years earlier, the year 1977 would undoubtedly see the cities engaged in rebuilding, some on entirely new sites and some in the older areas. The population of the cities, of course, would be much diminished, as would the population of the nation. Probably, there would be even a lesser number of people in the smaller communities of the United States owing to the ensuing starvation and epidemics that would take place if people were removed wholesale from the larger cities and if those cities were destroyed.

## Effects of Atomic War

The result of an atomic war could not help but mean radical changes of government with people of diverse cultures and backgrounds scattered in new locations. It is interesting to speculate on what changes would occur. It is entirely possible that the people of the United States could not resist the movements of people from more overcrowded parts of the world to settle into the nation in considerable numbers. In the matter of construction, such rebuilding which would take place would perhaps, in its initial phases, be more or less haphazard. As for transportation, undoubtedly there would be fewer automobiles since as a result of an atomic war, won or lost, the United States certainly would not enjoy the lion's share of the world's gasoline and oil resources. There is the probable increased use of atomic power, but even with this power source undoubtedly there would be a lower standard of living in urban areas and a considerable disarrangement of the transit systems which make large cities possible.

It is my opinion that a federal system of government would survive a world clash because the challenge to the powers of the states in the great urban areas would no longer exist. The disarrangement and chaotic conditions of the federal government as a result of atomic warfare would force more responsibility on state governments, at least temporarily. However, if the United States survived without being conquered or overrun either by an attacking enemy or by other nations which were relatively uninjured in an atomic war and which would seize control of a shaky government, then it is conceivable that the federal government might reassert its authority over the state governments. It is also possible that southern states faced with the inability to deal with the Negro question might seek to develop a regional government apart from the rest of the United States.

A course of action worth considering as a result of an atomic war is that the federal government might become more seriously concerned about the great urban areas, and by constitutional change or other amendment take these areas away from the jurisdiction of state governments and make them responsible directly to the federal government. This would be done to provide proper planning, dispersal of population and industry, and proper construction in urban areas to overcome the defects which became plain as a result of atomic attack.

To sum up: Under the assumption that there would be an atomic attack, the present impact of urbanism on the federal system is to place a problem before state governments and the federal governments which it is impossible for these governments to solve because of political factors. This condition results in the vulnerability of the United States to the point of possible destruction of many of its people and their industries and to the possible end of the United States as an independent government.

## Effects of the Cold War

The second assumption we can make on the future of cities is that they will persist at least until 1977 without an atomic attack, but under a constant threat of such a condition occurring. Even under this threat, a great increase in population will occur in the urban centers of the United States; these centers will become much larger and more numerous. Many urban areas now separated by open country will become one continuous set of contiguous urban communities. The pressures of a large population and the need for critical services such as water and sewer in these areas will undoubtedly promote the creation of the metropolitan concept of government.

The unwillingness of state legislatures to face the growth of urban areas will impel certain urban groups to continue to seek grants in aid from the federal government. If the situation is bad enough, there may be attempts to have the major metropolitan areas made special wards of the federal government for certain purposes. As the metropolitan growth occurs, it is likely that hostility between the state governments and the central cities may grow. The political cleavage between the two, urban areas and state governments, will influence elections of the United States during the next two decades.

The need for furnishing special units of government to deal with regional sewer, water and traffic problems will introduce great complexities into the laws of state governments. Since state governments do not desire to see the growth of the political power of metropolitan areas, they will persist in seeking to fragment the metropolitan areas into urban and suburban conflicting groups as a means of dividing and ruling.

One can expect, also, that there will be a continued stratification of population in the urban areas with the wealthy and the people of white ancestry moving to the suburban areas where a kind of economic caste system will develop. People of colored ancestry may continue to move from the rural South into the core cities of metropolitan areas. This situation, in which the bloc of Negro voters in central cities grows greater, will further promote the desire of the controllers of state governments to isolate the central cities in metropolitan areas and to choke off their growing political strength.

The possibility in some areas of central governments being greatly influenced by Negro voting blocs would undoubtedly materialize in many cities in the next two decades. The government of the urban areas, therefore, in the northern part of the United States will be directly subjected to the policies of the southern states with regard to migrating Negro minorities. The presence of such blocs will bring demands for housing, fair-employment practices, civil rights, and welfare legislation. Other people, too, will continue to crowd into the cities to enjoy the convenience of living and the high wages that are to be found there.

## Welfare State vs. Private Enterprise

The growth of urbanism will also tend to promote the conflict between public ownership and social welfare ideas and the concepts of private enterprise. Large numbers of people who are wage earners without any security other than their physical strength will tend to promote legislation which will guarantee their welfare and their security even in times of unemployment. This type of legislation, being considered hostile by the rural and suburban citizens, will result in struggles between the urban and the rural forces in the state legislatures and will spill over into the Congress. This same ideological conflict carried on in the field of housing will mean that the opponents of municipal housing will continue to be vigorous. As a result, there will be a constant shortage of adequate housing for urban residents of the United States since private enterprise will not be able to supply the urban population with adequate low-cost shelter because of fence-me-in economic laws.

The creation of express roads through the major cities will foster the spread of suburbanism. Within these cities there will be a development, though on a limited scale, of homogeneous, easily identifiable communities in the older areas. Some of these will be desirable; others will merely be unredeveloped slum areas bounded by trafficways which set them apart from surrounding communities. Out of each of these areas certain identifiable political yearnings will come. If urban redevelopment results in a mass dispossession of many small owners and the creation of a large tenantry, it is possible that federal and state laws will reflect the pressure of the tenants against the landlords.

The great growth of population without a proper expansion of resources to feed it and to provide it with fresh air and water may cause a significant deterioration in the standard of living for many people. A difficult problem will arise in the attempt to tax for educational purposes because of the larger number of children. It is possible that a resistance to property taxes for education will become so strong that the educational program of the nation will have to be seriously diminished.

The increased use of mechanical devices will also bring a rash of laws necessary to curtail their deleterious effects. Laws against improper uses of

motor vehicles, against noise, dirt, and unsanitary conditions will undoubtedly result in the further concentration of population. Most of these
laws will be developed in state legislatures but only after a resistance from
the rural people who cannot conceive of the need for such laws.

Partly because the urban needs will be so great and the urban communities will put pressure on the federal government to solve these needs,
state legislatures may make grudging concessions to the urban problems.
However, it is not likely that state legislatures will bow in any direction
toward legislation which might be described as socialistic if they can help
it. In addition, there will be constant agitation in state legislatures to dis-
mantle all of the operations of the federal government except those dealing
with the development of military forces for an attack.

The increase in population in the urban centers may also put a strain on
the agriculture of the United States, and it is entirely possible that unless
there is some better planning of agricultural development and water resources,
the urban areas may suffer shortages of essential supplies some time within
the next two decades. Even without the threat of atomic warfare, it is entirely
possible that there may be recessions in business which will have their
repercussions particularly on the urban communities and bring forth from
them a demand for federal social legislation rather than state legislation to
alleviate the conditions of unemployment.

The total results, therefore, of the pattern from 1957 to 1977, if the
nation lives at uneasy peace with Russia, will be to diminish the strength
of the state legislatures and to increase the strength of the federal government
because of the pressures of urban living.

## Group Conflicts

Over the next twenty years certain struggles between different groups in
the great urban areas will also have their reflection on the federal system.
The first of these is the struggle between two economic groups which are
able to finance elections to gain a dominant hand in the voice of the communities. The one is a group represented by owners and management, most
of whom are suburban dwellers, and the other is that reflected in organized
labor.

There will be an attempt by both groups to attain ascendency in the government in metropolitan areas. Since most of the management people live
in the suburbs, they will devote their attention particularly to changing state
laws which will permit them to control the destinies of the central city by
remote control or through special districts of government. In this action they
will have the support of the rural legislators.

The labor movement will attempt to resist this move by maintaining
control of the central cities independent of the legislatures. If the legislatures
invade this control of the central cities too extensively, it is entirely pos-

sible that labor-elected city representatives will seek relief and protection from the federal government.

A second struggle will take place on the part of organized supporters of vice, gambling, and crime to gain control of the central areas. The central cities are oftentimes regarded as "play spots," and there is a tendency for local officials to wink at organized vice and crime in certain districts of their cities. This leads to the flourishing of gangs and organized hoodlums; and in most cities these organized hoodlums, working either through the management or labor groups, and sometimes working through both, have been enabled to control city government with the resulting deterioration of government and wholesale corruption.

This type of struggle will be intensified in the future because some people's appetite for vice and gambling will not be appreciably diminished. If the organized criminal elements gain control of the cities, they will use the same tactics and techniques to gain control of state governments. They are completely impartial as to their connections and are equally at home among management representatives as with labor representatives. They will "work" either group to gain control as conditions may require.

In many places, the organized criminal elements are working in close liaison with so-called leaders of respectable business. In other places, they have worked their way into influential positions in the central labor bodies. Federal legislation may be directed to overcome this problem because the state governments are often helpless, unable to act, or unaware of the problem.

MIGRATING GROUPS

The third major conflict which may find its reflection in the federal system is the conflict between migrating peoples, particularly between peoples of substantially diverse cultural background such as the southern Negro and the northern white of European extraction, or the Puerto Rican and the northern white. The great influx of Negroes into the northern areas, for the present, may increase the desire of the northern political leaders to call for increased activity in civil rights and fair employment practices. But it is possible that in the long run there may be a segregated caste system developed as the northern whites seek to withdraw from contact with the Negro community. This withdrawal will occur when the mental image that the northern white has of a Negro as a harassed and relatively helpless person is changed to an image of the Negro as a brutal attacker of women on the streets, one given to the use of narcotics, a brawler, and a slovenly person. Thus, by a relocation of the Negro population from the rural South to the northern cities there may be a greater tendency in the North to follow the pattern of the southern states, and this in turn would have its subtle reflections in the federal system.

Another problem which may have its bearing in the federal government

is the growing number of young men who, kept apart from useful employment or from honest work necessary to support themselves, may readily lend
themselves to gang formations. These formations can be shrewdly mobilized
as a political force, even as youth movements in Germany were organized
by political leaders. Any depression, in which the younger persons are
deprived of money for automobiles and the pleasures which they are enjoying at the present time, might conceivably lead to a fascist development in
the United States because many young people, unaware of the facts of
economics, may follow a demagogue.


# HOME RULE FOR THE METROPOLIS!

## REXFORD G. TUGWELL


WE CANNOT HAVE STATES as they are at present constituted and have
metropolitan government. It is true that there are those who advocate states'
rights and at the same time favor metropolitan consolidation. But nothing
could be more illogical. Even illogicality, however, has its reasons. There is
a prevalent tenderness for state autonomy that long precedes, historically,
the perception that the great city is a necessity. Liberals and conservatives
alike—although for different reasons—fear a federal Moloch. And whenever they become excited about this they are apt to extol the state; it is
automatic to accept states' rights as the alternative to federal centralization.

President Eisenhower spoke of this with considerable emphasis in both
his Presidential campaigns and during his administration lent himself to a
serious movement for "decentralizing" federal functions. He undoubtedly
accepted this as a matter not worth close examination; and he appeared to
be very surprised when, at a Governors' Conference in 1957, his proposals
for getting ahead with an actual program were received with a good deal
of skepticism. The governors were no doubt in favor of more state autonomy,
but they thought the reversal of the long-time trend toward federal ag-
grandizement unlikely. In spite of this setback, the Republican administration
persisted to a degree that showed how deep-running conservative fears of
federal strength had become.

The City Managers Association, meeting in Washington in October of
1957, heard Mr. Robert E. Merriam, Assistant Director of the Budget, tell
them that it was "the Administration's hope to help them equip themselves
for coping with their difficulties *within the framework of the American
Federal System of Government.*" The reference was to the program for

This article is published for the first time in this book.

sloughing off to the states many federal functions.[1] Since they knew that it was this very framework that was choking the modern cities of which they were the operating heads, they must have wondered why Mr. Merriam—himself recently a city official and still more recently the author of a text on American government—seemed to feel that he was bringing them a message of encouragement. If there is one change the city officials would not care to see, it is more decentralization of federal functions to the states. To the extent that this "reform" prevails, their difficulties will deepen. They knew it; and Mr. Merriam must have known it too.

It is necessary to probe several American fears and to trace the struggle of various interests for the control of government if the curious notion that functional decentralization is actually achieved by increasing the powers of the states is to be understood. The states are neither social nor economic entities; they have no geographic existence; their limits do not correspond with commercial patterns; transportation systems overrun and ignore them; river systems are not contained in them; they have no relation to productive regions; and often the population of one or two of their metropolises will be considerably larger than that of the state itself.

Yet the cities—which do have a reason for existence—are legally the creatures of these entirely artificial constructs equipped with governments. Municipal charters are granted by them with such limitations and conditions as state lawmakers choose to impose. One of the longest-standing quarrels in this country is that between cities seeking freedom and state legislators seeking to restrict it. What gains the cities have made seem likely now to be jeopardized by the careless assumption of those who fear federal power that the only alternative is a strengthening of the powers of the states.

What is really essential is a reorganization of governmental structure to conform to social, economic, and geographic realities. This requires drastic downgrading of the states and equally drastic upgrading of regions and cities. Instead of new provisions for state aid, there ought to be region and city aids—that is to say, direct relations between the federal government and entities other than the states. This assumes that the cities themselves will discover their geographic personalities and be prepared to organize on a metropolitan scale. How to accomplish this with so many diverse interests in opposition is a baffling problem. If in the end it is done, it will be in spite of active resistance from many of those who should have been its supporters.

It is not too difficult to understand why powerful conservatives advocate the enlargement of state activities. It is because they regard the states as less formidable opponents than the federal government in the struggle between themselves and public authority for strategic controls in modern society. In contrast to the federal government, the states are small in size and cor-

---

1. Mr. Merriam's remarks are quoted from an account in the *Washington Post* of 23 October 1957, p. A13. The headline over the story was "Ike's States Rights Policy Told to City Managers."

respondingly weak; they are very often dominated by political machines able to bargain for favors; they are staffed by much less capable bureaucracies and so are more easily bullied by those they nominally regulate; their legislatures have majorities from rural areas with prejudices against cities; and they are apt to have executives who are conscious that their positions are staging bases for further advancement and who can use some skilled assistance and financial support.

But it would be a mistake not to recognize that there are other reasons than these. Liberals no less than conservatives actively advocate strengthening the states. The equalitarian and libertarian sentiments among Americans are strong and always have been strong. They were the moving power behind the Revolution; they motivated the Jeffersonian and Jacksonian movements; they determined that competitive free enterprise should be favored over state industry; and they have dominated the orthodox progressive outbreaks of our recent history. All these sentiments and prejudices call for resistance to strength at the center. And since there are fifty states, they furnish a convenient symbol for decentralization. Fifty is more than one. Then too, of course, there are areas of the country where states' rights have had ideological significance. The Civil War may have subdued the South, but it was no more convincing than force ever is.

Historians are often confronted with the necessity to explain how it is that apparently diverse and even hostile interests converge to form coalitions. There is one of these confluences here. The equalitarians are in agreement with their natural enemies—the financial and industrial interests—in demanding a reduction of federal strength and a decentralization of federal functions to the states. It was for this coalition that Robert E. Merriam spoke when he addressed the city managers. Merriam was once a Democrat and when he spoke, I am sure, regarded himself as a liberal. But he served a Republican administration that openly represented big business. In a way, the hostile forces would be said to come together and find a common purpose in Merriam himself. It is this joined force that will have to be met and worsted if there is to come about any such change as will allow the cities to break out of their constricting borders and find the scope and form required by their needs in the modern world.

Undoubtedly the most discouraging aspect of the future in this respect is the apparent willingness of everyone involved to accept the stereotypes. Hardly anyone any more speaks up against states' rights. And even those who plead for the cities either do not see where the obstacles lie or feel forced to accept them as they exist. The result is that even those who complain most bitterly about the situation offer solutions that they must know are no solutions at all, but only temporizing expedients whose utility is likely to have been already exhausted.

Consider, for instance, the Authority. This is a special-purpose institution operating under legislative authorization, and usually privately financed, although there are also publicly financed ones. Such Authorities are in effect municipalities, limited as to function but with a wider geographic scope than the cities. If they are privately financed, their capital comes from bonds, often revenue bonds, handled by underwriters and sold to the public. In this case their incomes are pledged for interest and amortization for a period of years. They perform services that were formerly expected of the city (or, sometimes, the state) and were free. They charge for this service whatever is necessary to meet their obligations. They are, therefore, put in a privileged position. Other agencies must compete for budget funds, but these Authorities are exempted from dependence on general revenues. Hard-pressed municipal officials resent this favoring of certain agencies over all the others; they have nevertheless felt forced to accept them as a way of getting done much needed projects otherwise impossible to finance.

The argument for them is that the tax they impose by charging fees is a direct one and falls only on those who make use of the facility. Apart from this argument from expediency (which is a doubtful one, since it assumes an indefinitely expansible income on the part of taxpayers, and certainly favors security investors over consumers), their usefulness in absorbing special powers from more than one state has been their most convincing support. For one purpose, at least, the Authority solves the problem of divided jurisdiction. It is sometimes contended that it shows the way to regional government. And it is true that the New York Port Authority, for instance, has been notably successful in developing certain facilities in its area. It administers the airports, the tunnels under the rivers, certain bridges, and some harbor facilities. But it would not have been invented except for the division of the metropolis between two states. It is thus an expedient. Its operations are vast; but even so, they constitute only a few of the many services expected of the cities.

To the extent that the Authority has succeeded, its success has been at the expense of the other services. If all municipal departments were thus to be made independent to issue bonds and charge fees for their services, those in the best position to impose the charges would be the ones most solvent. Others would fail to gain financing because investors would have no confidence in their ability to maintain sufficient revenue. And many of these services are so generalized that specific charges are wholly impracticable— parks, streets, sewers, lighting, police and fire protection, and many others. Furthermore, the need for facilities is not necessarily equated to people's willingness to pay for them. Individuals would not pay for many socially indispensable functions if they could escape the necessity.

It was for some such reason that a spreading movement to construct modern highways with private funds recently came to a sudden end. It was seen that it was likely to put certain parts of the interstate highway system in a favored position for the benefit of underwriters and investors. And the amount of revenue to be expected did not always correlate with the national desirability of the improvements. The pay-roads pre-empted the most-favored routes of the motorists. They thus gained a monopoly. There had been a long and popular tradition in this country that the linking of its various parts by highways was a public necessity. It was one way of making a nation out of vast expanses of hill and plain.

Highway Authorities were not interstate. They did not therefore offer any precedent, as did the New York Port Authority, for extension to other functions than road building and maintenance. But if they had, they would very possibly have offered a dangerous one. To allow agencies that—because of a favorable situation—can collect tolls to do so does make difficulties for others who are not in such a favorable position.

Another suggestion, not as yet tried anywhere, but often put forward, is federation. The model for this is something like the following: it is to be imagined that New York City and its surrounding municipalities in several states would work out among themselves a kind of constitution, leaving the constituent municipalities sovereign, but enumerating the powers and functions to be assigned to a central government. In this case the central organization can be imagined to be called Great Central East or Eastern Seabordia. It would have a legislature, an executive, and presumably a judiciary. It would derive its authority from ratification of its constitution by the state legislatures involved, and it would, in important respects, separate itself from those states and become a new governmental enclave.

The radical nature of this proposal becomes evident when the powers to be delegated are analyzed. Those who put it forward usually do so in the belief that it would be unlikely to encounter the same opposition as a proposal to create new states. Federation is pictured as a possible voluntary action on the part of the states—as was the authorization of the Port Authority by New York and New Jersey—blessed by, but hardly at all involving, federal authority.

This is certainly a possibility; and when considering it one should recall what the United States Constitution says about concurrence in the erection of new states:

> New States may be admitted by the Congress into this Union; but no new State shall be formed or erected within the Jurisdiction of any other state; nor any State be formed by the Junction of two or more States, without the consent of the Legislatures of the States concerned as well as of the Congress.

Thus any movement of a metropolis toward separation and statehood encounters two, three, or more formidable barriers, manned by those who have much to lose by giving consent. If the metropolis happens to fall wholly within one state, its sponsors would have to persuade first the legislature of the state and then the Congress of the United States; if it extended into more than one state, as many do, there would be additional legislatures to persuade. When one considers what the states would be giving up, the potential difficulties appear so great that nothing short of genuine crisis would justify the effort involved. A new-state movement would certainly be one of those generation-long efforts of citizens' committees and academic advocates such as have sometimes resulted in governmental changes in the past—the direct election of senators, for instance, or the change in electoral procedures. Meanwhile the present difficulties would go on proliferating

But even if the constitutional question is avoided, the prospect of federation without the actual erection of new states seems hardly less difficult than the question whether a new state had in effect been erected by subterfuge. The states now have absolute authority over their creatures, the cities. This is modified in practice. Whatever limits the state constitution places on the powers of the legislature constitute whatever strength the city representatives may have in the state legislature. It is conceivable that, slowly and grudgingly, the preponderance of urban population might establish a majority in the legislature through successive reapportionments, or that in some convention for revising the constitution it might be so amended that the movement would be facilitated. That this might occur in two or more states within a reasonable time—say a decade—is also conceivable. But it must be admitted that it stretches probability.

Such a development might have been much easier from the situation in the 1920's than from that of the 1960's. State aid had of course begun by 1920; but it was by no means so large a proportion of state expenditures. The agricultural college and experiment station and the county agent system have since been enlarged by the enormous bureaucracy that administers the conservation, crop control, insurance, and loan activities paid for by the federal government. Much the same thing is true of federal aid for roads, for hospitals, and for other assisting funds; they have expanded beyond recognition from what existed before the New Deal. And this is to say nothing of that part of the Social Security system which was entrusted to the states for administration.

It was sometimes pointed out while these policies were being argued out that the states were being given a formidable infusion of strength and importance at a time when it had begun to seem that they might wither away and become no more than vestigial reminders of a simpler past. If they had continued to decline, a logical administrative reorganization might in the course of time have become much easier. For it was not only the crisis in metropolitan affairs that seemed to require such a change. To mention no others, consider the implications of TVA if it had gone the way that seemed indicated at its beginning. It is significant that this development was arrested too, and that no other TVA's followed the first.

New Deal support for the states did not originate in any belief that it would improve the administration of the agencies involved. It was indeed recognized that the decentralization entailed a certain cost. But the cost was considered worth what was to be gained. This, when it is realistically analyzed, has to be identified as conformity to a stereotype or theory—the one already mentioned. In this theory big organizations—the federal establishment being the biggest of all—are considered to be inherently malevolent. And this is true whether they are governmental or private. The private ones are to be broken up by antitrust efforts; the public ones are to be checked by enlarging the powers and duties of the states. The irony of this is that it can only be accomplished by using the power of the federal government to emasculate itself and to go on doing it year after year.

As a principle of administration, decentralization is a recognized necessity. The problem of finding the proper division between the over-all and the more detailed functions, as well as that of separating policy making from execution, are matters that have engaged the talents of theorists and practitioners alike since the growth of scale became formidable in the nineteenth century. And if enough about it were known it would be found, no doubt, to have been considered earnestly by those responsible for administering the earliest empires. But it was not solved earlier, and it will not be solved in the United States, by resorts to division of function on the basis of a privileged principle.

Still, it is in this context that the feasibility of federation as a possible step short of state reorganization has to be considered. Would the states be willing to give up some of the powers they now possess over the cities within their jurisdictions by making it possible for the various municipalities within the metropolis to federate? If New York itself, Jersey City, Newark, Trenton, Bridgeport, Yonkers and the other municipalities within, say, a fifty-mile radius of Manhattan were to make a proposal to the states of New York, New Jersey, and Connecticut, what would they propose?

They would certainly ask that they should be freed from the financial limitations imposed by the states—that they be allowed to lay their own taxes and pay their own expenses. They would also ask that they be allowed to have direct relationships with the federal government. Federal aid, for instance, would no longer be channeled to them through the states. And this implies that they would ask for much more autonomy in other matters having to do with education, health, welfare, recreation, justice, and so on.

It will be seen that if the states involved allowed the New York Confederation—Eastern Seabordia—these freedoms, this consent would require the revision of a whole complex of laws, of both states and the federal government, that are adjusted to the present principle of federal aid. It would no longer be true to say, as political scientists have always said in the past, that, so far as the federal government is concerned, the cities do not exist. Many direct relationships would be set up.

It seems obvious that the real differences between state-permitted federation and the complete acceptance of the revisionist principle are very slight ones—much less conspicuous than the differences between the present situation and federation. The argument for the method of federation rests on the avoidance of Constitutional amendment with its formidable barriers. The states were certainly intended by the writers of the Constitution to be invulnerable. They have not always been so; West Virginia was abstracted from Virginia; and certain Western territories were made states in spite of titles to them held by the New England commonwealths. There are precedents. But obviously they are not very relevant in modern circumstances.

It would seem that the change to regional and metropolitan autonomy and the breaking up of the states would have to rest on the imperatives of logic and necessity. This is certainly not to argue that it may happen soon or that it may happen at all. Logic is notoriously weak in the management of public affairs; and necessity is often distorted. The stereotype will be defended bitterly both by those with a vested interest in it and by those who regard it as a bulwark of liberty. I would argue for the change; but I would not do so with much hope.

# CITIES IN THE 1960 PARTY PLATFORMS

## CLAYTON KNOWLES

THE DEMOCRATIC PLATFORM for the 1960 Presidential campaign deals with the problems of the cities and their suburbs as a major national issue.

Comprehensive in treatment and specific in detail, it pledges the party to "give the city dweller a voice at the Cabinet table by bringing together within a single department programs concerned with urban and metropolitan affairs."

The platform thus supports the creation of a Department of Urban Affairs, which influential national organizations have urged.

It also frankly acknowledges Federal interest and involvement in metropolitan problems, like urban renewal and slum clearance, water supply and area planning, which are "inter-state and regional in scope."

The Republican platform, in contrast, discusses urban problems in more general language in a brief, 225-word section on "Housing."

It states the objective of "a decent home in a suitable environment for every American" and, toward this end, pledges:

> Continued effort to clear slums and promote rebuilding, rehabilitation and conservation of our cities.
>
> New programs to stimulate development of specialized types of housing, such as those for the elderly and nursing homes.
>
> A program of research and demonstration aimed at finding ways to reduce housing costs, including support of efforts to modernize and improve local building codes.
>
> Adequate authority for the Federal housing agencies to assist the flow of mortgage credit into private housing, with emphasis on homes for middle and lower-income families and including assistance in urban residential areas.
>
> A stepped-up program to assist in urban planning, designed to assure far-sighted and wise use of land and to coordinate mass transportation and other vital facilities in our metropolitan areas.

The detail of Democratic treatment is pointed up by the fact that, while dealing in considerable detail with the metropolitan problem in a 500-word section on "Cities and their Suburbs," it goes into further specifics in sections on "Housing," "Transportation" and "Water and Air Pollution."

Reprinted from *New York Times*, August 7, 1960, by permission of the publisher.

The Democratic platform promises "a ten-year action program to restore our cities and provide for balanced suburban development." It pledges:

1. The elimination of slums and blight and the restoration of cities and depressed areas within the next ten years.

2. Federal aid for metropolitan area planning and community facility programs.

3. Federal aid for comprehensive metropolitan transportation programs, including bus and rail mass transit, commuter railroads as well as highway programs and construction of civil airports.

4. Federal aid in combating air and water pollution.

5. Expansion of park systems to meet the recreation needs of our growing population.

Fixing a "housing construction goal of more than 2,000,000 homes a year," the Democratic platform says the home-building industry "should be aided by special mortgage assistance, with low interest rates, long-term mortgage periods and reduced down payments." Where necessary, the platform urges direct government loans.

It states that the housing program for the most part should serve "middle and low income families who now live in substandard housing and are priced out of the market for decent homes."

In proposing Federal aid on metropolitan and regional problems, the Democratic platform maintains it can be done "without impairing local administration through unnecessary Federal interference or red tape."

The strong wording of the Democratic platform reflects the wishes of Senator John F. Kennedy, the party's Presidential candidate. Last December in an address before the American Municipal Association at Denver, he said:

"The cities of America, their problems, their future, their financing must rank at the top of any realistic list of 1960 campaign issues. This is the great, unspoken, overlooked, underplayed problem of our time."

With more than 70 per cent of the nation's population in 210 metropolitan areas across the country, Mr. Kennedy has complained that urban-suburban problems have been "brushed over lightly in party platforms."

A search of the files and inquiry at the office of Vice President Richard M. Nixon, Republican Presidential candidate, did not disclose any recent talks by him on the subject.

"Our files indicate he has not made any prepared talks on urban affairs in the past year," an office spokesman said. "He may have talked extemporaneously or from notes on the subject, though."

# A PROPER ROLE
# FOR THE FEDERAL GOVERNMENT

ROBERT H. CONNERY AND
RICHARD H. LEACH

AS THE FEDERAL GOVERNMENT moves to act on the metropolitan area problem, it begins with a severe handicap. It lacks knowledge, first of all, of the extent and complexity of the problem the nation faces. Not only is there no basis of fact regarding the total impact of its many activities in metropolitan areas on which to build, but its statistical procedures are not designed to produce the raw data for metropolitan areas as such, from which the basic facts can be derived. Even in its collection of urban data, there are a number of obvious gaps. The definition of a standard metropolitan area used by the Bureau of the Census still needs to be revised. Even the new definition of a "Standard Metropolitan Statistical Area" is built on a county basis. But counties which impinge on metropolitan areas often have a vast hinterland of sparsely settled rural territory which is far from being metropolitan in any sense of the term. San Bernardino County in southern California is a good example. Whereas the western end of the county is in fact part of the Los Angeles urban complex, the eastern part runs two hundred miles back into the desert. Yet all of it, by the Bureau of the Census definition, is part of the Los Angeles metropolitan area.

Moreover, knowledge is lacking about what happens when a federal program is put into effect in a metropolitan area so far as the total resources and social structure of the community are concerned, and even less is known about the total effect of a series of federal programs on a single metropolitan area. This was pointed out emphatically in the Kestnbaum report. Part of the trouble results from not knowing exactly how much federal money is spent in individual metropolitan areas. These data are available in the files of the operating agencies, but have never been put together in terms of metropolitan areas. As a preliminary step, exact data should be gathered on federal expenditures in major metropolitan areas over the past decade. Subsequently, a study should be made of the total impact of federal programs on government in metropolitan areas.

Because exact data are lacking, as this study has repeatedly emphasized, all recommendations for action to solve metropolitan problems must be predicated on a great deal of assumption. Nor is it possible, for the same reason, to spell out in great detail what should be done. A more solid basis of factual knowledge than is now available would be required for such a project. The recommendations which follow are therefore based, of necessity, on the facts which are most clearly evident.

There is reason to believe that federal programs are piling up on each other faster than metropolitan areas can digest them. Each is planned separately, and there is no correlation among them. Programs are launched in isolation, without reference to their impact on the areas to which they are directed. As a consequence, federal programs are badly co-ordinated so far as metropolitan areas are concerned, both among themselves and in terms of state and local programs in the same areas. Federal programs having a bearing on metropolitan problems should be re-examined in order to assure better co-ordination and to provide the maximum flexibility and a minimum of standardization as to detail and procedure.

Moreover, the federal government in its grant-in-aid programs should encourage the creation of larger units of government to fit present social and economic realities in metropolitan areas. In particular, it ought not to require the continued existence of outmoded local governmental units by limiting its grants to cities when action over a larger area is needed. The example set in the housing program, to provide assistance for broad over-all metropolitan planning, should be followed in other areas. The federal government should assist in the preparation of plans by providing technical aid, information, and financial assistance, and it should require all federal and federal grant-in-aid programs, including highways and recreation, as well as housing and urban renewal, to be related to comprehensive metropolitan plans.

Federal programs for the most part are concerned with unrelated physical things—buildings, highways, airports—but there is a magnificent unconcern about the people who are displaced by these activities. The elimination of slums, for example, is going on at such breakneck speed that many more people are left homeless than ever before, crowding is getting worse, and delinquency is increasing. To be sure, one cannot make omelets without breaking eggs, but the life of a community is as important as its physical development, and both should be taken into account. Moreover, it should be recognized that massive urban relocation breaks up long-established community patterns. Replacing slum dwellings with new and sterile housing projects which offer no encouragement to rebuilding community life will have serious repercussions on metropolitan living. The relocation of these displaced people and the solution of all the social problems their movement entails should be the joint responsibility of the federal government and the local communities.

In interstate metropolitan areas, the federal government should recognize its special responsibilities by offering incentives to the states involved to co-operate with one another and with the federal government in attacking particular problems on an area-wide basis. The states should be encouraged to make broader use of all sorts of co-operative arrangements, including interstate compacts, in attacking metropolitan area problems. Congress could do much to encourage the use of compacts by simplifying its own legislative procedures for dealing with them and by the passage of general permissive legislation. The federal government should give the nation a good example by speedily implementing the recommendations of the Bible Committee for the Washington metropolitan area. It should also grant the District of Columbia greater freedom to solve its own problems, and by a policy of self-restraint should refrain from constant interference with local policy formation in the District.

With regard to international metropolitan areas, the federal government should recognize that such areas have many of the same governmental problems that domestic metropolitan areas have, and it ought to facilitate the creation of local planning agencies or other appropriate devices for each of these areas. Moreover, since many problems of these areas will still have to be handled through ordinary diplomatic channels, the federal government should make certain that the International Commissions and the Department of State have personnel on their staffs who are familiar with metropolitan government and its problems.

Under the American system of government, unless the President provides leadership, no great amount of progress can be made in solving any problem. None of the recent presidents have been concerned with government in metropolitan areas; their neglect has affected both the legislative and the executive branches, and has been felt from top to bottom of the administrative pyramid and far beyond into the tentacles of the operating agencies. Presidential interest in metropolitan areas must be aroused before effective action can be expected. Lacking presidential leadership, Congress has been slow to appreciate the magnitude of the problem. Consequently, it has not given a high priority to considering ways in which the federal government could aid in solving it. Structural changes, such as those suggested below, can provide for better integration of federal programs, but mere structural change cannot make its maximum contribution until both the President and Congress have been made fully conscious of their responsibilities for action.

Urban needs have not received anything like the recognition that has been given to agriculture and the needs of rural areas because in many federal agencies there is a conspicuous lack of people with training and experience in the government problems of metropolitan areas. One of the reasons American agriculture has made the great strides it has in less than a century is that the federal government has recognized its importance by recruiting thousands of agricultural specialists. To date, not even the beginnings of anything comparable have been developed for metropolitan needs, although almost two-thirds of the population of the United States now live in metropolitan areas. The federal government does not lack skilled engineers to build urban highways or airports to serve urban areas, but it does lack personnel who are skilled in the general problems of urban government. Special urban units should be established and those already in existence should be strengthened in the federal agencies whose programs particularly concern metropolitan areas.

One of the structural changes which are needed is the establishment of a staff agency to furnish the President with continuous staff assistance on metropolitan problems. Stated briefly, a Council on Metropolitan Areas should be established by statute in the Executive Office of the President. The Council should consist of three to five full-time members, one of whom should be designated as chairman and be assigned broad administrative authority over the work of the Council. In addition to such day-to-day duties as the President might assign it, the Council should organize a program of continuing research on the impact of federal programs on metropolitan areas. Though the Council should have no authority to co-ordinate federal programs, it should have power to collect data, ask questions, and make recommendations to the President. It should keep abreast of developments in the field through the device of regional desks rather than by means of permanently established field offices. An advisory group representing private research bodies as well as state and local governmental units and interested professional groups should be appointed to consult with the Council in the performance of its duties.

The federal government's program for metropolitan areas should be firmly anchored in the structure of Congress as well as in the White House. This can best be accomplished by requiring the President to submit an annual report to Congress on metropolitan problems, just as he does on the economic state of the nation, and by creating an appropriate Committee on Metropolitan Problems to which the President's report could be referred for study and action. These devices have been used successfully with regard to economic matters, and they could be used with equal success here. The creation of such a committee, however, should not deter the present House Subcommittee on Intergovernmental Relations (the Fountain Subcommittee) from continuing its studies of intergovernmental problems in general, with special attention to the important problem of federal-state relations.

In addition to these general recommendations, there are actions which the federal government can take in relation to specific programs which would make its work in urban areas much more effective.

# WHY DECENTRALIZATION
# BY ORDER WON'T WORK

MORTON GRODZINS

OURS IS A GOVERNMENT of shared functions. There is no function of government for which federal, state, and local governments do not have some responsibility. The mixture of responsibilities varies, of course: the federal government, for example, has less to do with fire fighting than with police protection on the local scene; and the states and localities have less importance in the post office than in atomic energy development. But all areas of American government are involved in all functions. The federal system is not accurately symbolized by a neat layer cake of three distinct and separate planes. A far more realistic symbol is that of the marble cake. Wherever you slice through it you find an inseparable mixture of differently colored ingredients. There is no neat horizontal stratification. Vertical and diagonal lines almost obliterate the horizontal ones, and in some places there are unexpected whirls and an imperceptible merging of colors, so that it is difficult to tell where one ends and the other begins. So it is with federal, state, and local responsibilities in the chaotic marble cake of American government.

Repeated efforts have been made in recent years to devolve to the states and localities some of the functions that have been assumed by the federal government. Without exception these efforts have failed.[1] Passing laws and issuing executive orders, it is perfectly plain, will not change fundamentally the patterning of the marble cake. Why?

## History

In the first place, the history of the American governments is a history of shared functions. All nostalgic references to the days of state and local independence are based upon mythical views of the past, for there has in fact never been a time when federal, state, and local functions were separate and distinct. Government does more things in 1961 than it did in 1790 or 1861. But in terms of what government did then, there was as much sharing of

---

Adapted from a paper prepared for the Public Affairs Conference Center of the University of Chicago, 1961, by permission of the author and the Center.

1. For some details see Morton Grodzins, "The Federal System," in *Goals for Americans,* The Report of the President's Commission on National Goals (Englewood Cliffs, N.J.: Prentice Hall, Inc., 1960), pp. 265–284.

functions in 1790 and 1861 as there is today. Thus the effort to decentralize government through the ordered separation of functions is contrary to 170 years of experience.


## Politics


A second reason for the failure to decentralize government by order is inherent in the nature of American political parties. The political parties of this country are themselves highly decentralized. They respond to directives from bottom to top, rather than from top to bottom. Except during periods of crisis, not even the President of the United States requesting action from a congressman or senator can command the sort of accommodating response that, as a matter of course, follows requests from an individual, an interest group, or a mayor of a large city in the legislator's district. The legislator, of course, cannot fully meet all constituent requests; indeed, their very multiplicity, and their frequently conflicting character, are a liberating force, leaving room for individual judgment, discretion, and the expression of conviction. Nevertheless, the primary orientation of the vast majority of congressmen and senators is toward their constituency. Constituency, not party or President, is principally responsible for the legislator's election and re-election, and he therefore feels that accommodation to his constituency, rather than to party leaders, is his principal obligation. This is made easier because conflicts between constituency and party directives are rarely perceived as such. In the eyes of many members of Congress, what is good for the constituency is *ipso facto* good for the nation.

Thus, the parties are not, as they are in other countries, centralizing forces. On the contrary, they act to disperse power. And the significant point here is that they disperse power in favor of state and local governments.

I have described the actual mechanisms in another place.[2] Briefly, the parties can be seen as decentralizers in four ways. (1) They make possible the "multiple crack" attribute of American politics. That is to say, the loose party arrangements provide innumerable access points through which individuals, interest groups, and local and state governments take action to influence the processes of national legislation and administration. (2) The party arrangements are responsible for giving to state governments a role in national programs. It is remarkable how consistently in recent years the Congress has insisted that the states share responsibility in programs that, from constitutional and administrative considerations, might easily have been all-national programs. The local orientation of the members of Congress, which overrides the desires of national party leaders, is clearly responsible for this phenomenon. (3) The party system also makes possible the wide-

---

2. Grodzins, "American Political Parties and the American System," *Western Political Quarterly*, December, 1960.

spread, institutionalized interference of members of Congress in national administrative programs on behalf of local constituents (again including the state and local governments). On The Hill, this is called "case work." In the United States the bureaucracy is subject to an hour-by-hour scrutiny by members of the Congress. No aspect of procedure and no point of policy is free from inquiry. Any administrative decision by a national agency that is contrary, for example, to the desire of a mayor or governor is immediately subject to congressional inquiry which, if not satisfactorily answered, can in the end produce a meeting in a cabinet member's office, a full-scale congressional investigation, or a threat of reprisal through the appropriation or legislative process. (4) Finally, since the loose national parties cannot themselves supply the political support needed by administrators of national agencies, administrators are forced to seek their own support in Congress. This support must come from locally oriented members of the Congress. The result is that administrative policies must be made with great sensitivity to the desires of state and local governments and other local interests.

What does this have to do with decentralization by order? It means that there can be no such decentralization as long as the President cannot control a majority of the Congress, and he can rarely exercise this control as long as the parties remain in their decentralized state. The decentralization of parties indicates a decentralization of power that is strong enough to prevent a presidentially sponsored decentralization of administration. The analysis also shows that sharing functions in this fashion is also sharing power. States and localities, working through the parties, can assume that they will have an important role in many national programs; that is to say, there will be few all-federal domestic programs. The parties also give the peripheral governments significant influence in the administration of national programs, including those in which they have no formal role.

The influence of the federal government in state and local operations, made possible by its purse power and exercised through grants-in-aid, is more than balanced by the political power of the peripheral units, exercised through the multiple crack, the localism of legislators, their "case work," and the political role of federal administrators. Politics here is stronger than the purse, in part because the locally oriented Congress is also the final arbiter of federal expenditures. The states and localities are more influential in federal affairs than the federal government is in theirs. And this influence must be made a part of the equation when balancing the strength of state and local governments against the strength of the national government. Whatever their verbally expressed opposition to centralization, state and local officials do not in fact find federal activities a threat to their position because of their substantial control over those activities.

In sum, the nation's politics, misunderstood by those advocating decentralization by order, accounts in large part for the failure to achieve that sort of decentralization.

## The Difficulty of Dividing Functions: The Issue of "Closeness"

Another related reason for the failure of decentralization by order is the sheer difficulty of dividing functions between central and peripheral units without the division resulting in further centralization.

It is often claimed that local or state governments are "closer" to the people than the federal government, and are therefore the preferred instrument for public action. If one carefully examines this statement, it proves to be quite meaningless.

"Closeness" when applied to governments means many things. One meaning is the provision of services directly to the people. Another meaning is participation. A third is control: to say that local governments are closer to the people than the federal government is to say that citizens can control the former more easily and more completely than the latter. A fourth meaning is understanding, a fifth communication, a sixth identification. Thorough analysis of "closeness" would have to compare local, state, and federal governments with respect to these and other meanings of the term.

In few, if any, of these meanings are the state and local units "closer" to the people than the federal government. The big differences are between rural and urban areas; citizens in rural areas are "closer" (in many, but not all, meanings) to both the local and federal governments than are residents of big urban areas.

Consider, for example, "closeness" as the direct provision of services. All governments in the American system operate in direct contact with people at their places of residence and work, and in the important activities the units operate collaboratively. It cannot even be said that the local units provide the most important local services, for the important services are those of shared responsibility. Where it is possible to recognize primary responsibilities, the greater importance of local government does not at all emerge.

Where in the American system is the government closest to the people as a provider of services? The answer is clearly neither the local nor federal government in urban areas and not even local government in rural areas. Rather, it is the federal government in rural areas that is closest to the people (as a provider of services).

The farm sector of the population receives a wider range of governmental services than any other population group. These services are largely inspired by federal legislation and largely financed with federal funds. From the point of view of services rendered, the federal government is clearly "closest" to the farm population. Outside of institutionalized persons and those dependent upon relief, the American farmer receives at first hand more governmental services than any other American. And while he receives these services as the consequence of collaboration among all governments, the federal government plays the key role.

The full analysis of all meanings of closeness would not establish that local governments are in significant ways "closest" to the people.

## The Difficulty of Dividing Functions: Issues of Logic

Nor does it help, on grounds of logic, to attempt a division of federal and state (or local) functions. Indeed, such a division would probably result in putting virtually all functions in the hands of the national government.

The logical difficulty of dividing functions can be seen in the recommendation of President Eisenhower's powerful Federal-State Action Committee (1957–59) for turning over all responsibility for constructing sewage plants to the states and localities. The Committee's reason for recommending this program, rather than others, was only a simple affirmation:

> The Joint Federal-State Action Committee holds that local waste-treatment facilities are primarily a local concern and the construction should be primarily a local or State financial responsibility. . . . There is no evidence to demonstrate the continuing need for the present Federal subsidy of an essentially local responsibility.[3]

This sort of language was necessary because no more reasoned argument was possible. There is no way to distinguish, for example, the "localness" of sewage-treatment plants from the "nationalness" of, say, grants for public health. Sewage-treatment plants, no less than public-health programs, are aimed at increasing public health and safety. Where there are no adequate plants, the untreated sewage creates health hazards, including higher infant-mortality rates. This sewage, when dumped into streams (the usual practice), creates in many cases interstate hazards to health and safety. Every indicator of "localness" attributed to sewage-treatment plants can also be attributed to public-health programs. And every attribute of "nationalness" in one is also found in the other.

A detailed analysis would show that any division of functions, on the line of their "local" or "national" character, would leave precious few activities in the local category. Automobile safety, for example, is now largely a state and local (and private) responsibility. Automobile deaths approach 40,000 annually, while injuries exceed 1,500,000. Before any given week end, Dwight Waldo recently observed, it can be safely predicted that fifteen people will be killed by automobiles in Northern California. If a similar number of deaths were the result of an airplane crash, several teams of federal officers, operating under a number of federal statutes, would be combing the area in order to prevent further deaths. But there are no federal officers on the scene to prevent further auto deaths, not even if it be shown that some fatalities in California are caused by drivers licensed in New York. In a rational division of responsibilities, assuming that they have to be all

---

3. *Progress Report No. 1* (December, 1957), p. 6.

federal or all state-local, would automobile safety remain in the state-local category? Clearly it would not.

This sort of analysis can be applied to a number of fields in which states and localities have important, if not exclusive, responsibility. It is hard to find any area in which the states and localities would remain in control, if a firm division of functions were to take place. Not even education would be an exception. Pseudohistorical considerations, outworn conceptions of "closeness," and fears of an American brand of totalitarianism would argue for an exclusive state-local control of primary and secondary education. But if the choice had to be made, inequities of state resources, disparities in educational facilities and results, the gap between actual and potential educational services, and, above all, the adverse national consequences that might follow long-term inadequacies of state-local control would almost certainly establish education as the exclusive concern of the national government.

The clear conclusion is that widespread separation of functions would reduce states and localities to institutions of utter unimportance. They can no longer sustain the claim that they are closer to the people. Their strength has never been a strength of isolation. Their future depends upon their continued ability to assume important roles in the widening scope of public service and regulation. Their future, in short, depends upon the continuation of shared responsibilities in the American federal system.

## Decentralization via Strengthening State Governments

The strength of state governments is not often measured in terms of the states' influence on national programs. Rather their strength is most frequently discussed in terms of state independence, or at least of fiscal and administrative power sufficient to carry out their own functions. It is often held that federal programs are the result of a failure by the states to meet their own responsibilities. "By using their power to strengthen their own governments and those of their subdivisions," the Kestnbaum Commission said, "the states can relieve much of the pressure for, and generate a strong counterpressure against, improper expansions of National action." A distinguished scholar of American politics, V. O. Key, has expressed the same point, although somewhat more guardedly. He considers deficiencies of representation in state legislatures, constitutional restrictions on state power, and state political systems as a "centralizing factor in the federal system."

> Evidently the organization of state politics builds into the government system a more or less purely political factor that contributes to federal centralization. The combination of party system and the structure of representation in most of the states incapacitates the states and diverts demands for political action to Washington.[4]

---

4. V. O. Key, *American State Politics* (Alfred A. Knopf, 1956), pp. 81, 266–267.

The simplicity of the argument is persuasive. But that does not make it correct. There is no doubt that the inability or unwillingness of state legislatures and executives to plan a national airport program led to federal grants in that field. But could the states be expected to design and finance such a program? The same sort of question could be asked with respect to housing and urban renewal, the second conspicuous federal-local program of the postwar era. (In both fields, incidentally, the states are given the chance to assume important responsibilities.) The great expansion of federal aid programs came during the depression. Certainly it can be said that the federal government went into the business of welfare on a wholesale scale because the states were unable to do the job. Was state inability the result of the ineffectiveness of state political parties, inequities of legislative representation, and outmoded constitutions? Or was it the result of a catastrophic depression? The former factors may have had some effect, but they are minor compared with the devastating impact of the depression on state income. And the depression would have required action from the federal government (with its virtually unlimited borrowing power) in new fields whatever the status of the states' political parties or the modernity of their constitutional arrangement.

Furthermore, it can be empirically demonstrated that expansion of national programs has not always followed the *failure* of state programs; the nation has also assumed responsibility following the demonstrated *success* of state programs. Thus requirements for health and safety in mining and manufacturing, the maintenance of minimum wages, unemployment compensation, aid to the aged and blind, and even the building of roads, were all undertaken, more or less successfully, by some states before they were assumed as national functions. So the states can lose power both ways. The national government steps in as an emulator when the states produce useful innovations, making national programs of state successes; and it steps in when crisis is created as the consequence of State failure, making national programs of state inadequacies.

The role of the national government as an emulator is fostered by the nationwide communication network and the nationwide political process, which produce public demands for national minimum standards. The achievement of such standards in some states raises the goal of reaching them in all states. Many reasons exist for this tendency. Citizens of the active states feel that they are pricing themselves out of the market with their higher tax rates. Those in the laggard states can find specific points of comparison to demonstrate that their services are unsatisfactory. National fiscal aid may be essential for the economically disadvantaged states. State legislatures may be less congenial to a given program than the national Congress. Combinations of these and other causes mean that national programs will continue to come into being although, and even because, some states carry out those programs with high standards. The only way to avoid this sort of expansion by the national government would be if all fifty states were politically, fiscally, and administratively able to undertake, more or less simultaneously, a given program at acceptable national standards. This is not likely to happen.

If both state failures and state successes produce national programs, it must be added that neither of those mechanisms is the most important reason for the expansion of the central government. This expansion has been produced primarily by the dangers of the twentieth century. (War, defense, and related items constitute more than 80 per cent of the federal budget, and federal increases of nondefense activities lag far behind expenditure increases by the states and localities.) War items aside, the free votes of a free people have sustained federal programs in such areas as public welfare, highway, airports, hospitals and public health, agriculture, schools, and housing and urban redevelopment, to name only some of the largest grant-in-aid programs. The plain fact is that large population groups are better represented in the constituencies of the President and Congress than they are in the constituencies of governors and state legislatures. No realistic program of erasing inequities of representation in state legislatures can significantly alter this fact. Only those who hold that the federal government is something to be feared would wish to make the federal government unresponsive to those national needs expressed through the democratic process, needs which by their very nature will not, and cannot, be met by state action.

In sum, strong as well as weak states direct "demands for political action to Washington." More important, the ability of the central government to meet citizen needs that cannot be met by either strong or weak states, whatever those adjectives mean, also accounts for the expansion, as well as for the very existence, of the federal government. Strengthening states, in the sense of building more effective parties and of producing legislatures and executives who have a readiness and capacity for action, may indeed prevent an occasional program from being taken up by the federal government. But the total possible effect can only be insignificant. The only way to produce a significant decline in federal programs, new and old, would be to induce citizens to demand fewer activities from all governments. (The cry, "Strengthen the states," in many cases only means "Decrease all governmental activity.") This is an unlikely development in an age of universal literacy, quick communications, and heightened sensitivities to material factors in the good life as well as to the political appeals of an alternative political system. One can conclude that strengthening the states so that they can perform independent functions and thereby prevent federal expansion is a project that cannot succeed.

Historical trend lines, the impetus of technology, and the demands of citizenry are all in the direction of central action. The wonder is not that the central government has done so much, but rather that it has done so little. The parties, reflecting the nation's social structure, have at once slowed up centralization and given the states (and localities) important responsibilities in central government programs. Furthermore, political strength is no fixed quantum. Increasing one institution's power need not decrease the power of another in the same system. Indeed, the centralization that has taken place in the United States has also strengthened the states—with respect to personnel practices, budgeting, the governors' power, citizens' interest, and the scope of state action—as every impartial study of federal aid has shown.[5]

In summary, the argument that weak state governments make for national centralization is far more false than true. The states remain strong and active partners in the federal system. They do so in large part because of their power within federal programs and because of the strengthening effects that federal-state programs have on state institutions. The important reason for further strengthening state institutions is to make them more effective innovators and even stronger partners in a governmental system of shared responsibilities.

## Two Kinds of Decentralization

Those who attempt to decentralize by order are far more likely to produce centralization by order. In so doing they would destroy the decentralization that already exists in the United States.

The circumstances making possible a decentralization by a decision of central officials are simple to specify. What is principally needed is a President and a congressional majority of the same party, with the President consistently able to command a majority of the Congress through the control of his party. Under such an arrangement, a recommendation by a committee of cabinet members and governors to devolve functions to the states could, if strongly backed by the President, be readily implemented. Party control of the central government and the President's control of Congress through his party are the essentials. In other words, *party centralization* must precede *governmental decentralization by order*.

But a centralized party pledged to decentralization—that is, to minimizing central government activities—can hardly be or remain a majority party in the twentieth century. The power to decentralize by order must, by its very nature, also be the power to centralize by order. Centralized majority parties are far more likely to opt in favor of centralization than decentralization. At least this has been the history, during the past century, of both our own nation and every other democracy.

Decentralization by order must be contrasted with another sort of decentralization. This is the decentralization that exists as the result of independent centers of power and that operates through the chaos of American political processes and political institutions. It may be called decentralization

5. See, for example, *The Impact of Federal Grants-in-Aid on the Structure and Functions of State and Local Governments* (a study submitted to the Commission on Intergovernmental Relations covering 25 states), by the Governmental Affairs Institute (Washington, 1955); and the report of the New York Temporary Commission on the Fiscal Affairs of State Government (the Bird Commission) (Albany, 1955), especially Vol. II, pp. 431–672.

by mild chaos. It is less tidy and noisier than an ordered decentralization. But it is not dependent upon the action of central bodies, and its existence is not at the mercy of changing parties or of changing party policy.

If decentralization is a desirable end, decentralization by mild chaos is far preferable to decentralization by order. The former is built upon genuine points of political strength. It is more permanent. Most important, it is a decentralization of genuinely shared power, as well as of shared functions. Decentralization by order might maintain a sharing of administration, but it cannot, because of its nature, maintain a sharing of political power. An ordered decentralization depends upon a central power which, by the very act of ordering decentralization, must drastically diminish, if not obliterate, the political power of the peripheral units of government.

Finally, it should be clear that, because of the very existence of the chaos in American politics, a President in this country does not have consistent control of his Congress. The power of the President is often contested by the powers made manifest through the undisciplined parties of individuals, interest groups, and states and localities. And the President is not always the winner. President Eisenhower was not the winner in his several proposals to devolve federal functions to the states. (His situation was complicated by the fact that his party was a minority of the Congress, but the results would almost certainly have been the same if he had had a majority.) He lost because his proposals were contested by many governors, many mayors, their professional organizations, and a number of other groups; and the party system allowed these protests to be elevated over the decision of the President.

Thus the strength of states and localities in the federal system is evidenced in the failure to decentralize by order. Successful decentralization by order would mean the end of decentralization by chaos, the decline of state and local power, and the death of America's undisciplined parties. Decentralization by order would thus indicate profound changes in the nation's political style and its supporting social structure.

# III

## THE MACHINE AND ITS REFORM

A "machine" is a party organization held together and motivated by desire for personal gain rather than by political principle or ideology. To the poor in the slums, who are its chief support at the polls, it is a source of jobs, petty favors, and protection. To its precinct and ward workers, it is a source of soft jobs, careers in minor elective office, and favors—an "in"—at city hall. To the few who control it, it is a way of making money.

Perhaps the machine should be spoken of in the past tense. Chicago is the only large city still run by one, and (as a reading in Section V shows) the character of that machine is changing rapidly. Fragments of machines survive in various stages of deterioration in many cities. Some of these have a good deal of vitality and power, even though not enough to take control of the city, and it is not altogether out of the question that a change of conditions—the onset of a major depression, for example—might return them to power in a few central cities where the number of low-income Negroes, Puerto Ricans, and white hillbillies is very large. As a general phenomenon of urban politics, however, the machine is a thing of the past. The immediate causes of its decline were the introduction of merit systems (which eliminated most of the patronage at the disposal of the bosses), full employment and rising national income (which vastly depreciated the value of such patronage as remained), the development of professionalized welfare services under the New Deal, and the structural reorganization of city governments. But a more general and long-term cause was the changing class character of the urban electorate. Middle-class people do not want and will not tolerate the boss and his "gravy train," and they have recently come to be in the majority in almost every city.

For a long time the machine was a conspicuous and powerful institution in American life. Between the Civil War and the Second World War all large cities and many small ones were at one time or another in the grip of machines. The bosses of the big city machines were leading figures in state and national politics. Whatever its present or future role, the machine is well worth study because of the part it has played in our history.

There is, however, a further and perhaps more important reason for studying it. Every political party (like every other formal organization) must maintain what Chester I. Barnard calls an "equilibrium of incentives." That is, it must offer a combination of inducements (in the case of the machine, "friendship," jobs, favors, protection, money) that will elicit from various classes of actors (voters, precinct captains, ward leaders, elective officials) the actions the organization requires; it must then use these actions to replenish its supply of inducements so that it may elicit more actions, and so on. Because of its heavy reliance upon personal, material inducements, the machine represents an extreme—and therefore analytically interesting—type of organization. Analysis of the extreme type is likely to be productive of insights into the "equilibrium of incentives" of other kinds of party organization, including those that are very unlike it. All of the readings of this section contribute in some way to an understanding of the machine as a system of incentives.

The first two readings offer general views of the machine. Martin Meyerson and Edward C. Banfield describe the Chicago machine as it was during the transitional period between the retirement of Mayor Kelly and the rise of Mayor Daley. Lord Bryce's classic account is of machines as they were in many large cities at the turn of the century. The reader will find that the Chicago machine of the mid-1950's was strikingly like its predecessors.

George Washington Plunkitt, who started life as a butcher boy and became a millionaire during forty years of service as a Tammany officeholder, explains how the machine gets votes. The secret is that it asks for something of little or no value to the donor: note that Plunkitt's cousin Tommy "didn't take any particular interest in politics" and that his vote was therefore Plunkitt's for the asking. The Plunkitt reading incidentally conveys an impression of the amiable cynicism of the professional machine politician; perhaps William L. Riordan, the newspaperman who edited Plunkitt, gilded the lily a bit. In the next reading, Oscar Handlin, an historian, describes the bond between the immigrant and the ward boss. He says that the control of the boss rested on several grounds: the jobs at his disposal, the feelings of group loyalty that were focused upon him, his social role as a spokesman for the immigrant, and his having favors to give and being fair in the giving of them.

The next three readings describe the internal economy of the machine at a higher level of hierarchy. Frank R. Kent, for many years a writer for the Baltimore *Sun,* discusses two aspects of the mechanics of control: the use of primary elections and the picking of the ticket. Edward J. Flynn, a Bronx boss who helped to elect and re-elect Franklin D. Roosevelt, explains and attempts to justify the use of job patronage. William Foote Whyte, a sociologist, tells how the politician uses his stock of resources to create the largest possible amount of support, how he uses the support to augment his influence, how he sells the influence for cash to buy more support, and so on in the endless cycle of organizational maintenance.

Corrupt and wasteful as it was, the machine served some socially valuable functions. Robert K. Merton, a sociologist, says that to understand its role we must look at the social circumstances that prevent other institutions from fulfilling essential social functions (the "structural context") and at the subgroups whose needs would remain unfulfilled if it were not for latent (i.e. unintended and unrecognized) functions performed by the machine. He lists several of these. The machine, he says, was an antidote to the constitutional dispersal of power. It humanized and personalized assistance to the needy. It gave business, including illicit business, the privileges it needed to survive. It provided a route of social mobility for some to whom other routes were closed. Unless due recognition is given to the importance of these and other functions, Merton warns, attempts at reform are likely to be "social ritual rather than social engineering."

How to eliminate the machine and make democracy work has been the subject of a great deal of theory, a representative sample of which is presented in the second half of this section. Some of the theorists of reform anticipated Merton's functional approach. Thus Henry Jones Ford, writing more than half a century before Merton, makes much of the constitutional dispersal of power. The cities are corrupt, he says, because the executive and legislative functions are disconnected; corruption, under the circumstances, is an indispensable mechanism for overcoming an otherwise unworkable decentralization. Lincoln Steffens, the best known of the muckraking journalists, emphasizes another latent function of the machine, that of affording privileges to business, especially legitimate business. Politicians, he said, are corrupt because they are bribed by businessmen; businessmen offer bribes because they "have to." The cure, manifestly, was to change the system (the structural context, as Merton would say). "Abolish privilege" was the advice that Steffens, a man who prided himself on his realism, gave. Jane Addams, the founder of Hull House, wrote informatively of the way the machine humanized assistance to the needy and gave opportunities for social mobility. In the pages reprinted here, she dwells on a related theme: the difference between the moral perspectives of the lower and the middle classes. The machine politician, she says, personifies the lower-class ideal of moral goodness, an ideal lacking sophistication because it is "individual" rather than "social" in reference. Perhaps exemplifying the moral standards of a class is still another social function of the machine.

# A MACHINE AT WORK

## MARTIN MEYERSON AND
## EDWARD C. BANFIELD

THE CITY COUNCIL, the body which would have to pass upon any sites proposed by the Authority, consisted of 50 aldermen, with the mayor as presiding officer. The aldermen were elected for four-year terms from wards of roughly 25,000 to 65,000 registered voters, only about a third of whom usually voted in aldermanic elections. (The number who voted in mayoralty elections was about twice as great.) Nominally the office of alderman was non-partisan. Actually, however, no one could win an election without the support of a powerful organization and (with some rare exceptions) the only powerful political organizations in the wards were the Democratic and Republican parties. An alderman who did not have the support of his party "machine" ordinarily had no hope of reelection.

The Democratic "machine" had ruled Chicago since 1923. Catholics were in control of it; since 1930, with a few exceptions, they had held the major city offices: the mayor, city treasurer, county clerk, more than half of the county commissioners, and two-thirds of the aldermen were Catholics.[1] And among the Catholics it was those of Irish extraction who were dominant in politics: one-third of the Council, including most of its leaders, were Irish-Catholics. The other aldermen were mostly of Polish, Italian, Bohemian, Lithuanian, Slovak, or Greek extraction (in descending order of importance, these were the principal nationality groups in the Democratic party) or of German extraction (these were Republicans).[2] A few aldermen were Jews (unlike the Poles, Italians, and other ethnic minorities, the Jews did not usually endeavor to be recognized as a group on the party slate or in the award of patronage).[3] Two were Negroes. The numerical importance of the Irish in the Council was to be accounted for not so much by their num-

---

Reprinted from *Politics, Planning, and the Public Interest* (Glencoe: The Free Press, 1955), pp. 64–75.

1. William R. Gable, "The Chicago City Council: A Study of Urban Politics and Legislation," unpublished dissertation, Department of Political Science, University of Chicago, Chicago, 1953, p. 13.

2. John P. White, "Lithuanians and the Democratic Party, A Case Study of Nationality Politics in Chicago and Cook County," unpublished Ph.D. dissertation, Political Science Department, University of Chicago, Chicago, 1953, p. 25.

3. *Ibid.*, p. 28.

bers in the electorate as by the fact that in wards where no one ethnic group had a clear majority they made the most acceptable compromise candidates. As one politician explained to an interviewer, "A Lithuanian won't vote for a Pole, and a Pole won't vote for a Lithuanian. A German won't vote for either of them—but all three will vote for a 'Turkey' (Irishman)."[4]

A few of the aldermen aspired to higher political office, especially (among those who were lawyers) to judgeships, but most of them were in the business of being aldermen as other men are in the business of selling shoes. Being an alderman was supposed to be a full-time occupation, but the salary was only $5,000, so most aldermen supplemented their salaries by selling something—most often insurance or legal service (more than half of them were lawyers). Being an alderman was, of course, very good for business.

Ordinarily, even if he were so inclined, an alderman could not concern himself deeply with the larger issues of city government or take a city-wide view of important problems. If he wanted to stay in office, he had to devote all of his available time and attention to the affairs of the groups that made up his ward. He was in the Council to look after the special interests of his ward and to do favors for his constituents: to get streets repaired, to have a playground installed, to change the zoning law, to represent irate parents before the school authorities, and so on. In addition to activities of this kind, he had to take an interest in the social life of his ward—to appear at weddings, funerals, and neighborhood occasions, and to say a few well chosen words and make a small donation when called upon. If he had any time left, he might think about the problems of the city as a whole. But whatever he thought, he was expected to work for his ward first.

From a formal standpoint, the 50 aldermen governed Chicago.[5] The Council made appropriations for all municipal purposes, it awarded franchises to and regulated the rates of public utility companies, it passed on appointments presented by the mayor, and (within the authority given it by the state) it could create new city departments at will. The mayor could send or read messages to the Council, he could vote when there was a tie (or when more than one-half of the aldermen had already voted for a measure), and he had a veto (including an item veto over appropriations

---

4. *Ibid.*, p. 64. A candidate's ethnicity was often a decisive asset or liability; in mixed wards he was most fortunate if his name was such that he could be presented as belonging to more than one ethnic or nationality group. Thus, Alderman Benjamin M. Becker's ward committeeman introduced him to voters of German extraction as of German extraction, stressed to voters of Swedish origin that Becker's wife had lived in Sweden and must have Swedish blood herself, pointed out to Catholics that Becker was a graduate of the DePaul University College of Law and a teacher there (thus implying that he was a Catholic), and presented him to Jews as a Jew. If the Catholics were fooled, no great injustice was done, for Becker's predecessor as alderman for many years was Dr. Joseph Ross, a Catholic whom the Jews assumed was a Jew. [Interview document.]

5. The city could exercise only those powers doled out to it by the state legislature, however, and so it might be more accurate to say that the city was governed by the state. See Barnet Hodes, "The Illinois Constitution and Home Rule for Chicago," 15 *Chicago Law Review* 78 (1947).

acts) which could be overridden by a two-thirds vote. In principle, each alderman was the independent agent of his ward. From a formal standpoint, then, the Council was a good deal like a league of independent nations presided over by a secretary-general.

In fact, however, there existed two sets of informal controls by which the aldermen's independence was very much limited and qualified. One set of controls was the leadership of the Council itself. Half a dozen of the most powerful Democratic aldermen—the "Big Boys," they were sometimes called—working usually with the mayor, effectively controlled the whole Council when matters of interest to them or to the mayor were at stake. They did this in part by controlling committee assignments. Unless an alderman could get on an important committee, his power in the Council was small. And unless he cooperated with the chairmen of the important committees and especially with the chairman of the Finance Committee (whose salary was $8,500, who was provided a limousine with a police chauffeur, and who had an office second only to the mayor's in splendor), he could not hope to get anything done for his ward. Any measure that required an appropriation had to go to the Finance Committee, and so, as one alderman explained, the chairman of that committee "sits at the gate of accomplishment for any alderman. . . ."[6] Indeed, if an alderman fell foul of the Finance Committee chairman or of any of the "Big Boys" he might be punished by having some city service to his ward reduced or suspended. On the other hand, even if he were a Republican, he could expect generous treatment from the leadership if he "played ball."

The other set of informal controls operated through the party or machine. An alderman had to stay in favor with his ward committeeman—i.e., the party leader in his ward—or else be the committeeman himself. The ward committeeman made all of the important decisions for the party within the ward. The committeeman was elected in the primary every four years (usually he could keep an opponent off the ballot by raising technical objections to his petitions) and so his power rested in part upon a legal foundation. From a legal standpoint, he was entitled to receive and disburse party funds, to manage campaigns, and to represent the leaders of the party within the ward. In fact he was commonly the "boss" of the ward; the party organization in the ward "belonged" to him. He decided who would run on the party's ticket within the ward, he appointed and dismissed precinct captains at will, and he dispensed patronage. As a member of the City and County Central Committees of his party, he participated in selecting its candidates for all city, county, and state offices and for Congress. (Half of Illinois' 26 Congressional districts were in greater Chicago.) In each of the party governing bodies his vote was in proportion to the total primary vote for his party in the last election; this of course gave him an incentive to "turn in" the biggest vote possible.

---

6. Interview document.

No salary went with the office of committeeman, but most of the committeemen held one or more public jobs and some of them ran businesses which were profitable because of their political connections.

William J. Connors, Democratic boss of the 42nd ward (the district described by Zorbaugh in *The Gold Coast and the Slum*),[7] may be taken as reasonably representative of at least some other ward committeemen. In 1950 Connors, who was in the insurance business, was on the public payroll in two capacities: as a state senator and as a bailiff of Municipal Court. His way of running his ward was described as follows:

> That Connors provides well for his workers is undeniable. Not only does he have a great many jobs to distribute, but he is a source of funds if any of his men need to borrow. He supports them when they are in difficulty with the law, as sometimes happens, and takes an interest in their family affairs. His relationship with them is that of a benevolent despot. He holds the power to withdraw their source of livelihood and to banish them from active work in the party and from their power positions in the community. He is the sole dispenser of the campaign funds from the party superstructure and the candidates. He may establish the assessments of the jobholders at any rate he desires without consulting them. He makes the party commitments to the county and city organs without a canvass of the captains' opinions and then demands complete obedience to these decisions. He may move a captain from one precinct to another at his discretion and is, of course, the sole source of patronage distribution.
>
> The committeeman generals his workers much like a military leader might. He plots the strategy of the campaign, estimates the difficulties that may be encountered, and decides the amount and allocation of money to be spent. He shifts captains from one point to another when called for. He attempts to build good precincts over a long period of time. Such building requires several years and may involve extensive trials and changes. Jobs are distributed not only on the basis of the effectiveness of the captain but in regard to the total effects such distribution may have. It happens occasionally that a strong Democratic captain has a smaller number of jobs allotted to him than one who is attempting to build up a Democratic precinct in the face of strong Republican competition. Thus in one precinct which casts a heavy Democratic vote, there are only two jobs besides the captain's, while another precinct that turns in only a slight Democratic majority is staffed by nine jobholders in addition to the captain.
>
> The committee respects the unity of the precinct organization and the authority of the captain and his workers. As long as the captain's activities are successful and his conduct does not threaten the party's vote-getting power, Connors does not interfere with the internal structure. The captain selects his own assistants and nominates his choices to receive public jobs. He assumes the responsibility for building an effective precinct organization. He decides how party funds allocated to him will be distributed and to a certain extent how they will be obtained. He and his men must share the responsibility of contributing whatever additional money is necessary beyond that sent from the party's headquarters. Connors respects the autonomy of the captain in this area of personal influence. Captains may or may not dis-

7. Harvey W. Zorbaugh, *The Gold Coast and the Slum*, University of Chicago Press, Chicago, 1929, p. 287.

tribute campaign literature, pay cash for votes, engage in fraudulent activities, or arrange precinct meetings of the voters. The only important check on the captain's conduct is the final tabulation of votes at each election.[8]

Any ward committeeman who cared to could have himself nominated alderman. If he chose not to run for office himself (like Connors, he might prefer to be on the public payroll in another capacity), he made sure that the candidate was someone who would work closely with him in ward affairs and offer no challenge to his control of the organization. "Naturally," an alderman once explained, "he (the ward committeeman) doesn't want to get a man who will build himself into a power so he can take the organization away from the committeeman. If the alderman doesn't do what the ward committeeman wants him to do, then the committeeman will dump him at the next election."[9] Some committeemen treated their aldermen as errand boys, others paid little attention to them, and still others treated them as friends, partners, and collaborators.[10]

If an alderman became powerful enough, he might unseat his committeeman and become the ward boss himself. But even in this case he could not be independent of the machine. The leaders of the Central Committee could bring him into line by withholding patronage or discharging public employees from his ward, by denying him financial support from the party's general coffers at election time, or by allowing an investigation of graft and corruption to take place in his ward. If it saw fit, the Central Committee could destroy a ward organization—and thus a ward committeeman— by these means, but it could do so, of course, only at the cost of impairing, at least temporarily, the effectiveness of the machine. Since its purpose was to win elections, a major concern of the machine was "harmony." Only if a committeeman failed to support the party's slate was he likely to be disciplined severely. If they wanted a favor from him, party leaders would offer him a favor—usually patronage—in return.

To increase their power vis-à-vis the Central Committee leadership, ward committeemen formed factional alliances or "blocs." Usually these alignments were on a geographical basis—thus, for example, there were South Side and West Side blocs of ward committeemen.

In order to maintain itself and to accomplish its purposes, any organization must offer incentives of the kinds and amounts that are necessary to elicit the contributions of activity it requires. It must then use these contributions of activity so as to secure a renewed supply of resources from which further incentives may be provided—it must, in other words, maintain what

8. Leonardo Neher, "The Political Parties in Chicago's 42nd Ward," unpublished dissertation, Department of Political Science, University of Chicago, Chicago, 1952, pp. 65–66.

9. W. R. Gable, op. cit., p. 74.

10. James A. Rust, "The Ward Committeeman in Chicago," unpublished dissertation, Department of Political Science, University of Chicago, Chicago, 1953, p. 56.

Chester Barnard has called an "economy of incentives" or else cease to exist.[11]

In Chicago a political machine distributed "gravy" to its officials, its financial backers, and to the voters. In this way it induced them to contribute the activity it required—to ring doorbells on election day, to give cash, and to go to the polls and vote for its candidates—and in this way it gained possession, through its control of the city or county government, of a renewed supply of "gravy."

As the word "gravy" suggests, the incentives upon which the machines relied were mainly material. Some prestige attached to being a ward politician; there was "fun" in playing the political "game"; there was satisfaction in being "on the inside"; and sometimes there was even an ideological commitment to an issue, the party, or a candidate. But these non-material incentives were not ordinarily strong enough to elicit the amount and kind of activity that a machine required from its workers. "What I look for in a prospective captain," a ward committeeman told an interviewer, "is a young person—man or woman—who is interested in getting some material return out of his political activity. I much prefer this type to the type that is enthused about the 'party cause' or all 'hot' on a particular issue. Enthusiasm for causes is short-lived, but the necessity of making a living is permanent."[12]

The "material return" that the party offered a worker was generally a job on the public payroll. Committeeman Connors, for example, had at his disposal in 1952 an estimated 350 to 500 jobs and the total public payroll to Democratic workers in his ward was conservatively estimated at $1,-320,000.[13]

Although jobs were the most visible of the material returns the party gave its workers, other opportunities to make money may have been more valuable. An alderman or committeeman who was a lawyer, an insurance man, or a tavern owner could expect to profit greatly from his association with the party. Whether he was profiting lawfully or unlawfully it was often impossible to tell. Alderman Sain and his ward committeeman, County Commissioner John J. Touhy, for example, were partners in an insurance business. "We handle a lot of business, no question about it," Touhy once blandly told a reporter. "I assume its just good business in the ward to carry insurance with us."[14]

---

11. Chester I. Barnard, *The Functions of the Executive,* Harvard University Press, Cambridge, 1938, Ch. XL. Barnard discusses the special case of the political organization on pp. 156–157.

12. H. Dicken Cherry, "Effective Precinct Organization," unpublished dissertation, Department of Political Science, University of Chicago, Chicago, 1952.

13. Leonardo Neher, *op. cit.,* p. 76.

14. *Chicago Daily News,* August 27, 1949. Some years earlier the *Chicago Daily News* compiled a list of the ordinances introduced by Sain over a five-month period and then inquired of the people who were specially benefited by these ordinances whether they had recently bought insurance of the firm of Touhy and Sain. It turned out that many of them had. (September 24, 1940.)

Even with the voters the machine did not make its appeal on the basis of issues or ideology. It offered them certain non-material incentives—chiefly the friendship and protection of its precinct captains—but in the main with them, as with the party workers, it relied upon "gravy." Just as it gave its workers jobs and opportunities to make money in exchange for their services, so it gave its loyal voters "favors"—special services and preferential treatment at the hands of its members and dependents who held city or county jobs—in exchange for their votes.

The party's agent in exchanging friendship and favors for votes was the precinct captain.[15] In 1950 a representative captain described his work as follows:

> I am a lawyer and prosecuting attorney for the City. I have spent 19 years in precinct work and have lived and worked in my present precinct for three and a half years.
>
> I try to establish a relationship of personal obligation with my people, mostly small shopkeepers and eighty per cent Jewish. I spend two or three evenings a week all year round visiting people, playing cards, talking, and helping them with their problems. My wife doesn't like this, but it is in my blood now. I know ninety per cent of my people by their names.
>
> Actually I consider myself a social worker for my precinct. I help my people get relief and driveway permits. I help them on unfair parking fines and property assessments. The last is most effective in my neighborhood.
>
> The only return I ask is that they register and vote. If they have their own opinions on certain top offices, I just ask them to vote my way on lower offices where they usually have no preferences anyway.
>
> I never take leaflets or mention issues or conduct rallies in my precinct. After all, this is a question of personal friendship between me and my neighbors. I had 260 promises for Korshak in this primary.
>
> On election day I had forty or fifty people help me because this was a "hot" campaign. All they had to do was to get out their own family and friends. I used to lease an apartment near the poll where I gave out drinks and cigars, but I don't do this any more.
>
> I stayed inside the poll most of election day, especially during the vote counting. If something went wrong, you could have heard me yell all over the precinct. Actually there isn't as much fraud now as there used to be.
>
> Abner (the PAC candidate) was not really a threat in my precinct. He had seven workers but they contacted only their friends. No one feels obligated to them and they worked only during the campaign. Abner's campaigners were naive. They expected to influence people by issues, and they relied on leaflets and newspaper publicity which is not effective.

---

15. In a vivid account by David Gutmann, the Chicago precinct captain is described as a "salesman." "Mr. Dolin [the precinct captain] is a go-between between his party, which has services and favors to sell the public in exchange for the public's votes, and the public, or at least the segments of it which are willing to exchange their votes for services—often enough to swing a close election. In this relationship the vote stands for currency, the party is the manufacturer or the supplier, the public is the consumer, and Mr. Dolin the door-to-door salesman. . . . To the party the vote has 'commodity' or exchange value, in that it represents a fraction of the total sum of votes needed by the party to gain exclusive control over the 'tons' of patronage whereby it holds power, and to gain access to the financial resources of the community." [David Gutmann, "Big-Town Politics: Grass-Roots Level," *Commentary*, 17:1, February 1954, p. 155.]

Besides, Abner (Negro) is not hard to beat in a white precinct. I just carried a picture of both candidates around with me.

I can control my primary vote for sure because I can make the party regulars come out. I don't encourage a high vote here, just a sure vote. In the general election there is much more independent voting, and I can't be sure of control.[16]

In the conservation areas, especially, the precinct captain was often active in the neighborhood improvement association and a leader in efforts to keep "undesirable people" out of the neighborhood. An interviewer who spoke to 30 precinct captains in 1951 found that 16 of them had been approached by voters who wanted help in preventing Negroes and Jews from moving into the neighborhood. Some of these captains invented slogans and ran campaigns on an issue such as: "The ———————— neighborhood is a good clean neighborhood. Let's keep it that way!" A captain was likely to learn about it almost immediately if a landlord rented to an "undesirable"; very often the captain would go to the landlord to urge in the name of civic pride that he discriminate and to point out that property values would decline if he did not.

In heavily Democratic precincts the owners of rooming houses sometimes consulted with their precinct captains about new roomers and assisted the party workers with their canvass at election time. In some cases these owners refused to permit Republican workers to enter their buildings. The loyalty of the rooming house owner to the Democratic party was not a matter of ideology: the owner who did not cooperate with the precinct captain could expect a visit from the city building inspector the next day.[17]

In addition to the services of party workers and voters, the machine needed cash. (It usually cost about $40,000 to elect an alderman.) This it raised by assessing the salaries of people who owed their jobs to the party, from the proceeds of ward-sponsored affairs such as picnics, boxing matches, and golf days, and in contributions from individuals and organizations who wanted to be on good terms with the party or, perhaps, even to help its candidates win.[18] These were all considered legitimate sources of revenue. In some wards, however, money was raised by promising favors or threatening injury to business interests, especially to those interests—e.g., taverns, hotels, and nightclubs—which were subject to inspection and licensing laws. Business people who wanted favors—a change in the zoning law, a permit to operate a tavern, a tax adjustment, and so on—were expected to pay for them in cash. In some wards there was even said to be a fixed schedule of prices for such favors. Whether the money so received went to support the party or to support personally the ward committeeman, the alderman, and their cronies was seldom clear; indeed, in many wards no real distinction

16. Quoted in Fay Calkins, *The CIO and the Democratic Party*, University of Chicago Press, Chicago, 1952, pp. 67–68.

17. H. D. Cherry, *op. cit.*, pp. 67–68.

18. Neher, *op. cit.*, p. 92.

could be made between the coffers of the party and the pockets of the boss: the ward organization "belonged" to the boss.[19]

The most profitable favors were of course those done for illegal enterprises. In giving protection to gambling joints, unlawful taverns, and houses of prostitution some politicians joined with racketeers to form a criminal syndicate.[20] A by-product of their activity was the systematic corruption of the police force; in one way or another officers were either bribed or discouraged from doing their duty. "After you find out how many places are protected by the ward politicians," a patrolman of long service told an investigator, "you just stay out of the way so you won't be around when something happens."[21]

The machines were most effective in delivering votes in the precincts where they were most corrupt. In general, these were in the "skid-row" districts and the slums, where votes were cheapest and illegal activities most numerous. The "river wards" in the decaying center and on the West Side of the city were the most solidly organized and the most corrupt. Here "social absenteeism"—the departure of socially articulate leaders of the community —had reached such a point that the machine politicians had the field to themselves.[22] It was almost unthinkable that an alderman in one of these wards might lose at the polls because he took an unpopular stand on an issue. If he lost, it was because his committeeman "dumped" him, because the committeeman sold out to the opposition, or because the opposition managed to build a more powerful machine, but it was not because the voters disliked his stand on any issues. These "river wards" were in sharp contrast to the so-called "newspaper wards" particularly on the North Side where voters usually split the ticket in the way a newspaper advised. The aldermen in the "river wards" could afford to be contemptuous of the newspapers; in their wards editorials were words wasted.

---

19. If he thought the transaction was likely to be profitable, the ward boss might sell the services of his organization to the opposition. He might be criticized for doing this, but he was not likely to be unseated; after all, the organization "belonged" to him.

20. ". . . the criminal syndicate," according to Aaron Kohn, chief investigator for the Emergency Crime Committee of the City Council, "can be described as consisting of political officials, having the power and responsibility to enforce the laws, who maliciously withhold that power in exchange for money and support from hoodlums, vice operators, professional gamblers, and other community enemies, to aid them in their political ambitions." Independent Voters of Illinois, *The Kohn Report; Crime and Politics in Chicago,* Chicago, 1953, p. iii. However, after two months' inquiry a grand jury in the Spring of 1954 gave up its efforts to uncover specific links between crime and politics in Chicago. "If an alliance exists," the jurors said, "it might be disclosed with funds to conduct undercover work. . . ." *Chicago Sun-Times,* May 1, 1954.

21. Independent Voters of Illinois, *The Kohn Report; Crime and Politics in Chicago,* Chicago, 1953, p. 10.

22. See the discussion of social absenteeism in Morris Janowitz, *The Community Press in an Urban Setting,* The Free Press, Glencoe, Illinois, 1952, p. 214. Janowitz notes that social absenteeism contributes to the decay of the ideological element in politics, thus creating "a new kind of hoodlumism in politics" and making possible sudden shifts from one party to another which have no significance in terms of the traditional political allegiances.

Although corruption in varying degrees was widespread in both parties, it was by no means universal in either. Some Democratic and some Republican wards were probably almost entirely "clean" and even in wards which were not "clean" there were aldermen and other officials who were not parties to the "deals" that were made in the back rooms. The honest aldermen, however, got little credit or encouragement from the voters. Many people seemed to think that all politicians were corrupt and that if an alderman did not use his office for personal profit it was because he was a fool. When a North Side alderman bought his boy a football suit and helmet the other children in the neighborhood said, "Look at the alderman's son," suggesting ill-gotten funds. The alderman himself drove a two-year-old Dodge instead of the Cadillac that he could well afford, but even this did not convince his constituents that he was honest.[23] This widespread cynicism tended, perhaps, to give the aldermen a low conception of their calling and to encourage irresponsibility on their part.

Some of the honest men, the Mayor among them, did less than they might have done to put a stop to corruption. The fact was that they needed for themselves or for their party the support of the powerful bosses in the corrupt wards. So, for that matter, did many other interests, both liberal and conservative, in city, state, and nation.

# RINGS AND BOSSES

## JAMES BRYCE

THE READER WILL ASK, How is the Machine run? What are the inner springs that move it? What is the source of the power the committees wield? What force of cohesion keeps leaders and followers together? What kind of government prevails among this army of professional politicians?

The source of power and the cohesive force is the desire for office, and for office as a means of gain. This one cause is sufficient to account for everything, when it acts, as it does in these cities, under the condition of the suffrage of a host of ignorant and pliable voters.

Those who in great cities form the committees and work the machine are persons whose chief aim in life is to make their living by office. Such a man generally begins by acquiring influence among a knot of voters who live in his

23. Interview document. As this study went to press a committee of the Chicago Bar Association filed charges against this very alderman after the *Sun-Times* had accused him of fee-splitting in zoning cases.
Reprinted from *The American Commonwealth* (London and New York: Macmillan & Company, 1889), Vol. II, Ch. 63.

neighbourhood, or work under the same employer, or frequent the same grogshop or beer saloon, which perhaps he keeps himself. He becomes a member of his primary, attends regularly, attaches himself to some leader in that body, and is forward to render service by voting as his leader wishes, and by doing duty at elections. He has entered the large and active class called, technically, "workers," or more affectionately, "the Boys." Soon he becomes conspicuous in the primary, being recognized as controlling the votes of others —"owning them" is the technical term—and is chosen delegate to a convention. Loyalty to the party there and continued service at elections mark him out for further promotion. He is appointed to some petty office in one of the city departments, and presently is himself nominated for an elective office. By this time he has also found his way on to the ward committee, whence by degrees he rises to sit on the central committee, having carefully nursed his local connection and surrounded himself with a band of adherents, who are called his "heelers," and whose loyalty to him in the primary, secured by the hope of "something good," gives weight to his words. Once a member of the central committee he discovers what everybody who gets on in the world discovers sooner or later, by how few persons the world is governed. He is one of a small knot of persons who pull the wires for the whole city, controlling the primaries, selecting candidates, "running" conventions, organizing elections, treating on behalf of the party in the city with the leaders of the party in the State. Each of this knot, which is probably smaller than the committee, because every committee includes some ciphers put on to support a leader, and which may include one or two strong men not on the committee, has acquired in his upward course a knowledge of men and their weaknesses, a familiarity with the wheels, shafts, and bands of the party machine, together with a skill in working it. Each can command some primaries, each has attached to himself a group of dependents who owe some place to him, or hope for some place from him. The aim of the knot is not only to get good posts for themselves, but to rivet their yoke upon the city by garrisoning the departments with their own creatures, and so controlling elections to the State legislature that they can procure such statutes as they desire, and prevent the passing of statutes likely to expose or injure them. They cement their dominion by combination, each placing his influence at the disposal of the others, and settle all important measures in secret conclave.

Such a combination is called a Ring.

The power of such a combination is immense, for it ramifies over the whole city. There are, in New York City, for instance, over ten thousand persons employed by the city authorities, all dismissible by their superiors at short notice and without cause assigned. There are two thousand five hundred persons employed in the Custom-House, Post-Office, and other branches of the Federal service, most of whom are similarly dismissible by the proper Federal authority; and there are also State servants, responsible to and dismissible by the State authority. If the same party happens to be supreme in city politics, in the Federal government, and in the State government, all this army of employés is expected to work for the party leaders of the city, in city primaries, conventions, and elections, and is virtually amenable to the orders of these leaders.[1] If the other party holds the reins of Federal government, or of both the Federal government and State government, then the city wirepullers have at any rate their own ten thousand or more, while other thousands swell the army of "workers" for the opposite party. Add those who expect to get offices, and it will be seen how great and how disciplined a force is available to garrison the city and how effective it becomes under strict discipline. Yet it is not larger than is needed, for the work is heavy. *Tantae molis erat Romanam condere gentem.*

In a Ring there is usually some one person who holds more strings in his hand than do the others. Like them he has worked himself up to power from small beginnings, gradually extending the range of his influence over the mass of workers, and knitting close bonds with influential men outside as well as inside politics, perhaps with great financiers or railway magnates, whom he can oblige, and who can furnish him with funds. At length his superior skill, courage, and force of will make him, as such gifts always do make their possessor, dominant among his fellows. An army led by a council seldom conquers: it must have a commander-in-chief, who settles disputes, decides in emergencies, inspires fear or attachment. The head of the Ring is such a general. He dispenses places, rewards the loyal, punishes the mutinous, concocts schemes, negotiates treaties. He generally avoids publicity, preferring the substance to the pomp of power, and is all the more dangerous because he sits, like a spider, hidden in the midst of his web. He is a Boss.

Although the career I have sketched is that whereby most Bosses have risen to greatness, some attain it by a shorter path. There have been brilliant instances of persons stepping at once on to the higher rungs of the ladder in virtue of their audacity and energy, especially if coupled with oratorical power. The first theatre of such a man's successes may have been the stump rather than the primary: he will then become potent in conventions, and either by hectoring or by plausible address, for both have their value, spring into popular favour, and make himself necessary to the party managers. It is of course a gain to a Ring to have among them a man of popular gifts, because he helps to conceal the odious features of their rule, gilding it by his rhetoric, and winning the applause of the masses who stand outside the circle of workers. However, the position of the rhetorical boss is less firmly rooted than that of the intriguing boss, and there have been instances of his suddenly falling to rise no more.

A great city is the best soil for the growth of a Boss, because it contains the largest masses of manageable voters as well as numerous offices, and plentiful opportunities for jobbing. But a whole State sometimes falls under the dominion of one intriguer. To govern so large a territory needs high

---

1. Assuming, as one usually may, that the city leaders are on good terms with the Federal and State party managers.

abilities; and the State boss is always an able man, somewhat more of a politician, in the European sense, than a city boss need be. He dictates State nominations, and through his lieutenants controls State and sometimes Congressional conventions, being in diplomatic relations with the chief city bosses and local rings in different parts of the State. His power over them mainly springs from his influence with the Federal executive and in Congress. He is usually, almost necessarily, a member of Congress, probably a senator, and can procure, or at any rate can hinder, such legislation as the local leaders desire or dislike. The President cannot ignore him, and the President's ministers, however little they may like him, find it worth while to gratify him with Federal appointments for persons he recommends, because the local votes he controls may make all the difference to their own prospects of getting some day a nomination for the presidency. Thus he uses his Congressional position to secure State influence, and his State influence to strengthen his Federal position. Sometimes however he is rebuffed by the powers at Washington and then his State thanes fly from him. Sometimes he quarrels with a powerful city boss, and then honest men come by their own.

It must not be supposed that the members of Rings, or the great Boss himself, are wicked men. They are the offspring of a system. Their morality is that of their surroundings. They see a door open to wealth and power, and they walk in. The obligations of patriotism or duty to the public are not disregarded by them, for these obligations have never been present to their minds. A State boss is usually a native American and a person of some education, who avoids the grosser forms of corruption, though he has to wink at them when practised by his friends. He may be a man of personal integrity.[2] A city boss is often of foreign birth and humble origin; he has grown up in an atmosphere of oaths and cocktails: ideas of honour and purity are as strange to him as ideas about the nature of the currency and the incidence of taxation: politics is merely a means for getting and distributing places. "What," said an ingenuous delegate at one of the National Conventions at Chicago in 1880, "what are we here for except the offices?" It is no wonder if he helps himself from the city treasury and allows his minions to do so. Sometimes he does not rob, and, like Clive, wonders at his own moderation. And even he improves as he rises in the world. Like a tree growing out of a dust heap, the higher he gets, the cleaner do his boughs and leaves become. America is a country where vulgarity is scaled off more easily than in England, and where the general air of good nature softens the asperities of power. Some city bosses are men from whose decorous exterior and unobtrusive manners no one would divine either their sordid beginnings or their noxious trade. As for the State boss, whose talents are probably greater to begin with, he must be of very coarse metal if he does not take a polish from the society of Washington.

A city Ring works somewhat as follows. When the annual or biennial

---

2. So too a rural boss is often quite pure, and blameworthy rather for his intriguing methods than for his aims.

city or State elections come round, its members meet to discuss the apportionment of offices. Each may desire something for himself, unless indeed he is
already fully provided for, and anyhow desires something for his friends. The
common sort are provided for with small places in the gift of some official,
down to the place of a policeman or doorkeeper or messenger, which is
thought good enough for a common "ward worker." Better men receive clerk-
ships or the promise of a place in the custom-house or post-office to be obtained from the Federal authorities. Men still more important aspire to the
elective posts, seats in the State legislature, a city aldermanship or commissionership, perhaps even a seat in Congress. All the posts that will have to be
filled at the coming elections are considered with the object of bringing out a
party ticket, *i.e.* a list of candidates to be supported by the party at the polls
when its various nominations have been successfully run through the proper
conventions. Some leading man, or probably the Boss himself, sketches out
an allotment of places; and when this allotment has been worked out fully,
it results in a Slate, *i.e.* a complete draft list of candidates to be proposed for
the various offices.[3] It may happen that the slate does not meet everybody's
wishes. Some member of the ring or some local boss—most members of a
ring are bosses each in his own district, as the members of a cabinet are heads
of the departments of state, or as the cardinals are bishops of dioceses near
Rome and priests and deacons of her parish churches—may complain that
he and his friends have not been adequately provided for, and may demand
more. In that case the slate will probably be modified a little to ensure good
feeling and content; and will then be presented to the Convention.

But there is sometimes a more serious difficulty to surmount. A party in a
State or city may be divided into two or more factions. Success in the election
will be possible only by uniting these factions upon the same nominees for
office. Occasionally the factions may each make its list and then come together in the party convention to fight out their differences. But the more
prudent course is for the chiefs of each faction to arrange matters in a private
conference. Each comes wishing to get the most he can for his clansmen,
but feels the need for a compromise. By a process of "dickering" (*i.e.* bargaining by way of barter), various offers and suggestions being made all round,
a list is settled on which the high contracting parties agree. This is a Deal,
or Trade, a treaty which terminates hostilities for the time, and brings about
"harmony." The list so settled is now a Slate, unless some discontented
magnate objects and threatens to withdraw. To do so is called "breaking the
slate." If such a "sore-head" persists, a schism may follow, with horrible

---

3. A pleasant story is told of a former Boss of New York State, who sat with his
vassals just before the convention, preparing the Slate. There were half a dozen or
more State offices for which nominations were to be made. The names were with
deliberation selected and set down, with the exception of the very unimportant place
of State Prison Inspector. One of his subordinates ventured to call the attention of
the Boss to what he supposed to be an inadvertence, and asked who was to be the
man for that place, to which the great man answered, with an indulgent smile, "I
guess we will leave *that* to the convention."

disaster to the party; but usually a new slate is prepared and finally agreed upon. The accepted Slate is now ready to be turned by the Machine into a Ticket, and nothing further remains but the comparatively easy process of getting the proper delegates chosen by packed primaries, and running the various parts of the ticket through the conventions to which the respective nominations belong. Internal dissension among the chiefs is the one great danger; the party must at all hazards be kept together, for the power of a united party is enormous. It has not only a large but a thoroughly trained and disciplined army in its office-holders and office-seekers; and it can concentrate its force upon any point where opposition is threatened to the regular party nomination.[4] All these office-holders and office-seekers have not only the spirit of self-interest to rouse them, but the bridle of fear to check any stirrings of independence. Discipline is very strict in this army. Even city politicians must have a moral code and moral standard. It is not the code of an ordinary unprofessional citizen. It does not forbid falsehood, or malversation, or ballot stuffing, or "repeating." But it denounces apathy or cowardice, disobedience, and above all, treason to the party. Its typical virtue is "solidity," unity of heart, mind, and effort among the workers, unquestioning loyalty to the party leaders, and devotion to the party ticket. He who takes his own course is a Kicker or Bolter; and is punished not only sternly but vindictively. The path of promotion is closed to him; he is turned out of the primary, and forbidden to hope for a delegacy to a convention; he is dismissed from any office he holds which the Ring can command. Dark stories are even told of a secret police which will pursue the culprit who has betrayed his party, and of mysterious disappearances of men whose testimony against the Ring was feared. Whether there is any foundation for such tales I do not undertake to say. But true it is that the bond between the party chiefs and their followers is very close and very seldom broken. What the client was to his patron at Rome, what the vassal was to his lord in the Middle Ages, that the heelers and workers are to their boss in these great transatlantic cities. They render a personal feudal service, which their suzerain repays with the gift of a livelihood; and the relation is all the more cordial because the lord bestows what costs him nothing, while the vassal feels that he can keep his post only by the favour of the lord.

European readers must again be cautioned against drawing for themselves too dark a picture of the Boss. He is not a demon. He is not regarded with horror even by those "good citizens" who strive to shake off his yoke. He is not necessarily either corrupt or mendacious, though he grasps at place, power, and wealth. He is a leader to whom certain peculiar social and political conditions have given a character dissimilar from the party leaders whom Europe knows. It is worth while to point out in what the dissimilarity consists.

A Boss needs fewer showy gifts than a European demagogue. His spe-

---

4. As for instance by packing the primaries with its adherents from other districts, whom a partisan chairman or committee will suffer to be present and perhaps to vote.

cial theatre is neither the halls of the legislature nor the platform, but the committee-room. A power of rough and ready repartee, or a turn for florid declamation, will help him; but he can dispense with both. What he needs are the arts of intrigue and that knowledge of men which teaches him when to bully, when to cajole, whom to attract by the hope of gain, whom by appeals to party loyalty. Nor are so-called "social gifts" unimportant. The lower sort of city politicians congregate in clubs and bar-rooms; and as much of the cohesive strength of the smaller party organizations arises from their being also social bodies, so also much of the power which liquor dealers exercise is due to the fact that "heelers" and "workers" spend their evenings in drinking places, and that meetings for political purposes are held there. Of the 1007 primaries and conventions of all parties held in New York City preparatory to the elections of 1884, 633 took place in liquor saloons. A Boss ought therefore to be hail fellow well met with those who frequent these places, not fastidious in his tastes, fond of a drink and willing to stand one, jovial in manners, and ready to oblige even a humble friend.

The aim of a Boss is not so much fame as power, and not so much power over the conduct of affairs as over persons. Patronage is the sort of power he seeks, patronage understood in the largest sense in which it covers the disposal of lucrative contracts and other modes of enrichment as well as salaried places. The dependants who surround him desire wealth, or at least a livelihood; his business is to find this for them, and in doing so he strengthens his own position.[5] It is as the bestower of riches that he holds his position, like the leader of a band of condottieri in the fifteenth century.

The interest of a Boss in political questions is usually quite secondary. Here and there one may be found who is a politician in the European sense, who, whether sincerely or not, purports and professes to be interested in some principle or measure affecting the welfare of the country. But the attachment of the ringster is usually given wholly to the concrete party, that is to the men who compose it, regarded as office-holders or office-seekers; and there is often not even a profession of zeal for any party doctrine. As a noted politician happily observed to a friend of mine, "You know, Mr. R., there are no politics in politics." Among bosses, therefore, there is little warmth of party spirit. The typical boss regards the boss of the other party much as counsel for the plaintiff regards counsel for the defendant. They are pro-

---

5. "A Boss is able to procure positions for many of his henchmen on horse-railroads, the elevated roads, quarry works, etc. Great corporations are peculiarly subject to the attacks of demagogues, and they find it greatly to their interest to be on good terms with the leader in each district who controls the vote of the assemblyman and alderman; and therefore the former is pretty sure that a letter of recommendation from him on behalf of any applicant for work will receive most favourable consideration. The leader also is continually helping his supporters out of difficulties, pecuniary and otherwise: he lends them a dollar now and then, helps out, when possible, such of their kinsmen as get into the clutches of the law, gets a hold over such of them as have done wrong and are afraid of being exposed, and learns to mix bullying judiciously with the rendering of service."—Mr. Theodore Roosevelt, in an article in the *Century* magazine for November 1886.

fessionally opposed, but not necessarily personally hostile. Between bosses there need be no more enmity than results from the fact that the one has got what the other wishes to have. Accordingly it sometimes happens that there is a good understanding between the chiefs of opposite parties in cities; they will even go the length of making (of course secretly) a joint "deal," *i.e.* of arranging for a distribution of offices whereby some of the friends of one shall get places, the residue being left for the friends of the other. A well-organized city party has usually a disposable vote which can be so cast under the directions of the managers as to effect this, or any other desired result. The appearance of hostility must, of course, be maintained for the benefit of the public; but as it is for the interest of both parties to make and keep these private bargains, they are usually kept when made, though of course it is seldom possible to prove the fact.

The real hostility of the Boss is not to the opposite party, but to other factions within his own party. Often he has a rival leading some other organization, and demanding, in respect of the votes which that organization controls, a share of the good things going. The greatest cities can support more than one faction within the same party; thus New York has long had three democratic organizations, two of which are powerful and often angrily hostile. If neither can crush the other, it finds itself obliged to treat, and to consent to lose part of the spoils to its rival. Still more bitter, however, is the hatred of Boss and Ring towards those members of the party who do not desire and are not to be appeased by a share of the spoils, but who agitate for what they call reform. They are natural and permanent enemies; nothing but the extinction of the Boss himself and of bossdom altogether will satisfy them. They are moreover the common enemies of both parties, that is, of bossdom in both parties. Hence in the ring-governed cities professionals of both parties will sometimes unite against the reformers, or will rather let their opponents secure a place than win it for themselves by the help of the "independent vote." Devotion to "party government," as they understand it, can hardly go farther.

This great army of workers is mobilized for elections, the methods of which form a wide and instructive department of political science. Here I have to refer only to their financial side, because that is intimately connected with the Machine. Elections need money, in America a great deal of money. Where, then, does the money come from, seeing that the politicians themselves belong to, or emerge from, a needy class?

The revenues of a Ring, that is, their collective, or, as one may say, corporate revenues, available for party purposes, flow from five sources.

I. The first is public subscriptions. For important elections such as the biennial elections of State officers, or perhaps for that of the State legislature, a "campaign fund," as it is called, is raised by an appeal to wealthy members of the party. So strong is party feeling that many respond, even though they suspect the men who compose the Ring, disapprove its methods, and have no great liking for the candidates.

II. Contributions are sometimes privately obtained from rich men who, though not directly connected with the Ring, may expect something from its action. Contractors, for instance, have an interest in getting pieces of work from the city authorities. Railroad men have an interest in preventing State legislation hostile to their lines. Both, therefore, may be willing to help those who can so effectively help them. This source of income is only available for important elections. Its incidental mischief in enabling wealth to control a legislature through a Ring is serious.

III. An exceptionally audacious Ring will sometimes make an appropriation from the city or (more rarely) from the State treasury for the purposes not of the city or the State, but of its own election funds. It is not thought necessary to bring such an appropriation[6] into the regular accounts to be laid before the public; in fact, pains are taken to prevent the item from appearing, and the accounts have often to be manipulated for that purpose. The justification, if any, of conduct not authorized by the law, must be sought in precedent, in the belief that the other side would do the same, and in the benefits which the Ring expects to confer upon the city it administers. It is a method of course available only when Ring officials have the control of the public funds, and cannot be resorted to by an opposition.

IV. A tax is levied upon the office-holders of the party, varying from one to four or even five per cent upon the amount of their annual salaries. The aggregate annual salaries of the city officials in New York City amount to $11,000,000 (£2,200,000 sterling), and those of the two thousand five five hundred Federal officials, who, if of the same party, might also be required to contribute,[7] to $2,500,000 (£500,000 sterling). An assessment at two per cent on these amounts would produce over £45,000 and £10,000 respectively, quite a respectable sum for election expenses.[8] Even policemen in cities, even office boys, and workmen in Federal dockyards, have been assessed by their respective parties. As a tenant had in the days of feudalism to make occasional money payments to his lord in addition to the military service he rendered, so now the American vassal must render his aids in money as well as give knightly service at the primaries, in the canvass, at the polls. His liabilities are indeed heavier than those of the feudal tenant, for the latter could relieve himself from duty in the field by the payment of

---

6. The practice of openly taking from Parliament a sum for secret service money, which was usually applied by the government in power for electioneering purposes, has just been finally extinguished (1887) in England. A sum is still voted for foreign secret service. In England, however, the money was regularly voted each session for the purpose, and though no account was rendered, it was well understood how it went.

7. Federal officials, would, as a rule, contribute only to the fund for Federal elections; but when the contest covered both Federal and city offices the funds would be apt to be blended.

8. To make the calculation complete we should have to reckon in also the State officials and assessments payable by them.

scutage, while under the Machine a money payment never discharges from the obligation to serve in the army of "workers." As in the days of the Anglo-Norman kings, forfeiture and the being proclaimed as "nithing" is the penalty for failure to discharge the duties by which the vassal holds. Efforts which began with an order issued by President Hayes in 1877 applying to Federal offices, have lately been made to prevent by administrative action and by legislation the levying of this tribute on officials, but they have not as yet proved completely successful, for the subordinate fears to offend his superiors.

V. Another useful expedient has been borrowed from European monarchies in the sale of nominations and occasionally of offices themselves.[9] A person who seeks to be nominated as candidate for one of the more important offices, such as a judgeship or a seat in the State Senate, or in Congress, is often required to contribute to the election fund a sum proportioned to the importance of the place he seeks, the excuse given for the practice being the cost of elections; and the same principle is occasionally applied to the gift of non-elective offices, the right of appointing to which is vested in some official member of a Ring—*e.g.* a mayor. The price of a nomination for a seat in the State legislature is said to run from $500 up to $1000, and for one of the better judgeships as high as $5000; but this is largely matter of conjecture.[10] Of course much less will be given if the prospects of carrying the election are doubtful: the prices quoted must be taken to represent cases where the party majority makes success certain. Naturally, the salaries of officials have to be raised in order to enable them to bear this charge, so that in the long run it may be thrown upon the public; and a recent eminent boss of New York City defended, before a committee of the legislature, the large salaries paid to aldermen, on the ground that "heavy demands were made on them by their party."

---

9. As judicial places were sold under the old French monarchy, and commissions in the army in England till sixteen years ago.

10. "A judgeship," says Mr. F. W. Whitridge, "costs in New York about $15,000; the district attorneyship the same; for a nomination to Congress the price is about $4000, though this is variable; an aldermanic nomination is worth $1500, and that for the Assembly from $600 to $1500. The amount realized from these assessments cannot be exactly estimated, but the amount raised by Tammany Hall, which is the most complete political organization, may be fixed very nearly at $125,000 (£25,000). This amount is collected and expended by a small executive committee who keep no accounts and are responsible only to each other."—Article "Assessments," in *Amer. Cyclop. of Political Science.*

# HOW TO GET A POLITICAL FOLLOWING

## GEORGE WASHINGTON PLUNKITT
### Recorded by WILLIAM L. RIORDAN

"THERE'S THOUSANDS of young men in this city who will go to the polls for the first time next November. Among them will be many who have watched the careers of successful men in politics, and who are longin' to make names and fortunes for themselves at the same game. It is to these youths that I want to give advice. First, let me say that I am in a position to give what the courts call expert testimony on the subject. I don't think you can easily find a better example than I am of success in politics. After forty years' experience at the game I am—well, I'm George Washington Plunkitt. Everybody knows what figure I cut in the greatest organization on earth, and if you hear people say that I've laid away a million or so since I was a butcher's boy in Washington Market, don't come to me for an indignant denial. I'm pretty comfortable, thank you.

"Now, havin' qualified as an expert, as the lawyers say, I am goin' to give advice free to the young men who are goin' to cast their first votes, and who are lookin' forward to political glory and lots of cash. Some young men think they can learn how to be successful in politics from books, and they cram their heads with all sorts of college rot. They couldn't make a bigger mistake. Now, understand me, I ain't sayin' nothin' against colleges. I guess they'll have to exist as long as there's bookworms, and I suppose they do some good in a certain way, but they don't count in politics. In fact, a young man who has gone through the college course is handicapped at the outset. He may succeed in politics, but the chances are 100 to 1 against him.

"Another mistake; some young men think that the best way to prepare for the political game is to practise speakin' and becomin' orators. That's all wrong. We've got some orators in Tammany Hall, but they're chiefly ornamental. You never heard of Charlie Murphy delivering a speech, did you? Or Richard Croker, or John Kelly, or any other man who has been a real power in the organization? Look at the thirty-six district leaders of Tammany Hall to-day. How many of them travel on their tongues? Maybe one or two, and they don't count when business is doin' at Tammany Hall. The men who rule have practised keepin' their tongues still, not exercisin' them. So you want to drop the orator idea unless you mean to go into politics just to perform the sky-rocket act.

Reprinted from *Plunkitt of Tammany Hall* (New York: McClure Philips & Co., 1905), pp. 11–18 and 46–53.

"Now, I've told you what not to do; I guess I can explain best what to do to succeed in politics by tellin' you what I did. After goin' through the apprenticeship of the business while I was a boy by workin' around the district headquarters and hustlin' about the polls on election day, I set out when I cast my first vote to win fame and money in New York city politics. Did I offer my services to the district leader as a stump-speaker? Not much. The woods are always full of speakers. Did I get up a book on municipal government and show it to the leader? I wasn't such a fool. What I did was to get some marketable goods before goin' to the leaders. What do I mean by marketable goods? Let me tell you: I had a cousin, a young man who didn't take any particular interest in politics. I went to him and said: 'Tommy, I'm goin' to be a politician, and I want to get a followin'; can I count on you?' He said: 'Sure, George.' That's how I started in business. I got a marketable commodity—one vote. Then I went to the district leader and told him I could command two votes on election day, Tommy's and my own. He smiled on me and told me to go ahead. If I had offered him a speech or a bookful of learnin', he would have said, 'Oh, forget it!'

"That was beginnin' business in a small way, wasn't it? But that is the only way to become a real lastin' statesman. I soon branched out. Two young men in the flat next to mine were school friends. I went to them, just as I went to Tommy, and they agreed to stand by me. Then I had a followin' of three voters and I began to get a bit chesty. Whenever I dropped into district headquarters, everybody shook hands with me, and the leader one day honored me by lightin' a match for my cigar. And so it went on like a snowball rollin' down a hill. I worked the flat-house that I lived in from the basement to the top floor, and I got about a dozen young men to follow me. Then I tackled the next house and so on down the block and around the corner. Before long I had sixty men back of me, and formed the George Washington Plunkitt Association.

"What did the district leader say then when I called at headquarters? I didn't have to call at headquarters. He came after me and said: 'George, what do you want? If you don't see what you want, ask for it. Wouldn't you like to have a job or two in the departments for your friends?' I said: 'I'll think it over; I haven't yet decided what the George Washington Plunkitt Association will do in the next campaign.' You ought to have seen how I was courted and petted then by the leaders of the rival organizations. I had marketable goods and there was bids for them from all sides, and I was a risin' man in politics. As time went on, and my association grew, I thought I would like to go to the Assembly. I just had to hint at what I wanted, and three different organizations offered me the nomination. Afterwards, I went to the Board of Aldermen, then to the State Senate, then became leader of the district, and so on up and up till I became a statesman.

"That is the way and the only way to make a lastin' success in politics. If you are goin' to cast your first vote next November and want to go into politics, do as I did. Get a followin', if it's only one man, and then go to the district leader and say: 'I want to join the organization. I've got one man who'll follow me through thick and thin.' The leader won't laugh at your one-man followin'. He'll shake your hand warmly, offer to propose you for membership in his club, take you down to the corner for a drink and ask you to call again. But go to him and say: 'I took first prize at college in Aristotle; I can recite all Shakspere forwards and backwards; there ain't nothin' in science that ain't as familiar to me as blockades on the elevated roads and I'm the real thing in the way of silver-tongued orators.' What will he answer? He'll probably say: 'I guess you are not to blame for your misfortunes, but we have no use for you here.' "

## To Hold Your District—Study Human Nature and Act Accordin'

"There's only one way to hold a district; you must study human nature and act accordin'. You can't study human nature in books. Books is a hindrance more than anything else. If you have been to college, so much the worse for you. You'll have to unlearn all you learned before you can get right down to human nature, and unlearnin' takes a lot of time. Some men can never forget what they learned at college. Such men may get to be district leaders by a fluke, but they never last.

"To learn real human nature you have to go among the people, see them and be seen. I know every man, woman, and child in the Fifteenth District, except them that's been born this summer—and I know some of them, too. I know what they like and what they don't like, what they are strong at and what they are weak in, and I reach them by approachin' at the right side.

"For instance, here's how I gather in the young men. I hear of a young feller that's proud of his voice, thinks that he can sing fine. I ask him to come around to Washington Hall and join our Glee Club. He comes and sings, and he's a follower of Plunkitt for life. Another young feller gains a reputation as a base-ball player in a vacant lot. I bring him into our base-ball club. That fixes him. You'll find him workin' for my ticket at the polls next election day. Then there's the feller that likes rowin' on the river, the young feller that makes a name as a waltzer on his block, the young feller that's handy with his dukes—I rope them all in by givin' them opportunities to show themselves off. I don't trouble them with political arguments. I just study human nature and act accordin'.

"But you may say this game won't work with the high-toned fellers, the fellers that go through college and then join the Citizens' Union. Of course it wouldn't work. I have a special treatment for them. I ain't like the patent medicine man that gives the same medicine for all diseases. The Citizens' Union kind of a young man! I love him! He's the daintiest morsel of the lot, and he don't often escape me.

"Before telling you how I catch him, let me mention that before the election last year, the Citizens' Union said they had four hundred or five hundred enrolled voters in my district. They had a lovely headquarters, too, beautiful roll-top desks and the cutest rugs in the world. If I was accused of havin' contributed to fix up the nest for them, I wouldn't deny it under oath. What do I mean by that? Never mind. You can guess from the sequel, if you're sharp.

"Well, election day came. The Citizens' Union's candidate for Senator, who ran against me, just polled five votes in the district, while I polled something more than 14,000 votes. What became of the 400 or 500 Citizens' Union enrolled voters in my district? Some people guessed that many of them were good Plunkitt men all along and worked with the Cits just to bring them into the Plunkitt camp by election day. You can guess that way, too, if you want to. I never contradict stories about me, especially in hot weather. I just call your attention to the fact that on last election day 395 Citizens' Union enrolled voters in my district were missin' and unaccounted for.

"I tell you frankly, though, how I have captured some of the Citizens' Union's young men. I have a plan that never fails. I watch the City Record to see when there's civil service examinations for good things. Then I take my young Cit in hand, tell him all about the good thing and get him worked up till he goes and takes an examination. I don't bother about him any more. It's a cinch that he comes back to me in a few days and asks to join Tammany Hall. Come over to Washington Hall some night and I'll show you a list of names on our rolls marked 'C.S.' which means, 'bucked up against civil service.'

"As to the older voters, I reach them, too. No, I don't send them campaign literature. That's rot. People can get all the political stuff they want to read—and a good deal more, too—in the papers. Who reads speeches, nowadays, anyhow? It's bad enough to listen to them. You ain't goin' to gain any votes by stuffin' the letter boxes with campaign documents. Like as not you'll lose votes, for there's nothin' a man hates more than to hear the letter-carrier ring his bell and go to the letter-box expectin' to find a letter he was lookin' for, and find only a lot of printed politics. I met a man this very mornin' who told me he voted the Democratic State ticket last year just because the Republicans kept crammin' his letter-box with campaign documents.

"What tells in holdin' your grip on your district is to go right down among the poor families and help them in the different ways they need help. I've got a regular system for this. If there's a fire in Ninth, Tenth, or Eleventh Avenue, for example, any hour of the day or night, I'm usually there with some of my election district captains as soon as the fire-engines. If a family is burned out I don't ask whether they are Republicans or Democrats, and I don't refer them to the Charity Organization Society, which would investigate their case in a month or two and decide they were worthy of help about the time they are dead from starvation. I just get quarters for them, buy clothes for them if their clothes were burned up, and fix them up till they get things runnin' again. It's philanthropy, but it's politics, too—mighty good politics. Who can tell how many votes one of these fires bring me? The poor are the most grateful people in the world, and, let me tell you, they have more friends in their neighborhoods than the rich have in theirs.

"If there's a family in my district in want I know it before the charitable societies do, and me and my men are first on the ground. I have a special corps to look up such cases. The consequence is that the poor look up to George W. Plunkitt as a father, come to him in trouble—and don't forget him on election day.

"Another thing, I can always get a job for a deservin' man. I make it a point to keep on the track of jobs, and it seldom happens that I don't have a few up my sleeve ready for use. I know every big employer in the district and in the whole city, for that matter, and they ain't in the habit of sayin' no to me when I ask them for a job.

"And the children—the little roses of the district! Do I forget them? Oh, no! They know me, every one of them, and they know that a sight of Uncle George and candy means the same thing. Some of them are the best kind of vote-getters. I'll tell you a case. Last year a little Eleventh Avenue rosebud whose father is a Republican, caught hold of his whiskers on election day and said she wouldn't let go till he'd promise to vote for me. And she didn't.

# THE ATTACHMENT OF THE IMMIGRANT TO THE BOSS

### OSCAR HANDLIN

AS A BOY in Brooklyn, "Hughey" McLaughlin was already a leader among his cronies. Big and strong, handy with his fists in a fight, he commanded the respect of the lads who hung around the firehouse. One employment after another was not quite to his taste; but in the neighborhood he was well known, and favorably. In 1855 his opportunity came. Taken on at the Navy Yard, he was put in charge of a group of workers, a gang, with the title of Boss Laborer, soon shortened to Boss.

These were the essential elements. To hold his own position it was necessary that he retain the favor of the political authority that appointed him. He did so by the ability to deliver a certain number of votes. And he was able to deliver those votes because he controlled a fund of desirable jobs. In time, McLaughlin extended the scope of his operations from the Navy

Reprinted from *The Uprooted* by Oscar Handlin, pp. 209–217, by permission of Little, Brown & Co. Copyright 1951, by Oscar Handlin.

Yard to the whole municipality. The relationship between votes and jobs remained the same.

Throughout the country in the great cities, other bosses became the heads of other gangs. Some had assembled followings as foremen or contractors, others by growing up in a district where they exercised continuing leadership as a gang of boys grew up to be a gang of voters. Everywhere the connection between these allegiances and the opportunity to work was plain. In an economy that condemned the immigrants to unskilled labor a large percentage of the available jobs were directly or indirectly dependent upon political favor. Aqueducts and streets the city built for itself; trolley, gas, telegraph, and electric lines were laid by companies franchised by the city; and every structure, as it went up, was inspected by the city. One pair of hands was much like another when it held the shovel; the employers of unskilled labor were wise enough to treat indulgently the wishes of the municipal officials in whose power it was to let contracts or grant permits.

The job was at the center of the boss's attractiveness. But he was also able to call forth a more general sense of attachment. Often the feelings of group loyalty focused upon him. He was a member of many associations, made friends on every block. In the columns of their own newspapers his name appeared frequently. His achievements cast their reflected glory on the whole community and he in turn shared its sense of solidarity. In that respect he stood at an advantage over every competitor for the immigrants' leadership. He had sprung from among them and substantially remained one with them.

Furthermore, he spoke for them. After the Civil War as the national parties in election after election chewed over the same stale issues, a great dullness settled down over their campaigns. Few people cared to take the trouble to distinguish how the position of the Democrats differed from that of the Republicans on civil service reform or the tariff. Few even bothered to learn what those problems were about. These were remote and abstract questions that did not directly touch on their own lives. The immigrant might sometimes read an article on such a matter in his newspaper but was less likely to be persuaded by any intrinsic ideas on the subject than by the character of the persuader. If a trusted source said that when a Democrat is President misery comes, that if the Republicans win the factories will open, the new citizen was likely to accept the statement without cavil.

The local issues were the important ones. Whether there should be a new public bathhouse in Ward Twelve, whether the city should hire extra laborers, seemed questions of no moment to the party statesmen. To the residents of the tenement districts they were critical; and in these matters the ward boss saw eye to eye with them. *Jim gets things done!* They could see the evidence themselves, knew the difference it made in their own existence.

The boss took command of the group in political matters. The old-line nationalist leaders still commanded the respect of their fellow countrymen but could not compete with the boss for votes. That fact Bourke Cockran discovered, in New York, when he met the opposition of Croker of Tammany Hall. Patrick Collins learned the same lesson in Boston, and an identical moral was pointed in other cities throughout the country. The machine gave form to the immigrant vote.

The ambitious politician, however, could not get very far if his power rested only on the loyalty of a bloc of immigrant followers. The instability of settlement prevented the consolidation of control on that basis. Tammany could not be sure how long its dominance of the East Side wards would last, or Lomasney in Boston of the West End, when the original Irish residents moved out and their place was taken by Jews and Italians. The successful chieftains were those who expanded their roles beyond the little group within which they had grown to power.

Hugh McLaughlin had perceived this. In his White House Saloon or in his office on Willoughby Street, he had made himself available to all comers. On the corner in Boston where his boyhood gang had whiled away the time, Martin Lomasney built the Hendricks Club. By the century's end, behind the whitened windows of an empty store, in the back room of a saloon, upstairs above the dance hall—under a variety of designations there was in every ward a place where a man could go and see the boss, or see someone who would in turn see the boss.

*I think that there's got to be in every ward a guy that any bloke can go to when he's in trouble and get help—not justice and the law, but help, no matter what he's done.* The old man reminisces as the incidents of a long career come back. What requests had not been made of him! And often enough he'd stepped in without waiting to be asked. Time and again one of the boys would let him know: the poor fellow had allowed his payments to lapse and now the widow had not the burial money; or, the furniture was being put out in the street and them with no place to go and the wife ailing at that. Baskets at Christmas, picnics, boat rides on the river or lake, and a ready purse at the mention of any charitable collection—these were all within his realm of obligations.

But mostly he had intervened at the points at which his people encountered the difficulties of the law. Between the rigid, impersonal rulings of the statute and the human failings of those ignorant of its complexities he stood as mediator. The poor lad who had an extra glass and by some half-remembered encounter ended the night in jail, the shopkeeper whose stand edged beyond the legal limit onto the sidewalk, turned to him whose contact set matters straight. They had all sat there explaining their troubles, the liquor dealer and the peddler worried about licenses, the contractor and the real-estate owner involved in deals with the city. They had come to him because they knew he was *fair* with his *favors*.

Those vain fools up on the hill had laughed and then seethed with indignation when he had torn the legislature apart so that wretched Italian could vend his peanuts on the grounds. The fulminations against "peanut politics" had been all to the good. They had confirmed the popular impression that he championed the little men against the big, the humble against the proud. Hundreds who themselves never had the occasion to turn to him firmly believed in his accessibility. The image, his own and theirs, was that of the kindly overlord, the feudal noble translated from the manor to the ward— above the law and therefore capable, if properly approached, of doing better justice than the law.

There was a price, of course. An exception made for one lawbreaker could be made for another; if the frightened peddler could get off, so too could the swaggering tough. After all, the turkeys in the baskets, the bubbling kegs of beer at the ends of the long picnic tables, all cost money. Whose money?

There were persons who would pay the bill. The thriving gambling industry of the 1870's stood on a tenuous relationship with the police. With expanded operations and greater capital investments, the operators of the keno, faro, and policy games could not tolerate a situation in which they were at the mercy of the extortions of every precinct lieutenant and his underlings. Nor would saloonkeepers willingly expose themselves to the assaults of temperance fanatics with their zealous insistence upon awkward closing hours or even upon total prohibition. An accommodating boss like Mike McDonald in Chicago provided protection in return for moderate occasional contributions from some two thousand gamblers in Chicago.

This source of support was not very secure, however. With time, the big promoters moved into the shadowland of legality and became less dependent upon protection. Some advanced to the ownership of bucket shops or indeed to the dignity of brokerage offices; others began to make book on horse racing and prize fighting, now legitimate enterprises. The older forms of speculation catered increasingly to the less profitable poor and were left to the attention of the petty promoter, from whom not much could be drawn in the ways of assessments.

Some bosses and their wives were, at the same time, stricken with social aspirations. Having made their way in the world, they wanted the visible symbols of having done so. Mike McDonald had made Carter Harrison mayor. Why should not the one be as respectable as the other? Unfortunately there were limits to the enjoyment of success; when McDonald moved to a fine suburb and began to play the gentleman, he lost his following and was unseated by Bathhouse John Coughlin and Hinky Dink Mike Kenna, two ungentle characters still close to the source of the votes.

If it was unsafe to desert one's proper district, at least some leaders hoped to surround themselves with other forms of respectability. They preferred not to deal with gamblers and saloonkeepers, but with nice people. And by this time there were some nice people quite eager to deal with the wielders of political influence. The perspicacious boss could become the familiar of the banker and the traction magnate, be taken to lunch in a good club (though not made a member), and puff his chest in the company of the financially mighty. Within the grant of government in these years were all sorts of profitable franchises, for laying trolley tracks, for building subways and electric and water lines, for the disposing of garbage. The interests concerned with these privileges were willing to aid the co-operative politician, aid to such an extent that he would not any longer be dependent on his emoluments from faro or overhours beer. The New York Dutch had a word for it, *boedel.*

Boodle was honest graft. When they floated the gas company they set aside a block of shares for the good fellows. No cash down—their credit was good. When the franchise came through and the stock prices rose in the market, the shares could be sold, the original purchase price paid, and a tidy balance would be left for the deserving. Or even if the capitalists were forced to lay out a flat sum without these complexities, that didn't hurt anyone. Such practices were not too far from the ordinary practices of legitimate business to offend any but the most tender consciences. Occasional revelations by shocked reformers did not alienate the boss's constituency; they merely endowed him with the additional romantic aspects of a Robin Hood.

Rivalry, not moral disapproval, provoked the serious troubles. In many matters the municipality shared jurisdiction with the state; and in the halls of the legislature, the city machines ran head-on into collision with the politicians who had long operated on a statewide basis. These men had not the assistance of the formal organization of the machine, but they had earlier consolidated their positions through alliances of key officeholders. Generally they were native American, as was the bulk of their following; and they drew their support from the farming areas and from the small towns. In most parts of the country they had the advantage of an anachronistic distribution of power which favored the rural at the expense of the urban districts. Years of bitter struggle followed the appearance of the immigrant organizations, as the state party chieftains attempted to mobilize minority national blocs to undermine the authority of their metropolitan competitors. In New York and Massachusetts, for instance, the Republicans attempted to woo the Italians and Jews to break the hold of the Irish Democrats on the city vote.

In time, however, there was an accommodation. Spheres of influence were defined and divided. Live and let live. Perhaps the appearance on the scene after 1900 of a crew of miscellaneous reformers and liberal independents drove the various manipulators of power into a union of convenience. In any case, shortly after 1910 the old acerbity was dulled and an era of more peaceful relationships ensued.

# HOW THE BOSS RUNS
# THE ORGANIZATION

FRANK R. KENT

## The Importance of Primaries

RIGHT HERE is the place to explain exactly why the primaries are so much more vital than the general election to the precinct executive.

The same reasons that make this statement apply to the precinct executive, make it equally apply to the ward executive, the district leader, the boss, the machine as an entirety, and the country as a whole.

Unless these facts are clearly understood at the start, there can be no real grasp of machine power, methods, and control. No political knowledge is worth anything unless they are comprehended.

To think that the general election is more important than the primary election, as most voters do, is to magnify the wrong side of the political picture. It ought to be reversed, and instead of, as now, many more voters voting in the general election than in the primaries, the public interest should be concentrated on the primaries first, and the general election second. As things stand to-day, the popular tendency is to regard primaries as the particular concern of the politicians, and not of real interest to the average voter. The result is that often an absurdly small proportion of the qualified voters participate in the primaries.

There could not be a greater mistake. This lack of appreciation of what the primaries really mean, and the general neglect to participate in them, plays directly into the hands of the machine. It makes it ridiculously easy for the machine, through the precinct executives, to control the situation. It actually permits the machine to run the country.

The reasons this is true are simple enough. Primaries are really the key to politics. There is no way for party candidates to get on the general election ballot except through the primaries. Primaries are the exclusive gate through which all party candidates must pass. Control of that gate in any community means control of the political situation in that community. It makes no difference whether the candidates who pass through that gate are knocked down in the general election or not, the next set of candidates must pass through the primary gate just the same. It ought to be plain, then, that so long as the machine controls the primaries, it is in a position to limit the

Reprinted from The Great Game of Politics by Frank R. Kent (New York: Doubleday & Company, 1923), pp. 6–13 and 103–111. Copyright 1923. Doubleday & Company. Reprinted by permission of the publisher.

choice of the voters in the general election to its choice in the primaries. That is the real secret of its power, and, so long as it holds that power, it cannot be put out of business. Defeating its candidates in the general election not only does not break its grip, it often does not make even a dent in it. It can and does continue to function after a general election defeat just as it did before. The only place a machine can be beaten is in the primaries. So long as it can nominate its candidates, so long is it an unbeaten machine. This is a government by parties, and under our system parties are essential to government. In all the states the two big parties—the Democratic and Republican—are recognized by law. These laws provide that these parties shall hold primaries, which are preliminary elections, participated in exclusively by party voters, for the purpose of nominating party candidates. The only way in which candidates may get on the ballot at the general election, other than through direct nomination in the primaries, or through nominations by conventions composed of delegates chosen in the primaries, is by petition signed by a designated number of voters. This gives a candidate a place on the ballot as an "outsider" and is rarely resorted to because of the extremely small chances of success of such candidate. Nothing short of a political tidal wave or revolution can carry an independent candidate to success. He may pull sufficient votes from one side or the other to bring about the defeat of one of the regular party nominees, but his own election is a thing so rare as to be almost negligible.

The fact that I wish to drive home now is that all over the country 99 per cent of all candidates for all offices are nominated as a result of primaries. The obvious and inescapable deduction is that in 99 per cent of all elections, the choice of the voters in the general election is limited to the choice of the voters in the primary elections. When the full significance of that statement sinks in, the tremendous importance of the primaries will be better appreciated. It ought to be clear that the man who votes in the general election and not in the primaries loses at least 50 per cent of the value and effectiveness of his vote as compared to the man who votes in both. Before a candidate for any office can be elected, except the rare independents who escape the primaries and go on the general ballot by petition, he must first be nominated. In 99 per cent of the cases, nominations are made in the primaries. In 1 per cent of them they are made by petition. In the face of these facts, it would appear distinctly in the interest of every voter to be a primary election voter. The truth is, however, that the one class that regularly votes in the primaries is the machine voters—and, of course, they control, and always will control, under these conditions.

It is not too much to say that the great bulk of the men holding municipal, state, and federal offices throughout the country to-day were elected or appointed to these offices because of the support of the party organizations or machines. They are exactly the same thing. There are in the United States more than 2,000,000 political jobholders of one kind or another. They range all the way from the President of the United States to the city street sweeper.

Nearly all of these are strictly organization men. Practically all of them vote strictly party tickets with unvaring regularity. Moreover, through family or other ties, every one of them is able to influence from two to ten votes beside his own. Some of them, of course, control a great many more. Five is the average. This means a powerful army. It is a lot of votes. They are divided between Republicans and Democrats, but the number is great enough to give each an exceedingly formidable force. They constitute the shock troops of the organization—the rank and file of the machines.

The potent thing politically about these machine men is that they vote. That is the real secret of machine power. They do not talk politics and then fail to register. Nor do they register and then fail to vote. Nor do they, when they vote, spoil their ballots. Every election day, regardless of wind or weather, "hell or high water," they march to the polls, cast their straight organization ballots, and they are counted. As voters they are 100 per cent effective. Besides, they see that the voters they are supposed to influence or control likewise go to the polls. Voting is a business matter with them and they attend to it.

But the overwhelming big thing is that they are primary-election voters— not merely general-election voters. No clear comprehension of politics can possibly be had until these basic facts are grasped:

First, all candidates of the two great parties must first be nominated as a result of primaries. There is no other way for them to get on the ballot.

Second, it is more important to the machine to nominate its candidates than to elect them.

Third, that the primaries are the instrument that gives the organization its legal status, and that it is, therefore, the only instrument through which it can be destroyed.

Fourth, that in the general election, the two party machines compete in getting the vote to the polls, and thus largely nullify each other's effectiveness. In the primaries the machines have no organized competition. Hence they become enormously effective and, so long as the average voter fails to participate, are practically invincible.

Fifth, in nearly all states, Republicans are barred from voting in Democratic primaries and Democrats must keep out of Republican primaries, which means that each party machine in the primaries is free from conflict with the other party machine.

Sixth, not only are the nominations made in the primaries, but members of the state central committee, control of which is the key to the whole machine, are elected in the primaries.

This is not the place to go into a detailed account of primary election variations in the different states. Some data concerning exceptions to the general rules here laid down are given in the Appendix to this book, but in the main the statements made in this chapter apply to the country as a whole.

When these things are considered, it ought to be plain why the primaries are so vital to the machine, and why it is a matter of political life and death to the precinct executive to carry his precinct in the primaries. The machine can lose its candidate time after time in the general election without greatly diminishing its strength or loosing the grip of its leaders. Of course, it is disheartening to the rank and file and it greatly lessens the number and quality of the political pies for distribution to the faithful. It could not be kept up too long without causing a revolt in the organization, but, I repeat, the machine cannot be smashed by defeating its candidate at the election.

But if it loses in the primaries, it is out of business. Any organization that cannot carry the primary election is a defunct organization. It either politically disappears or it makes peace and amalgamates with the faction that defeated it. In rare cases it waits for the wind of public sentiment that blew it over to die down, picks up the pieces, and crawls back into the saddle. But no political machine or precinct executive could possibly survive two primary defeats.

Apart from the lack of competition, it must be evident that the reason the machine is so much more potent in the primaries is that the total number of voters is so much smaller. The smaller the vote the more dominant the machine. Only the voters of one party are permitted to vote in that party's primaries. All the members of any political machine are members of one party, and they all vote. Hence, in the primaries the machine polls its full strength, while the number of voters outside of the machine who can vote is very much cut down. It ought to be plain that every party voter outside of the machine who refrains from voting in the primaries adds to the strength of the precinct executive—which means the machine—by just that much.

It also ought to be plain that the man who poses as an independent in politics and declines to affiliate with either party, thus disqualifying himself as a primary voter, has greatly lessened his individual importance as a political factor as well as added to the strength of the machine.

He can be as independent as he pleases in the general election. He can refuse to vote for the party nominees if they do not suit him, but if he does not vote in the primaries, those who do are picking the men for whom he must vote, for or against, in the general election.

Boiled down, it comes to this: so long as the primaries are controlled by machines, the general-election voter, no matter how independent he may be, 99 per cent of the time is limited in his choice to two machine selections. There is no getting away from that fact.

## Picking the Ticket

Placing just as much of his machine as he possibly can on the payroll is the primary purpose of the boss.

That is the fundamental idea back of a political organization. That is its *raison d'être*. All the labour and expense of building it up, all the time and trouble of controlling the primaries, all the fighting and working to elect the ticket after it has been nominated, from the machine standpoint, would be aimless and futile and foolish, if success were not to be rewarded with something more than the mere satisfaction of winning. If, after the machine has sweated, fought, and bled to nominate and elect a set of party candidates, somebody else is to get the jobs—why, what is the use?

Political organizations run politics because of the lack of active interest and clear understanding upon the part of the ordinary citizen. This general political inertia, these hazy and confused political ideas, this tendency to think of politics as something low and slimy, which ought to be left to the politicians—particularly the primaries—these are the things that make machines possible and powerful. In proportion as the average voter becomes interested and informed, the bulk and power of the machine decreases.

Under our party system, as has been shown, some sort of unofficial organization is essential to the orderly conduct of elections and the proper functioning of the Government. There has to be some human agency to do the actual party work of filling tickets, arranging details, providing election officials, bringing forward candidates, preparing for registration. These things do not do themselves. Nor can the state do them all. They call for voluntary activity upon the part of some one—and those who volunteer naturally form an organization and develop leaders. The whole thing is human and natural and inevitable. Nor can it be expected that the men who take over this work do so from patriotic or public-spirited motives. They take it over from purely practical and selfish motives and because there is an opportunity there for place, power, and money.

The point is that, although an organization of some sort is essential, under ideal conditions, with every citizen politically informed, and active enough to vote, the organization would be a simple, slender, inexpensive affair, easy to reward through proper patronage recognition without imposing a real burden on the taxpayers. Under existing conditions, with the voters lax, uninformed, inactive, and numerously not voting in every community—particularly in the primaries—the machine grows great and powerful, tremendously costly to the taxpayers, and develops bosses who are able to demand and get a far larger proportion of the positions under city, state, and federal governments than is good for them, for the state, the city or the country. The basic truth is that the boss will go just so far in the patronage matter as he can—and the distance he can go is exactly measured by the indifference of the voters. Under conditions as they exist to-day in the big cities of the country, he goes very far, indeed. It becomes his chief occupation—this placing of his followers on the public payroll.

But that is not all he has to do. There are two things expected of him as boss—the nomination in the primaries of candidates friendly to the organization and the election of these candidates. It is here that the boss shows his quality. So long as more than half the qualified voters fail to vote, the kind of machine described in these pages has the power to put over in the primaries practically any one it wants. It would be possible, for instance, in either New York, Philadelphia, Chicago, Boston, Baltimore, St. Louis, or Cleveland for the bosses to nominate almost any old "Muldoon" for mayor that they might choose—but electing him is another matter. There is no sense in putting up a candidate in the primaries merely to have him knocked down in the general election.

It is true that, so long as he holds control of the primaries, the boss still has his machine, but no machine will indefinitely follow a funeral director— and no boss not a fool would deliberately court defeat through a too-brazen exhibition of primary power. What he does is to try so to load the ticket in the primary with the precise proportion of "Muldoons" that can get by in the general election—but no more. Almost always, in the framing of the ticket which the machine supports in the primary, the boss looks for men of sufficient standing and independence not only to command a certain degree of public respect and support but also to enable him to nominate "Muldoons" for the bulk of the places without arousing a dangerous popular resentment.

It is a matter of judgment. The boss wants a ticket that will win, but, at the same time, he wants candidates, who when they win, will not turn around and kick him and his machine out of the City Hall. How far he has to go in taking chances with independent men on the machine ticket depends upon the strength of his party in the city, the temper of the people, and the weight, disposition, and force of the newspapers. It has been shown how the nominations for the legislatures, the city councils, and the smaller or more numerous officers are made through the ward executives—and how it is easy in these instances to "get by" with tried and true deliverable machine men.

It is when it comes to picking the head of the ticket—the candidates for mayor or governor or judge—that the boss uses care and judgment. It is by the head of the ticket usually that the public judge the whole thing. If the head of the ticket is a good, strong man of standing and known integrity, or if some of the more conspicuous of the candidates are of this type, the rest of the ticket can be and is with impunity loaded down with "Muldoons."

In political circles this practice of putting a few of the conspicuously higher type on to leaven the organization loaf is known as "perfuming the ticket" or putting a "clean collar on the dirty shirt." In other words, the machine ticket is as clean as—and no cleaner than—the sentiment of the people of the community compels it to be. That is to say once more what has already been said in these pages a number of times—the quality of the ticket is exactly measured by the tolerance of the voters. Everything about the machine—everything in politics—is measured by this same yardstick, and it cannot be said too often. It is the heart of the whole thing from beginning to end.

There are various ways in which the boss, or bosses—because in some cities like Philadelphia and Norfolk the machine is run by a little oligarchic group of bosses, rather than by one man—get the "clean collar" or "perfumery." Sometimes he has nothing at all to do with bringing the candidate out, but places his machine behind a man who announces himself, without reference to the boss or the machine, but who looks like the strongest proposition in sight, and a dangerous one to beat in the primaries. It may be a matter of expediency, or to avoid a bruising fight, or to placate popular sentiment, or purely a question of finances.

Sometimes the boss manœuvres the appointment of a group of prominent business men affiliated with the party, who canvass the field and induce some respectable citizen to enter with the assurance of a machine support, which leaves him unpledged and uncompromised. Sometimes the man thus chosen is friendly to the machine; sometimes not. There are no rules about this part of the game. It is purely a matter of what can be done, and depends upon the character of the candidate, the exigencies of the situation, the necessities of the machine, the political complexion of the community. There are times and places when the boss can himself inspire a mayoralty candidacy without the necessity of a camouflaged committee or any other set of false whiskers. The disadvantage of this, however, is that it is apt to make the boss and the machine more directly the campaign issue than is safe.

This fact may be set down as sure—whatever way the boss may get his candidate, he tries to pick one whom he can elect.

Right here it ought, in fairness to the boss, to be said that, even if he had a free hand and did not operate under the restraint of public sentiment, in only rare cases would he go the limit in putting up wholly unfit or really bad men for conspicuous places. The boss may, and often does, live like a leech, on the public purse, but, in spite of being a boss, he is also a citizen of his community, and there are mighty few of them who have not some sort of civic sense of right and wrong. His is not at all the civic view of the reformer, perhaps, but it is a distinct civic sense just the same. It is an unusual boss who does not take pride when his machine-made mayor turns out to be a good public official, and equally unusual that he is not disgusted when he commits some disgraceful or scandalous act.

There have been instances in most cities where the boss has sold out to the other side, "laid down" or "thrown the election," but they are rare. Often machines coöperate and help one another in the primaries. That is sensible and easy, but it is neither sensible nor easy in the general election. In the first place, the ward and precinct executives, very many of whom are decent fellows who play the game on the level, according to their lights, revolt against treachery. In the second place, if there is a chance to win they want to win, because to lose means hard times and no jobs. In the third place, the boss cannot "throw an election" without a good many people knowing about it and raising a howl that may split his machine.

Some of the cogs in the machine in a hard fight, with money on both sides, go crooked. District leaders and executives of the lower type may jump the track, but rarely the boss, and when there is treachery in the ranks it is sternly punished by the boss. All of this does not prevent an occasional general "sell out," but in these days it is rapidly getting almost as dangerous to "buy" as well as to "sell." Men are apt to hesitate before they give to the necessarily unscrupulous person with whom they must deal the power such knowledge affords him.

Now, when the boss gets his "clean collar" it is the simplest and easiest thing imaginable to swing the machine back of him. The balance of the ticket has been made up through recommendations of the ward executives and district leaders, by giving recognition to the various elements with voting strength sufficient to make it inexpedient to ignore them, or to individuals powerful enough to compel recognition, and to sections of the city which will resent being left unrepresented on the ticket. In some cases candidates are put on because of their ability, or the ability of their friends, to contribute to the campaign fund, and sometimes for purely personal reasons. Sometimes, too, it is a matter of luck with a candidate—lack of opposition, or a last-minute demand for a man. Take any machine ticket in any city and it is a queer conglomeration containing some of the best and some of the worst types in town—and put there through all sorts of influence and for all sorts of reasons

When it is completed the boss closes the gate and "sends the word down the line." All this consists of is a curt phrase to the ward executives and the district leaders as they come in to see him at headquarters.

"It's Smith," says the boss, or "It's Jones," "go to it." In many cases, that is all he does say. Sometimes after the "It's Smith," the boss says, "What can you do down your way?" or "What will your ward give?" or "You ought to give him 1,000 majority," or some such thing. The ward executive is likely to reply, "All right, boss," and get out, or he may tell the boss about the sentiment of his people or express his judgment as to the selection's strength or weakness in his ward or district, but it is always an exceedingly brief conversation. There is no argument. What the boss says goes.

A bolter is an extremely rare bird in a well-run machine with a real boss. Once he gets the "word" the ward executive or district leader hurries off, calls a meeting of his ward club, and passes the "word" along that night to his precinct executives. Inside of twenty-four hours after the boss decides the whole machine, from top to bottom, has got the "word" and begins to function. The ward clubs meet and indorse the ticket, the business of lining up the office-holders begins, the candidates open up headquarters and the campaign is under way.

Sometimes the boss decides weeks in advance. Sometimes it is only a few days before the primaries when the decision is given out, but it makes no difference—the machine can be swung in line just the same. The executives prefer to know as far ahead as possible, because it gives a better chance to iron out the rough spots, and checks freelance candidates from tying up and committing precinct executives, and making inroads on the organization forces. But the manner in which, at short notice, the vast bulk of the machine workers can be swung in behind the boss's candidate is a marvellous illustration of discipline, when the looseness of the organization construction is considered and the varieties of human beings taken into account.

# HOW THE SPOILS SYSTEM WORKS

## E D W A R D   J.   F L Y N N

THE "SPOILS SYSTEM" is invariably associated with "machines." Very well, then, suppose you do away with machines. Without them you, the reader, as an "average" voter interested only in good government, would have to devise some alternative means of discovering, before each election, the men and women best qualified for public office. Could you, out of your present knowledge, choose a city-wide slate on which your neighbors could agree?

Obviously you would have to talk things over with your neighbors. But since every New Yorker has eight million "neighbors," and since the city boasts no hall that will accommodate eight million persons, even if they would turn out, doesn't this suggest some system of representation? Who would represent your building at the block meeting? your block at the inevitable and interminable series of district meetings to iron out differences that would be bound to arise? Would you be willing to drop your business every two years to devote full time to attending meetings, canvassing potential candidates, canvassing voters from door to door, raising the indispensable campaign funds? Of course you wouldn't. One evening of it would convince you that politics is a full-time job, not a hobby.

So you would simply turn for representation to some other group of full-time politicians, men and women whose claim on your confidence stemmed from nothing more substantial than that they were at the moment out of office and, therefore, presumably "pure." There are always two such groups waiting patiently at the political stage door for your signal of distress: the "other party," which in New York City is the Republican party; and the motley mob of political hacks that cluster periodically about benign old jurists and smart young boy gang-busters who raise the flag of "Fusion."

From *You're the Boss* by Edward J. Flynn (New York: Viking Press, 1947), pp. 20–26. Copyright 1947 by The Viking Press, Inc. and reprinted by their permission

I will not insult the reader's intelligence by laboring the fact that whenever these two groups get together and win an election, they promptly set up a "spoils system" all their own. But I would like to ask the reader what would happen if he and a lot of his neighbors did what I said they would not do: went out and set up an *ad hoc* machine to win one election. Wouldn't you say to one another, "Now we'd better keep this thing together somehow for two years from now, to make sure those scoundrels we just turned out don't sneak back in"?

And just how do you keep a machine together? I think I may be pardoned for assuming that I am a qualified witness on this subject.

As with any machine, it is the motor that keeps it going. The component parts of a political machine are the active workers within the party. It is probably the least complicated of mechanisms, and its foundation is the Election District Captain. Each Leader uses his Captains as reporters. The workers within the Election Districts bring to the Captains all sorts of entreaties—a boy may be in trouble, someone may be out of work, someone may have run afoul of the law in a minor way, someone may want civil service promotion. (And, remember, that to ninety-nine out of a hundred voters these personal matters are more important than what is happening in Paris, or the tariff, or even new sewers. Whether they should or shouldn't be is beside the point. They just are.)

The Captains take up such requests with the District Leader. The District Leader tries to do something. I think I may truthfully say that, no matter how minor or downright silly a petition may seem, a Bronx voter is always given the time and courteous attention of his Leader. For there is no one who comes to the party asking for help, or to offer a suggestion, who does not himself think that he or she is important. If he is made to feel welcome, his allegiance most often stays with the party. The Leader who does not realize this, does not practice what his candidates constantly preach about the importance of the common man, soon becomes unpopular, and ultimately has to be replaced.

If a District Leader is unable to help, the inquiry is then passed on to the County Committee. The County Committee, in turn, does what it can. There is a filing system at Bronx County headquarters, inaugurated when I first became Chairman, where all requests from Leaders are put on cards. It is the duty of two or three men to go through the files periodically and see that nothing is overlooked. When a matter has been taken care of, or has reached the stage where nothing more can be done, the card is put in an inactive file. Always before this is done, however, every effort is made to achieve some sort of satisfactory result. Naturally, the District Leaders and Captains feel that because of such attention to their constituents they can go back to the persons helped and ask reciprocal support for the organization.

There is a popular notion that all District Captains have "political" jobs which support them. Bronx County has seventeen hundred Captains, and only a hundred and forty-two of them have political positions. Most of our Captains earn more in private industry than any but a few top political jobs pay. Captains are Captains for a variety of reasons. Some like the excitement of working with a political party. Some have their egos satisfied by the distinction it gives them among their neighbors. Some hope for promotion within the party. Some (but all too few) work because they have made a study of party politics and principles and believe in them. Whatever the reason, the fact remains that most Captains receive nothing more than the glory that goes with the title. And they receive no cash, except a small amount—perhaps from twenty to fifty dollars—for expenses on election day. (I ought to say just here that by "expenses" I do not mean the purchase of votes. We have pretty alert Republican poll-watchers in the Bronx and, anyway, we've never had to buy votes.)

Still, it would be nonsense to pretend that devotion and personal ego are all that hold a machine together. In Bronx County there are one hundred and sixty-five "exempt" positions (excluding federal ones), which simply means that the appointments can be made without civil service examinations. Naturally, many party workers wish to obtain these positions. An example is the State District Attorney's office. It is the heart of the county government. The organization invariably nominates for it men who have shown themselves to be honest and efficient. Further, the organization sees to it that when the time comes for promotion, the District Attorney is nominated for a place on the State Supreme Court bench. (As a result of this policy, the Bronx has a number of justices in that court.)

In the State District Attorney's office are a number of Assistant District Attorneys. All these men and women are members of the regular Democratic organization. They are appointed in this manner: A vacancy occurs for Assistant District Attorney because someone has resigned, retired, or died. Since he would not have had the position if he were not an organization man, he must have come from an Assembly District presided over by one of the Executive Members. If the vacancy is in one of the higher brackets, the District Attorney makes step promotions within the office, giving an increase in salary to all the Assistant District Attorneys who were below the man who left. This in turn leaves a staff vacancy with a minimum salary. The District Attorney then sends for the Leader in whose district the vacancy occurred and asks him to submit names of lawyers who would be qualified for appointment to the vacancy. The qualifications and honesty of all persons recommended are investigated. If none meets the standard, the District Attorney asks for more names, until he finds a satisfactory one.

The Leader is satisfied, because he has been able to help a young lawyer in his district. It creates good feeling all the way down the line in the party, because a qualified young man has been given a chance in his profession, and others hope for the same consideration in the future. (I might say that while this system is followed religiously in the Bronx, it is not used consistently by a great many other political machines.) Employees of the District Attorney's office are, for the most part, lawyers. A young man starting out in the practice of law, or even an older man who has been practicing for some time, is eager for the experience or prestige an appointment as Assistant District Attorney would bring. With that in mind, he joins the district group and makes himself active. Thus, when an opportunity comes for an appointment to the District Attorney's office, he is in a position to be considered. Further, most lawyers aspire to be judges. If a man does not take an energetic role in party activities, he cannot expect to gratify this ambition. Therefore the great majority of lawyers join the organization and are active in anticipation of political preferment in the District Attorney's office and eventual election or appointment to some place on the bench; or, failing that, some other public office the County Committee might obtain for them. The appointments are few, but the hopes are many.

There are, of course, many lawyers who do not want political appointment, but who have law practices that take them into various courts. Because they are members of the organization, they have an opportunity to meet and become acquainted with the judges who are sitting. These judges often make appointments of referees or receivers, sometimes to the profit of the appointee. One can (and in the Bronx we do) frown on any attempt to influence a judge to commit an improper act without minimizing the part that personal friendships play in such matters as appointments.

Members of the organization, in order to prove their strength in the district, are constantly bringing new people to join the activities of the organization. By this means they may work toward nomination to either branch of the State Legislature or the Congress of the United States. To obtain such a nomination, a person must have a record of service to the organization. The more popular a man becomes within his district, the more likely he is to obtain political preferment.

There are many businessmen who, while their businesses have no actual connection with either government or politics, feel that having a "friend at court" in a political position may at some time be helpful to them. This does not necessarily mean that they hope to obtain illegal favors. Many things can be done for them that are not wrong. At times business concerns are cited for minor violations. Where discretion is indicated, having a friend at court harms no one.

All this is what keeps a political organization going. It is the "spoils system" in operation. But as we cannot have government without elections, elections without organizations, or organizations without a "spoils system" to keep them going, it is obviously more than a pat catch phrase. The "spoils system" is not new, nor was it invented by any political party in this country. Its origins go back into the reaches of antiquity. "To the victor belongs the spoils" has always been the axiom of war, whether between nations or between individuals. If it is immoral, then man is immoral.

For man is endowed from birth with the will to win. Fundamentally the urge to win is the desire to enjoy the fruits of victory. The measure of a political party's success is the triumph of the platform on which it stands and the principles it espouses. The people of a political division have spoken, and by their vote they have placed responsibility in the hands of one or the other major political party. What should that party do? Should it permit government to continue to be administered by the political party the people have decided they no longer want in power? Should it leave in office men who opposed the principles the people have embraced?

There is no such thing as nonpartisanship. If there were, there would be no need for elections. The phrase "nonpartisanship" has a high moral tone. It is used by men running for public office to attract votes, but deep down in their hearts these men know that it is only a word without real meaning. There is, and always must be, honest disagreement. All of us have our likes and dislikes. And that is the genesis of partnership. It explains why in filling the sixty-two of the sixty-seven jobs in the Sheriff's office that were political appointments, I considered the party's interests, and my own. . . .

I cannot resist one last observation on the "spoils system"—because there is something about the clamor against it that puzzles me, and always has. There is a fight for control of a corporation. A group of stockholders is dissatisfied with the management. A battle of proxies takes place, and the group in opposition to the management succeeds in controlling the voting stock. They vote the stock. Do they leave their defeated enemies in control? If they did, they would have wasted the effort to wrest control from them in the first place. No, they throw the losers out. What puzzles me is this: why does something that in business circles is called plain common sense become something sinister called the "spoils system" when applied to the biggest business in the land—government?

# THE NATURE OF POLITICAL OBLIGATIONS

## WILLIAM FOOTE WHYTE

THE CORNERVILLE POLITICAL ORGANIZATION can best be described as a system of reciprocal personal obligations The nature of the obligations may be understood by observing the situations in which they arise, the

Reprinted from *Street Corner Society* by William Foote Whyte (Chicago: University of Chicago Press, 1943), pp. 240–246, by permission of The University of Chicago Press.

actions which create them, and the actions which are required to discharge them.

Everyone recognizes that when a politician does a favor for a constituent, the constituent becomes obligated to the politician. Depending upon the importance of the favor, the obligation may be discharged by voting for the politician or by performing more important services for him. The politician need not bring the whole weight of his personal influence to bear in obtaining each favor for his constituents. When dealing with authorities, the person who speaks English poorly or not at all has an obvious need for an interpreter, and even the corner boy who has grown up speaking English tends to be inarticulate when he is out of his own sphere. Besides, the uninitiated do not understand the complex organization of government and do not know how to find the channels through which they can obtain action. In some cases the constituent has an undeniable claim to a certain benefit and may secure it simply by appearing before the proper authority and stating his case. Nevertheless, the person who does not know where to go or how to speak for himself must ask for a guide and spokesman, and the politician who serves in that capacity performs a real service, which results in the creation of an obligation.

The politician becomes obligated to those who support his campaign, and the high cost of political activity tends to put a premium on financial support. The more the politician can contribute to the support of his own political activity, the freer he will be from this particular type of obligation. This may account for the fact that the undertaker-politician is less closely tied to the racketeers than is the lawyer-politician, for whom the racketeers are the most important clients as well as the largest campaign contributors.

Discussion of the campaign indicates the different ways in which money may be spent but does not show how the politician decides into which particular channels to pour his funds. In practice the politician spends most of his money in areas where he lacks popular support.

Fiumara's campaign of 1937 provides an illustration of this sort of behavior. For years Joseph Maloney had been so firmly intrenched as alderman that most Italian politicians concentrated their attention upon other offices. At this time Fiumara was just another undertaker to the voters of the ward. When he opened his campaign, he set about winning over the various Italian and other non-Irish groups. He paid clubs for their indorsements and in addition financed election parties in their quarters. He gave out money to be spent in his interest. His expenditures, locally reported as $6,400, was unparalleled in the history of Ward 4 aldermanic contests, and some of it may have been wasted, but it served to establish Fiumara as Boss Maloney's chief rival for the office. In his first campaign Fiumara polled over three thousand votes and ran second to Maloney. Without such lavish financing, Fiumara would have been only one more minor competitor, and he would have had no chance to defeat the Cleveland Club boss in 1939.

Even so free a spender as Fiumara does not spread his money evenly. He tries to win as much Italian support as he can without spending money. In the election of 1939 most of the Fiumara poll workers in Cornerville served as volunteers. Maloney and Kelly, who had little support in Cornerville, paid five dollars each to their poll workers in that section. That is the situation in general. Where a politician has established a chain of personal obligations, he spends little, and where he lacks such a chain he concentrates his funds.

The politician who must pay cash for a large proportion of his support may offset this by charging his constituents for favors. This practice has become increasingly common.

In order to get a job, to have a case fixed, or to obtain some other favor, one is required to pay a sum of money which varies with the importance of the favor. The ward politician does not keep all this himself. He must pay someone who has the power to grant the favor. If it is an important favor which must be performed by a man near the top of the political hierarchy, the money passes through an intermediary. The ward politician pays the "bag man," who turns the money over to the "big shot." All important politicians who operate according to this system have trusted friends who serve as graft collectors in order to protect their superiors from prosecution. It is understood in Cornerville that the constituent's money is not paid in full to the big shot. The ward politician takes his "cut" and the bag man does likewise. If the favor is performed, the constituent is not expected to interest himself in the fate of his money. Not all Ward 4 politicians work on this basis. There are some, like George Ravello, who refuse to accept cash payment for their political services.

The nature of the obligations existing between politicians and their constituents depends upon whether the services performed on either side are paid for or furnished free of charge. The constituent who pays for a favor feels less obligated than the one who is not charged. Money need not entirely destroy the basis of personal obligation. That depends to a certain extent upon the size of the payment and the importance of the favor. The constituent may say to himself: "I paid the politician for getting me a job, but, still, jobs are in demand; there are plenty of others who would have paid what I did and more for this job; the politician was a good fellow to do this for me, and I'll be with him at the next election." Nevertheless, the obligation is not so secure when money passes from constituent to politician.

As Joseph Maloney expressed it in attacking his rival, Mike Kelly, in the campaign of 1939:

> There is one candidate that has promised at least two hundred jobs. How is he going to deliver them? He's got men with him, yes, they've all got their price, but they should realize that when they get their price the obligation is discharged.

One of the corner boys expressed his opinion in this way:

> Sometimes them politicians want to give you money if you work for them. Then when you come up to them after for a job, they say, "What's the matter, didn't I pay you?". . . . If you're smart, you don't take the money, and then maybe you got a chance to get something.

Many take the opposite view. Tony Cataldo, Carlo, and several other members of the Cornerville S. and A. held that the corner boys should recognize that they were not going to get anything after the election anyway and that therefore they should demand cash in advance. The politician would then not be obligated to them for their support, but, if they had received the money, they would be satisfied.

If the politician uses money to secure a large part of his support, he frees himself from his obligations to those constituents. Lacking strong personal ties, they may turn against him after the election, but in the next campaign he can win them over with money once more, or, if they desert him permanently, he can find other groups which will respond to the same incentive.

The effectiveness of cash payments in securing votes should not be over-emphasized. The corner boys' attitude toward money in politics is something like this: Politics is a racket; the politician is just trying to use us to get something for himself; we might as well promise him anything and get all we can out of him; then we'll do what we want to do anyway. In this connection it is pertinent to recall the speech made in the Cornerville S. and A. Club by the Fiumara supporter who advised the boys: "Don't be chumps. Take their dough. You can use it, but then go in and vote for Fiumara." The political obligation depends not alone upon a favor done by the politician but upon the personal contacts between the politician and his constituents. Where these are lacking, money cannot fill the gap.

This discussion should not give the impression that the politician is free to select his course of action. If he has not been able to establish a sufficiently extensive network of obligations before the campaign, he will have to use money freely in order to win support. If, when elected, he cannot raise sufficient funds in other ways, he may have to take money for the favors he does. Since many of his superiors operate on a cash basis, he may be forced to do likewise. One of the reasons given for George Ravello's failure to secure more jobs and favors for his constituents was his unwillingness to arrange for their purchase. In his first term he asked certain big shots for favors and was told that they could be had for a price. When word got around that Ravello would not pay, the big shots simply told him that the favors could not be done.

This does not mean that all important favors must be paid for. The relations between politicians, like those between the politician and his constituents, are based upon personal nonfinancial obligations as well as upon cash payments. By refusing to pay cash, the politician cuts himself off from some but not all the available favors.

According to Cornerville standards, the politician who does a favor for friendship is considered morally superior to one who does it for money. Similarly, the constituent who shows his devotion to the candidate's cause by contributing freely to his campaign fund is superior to the man who tries to buy a special favor. Favors should be reciprocated out of personal loyalty, as they are in the corner gang.

Although political organizations have changed profoundly in recent years, most Cornerville people continue to believe in these standards. Still, cash in advance has a powerful appeal, and people do not always support the candidate for whom they have the most respect. Since more and more of the ward candidates have taken to a cash basis, their constituents have less choice in the matter of obtaining favors. They feel that it is better to pay for a favor than to get no favor at all.

So far, obligations and favors have been discussed in personal terms. It is believed in Cornerville as well as elsewhere that the politician has an obligation to his community to secure parks, playgrounds, and other improvements contributing to the general welfare. Cornerville people complain bitterly that their representatives have failed to meet this obligation. Brief inspection is all that is needed to convince one that the district has fared worse than others in obtaining such improvements.

Cornerville people have a variety of explanations for this condition. They say that the politicians sell them out, that the politicians are not interested in improving the district, or that they do not want to do too much for fear that the people will be able to get along without them. These expressions of sentiment throw little light upon the question. We should not expect a politician who sincerely desires to obtain improvements to lose interest in this goal as soon as he is elected. Even if he were only interested in graft, there can be more graft in a public improvement project than in anything else.

Evidently, the explanation must be made in different terms. The politician-constituent and politician-politician personal relations provide a clue.

It would be pleasing to people in general to have public improvements, but the political structure is not based upon people in general. The politician has obligations to particular people, and he maintains his organization by discharging a certain number of these obligations.

The politician must concentrate his efforts where there are the most pressing demands. If a man wants three things—to keep out of jail, to get a job, and to have new play space for his children—he will not ask for them all at once. First, he wants to secure his freedom and then a means of obtaining money. If the politician can do these favors for him, he will be satisfied and probably will not mention the park at all, for the constituents realize that what they can ask from a politician depends upon what they can do for him.

The constituents feel that people in general have a right to community improvements and therefore they do not look upon them as personal favors. The man who has a job and has no trouble with the law does not make the effort to establish close personal relations with the politician in order to obtain community improvements.

When he is asked to fix a pinch for a corner boy or to use his influence to protect the racketeers, the politician must make the connections with the police and the district attorney which such action requires. The closest possible connections with these people will not aid him toward obtaining community improvements because they have no jurisdiction in such matters. When he is asked to get a man on the relief rolls, he must make connections with the authorities who handle such matters, and they also have nothing to do with initiating community improvements. When he is asked to get a man a political job, he must try to make connections with the important figures in the administration, and there he comes into contact with the people who have power over improvements. But he cannot ask for everything. It is well understood in politics that one politician cannot ask a great deal of another unless he can perform important services in return. If he asks too much, the connection breaks down, and he can get nothing.

# THE LATENT FUNCTIONS
# OF THE MACHINE

## ROBERT K. MERTON

. . . IN LARGE SECTORS of the American population, the political machine or the "political racket" are judged as unequivocally "bad" and "undesirable." The grounds for such moral judgment vary somewhat, but they consist substantially in pointing out that political machines violate moral codes: political patronage violates the code of selecting personnel on the basis of impersonal qualifications rather than on grounds of party loyalty or contributions to the party war-chest; bossism violates the code that votes should be based on individual appraisal of the qualifications of candidates and of political issues, and not on abiding loyalty to a feudal leader; bribery and "honest graft" obviously offend the proprieties of property; "protection" for crime clearly violates the law and the mores; and so on.

Reprinted from *Social Theory and Social Structure* (rev. ed.; Glencoe: The Free Press, 1957), pp. 71–81.

In view of these manifold respects in which political machines, in varying degrees, run counter to the mores and at times to the law, it becomes pertinent to inquire how they manage to continue in operation. The familiar "explanations" for the continuance of the political machine are not here in point. To be sure, it may well be that if "respectable citizenry" would carry through their political obligations, if the electorate were to be alert and enlightened; if the number of elective officers were substantially reduced from the dozens, even hundreds, which the average voter is now expected to appraise in the course of local, county, state and national elections, if the electorate were activated by the "wealthy and educated classes without whose participation," as the not-always democratically oriented Bryce put it, "the best-framed government must speedily degenerate," if these and a plethora of similar changes in political structure were introduced, perhaps the "evils" of the political machine would indeed be exorcized. But it should be noted that these changes are not typically introduced, that political machines have the phoenix-like quality of arising strong and unspoiled from their ashes, that, in short, this structure exhibits a notable vitality in many areas of American political life.

Proceeding from the functional view, therefore, that we should *ordinarily* (not invariably) expect persistent social patterns and social structures to perform positive functions *which are at the time not adequately fulfilled by other existing patterns and structures,* the thought occurs that perhaps this publicly maligned organization is, *under present conditions,* satisfying basic latent functions. A brief examination of current analyses of this type of structure may also serve to illustrate additional problems of functional analysis.

*Some Functions of the Political Machine.* Without presuming to enter into the variations of detail marking different political machines—a Tweed, Vare, Crump, Flynn, Hague are by no means identical types of bosses—we can briefly examine the functions more or less common to the political machine, as a generic type of social organization. We neither attempt to itemize all the diverse functions of the political machine nor imply that all these functions are similarly fulfilled by each and every machine.

The key structural function of the Boss is to organize, centralize and maintain in good working condition "the scattered fragments of power" which are at present dispersed through our political organization. By this centralized organization of political power, the boss and his apparatus can satisfy the needs of diverse subgroups in the larger community which are not adequately satisfied by legally devised and culturally approved social structures.

To understand the role of bossism and the machine, therefore, we must look at two types of sociological variables: (1) the *structural context* which makes it difficult, if not impossible, for morally approved structures to fulfill essential social functions, thus leaving the door open for political machines (or their structural equivalents) to fulfill these functions and (2) the subgroups whose distinctive needs are left unsatisfied, except for the latent functions which the machine in fact fulfills.

*Structural Context:* The constitutional framework of American political organization specifically precludes the legal possibility of highly centralized power and, it has been noted, thus "discourages the growth of effective and responsible leadership. The framers of the Constitution, as Woodrow Wilson observed, set up the check and balance system 'to keep government at a sort of mechanical equipoise by means of a standing amicable contest among its several organic parts.' They distrusted power as dangerous to liberty: and therefore they spread it thin and erected barriers against its concentration." This dispersion of power is found not only at the national level but in local areas as well. "As a consequence," Sait goes on to observe, "when *the people or particular groups* among them demanded positive action, no one had adequate authority to act. The machine provided an antidote."[1]

The constitutional dispersion of power not only makes for difficulty of effective decision and action but when action does occur it is defined and hemmed in by legalistic considerations. In consequence, there develops "a much *more human system* of partisan government, whose chief object soon became the circumvention of government by law. . . . The lawlessness of the extra-official democracy was merely the counterpoise of the legalism of the official democracy. The lawyer having been permitted to subordinate democracy to the Law, the Boss had to be called in to extricate the victim, which he did after a fashion and for a consideration."[2]

Officially, political power is dispersed. Various well-known expedients were devised for this manifest objective. Not only was there the familiar separation of powers among the several branches of the government but, in some measure, tenure in each office was limited, rotation in office approved. And the scope of power inherent in each office was severely circumscribed. Yet, observes Sait in rigorously functional terms, "Leadership is necessary; and *since* it does not develop readily within the constitutional framework, the Boss provides it in a crude and irresponsible form from the outside."[3]

Put in more generalized terms, *the functional deficiencies of the official structure generate an alternative (unofficial) structure to fulfill existing needs somewhat more effectively.* Whatever its specific historical origins, the political machine persists as an apparatus for satisfying otherwise unfulfilled needs of diverse groups in the population. By turning to a few of these subgroups and their characteristic needs, we shall be led at once to a range of latent functions of the political machine.

*Functions of the Political Machine for Diverse Subgroups.* It is well

---

1. Edward M. Sait, "Machine, Political," *Encyclopedia of the Social Sciences,* IX, 658b [italics supplied].
2. Herbert Croly, *Progressive Democracy* (New York, 1914), p. 254, cited by Sait, *op. cit.,* 658b.
3. Sait, *op. cit.,* 659a.

known that one source of strength of the political machine derives from its roots in the local community and the neighborhood. The political machine does not regard the electorate as a vague, undifferentiated mass of voters. With a keen sociological intuition, the machine recognizes that the voter is primarily a man living in a specific neighborhood, with specific personal problems and personal wants. Public issues are abstract and remote; private problems are extremely concrete and immediate. It is not through the generalized appeal to large public concerns that the machine operates, but through the direct, quasi-feudal relationships between local representatives of the machine and voters in their neighborhood. Elections are won in the precinct.

The machine welds its link with ordinary men and women by elaborate networks of personal relations. Politics is transformed into personal ties. The precinct captain "must be a friend to every man, assuming if he does not feel sympathy with the unfortunate, and utilizing in his good works the resources which the boss puts at his disposal."[4] The precinct captain is forever a friend in need. In our prevailingly impersonal society, the machine, through its local agents, fulfills the important social *function of humanizing and personalizing all manner of assistance* to those in need. Foodbaskets and jobs, legal and extra-legal advice, setting to rights minor scrapes with the law, helping the bright poor boy to a political scholarship in a local college, looking after the bereaved—the whole range of crises when a feller needs a friend, and, above all, a friend who knows the score and who can do something about it—all these find the ever-helpful precinct captain available in the pinch.

To assess this function of the political machine adequately, it is important to note not only the fact that aid *is* provided but *the manner in which it is provided*. After all, other agencies do exist for dispensing such assistance. Welfare agencies, settlement houses, legal aid clinics, medical aid in free hospitals, public relief departments, immigration authorities—these and a multitude of other organizations are available to provide the most varied types of assistance. But in contrast to the professional techniques of the welfare worker which may typically represent in the mind of the recipient the cold, bureaucratic dispensation of limited aid following upon detailed investigation of *legal* claims to aid of the "client," are the unprofessional techniques of the precinct captain who asks no questions, exacts no compliance with legal rules of eligibility and does not "snoop" into private affairs.

For many, the loss of "self-respect" is too high a price for legalized assistance. In contrast to the gulf between the settlement house workers who so often come from a different social class, educational background and ethnic group, the precinct worker is "just one of us," who understands what it's all about. The condescending lady bountiful can hardly compete with the understanding friend in need. In *this struggle between alternative structures*

4. *Ibid.*

*for fulfilling the nominally same function* of providing aid and support to those who need it, it is clearly the machine politician who is better integrated with the groups which he serves than the impersonal, professionalized, socially distant and legally constrained welfare worker. And since the politician can at times influence and manipulate the official organizations for the dispensation of assistance, whereas the welfare worker has practically no influence on the political machine, this only adds to his greater effectiveness. More colloquially and also, perhaps, more incisively, it was the Boston ward-leader, Martin Lomasny, who described this essential function to the curious Lincoln Steffens: "I think," said Lomasny, "that there's got to be in every ward somebody that any bloke can come to—no matter what he's done—and get help. *Help, you understand; none of your law and justice, but help.*"[5]

The "deprived classes," then, constitute one subgroup for whom the political machine clearly satisfies wants not adequately satisfied in the same fashion by the legitimate social structure.

For a second subgroup, that of business (primarily "big" business but also "small") the political boss serves the function of providing those political privileges which entail immediate economic gains. Business corporations, among which the public utilities (railroads, local transportation companies, communications corporations, electric light) are simply the most conspicuous in this regard, seek special political dispensations which will enable them to stabilize their situation and to near their objective of maximizing profits. Interestingly enough, corporations often want to avoid a chaos of uncontrolled competition. They want the greater security of an economic czar who controls, regulates and organizes competition, providing this czar is not a public official with his decisions subject to public scrutiny and public control. (The latter would be "government control," and hence taboo.) The political boss fulfills these requirements admirably.

Examined for a moment apart from any "moral" considerations, the political apparatus of the Boss is effectively designed to perform these functions with a minimum of inefficiency. Holding the strings of diverse governmental divisions, bureaus and agencies in his competent hands, the Boss rationalizes the relations between public and private business. He serves as the business community's ambassador in the otherwise alien (and sometimes unfriendly) realm of government. And, in strict business-like terms, he is well-paid for his economic services to his respectable business clients. In an article entitled, "An Apology to Graft," Steffens suggested that "Our economic system, which held up riches, power and acclaim as prizes to men bold enough and able enough to buy corruptly timber, mines, oil fields and franchises and 'get away with it,' was at fault."[6] And, in a conference with

---

5. *The Autobiography of Lincoln Steffens* (Chautauqua, N.Y.: Chautauqua Press, 1931), 618.
6. *Autobiography of Lincoln Steffens*, 570.

a hundred or so of Los Angeles business leaders, he described a fact well known to all of them: the Boss and his machine were an *integral part* of the organization of the economy. "You cannot build or operate a railroad, or a street railway, gas, water, or power company, develop and operate a mine, or get forests and cut timber on a large scale, or run any privileged business, without corrupting or joining in the corruption of the government. You tell me privately that you must, and here I am telling you semi-publicly that you must. And that is so all over the country. And that means that we have an organization of society in which, *for some reason,* you and your kind, the ablest, most intelligent, most imaginative, daring, and resourceful leaders of society, are and must be against society and its laws and its all-around growth."[7]

Since the demand for the services of special privileges are built into the structure of the society, the Boss fulfills diverse functions for this second subgroup of business-seeking-privilege. These "needs" of business, as presently constituted, are not adequately provided for by "conventional" and "culturally approved" social structures; consequently, the extra-legal but more-or-less efficient organization of the political machine comes to provide these services. To adopt an *exclusively* moral attitude toward the "corrupt political machine" is to lose sight of the very structural conditions which generate the "evil" that is so bitterly attacked. To adopt a functional outlook on the political machine is not to provide an apologia, but a more solid base for modifying or eliminating the machine, *providing* specific structural arrangements are introduced either for eliminating these effective demands of the business community or, if that is the objective, of satisfying these demands through alternative means.

A third set of distinctive functions fulfilled by the political machine for a special subgroup is that of providing alternative channels of social mobility for those otherwise excluded from the more conventional avenues for personal "advancement." Both the sources of this special "need" (for social mobility) and the respect in which the political machine comes to help satisfy this need can be understood by examining the structure of the larger culture and society. As is well known, the American culture lays enormous emphasis on money and power as a "success" goal legitimate for all members of the society. By no means alone in our inventory of cultural goals, it still remains among the most heavily endowed with positive affect and value. However, certain subgroups and certain ecological areas are notable for the relative absence of opportunity for achieving these (monetary and power) types of success. They constitute, in short, sub-populations where "the cultural emphasis upon pecuniary success has been absorbed, but where there is *little access to conventional and legitimate* means for attaining such success. The conventional occupational opportunities of persons in (such areas)

---

7. *Ibid.,* 572–573.

are almost completely limited to manual labor. Given our cultural stigmatization of manual labor, and its correlate, the prestige of white-collar work, it is clear that the result is a tendency to achieve these culturally approved objectives *through whatever means are possible*. These people are on the one hand, "asked to orient their conduct toward the prospect of accumulating wealth [and power] and, on the other, they are largely denied effective opportunities to do so institutionally."

It is within this context of social structure that the political machine fulfills the basic function of providing avenues of social mobility for the otherwise disadvantaged. Within this context, even the corrupt political machine and the racket "represent the triumph of amoral intelligence over morally prescribed 'failure' when the channels of vertical mobility are closed or narrowed *in a society which places a high premium on economic affluence, [power] and social ascent for all its members*."[8] As one sociologist has noted on the basis of several years of close observation in a "slum area":

> The sociologist who dismisses racket and political organizations as deviations from desirable standards thereby neglects some of the major elements of slum life. . . . *He does not discover the functions they perform for the members* [of the groupings in the slum]. The Irish and later immigrant peoples have had the greatest difficulty in finding places for themselves in our urban social and economic structure. Does anyone believe that the immigrants and their children could have achieved their present degree of social mobility without gaining control of the political organization of some of our largest cities? The same is true of the racket organization. *Politics and the rackets have furnished an important means of social mobility for individuals, who, because of ethnic background and low class position*, are blocked from advancement in the "respectable" channels.[9]

This, then represents a third type of function performed for a distinctive subgroup. This function, it may be noted in passing, is fulfilled by the *sheer* existence and operation of the political machine, for it is in the machine itself that these individuals and subgroups find their culturally induced needs more or less satisfied. It refers to the services which the political apparatus provides for its own personnel. But seen in the wider social context we have set forth, it no longer appears as *merely* a means of self-aggrandizement for profit-hungry and power-hungry *individuals*, but as an organized provision for *subgroups* otherwise excluded or restricted from the race for "getting ahead."

Just as the political machine performs services for "legitimate" business, so it operates to perform not dissimilar services for "illegitimate" business: vice, crime and rackets. Once again, the basic sociological role of the machine in this respect can be more fully appreciated only if one temporarily abandons attitudes of moral indignation, to examine with all moral in-

---

8. Merton, *op. cit.*, 146.
9. William F. Whyte, "Social Organization in the Slums," *American Sociological Review*, Feb. 1943, 8, 34–39 (italics supplied).

nocence the actual workings of the organization. In this light, it at once appears that the subgroup of the professional criminal, racketeer, gambler, has basic similarities of organization, demands and operation to the subgroup of the industrialist, man of business, speculator. If there is a Lumber King or an Oil King, there is also a Vice King or a Racket King. If expansive legitimate business organizes administrative and financial syndicates to "rationalize" and to "integrate" diverse areas of production and business enterprise, so expansive rackets and crime organize syndicates to bring order to the otherwise chaotic areas of production of illicit goods and services. If legitimate business regards the proliferation of small enterprises as wasteful and inefficient, substituting, for example, the giant chain stores for the hundreds of corner groceries, so illegitimate business adopts the same businesslike attitude, and syndicates crime and vice.

Finally, and in many respects, most important, is the basic similarity, if not near-identity, of the economic role of "legitimate" business and "illegitimate" business. *Both are in some degree concerned with the provision of goods and services for which there is an economic demand.* Morals aside, they are both business, industrial and professional enterprises, dispensing goods and services which some people want, for which there is a market in which goods and services are transformed into commodities. And, in a prevalently market society, we should expect appropriate enterprises to arise whenever there is a market demand for given goods or services.

As is well known, vice, crime and the rackets *are* "big business." Consider only that there have been estimated to be about 500,000 professional prostitutes in the United States, and compare this with the approximately 200,000 physicians and 200,000 nurses. It is difficult to estimate which have the larger clientele: the professional men and women of medicine or the professional men and women of vice. It is, of course, difficult to estimate the economic assets, income, profits and dividends of illicit gambling in this country and to compare it with the economic assets, income, profits and dividends of, say, the shoe industry, but it is altogether possible that the two industries are about on a par. No precise figures exist on the annual expenditures on illicit narcotics, and it is probable that these are less than the expenditures on candy, but it is also probable that they are larger than the expenditure on books.

It takes but a moment's thought to recognize that, *in strictly economic terms,* there is no relevant difference between the provision of licit and of illicit goods and services. The liquor traffic illustrates this perfectly. It would be peculiar to argue that prior to 1920 (when the 18th amendment became effective), the provision of liquor constituted an economic service, that from 1920 to 1933, its production and sale no longer constituted an economic service dispensed in a market, and that from 1934 to the present, it once again took on a serviceable aspect. Or, it would be *economically* (not morally) absurd to suggest that the sale of bootlegged liquor in the dry state of Kansas is less a response to a market demand than the sale of publicly manufactured liquor in the neighboring wet state of Missouri. Examples of this sort can of course be multiplied many times over. Can it be held that in European countries, with registered and legalized prostitution, the prostitute contributes an economic service, whereas in this country, lacking legal sanction, the prostitute provides no such service? Or that the professional abortionist is in the economic market where he has approved legal status and that he is out of the economic market where he is legally taboo? Or that gambling satisfies a specific demand for entertainment in Nevada, where it is one of the largest business enterprises of the largest city in the state, but that it differs essentially in this respect from movie houses in the neighboring state of California?

The failure to recognize that these businesses are only *morally* and not *economically* distinguishable from "legitimate" businesses has led to badly scrambled analysis. Once the economic identity of the two is recognized, we may anticipate that if the political machine performs functions for "legitimate big business" it will be all the more likely to perform not dissimilar functions for "illegitimate big business." And, of course, such is often the case.

The distinctive function of the political machine for their criminal, vice and racket clientele is to enable them to operate in satisfying the economic demands of a large market without due interference from the government. Just as big business may contribute funds to the political party war-chest to ensure a minimum of governmental interference, so with big rackets and big crime. In both instances, the political machine can, in varying degrees, provide "protection." In both instances, many features of the structural context are identical: (1) market demands for goods and services; (2) the operators' concern with maximizing gains from their enterprises; (3) the need for partial control of government which might otherwise interfere with these activities of businessmen; (4) the need for an efficient, powerful and centralized agency to provide an effective liaison of "business" with government.

Without assuming that the foregoing pages exhaust either the range of functions or the range of subgroups served by the political machine, we can at least see that *it presently fulfills some functions for these diverse subgroups which are not adequately fulfilled by culturally approved or more conventional structures.*

Several additional implications of the functional analysis of the political machine can be mentioned here only in passing, although they obviously require to be developed at length. First, the foregoing analysis has direct implications for *social engineering.* It helps explain why the periodic efforts at "political reform," "turning the rascals out" and "cleaning political house" are typically short-lived and ineffectual. It exemplifies a basic theorem: *any attempt to eliminate an existing social structure without providing adequate alternative structures for fulfilling the functions previously fulfilled by the abolished organization is doomed to failure.* (Needless to say, this theorem has much wider bearing than the one instance of the political machine.) When "political reform" confines itself to the manifest task of "turning the rascals out," it is engaging in little more than sociological magic. The reform may for a time bring new figures into the political limelight; it may serve the casual social function of re-assuring the electorate that the moral virtues remain intact and will ultimately triumph; it may actually effect a turnover in the personnel of the political machine; it may even, for a time, so curb the activities of the machine as to leave unsatisfied the many needs it has previously fulfilled. But, inevitably, unless the reform also involves a "re-forming" of the social and political structure such that the existing needs are satisfied by alternative structures or unless it involves a change which eliminates these needs altogether, the political machine will return to its integral place in the social scheme of things. *To seek social change, without due recognition of the manifest and latent functions performed by the social organization undergoing change, is to indulge in social ritual rather than social engineering.* The concepts of manifest and latent functions (or their equivalents) are indispensable elements in the theoretic repertoire of the social engineer. In this crucial sense, these concepts are not "merely" theoretical (in the abusive sense of the term), but are eminently practical. In the deliberate enactment of social change, they can be ignored only at the price of considerably heightening the risk of failure.

A second implication of our analysis of the political machine also has a bearing upon areas wider than the one we have considered. The "paradox" has often been noted that the supporters of the political machine include both the "respectable" business class elements who are, of course, opposed to the criminal or racketeer and the distinctly "unrespectable" elements of the underworld. And, at first appearance, this is cited as an instance of very strange bedfellows. The learned judge is not infrequently called upon to sentence the very racketeer beside whom he sat the night before at an informal dinner of the political bigwigs. The district attorney jostles the exonerated convict on his way to the back room where the Boss has called a meeting. The big business man may complain almost as bitterly as the big racketeer about the "extortionate" contributions to the party fund demanded by the Boss. Social opposites meet—in the smoke-filled room of the successful politician.

In the light of a functional analysis all this of course no longer seems paradoxical. Since the machine serves both the businessman and the criminal man, the two seemingly antipodal groups intersect. This points to a more general theorem: *the social functions of an organization help determine the structure (including the recruitment of personnel involved in the structure), just as the structure helps determine the effectiveness with which the functions are fulfilled.* In terms of social status, the business group and the criminal group are indeed poles apart. But status does not fully determine behavior and the inter-relations between groups. Functions modify these relations. Given their distinctive needs, the several subgroups in the large society are "integrated," whatever their personal desires or intentions, by the centralizing structure which serves these several needs. In a phrase with many implications which require further study, *structure affects function and function affects structure.*

# SEPARATION OF POWERS
# NECESSITATES CORRUPTION

## HENRY JONES FORD

THAT THE CORRUPTION of local politics is the natural outcome of democratic institutions is the explanation one is apt to get in private talk with party managers. It is not propounded as a theory, but frankly recognized as a condition which must be dealt with on the principle that what can't be cured must be endured. Good and bad go together in most of the affairs of life, and democratic government is no exception to the general rule. It is in the main good, because it secures attention to the wants and desires of the common people, but at the same time it subjects the transactions of government to the play of their passions and appetites. Despite the railing of purists and idealists, the general result is not so bad; the public business in one way or another does get on and social interests are tolerably well protected. It is true that a great deal of grafting goes on, but if there is a strong boss and a solid machine it is kept within bounds and business interests can know just what they can depend upon. It costs a great deal of money to run politics, and in one way or another the public offices must meet the cost of filling them under the system of popular election. The best and really cheapest way of treating the problem is through the boss system, which controls the selection of candidates and determines public policy by putting it upon a business basis.

This opinion is held not only by party managers but also prevails among hard-headed business men who face facts as they find them. They support ring rule as a practical necessity; that is to say, they believe that some sort of a firm political control superior to and exercising authority over the regular constitution of municipal government is necessary to prevent the government from being simply almoner and pander to the mob, and to make it considerate of business and social interests about which the ordinary run of people know little and care less. Unless there is a boss, government lacks consistency and purpose; there are no settled conditions upon which enterprise can rest; no competent authority with which business interests can negotiate. The occasional interregnums which occur between the downfall of one boss

Reprinted from *Annals of the American Academy of Political and Social Science,* March, 1904, pp. 202–203 and 207–216, where it appeared under the title, "Principles of Municipal Organization."

and the rise of another are always a period of political demoralization and contention. While not enunciated as a distinct principal, yet the tone of comment one hears in discussion of municipal politics among practical men of affairs implies that corruption is the natural defence of society under democratic conditions of government.

It must be admitted that close contact with actual conditions is apt to lead to practical conclusion of this kind. No one who ever knew a boss as he is can doubt that he constantly acts under stress of circumstances which he did not create and which his disappearance would not remove. The individual boss frequently disappears; the boss system remains and is a normal characteristic of American municipal politics. The combinations which the boss makes and by which he maintains his ascendency are his own, but he must play the game on the board and with the pieces he finds. I have heard a boss speak in tones of unfeigned scorn of city councilmen who were reputed to be his own agents. When asked why he took up with such people, he described the posture of politics in their wards to show that in joining interests with them he had done the best he could under the circumstances. The poor material furnished by the working of local representation is not unfrequently a subject of remark in the private talk of a boss, but without complaint, for it is the characteristic of the type and the secret of its strength to respond with simple directness to actual conditions, and to base measures on the realities. It is proof of great efficiency of character when a boss is able to maintain himself upon his slippery throne.

The notion that democratic politics are necessarily vile has abundant philosophic support. It pervades the Federalist and was fairly rampant in the convention which framed the Constitution of the United States. If one consults Calhoun's analysis of the tendencies of "the government of the numerical majority," his prophecy seems startling in its accurate anticipation of the present evils of our politics. As an exercise in dialectics it would be possible to produce a copious thesis in support of Talleyrand's cynical definition of democracy as an aristocracy of blackguards, but there would be a fatal flaw in the argument. For one thing, the marked difference which exists in this country between national and municipal administration, which have a common base in the character of the people, would not be accounted for. Dialectic skill might perhaps get around that, but the working of democratic institutions elsewhere furnishes facts absolutely irreconcilable with the thesis. If corruption is a character mark of democracy, why is it not displayed in the municipal institutions of Canada, England, Switzerland, and Australia? They are far more democratic than those of this country; the policy of government is immediately subject to popular control; checks which we think necessary to guard against results of popular impulse do not exist; mayors have no veto power and all power is amassed in the city council. but there is no boss system, no machine to run the administration, and honesty is the normal characteristic of the system. Although there is complaint as to the character and tendencies of municipal government, it does not relate to integrity of administration but to its scope and purpose. That democratic government should be successful in securing a faithful steward-ship of public resources is assumed as a natural consequence of the system; where it works badly is in the ideas it engenders of the social application of these resources, and some alarm is expressed as to the results of the tend-ency of municipal government to enlarge its functions. Not content with managing markets, water supply, lighting, and street railways, it is taking on lodging-houses and even dance-halls. . . .

## Defect in the Organization of Government

We now take up . . . the possibility that the cause of failure may be defect in the organization of government. On first thought it might seem to be impracticable to submit this hypothesis to the test of facts, so many ex-periments have been tried in municipal charters and so many varieties exist. Upon this score alone one might feel justified in rejecting the supposition off-hand, since if the trouble lay in defect of organization surely it would have been gotten at in the course of so much anxious effort. We are, however, bound by our plan to discard all assumptions and to proceed with scientific precision. Since American varieties of municipal government unite in common failure, we need not consider them in detail. Whatever the cause may be, it is generic. Furthermore, we must conclude that this generic cause will manifest itself as a generic difference when American municipal govern-ment is compared with municipal government in other civilized countries. Now when the comparison is made, what generic difference appears? Nearly all cities here and abroad have their own peculiarities, and a survey of the general field reveals great variety of organization. The only difference which appears to be generic is this, that whereas everywhere else the executive and legislative departments are connected, in the United States they are disconnected. It further appears that whatever evils or defects may accompany the connection of the executive and legislative departments in one organ of municipal sovereignty, the boss system is unknown wherever that principle of organization obtains, no matter in what country we look for examples. It is a phenomenon characteristic of and peculiar to municipal government organized upon the principle of separating the executive and legislative functions by embodying them in distinct organs of authority. The logical conclusion is that the principle of corruption in American municipal government is this disconnection of the executive and legislative functions.

On reaching this conclusion one instinctively revolts from it, because it seems to attack the fundamental principle of American constitutional law,—the principle of the separation of the powers of government. Moreover, one finds that the idea which pervades theories of municipal reform is the necessity of sharper division and more effectual separation of the executive and legislative functions. This idea is the cardinal principle of reform advocated in the municipal programme adopted by the National Municipal League, and so high an authority as Professor Goodwin argues that it is a principle based upon the laws of psychology, governing all conscious activities. It would seem to be a supposition too monstrous to be entertained that the whole theory upon which American institutions of government are founded is malign, and that the anxious studies of reformers have so grievously miscarried as to prompt them to select the fundamental case of corruption as the cardinal principle of municipal organization. But, on the other hand, the conclusion in which our inquiry has resulted has been reached by logical inference, so that the need is suggested of close scrutiny to determine whether the apparent conflict really exists.

## Separation of the Powers of Government

What is meant by the separation of the powers of government? If it means simply that the executive, legislative, and judicial powers shall be separately constituted, there is no radical divergence between American institutions and those of other civilized countries. The generic difference which has been noted lies in this: outside of the United States it is the practice to join together in one organ of government and thus indissolubly connect in their operations the separately constituted powers of government; in the United States it is the practice not only to constitute these powers separately, but also to disconnect them in their operation by embodying them in separate organs of government. For instance, in Toronto the people elect a mayor to be head of the executive government; they also elect a board of controllers upon a general ticket to represent the community as a whole, and in addition members of the city council are elected in every ward to represent the interests of locality. Each of these separately constituted bodies have their special powers and functions which are sharply defined, but they meet and act together as the city council, the organ of municipal sovereignty, whose determinations are final and conclusive. The mayor presides, but he has only his own vote, and has no veto power. He does not even appoint the committees, that being the province of the ward representatives; but the mayor is *ex officio* a member of the board of controllers and of every committee. The controllers, as representatives of the community as a whole, are the medium through which the reports of council committee are submitted to the city council, and the recommendations of the controllers form the subject of legislative action. All appointments to office in the service of the corporation are made by the nomination of the mayor and controllers subject to the approval of the city council. At every point in the organization of the city government the executive and legislative functions, while separate and distinct in constitution, are connected so that they operate as a reciprocal control. While the means by which the executive authority and the legislative authority is separately constituted varies in different countries, the usual English and Swiss practice being to form the executive administration through the action of the legislative body, yet the two functions are always sharply distinguished and separately constituted, but are at the same time invariably connected.

In the United States the authority of the mayor is not only separate and distinct from that of the legislative branch, but is altogether disconnected by being made also a separate organ of government. The legislative authority is embodied in the city council, organized as a separate organ of government. In many cities it is divided into two branches so that one may be a check upon the other, and a further check is provided by giving the mayor a veto over the acts of the city council. It is frequently the case that such offices as those of treasurer and controller are separately constituted and independently organized. The process of separate organization is in some cases— as, for instance, in Ohio municipal corporations—carried out to such an extent that important branches of executive authority, such as police control, fire department administration, and the management of public works, are separately embodied.


## The Views of the Fathers


The essential difference between the two systems in organic principle is not in the separate constitution of different powers of government, but in the fact that one system connects them while the other disconnects them. Is it contrary to the principles of the separation of powers to connect them? It is generally assumed that it is. While the point was not considered in the discussion attending the adoption of the programme of the National Municipal League, the tone of the discussion and the recommendations made assume that this principle requires the embodiment of executive and legislative authority in separate organs of government. Nevertheless, there is conclusive evidence that no such assumption was made by the framers of the Constitution of the United States, and indeed, that it is contrary to their ideas of the meaning of the principle of the separation of the powers. Their ideas are not to be inferred from the relations between the executive and the legislative departments as they now stand in our national government, for, as is well known to students of our constitutional history, they contemplated a much closer connection than that which now exists. It fortunately happens that this very point was discussed in the *Federalist*. In numbers 47 and 48 Madison argues that the principle of the separation of powers "does not require that the legislative, executive, and judiciary departments should be

wholly unconnected with each other." Not content with this negative statement of the case, he goes on to say that "unless these departments be so
far connected and blended as to give to each a constitutional control over the
others, the degree of separation which the maxim requires, as essential to a
free government, can never in practice be duly maintained." The profound
truth of this observation is conspicuously attested by the present condition of
government in this country. Any one possessing insight into actual conditions
knows that executive and legislative functions are not really separate in
practice. Members of legislative and city councils habitually extort surrender
to them of executive function, especially as regards appointments to office, and
are enabled to do so because the executive department, being disconnected
from the legislative department, has no way of securing consideration of
public business save by the favor of members. The same is true as regards
the national government also, but presidential authority is a force of such
high tension that it tends to establish a regular connection although subject
to interruptions which cause jarring vibrations through the whole frame of
government. The connection is, however, sufficiently constant to preserve the
national government from the system of boss control which is the natural
adjunct of state and municipal government. When those functions of government whose concerted action is essential to administration are connected,
there is no room for the boss system, and it has never been developed under
such circumstances. The conditions are such that actual control can be
developed only inside the formal constitution of government and not outside of it. Hence in the municipal institutions of other countries having
fairly representative institutions there appears, instead of the irresponsible
boss ruling from the outside by combinations of class interest, the responsible leader basing his control upon the support of public opinion. The
variation in the practical application of the principle of separate powers which
has such disastrous results in the United States, so far from being constitutional doctrine, is the result of departure from it, and the consequence
has been just as Madison predicted,—the destruction of constitutional separation in actual practice.

## The Psychological Basis

Let us now proceed to consider the principle itself, to see whether
analysis of its nature will enable us to determine how it should be construed. Professor Goodnow has suggested that it has a psychological foundation. He says:

"It is a distinction based upon a sound psychology. In the case of a
single sentient being the will must be formulated, if not expressed, before
its execution is possible. In the case of political bodies, which are more and
more coming to be recognized as subject to psychological law, not only

must the will or policy be formulated before it can be executed, but also the very complexity of their operations makes it almost impossible to intrust the same authority as well with the execution as with the determination of the public policy."[1]

Following out this line of reasoning, which is extremely valuable and suggestive, Professor Goodnow distinguishes between the formation of policy, which he regards as the legislative function, and the execution of policy or the administration function, and he concludes that these two functions should be separately constituted in any proper organization of government. "The failure to distinguish legislation from administration" he considers to be the root of trouble in our municipal institutions. The proper connection of these functions is not considered, but the subject is treated in a way which assumes that separation means also disconnection. This assumption, moreover, affects the statement of psychological principle which appears to have been unconsciously warped to fit the case. If we consider the volitional process it will be seen that while there is a separation of function it is not exactly such as Professor Goodnow has delineated. A man sees something he would like to buy, doubts whether he can afford it, decides to gratify his inclination, and makes the purchase. The totality of his action is made up of volitional and inhibitory impulses, but his resolution and the execution thereof are both stages of volition. The will participates in what Professor Goodnow designates as the policy-forming function, which, psychologically speaking, is not a function at all, but a process in which the volitional and inhibitory impulses participate in conjunction. The distinction suggested by psychological law is not between administration and legislation, but between administration and control, corresponding to the volitional and inhibitory functions of mental activity, and as those functions meet together in determinations of conduct, so administration and control should be connected in legislation.

If the organization of municipal government outside of the United States be examined, it will be found that it conforms to these psychological principles. Administration and control are separately constituted, but meet together in the city council. In practice, administrative experience furnishes the legislative impulse. The organs of administration conceive and mature the legislative proposals, a process conforming to the psychological law that perception is developed through the agency of special organs. The administration submits its legislative proposals to the city council, representing the function of control, assists deliberation by explanation and advice, and thus determinations of conduct are reached in strict conformity to psychological law, through the interaction of the volitional and inhibitory functions.

We have all about us illustrations of the same principle in the business world. There administration and control are invariably connected, distinguished as the management and the directory, which meet in determina-

---

1. *A Municipal Programme.* The Macmillan Co., page 74.

tion of policy. It is the function of the management to plan the operations of the concern as well as execute them, subject to the approval of the board of directors. Is it a question of entering a new field, adopting new processes, enlarging the plant, providing fresh capital? The management conceives and formulates the measures and submits them to the board of directors for approval. What may be called the legislative initiative of the management is justly regarded as its most important and valuable function.

If, however, the organic connection of the separately constituted functions of administration and control is a principle founded upon psychological law, it must be immutable in its operation, whether or not it be recognized or provided for in the intentional structure of government. Although the generic type of American municipal institutions violates that principle, yet if the principle is sound the actual operations of government should conform to it. That is invariably what we do see if able to see things as they really are. The vital principle of the boss system is that it furnishes this connection between the executive and legislative departments. It has grown up in satisfaction of practical necessities of government, and it is peculiar to our institutions because they disconnect what must in some way or another be joined in carrying on administration. This is the secret of the normal tendency of municipal government towards corruption; it is so constituted that it cannot be carried on without corruption. In the national government this tendency is mitigated by the fact that executive authority has escaped the disintegration to which it has been subjected in State and municipal government. Functions which in the latter are separately constituted are in the national government united in one executive authority, making it so massive that it attracts legislative initiative despite the formal disconnection, and "the policy of the administration" is ordinarily the informing principle of legislative activity, but in this field also defect of regular connection is the source of continual evil.


## The Course of Improvement


In further illustration of the operation of this principle despite failure to recognize it, observe that such reforms of municipal government as have resulted in real improvement have really connected the executive and legislative powers. The New York and Baltimore city charters are typical examples of this process. Both the formulation of public policy and the execution of public policy have been concentrated in the executive department which fixes the tax levy, frames the appropriations, determines the conditions and terms of legislative grants, and in general decides upon ways and means. A pretence is made of retaining the usual disconnection through the separate organization of the city council, but it has become an atrophied organ of government. While there is a formal reference to the city council of the determinations of the governing body, yet its authority is so reduced that all it amounts to is a limited veto power. It has become the practice of the New York city council to treat its authority frankly as such, allowing appropriations to become law by lapse of the time in which the city council has power to act, and interfering only for the purpose of negativing some particular appropriation when exertions of political influence temporarily energize council proceedings. The practical benefits of the system causes its violation of traditional theory to be ignored. The enormous gains it makes for the public in the granting of franchises has excited general notice and has stirred up angry agitations for like benefits in other cities, which, however, they will never secure until they adopt like methods. These gains are essentially economies introduced by dispensing with the boss and the machine as the basis of administrative connection. By abolishing their office, its emoluments have been turned into the public treasury. There is, however, a principle of evil still at work, in that the system, although a vast improvement over the old one, aggrandizes the administrative function at the expense of the function of control, which, lacking adequate expression in the organs of government, tends to pass outside of them to become part of the inorganic mass of public opinion, confused with popular prejudice and ignorance, operating blindly and spasmodically upon the conduct of government, and exposing it to violent alternations in character and tendency.

## Summary of Conclusions Reached

In view of all these considerations, we must conclude that the truly remarkable thing about American institutions of government is not that they work so badly as that they should work so well. Owing to misconceptions which have hardened into political superstition our institutions have been subjected to conditions violating principles of government universally recognized and usually correctly applied except in the administration of public affairs. That with such defective organization a tolerable degree of administrative efficiency has been secured, is the strongest possible proof of the great capacity of American character. This opinion is corroborated by the weighty authority of Bagehot, whose writings evince a rare combination of business sagacity and political insight. He remarked: "The Americans now extol their institutions, and so defraud themselves of their due praise; but if they had not a genius for politics, if they had not a moderation in action singularly curious where superficial speech is so violent, if they had not a regard for laws such as no great people have yet evinced, and infinitely surpassing ours, the multiplicity of authorities in the American constitution would long ago have brought it to a bad end."[2] The particular reference is to the organization of the national government, but it applies

2. *The English Constitution.* Walter Bagehot. Chapter VIII.

to all our institutions of government. The chief agency of the moderating influence which makes actual results endurable is that very spirit of commercialism against which sentimentalists are in the habit of inveighing. It establishes connections of interest which enfold the organs of government, and while it imparts to government a plutocratic character it interposes defences against disorder. When our institutions are imitated by countries in which the spirit of commercialism is not sufficiently developed to acquire political ascendency, chronic disorder is the result. In this way our political example has been a source of immense mischief in the politics of Central and South America. For the same reason, municipal institutions of the American type introduced into Porto Rico and the Philippines, where the commercial spirit is not strong and masterful enough to govern by corruption, will tend to generate fraud and violence as their political adjuncts. This may be asserted with the certainty of scientific deduction.

The results of our extended inquiry may be summarized as follows: The bad operation of American municipal government is due not to defect of popular character, but to defect in the organization of government. The organic defect lies in the fact that the executive and legislative departments, in addition to being separately constituted, are also disconnected, and this very disconnection has prevented in practice the degree of separation in their functions which their integrity requires, a consequence precisely what Madison predicted if separate powers are not duly connected in their operation. The remedy is therefore to be found in establishing a proper connection between the executive and the legislative organs of government, so as to make the functions of administration and control coextensive. No arrangement can secure this short of one which gives the executive department complete legislative initiative, and at the same time secures to the legislative department complete supervision over all administrative transactions. If this be accomplished, nominal relations or divisions are unimportant.

# WHO, OR WHAT, STARTED THE EVIL?

## LINCOLN STEFFENS

SAN FRANCISCO learned nothing from the graft prosecution, nothing but facts—no lessons that were applied either economically or politically. The fighting passion persisted. Francis J. Heney was hated and admired as a fighter and highly respected as a lawyer, but his practice was so damaged

Reprinted from *The Autobiography of Lincoln Steffens*, pp. 570–574, copyright, 1931, by Harcourt, Brace & World, Inc.; renewed, 1959, by Peter Steffens. Reprinted by permission of the publishers.

by the fear of the prejudice of the courts against him that he had to remove his office to Los Angeles. Fremont Older was punished by business men through his paper. The circulation had gone up and continued to grow as his change of policy from righteous wrath to mercy for the under dog became clear. Its advertising suffered, and his personal standing as an editor was attacked privately by the business men who finally drove the owners to get rid of him. Hearst called Older to his rival evening paper, the *Call*, which immediately began to rise till it passed and finally absorbed the *Bulletin*. William J. Burns had proved himself to the men he called sons of bitches so that when he organized a national detective bureau they joined it as subscribers. Hiram Johnson, as governor, put the railroad out of power for a while; he gave one of the most efficient administrations any State has ever had, was re-elected, and then went to the U.S. Senate as the political reform boss of California. But there was no fundamental reform in the city or the State.

Were exposures useless? I could not at that time believe this. I went back to my theory that it was the threat of punishment which, by forcing men to defend themselves, put them in a state of mind where they could not see straight and learn. I wrote an article entitled "An Apology for Graft," showing that our economic system, which held up riches, power and acclaim as prizes to men bold enough and able enough to buy corruptly timber, mines, oil fields, and franchises and "get away with it," was at fault, and that San Francisco's graft trials showed that; and showed that we should change the system and meanwhile let the crooks go, who would confess and tell us the truth. The only reaction I got from the article was the wonder of good citizens and liberals whether I had sold out and gone back on reform!

Then it occurred to me to go to Los Angeles to see if that city had learned anything from the sight of San Francisco exposed. No one down there had been threatened with punishment; they had only to look on and see themselves in the fix of the San Franciscans. I called on Dr. John R. Haynes, a rich, very kind veteran reformer, who understands economics and men pretty well. He took me into the swell Jonathan Club, introduced me to some public service corporation men; others that I knew came up, and soon there was a group of "knowing" Los Angeles business leaders deploring the conditions of politics and business in San Francisco. They were cheerful about it. There was a self-congratulatory note in their grief at the shame of San Francisco, poor San Francisco. Los Angeles was, fortunately, not like that. I thought they were joking.

"Wait a moment," I said. "You have been having your sport with me, a San Franciscan. It's my turn now. You know, don't you; I know you know, and you know that I know, that Los Angeles is in the same condition as San Francisco. The only difference is that San Francisco has been, and Los Angeles has not been, shown up."

Silence. Uneasiness, but no denial. I waited for the street railway or gas men to think, and one of them did mutter something about "another difference, San Francisco had a Labor government."

"Labor government!" I exclaimed, and I reminded them that that Labor government had sold out to capital and represented business.

Again no denial, only silence. They knew. They had forgotten. They wished to forget, to ignore what they knew. They had no fear of punishment, but they had learned no more from the experience of San Francisco than the San Franciscans had.

"I'll tell you what I'll do," I said into their silence. "If you will call a closed meeting somewhere soon and invite only yourselves, and your wives, and your associates, fellow directors, managers, attorneys, and—and your priests and their wives, no outsiders at all—I will show you that you yourselves should want, at the least, the public ownership of all public utilities and natural resources."

They laughed; it was partly the laugh of relief. The tension of my accusations had been unclublike. They laughed and we broke up, but they accepted my challenge. They would have a little dinner and eat me up.

Dr. Haynes managed the affair very well. He had the right kind of people there, some hundred or more. No outsiders. Nobody to enjoy and spoil the debate by making us conscious of a contest. It was a conversation. The arrangement was that I was to state my thesis and argument in a short twenty minutes, after which any one of the company might challenge any point of mine, preferably in the form of a question. But I asked leave to answer each question before another spoke. No objections.

I restated my thesis. My argument was a narrative, my own story. I had gone forth, thinking what they thought, that bad men caused bad government, especially politicians. Having to see them for information, I found politicians to be not bad men; they were pretty good fellows. They blamed the bad business men who, they said, bribed them.

Who, then, were those bad business men? They named them, each in his city, and as I saw them they were not bad, but they were always in the same businesses. Regardless of character, education, and station, the people in these businesses were in the corruption of politics and the resistance to reform. This suggested that it was these businesses, not the men in them, that were the cause of our evil. And that's what they told me. They did not like or wish or mean, they said they "had to" do evil. I could not for a long time believe this. It sounded like a weak excuse when a big, powerful captain of industry declared that the bad politicians "held him up" and struck him for a bribe or a contribution to a campaign fund. It was only after going through many cities and States and hearing always the same plea of compulsion that I was persuaded at last that it is true.

"You cannot build or operate a railroad," I said, "or a street railway, gas, water, or power company, develop and operate a mine, or get forests and cut timber on a large scale, or run any privileged business, without corrupting or joining in the corruption of the government. You tell me privately that you must, and here I am telling you semi-publicly that you must. And that is so all over the country. And that means that we have an organization of society in which, for some reason, you and your kind, the ablest, most intelligent, most imaginative, daring, and resourceful leaders of society, are and must be against society and its laws and its all-around growth."

My conclusion was that we all of us, they as well as I—they more than I—should seek to rid all individuals of those things that make them work against the greater, common welfare.

The first question from that company, and the last, was, "Who started the evil?" I reminded them that the question should be what, not who, and that everything they believed would be brought together by the answer. If it was some Thing that hurt us we could be Christians and forgive sinners; we could cease from punishing men and develop an environment in which men would be tempted to be good. No use; those business men wanted me to admit that the politicians made the conditions that business men were subject to. I related how the San Francisco banker, William H. Crocker, had argued that he had to do business under conditions as he found them, and I had reminded him that his father and the rest of the Big Four who built the Central Pacific Railroad were blamed by the politicians for corrupting the State and making the conditions he, the son and successor, "had to" continue.

Somebody mentioned the fear that government operation was always inefficient. I cited Seattle, where a publicly owned power plant was breaking down so often that there was an investigation, and they learned that the private competitors had paid certain political employees to sabotage the city's plant.

Another voice asked if the public operation of utilities would not put them into politics. To answer that, I turned to William Mulholland, the popular, highly respected engineer, who was the manager of the city's water system. He had been the manager when the water company was a private corporation, and it was notorious that he was then a very active and efficient politician. Everybody in that room knew that Mr. Mulholland had said over and over again that the change from private to public operation had got him and the business out of politics. When I passed the question of politics to him he did not have to answer. The whole company burst into laughter.

There were other questions, other arguments against business in politics, which I learned in college. But the ever-recurring question that night was Who? Who started it? Who is to be blamed and—punished? And at last, the Episcopal bishop of that diocese stated it in a form that suggested an answer. I was emphasizing the point that society really offers a prize for evil-doing: money, position, power. "Let's take down the offer of a reward," I said. "Let's abolish—privileges."

The bishop rose and very kindly, very courteously said that he felt that I was not meeting the minds of my hearers. "What we want to know," he said, "is who founded this system, who started it, not only in San Francisco and Los Angeles, in this or the last generation, but back, 'way back, in the beginning."

"Oh, I think I see," I said. "You want to fix the fault at the very start of things. Maybe we can, Bishop. Most people, you know, say it was Adam. But Adam, you remember, he said that it was Eve, the woman; she did it. And Eve said no, no, it wasn't she; it was the serpent. And that's where you clergy have stuck ever since. You blame that serpent, Satan. Now I come and I am trying to show you that it was, it is, the apple."

The bishop sat down. You could hear him sit down. For there was silence, a long moment, and in that silence the meeting adjourned.


# THE CLASS BASIS
# OF THE REFORM IDEAL

## JANE ADDAMS


IT IS DIFFICULT both to interpret sympathetically the motives and ideals of those who have acquired rules of conduct in experience widely different from our own, and also to take enough care in guarding the gains already made, and in valuing highly enough the imperfect good so painfully acquired and, at the best, so mixed with evil. This wide difference in daily experience exhibits itself in two distinct attitudes toward politics. The well-to-do men of the community think of politics as something off by itself; they may conscientiously recognize political duty as part of good citizenship, but political effort is not the expression of their moral or social life. As a result of this detachment, "reform movements," started by business men and the better element, are almost wholly occupied in the correction of political machinery and with a concern for the better method of administration, rather than with the ultimate purpose of securing the welfare of the people. They fix their attention so exclusively on methods that they fail to consider the final aims of city government. This accounts for the growing tendency to put more and more responsibility upon executive officers and appointed commissions at the expense of curtailing the power of the direct representatives of the voters. Reform movements tend to become negative and to lose

Reprinted from *Democracy and Social Ethics* (New York: The Macmillan Company, 1902), pp. 222–227, 257–260, and 266–271.

their educational value for the mass of the people. The reformers take the rôle of the opposition. They give themselves largely to criticisms of the present state of affairs, to writing and talking of what the future must be and of certain results which should be obtained. In trying to better matters, however, they have in mind only political achievements which they detach in a curious way from the rest of life, and they speak and write of the purification of politics as of a thing set apart from daily life.

On the other hand, the real leaders of the people are part of the entire life of the community which they control, and so far as they are representative at all, are giving a social expression to democracy. They are often politically corrupt, but in spite of this they are proceeding upon a sounder theory. Although they would be totally unable to give it abstract expression, they are really acting upon a formulation made by a shrewd English observer; namely, that, "after the enfranchisement of the masses, social ideals enter into political programmes, and they enter not as something which at best can be indirectly promoted by government, but as something which it is the chief business of government to advance directly."

Men living near to the masses of voters, and knowing them intimately, recognize this and act upon it; they minister directly to life and to social needs. They realize that the people as a whole are clamoring for social results, and they hold their power because they respond to that demand. They are corrupt and often do their work badly; but they at least avoid the mistake of a certain type of business men who are frightened by democracy, and have lost faith in the people. The two standards are similar to those seen at a popular exhibition of pictures where the cultivated people care most for the technique of a given painting, the moving mass for a subject that shall be domestic and human.

This difference may be illustrated by the writer's experience in a certain ward of Chicago, during three campaigns, when efforts were made to dislodge an alderman who had represented the ward for many years. In this ward there are gathered together fifty thousand people, representing a score of nationalities; the newly emigrated Latin, Teuton, Celt, Greek, and Slav who live there have little in common save the basic experiences which come to men in all countries and under all conditions. In order to make fifty thousand people, so heterogeneous in nationality, religion, and customs, agree upon any demand, it must be founded upon universal experiences which are perforce individual and not social.

An instinctive recognition of this on the part of the alderman makes it possible to understand the individualistic basis of his political success, but it remains extremely difficult to ascertain the reasons for the extreme leniency of judgment concerning the political corruption of which he is constantly guilty.

This leniency is only to be explained on the ground that his constituents greatly admire individual virtues, and that they are at the same time unable to perceive social outrages which the alderman may be committing. They thus free the alderman from blame because his corruption is social, and they honestly admire him as a great man and hero, because his individual acts are on the whole kindly and generous.

In certain stages of moral evolution, a man is incapable of action unless the results will benefit himself or some one of his acquaintances, and it is a long step in moral progress to set the good of the many before the interest of the few, and to be concerned for the welfare of a community without hope of an individual return. How far the selfish politician befools his constituents into believing that their interests are identical with his own; how far he presumes upon their inability to distinguish between the individual and social virtues, an inability which he himself shares with them; and how far he dazzles them by the sense of his greatness, and a conviction that they participate therein, it is difficult to determine. . . .

That the alderman has much to do with setting the standard of life and desirable prosperity may be illustrated by the following incident: During one of the campaigns a clever cartoonist drew a poster representing the successful alderman in portraiture drinking champagne at a table loaded with pretentious dishes and surrounded by revellers. In contradistinction was his opponent, a bricklayer, who sat upon a half-finished wall, eating a meagre dinner from a workingman's dinner-pail, and the passer-by was asked which type of representative he preferred, the presumption being that at least in a workingman's district the bricklayer would come out ahead. To the chagrin of the reformers, however, it was gradually discovered that, in the popular mind, a man who laid bricks and wore overalls was not nearly so desirable for an alderman as the man who drank champagne and wore a diamond in his shirt front. The district wished its representative "to stand up with the best of them," and certainly some of the constituents would have been ashamed to have been represented by a bricklayer. It is part of that general desire to appear well, the optimistic and thoroughly American belief, that even if a man is working with his hands to-day, he and his children will quite likely be in a better position in the swift coming to-morrow, and there is no need of being too closely associated with common working people. There is an honest absence of class consciousness, and a naïve belief that the kind of occupation quite largely determines social position. This is doubtless exaggerated in a neighborhood of foreign people by the fact that as each nationality becomes more adapted to American conditions, the scale of its occupation rises. Fifty years ago in America "a Dutchman" was used as a term of reproach, meaning a man whose language was not understood, and who performed menial tasks, digging sewers and building railroad embankments. Later the Irish did the same work in the community, but as quickly as possible handed it on to the Italians, to whom the name "dago" is said to cling as a result of the digging which the Irishman resigned to him. The Italian himself is at last waking up to this fact.

In a political speech recently made by an Italian padrone, he bitterly reproached the alderman for giving the-four-dollars-a-day "jobs" of sitting in an office to Irishmen and the-dollar-and-a-half-a-day "jobs" of sweeping the streets to the Italians. This general struggle to rise in life, to be at least politically represented by one of the best, as to occupation and social status, has also its negative side. We must remember that the imitative impulse plays an important part in life, and that the loss of social estimation, keenly felt by all of us, is perhaps most dreaded by the humblest, among whom freedom of individual conduct, the power to give only just weight to the opinion of neighbors, is but feebly developed. A form of constraint, gentle, but powerful, is afforded by the simple desire to do what others do, in order to share with them the approval of the community. Of course, the larger the number of people among whom an habitual mode of conduct obtains, the greater the constraint it puts upon the individual will. Thus it is that the political corruption of the city presses most heavily where it can be least resisted, and is most likely to be imitated. . . .

A reformer who really knew the people and their great human needs, who believed that it was the business of government to serve them, and who further recognized the educative power of a sense of responsibility, would possess a clew by which he might analyze the situation. He would find out what needs, which the alderman supplies are legitimate ones which the city itself could undertake, in counter-distinction to those which pander to the lower instincts of the constituency. A mother who eats her Christmas turkey in a reverent spirit of thankfulness to the alderman who gave it to her, might be gradually brought to a genuine sense of appreciation and gratitude to the city which supplies her little children with a Kindergarten, or, to the Board of Health which properly placarded a case of scarlet fever next door and spared her sleepless nights and wearing anxiety, as well as the money paid with such difficulty to the doctor and the druggist. The man who in his emotional gratitude almost kneels before a political friend who gets his boy out of jail might be made to see the kindness and good sense of the city authorities who provided the boy with a playground and reading room, where he might spend his hours of idleness and restlessness, and through which his temptations to petty crime might be averted. A man who is grateful to the alderman who sees that his gambling and racing are not interfered with, might learn to feel loyal and responsible to the city which supplied him with a gymnasium and swimming tank where manly and well-conducted sports are possible. The voter who is eager to serve the alderman at all times, because the tenure of his job is dependent upon aldermanic favor, might find great relief and pleasure in working for the city in which his place was secured by a well-administered civil service law.

After all, what the corrupt alderman demands from his followers and largely depends upon is a sense of loyalty, a standing-by the man who is good to you, who understands you, and who gets you out of trouble. All the social life of the voter from the time he was a little boy and played "craps" with his "own push," and not with some other "push," has been founded on this sense of loyalty and of standing in with his friends. Now that he is a man, he likes the sense of being inside a political organization, of being trusted with political gossip, of belonging to a set of fellows who understand things, and whose interests are being cared for by a strong friend in the city council itself. All this is perfectly legitimate, and all in the line of the development of a strong civic loyalty, if it were merely socialized and enlarged. . . .

Would it be dangerous to conclude that the corrupt politician himself, because he is democratic in method, is on a more ethical line of social development than the reformer, who believes that the people might be made over by "good citizens" and governed by "experts"? The former at least are engaged in that great moral effort of getting the mass to express itself, and of adding this mass energy and wisdom to the community as a whole.

The wide divergence of experience makes it difficult for the good citizen to understand this point of view, and many things conspire to make it hard for him to act upon it. He is more or less a victim to that curious feeling so often possessed by the good man, that the righteous do not need to be agreeable, that their goodness alone is sufficient, and that they can leave the arts and wiles of securing popular favor to the self-seeking. This results in a certain repellent manner, commonly regarded as the apparel of righteousness, and is further responsible for the fatal mistake of making the surroundings of "good influences" singularly unattractive; a mistake which really deserves a reprimand quite as severe as the equally reprehensible deed of making the surroundings of "evil influences" so beguiling. Both are akin to that state of mind which narrows the entrance into a wider morality to the eye of a needle, and accounts for the fact that new moral movements have ever and again been inaugurated by those who have found themselves in revolt against the conventionalized good.

# IV

## "GOOD GOVERNMENT"

---

"Good government" is put in quotation marks because for more than a hundred years it has been part of the jargon of the municipal reform movement. (In Lincoln Steffens' day reformers were called "goo-goos" by unregenerate boodlers because they used the words so much.) In the jargon, good government meant government that was honest, impartial, and efficient —the kind of government that would exist (so the reformers thought) once the machines were destroyed, "petty politicians" driven out, and public-spirited citizens like themselves elected to office. Good government in this sense was neither very democratic nor very much concerned with the needs and wishes of the low-income and low-status elements of the community. But whereas to the reformers the machine represented evil, good government represented virtue.

The ideal of "good government" was a class ideal, of course. As Jane Addams explained in a reading in the previous section, there is wide difference in the moral perspective of middle- and of lower-class voters. The lower class thinks of "goodness" in terms of some advantage for the individual or the family, whereas the middle class thinks of it in terms of the community or some larger abstract public. From the standpoint of the middle-class ethic, which is mainly that of native Yankee-Protestants and Jews, the task of government is to serve the "community as a whole." Implicit in this idea is the notion that the community is an entity that has ends or purposes different from those of the individuals who comprise it. In this view, the ends of individuals—indeed, of all private, local, or partial interests—should be subordinated to the "community as a whole." Therefore politics, instead of being a competitive struggle among partial interests, ought to be a cooperative search for the implications of communal interests. In this search the expert—one who is both disinterested and possessed of special technical qualifications—should play a leading, and perhaps a decisive, part.

It will be seen that this conception of politics implies an altogether different set of institutional arrangements than does the individualistic, lower-class conception. It implies nonpartisanship (for the interest of a party is less than, and therefore opposed to, that of the "community as a whole"), election at-large rather than on a ward basis, and a strong, independent executive who will ignore special interests and assert his "impartial" conception of the interest of the "community as a whole." The nonpartisan election system and the council-manager form of government are both expressions of these general principles. Proportional representation, which the promoters of the council-manager plan tried for a time to link with it, did not fit this underlying logic, and, as Don K. Price explains, never had the popularity of the other reforms.

The middle-class, Yankee-Protestant belief that government is mainly a matter of honest, impartial, and efficient pursuit of the interest of the "community as a whole" (and not at all one getting petty favors, protection, or advantage for one's family, ethnic group, or ward) leads, of course, to a conception of government as "administration," or the businesslike conduct of service functions, rather than as "politics," or the management of conflict. It is not surprising, therefore, to find a conservative like Andrew D. White (the first president of Cornell University) and a progressive like Brand Whitlock (a novelist who in 1905 became the first nonpartisan mayor of Toledo) both supporting nonpartisanship on the grounds that city affairs should be kept clear of state and national politics. Both of these men, it must be added, saw other advantages in nonpartisanship. White believed it would put affairs out of the reach of the city proletariat. Whitlock thought that, by eliminating the machine, it would make democracy work.

In practice, the nonpartisan system has by no means always kept the parties out of local elections. Robert L. Morlan, a political scientist, describes the actual working of a nonpartisan system in Minneapolis, one of the many cities where the parties, although without any formal standing, do a good deal of prompting and managing from the wings. Charles R. Adrian, another political scientist, tells what some of the consequences of nonpartisanship have been for the national parties, the recruitment of political personnel, the financing of elections, the content of election issues, and the quality and character of legislative bodies.

The relation of the city manager movement to the general doctrines of "good government" is explained by Don K. Price, now the Dean of the Littauer School at Harvard. He shows that the main motivation of the reformers was not to overturn the machine (cities that would accept the council-manager plan were likely to be middle-class ones that had no

machines) but rather to make government more effective and more democratic. It was a mistake, Price says, to think that the city manager could
"administer" policy, leaving the making of it to others. The most influential
spokesman for the point of view Price here attacks was the late Professor
Leonard D. White, who argued, in a book that did much to establish doctrine
about the city manager profession, that a city manager who attempted to
furnish the brains, enthusiasm, and leadership to decide policy for his city
would risk having his program rejected and his position weakened. Charles
R. Adrian brings some facts to bear upon this old dispute. Observations in
three cities that have had managers for more than twenty-five years, he says,
show that the managers have been leaders in policy matters—indeed, that
they could not help being so even when they tried—but that they have
preferred to attribute *innovations* in policy to others.

What Harold A. Stone, Don K. Price, and Kathryn H. Stone have to
say about the theory of the city manager plan in their "Three Fundamental
Principles" applies equally to nonpartisanship and may be taken as a general
account of the theory of the "good government" movement. Implicit is the
idea that the community has an interest "as a whole," that the main problem
of governmental organization is to give effective and consistent expression
to this interest, and that this is to be done by preventing "special interests"
from asserting themselves while at the same time giving "impartial experts"
—especially the city manager—a free hand. Charles A. Beard, the historian,
disputes the premises of this theory. Group conflict is inevitable in a major
city, he says, and issues are more frequently pretexts than causes of partisanship. His article is somewhat marred by a confusing use of the word "partisan." Apparently Beard thinks of nonpartisanship, not as a system in which
state and national parties play no part (the accepted meaning of the term),
but as one in which there are no factional groupings at all. This mis-
understanding makes it difficult to follow his criticism of nonpartisanship,
but it makes his criticism of the fundamentals of the "good government"
position all the more pertinent.

The three readings at the end of this section show that "good government" (the reformers' ideal) is not always good government (government
that is good by the standards of the ordinary citizen). John Bartlow Martin,
a magazine writer, shows how hard it is for many Americans to swallow
honesty, impartiality, and efficiency in local government, even when they
know that these are good for them. Rexford G. Tugwell asserts that former
Mayor La Guardia mismanaged New York in the name of "good government." Honesty, impartiality, and efficiency (this last in the narrow sense
of correct technical procedures) are not enough, he says, to insure the welfare of a great city. James E. Reichley, a novelist and political scientist, goes
much further in his criticism of "good government" as he found it in Philadelphia. In his view, the efforts of upper-class Protestant reformers have
emptied political life of much of its interest and meaning. This accounts for

the impermanence of reform and for its lack of real accomplishment. Excessive individualism, he says, has led the Protestant elite away from politics, one of men's natural interests. This conclusion is, of course, wholly at odds with the line of analysis in this introductory note. In this writer's opinion, the Protestant elite withdrew from city politics because the only kind of politics it thought moral—a politics of community rather than of individual or group interest—was impossible in the institutional and cultural setting of the large American city.

# MUNICIPAL AFFAIRS
# ARE NOT POLITICAL

ANDREW D. WHITE

WITHOUT THE SLIGHTEST EXAGGERATION we may assert that, with very few exceptions, the city governments of the United States are the worst in Christendom—the most expensive, the most inefficient, and the most corrupt. No one who has any considerable knowledge of our own country and of other countries can deny this. . . .

What is the cause of the difference between municipalities in the old world and in the new? I do not allow that their populations are better than ours. What accounts, then, for the better municipal development in their case and for the miserable results in our own? My answer is this: we are attempting to govern our cities upon a theory which has never been found to work practically in any part of the world. Various forms of it were tried in the great cities of antiquity and of the middle ages, especially in the mediæval republics of Italy, and without exception they ended in tyranny, confiscation, and bloodshed. The same theory has produced the worst results in various countries of modern Europe, down to a recent period.

What is this evil theory? It is simply that the city is a political body; that its interior affairs have to do with national political parties and issues. My fundamental contention is that a city is a corporation; that as a city it has nothing whatever to do with general political interests; that party political names and duties are utterly out of place there. The questions in a city are not political questions. They have reference to the laying out of streets; to the erection of buildings; to sanitary arrangements, sewerage, water supply, gas supply, electrical supply; to the control of franchises and the like; and to provisions for the public health and comfort in parks, boulevards, libraries, and museums. The work of a city being the creation and control of the city property, it should logically be managed as a piece of property by those who have created it, who have a title to it, or a real substantial part in it, and who can therefore feel strongly their duty to it. Under our theory that a city is a political body, a crowd of illiterate peasants, freshly raked in from Irish bogs, or Bohemian mines, or Italian robber nests, may exercise virtual con-

Reprinted from *Forum*, December, 1890, where it appeared under the title, "The Government of American Cities."

trol. How such men govern cities, we know too well; as a rule they are not alive even to their own most direct interests. . . .

The difference between foreign cities and ours, is that all these well-ordered cities in England, France, Germany, Italy, Switzerland, whether in monarchies or republics, accept this principle—that cities are corporations and not political bodies; that they are not concerned with matters of national policy; that national parties as such have nothing whatever to do with city questions. They base their city governments upon ascertained facts regarding human nature, and upon right reason. They try to conduct them upon the principles observed by honest and energetic men in business affairs. We, on the other hand, are putting ourselves upon a basis which has always failed and will always fail—the idea that a city is a political body, and therefore that it is to be ruled, in the long run, by a city proletariat mob, obeying national party cries.

What is our safety? The reader may possibly expect me, in logical consonance with the statement I have just made, to recommend that the city be treated strictly as a corporate body, and governed entirely by those who have a direct pecuniary interest in it. If so, he is mistaken. I am no doctrinaire; politics cannot be bent completely to logic—certainly not all at once. A wise, statesmanlike view would indicate a compromise between the political idea and the corporate idea. I would not break away entirely from the past, but I would build a better future upon what we may preserve from the past.

To this end I would still leave in existence the theory that the city is a political body, as regards the election of the mayor and common council. I would elect the mayor by the votes of the majority of all the citizens, as at present; I would elect the common council by a majority of all the votes of all the citizens; but instead of electing its members from the wards as at present—so that wards largely controlled by thieves and robbers can send thieves and robbers, and so that men who can carry their ward can control the city—I would elect the board of aldermen on a general ticket, just as the mayor is elected now, thus requiring candidates for the board to have a city reputation. So much for retaining the idea of the city as a political body. In addition to this, in consideration of the fact that the city is a corporation, I would have those owning property in it properly recognized. I would leave to them, and to them alone, the election of a board of control, without whose permission no franchise should be granted and no expenditure should be made. This should be the rule, but to this rule I am inclined to make one exception; I would allow the votes of the board of control, as regards expenditures for primary education, to be overridden by a two-thirds majority of the board of aldermen. I should do this because here alone does the city policy come into direct relations with the general political system of the nation at large. The main argument for the existence of our public schools is that they are an absolute necessity to the existence of our Republic; that without preliminary education a republic simply becomes an illiterate mob;

that if illiterate elements control, the destruction of the Republic is sure. On this ground, considering the public-school system as based upon a national political necessity, I would have an exception made regarding the expenditures for it, leaving in this matter a last resort to the political assembly of the people.

A theory resulting in a system virtually like this, has made the cities of Europe, whether in monarchies or republics, what they are, and has made it an honor in many foreign countries for the foremost citizens to serve in the common councils of their cities. Take one example: It has been my good fortune to know well Rudolf Von Gneist, councilor of the German Empire. My acquaintance with him began when it was my official duty to present to him a testimonial, in behalf of the government of the United States, for his services in settling the north-west boundary between the United States and Great Britain. The Emperor William was the nominal umpire; he made Von Gneist the real umpire—that shows Von Gneist's standing. He is also a leading professor of law in the University of Berlin, a member of the Imperial Parliament and of the Prussian Legislature, and the author of famous books, not only upon law, but upon the constitutional history of Germany and of England. This man has been, during a considerable time, a member of what we should call the board of aldermen of the city of Berlin, and he is proud to serve in that position. With him have been associated other men the most honored in various walks of life, and among these some of the greatest business men, renowned in all lands for their enterprise and their probity. Look through the councils of our cities, using any microscope you can find, and tell me how many such men you discern in them. Under the system I propose, it is, humanly speaking, certain that these better men would seek entrance into our city councils. Especially would this be the case if our citizens should, by and by, learn that it is better to have in the common council an honest man, though a Republican, than a scoundrel, though a Democrat; and better to have a man of ability and civic pride, though a Democrat, than a weak, yielding creature, though a Republican.

Some objections will be made. It will be said, first, that wealthy and well-to-do people do not do their duty in city matters; that if they should, they would have better city government. This is true to this extent, that even well-to-do men are in city politics strangely led away from their civic duties by fancied allegiance to national party men and party issues. But in other respects it is untrue; the vote of a single tenement house, managed by a professional politician, will neutralize the vote of an entire street of well-to-do citizens. Men in business soon find this out; they soon find that to work for political improvement under the present system is time and labor and self-respect thrown away. It may be also said that the proposal is impracticable. I ask, why? History does not show it to be impracticable; for we have before us, as I have shown, the practice of all other great civilized nations on earth, and especially of our principal sister republics.

But it will be said that "revolutions do not go backward." They did go backward in the great cities of Europe when these rid themselves of the old bad system that had at bottom the theory under which ours are managed, and when they entered into their new and better system. The same objection, that revolutions do not go backward, was made against any reform in the tenure of office of the governor and of the higher judiciary in the State of New York; and yet the revolution did go backward, that is, it went back out of doctrinaire folly into sound, substantial, common-sense statesmanship. In 1847 the State of New York so broke away from the old conservative moorings as to make all judgeships elective, with short terms, small pay, and wretched accommodations, and the same plan was pursued as regards the governor and other leading officials; but the State, some years since, very wisely went back to much of its former system—in short, made a revolution backward, if any one chooses to call it so—resuming the far better system of giving our governor and higher judges longer terms, larger salaries, better accommodations, and dignified surroundings. We see, then, that it is not true that steps in a wrong direction in a republic cannot be retraced. As they have been retraced in State affairs, so they may be in municipal affairs.

But it will be said that this change in city government involves a long struggle. It may or it may not. If it does, such a struggle is but part of the price which we pay for the maintenance of free institutions in town, State, and nation. For this struggle, I especially urge all men of light and leading to prepare themselves. As to the public at large, what is most needed in regard to municipal affairs, as in regard to public affairs generally, is the quiet, steady evolution of a knowledge of truth and of proper action in view of it. That truth, as regards city government, is simply the truth that municipal affairs are not political; that political parties as such have nothing to do with cities; that the men who import political considerations into municipal management are to be opposed. This being the case, the adoption of some such system as that which I have sketched would seem likely to prove fruitful of good.

# THE ABSURDITY OF PARTISANSHIP

## BRAND WHITLOCK

I HAVE SPOKEN of the Independents as though they were an authentic political party, when it was one of their basic principles to be no party at all. They were Republicans and Democrats who, in the revelation of Jones's

From *Forty Years of It* by Brand Whitlock, pp. 188-191, 193, and 203–205. Copyright, 1914, D. Appleton & Company. Reprinted by permission of the publisher Appleton-Century-Crofts, Inc.

[Golden Rule Jones, reform mayor of Toledo] death, had come to see that it was the partizan that was responsible for the evil political machines in American cities; they saw that by dividing themselves arbitrarily into parties, along national lines, by voting, almost automatically, their party tickets, ratifying nominations made for them they knew not how, they were but delivering over their city to the spoiler. As Republicans, proud of the traditions of that party, they had voted under the impression that they were voting for Lincoln; as Democrats they thought they were voting for Jefferson, or at least for Jackson, but they had discovered that they had been voting principally for the street railway company and the privileges allied with it in interest.

And more than all, they saw that in the amazing superstition of party regularity by which the partizan mind in that day was obsessed, they were voting for these interests no matter which ticket they supported, for the machine was not only partizan, it was bi-partizan, and the great conflict they waged at the polls was the most absurd sham battle that ever was fought. It seems almost incredible now that men's minds were ever so clouded, strange that they did not earlier discover how absurd was a system which, in order to enable them the more readily to subjugate themselves, actually printed little woodcuts of birds—roosters and eagles—at the heads of the tickets, so that they might the more easily and readily recognize their masters and deliver their suffrages over to them. It is an absurdity that is pretty well recognized in this country to-day, and the principle of separating municipal politics from national politics is all but established in law. Mr. James Bryce had pointed it out long before, but [former Mayor] Jones seemed to be almost the first among us to recognize it, and he probably had not read from Mr. Bryce; he deduced the principle from his own experience, and from his own consciousness, if not his own conscience. Perhaps he had some intimation of it from the Genius of These States, whose scornful laugh at that and other absurdities his great exemplar Walt Whitman could hear, echoed as from some mountain peak afar in the west. But it was no laughing matter in Toledo in those days. Men were accused of treason and sedition for deserting their parties; it made little difference which party a man belonged to; the insistence was on his belonging to a party; any party would suffice.

I have no intention, however, of discussing that principle now, but it was the point from which we had to start in our first campaign, the point from which all cities will have to start if they wish to be free. The task we faced was relatively greater than that which [former Mayor] Jones had faced; we had a full ticket in the field, a candidate for every city office and a man running for the council in every ward in town. Jones had run alone, and though he succeeded there was always a council and a coterie of municipal officials who represented the other interest in the community. Of course he had made our work possible by the labor he had done, great pioneer that he was. He had been his own platform, as any candidate after all must be, but with our large movement it was necessary to reduce our principles to some form and we tried to do this as simply as we could. We put forth our belief that local affairs should be separate from, and independent of, party politics, and that public officers should be selected on account of their honesty and efficiency, regardless of political affiliations; that the people should be more active in selecting their officials, and should not allow an office-seeker to bring about his own nomination; that the prices charged by public service corporations should be regulated by the council at stated intervals; and that all franchises for public utilities should first be submitted to a vote of the people, that the city should possess the legal right to acquire and maintain any public utility, when authorized so to do by direct vote of its people, that every franchise granted to public service corporations should contain an agreement that the city might purchase and take over its property at a fair price, whenever so voted by the people, and that no street railway franchise should be extended or granted, permitting more than three-cent fares, and unless it includes provisions for universal transfers, satisfactory service, and reasonable compensation for the use of bridges, and we demanded from the legislature home rule, the initiative and referendum and the recall.

Perhaps it was not such a little platform after all, but big indeed, I think, when one comes to consider its potentialities, and if anyone thinks it was easy to put its principles into practice, let him try it and see! It was drawn by that Johnson Thurston of whom I spoke, and by Oren Dunham and by Elisha B. Southard and others, citizens devoted to their town, and already with a prescience of the city spirit. They succeeded in compressing into those few lines all we know or need to know about municipal government, and ages hence our cities will still be falling short of the ideal they expressed on that little card. There were many who went with us in that first campaign who did not see all the implications of that statement of principles; none of us saw all of them of course. The movement had not only the strength but the weaknesses of all so-called reform movements in their initial stages. Those who were disappointed or disaffected or dissatisfied for personal reasons with the old party machines, no doubt found an opportunity for expression of their not too lofty sentiments, although later on when they saw that it was merely a tendency toward democracy they fell away, not because the movement had deserted its original ideals but because they at last understood them.

As I now look back on that first campaign, on the experience I had so much dreaded, the perspective has worked its magic, and the hardships and difficulties have faded away. . . .

There was no old gray Molly to jog about from one meeting to another, and if there had been, she could not have jogged fast enough for the necessities of that hour; and we established new precedents when Percy Jones, the son of the Golden Rule Mayor, drove me about at furious speed in his big touring car, the "Grey Ghost" the reporters called it, and it streaked through the night, with its siren singing, from place to place until I had spoken at half a dozen meetings. Every day at noon it wheeled up to the entrance of the factories and shops as the men were coming out for their

noon hour. And such meetings I believe were never held anywhere; there
was an inspiration as the men crowded about the car to hear the speeches;
they were not politicians, they were seeking nothing, they were interested in
their city; and in their faces, what is far above any of these considerations,
there was an eager interest in life, perhaps a certain hunger of life which in
so many of them, such were the conditions of their toil, was not satisfied. . . .

The one thing that marred these contacts was not only that one was so
powerless to help these men, but that one stood before them in an attitude
that somehow suggested to them, inevitably, from long habit and the pretense
of men who sought power for themselves, that one needed only to be placed
in a certain official relation to them, and to be addressed by a certain title,
to be able to help them. It was enough to make one ashamed, almost enough
to cause one to prefer that they should vote for someone else, and relieve one
from this dreadful self-consciousness, this dreadful responsibility.

And these were the people! These were they who had been so long
proscribed and exploited; they had borne a few of the favored of the fates
on their backs, and yet, bewildered, they were somehow expectant of that
good to come to them which had been promised in the words and phrases
by which their very acquiescence and subjugation had so mysteriously been
wrought—"Life, liberty and the pursuit of happiness."

Where? And for them, when? Not through the efforts of those who
employed cold phrases about "good" government, and "reform," and "business" administrations, and efficiency methods, and enforcement of the laws,
and law and order, and all that sort of thing, and class consciousness, and
economic, or any other interpretation of history, or through initiatives,
referendums and recalls. What good would any of these cold and precise
formulæ do them? Better perhaps the turkey at Thanksgiving, and the goose
at Christmas time which the old machine councilman from the ward gave
them; of course they themselves paid for them, but they did not know it,
and the councilman did not know it; he had bestowed them with the voice of
kindness, in the same hearty human spirit in which he came to the wedding
or the wake, or got the father a job, or the oldest son a parole from the work-
house, and rendered a thousand other little personal services. Perhaps Bath
House John and Hinky Dink were more nearly right after all than the cold
and formal and precise gentleman who denounced their records in the
council. For they were human, and the great problem is to make the government of a city human.

There were many, of course, even in our own movement, who were not
concerned about that; I was strongly rebuked by one of them once in that
very first campaign for declaring that we were no better than anyone else,
and that all the "good" men of the world could not do the people much good
even if they were elected to the city government for life. No, we may have
efficient governments in our cities, and honest governments, as we are beginning to have everywhere, and, happily, are more and more to have, but the
great emancipations will not come through the formulæ of Independents,

Socialists, or single-taxers, nor through Law and Order Leagues, nor Civic Associations. Down in their hearts these are not what the people want. What they want is a life that is fuller, more beautiful, more splendid and, above all, more human. And nobody can prepare it and hand it over to them. They must get it themselves; it must come up through them and out of them, through long and toilsome processes of development; for such is democracy.

# THE UNORGANIZED POLITICS
# OF MINNEAPOLIS

## ROBERT L. MORLAN

THE STUDENT of municipal politics in the United States today is being given an extremely one-sided picture of political organization and party activity, at least in so far as existing literature is concerned. Most of the writing on this subject seems to assume that, excepting only those cities under 100,000 population, the pattern is essentially that expounded so entertainingly by the immortal *Plunkitt of Tammany Hall* a half century ago.

The picture almost invariably presented is one of tight political hierarchies extending from a boss and the city or county central committee through ward executives, precinct leaders and multitudinous block workers, all welded into a highly efficient 365-day-a-year machine by the magic of patronage, and controlling votes largely through the familiar process of rendering personal service to the voters.

This is not to deny that extremely effective machines continue to flourish in some American cities but rather to challenge the traditional assumption that this is the way it is done everywhere. Operations of bosses and machines have often been sensational and hence have tended to attract the attention of those investigating the facts of local political life. Interesting and useful studies of bossism have resulted from these researches, but the focusing of attention in that direction has meant the virtual ignoring of cities with less spectacular politics.

Authors of general works on municipal government and politics have found their sources of material almost entirely limited to studies of highly organized cities—and have doubtless also been anxious to include in their texts as much colorful matter as possible. As a result, the politically loosely organized city has received either no attention or has been summarily passed off with a statement that in some small cities party organization is less comprehensive.

Reprinted from *National Municipal Review*, November, 1949, pp. 485–490.

There is, in fact, a tremendous variation in the comprehensiveness of party organization and in the extent of party activities in city wards. Machine strength is, of course, normally centered in the poorer wards, while in the more prosperous wards workers rarely engage in much more than a bit of pre-election activity. The minority party frequently maintains little if any organization in wards which are overwhelmingly of the opposite political faith, but it is also true that even the dominant party is often poorly organized in certain wards. The significant fact too commonly overlooked, however, is that there are some large cities as well as many smaller ones in which *neither* party has a strong organization in *any* ward.

It is time to re-examine our traditional concepts of city political organization, to get away from the universalities in which most of the writing in this field has dealt, and to recognize the fact that even in large municipalities political organization and activity vary all the way from highly concentrated control to loose and haphazard operation.

## An Unorganized City

Minneapolis, with a population of over half a million and a long history of volatile politics, is an excellent example of a major city loosely organized politically. Its situation may not be widespread, but it is significant as a striking deviation from a presumed norm, and one may speculate that it is not alone.[1]

It is often difficult for persons familiar with the politics of highly organized cities to believe that political activity in Minneapolis can actually be as "free and easy" as it is. The truth is that any interested person can step immediately into political work, that the average party ward meeting is for all practical purposes open to anyone, that in no ward is there a party organization adequately covering every precinct the year around, that many officers of both parties at the city, ward and precinct levels are practically neophytes in politics, and that the party organizations as such play minor roles in the selection and control of candidates and have almost negligible influence with city officials.

The ease with which a political amateur with a sense of direction may succeed in Minneapolis politics is strikingly illustrated by the career of former Mayor, now U.S. Senator, Hubert H. Humphrey. As a young college political science instructor with a "gift of gab," he was expounding his views on local politics one night in a typical campus bull session when someone brought him up short: "Humphrey, why don't you practice what you're always preaching about political participation, and see what you can do in this next city election?"

The upshot was that Hubert Humphrey, with hastily collected and almost

---

1. The situation in the other of the "Twin Cities," St. Paul, is essentially similar.

wholly amateur support, little money and organization, not only survived the nonpartisan primary in 1943 but also lost to the incumbent mayor in the final election by only 5,000 out of 115,000 votes. Gathering liberal and labor support in the interim, but still operating to a large degree with what was in effect his own organization, he came back to win in 1945 by the largest plurality any mayor has ever secured. In 1947 he swept every ward and the following year went on to defeat Senator Joseph H. Ball by a three to two margin. Never did he have behind him a tight ward and precinct organization even approximating the traditional type.

Part of the reason for this wide open situation is found in the fact that Minneapolis—as do all local units in Minnesota—elects its officials on a nonpartisan ballot although this of course does not mean that the parties take no part in municipal politics. Party organizations would exist for state and national affairs at any rate and, since essentially the same persons are interested in politics at all levels, it is hardly to be expected that they will remain aloof in municipal campaigns.

## Pressure Group Government

Campaigns are managed by volunteer committees for individual candidates, but the parties make endorsements instead of nominations, and in most cases they quite openly support their choices. Nevertheless, since the parties do not manage the campaigns of individual candidates and do not finance them except in the form of minor contributions, nonpartisanship in local elections is definitely a factor. It has resulted in government by pressure groups—labor unions, business associations, etc.—rather than by parties at the city level.

A further cause of party weakness is the almost complete absence of local patronage in the sense of jobs for loyal workers. The city merit system, although it has some shortcomings, covers almost all municipal employment and has been little abused in recent years.

Patronage in the sense of special favors in the expectation of future support is extensive, but it is centered almost entirely in the hands of the 26 aldermen and party officials as a rule have practically nothing to do with it. The aldermen, therefore, to that extent play the role which is normally played by party ward and precinct executives. Being relatively independent, they have tended to build up personal blocs of support with little thought for the parties whose support they receive. They consider themselves more dependent upon the support of powerful pressure groups and party organization has suffered as a consequence.

Political leaders say that a strong party organization not only lives upon patronage but cannot exist without it. Experience in Minneapolis lends credence to the argument. Persons with a sincere interest in politics and reasonably strong party convictions can be stirred by a cause long enough to work for brief periods before election, but they cannot be expected to devote themselves constantly to political activity unless the party has some control over them—or unless they are possessed of a Messianic zeal like that of the Communists.

Frank Kent, in his well known but occasionally inaccurate book, *The Great Game of Politics,* says categorically that eight out of ten ward executives are on the public payroll at good salaries. In Minneapolis, of the 26 ward chairmen serving the two major parties, only one is a city employee, and his is a position under the merit system for which he is in no way indebted to the party. Nor is it true that these officials are to any extent in businesses which stand to profit from political pull. Precinct executives in strongly organized cities often hold minor political jobs, yet in Minneapolis scarcely a handful who are public employees can be found.

One of the leading college textbooks on city government opens its discussion of party organization with a statement concerning the hierarchy of political organization, "at the base of which is the precinct committeeman or committee in each of the 130,000 precincts in the United States."[2] This statement is misleading, since it indicates that precinct committeemen actually exist in each of those precincts. Obviously there is nowhere near the full quota.

In Minneapolis alone, except perhaps in the weeks just preceding an important election, roughly 100 of the 634 possible precinct captaincies will be unfilled and not over half the remainder are filled by active party workers who can be depended upon at all times.

## Precinct Captains

The precinct executive, we are told, is a person who holds that position because he can control more votes than can any competitor, and who stays in power only so long as he can "deliver the goods." In the highly organized city the precinct executive must presumably devote a major portion of his time to politics. He must have information about virtually every voter in his precinct, know many of them personally and be able to swing enough votes to carry at least his party's primary. Traditionally he has been able to control votes largely by means of giving personal service in the form of jobs, assistance to those in trouble with the police, relief for the poor, etc. Kent insists that the precinct executive functions in this manner in nine-tenths of the precincts in every city.

As many of these services are becoming institutionalized, being handled at least in part by government employment bureaus and social welfare agencies, for example, the role of the precinct executive has become more and more that of a go-between and a cutter of red tape. But in the unorgan-

2. Charles M. Kneier, *City Government in the United States,* 1947, page 508.

ized city even this type of service is largely unknown. Minneapolis precinct captains lack the necessary political pull to do the job, even if they have the inclination. Few put any time on politics except in pre-election periods, when they distribute campaign literature from door to door, perhaps make a few phone calls on election day to remind persons to vote and assist in providing transportation to the polls. On rare occasions a few of the more earnest ones may do some doorbell ringing.

The average precinct captain has no personal political following and is unlikely to possess even such an elementary tool as a list of the registered voters of his precinct. He is not in the least concerned over the danger of a competitor developing sufficient strength to take over his job, for the job in most cases means nothing to him and he would be happy to be relieved of it.

"Every ward executive," says Frank Kent, "holds his position because he has the strength to hold it and for no other reason." He is, presumably, a little king in his ward. It is he who sits in the inner councils of the central party organization. It is he who wields influence at city hall, who appoints— or controls the election of—precinct executives and supervises their political activity. He has earned his position by hard work and fighting his way to the top.

The average ward executive in Minneapolis will hardly fit these specifications. Lawyers, labor leaders, business men, housewives—they devote only a relatively small portion of their time to politics and as a rule have but limited control over their ward organizations. As for influence at the city hall, they would be in vastly stronger positions as officers of the central labor union or the chamber of commerce. Not only do they have almost nothing to say in the selection of precinct executives but they can also do little more than request their cooperation once in office. That chairman is fortunate who is able to secure the attendance of over 50 per cent of his precinct captains at a meeting of the ward central committee.

## Few Ward Contests

Nor have these ward executives for the most part fought their way to the top. In many cases they had no opposition and have simply been asked to serve—in some instances there are minor skirmishes. The only real battles over these positions come when there is a struggle for control of the state or county organization. After all, the ward chairman gets nothing from his job except the satisfaction of serving the party cause, although it has occasionally been used as a stepping stone toward running for elective office. Certainly he is probably one of the most politically active persons in his ward but he is only rarely a political power.

Compared to the length of service required for a person to become a ward executive in a tightly organized city, many Minneapolis ward chairmen are virtually beginners in politics. The turnover is rapid and over half the current chairmen are new to the office within the past two years, while the oldest in point of service has been a chairman for twelve years.

The writer came to Minneapolis in the spring of 1946, in a few months became a precinct captain, and in the spring of 1948 was elected ward chairman for the majority party in one of the most active and most evenly divided wards in terms of party votes. The same year he was elected a delegate to both the county and state conventions of the party—altogether a totally inconceivable series of events for a well organized city.

In the highly organized city, meetings of a ward organization are essentially closed affairs, attended only by ward and precinct officers and a few other trusted workers.

Meetings of the ward organizations of both parties in Minneapolis are open to the public. Any interested person may attend and vote on all matters, helping to elect officials or delegates and to determine party policy. To be sure, an unknown person may be questioned about his party allegiance, and known members of an opposing party would not be permitted to participate, but the individual's word on the matter is usually accepted. At most he can merely be required to state either that he voted for a majority of the party's candidates at the last election or that he intends to do so at the next.

The practice in Minneapolis is to send meeting notices to all persons in the ward who have indicated reasonably active interest. Attendance is normally low and the ward and precinct officers are likely to constitute a sizable bloc. The fact is of little significance, however, since they are rarely if ever united upon any specific course of action in advance. A highly controversial issue may and often does bring out larger crowds, when all are given a chance to be heard and to participate in decisions. Groups with prearranged slates or programs of action are, of course, to be expected when anything of importance is at stake, but rarely is such a group made up of ward and precinct officers.

## Caucuses Routine Affairs

Biennial ward and precinct caucuses, the vehicle in Minnesota for election of local party officers and selection of delegates to county and state conventions, are subject to the same conditions as are regular ward meetings. Adherence to the party concerned is checked more rigidly, although legally the individual's statement is all that is required. At a time of intense factional strife these caucuses may be heavily attended, as was the case within the Democratic-Farmer-Labor party in 1948 when as many as six hundred persons jammed certain ward caucuses in Minneapolis. Normally, however, they are routine affairs, with few brisk contests.

The writer in the spring of 1948 was an observer at the precinct and ward caucuses of the Republican party in a ward where the vote is fairly evenly divided between the parties. All were held in a school gymnasium, with the ward caucus being convened after the precinct caucuses had completed their business. Out of 28 precincts there were eleven in which no one appeared for the precinct caucus. One person could have come and elected himself both precinct captain and delegate to the county convention—this happened in two other precincts. Moreover, a person with five followers could have controlled any precinct caucus, and this is not the exception but the rule.

Perhaps this loosely organized state of politics in Minneapolis is unique, or perhaps we have too long accepted the situation in a few tightly organized cities as being universal. Surely we have been too ready to accept without adequate investigation the statement that all cities are organized politically in such and such a manner. There are a great variety of local conditions existing within the pattern of certain fairly common structural arrangements. It is time to recognize the fact that there is, in larger cities as well as smaller ones, an unorganized as well as an organized style of municipal politics.

# SOME GENERAL CHARACTERISTICS
# OF NONPARTISAN ELECTIONS

## CHARLES R. ADRIAN

OUT OF THE MIDDLE-CLASS BUSINESSMAN'S "Efficiency and Economy Movement" that reached full strength in the second decade of the twentieth century came a series of innovations designed to place government "on a business basis" and to weaken the power of the political parties. The movement was inspired both by the example of the success of the corporate structure in trade and industry and by revulsion against the low standards of morality to be found in many sectors of political party activity around the turn of the century. The contemporary brand of politician had recently been exposed by the "muckrakers" and the prestige of the parties had reached a very low level.

Of the numerous ideas and mechanisms adopted as a result of the reform movement, one of the most unusual was that of election without party designation. Early in the twentieth century, under the theory that judges are neutral referees, not political officers, and that political activities should therefore be discouraged in the choosing of them, many communities initiated "nonpartisan" elections (the term that is usually applied) in the balloting for judicial posts. Next, using the argument that local officials should be

Reprinted from *American Political Science Review*, 46 (September, 1952), 766–776, by permission of the publisher and of the author.

businesslike administrators—there being no Republican way to pave a street and no Democratic way to lay a sewer—and that politics on the national scene have nothing in common with local problems, the movement spread to other offices. In a number of states various district, county, township, judicial, school, and city offices were made nonpartisan. And in 1913 largely as the result of a strange political accident, Minnesota not only made its county municipal offices nonpartisan, but extended the principle to the election of the state legislature.[1]

The principle lost much of its fascination for the public after the early years of the 'twenties, although it enjoyed some revival after Nebraska applied the method to the choice of its widely discussed unicameral legislature authorized in November, 1934.[2] In recent years the nonpartisan plan has not spread further but the fact that nearly one-half of the nation's voters are called upon to make some of their electoral choices from a nonpartisan ballot makes its nature and consequences matters of continuing importance for study.

As a term, "nonpartisanship" is at best somewhat ambiguous, and to the poorly informed voter it may be misleading. The expression cannot be said to denote the absence of adherence to factional or political interests. No matter how ephemeral the organizational structure, wherever men are elected to offices that require the making of *public policy* decisions, there are always persons and groups interested in getting certain candidates elected and in defeating others. All elections are partisan in the sense that people and groups take sides and struggle against one another for victory; and offices filled "without party designation" are partisan enough according to this meaning. As it is used in the United States, "nonpartisanship" actually describes a situation in which (1) public offices are filled without party designations being placed on the ballot and (2) the long ballot is used. (The Australian ballot, employed in many British Commonwealth elections, has no party designation, but the voter is ordinarily called upon to cast a single vote for a single office and presumably can hardly avoid knowing the political affiliation of the two or three candidates for the seat.)

While nonpartisan elections have not been given close study by many scholars, the materials available indicate that the system has certain characteristics which reappear wherever the plan is used. The purpose of this study is to submit some tentative propositions which seem to be characteristic of nonpartisanship. These propositions are based upon available empirical evi-

---

1. See Charles R. Adrian, "The Adoption of a Nonpartisan Legislature in Minnesota," in an issue of *Minnesota History*. For the spread of nonpartisanship on the state level, see C. C. Young, *The Legislature of California: Its Membership, Procedure and Work* (San Francisco, 1943), pp. 129–130.

2. Legislative nonpartisanship has been urged by various persons and groups in more than a dozen states, including especially California, Michigan, New York, and North Dakota. See Charles R. Adrian, "The Nonpartisan Legislature in Minnesota," unpubl. Ph.D. thesis (Minneapolis, 1950), Ch. 6. Later citations are to this work by this author.

dence, and all require verification through additional research. Owing to space limitations little evidence is actually presented here; personal observations and studies of the state legislatures of Minnesota[3] and Nebraska[4] and of the city councils of Minneapolis[5] and Detroit[6] have furnished most of the data suggesting the hypotheses.

Certain qualifications must be made in establishing a frame of reference. First, where comparisons with partisan situations are made, a general two-party system is presumed—not necessarily an "ideal" two-party system, but one in which members of one party may conceivably replace members of another party in office. In one-party situations, a quasi-nonpartisanship obtains that makes comparisons with nonpartisanship meaningless. In addition, where local, rather than general, parties are found, it is probable that some of the characteristics postulated for nonpartisanship would be valid while others would not. Second, what might be called an impersonal type of politics is presumed. Where elections are held in constituencies small enough to have government by personality, it would be unsafe to say that the material below is applicable.

The following are offered as propositions:

*1. Nonpartisanship serves to weaken the political parties in those areas where it is in effect.* This is what its creators intended that it should do. They felt that the established political parties, closely tied up with the system of spoils and other Jacksonian precepts, were not to be trusted. Ideally, they wanted to see the principles of "sound business management" applied to government, not by professional politicians, but by established and successful business men of the community.

The removal of the party label from certain parts of the ballot has resulted in the weakening of political party organizations for several reasons. The reduction in the number of offices to be filled by the parties has weakened them by making active participation in their activities less attractive to the citizen: with fewer elective or appointive jobs available as rewards, there is less incentive for the individual to give his energies. There is not even the incentive of seeking to influence party members in the many areas where the parties are no longer effective in the determination of policy. Furthermore, the removal of some or all of the state and local offices from the party ballot has served to cut away the local roots of the party; weak local

---

3. See Adrian's dissertation and the sources cited therein.

4. A wealth of material is available on the Nebraska legislature, dealing more with unicameralism than with nonpartisanship, however. Much of it has appeared over the years in the *National Municipal Review*. See Adrian, esp. pp. 331–353 and the bibliography.

5. Personal observations by the author supplied this data. There is no comprehensive study of the Minneapolis council.

6. See Maurice M. Ramsey, "Some Aspects of Non-Partisan Government in Detroit, 1918–1940," unpubl. Ph.D. thesis (Ann Arbor, 1944). The author also was again in a position to make personal observations.

organizations in turn have made effective campaigning difficult by removing the ordinary citizen from regular and frequent contact with the parties.[7]

Although, in states where nonpartisanship applies to an important sector of the ballot, the party organizations have been weak. This remains true, for example, in California, Michigan, Minnesota, Nebraska, and North Dakota;[8] and further evidence of the debilitating effect of nonpartisanship upon the established parties is to be found in the attitudes of professional politicians. When the system was first proposed in Minnesota, Republican leaders in large measure stood in opposition to the elimination of the party label.[9] While some Democrats at first believed that the party had nothing to lose in a situation in which it was already extremely weak, they later changed their mind, and leaders of all three of the state's major parties eventually took strong stands against the plan.[10] In Michigan, Democrats at first supported the nonpartisanship movement, but subsequently regretted their action.[11] Party leaders viewed nonpartisanship in the Nebraska legislature with apprehension.[12]

2. *Segration of political leaders strictly to either partisan or nonpartisan areas is the general rule.* The effect of this tendency upon Minnesota politics when the legislature of that state was removed from the party ballot is clearly described in the following quotation:

> The new law which requires county officers and members of the legislature to be elected as nonpartisans takes all of the vitality out of a party campaign. Heretofore it has been the county officers and legislative candidates who have paid most of the expenses and harrowed up the country for the benefit of state candidates. This year it is all different. Only two of the county offices have contests and as they are nonpartisan they are taking no part in the state campaign nor are they paving the way for the state contestants.[13]

---

7. For an extreme example, see John W. Lederle, "Political Party Organization in Detroit, 1920–1934," unpubl. M. A. thesis (Ann Arbor, 1934), and also Arthur Pound, *Detroit; Dynamic City* (New York, 1940). It should be noted, however, that party organization in Michigan has never been very strong; see Arthur C. Millspaugh, *Party Organization and Machinery in Michigan Since 1890* (Baltimore, 1917).

8. The rigidity of structure in a city with a high degree of political organization may delay the weakening effect, especially where nonpartisanship is grafted onto a "machine-governed" city, as was the case in Boston and in the city council in Chicago. In recent years party organizations have been weakened in both cities. The degree to which this has been caused by the long-range effect of nonpartisanship as against possible other causes, including the decline of the factors that made the nineteenth-century political boss possible, this writer is not prepared to say. Recent developments in Boston, in particular, would appear to support the general hypotheses expressed in this paper.

9. Adrian, p. 17.

10. *Ibid.*, Ch. 7 and *passim*. Today, some members of the conservative faction of the Republican Party, for special reasons, appear to be satisfied with the present arrangement (*ibid.*, pp. 377–378).

11. Ramsey, p. 161.

12. See Charles D. Green, "Nebraska Launches Unicameral," *State Government*, Vol. 10, pp. 3–5 (Jan., 1937); Robert L. Cochran, "Nebraska's Unicameral Adjourns," *ibid.*, p. 131 (July, 1937); and William E. Johnson, "Unicameralism Works," *ibid.*, Vol. 12, pp. 198, 207 (Nov., 1939).

13. *Fergus Falls Daily Journal*, Oct. 19, 1914, p. 2.

Here was a basic alteration in traditional campaign techniques. The local organizations had been the very heart of the political parties in Minnesota, but it now became necessary for the parties to establish regional campaign personnel separate from politicians on the local scene. (The obverse situation obtained as well: party state central committees immediately chose virtually to ignore legislative and county contests.) With some exceptions, as indicated below, parallel sets of office-seekers, aides, and organizations had to be created, with very little intercourse between them. This was the case in all four of the areas observed for this article; an individual who wished to become active in politics had to choose one road or the other.

3. *Channels for recruitment of candidates for partisan offices are restricted by nonpartisanship.* It is unusual for a successful nonpartisan politician to move up into higher partisan ranks. Thus the fact that personnel for the two ballots are kept largely separate creates a problem for the parties, which ordinarily use local and legislative positions as the training ground for higher offices.

The problem has not been acute in Minnesota (though certainly it is present), because a workable, particularly competive two-party system has in recent years provided impetus for recruitment of able personnel. But in Michigan where Detroit, most of its suburbs, and other cities have non-partisan elections, the system appears to have had a definitely adverse effect upon the quality of party personnel. This is particularly true of the Democratic party, which draws most of its strength in the state from the city of Detroit, and the results are especially apparent in the consistently low over-all quality of the Wayne County legislative delegation.

In exceptional circumstances an outstanding campaigner from non-partisan ranks will receive overtures from one or both political parties, but even in these rare cases there are many obstacles to success. For example, Edward J. Jeffries, Jr., the greatest vote-getter ever to serve as mayor of Detroit, was wooed by both major parties as a gubernatorial candidate, and after having served four terms as mayor (the longest tenure in the city's history), he filed for the Republican nomination for governor in 1946. He ran a poor fourth in a field of four.[14] Some members of the Minnesota legislature have looked fondly toward the governor's chair; but party regulars understandably take a dim view of bringing in candidates "from outside the party," and success is rare.[15] Since the overwhelming majority of the members of the Nebraska and Minnesota legislatures are inactive in the regular parties and so without chance for further advancement there, their services are not available for positions of higher party leadership. Similarly, almost no members of the Minneapolis or Detroit city councils have been active in

---

14. It should be added that his effort was made after his popularity in Detroit had waned somewhat.

15. For an elaboration on this point, see Adrian, pp. 397–404. These pages compare the situation in Minnesota just before and just after the establishment of nonpartisanship. The change in the political future of the Speaker of the House of Representatives is especially significant.

party affairs, and the same, with only a few exceptions, may be said of the mayors of the two cities. These office-holders are not available to the political parties, or, at the very least, the parties do not wish to avail themselves of their services.

4. *Channels for recruitment of candidates for nonpartisan offices are restricted by nonpartisanship.* The securing of active political party members to fill nonpartisan positions is difficult. In Minneapolis, a party regular seeking a nonpartisan council or mayoralty seat is at a disadvantage and seldom makes good, especially in the case of the former. In Detroit, where nonpartisanship has become a refuge of conservatism, any attempt by an active party member to penetrate into the city's nonpartisan elections, and especially an effort to carry along "partisan politics," is greeted by powerful and effective blasts from the newspapers and from the Detroit Citizens' League. And status as active party members almost invariably places legislative candidates at a disadvantage in Minnesota and Nebraska.

Occasionally it is possible for an active party member to enter the nonpartisan lists and sometimes even go on from there to higher positions within the party. Frank Murphy, the only mayor of Detroit to achieve national fame in the more than three decades since the city's present charter was adopted, was an active Democrat both before and after his tenure in the city hall. Murphy's election, however, was the result of a combination of unusual circumstances—including the recall in 1930 of the incumbent mayor, whose unethical behavior in office had temporarily weakened public confidence in some of the groups ordinarily most influential in choosing the chief executive, the extreme economic depression that affected Detroit even more than the rest of the nation and the very strong support given him by the *Detroit Times;* and Murphy made a strenuous effort to keep his partisan and nonpartisan political activities separate from one another.[16] A few other Detroit mayors have had loose party connections and one had served in Congress before becoming mayor, but that was in the earliest day of nonpartisanship in the city government.[17]

Hubert H. Humphrey, an active Democrat, became mayor of Minneapolis in 1945, but on a largely nonparty campaign to "clean up" the city and with support from the Republican Cowles newspapers. Very active in partisan affairs while mayor, he moved on from that position to the United States Senate, while his successor, who had never been active in partisan activities, returned to the customary nonpartisan pattern. It is also to be remembered that James Michael Curley was for a time head of both the nonpartisan city government and the Democratic party in Boston, although his once vast support was always more of a personal than a party matter.

Certainly cases of party actives successful in obtaining nonpartisan offices are always exceptional. The usual picture finds nonpartisan mayors rising

---

16. Ramsey, pp. 58–59.
17. In addition, Mayor James Couzens was appointed to fill a vacancy in the United States Senate in 1922; but he was not, and had not been, a Republican party regular, and he remained almost continuously at odds with party leaders (*ibid.,* p. 57).

from nonpartisan councils and nonpartisan councilmen coming from political obscurity—successfully reaching the council usually only after several tries have afforded the chance for the public to become familiar with their names.

5. *Limited new channels for recruitment of candidates for nonpartisan offices are opened by nonpartisanship.* Proponents of nonpartisanship have always argued that the system encourages many able, successful, well-known citizens of the community to run for office who would never become candidates under the traditional method since they would be unwilling to become entangled in the ordinary processes of party politics. There is evidence in all nonpartisan jurisdictions to support this contention. To be sure, the candidate under any elective system (except, perhaps, in very small communities with a purely personal type of government) must have a yen, or at least a tolerance, for electioneering; but many persons who have established reputations as business or professional men would fear the condescending attitudes often taken by Americans toward candidates who engage in party activities. These individuals sometimes can be persuaded to hold a nonpartisan office in the council or legislature as a civic duty. Such persuasion appears to be effective from time to time and probably helps bring many capable persons into law-making bodies or mayoralty offices.

Nonpartisanship does not, however, *insure* the filling of available seats from among the community's successful. The individual who has never "made good" at anything else, who is a perennial office-seeker, and who depends for a livelihood upon scraps from the political table—the "political hack" of the vernacular—is a familiar figure around the Minneapolis council table and certainly is not unknown in the Detroit council or the Minnesota and Nebraska legislatures.

6. *Segregation of funds for financing nonpartisan and partisan election campaigns is nearly complete.* Nonpartisanship has produced parallel financing systems. In Michigan this separation of funds is required by law,[18] but even in Minnesota, where rapport with the regular parties is close to being established, most individual candidates must shift for themselves. In that state, the Republicans, indirectly and *sub rosa,* give aid to certain needy candidates who agree to join the Conservative caucus in the legislature; but the Democratic Party has given no similar assistance, and the general practice in nonpartisan jurisdictions is for the individual candidate to seek out his own support. This is hardly surprising in light of the fact that political parties are almost never really rich and, needing money to support their own candidates, can scarcely be expected to give assistance to persons over whom they probably would exercise little or no control, granted election.[19]

18. To discourage direct party activities, Michigan law prohibits overt participation by parties in nonpartisan elections and forbids both party endorsements previous to election and the spending of party money on behalf of nonpartisan candidates. The law is so drawn as to be easily circumvented, but little evasion appears to take place. Minnesota, in contrast, has no such legal restrictions.

19. In this connection, see the quotation above (referred to by n. 13) from the *Fergus Falls Daily Journal.*

Individual financing has a tendency to confuse the voting public, leading many persons into believing that, while the political parties are beholden to those who pay their bills, nonpartisans are "independent." This naive belief is often encouraged in nonpartisan jurisdictions and results in a definitely undesirable development, for it means that the public is quite unaware of the nature of the commitments made by, or the type of support being given, a candidate. (The fact that state law may require the filing of a statement of campaign contributions does not fundamentally alter this situation.)

7. *Facilities for fund-raising by candidates for nonpartisan offices are restricted by nonpartisanship.* Under the traditional political system, the party carries on much of the financing burden as a staff function. If a candidate can secure organizational backing, he is free to carry on his campaign with little or no worry about the requisite funds: the party has machinery to care for this problem. On the other hand, the nonpartisan candidate is an individual who, when he first enters politics, has no organized support or money-raising mechanism. When he knows that he must spend his own money, or that of friends, or persuade an important interest group to give him aid, the burden of campaigning is made so heavy that the likelihood of an individual's trying to gain a seat is decreased. When this situation is combined with the discouraging advantage held by the incumbent (discussed below), it is not surprising that relatively few persons run for nonpartisan offices and that those who do become candidates do not, and cannot campaign extensively.[20]

8. *Nonpartisanship encourages the avoidance of issues of policy in campaigns.* Since voting "for the man" and other frontier concepts have kept American political parties from exercising responsibility, the lack of definite platforms and the failure to carry out concrete campaign promises under nonpartisanship have not been as apparent as would otherwise be the case. The system does not make campaigning upon issues profitable, but discourages it even more than does the present party system. Seldom does a nonpartisan candidate take a firm, widely-publicized stand upon the important issues of the day, and this is especially true if he is running for a seat in a collegial body.[21] He prefers to take no stand at all, or an ambiguous one, or to discuss irrelevancies. He would rather try to be all things to all people, depending upon a well-known political name, or upon religious, ethnic, or other ex-

---

20. This conclusion is based largely upon personal observations of the author. See also the comments of W. K. Kelsey in the *Detroit News,* Sept. 14, 1951, p. 30.

21. In the not untypical 1951 election for the Detroit council, perhaps two of the eighteen finalists in the run-off could be said to have campaigned energetically and clearly upon several major issues of the day. A few others made fairly definite positions known on one or two issues. Most candidates preferred ambiguity, generality, or silence upon these matters. One incumbent campaigned for "the perpetuation of our way of life," while another stood largely on the implicit platform that he had been an able shortstop on the Detroit Tigers' baseball club. A similar type of campaign regularly takes place in Minneapolis. For many illustrations from Minnesota legislative campaigns, see Adrian, pp. 187–235.

traneous associations.[22] In fact, fence-straddling is much more tempting than under the conventional election system, since in the latter the presence of a party label suggests some sort of "position" to the electorate. And since under nonpartisanship the voter seldom can associate a candidate with a position, he comes, as a last resort in his confusion, to choose "name" candidates. This means that there is a premium upon personal publicity; that the individual with newspaper backing often has an inordinate advantage; and that the *incumbent* nearly always (unless he has somehow managed to develop notoriety) is in a very strong position simply because his name has appeared more or less regularly before the public during his years in office.

9. *Nonpartisanship tends to frustrate protest voting.* This is so because the electorate, when disgruntled, tends to vote on a party basis and, of course, cannot do so without party labels. American politics is characterized by an "in" party versus an "out" party. Even if there is little philosophical cohesion within each, there is at least the label to serve as a guide for the voter. Under ordinary circumstances, the voter will accept the "in" group; but in times of grave dissatisfaction he can turn to the "out" party for the hope of relief. In nonpartisan jurisdictions, this is impossible. In the first place, there is no collectively identifiable "in" or "out" group. Whether or not there is within a legislative body a majority clique, caucus, or set indebted to the same interest groups, its members are to the voter, who seeks to hold them accountable, merely a collection of individual names. In the second place, if the voter seeks to "turn the rascals out," he has no guide for doing so. He may, if interested enough, determine the incumbents' names, but he usually has no way of knowing whether the opposing candidates will follow a policy of reform, or whatever it is that the voter desires. In partisan politics, the "out" party under such circumstances would promise changes akin to what the voter wanted and could be held accountable for producing them after the election. But the non-incumbent nonpartisan candidate usually prefers the middle-of-the-road; even if he makes definite commitments, his eventual voting behavior can be known to the individual voter only with the greatest difficulty, and under no circumstances need he bear responsibility for the acts of the body to which he belongs.

Although violent changes have taken place in partisan legislative bodies, as in the early day of the great depression, no similar drastic changes can be found in nonpartisan bodies. In 1931 the Michigan House of Representatives was under Republican control by a majority of ninety-eight to two; in 1933 the Democrats organized the House with a fifty-five to forty-five majority. A similar result took place in the Senate, where in 1931 the Republicans held a majority of thirty-one to one; two years later the Democrats were in control with an advantage of seventeen to fifteen.[23] Evidence of the effectiveness of

---

22. For a detailed description of a vicious use of extraneous associations in a municipal nonpartisan campaign, see Carl O. Smith and Stephen B. Sarasohn. "Hate Propaganda in Detroit," *Public Opinion Quarterly,* Vol. 10, pp. 24–52 (Spring, 1946).

23. *Michigan Legislative Handbook,* 1931–1933.

protest voting was even more spectacular in the state of Washington. There, the Republicans held a majority in the 1931 House of Representatives of ninety to eight. In 1935 the relative positions had been completely reversed and the Democrats were in control, ninety-one to eight. Similarly, in the 1931 Washington Senate the Republicans were in charge, forty-one to one; four years later the Democrats held a majority of thirty-seven to nine.[24] No such changes took place in the nonpartisan Minnesota legislature during the same period, despite drastic changes in the partisan state offices. In 1931 when the Farmer-Labor radical Floyd B. Olson was swept into the governorship, the House Liberals were too weak even to have a candidate for the speakership.[25] In 1933, fifty-eight per cent of the House and fifty-five per cent of the Senate were made up of incumbent holdovers from the previous conservative era. Olson never held a working majority in either house, although he won three consecutive decisive victories for himself. The voters apparently did not know how to give him a legislative majority.[26]

10. *Nonpartisanship produces a legislative body with a relatively high percentage of experienced members, making for conservatism.* This follows from the lack of provision for protest voting, the scarcity of campaigns based upon issues, and the resultant advantage given the incumbent as the voter casts about for a familiar name.

In Minnesota, nonpartisanship has produced a continuing trend toward a large number of holdovers from one legislature to the next.[27] In Nebraska, the trend has been striking and uninterrupted since the adoption of nonpartisanship[28] and in Detroit the incumbent's advantage has been one of the most definite characteristics of elections to the council.[29] In the 1951 Detroit election, in fact, all nine incumbents were returned to office. An incumbent in that city is rarely defeated so long as he contests for a seat.

A study of ten non-southern states made a number of years ago indicated

---

24. Leslie Lipson, *The American Governor; From Figurehead to Leader* (Chicago, 1939), p. 28.

25. See Adrian, pp. 116–123.

26. *Ibid.*, pp. 320–330, Table 13. Also see Arthur Naftalin, "The Failure of the Farmer-Labor Party to Capture Control of the Minnesota Legislature," *American Political Science Review*, Vol. 38, pp. 71–78 (Feb., 1944).

27. In the six elections for the House preceding the establishment of nonpartisanship, the percentage of holdovers averaged 36.8. In the six elections following, the holdovers averaged 50.9 per cent and the trend continued, reaching an all-time high of 77.9 per cent in the election of 1944. Senate elections followed a similar development. For complete data, see Adrian, pp. 236–243 and Table 13.

28. *Ibid.*, pp. 345–346, Table 18. In the six elections for the House preceding the establishment of nonpartisanship, the percentage of holdovers averaged 41.6; for the Senate, 46.9. In the six elections following, holdovers amounted to 56.2 per cent. The percentage followed an *uninterrupted* upward trend, reaching 62.7 per cent in the 1948 election. In each election since 1944, the percentage of holdovers has been higher than it ever was in *any* election under the partisan system. (Figures for 1950 are not available.)

29. Ramsey, pp. 86–92, 107, cites statistics demonstrating that "the public showed a marked preference for incumbents and lengthy tenure was frequent."

that Minnesota had a more experienced legislature than any except the most populous states, where the salary is outstanding (among state legislatures) and a high degree of political organization aids stability.[30] Unlike the situation in many state legislatures (as in the Michigan and Washington cases cited above), where first and second-term members must be called upon to shoulder committee chairmanships and other important positions, the Minnesota legislature has almost never had to place inexperienced persons in key positions. This is also true in the Nebraska legislature and in nonpartisan city councils.

The tendency to reëlect members of the policy-making body has helped to make nonpartisan organizations lean toward conservatism. As indicated above, traditional legislative bodies are often called upon to sacrifice experience for flexibility in the face of demands of the public. Sessions that result are often chaotic, but they are ordinarily productive and responsive. Under nonpartisanship, a much more conservative approach may be expected, and as a result there is a tendency for legislators to diverge from contemporary public thinking on issues.[31]

In Detroit, and to a lesser extent in Minneapolis, the vacuum caused by the absence of party labels as a guide for the voter has been partly filled by newspaper activity. Since daily newspapers are for the most part conservative, especially on local affairs, and since they have a disproportionate advantage in nonpartisan elections by the dissemination of all-important publicity, the conservative tendency of nonpartisan bodies is enhanced. (In legislative constituencies of rural Nebraska and Minnesota, newspapers are of less influence than they are in metropolitan areas, probably because of the more personal nature of a rural campaign.)

*11. There is no collective responsibility in a nonpartisan body.* This follows from the fact that there is no unifying organization or symbol. Each individual stands alone, responsible to his constituents for his own acts only, and for them but vaguely, since nonpartisan campaigns do not ordinarily center upon definite issues. Individual political behavior is not tempered by the fact that a political party has "a past to honor and a future to protect," in the words of a former Minnesota governor.

Without collective responsibility and a well-knit internal organization, a legislative body is likely to be lacking in a collective, comprehensive program. This often results either in a great deal of wasted motion and ineffective floundering or in the leadership's passing to an individual outside the legislative body who is in the public eye—the governor or mayor. In Nebraska, the former appears to have resulted,[32] while in Minnesota the governor has become the dominant policy-maker, taking away much of the potential

---

30. See Charles S. Hyneman, "Tenure and Turnover of Legislative Personnel," *Annals,* Vol. 195, pp. 21–31 (Jan., 1938).

31. For the difficulties experienced by Floyd B. Olson owing to this phenomenon, see Adrian, pp. 273–289.

32. *Ibid.,* pp. 337–338, 350–352, and the sources there cited.

legislative leadership.[33] In Detroit, the mayor has completely overshadowed the council in policy leadership—aided, to be sure, by the fact that the city has a strong-mayor form of organization.

Without collective responsibility, no one, except possibly the governor, is answerable for the budget in Nebraska or Minnesota. The individual legislator can always, and frequently does, assert that he voted for those items of interest to his district, while disclaiming responsibility for the budget as a whole, or for the legislative pork barrel. From the beginning of legislative nonpartisanship in Minnesota, claims have been made that the system encourages excessive legislative expenditures and logrolling for this reason. The writer has heard similar charges voiced against the Minneapolis and even the Detroit councils, although the fact that the latter is elected at large probably mitigates the tendency there. The Nebraska legislature has been charged with being a "fraternity of tolerance" because of vote trading and pork barreling.[34] Nonpartisan legislatures could hardly be called unique in this respect, but the lack of a party answerable for padding of the budget surely places legislators in sore temptation.

It should be noted that although the Minnesota legislature is organized into two caucuses, "Liberal" and "Conservative" to which nearly all members nominally belong, these two groups do not bear collective responsibility for legislative actions. Caucus labels do not appear on the ballot, and the voter often finds it very difficult to discover the allegiance of a non-incumbent candidate, especially since membership is largely optional and often is not announced publicly until after election. Furthermore, caucuses do not directly parallel the two major parties and are not party adjuncts; caucus membership may be very nominal; and both caucuses are without effective methods of disciplining "members."

The twenty-six member Minneapolis city council is likewise divided into two caucuses, "Liberal" and "Progressive," but the same statements may be made about this structural arrangement as have been made concerning the Minnesota legislative caucuses. The Nebraska legislature, in a proper respecting of the spirit of nonpartisanship, does not have caucus organizations, while the Detroit and many other nonpartisan city councils are too small to have even a nominal bifurcation.

---

33. *Ibid.,* Ch. 5.
34. See Richard C. Spencer, "Nebraska Idea Fifteen Years Old," *National Municipal Review,* Vol. 39, p. 86 (Feb., 1950).

# THE PROMOTION OF THE
# CITY MANAGER PLAN

DON K. PRICE

IT WOULD HAVE BEEN amusing to write the history of the city manager plan in terms of symbols and publicity techniques alone. By looking at only one aspect of the history of the plan, the narrator could show most plausibly how the hand that manipulates the symbols rules the world. For example—

The city manager plan, the form of municipal government under which an elected council appoints and may remove an over-all chief administrator, was invented and most effectively promoted not by an experienced public official, and not by any seasoned student of political science, but by a young advertising man who, as he remarked years later in a reminiscent mood, had the knack of "simplifying things until they were no longer so." This young man, Mr. Richard S. Childs, started the Short Ballot Organization as a part-time hobby, with the assistance of a gentleman who had written a book on Congressional Government without ever setting foot in the United States Capitol—Mr. Woodrow Wilson. Mr. Childs found the "commission government" movement well under way, and so he proposed the new idea, part of which was borrowed from a small Virginia city, as the most modern version of the commission plan, and perhaps with his tongue in his cheek, stoutly defended the new idea against the charge of unorthodoxy. At the same time, he fused the symbols of Big Business with those of the New Freedom— "business corporation," "board of directors," "popular government," "political responsibility."

To continue with this factually accurate but completely unbalanced story: Articles signed or ghost-written by Mr. Childs began to appear in leaflets or magazines throughout the country. They made much of the new municipal official whose name itself was a slogan, consciously chosen as such—the city manager. A charter that Mr. Childs had a draftsman prepare for the city of Lockport, New York, although never put into effect, was inserted on *pink* paper in Mr. Charles A. Beard's otherwise colorless *Loose-leaf Digest of Short Ballot Charters*. Newspapers and magazines about the country began to report the city manager plan as if it were actually in operation, and phrases

Reprinted from *Public Opinion Quarterly*, 5, No. 4 (Winter, 1941), 563–578, by permission of the publisher and the author.

from Mr. Childs' pamphlets found their way into editorials and after-dinner speeches and became a part of the stock-in-trade of the municipal reform movement. And thus hundreds of cities were led to adopt the city manager plan by a man who remained so inconspicuous that no one at the first convention of city managers that he attended had ever heard of him.

But students of public opinion do not need to be told this story, for they know already that symbols and publicity techniques are useful in promotional campaigns. The significant story is another one: how some symbols were in harmony with the essential nature of the plan and therefore furthered its acceptance, while other symbols handicapped the plan, even though they were used by those who sought to promote it, because they were not suited to the plan's original purpose, and those who used them did not believe in that purpose.

The inventor of the city manager plan was, in the current phrase, a manipulator of symbols. He recognized that "any idea that is to be widely spread and remembered must be condensed to a catch-phrase first, even if such reduction means lopping off many of its vital ramifications and making it false in many of its natural applications." But at the same time, he was deeply concerned with the fundamental structure of government and was convinced that the structure itself could do much to facilitate or impede the effectiveness of public opinion.

Mr. Childs' principal contribution was not the invention and popularization of new symbols. Most of the original symbols of the city manager plan had already been used by advocates of commission government. What Mr. Childs did was to add substance to the symbols, by proposing a structural change in conformity with their essential spirit. Commission government, its advocates said, was "just like a corporation with its board of directors." Mr. Childs saw that this "catch phrase has converted whole cities," but remarked that the commission would not be like a board of directors until it would "appoint a manager who in turn would hire the departmental heads, reporting regularly to the commission and submitting to it only broad matters of policy." The city manager or commission-manager plan was Mr. Childs' effort to make the commission do so.

## To Make Public Opinion Effective

Mr. Childs intended the city manager plan to make public opinion effective in municipal affairs. He saw two obstacles to the effectiveness of public opinion—first, that the public was trying to choose too many public officials; second, that municipal governments had to work under intricate systems of checks and balances and legalistic procedures, all of which could be used as barricades by those who wished to fight rear-guard actions against government. To overcome the first obstacle he proposed the "short ballot"; to overcome the second, he proposed a brief charter that simply gave a single small council full control of the city government, with all legislative powers and the power to control the administration of its ordinances by hiring and firing its chief administrative official. Public opinion, he thought, would be most effective if the electorate delegated to a governing body the job of enacting policies, and if the governing body delegated to an expert administrator the job of putting those policies into effect.

The two principal symbols of the city manager plan were based on positive ideas. The adoption of these ideas provided more workable methods for the expression of public opinion on the primary questions, those which public opinion was solely qualified to answer, and discouraged the expression of public opinion on matters in which public opinion would be irrelevant, incompetent, and immaterial.

The first symbol was the "business corporation." It was easy to point to the typical, or at any rate the ideal, business corporation, purposeful in its policies, efficient in its administration, and then in contrast show how the municipal corporation was directed without a program and managed without vigor. The proposal to have the municipality run like a private business meant the abolition of the double standard between business and government that had existed so long in American political thought; the city government was no longer to be tied up in legal red tape, with the selection of all its employees and the spending of each of its dollars subject to ratification by either popular vote, or by several committees or independently elected officials. The city government was no longer to be a parochial institution; like modern business, it was to draw on the entire nation for personnel, purchases, and ideas. The city government, in short, was to become a working institution, controlled by a board of directors who would have plenty of power and discretion from election to election.

The second of these symbols was the manager himself. The word "manager" suggested common sense, energy, leadership, and a preoccupation with results rather than forms and procedures. It implied responsibility to an appointing authority and expertness at a task. Above all, it signified general authority and responsibility for the ways in which policies were effected, and for the choice and control of employees.

## The Effects of These Symbols

It is unnecessary to review in detail the effect of these symbols. Wherever an organized effort was being made to improve local government, their appeal was felt. The city manager plan became a movement, and, as its originator expected, the superficial aspects of the movement were sometimes adopted without its substance. In one small city, for example, where the public works director was known as the city commissioner, the city council adopted a resolution that ran substantially as follows:

WHEREAS it is getting to be the fashion for up-to-date cities to have city managers, and WHEREAS it will make . . . City look like an up-to-date city to have a city manager; therefore, be it *Resolved* that the title of the present city commissioner be changed to city manager.

The principal symbols of the city manager plan were in harmony with the idea that government should be strengthened and made capable of rendering service, rather than weakened to prevent it from doing harm. It was therefore appropriate, no matter how illogical it seemed to some of the leaders of the good government movement, that local campaigners for the adoption of the city manager plan usually put their greatest emphasis on the accomplishment of some specific objective—such as the enforcement of moral regulations or the construction of streets and parks—that was quite distinct from the proposal to change the structure of the government.

Few cities cared what their municipal organization charts looked like, and few people in them cared very much whether municipal employees were selected for merit or by patronage. On the other hand, it often became clear to municipal leaders that the community could not achieve its objective—any important objective—if the structure of government did not permit the city to take two steps: first, organize a majority to make a decision; second, enable that majority to protect against the obstructive tactics of the minority those who put the decision into effect.

Lynchburg, Virginia, had a bicameral council elected by wards: on one occasion it had taken ten months of parliamentary maneuvering to get a $500 sidewalk built, although twenty-one of the twenty-four elected representatives had approved the project from the beginning. The leading advocates of a street paving program in Lynchburg wanted the city manager plan for what it would enable them to do; it was perfectly sensible for the community to emphasize its ultimate purpose, rather than its intermediary purpose, in considering the adoption of the city manager plan.

The interest in general policy was closely accompanied by an interest in personalities in most of these campaigns for the adoption of the city manager plan. As the arguments and discussions of the average campaign clearly indicated, the voters wanted to take one group of leaders out of power and put another group in, and were more interested in doing so than in the details of the charter for which they were voting.

This was not true in cities like Lynchburg, which had managed to keep its community leadership on the city council by continuing to attach more prestige to municipal service than to commercial success. But elsewhere it was quite obvious that the community could accomplish nothing unless it not only simplified its municipal structure, but changed its mind about the worth of municipal political leadership and put its most esteemed men and effective leaders into municipal office.

For this purpose, the proposal to make government "nonpolitical" under the city manager plan was a symbol of the greatest importance in those cities where "politics" had been lowest in connotation and in practice. A businessman of importance could not be induced to take part in "politics," but he might be drafted for a position on the municipal council if he were assured that the municipality was to be managed like a business corporation.

## How It Worked

In practice, it was not often the business magnate or the large employer who was drafted for councilmanic service, but citizens who were neither employers nor labor—professional men, salaried executives, small businessmen—who as leaders in church, service club, or lodge would undertake community responsibility only if the curse of "politics" were removed. And in common usage, the antithesis of politics was "business."

The antithesis of "business" in some industrial communities was also "labor." Organized labor in most American cities was not especially interested in increasing governmental services during the 1920's. Its members, or at least its leaders, were usually skilled tradesmen, homeowners and taxpayers, who were not at all eager to help pay for public works to gratify the pride of the Chamber of Commerce, or for social services to further the health and welfare of the very poor. The city manager movement made no very positive appeal to trades unions, which sometimes supported the city manager plan, but were more often lukewarm or actually in opposition.

Chambers of commerce appealed in the average towns to the type of local businessman who was willing to work collectively with his fellows and to exchange ideas with other cities. The same type of businessman took to the city manager plan. (My personal hunch is that the interest and influence of the local businessman in municipal affairs have been reduced in many cities by the displacement of the small independent businessman by the branch manager of the national corporation, and by the movement of community leaders into suburbs outside of the limits of the city where they do business; this hunch needs to be proved or disproved by more systematic observation.) The American City Bureau, an institution which trained civic workers and secretaries for chambers of commerce, taught them the superiority of the city manager plan. The United States Chamber of Commerce publicized it, though never taking a formal stand on the matter.

The American Federation of Labor headquarters, although it too has never taken an official stand, has usually answered inquiries about the city manager plan from its locals with rather discouraging advice. It once, for example, referred to the symbol that, by branding as an "alien" the city manager who is not a resident when appointed, has had the greatest adverse effect on the growth of the profession. The manager, it said, "is generally selected from another state and therefore has no conception of the sentiment among the people regarding their desires as to how the city shall be conducted." It is curious that this prejudice against hiring a city manager from out of town should exist, unless it can be explained on the grounds of the belief that the public payroll—except for school superintendents—should be reserved for neighbors of the taxpayer, for there is usually little prejudice against out-of-town ministers or labor union organizers.

In spite of all this, the student of political science, and more especially the student of economics, is likely to read far too great a flavor of industrial dispute into municipal politics. The contest in municipal politics is often one side of the tracks against the other; occasionally it is one nationality or one denomination against another. But even in a town like Jackson, Michigan, which before the first World War had a strong Socialist movement in those wards which were predominantly German, Irish, and Polish, Democratic, Catholic, and "wet," and where the factory owners all lived in wards that were predominantly Republican, Protestant, British in national origin, and prohibitionist, the issue over the city manager plan had nothing to do with the traditional issue between "conservative" and "radical." Time after time in such cities, research on the history of the city manager plan showed, the so-called "businessmen's" group got a new city manager who introduced new social services, while the representatives of the "across the tracks" section ridiculed social welfare programs and opposed the idea of expert administration. At the same time, the title "manager" had probably had a rather favorable connotation among workingmen, who objected to it no more than to that of the Sunday School "superintendent." Recognizing that the title "manager" was a plus symbol, the leaders of the opposition to the city manager plan have always had to call the manager something else—in the old days, "czar," in more recent years, "dictator."

The connotation of the symbols which connect the city manager plan with "business" has probably become less favorable during the past decade. The prestige of the businessman and business ideas in government has been pretty badly battered, but the original symbols are probably still useful except in communities that have seen acute industrial disputes.

The city manager plan has become snarled in its own symbols less often because their connotation has changed for the worse than because many of its supporters have not believed in its original and fundamental ideas.

## What City Government Should Do

Back of the symbol of the business corporation was the idea that the city government should do an important job and a productive job rather than confine itself to regulatory functions and ceremonial. Back of the symbol of the manager there was the idea that the city government should go about its job with a primary emphasis on results rather than on ritual and procedure. And back of both of these ideas was the primary approach of the original sponsors of the plan: "Good government is not our object. The short ballot movement is a contest for *popular* government." The original advocates of the city manager plan were not proposing to lower tax rates, to introduce a merit system, to destroy the influence of national parties in local affairs, to make administration more efficient—they were proposing primarily to make city government more democratic, to make "every man a politician."

Instead of advocating the city manager plan as a vehicle for expanding and vitalizing the social services of the municipality, in many a city its supporters have handicapped it by implying that "business-like government" would be cheap government, and by making extravagant promises of reductions in expenditures and tax rates without waiting to discover whether or not a business-like investigation would show a need for an increase in capital investment and maintenance expenditures. Such promises had little appeal to begin with, and handicapped the city manager plan after its installation in two ways. First, many a city manager found himself being attacked as a cold-hearted economizer, a boss with "ice water veins," even if he were actually instituting new social services and persuading a surprised council that it should spend more money rather than less. Second, many a property owner supported the city manager plan to get taxes reduced and withdrew his support when he found that they were not.

Instead of emphasizing the positive virtues of the city manager plan, many of its supporters have made the error of proposing it as a means of abolishing machine or boss rule in cities that never had machines or bosses. The symbol of the boss is an inviting target for the attack of reformers, especially when it is taken straight from the classic mythology of Thomas Nast: fat paunch, checked suit, big cigar, and all. The idea of a machine, although a little less tangible, will do well enough. But it is doubtful strategy to label as a machine the "city hall crowd" that happens to hold office at the moment, regardless of whether it has a continuous and cohesive organization, or to label as a boss an amateur politician who likes to get jobs for his friends or fix their parking tickets. The voter, especially in a small city, is too likely to know the man in question as a deacon in his church who has a fondness for getting about with the boys, and to dismiss the labeller as an officious busybody.

The second fundamental idea on which the manager plan was originally based—the idea of emphasizing first the job to be done and second the discretion to be given the governing board and its appointee in doing that job—has been violated by supporters of the manager plan who have insisted on emphasizing procedure rather than purpose in the arguments that they have presented to the public. They have done so in three ways.

## Rule of Political Etiquette

First, they have tried to impose on the city manager a most un-American rule of political etiquette. They have promised that under the city manager plan the city manager would not only refrain from taking part in political campaigns, i.e., contests for public office, but would not be connected in any way with factional disputes and would not undertake to promote policies. Those who did so were following such expert opinions as that of I. G. (now Sir Gwilym) Gibbon, then assistant secretary to the British Ministry of Health, who warned the city managers in 1925 that the future of the whole movement was imperiled by the incursion of city managers into matters of policy, because by becoming identified with questions of policy they risked discharge when policies changed.

Generally speaking, this idea has never taken root in America. In Great Britain, the civil servant, like Jeeves, takes pride in carrying out with discreet reserve the whims of his elected masters, and in offering advice only confidentially on request. But in the United States, Bertie Wooster's Jeeves is not as close to the popular ideal of a servant as is Jack Benny's Rochester. The public admiration of the city manager who is not afraid to disagree with the council that appoints him has been so marked that it has occasionally, I suspect, led certain managers to make an unmannerly show of their "independence." But the council's privilege of discharging the city manager at will has held such tendencies in check pretty effectively.

In city after city where the manager plan was studied, it was clear that the manager was less likely to get fired for advocating a policy than for administering one; less for proposing a bond issue or a health program than for firing somebody's cousin, or collecting somebody's taxes, or refusing someone a building permit. The city managers who held their jobs in the face of early political turmoil were those who, with their council's approval, led their communities into popular new policies and distinguished themselves as much by their leadership as by their operating efficiency.

It was inevitable that the city manager would become identified with policies and would be unable to observe the principle of anonymity. He had to make recommendations to the council and no one could keep gossip and newspaper reporters from picturing him rather than his superiors, the council members, as responsible for the measures that they adopted. It has therefore been a mistake for advocates of the city manager plan to assure the public in advance that the city manager will not become involved in disputes over policies, and to give the opposition the argument that he ought not to do so.

## The City Manager Charter

Second, too many advocates of the city manager plan, because of their interest in "good government," have rejected the original idea of emphasizing purpose and leadership rather than procedures and checks and balances, and have put far too much reliance on the city manager charter. Almost invariably excessive emphasis on charter provisions defining procedures under the city manager plan has led to or been a result of weak councilmanic leadership. It is hard to persuade the public at once to support a political leader and to support provisions that imply a distrust of him.

As a matter of practical strategy, it should be obvious that a charter may be a prerequisite, but it cannot be a guarantee, of city manager government. For the essential theory of the city manager plan, and an effective feature of every city manager charter, is that the city manager shall be continuously responsible to the council and shall serve at its pleasure. The relationship between council and manager is so intimate that it is generally impossible to prove whether the manager is using his own judgment in taking an administrative action or is acting under coercion or threat by the council or some of its members, or whether the council in adopting a policy is following the ideas originated by its members or the advice of the city manager. A manager may be discharged merely for doing his legal duty and the courts will not interfere. Yet in city after city the charter has been set up as the principal symbol of city manager government; indeed in Cincinnati the plan is popularly known as "charter government."

In consequence, a great deal of energy has usually been devoted to talking about the charter, and too little energy and leadership have gone into service on the council. In San Diego, this tendency was carried to its logical conclusion. After four years of expensive and arduous effort at charter drafting, the reform group that got the city manager charter enacted refused to enlist or support candidates for the council, hoping, as its leader explained privately, that "the public may be aroused by the time the campaign is over to a point of a lack of confidence in those [councilmen] elected, and that they will then be in a mood to place their hopes in the city manager."

The reform group then tried to get the councilmen to delegate authority freely to the city manager by acting as a sort of unofficial supreme court, looking on the "city manager formula" in the charter as a municipal constitution; they tried to defend the city manager's control over personnel, for example, primarily in order to keep the council from misusing its influence over appointments.

The reform group discovered by experience what too few cities have been told as they adopted the city manager plan: that it is useful as a system to enable elected representatives to get something done, but it is useless as tactics to keep them from doing the wrong things. In short, it is impossible to enforce the proper confidential relationship between master and servant by publicity, and the city manager is very definitely in the position of servant to the council—as the San Diego council proved to the reform group in question by firing four managers in less than three years and giving none of them a chance to do a job.

The early publicity for the city manager plan made a sharp distinction between the scope of the work that the city council ought to permit the manager to do and the scope of the powers granted him by the charter. The theorists who invented the city manager did not want him to be a mere routine clerk; on the contrary they wanted him to exercise broad discretion in the administration of policies and to help to formulate new policies of social welfare and municipal enterprise. But thinking of the council's ability to discharge the city manager at will—the primary feature of the city manager plan—they wanted to make it clear that the manager would be given administrative powers because the council would want to get a good job done, not at all because the charter said so. And they explicitly insisted that a city manager charter should not restrict the council's authority over administrative matters.

In the early publicity for the plan, the charter was considered mainly as a device to free the council from existing legal restrictions so that it could employ a manager and delegate power to him. The first city persuaded by this publicity adopted a one-sentence "charter," an optional law empowering the council to "employ a male person of sound discretion and of good moral character not of their number of such salary and upon such terms as they may decide, who shall be subject to such rules and regulations as may be provided by said councilmen." And in the state where the city manager plan has made the greatest progress—I am referring to Virginia, where 21 of the 29 cities of more than 5,000 population have adopted the plan—the usual legal procedure has been for a city to adopt the state optional law. This law (which merely states in a few brief paragraphs that the city council shall be the legislative body and the city manager shall be its chief executive officer, holding office at its pleasure, and which otherwise has no effect on the municipality) contains none of the gadgets which have been added to so many "home rule" charters as integral parts of the city manager plan.

In too many cities advocates of the city manager plan, desiring primarily to hamstring the politician, have thought of the essential features of the plan as secondary to such gadgets as election by proportional representation, prohibitions of political activity on the part of employees and of employment for political reasons, or a charter provision forbidding councilmen on penalty of fine, imprisonment, and removal from office, to interfere with the administrative work or appointments of the city manager.

## Proportional Representation

But of all these the greatest handicap to the promotion of the city manager plan has been proportional representation. P.R. and the city manager plan have no essential relationship; the city manager plan, indeed, is peculiarly ill-suited to P.R. Under the city manager plan, if there is any political division at all within the council, it is peculiarly necessary to have a consistent majority. For under this plan the council is not only a legislature, but a governing or an executive board, which will not work through its executive officer—the city manager—unless its members, or a majority of them, have confidence in him. If P.R., as its logic intends, brings to the council representatives of all groups, and assures them that they can keep their seats if they maintain minority support, the city manager will be in a most difficult position. If there is no coherent majority, but only shifting alliances of members who are *consciously* group representatives, the manager is likely to antagonize each of them in turn if he attempts in any way to provide administrative leadership.

A "strong mayor" may have enough legal authority and political independence to preserve a degree of administrative integration and order even if his council runs off in different directions after different policies; a city manager, being responsible to the council, can do nothing of the sort. If there are factions in the city so antagonistic that they will not ally themselves during a campaign, it is exceedingly dangerous to assure them seats in the council and expect them to unite in favor of an administrative program after the election. The story of ward elections under the city manager plan shows clearly how easy it is for a minority group—if sure of a seat or two on the council—to disrupt municipal administration, and to wreck a reform or policies that have majority support.

Regardless of the merits of P.R., however, to connect it with the city manager plan is to check the spread of the city manager plan. The American Proportional Representation League worked for twenty-two years without effect, until it began to concentrate its efforts on cities considering the manager plan. Since then about five hundred cities have adopted the manager plan, but less than a dozen of them—in spite of the virtual consolidation of the city manager and P.R. movements—have been induced to try P.R. The comparative popularity of the two devices leads to the conclusion that the city manager plan is relatively popular, and that it would be accepted much more readily alone than in combination with P.R.

What has been the effect on public opinion of the emphasis on charter detail? The answer to this question cannot be quantitative. It cannot be expressed in terms of number of votes for or against charters, or for and against "reform" councilmen. A statement in such terms, whether accurate or not, would be irrelevant, for two reasons. First, the spread of the city manager plan has been checked most effectively not by defeats in charter elections, but by the failure of state legislatures to empower cities to consider the city manager plan. Second, important changes after the adoption of the city manager charter were not brought about by charter changes, or by the election of the same men who had been thrown out by "reform." Public opinion changed in a different way; it did not decide to go back to the old system, it merely lost interest in the city manager plan as the leading reformers lost their zeal. The leading reformers, in turn, cooled off because their interest had been in the charter and in a pattern prescribed in detail by its provisions, and when they saw that the pattern was not being followed as they had planned, they were inclined to voice their distaste for "politics" and drop the matter. And thus a "drafted" council and its city manager would be left without support, simply holding the charter. And after the next election, the city manager plan, which consists in the willingness and ability of the council to delegate administrative authority rather than in any charter provisions, would be quickly abandoned without the change of so much as a comma in the existing law.

It is customary to talk about an invariable "cycle" of reform and corruption in municipal politics, and to deplore the decline in "citizen interest" and the persistence of "sinister influences" that make the downswing of the cycle inevitable. This point of view is a stock excuse of those who try to sell the public political prayer-wheels, or gadgets that will make sure that the voters will want what the salesman thinks they ought to want. For there is available the story of city after city that for many years has had no municipal political machine, no organized corruption, and a fair degree of community coherence; the evidence suggests strongly that the voters are likely to give sustained support to public-spirited political leaders who are willing to adopt rules for the game of local government that facilitate rather than impede the effectiveness of public opinion.

There is no question that the city manager, like other public officials today, needs to have a weighty sense of responsibility to the ideal of his profession, to the integrity of its purpose, and to the effectiveness of its techniques. This is the responsibility which Professor Friedrich has called "functional responsibility." It is significant that the municipal administrators who as a group have developed the strongest sense of functional responsibility have been those who have been subjected to the most immediate and stringent political responsibility—the city managers.

It was unfortunate for the city manager plan and for American local government in general that in so many cities the promotion of the plan was taken over by those who attached the wrong symbols to it—symbols that were inconsistent with its fundamental structure. For they made it a movement of "reform" and a procedural pattern; they hopelessly confused many persons about the relationship of the city manager to public opinion and the democratic process; and by trying to strengthen the city manager's functional responsibility at the expense of his political responsibility, they damaged both without improving either.

They have not completely succeeded, for the city manager plan has done well in spite of its friends, as the improvements that it has effected in nearly five hundred American cities indicate. City after city has forgotten the catchwords for which it adopted the city manager plan and the disillusion which followed, and has retained that plan as a system of responsible government which encourages the expert executive to make the greatest possible contribution to policy and administration without even momentary immunity from political responsibility.

# THE ROLE OF THE CITY MANAGER

## LEONARD D. WHITE

EVERY GENERATION is swept along on the tides of deep-flowing currents, which, unperceived by most men, silently govern the direction of events. The forms and methods of our government—city, state, and national—are ceaselessly modified in a thousand particulars but in a general sequence which reflects the primary drift of the time. To survey the city manager in the large and attempt to grasp the inner significance of his work and position, it is therefore essential to have in mind at least the more obvious of the underlying tendencies of the age.

In any enumeration of these tendencies the steady growth of urban population must be included. The people of the United States are already, and are destined to become in greater measure, city-dwellers—cliff-dwellers of the modern world. The government of the people of the United States is destined to be the government of municipalities. The government of municipalities, especially the larger range, presents in the sharpest form most of the problems of modern democracy and raises insistently the question whether local government can rest on a popular base and hold high standards of operating efficiency.

The course of modern municipal government also reflects the growing conviction of the people of the United States (1) that they must effectively control, and in increasing measure own and operate, the public utilities; and (2) that they can use their government to render service on a scale as yet untouched. This concept of the function of municipal government is crystallizing as rapidly as confidence in the city government is established. The city is understood to be not merely an organization for purposes of construction, to build and maintain pavement, sidewalk, sewers, water pipe, and police stations; it is understood also to exist for the purpose of securing as far as possible the conditions of the good life for its inhabitants. In this larger range of duties co-operate the church, the school, and the municipal government. Education, formal and informal, recreation, reading, the organization of community groups, music, the arts, and loyalty to the general interest of the city are all struggling up into the consciousness of the public authorities as subjects with which they must concern themselves if they are to discharge their full duty to the city.

Having become now the dominant type of local government, and faced with a constantly enlarging program of municipal activity, how are the

Reprinted from *The City Manager* by Leonard D. White (Chicago: The University of Chicago Press, 1927), pp. 292–302, by permission of The University of Chicago Press.

American cities responding to their opportunities? In what way is the structure of municipal institutions being adapted to the greater strain constantly put upon it? The adaptations which the twentieth century has witnessed in the cities are to a considerable extent paralleled by corresponding movements in the state, and even in the national government.

Of these, one of the clearest is the tendency to bring together in the hands of one person the responsibility for the administrative affairs of government. In the United States the director of the Bureau of the Budget is making the president's control of administration effective; in the states, the Illinois Civil Code has led the way in concentrating power in the hands of the governor; in the cities the growth of the strong mayor plan (Boston, New York, Philadelphia) and of the council-manager plan all point in the same direction. The unco-ordinated, disorganized many-headed administrative systems of the states and of the cities seem to be on their way to disappearance.

Parallel with this movement is the tendency to allow the chief executive a relatively free hand in dealing with the business affairs of the government. The American people distrust the business ability of their elected representatives, especially when acting collectively in a political situation. They view with satisfaction a strong executive, who not only takes the leadership of the council or assembly but who insists on being master in his own house.

This point of view coincides with a gradually emerging preference for a non-partisan administration. This preference is hardly to be discovered in some cities and states, but a broad survey of the course of events of the twentieth century can hardly fail to convince one that the spoils system is gradually receding. Higher standards of official integrity, impartiality, and loyalty are reached decade by decade, however great the variation may be from place to place.

These changes are proceeding along with another profound alteration in our public affairs, the decline of the organized political party. The "machine" has all but disappeared in the small- and medium-sized cities. The state "machine" has gone in many of the western commonwealths. The field is open to a new type of political organization in which idea and ideals are stressed, appointments and contracts neglected. This transformation deserves much more careful study than has been given it, for its consequences are likely to be of great importance.

The conditions of life in America are now such that these changes seem almost inevitable. Governmental problems have become intricate and even more insistent. They call for solution with the aid of science, not with the wisdom of a ward politician. The amazing mobility of the American people leaves no community a law unto itself; each and all are responsible for their own good government to the larger whole of which they are a part. What the whole world is witnessing is the emergence of government by experts, by men and women who are trained technicians highly specialized to perform some service by scientific methods. It is indeed a fair question whether we shall not be forced to reinterpret American government as a means for utilizing the services of experts in the performance of ends democratically defined.

The council-manager plan has an intimate relation to these fundamental tendencies. It is the most perfect expression which the American people have yet evolved of the need for combining efficient administration with adequate popular control. The council, elected for a term of two or four years, sometimes by wards and sometimes at large, representing the voters with whatever fulness the voters demand, holds complete and undivided power over the whole city government. It determines the metes and bounds of city policy; it appropriates the necessary funds; it selects the city manager; and it can remove him at will. There is no separation of power, for all power is in the hands of the council, the direct representatives of the voters. To insure effective and continuing popular control, many cities have adopted the recall with respect to the council—and Dayton with respect to the manager. These arrangements give no valid reason for disputing the essential democracy of the council-manager plan.

The voters, however, do not elect directly, nor do they usually have the power to recall directly, the manager. The operating executive is chosen by a delegate body. American experience shows with sufficient clearness that we cannot expect to maintain high standards of administrative ability in an elective office. Waiving the question whether the voters can be depended upon, year in and year out, to select the best administrative ability, it is perfectly certain that the best executive brains will not be interested in an office to secure which requires the embarrassments of a political campaign, and the tenure of which is liable to interruption by the hazards of later campaigns at the intervals of two or four years. It is true that we cannot depend upon a city council always to make the wisest choice, but it seems clear that the likelihood of having high ability to choose from and of a satisfactory choice are greater when this duty is performed by the council rather than by the voters. This is indeed one of the fundamental advantages of the manager plan. Most city managers could not and would not be elected to the office of mayor, but they have no hesitation in accepting the lesser hazards of the manager's office.

By establishing the confidence of the voters in the integrity and efficiency of the city government, the managers are steadily developing new opportunities to serve the people. It appears in an earlier chapter that the managers are not of one mind concerning the extent of their service to the citizens of their community; but as they succeed, and to the measure of their success, they and their councils will be swept along by a growing desire to utilize in greater and greater degree the service of an efficient municipal government.

The office of manager is a typical specimen of the modern conception of integrated consolidated administrative power. The manager has in full measure the administrative power which the reconstruction of our state and national governments is seeking to acquire for the governors and the president.

The professional manager is himself an expert. He understands the need for experts in the conduct of municipal government. He knows the necessity of allowing experts a substantially free hand in carrying on their specialty and leaves them substantial freedom. He is willing to protect the expert from political or other influence. He is not blind to the necessity of opening up freedom of movement for the expert from city to city, for his own future depends on this same freedom. In short, the effective utilization of expert, trained, and professional service is a characteristic sign of the manager-governed cities.

The manager is profiting by the decline of partisanship and is contributing to the elimination of spoils politics and hidden influence. This unrecognized change in municipal life is sweeping at full tide through the manager cities. There has not been an important political campaign in Winnetka, Illinois, since Manager Woolhiser took charge a decade ago. While differences of opinion are inevitable in most communities and will inevitably crystallize in parties, temporary or permanent, bringing about sharp clashes at the elections, the political life of the American city of the future seems likely to be relatively devoid of the unscrupulous personal "politics" of the past. The managers on the whole are pulling in the center of the stream in this respect.

In fact, as one observes the significant tendencies of the twentieth century in public affairs, one feels that the managers are unconsciously perhaps, but none the less truly, marking out the clear pattern to which certainly municipal government, if not county and state, will conform. The manager movement is the product of deep-lying physical and psychological forces which are bound to affect all levels of government, but, although a product of these forces, they are now serving to intensify them. The American people have a deep conviction that their business organizations and methods are uniquely successful, and they readily understand the resemblance between the city manager and the general superintendent. The council-manager plan seems to be the application of American business methods to government, a practical answer to the demand for more business in government.

The council-manager plan has passed beyond the experimental stage, but it has not, and probably never will, reach the point when problems of great importance and difficulty will not confront it. Some of these problems will be presented by the environment in which manager government finds itself, the character of the town and its principal figures, the quality of its newspapers, chamber of commerce or labor unions; others will be set by the character and quality of the councils; still others by the ability and purposes of the managers themselves. As a student surveys the scene at the end of nearly two decades' experience with the manager plan, he may readily discover present problems of the greatest significance, some of them fraught with the most serious consequences to the manager movement. . . .

The failure of the city council is one of the most startling weaknesses of the council-manager plan. Making exception of the first council elected under the manager plan and of a few residential cities like East Cleveland or Winnetka, the failure of the council to measure up to its responsibilities is widespread. The first council elected under the new régime is likely to be satisfactory; but before many years have passed an insidious process of decline sets in. The old crowd regains its courage and persistently prepares the way to elect one of its representatives to the council, then two, finally a majority. The "business men" meanwhile find that their personal affairs cannot be neglected too long; they insist on being replaced by others; and they seldom display the tenacity or the ingenuity of the professionals who make politics their business.

Manager Carr complained once that the greatest weakness of the manager plan was that there was no organized body back of it. There is usually organized opposition to it, and this opposition rightly understands that control of the council will give absolute control of the city government. In some cities the reaction against "politician government" has been so thorough that it seems unlikely that it can be restored; but, viewing the country at large, it is clearly an unsettled question whether the desire for non-partisan, scientific city government has a commanding position in the minds and hearts of the American voter. In the smaller cities the answer seems fairly clear; but in the larger cities many an engagement will be fought before the ultimate triumph of modern ideals of government is assured.

Apart from the political phase of this situation is another of perhaps equal importance. The decline of the council is not only usually a reversion to politics; it involves also a loss in ability and foresight and capacity for leadership. No organization, however perfect, will function to give good government unless it is manned by men who can breathe into it the will and vision of good government. A council composed of men without a broad vision of the opportunities and needs of city government, lacking the courage to take the initiative, devoid of the will to discharge their duties intelligently, and unable to assume the leadership of their community, can nullify the efforts of the best manager in the country—or drive him to assume their responsibilities. It is unfortunately true that the majorities in many city councils in council-manager cities are composed of such men. There is a continuing danger that the preoccupation of business men with their affairs and the unwillingness of civic leaders to accept the often unpleasant duties of a campaign will hold the level of council ability at far too low a level. The council-manager plan will not show clear-cut superiority as long as it is forced to labor under this handicap; and vice versa, the mayor-council plan will not demonstrate its potential promise until the voters select a different type of representative in the councils.

All this means perhaps no more than to say that the performance of the manager is fundamentally conditioned by the kind of a council with which he has to work; but it should be understood that the first years of the council-manager plan are likely to be the best unless constant effort is made to hold up the level of ability in the council. It is hardly too much to say that the council is the real problem in the manager city.

A second hazard facing the manager movement is to be found in the adventuresome spirit of many managers, especially those new to the game. These aggressive personalities seek not only to give good administration, but also to furnish the brains, enthusiasm, and leadership in deciding what shall be the policy or program of the city. . . . The temptation to follow this path is intensified by the unwillingness or inability of the council to supply effective leadership. This course is one which, if persisted in, will sound the death knell of the manager plan as now conceived, for a manager who undertakes civic leadership stakes his position on the acceptance of his program by the voters. If his program is rejected, and no man can supply effective leadership without openly courting the possibility of rejection, he sacrifices his position as manager. Moreover by entering the area of public opinion and identifying himself with a policy or program, he allies himself with one group of citizens and against another and incurs ill will which is bound to be transferred to the purely administrative phases of his work.

It ought to be possible in this country to separate politics from administration. Sound administration can develop and continue only if this separation can be achieved. For a century they have been confused, with evil results beyond measure. The managers have an unparalleled opportunity and a deep obligation to teach the American people by their precept and conduct that their job is to administer the affairs of the city with integrity and efficiency and loyalty to the council, without participating in or allowing their work to be affected by contending programs or partisans. Their duties with regard to the policy of the city are properly restricted to recommendations to the council and to supplying information to citizens upon request. They have a duty on their own initiative to keep the city informed on the administrative program and achievements, but can hardly go beyond this to dabble in the public advocacy of an unsettled policy. Mr. I. G. Gibbon, an English authority on local government, was well within the truth when he wrote,

> The manager often becomes not only the initiator but also the public advocate of policy. . . . This indicates the chief danger of the whole system. The manager, if he dabbles in policy, if he becomes to the electorate a prominent, perhaps the most prominent, representative of particular measures, marches beyond his intended beat, and he, and the system of which he is a pattern, may suffer disaster with the particular policy which is advocated.

A third hazard which faces the manager is the inclination of American cities to prefer local men. This is a matter of fundamental importance, the significance of which has been obscured by reason of the rapid expansion of the movement and the momentary creation of a large number of new positions. This frontier is doomed, and probably in the not far-distant future. As the number of manager towns becomes stable, the number of initial appointments will dwindle and eventually disappear. Examination of the figures presented in an earlier chapter demonstrates that as the order of appointment moves from first to second and third and fourth, the proportion of outside appointments declines. But in ten years most of the manager towns will be in their fourth or fifth or sixth appointment. The evidence now available indicates a most unfortunate progressive restriction of the opportunity for a manager to be promoted from city to city.

If this restriction coincides with a persistent attempt of the manager to concern himself with policy, the outcome is almost inevitable. A local manager, who is also a community leader, is the counterpart of the strong mayor; and it would not be long before the people would insist on electing the official who takes the lead in advocating policy. This would mean a reversion to the strong mayor plan of city government.

# THE CITY MANAGER AS A LEADER

## CHARLES R. ADRIAN

THIS IS A REPORT on a continuing study of policy leadership in three middle-sized council-manager cities. All three cities are in the 50,000 to 80,000 population range, are in Michigan, and have been council-manager cities for over twenty-five years. The study covers the period of the calendar years 1953 to 1957. The manager in each city had been in office before the beginning of this period and remained in office throughout the period.[1]

None of the cities is within the six counties of the Detroit metropolitan area. Cities A and B are manufacturing cities with a fairly slow population growth; city C, also predominantly a manufacturing city, has grown somewhat more rapidly. All have nonpartisan elections. Labor is organized in the three cities but has been of little influence in the selection of the council in cities A and B. City C had one AFL and CIO endorsee elected to the council during the period studied; two other councilmen were given limited labor endorsement.

Reprinted from *Public Administration Review* (American Society for Public Administration, 6042 Kimbark Avenue, Chicago 37), 18, No. 3 (Summer, 1958), 208–213, where it appeared under the title "Leadership and Decision-Making in Manager Cities, a Study of Three Communities," by permission of the publisher and the author.

1. I wish to extend special thanks to William Cottrell, graduate Falk fellow at Michigan State University, for his able and considerable assistance in the collection of data for this paper. Concerning the research method used: council records and newspaper accounts were examined to determine the issues that were taken up by the city councils during the five-year period; newspaper stories were used to delineate the public roles played by the various individuals involved in the development of public policy toward each issue. Informants in each community helped to clarify the nonpublic roles played by these persons.

Tentative conclusions reached in this preliminary report indicate that the manager and his administration are the principal sources of policy innovation and leadership in council-manager cities, even though the manager seeks to avoid a public posture of policy leadership; that the manager has resources and techniques that enable him to withstand even strong attempts by some councilmen to take policy leadership away from him; that nonofficial groups provide a greater amount of leadership in council-manager cities than is allowed for in the theory of the plan; and that this leadership is a result of councilmanic leadership falling short of the idealized role assigned to it by the theory. Councilmen who do seek to lead place their political careers in greater jeopardy than do other councilmen. It is also found that there were few important issues confronting city councils in middle-sized cities and that even some of these were settled with little conflict, particularly those where few solutions seemed to be available.

## The Manager Plan

The basic idea of the council-manager plan is well known: an elective council of laymen is to make policy and a professional administration under a chief administrative officer selected by, and responsible to, the council is to carry out policy. It is not necessary to comment here on the fact that this approach to organization seems to imply the acceptance of the dichotomy which was held, some years ago, to exist between policy and administration. Practicing city managers quickly learned that they could not avoid taking leadership in policy-making. (The tempests created in academicians' teapots when the idea was presented that politics and administration cannot be separated were of little or no interest to managers and their subordinates who must have discovered the necessary interrelationship of the two about the time that the first manager was appointed in 1908.) Summarizing some studies which were made about twenty years ago, Stone, Price, and Stone noted that:

> It is generally impossible for a city manager to escape being a leader in matters of policy, for it is an essential part of his administrative job to make recommendations. The most important municipal policy is embodied in the budget, and the city manager, of course, must prepare and propose the budget. The city manager's recommendation on an important policy, even if he makes it in an executive session of the council, is usually a matter of common knowledge.[2]

Thus, while it was recognized no doubt almost at once that the manager would have to be a policy leader, he was also expected to do this in a discreet

---

2. Harold A. Stone, Don K. Price, and Kathryn H. Stone, *City Manager Government in the United States* (Public Administration Service, 1940), p. 243. See also, Steve Matthews, "Types of Managerial Leadership," 39 *Public Management* 50–53 (March, 1957).

manner. The code of ethics of the International City Managers' Association enjoins each manager to further "positive decisions on policy by the council instead of passive acceptance of his recommendations," and to give formal credit for policy decisions to the council. (The code, with some modifications, dates from 1924.)

Thus, the role of the manager was conceived realistically decades ago and is well described in the study by Stone, Price, and Stone. On the other hand, neither that study nor other writings on the council-manager plan have paid very much attention to the role of other individuals and groups in the municipal policy-making process: the mayor, the council, and interest groups confronting the manager and the council between election campaigns. It is principally to these areas that this paper is addressed.

## Scarcity of Issues

A study of the role of various groups and actors in the making of municipal public policy is handicapped to some extent by the relative scarcity of issues that could be classified as important. Most of the work of the council appears to consist of routine approval of recommendations from the city manager or his staff; these actions are routine because they fit within general policy already well established.

Judged on the basis of the amount of controversy engendered, the time required to achieve a policy decision by the council, and the amount of space devoted to the issue by the local press, the number of important issues coming before the councils of the three cities averaged about two per year. There was little variation among the cities on this point. It should be noted, however, that an issue may be divided into a number of parts and take many forms. A major conflict between the manager and one of the councilmen in City C, for example, was raised as a background issue in connection with almost every other councilmanic discussion during the period of the controversy.

## The Role of the Manager

In all three cities studied, the manager played the social role expected of him by his professional organizations. In each case, he avoided taking a public role of policy innovator, except at the specific request of the council or in cases involving matters on which he could be considered a technical expert (e.g., on the effect of allowing a bank to install a drive-up window or of a proposed shuffling of administrative agencies).

If we assume, along with Herbert Simon,[3] that major decisions are almost

---

3. *Administrative Behavior* (2d ed., Macmillan Co., 1957).

always made through a "composite process" involving many people, so that no single person is wholly responsible for the final product, it becomes advantageous to view the policy-making process as one in which individual roles are specialized. Since the leader, according to Simon, is a person "who is able to unite people in pursuit of a goal," alternative goals must first be perceived by someone. This is done through a precedent role of *policy innovation*, by which I mean the development of ideas, plans, or procedures that may be presented as alternative choices to the decision-makers. A decision might be said, for purposes of this article, to refer to the selection of an idea, plan, or procedure from among the perceived choices. Many decisions must be made in the development of a policy. To name only a few, the innovators of policy must decide whether their incipient suggestions are worthy of development and subsequent presentation for consideration by the leaders. Each leader must decide upon a policy from among what may be several proposals coming from a single individual or agency or from more than one agency. Once the manager or other leader has decided upon a proposal, he will seek to secure its acceptance. The governing body must then choose a proposal presented by one leader or must consolidate the proposals of two or more leaders. Final acceptance by the council gives the policy legitimacy. Of course, the council may veto all proposals, which would then force a reconsideration of the earlier decisions by other actors.

In the council-manager cities studied, the manager presented and sometimes strongly defended policy proposals that had originated largely from one of his own agencies (e.g., the police department on parking policies), from an advisory group (e.g., the planning commission which developed urban renewal plans), from study committees of lay citizens (e.g., citizens seeking to prevent the breakdown of public transportation), or private groups (e.g., downtown merchants interested in off-street parking).[4] There appeared to be a psychological advantage to the manager if he could place himself in the position of defending a policy developed by these individuals or groups.[5] He would take a strong stand, but would use the protective coloration of saying, "professional planners tell me. . . ." He would, in other words, take a public position of *leadership* in policy matters, but preferred to attribute policy *innovation* to technical experts or citizens groups.

Although managers in all cities appeared to exercise considerable skill in avoiding a public appearance of being the tail that wags the dog, in two cities they were accused of seeking to "control" the mayor or council.

---

4. In City C, however, the manager was in the position of presenting an off-street parking plan that was strongly opposed by the downtown merchants and parking lot owners. The opponents were able to delay but not prevent the adoption of the plan developed by the manager and his staff.

5. One manager (not from Cities A, B, or C) pointed out in an interview that his office is one from which "trial balloons" can be sent up. If a proposed policy is greeted with general disfavor, the council can reject "the manager's suggestion"—he takes the blame regardless of where the idea may have originated. If the proposal is well received, councilmen accept it as their own.

In City C, the manager had to overcome major opposition which, for a short while, actually held majority control of the council. The manager chose to wait out the opposition, almost succeeded in keeping from being quoted in the newspapers concerning his own views on the conflict, and eventually weaned the mayor from the opposition, thus making his supporters on the council a majority. In City B, two councilmen, elected to office late in the five-year period studied, accused the manager of policy domination and voted against proposals that had his blessing, but there appears to have been no support for the two men from other councilmen. In an election toward the end of the period studied, a little-known candidate, seeking to join them, failed to secure nomination.

## The Role of the Mayor

What of the mayor as a leader? In two of the cities studied, the mayor did not play a special leadership role. In one, he was elected by the council; in the other he was directly elected. In the third city, the mayor was the councilman receiving the largest number of votes. An individual of high prestige both among the public and on the council was regularly elected mayor through the period studied. Because of his high status, he appears to have been deferred to by other councilmen and his views were respected. His leadership was rather inconspicious, however, and he did not play the role of policy innovator, or of a chaperon of legislation through the council.[6]

In the thirty issues of importance during the five-year period, the mayor was a principal leader on only two, both of them in City B. The mayor in this case was an elderly man who had held his office for many years. He was chief spokesman on the council for an unsuccessful proposal for a metropolitan area hospital authority, although the plan had first been worked out by a citizen group which strongly supported it. A new city hall for the community was a matter close to his heart, but he was opposed by the chamber of commerce and the taxpayers group which thought the plan extravagant and unnecessary. Although the mayor had the support of the manager and of the planning commission, the council finally accepted the plan of the economy groups.

It is impossible to conclude whether the manner by which the mayor was selected affected his role as a policy leader. In general, there was not much reason to believe that the office of mayor, as such, was prestigious enough to give the incumbent a significant advantage over other potential leaders.

---

6. In one of the cities, the office of city attorney was elective. The incumbent played a definite policy-making role independent of the manager. In the two cities where the attorney was appointed, his role was much less important.

## The Role of the Council

Members of the council did not emerge as either general policy in-novators or as general policy leaders. The individual councilman, rather, was likely to assume leadership in connection with a specific issue or function of government. He developed pet interests or came to know one area of municipal activity especially well and concentrated upon that.

There was one exception: a councilman who acted as a leader both in the general development of policy and in seeking support for policies first presented by some other individual or group (Councilman n in City A). To this case might be added another, somewhat similar. In City C, one councilman definitely acted as the leader of the opposition to the manager, regardless of the particular policy issue under discussion. His leadership, with a few exceptions, was of a negative sort, however. Since the conflict over the management began almost at the outset of the period covered by this study, it is impossible to say if this councilman could also have served as a con-structive policy leader under other conditions.

While a councilman might concentrate upon a particular aspect of municipal policy, it was found to be dangerous for him to seek to make some specific issue a *cause célèbre*. If he chose to do so, he immediately subjected himself to greater public attention and scrutiny than was the case for the typical councilman, and he risked a defeat on the issue which could in turn have disastrous political consequences for him. There is danger in leadership, relative safety in conformity and anonymity. The study indicated that councilmen were aware of this.

In the five-year period covered, there were two incidents in which council-men chose to make major controversies out of particular issues, and in each case the councilman was defeated in his try for re-election. In City A, Councilman m, who had served continuously for a quarter of a century and who came from one of the city's high prestige families, chose to take the lead in a full defense of municipal ownership of the light plant. The plant, long owned by the city, competed with a private utility. It served relatively few customers and costs were higher than those of the private company. As a result, patronage was falling and unit cost rising. Shortly after a new councilman took office, he began a campaign for the sale of the light plant to the private utility. His proposal was immediately and vigorously opposed by Councilman m. The issue was carried along at council meetings, through referendums and into court before it was finally settled in favor of sale to the private company. When Councilman m ran for re-election, he was de-feated. He lost again two years later. (The referendums on the issue indi-cated that he was on the unpopular side of the controversy.)

Another case, in City C, involved the leader of a group opposing the city manager and his policies. Councilman y in this case was hostile to the manager at the beginning of the period studied. It took him some time, however, to organize a bloc. After an election, he picked up two new council members. When the mayor joined with him on two important issues, involving the dismissal of two employees and wage and salary policies, Councilman y had a 4-3 majority on the council. The local newspaper speculated on the possible resignation of the manager. The manager apparently decided to wait for further developments and for public opinion to become crystallized. He neither fought back nor made plans for resignation. Later, he became ill and and the mayor acted in his stead for a few weeks. Shortly after, the mayor began to support the pro-manager group under Councilman z's leadership. This switch produced a new one-vote majority in support of the administration and talk of the manager's resignation stopped. A hard fought election campaign followed in which the issues included the question of wage and salary policy, support for the principle of the council-manager plan (all groups claimed to support it, but Councilman y was accused of seeking to sabotage it), and support for the incumbent manager. Councilman y was defeated for re-election by one of the city's leading industrialists, a supporter of the manager.

## Leadership on Important Issues

Since in both policy innovation and leadership, the role of the councilmen was a relatively modest one, it is necessary to look elsewhere for the actors who played these parts. They were the manager, the members of his administration, and the leaders of interest groups.

Not all issues that were regarded in the community as being important involved intense controversy. In the case of some significant community problems, only one plausible solution was offered. In others, no councilman seemed to see any political advantage in presenting alternative solutions.

When the bus companies came to the councils from time to time asking for fare increases, each councilman would deplore the trend toward higher fares and poorer service, but since the only discernible alternative to refusing the rate increase was a discontinuance of service, almost all councilmen voted in favor of the request. In each of the cities, study committees of lay citizens were appointed to seek solutions to the bus problem. In two cities, they recommended that the city lease the lines and then hire the bus company to run them, thus avoiding certain taxes. In the third city, the committee found another bus company to operate in the city when the existing company sought to withdraw. In each case, the council gratefully, and with little discussion, accepted the proposed solutions. Although the operation of the bus lines was considered vital to each community, a crisis situation was solved in each of them with little or no conflict.

In cases where controversy did exist, as Table 1 indicates, leadership in favor of a proposal was most likely to come from the administration, with outside groups the second most likely source. In fact, nearly all the really significant issues derived their leadership from these two sources. (The cases are too few to attempt to correlate the types of issues with the sources of leadership.) Councilmanic leadership came in annexation proposals, in seeking to make suburbs "pay their own way," and in revolts against the manager. Only in the proposal to sell City A's light plant and in a water supply revenue bond plan in City B did a councilman provide the leadership. In the second case, he had strong administration backing. Issues involving sharp conflict were rarely resolved as the result of leadership coming from the governing body.

In contrast to the leadership *for* proposals, councilmen did lead in opposition to proposals more often than did persons in any other category. Most of the opposition was aimed either against the manager or against expanded services or capital outlay. A good bit of it was nonconstructive and perfunctory. The picture of the council, in summary, was one of a largely passive body granting or withholding its approval in the name of the community when presented with proposals from a leadership outside itself.

### Table 1

### Leadership on Municipal Issues in Three Michigan Cities

| Source of Leadership | In Favor | Opposed |
|---|---|---|
| Administration | 15 | — |
| Mayor | 2 | — |
| Councilmen | 7 | 15 |
| Outside Groups | 10 | 7 |

Note: The table covers the 30 important municipal issues discussed during the years 1953-57. Because leadership was shared in several and lacking in others, the totals do not equal 30.

Nonofficial leadership was important in the case of two types of issues in addition to those that were regarded as "hot potatoes" and so treated gingerly by elected officials. The first type included those submitted by both neighborhood and downtown businessmen seeking municipal assistance in solving their problems. The second included the public transportation problems which, in all three cities, were turned over to citizens committees to bring in recommendations. The first is the kind of interest group activity commonplace before legislative bodies at all levels of government. The second offers something of a puzzle, however. It would seem likely that the solution to the bus problem in each city was one that might have been pushed by almost any councilman, and to his political advantage. Yet, this was not the pattern. Possibly councilmen feared that any solution would also involve increased rates or the necessity of the city buying the transportation system—a solution that seemed unpopular in each city. Possibly controversy was anticipated that never materialized.

It might be noted that the important policy and leadership role of the manager, of his administration, and of leaders of nonofficial groups differs from the pattern intended in the original theory of the council-manager plan. That theory assumed that able, respected leaders of the community would be willing to serve on councils and would take responsibility for policy decisions in government as they did in their businesses. While the typical councilman in the three cities studied gave the impression of being a sufficiently competent person, it seems clear enough that he was not willing to assume a public leadership role under circumstances where he might thereby be plunged into controversy. The politician in the council-manager city, though he may be an amateur, thus follows the traditional practice of American politicians and seeks to avoid taking sides in closely matched battles.

## Suggested Areas for Further Study

A study covering a span of only five years in three cities is scarcely sufficient to serve as a basis for firm generalizations. It is, however, possible for certain tentative hypotheses to be offered from the work reported on here and these may properly provide a basis for further investigation. The following seven hypotheses appear to be most worthy of further inquiry:

1. There will be relatively few issues coming before the council that will be regarded by councilmen, the manager, or the press as involving important, nonroutine decisions.

2. A manager will avoid taking public positions as a policy innovator on items of major importance, but will serve as a leader in presenting and publicly defending policy recommendations developed within the administrative departments, the advisory boards and commissions, study committees of lay citizens, or private groups.

3. The mayor is not chosen on the basis of leadership ability or willingness to play a leadership role and he is, therefore, no more likely to serve as a policy leader than is any other councilman.

4. A councilman is likely to assume leadership in connection with a specific function of government, but not as a general policy leader.

5. A councilman who chooses to make some specific issue a *cause célèbre* thereby becomes subject to greater public attention and scrutiny than is the case with the typical councilman and, if he fails in his objective, runs serious risk of defeat in the following election.

6. Important issues, measured by the consequences of failure to act, may involve little controversy if no alternative solutions are perceived, or if no political advantage is seen in the advancement of alternative solutions.

7. When issues are regarded as being important, but when possible solutions are controversial, or many plausible solutions are discernible, the alter-

native finally selected is likely to come from the administration or from a group outside of the local government structure.

Further inquiry into these hypotheses should help to expand our areas of knowledge about local government and the characteristics of the public policy-making process.

# THREE FUNDAMENTAL PRINCIPLES

## HAROLD A. STONE, DON K. PRICE, AND KATHRYN H. STONE

THE LEADING ADVOCATES of the city manager plan in nearly every city had a general purpose in common: to have the city government devote its energies more effectively toward getting work done for the community and toward wasting less of its money and effort on incidental or factional purposes. To achieve their purpose, they proposed three ideas—the three principal political ideas that characterized the city manager movement. Each of these ideas was reflected or embodied in one of the three fundamental principles of the city manager form of government.

First, there was the idea that the most capable and public-spirited citizens should serve on the governing body as representatives of the city at large, to determine policies for the benefit of the community as a whole, rather than for any party, faction, or neighborhood. This idea was embodied in the non-partisan ballot and in the system of election at large of a small council.

Second, there was the idea that municipal administration should be delegated to a thoroughly competent, trained executive, who should get and hold his job on his executive ability alone and should be given a status and salary comparable to that of an executive in charge of a private corporation. This idea was embodied in the concentration of administrative authority in the city manager.

Third, there was the idea that the voters should hold only the councilmen politically responsible and should give the city manager a status of permanence and neutrality in political controversy. This idea was embodied in the unification of powers in the council as a body comprising the only elected officials in the city government.

No matter how many different immediate objectives characterized the campaigns for city manager government, the city manager movement was motivated by these ideas. In cities that were accustomed to partisan patronage, the advocates of the city manager plan expressed them in terms of a crusading appeal for the elimination of partisan influence in municipal administration and for an increase in the influence of technical experts. In other cities there was no such public appeal; members of the governing body simply decided

Reprinted from *City Manager Government in the United States* (Chicago: Public Administration Service, 1940), pp. 236–242.

to get a city manager in order to get their job done better. In other words, the objectives of the city manager movement were pretty much the same in all these cities, although its advocates had to adapt their tactics to different local conditions.

Then why did different cities have such sharply different experiences with the plan? Why did some cities have violent political disagreements over the adoption of the plan and then drag the city manager into political controversy, while other cities adopted the plan quietly and allowed their managers to lead a relatively peaceful existence? It was not—in the main—because one city had a charter that was superior in certain details to that of another or because the leaders of the city manager movement in that city adopted superior tactics. It was because of a great difference between the cities in the political ideas or attitudes of the rank and file of the voters.

Respected community leaders were able to induce the generally uninterested voters in all these cities to support a change to the city manager plan. Then in one city such voters would continue to support the ideas of the city manager plan because those ideas were in harmony with their established habits; in the other city the uninterested voters would follow dissatisfied political leaders in a reaction against the unfamiliar ideas. Thus, the cities in which the city manager plan operated most smoothly were the cities in which its fundamental ideas were accepted without a conflict. . . .

On the other hand, the cities in which the possibilities of the new form of government were not fully realized were those in which the ideas of the city manager movement came into conflict with traditional political ideas. In such cities some of these ideas that contributed to the reaction against the city manager movement were held by leading advocates of the city manager plan. This reaction, which developed several years after the establishment of the plan in most of the so-called Machine-Ridden and Faction-Ridden cities . . . , was by no means caused entirely by the selfish material interests of professional politicians. The reaction was instigated by such politicians in some cities, but not in all of them. Nevertheless, in all cities in these two groups the success of the reaction depended on popular support, which could be organized only where the reaction was in harmony with popular political ideas—ideas which the reader, according to his point of view, may call either ideals or prejudices.

The adoption of the city manager plan brought about improvements in the political leadership of municipalities in two ways. First, it broadened the possibilities of municipal politics. Second, it heightened the prestige of the councilmanic office and thus led men of greater ability and reputation to be willing to serve as councilmen.

The first type of improvement came about in all groups of cities. In a municipal organization that included no administrators of ability and performed none but the minimum routine functions, the political leader at best was a dignified but negative participant; at worst he was a grafter. An effective organization under an expert manager, on the other hand, broadened the political leader's scope; he could promote more positive municipal policies because their effective execution had become a possibility.

This contrast is stated in extreme terms, but the general improvement in administrative machinery under the city manager plan certainly changed the function of the political leader to some extent in nearly every community, no matter what its former political tradition. In Lynchburg the councilmen gave less time to detailed supervision of public works and to parliamentary red tape and were considering city planning and co-operation with the state municipal league; in Austin they forgot the old neighborhood factionalism and promoted housing projects in Mexican districts; in Rochester they paid less attention to patronage and more to transportation facilities and to the industrial development of the city.

In the increase in the prestige of the councilmanic office and in the improvement in the ability and the reputation of councilmen the changes were less uniform. Some cities that adopted the manager plan had long been accustomed to electing the community leaders of the greatest prestige and public spirit to their governing bodies, and the change in the form of government did not affect this habit. In these cities, a councilmanic election was not a contest between factions that were interested either in patronage or in special policies. It was an expression by the community of confidence in its leaders, who served for the prestige of the office and from a sense of civic responsibility rather than from a desire to further the interest of any group. But no one group—economic, religious, or political—maintained a monopoly on municipal affairs. Voters, in choosing councilmen, thought more of the general prestige of candidates in the community than of their membership in any faction. Councilmen, as a result, tended to think more of the community as a whole and less of factional interests in making their decisions.

This was the state of affairs which leaders of the city manager movement wanted to bring about in the other cities that adopted the city manager plan. . . . In these cities politics had not attracted the community leaders of the greatest public spirit and prestige, and members of the governing body had served their factions rather than the community as a whole. Since the subject matter of municipal government was largely routine business, factional competition was based, not on broad policy, but on special favors and patronage.

The leaders in the city manager movement in these cities, seeking to have the affairs of the municipal government administered impartially for the community rather than for the benefit of factional groups, formed a citizens' association and drafted as councilmanic candidates men who were accustomed to taking the lead in other community institutions—churches, schools, service clubs and commercial organizations, labor unions, and other organizations which enlisted unpaid leaders. Some candidates were professional men, a few were workingmen, and many were business executives or men engaged in independent commercial enterprises. Their common quality was that they possessed the respect of the community. But in these cities the idea that the community should delegate control of municipal affairs to its most respected citizens and should permit them to direct the administration of the government without giving factional followers special favors was not supported by tradition or by general sentiment. The impartial administration of the government aroused resentment among those who had been accustomed to exceptional treatment, and the resentment was directed at the symbol of the new regime—the city manager.

## The Theory of Group Representation on the Council

In the reaction against the city manager plan, which usually produced a conspicuous decline in the prestige of the council, one of the arguments most frequently used was that various groups—geographical, racial, political, social—ought to be represented on the council. The leaders of the political reaction against the first council and the first city manager made the councilmen out to be, not merely respected community leaders, but businessmen who had little regard for the common people. The reactionary leaders argued that a small council consisting mainly of men who were successful community leaders was unrepresentative of the city and therefore undemocratic. By this argument they proposed that the voters should restore to office the traditional political leaders of the city or even that the charter should be amended to enlarge the council and to restore the system of election by wards. This argument was often used by factional leaders who were seeking any stick with which to beat the reformers. Nevertheless, it probably carried considerable weight with the rank and file of the voters, who thought of representation in terms of groups because they were accustomed to pay more attention to factional purposes than to community purposes in municipal politics.

In some cities, of course, leaders in the city manager movements, conforming to local habits, formed factions of their own, and used their control of the local government to keep their friends in office and their enemies out—regardless of the desire of either of them to cooperate for the welfare of the community. The existence of strong political animosities made it difficult for those who wanted to establish impartial administration to be impartial; until a united community spirit developed, every one of their actions was interpreted according to its effect on the factional controversy. Under these conditions an electoral system that would have guaranteed each political faction seats in the city council would have tended to defeat the will of the majority, which had affirmed itself in favor of impartial administration. Different factions did not want representation in order to participate in the discussion of policy which should then be administered impartially; they wanted representation in order to be able to bargain for special favors and to be able to obstruct those who were trying to put into effect the new system of government.

The original advocates of the city manager plan were not in every city the only leaders who could be trusted to operate it properly. On the contrary, the reformers who put it into effect were not always best able to maintain popular support for its principles. As long as they held office, the plan might be identified with them alone and might not be accepted by the city as a whole; the plan might be put on a stable basis only by the election to the council of leaders who had formerly opposed the plan. To have the city government run smoothly, it was sometimes better to have all self-conscious social groups represented on the council—as long as their representation depended on the sanction of the community as a whole and as soon as they thought in city-wide, not ward or factional, terms.

Under election at large all groups could be represented so long as they were willing to cooperate in a program approved by the majority; under a group representation system of election, each faction could retain its councilmanic seats even if it was willfully sabotaging the policies of the administration. The theory of group representation was accepted by a great many advocates of the city manager plan, as well as by its opponents. In practice it was most often embodied in a system of election by wards; in theory, it was embodied in the system of proportional representation, which was recommended by the Model Charter as an alternative that was preferred to election at large and as an improvement on election by districts.


## Assumptions Underlying the Theory of Group Representation

The whole idea of group representation depends upon certain assumptions that are not truly applicable to city government and overlooks what is usually the most important issue of municipal politics. It assumes that the policy determined by the council will depend more on what groups or factions the councilmen belong to than on how much public spirit and intelligence the councilmen have. A councilman elected by the votes of a neighborhood of underprivileged citizens, according to this theory, should be more active in promoting that neighborhood's welfare than a councilman elected at large or by some other group of voters. In the cities covered by this survey, however, real changes in municipal policy were rarely brought about by competition among self-interested political groups. The most conspicuous changes were not made by representatives acting on mandates from a group of their constituents that stood to benefit by the new policies; on the contrary, they were made by leaders of the community as a whole, acting out of public spirit on the proposals of a trained administrator. For example, there were the inaugurations of the comprehensive health, recreation, and welfare programs in Dayton, in Austin, and in Janesville. These programs were established on the recommendations of city managers by councilmen, most of whom were well-to-do and important businessmen, in the face of bitter political attacks from the traditional political leaders of the lower-income neighborhoods, the very neighborhoods that needed the new programs most.

The idea that various groups ought to have representatives on the council to look after their interests overlooks what is usually the most important issue of municipal politics. In many cities the greatest issue, and the greatest conflict of interests, was between those who supported a system of partisan patronage and those who demanded impartial administration. The interests of any social or economic group may often be more greatly affected by the quality of administration of noncontroversial municipal policies than by the decision—one way or the other—of the controversial issues. The competition of municipal political factions did little in these cities to bring about democratic control of policies. On the other hand, it did a great deal to destroy the prestige of local government and to subordinate its fundamental purpose of community services to factional interests. The idea of group or neighborhood representation was one of the great handicaps to the election of public-spirited representatives for the city as a whole under the city manager plan.

# GROUP CONFLICT IS INEVITABLE IN A MAJOR CITY

## CHARLES A. BEARD

IF I WERE to make an excursion into utopian politics and sketch a new "City of the Sun," assigning to political parties their proper place in my dream-made republic, I should start out by saying with the great chief justice, John Marshall, that nothing more debases and pollutes the human mind than partisan politics. When we see men otherwise just and fair in their judgments vilifying, maligning, and slandering their opponents, even in unimportant political campaigns, those of us who are not enamoured of billingsgate are moved to exclaim that political parties have no place at all in a rational society. But this would be a vain flying in the face of the hard and unpleasant facts of life and a vain longing for the impossible.

Viewing the subject from a practical angle we may inquire whether the issues which divide men and women into national parties are issues which have any relation to municipal questions as such. The facile reformer usually answers in the negative. It is true that there seems to be no connection between ship subsidies, tariff, labor legislation, farm loans, and kindred matters and the problems that arise in our great urban centres. Superficially

Reprinted from *National Municipal Review*, 6, No. 2 (March, 1917), 201–206, where it appeared under the title "Political Parties in City Government: A Reconsideration of Old Viewpoints."

there is none. But I cannot be too emphatic when I say that not a single one of our really serious municipal questions—poverty, high cost of living, over-crowding, unemployment, low standards of life, physical degeneracy—can be solved, can be even approached by municipalities without the co-operation of the state and national government, and the solution of these problems calls for state and national parties. No big vision of this mighty nation as it is to be can exclude from its range an economy which is both urban and rural, one and truly indivisible.

Of course, speaking practically there is no real division between the Republican and the Democrats on municipal issues. The usual slogans of economy, efficiency, and good management are accepted by both of them. No party is willing to advocate waste, inefficiency, and bad management. The Socialist party is the only party that has a complete program of public economy which includes national and state and city issues. That is a program of collectivism, public ownership and operation of the great utilities or economic processes upon which all depend for a livelihood. We may or may not approve of that program, but we cannot deny that it is a consistent municipal, state, and national program. Neither can we deny that the Socialists are both logical and sound, from their point of view, when they insist upon maintaining a municipal party organization and linking it up with the state and national organization. Insisting that not a single great problem of social economy is purely or even primarily municipal, the Socialists rightly stick to a unified party organization. Up to the present time, however, they have been almost negligible factors in most of our great cities, and as we are not here concerned with prophecy or speculation we may leave them out of account.

I have said above that there is no real division between the Republicans and Democrats on municipal issues, but I do not mean that issues create parties. On the contrary I think the causes of party division lie deeper than superficial paper declarations of party principles. Issues are more frequently pretexts than causes of partisanship. That profound statesman, Alexander Hamilton, said in the convention that framed the constitution of the United States: "All communities divide themselves into the few and the many. The first are the rich and the well-born, the other the mass of the people." I think we have in that laconic statement more information on the place of political parties in municipal government than in all the literature that has been issued by the reformers since the foundation of this republic. Disparity in the kinds and distribution of property, as the father of our constitution, James Madison, said, is the most fundamental cause of parties and factions in all ages and all places.

Of other cities I have little knowledge, but I know something about the history of parties in the city of New York, from the days of Jefferson to the days of Mitchel. By a long and painstaking study of election returns, ward maps, occupations, and wealth distribution, I arrived at the conclusion that the first great party division in New York city—that between the Federalists and the Jeffersonian Republicans—was a division between "wealth and talents" on the one hand and the masses on the other hand. Anyone interested in the facts will find them on pp. 383–387 of my *Economic Origins of Jeffersonian Democracy*. The studies I made for that work have been carried forward with great skill, accuracy and ingenuity by one of my colleagues, Mr. Dixon R. Fox, who has now completed the maps of the elections by wards down until 1840. He finds that in every great contest the "wealth and talents" were in the main with the Federalists or later the Whigs, while the masses were Democrats. I believe that fundamental division exists to-day in our great northern cities. I do not mean to say that there are not wealth and talents in the Democratic party, but I do contend that the center of gravity of wealth is on the Republican side while the center of gravity of poverty is on the Democratic side. Anyone who wants official confirmation of this view may read President Wilson's *New Freedom*.

Of course in the smaller cities like Des Moines, Iowa, or Dayton, Ohio, where the area of the great industrial proletariat is not large and where distinctions of group and class are not marked, the materials for party divisions are not so obvious and so persistent. In the south cities are few and new, and there are special problems. As Plato and Aristotle long ago pointed out where there is similarity and approximate equality of property interests, there unity and stability may take the place of divisions and contests. To anyone really interested in the profound philosophical problem set by the theme of my paper I commend a long and prayerful study of Aristotle's *Politics*. There he will find more genuine information on the subject than in all the books that have ever been written on American government. Speaking, therefore, not as a prophet or an advocate, I should say that parties are inevitable and unavoidable in modern society.

By that I do not mean to say that the corruption and excesses which have characterized political organizations in our great cities will continue unabated. On the contrary, I look forward with confidence to a diminution in corruption, partly on account of the increasing number of independent voters who cannot be counted upon to follow slavishly the dictates of leaders, but mainly on account of the fact that the opportunities for corruption are now materially reduced. There will be no more boards of "forty thieves" in New York disposing of Broadway franchises, not because we are better than our fathers but because the Broadway franchise has been disposed of and made perpetual. With more than 95 per cent of our surface railway franchises granted in perpetuity in New York city we may feel reasonably secure from the attacks of franchise grabbers masked as party organizations.

In other words, to use academic terminology, the law of diminishing returns has set in against municipal corruption in its grosser forms, and so we may expect to see an increasing number of the so-called "interests" becoming good and non-partisan. They are like Great Britain. Having possession of the earth, she is for peace and the *status quo*. Certain financial groups in New York that formerly looked with kindly toleration on Tammany, having "got theirs," are now for efficiency and economy. Providence works in mysterious ways His wonders to perform, and those who are weary of Tweed rings and gas scandals may look forward with confidence and hope. The age of great graft in our cities is over; we have eaten our cake. We shall be bothered with petty graft, but that is not so dangerous to public morals. But we shall have parties for such a long time in the future that we need not make our last will and testament now.

If this analysis is correct then those of us who dwell in large cities must arrange to live and work with parties. Rural villages may experiment with "non-partisanship." From what I can gather from newspapers and gossip with visitors from non-partisanship cities of any size, the abolition of city parties by statutory devices is a delusion. Perhaps some of the delegates from Boston will inform us whether there are any Democrats or Republicans in the city government there. Of course some one will rise up from Dayton and tell us that utopia is there, but some of us skeptics from the east must be pardoned if we do not rewrite our entire political science in the light of three years' experience of an Ohio city, whose population is about equal to the annual increment in the population of New York. I know of nothing more amusing than the report of the first trial of the "new non-partisan election system" in San Francisco, reported by the *National Municipal Review* in its first number. The reporter told us that the results of the same were "generally considered satisfactory," and then proceeded: "A candidate has but to secure ten electors to take the sponsor's oath, to get his name printed on the primary ballot. No candidate succeeded, however, unless he was backed by a large organization. Six such organizations took part in the contest: the municipal conference, the good government league, the Republican, Democratic, Union Labor, and Socialist parties. The first four combined on James Rolph, Jr., a prominent shipowner, as a candidate for mayor and had many other candidates in common. The Union Labor party put forward Mayor McCarthy and a straight ticket. The Socialists named Wm. McDevitt." Surely an Irishman wrote this account of a "genuine, non-partisan" election under a non-partisan law.

In fact, I am prepared to defend the thesis that non-partisanship has not worked, does not work, and will not work in any major city in the United States. We have plenty of non-partisan election laws designed to smash party organizations. We also have direct primary laws designed to take nomination out of the hands of party leaders. I think these laws have in many instances put a wholesome fear in the minds of political leaders, but I do not believe that they have permanently reduced the power of the expert political minority that manages public affairs.

To come right down to practical conclusions, I should make the following summary: (1) that the causes of parties lie deeper than election laws or most so-called issues; (2) that the causes of parties being social and economic, we must expect the continued existence of party organizations in our municipal affairs; (3) that the task before the reformer is not the enactment of non-partisan laws but the development of legislation and public opinion which will make parties responsible for their conduct of municipal government; (4) that fusion is a temporary process better calculated to frighten and educate party leaders than to develop a unified and well-planned city administration; (5) the independent, self-directing citizens are relatively few in any community or party but education will widen that number and from them we may expect a check upon the party extravagance which has disgraced so many of our cities; (6) that men who want wise and just government in cities are likely to do as much good by co-operating with parties and insisting upon the establishment of sound party policies and genuine party responsibility as they are by running to the legislature for new non-partisan election laws; (7) that there is a power, not in legislation, that worketh for righteousness.

# THE TOWN THAT TRIED "GOOD GOVERNMENT"

### JOHN BARTLOW MARTIN

OVER THE YEARS, Peoria, Illinois, has been known as a steamboat town, a whisky town, a railroad town, a river town, a convention town, a wide-open town. At one time it seemed less a city than a vaudeville joke. Renowned for its gambling, prostitution and political corruption, it was accounted almost a classic case of American municipal decay.

Two years ago the citizens voted to get rid of the old aldermanic form of government and to install the city-manager plan. The new administration assiduously scrubbed the city clean, amid loud praise. And then, in an election a few months ago, the people issued a somewhat murky mandate that seemed to indicate they thought maybe reform wasn't so good after all. Why and how did all this come about?

On a hot day in June, down by the edge of the Illinois River, where diesels honk in the railroad yards and men make earth movers in clangorous factories, heat and smoke and the stench from the stockyards press down on the gray cottages and broken streets in the section of town know as The Valley. High on The Bluff and farther out in The Knolls, the air is cleaner and traffic moves quietly past the mansions along Moss Avenue. Peoria is built on steep-rising hills above the Illinois River, and it is sharply divided into The Valley and The Bluff—the workers in The Valley, the owners on The Bluff.

Tall office buildings rise near the courthouse, set on a bench of land above the river, and out in the wide one-way street a neat policeman prowls up and down, chalking the tires of parked automobiles. ("We're pushing our chalking program vigorously," says the young man in the city administration who is giving me a conducted tour.)

The City Hall was built in 1897–99, and the copper on its dome is peeling away, and water has come through the roof, cracking the ceiling of the grimy council chamber. The new administration has cleaned the tobacco juice of years from the marble walls of the first-floor hallways, has auctioned off the old spittoons, has put fluorescent lights and brand-new steel desks and business machines into the ancient offices.

Across the street from City Hall is a parking lot where once stood the headquarters of the gambling syndicate—a gambling casino, an accounting office and a tavern. Citizens who received traffic tickets used to go into the tavern and drop the tickets into a little box, and on Friday someone would go over to City Hall and fix all the tickets. And from this headquarters, too, the gamblers brought their monthly tribute, paid directly into the city treasury— as much as $69,000 in one year.

"The town is down"—everyone says so. No more organized gambling, no more organized prostitution. The bars, once crowded, are almost deserted. The three large gambling casinos near City Hall which for years offered craps, poker, roulette and horse betting are closed. Slot machines have disappeared. The houses on The Line, the red-light district famed through-out the Midwest, are dark. A bartender says, "This used to be the best town in the country. Then we got a reform administration. Now it ain't worth a damn."

Students of local lore trace Peoria's predilection for frontier-style living to the roistering steamboat days. The town's recent history has been en-livened by gunplay and the periodic bombing of the homes of law-enforce-ment officials. Peorians talk about corruption the way people elsewhere talk about baseball.

Off and on, Ed Woodruff was Peoria's mayor for twenty-four years. An old-timer politician recalls fondly, "Old Ed Woodruff. There was a man that was a liberal. What made the town a wide-open liberal town was that Ed Woodruff started in 1903 and lasted till 1945. If some reformer got in for a while and the town was slowed up a little, he'd get back in and open her up. He poured out the jobs and seen that everybody made a little money and catered to The Valley and never paid any attention to the Association of Commerce. He never took a quarter himself. 'Course, he didn't mind his friends makin' some of it. And he made the gamblers bring it in at campaign time. But, hell, they overdid it. They put slot machines in drugstores and school zones and groceries and beauty parlors.

"Old Ed had an old houseboat called the Bumboat hauled up on the bank of the river, and he and his cronies used to run the city from it. That was where they chopped the heads off"—that is, dispensed patronage. "They'd go down there and they'd eat and drink and—you know, decide the city policies. He was a tough Republican, but he'd play with them Democrats. He didn't bar any holts."

There were no application forms for city jobs till the present administra-tion came in. Excluding firemen and police, the city employed about 200 people, and they were swept out when the mayor's office changed hands. Even policemen were fired and replaced with friends of politicians. Who ran the police force? "Well," says a veteran policeman, "there were twenty-two aldermen. And each alderman had five friends. How many's that? About a hundred and ten?"

The present chief says, "I run the police department."

In 1951 the state legislature authorized Peoria to adopt the city-manager plan if it wished. Civic groups formed the Peorians for Council-Manager. They say that membership was open to the public, but PCM critics say PCM was a closed corporation. Mostly, PCM was led by men who live on The Bluff and represent the business interests of Peoria.

One of its young leaders, Joe Kelly, a customer's man in a stock-brokerage firm, a big, crew-cut man of thirty-two, has said, "They were all just good citizens sold on the idea of the need for the cleanup of the city—bad streets, bad lighting, plus the general decrepitness of the city. The president of PCM and the campaign manager were both leading Jaycees. One was voted The Outstanding Young Man of 1951. We put out literature. We set up a speakers' bureau and talked to five hundred organizations. The opposition was terrific." It came from organized labor and old-fashioned politicians. But the plan was adopted, 15,000 to 7000.

The next step was to elect a mayor and eight councilmen in nonpartisan balloting. PCM decided to endorse candidates.

Kelly has said, "Not everybody thought we should. But there has to be some group to get good people to run for government. If not, the government will fall back to the grafters and crooks. To get a top industrialist or any honest man to run for public office is very, very hard. They won't subject themselves to politics."

For mayor PCM slated Robert Morgan, an upright man of forty-three, long active in civic affairs, a brother of the president of PCM and himself a leading lawyer who represents corporations in their dealings with labor unions. For councilmen PCM slated the president of the LeTourneau earth-moving-equipment-manufacturing company, the comptroller of a washing-machine company, the employee-relations manager of Caterpillar Tractor, a merchant, a mover, a newspaper distributor, the president of the Women's Civic Federation, and a banker.

Independent candidates filed against them. The campaign was noisy. PCM was accused of being a machine, trying to run the city. But PCM elected the mayor and five councilmen, giving it a 6–3 majority in council.

Council, taking office in May of 1953, hired as the new city manager George Bean. Bean, a professional city manager of seventeen years' experience, was then managing Grand Rapids, Michigan, and could not come to Peoria till July. Mayor Morgan and council, however, lost no time in commencing reform.

Mayor Morgan recalls, "The job of sewer superintendent had for years been a sinecure for the retired head of the bricklayers union. We called him in and asked what his duties were. He said, 'I help Mr. Kosanovich.' Kosanovich was his assistant. We asked when he helped him. 'When he needs help.' So we just cut off his job and elevated Kosanovich. That made the brick-layers mad, of course." They also appointed a new police chief, fire chief, comptroller and street superintendent. And Mayor Morgan ordered the police to begin raiding gambling games and brothels.

Actually, big-time organized gambling had already stopped, ruined by political turnover, the enactment of a Federal law taxing gamblers, and the murder of the head of the gambling syndicate. Under Mayor Morgan the police closed the surviving poker games and lotteries. Prostitution, however, was still running wide open. "We had to root 'em out," police chief Frank Evans recalls. They made more than fifty raids on brothels.

The court fined the keeper and the inmates $200 apiece. This was costly; a raid might cost a madam $1800. (Fines have totaled about $25,000.) Moreover, after the police raided a house three times the city asked the state's attorney to obtain an injunction padlocking the house permanently as a public nuisance. Once somebody planted a dynamite bomb at the mayor's house and blew a hole in the foundation. But the police raids continued. Soon The Line was down. The police think a call-girl operation has begun. Now and then, they find a girl in a car or a tavern.

Such furtive operations do far less damage than a wide-open Line: they do not corrupt officials or spread disease. The month the raids started, 130 new venereal-disease cases were reported in Peoria, and the average for the preceding two years had been eighty-eight new cases a month. In 1955 it has been twenty-six.

When Manager Bean arrived he found the city's affairs in a deplorable state. This did not surprise him.

Bean, a tall, red-haired man of fifty-five, said recently, "The city-manager plan is a tool that desperate people reach for when everything else has broken down. Peoria's services were ineffective. There was a big backlog of needed physical improvements after forty years of neglect, and the city was broke—we had three hundred thousand dollars in unpaid bills. The budget had been unbalanced since 1948."

One of Bean's aids recalls, "Nearly all the department heads were about sixty-five years old. Everything was obsolete. They were using old incandescent lamps in the drafting department; I worked there awhile and kept getting headaches from the poor lighting. Some department heads never got to travel around to see what other cities were doing."

William Sommers, the new personnel officer, says, "In the old days the aldermen would hire men for the street department, then lay them off, mostly old men, couldn't work anywhere else, old winos, helpless drifters. So the street department was really a kind of relief agency. I felt sorry for the old guys. But you can't run a street department that way. We've been building up personnel files. We introduced physical examination, probationary six months' period, progress reports, training program and a merit system."

Manager Bean began his work in Peoria by recruiting a professional staff. All five of his recruits were young and all but one came from outside Peoria. Jake Dumelle was twenty-eight when he became Bean's administrative assistant, a mechanical engineer with a degree in public administration who had been assistant to another city manager. Dumelle brought in a classmate, Roy Anderson, a thirty-year-old certified public accountant, to replace the city comptroller. William Sommers, with a graduate degree from Harvard in public administration and experience with the Colorado Municipal League, became personnel officer at the age of twenty-seven. Dean DuBoff, an architect just out of the Navy, was the only local man; he became director of inspections. The youngest of all was Dan Hanson, who, at twenty-four, was hired away from the Chicago Motor Club to become Peoria's first traffic engineer.

The young administrators are bouncy and bright and eager. One of them said recently, "It's surprising how much we get done at staff meetings, considering the number of prima donnas there are among us." On an average they possess two college degrees each. Their average age is now twenty-nine, all but Dumelle are married. They sometimes refer to themselves as "the crew-cuts."

Watching them at work, you get the impression they care more deeply about the city than many people who have lived here all their lives. Their youth and eagerness have led them to make some "boners," as they term them. Manager Bean has said, "Young people tend to go too fast." Once the traffic engineer, Dan Hanson, began enforcing the parking-meter ordinance on Monday until nine o'clock at night, something that hadn't been done for years. Police handed out 300 tickets in one night. Amid loud public outcry, council changed the ordinance.

Dumelle recalls, "Once council bought some parking meters to be paid for at two thousand dollars a month out of revenue. The comptroller thought this was silly and asked the manufacturer for a five per cent discount for cash, got it, issued tax-anticipation warrants, and paid them off. Council didn't find out about it till the end of the year. The comptroller hadn't consulted them and they were indignant. He couldn't understand that as a private CPA he had had only one boss, but now, as a public official, he had more than a hundred thousand. A lot of public relations is needed in this work. You get in a town like this, you can't change it all overnight."

When Hanson, the traffic engineer, came to Peoria he spent six months compiling facts about traffic—accident statistics, law violations, traffic flow—then waded in. He installed new street-name signs throughout the city. He adopted a city-wide through-street plan. He changed bus routes. He painted forty-five miles of center stripes and lanes. Perhaps his biggest job was removing a lot of stop signs.

Hanson said recently, "Under the old form of government, aldermen were deluged with requests for stop signs. Stop signs were erected at every place where a near miss occurred, or where there was a school, or where the alderman's wife was involved in an accident. The city has sixteen hundred street intersections and it had over thirteen hundred stop signs. We went to the council with a plan to remove three hundred and ten signs. They adopted it. Since then we've had only three petitions asking that signs be reinstalled."

A blond young man, crew-cut, pink-cheeked, short and compact, Hanson spends as much time as he can driving around and looking for traffic trouble spots. One day recently he left the downtown district and headed up The Bluff on Knoxville Avenue, traffic swirling smoothly along on new pavement, and he said, "Along here is the first place in the city that we installed rush-hour parking control. They'd tried it several years ago and it lasted thirty days—too many complaints from the neighbors. When we got ready to do it, the captain of traffic and I went to every house along here, door to door, and explained why it was necessary. We've had very few complaints."

Driving on, Hanson pointed to a set of traffic lights and said, "Here's a new intersection we synchronized. We put in green arrows to let them turn on the red and head for downtown; then we laned it off-center to give 'em room to turn, and we took off parking on one side. That's the kind of stuff we're always looking for."

In an outlying neighborhood, seeing a motorcycle policeman lying in wait for stop-sign violators, he said, "He's not there just because he happens to live nearby or anything. He's there because they've analyzed the accident reports of several months and found that they were caused by stop-sign violation at about this time of day. It's really scientific now."

Enforcement and engineering were getting results. Last year only three people were killed in traffic accidents—fewer than ever before. Injuries and accidents declined. In 1953 the National Safety Council ranked Peoria's traffic-safety program forty-third out of fifty cities. Last year it ranked third. "So," Hanson said, "we feel something's beginning to happen. Of course, it's slow. You can't move any faster than the town will let you."

At the end of its first year in office the new administration issued a report to the people, pointing proudly to its achievements. Peoria had been termed an "All-American City" by the National Municipal League. The administration had improved the city's housekeeping, bought new equipment, bought a new police headquarters, improved law enforcement, cut accidents, taken politics out of city service, and balanced the budget. It had balanced its current budget by funding $300,000 of unpaid bills, by re-enacting a city vehicle license which the outgoing aldermen had repealed, and by imposing a new cigarette tax.

But it still had not solved its basic financial problem. The city badly needed $20,000,000 worth of new streets and sewers and other capital improvements. To raise the money the council submitted to the people a proposal to levy a one-half-cent city sales tax. It promised to cut back the property tax and take off the vehicle license and cigarette tax. But labor viewed this as an attempt to shift the tax burden to the workingman. And the Association of Commerce objected that a city sales tax would drive shoppers out of the city. The proposal was beaten 4 to 1.

How did Peorians like their new government? Most of them liked the vice and gambling cleanup, though some felt nostalgia for the old days. They liked the housekeeping improvements in general, though many grumbled specifically about the streets. Many said they didn't know whom to complain to, now that councilmen were not elected from wards. Some said the new administration's innovations had been abrupt and arbitrary. Some said the new regime was too costly and had raised taxes; they complained about Bean's $18,000 salary and about "the outsiders" he had imported to run the city.

Organized opposition came from tavern-keepers who felt the cleanup kept big conventions away and hurt day-to-day business, and from organized labor. The state federation of Labor has long officially opposed the city-manager plan as not being representative government. Labor was not included in the original PCM which brought the manager plan to Peoria.

The new administration fired a city painting contractor and merely hired a painter; this antagonized the union. The administration ended "labor patronage"—took the job of sewer superintendent away from the bricklayers union, the job of building commissioner away from the carpenters union. It bought cigarette-tax stamps from a nonunion company, offending the printers union. It bought prison-made traffic signs.

Dick Estep, who speaks for the AFL, complains bitterly about PCM. "They sold the people on the idea that this type of government was going to be independent. No politics at all. But PCM has a slate, it has a treasury, it has officers—to me, it's just a political party." And Coy Lutes, of the United Auto Workers (CIO), said, "We're not against the manager form as such, but only against the way in Peoria it has been packed with management people. They are all antilabor to start out with."

The administration faced its first test in the councilmanic election of 1955. Four councilmen had to stand for re-election. Three of them originally had been supported by PCM; the fourth, a labor man, had not. This time PCM endorsed them all. The labor man promptly renounced PCM support. PCM began running ads praising him; he ran ads denouncing PCM. Otherwise the campaign was quiet until the last couple of weeks. Then all the independents began attacking PCM. An organization called Peorians for Peoria sprang up to aid the independents. Its cartoons caricatured Bean. Its ads kept asking: "Who Is Mr. Syndicate?" and hinting that Bean was "Mr. Syndicate" and was involved in some devious plot of an unspecified nature. It said, "Mr. Syndicate Ordered IT for Grand Rapids and Now Peoria," not saying what "IT" was. Voters were urged to "watch tomorrow's newspapers for details" and to "Save Peoria" on April fifth.

PCM disdained to answer any of this. Its ads simply praised the incumbents and recalled the bad old days of the aldermanic system: "inefficiency," "waste," "payroll padding," "graft," "shady deals." One of the independent candidates, James J. Manning, a shrewd, genial former alderman who had become a symbol of the old regime, promptly ran an ad listing numerous members of the old regime and asking whether PCM was accusing these "distinguished Peorians" of chicanery.

Nearly everyone expected the PCM candidates to sail through. So, when the blow fell, it was a heavy one. Not a single PCM man won except the labor man who had repudiated PCM endorsement.

What had happened? Almost nobody interpreted the election as a repudiation of the city-manager plan itself. Most people, PCM and labor leaders alike, thought the election indicated resentment of "PCM domination." Mayor Morgan attributed the result to the small vote—"the aginners always get out and vote." The vote was indeed very light—only 41 per cent of the registration. But it was light all over town and one of the elected councilmen said, "If The Valley had got out and voted, we'd have beaten 'em worse." How did he account for the light vote? "It's the same all over the country. The people figure why should they vote; they got a nice big house, nice big car, they got television, they got everything they want, they got money." He found the people's mandate somewhat cloudy. "The people definitely want a change. You've got to change something." Probably, he thought, they wanted better streets and alleys and more stop signs.

After the election, many people expected that Bean would be fired forthwith. Citizens bought chances in a pool, betting on the day of the month the city manager would be fired. The night the new council was inaugurated a sizable crowd turned out. But Bean wasn't fired, and four months later he still hadn't been.

Council, however, adopted a resolution asserting its authority over the manager and its sole power to determine policy and limiting the manager's authority to administering council's policies. Council established committees to "investigate" city problems. The independents say that formerely one or two PCM councilmen, meeting secretly with Bean, made major policy decisions and presented them to council for rubber-stamp approval. They insist that they will scrutinize the city's every act and return government to the people.

They have certainly worked at it. The former council had met only twice a month, and then only briefly; the new council holds long meetings twice a week or oftener. Council voted to "adopt a policy of having windows of city buildings washed every two months." Council voted to reinstall stop signs at one intersection whence Hanson had removed them. Council spent weeks studying the comparative merits of a brass pump and a cast-iron pump on a new fire truck. As a consequence of this attention to detail, business is transacted slowly and major problems tend to pile up.

Bean appears to have adopted a strategy of asking council's guidance before making the most unimportant decision. Possibly he hopes to bore council to death, so that it will restore to him some of his duller prerogatives. Council leadership has developed upon two holdover anti-PCM councilmen —Robert McCord, an attorney; and Myrna Harms, a young woman of considerable charm. At almost every council meeting one of them takes a pot shot from the floor at Bean or PCM. Recently, Mrs. Harms' criticism of fire-department purchasing blew up a scandal that resulted in a vitriolic dispute between Mrs. Harms and Mayor Morgan, the indictment of the fire chief, and a councilmanic vote of confidence on Manager Bean, which he survived, 6–3.

Bean, a hotheaded, upright man, has tried to avoid brawling with his critics. He said recently that the manager plan functions best in cities where the manager and council feel a mutual confidence. That this is no longer so in Peoria disturbs him, not only because he is involved but because the plan itself is involved.

Why has a government so widely acclaimed aroused so much opposition? Some has been aroused by councilmanic headline hunting. But PCM invited opposition at the outset by failing to embrace all segments of the city, including labor. PCM was blinded by its mistrust of politicians. It blamed all the city's woes on them and said that ousting them would solve all problems. It forgot that politicians perform a real service: they respond to the people's wishes. PCM leaders neglected to do this. The councilmen, enthusiastic about the plan and anxious to make progress rapidly, were too eager to hand over responsibility to the manager. The administrators reckoned too much with slide rules and too little with people. Their determination to solve the city's financial problem led them to propose the unpopular sales tax. And yet surprisingly few people in Peoria seem to think the manager plan is on the way out. Many people, however, do think the city may return to the ward system of electing councilmen, to meet the most widespread objection to the plan: people feel their government is remote.

Recently the state legislature authorized council to enact a one-half-cent city sales tax without referendum, and it did so, repealing the vehicle and cigarette taxes. The new tax solves Peoria's financial problem. It will mean better streets and sewers. But it is still an unpopular tax.

The election demoralized Bean's aids. Councilmen talked of abolishing some of their jobs. Recently, however, the staff has taken heart. One of them said, "At first the election seemed a repudiation of everything we stood for. But maybe it was good for us. We experts have a tendency to take ourselves too seriously, to think that 'papa knows best,' to just go ahead and do things. In administrative government you forget that politics underlies everything in a democracy."

# LA GUARDIA: "GOOD GOVERNMENT" CAN BE MISMANAGEMENT

## REXFORD G. TUGWELL

THERE HAD BEEN REFORM MAYORS before La Guardia, even in New York City; by his time historians had made up their minds why these re-

Reprinted from *The Art of Politics* by Rexford G. Tugwell (New York: Doubleday and Company, Inc., 1958), pp. 27–33 and 103–104. Copyright © 1958 by Rexford G. Tugwell. Reprinted by permission of Doubleday and Company, Inc.

formers had been comparative failures: they had not created machines. When the first fervor of reformism had passed, the bosses of the old parties had simply taken charge again by default. There was no one else to perform a necessary function. So far as there was wisdom from other instances, it was to the same effect. Steffens, again, was full of it; and the one competent littérateur among modern municipal reformers, Brand Whitlock, had the same, or about the same, deduction to offer. La Guardia should therefore have concentrated on building a machine, in opposition to that of the bosses, which would have furnished support for himself and made his reforms more permanent. But this is precisely what he did not do, never thought of doing, and, as part of his public attitudinizing, strenuously denounced. The machine was to be La Guardia, as it had been Tom Johnson, Hunt, Jones, Mitchel, Heney, Blankenburg, and other reformers before him. All of them had failed to do more than upset the bosses temporarily, but all had had picturesque careers. I could recall, from my undergraduate days at the University of Pennsylvania, Blankenburg riding down Market Street in Philadelphia on a white horse which was symbolic of crusading purity. At the time I was stirred. But my recollections included disillusion. His reforms disappeared with him after the next election, much as snowdrifts melt in a warm spring wind.

Was La Guardia conscious that he inherited and was the responsible contemporary repository of a reformist tradition? More important, was he conscious that none of his predecessors had "succeeded"—that none had done more than, for the moment, to channel through a group of honest administrators the business of the city? These are not easy questions to answer, but some light is thrown on them by asking the associated question that can with some confidence be answered: Do the incidents of his administration seem to show that there was a rule to which they conformed?

In the first place, La Guardia left the city government better structured than he found it. In the second place, however, the better government was not proof against the mishandling of later mayors—or even against his own. And as to his own mishandling, it is not difficult to demonstrate that he himself was the best exponent of methods for evading the intentions of the City Charter. There was no limitation on himself that he tolerated gracefully and hardly any that he did not break through whenever it became irksome. And very often no more needed to be involved than mere caprice to cause an outbreak of temper, a fracture of regulations, and subsequent virtuous preening as a man whose care for his responsibilities transcended red tape, bureaucratic obstruction, and stifling inertia. There was no sense in him of the value of precedent, of the utility of unexceptionable behavior. He was a one-man government and not to be held to the conduct expected of others. So long as he was there, no limitations were necessary or even tolerable.

Also, it is a sad truth that when he was through, La Guardia left a bankrupt city. On the day his successor, William O'Dwyer, took office several hundred million dollars had to be found to meet pressing obligations not provided for by La Guardia. Debts were falling due; but also, although the city was equipped as never before with public facilities—especially parks and parkways—the adequate maintenance and operation of these pleasant appurtenances had not been budgeted. Not only were the new parks, parkways, playgrounds, and recreation facilities already falling into neglect, all the streets were dirty, garbage was not being effectively collected, children were either not able to go to school or could go only part time, vast hospitals were inadequately staffed and tended—the whole of the city machinery was breaking down from sheer lack of funds. This debacle was in no small part traceable to La Guardia's carelessness in allowing the city's tax base to attenuate. Suburbs outside his jurisdiction had absorbed many of the large taxpayers—a movement facilitated by the expensive parkways—and there had been an increase rather than a diminution of expenses to be met with shrunken income. Old facilities had to be maintained even when new ones in fringe neighborhoods still within the city were being built and staffed.

During most of La Guardia's regime municipal revenue had been supplemented by federal funds—notably from the Works Progress Administration and its predecessor organizations. In 1938, for instance, when I had occasion to examine the matter (as chairman of the City Planning Commission) *slightly more than half* of those expenses were being met from federal or state allocations. There was an end to this as the long depression faded out and war approached. Unemployment was no longer an excuse for asking Washington to support the city. And numerous enlarged facilities, built with relief labor, remained to be supported from revenues cut just about in half. No wonder Mayor O'Dwyer was aghast when he first surveyed the problem he had to meet.

All this is said to show that even a good government can be mismanaged by the most honest of administrators. La Guardia never allowed a cent to be stolen, a favor to be given at city expense, or a compromise he knew to be a losing one to be made with private interests. But when his regime was over, the city's debt to the bankers was larger than it had ever been before, and it consequently carried a burden of interest which in itself would almost have met a reasonable ordinary budget. The only advance toward municipal ownership of utilities had been the taking over of the subways. This was done, strangely enough, at the instance of the financiers, who in former years had propagandized expensively to the effect that there were deep socialistic dangers in such a move. But when subways became unprofitable it was no longer socialistic for the city to take them over. For a system with negative earning power, several hundred millions was paid. This sum committed the city for the next decade and a half—until an Authority was established in a later crisis of virtual bankruptcy under Mayor Impellitteri—to the assumption of an operating deficit ranging up to a hundred million annually which otherwise might have had to be met by the sellers. There was also the interest on all those bonds!

It was obvious from the time when the subways first began to lose, although there were long delays while politicians maneuvered around the issue, that fares would have to be at least doubled. La Guardia was gone, however, long before this public admission finally had to be made. It was not a profitable deal for the city. How La Guardia really felt about it, he did not say. He can hardly have been proud of the result; but if he had had to argue the matter he most probably would have contended that expediency had controlled his action. And he would have thought that a quite sufficient justification.

New Yorkers, in later decades, after experience with O'Dwyer and Impellitteri, looked back to La Guardia with growing nostalgia. A majority of them had been amused by him, felt tolerantly possessive about him, and often said to themselves that anyway he was honest. And he was; they were right. Not one in a million realized how he had pledged them to the bankers, permanently increased the cost of their utilities, and made municipal bankruptcy inevitable; and even if they had they would by then have wanted him back. They only knew that he had been energetic, vigilant in their interest, and, in spite of his sometimes overflamboyant behavior, really dedicated. He was against bosses, crooks, graft, and bureaucrats. They liked that.

Then there was the City Charter of 1936. This made New York's the most effectively constituted of all city governments, past or present. It was an amazing as well as a marvelous achievement. It embodied all—or most— of the devices and arrangements for which theorists and practitioners alike had for a generation been longing. It made the executive powerful but responsible; it confined the legislature (the old Board of Aldermen, now the City Council) to its proper sphere and made logrolling and capricious interference with the executive next to impossible; it provided for long- and short-range planning; it possessed built-in devices for insuring honesty and the careful selection of personnel; it arranged for policy-making at the proper level and with the proper participation, and it gave the city an almost adequate home rule.

La Guardia did not participate in writing this Charter, but when he had finished campaigning for it he had made it his own. He was the first mayor under it and began the shaping of its traditions. There is a great deal to be said about this that would be too detailed for the purpose here. There is reason to believe that he really had understood only the main features, so that when he came to administering it he felt compelled to attenuate some of its best provisions when they proved to be limitations on his own freedom of action. But the most significant fact is that a long effort by New York's most devoted citizens issued in a document that La Guardia adopted before the electorate. This identified him further as a good-government man in the tradition of the municipal reformers—a role he obviously felt himself appointed to play.

The new Charter suited him in one large aspect—it centralized power in himself as mayor. But it irked him in other ways. It interfered with his willful judgments; and no more intolerant public man ever functioned in

America—where there has been a succession of obstreperous ones. And when this happened he recognized none of its limitations, most of which were inherent in a government of separated powers.

When La Guardia was gone the Charter remained. It was not so good an operating guide because of him as it would have been had he been more devoted to its principles—he had established some dangerous precedents—yet the residue of credit is considerable. And in all his subsequent machinations to escape from the net woven about him by the provisions of the Charter, he never acknowledged a reversal of his devotion to it. Even serious breaches in its principles he sought to make appear as "improvements." When this interpretation was not accepted by his friends he often became exaggeratedly angry and sometimes accused them of betrayals much more honestly attributable to himself. There were, indeed, many subtractions to be made from the La Guardia reputation as a reformer, and none knew so well what they were as those close to him. They suffered most from his struggles in the net of restrictions required by honest and efficient government.

This side of La Guardia could not be kept secret; but surprisingly little of it reached the public. Loyalty was very characteristic of the substantial citizens who were his sponsors and supporters. They had to deal with a willful, sometimes irresponsible, individual in a position of great—and deliberately enhanced—power; but they had looked a long time for even so imperfect an embodiment of their civic ideals. And to the public he was always the enemy of spoils and of corruption even while his antics seemed slightly ridiculous. In the middle of his career, as I talked with many of his partisans, I discovered that they had not come to any satisfactory conclusions. Some said they thought he had no interest at all in good government. It had merely been a convenient way to get the Fusion nomination and to set up a properly striking contrast with the preceding boss-controlled mayors. Most, however, had quite a different view. They regarded the difficult mayor as a spoiled child suddenly able to impose his will on those around him but basically responsible and with a set toward running the city as a public service institution. As such it had to have honest police and inspection services (the locus of most municipal corruption); it had to perform such duties as putting out fires, furnishing water, and providing schools, hospitals, and playgrounds; and all this must be done better than it had ever been done before. All the La Guardia performances were, in this view, merely calculated to mark him as the embodiment of these aspirations. Notoriety and a reputation for crusading would continue in power the regime that accomplished these things.

This was the view I came to take. It was very hard to get along with him as Mayor. It was more difficult for those who were his associates or subordinates than for his citizen supporters, because he was so often unfeeling, so unwilling to explore facts, and so apt to demand undeserved loyalty in specific and inappropriate instances. We were often on the receiving end of his famous temper, and to the more sensitive or vulnerable this made continuation of work with him impossible. But this, in itself, is not the point here, except as it bears on the question whether his outstanding success was owed in any measure to, or was achieved in spite of, his faults as a chief and as a member of the political profession.

That he invariably knew what he was doing, I became convinced. His tempers were mostly synthetic—to gain a point, to effect a subjection, to exhibit himself in a righteous role. They were part of a whole acting scheme that also included the reward of virtue in conspicuous instances, preferably for the heroism of police or firemen; the treatment with obvious contempt of most associates so that they should share none of his credit with the public; the spectacular emphasis on his jealous direction of city affairs—he raced to fires in helmet and boots, took credit for all the favors flowing from Washington (one reason he petted Robert Moses was that, as a Republican and an old feuder with Roosevelt, Moses obviously had no influence in Albany or Washington), and intervened in time to center attention on himself whenever there was any clear political profit in anything going on—the settlement of a labor dispute, the location of a housing project, a school, or an extension of the rapid transit lines.

In a technical way, all of this is important, just as it was important in the careers of his predecessors. I am quite certain that he, however, as well as they, invented the method for himself and made his own variations on a role that may seem to have been studied but was not. If political observers are struck with the similarities in the careers of some dozen American reform Mayors, they must remember what kind of person it takes to assume and carry out, over a full career, the character necessary to spectacular local leadership. Nothing learned from books or from the study of precedents could produce what New Yorkers recognize as La Guardiaism. And it is impossible to think that a student of government would imagine himself as a La Guardia and study consciously to attain La Guardia's public position. They might want to, and study to, become Mayor; but La Guardia screaming at a meeting of subordinates, running to a midnight fire, scheming to double-cross an associate in such a way as to get public credit—these are not admirable attributes to imitate. They were, however, essential ingredients of the living and acting La Guardia. It was also part of the La Guardia essence that it all came to far less than it might have, because he sabotaged his own charter and failed to map a strategy that would keep his city solvent. In the end he was succeeded by an organization Democrat. If a rule were being made for students to follow, La Guardia, the reformer, if all his characteristics were essential, would be something less than a reasonable example—so much less than reasonable that there cannot actually have been any rule. And if it does not exist, it cannot be followed. . . .

Very possibly I exaggerate La Guardia's incompetence in administration; it was less incompetence, really, than perverseness. Or it may be that he could not believe housekeeping tasks to be important. Or again he may have felt the lack in them of the spectacular for which he thirsted. Yet again, he may

have sensed the wastage of great talents for one occupation on another occupation for which they were unsuited, without proceeding to an understanding that something remedial could be done about it that would enhance,
not diminish his prestige. He certainly worked very hard and was as earnest
as a man could be. Also, he was always fascinated by details, even if without
any competence in their disposal. It made him genuinely happy to feel that
his municipal organization was giving good service, something everyone
understood. So he cannot have been quite so bad as those who had to work
with him thought he was. The record of his administration is one of considerable progress, especially in public works. Many projects had been talked
about for years and deferred time after time as Tammany Mayors fell farther
and farther into fiscal chaos. Most of the old ones and many new ones were
undertaken and promptly carried through, some under the direction of the
redoubtable Robert Moses, but many under other auspices. The difficulty
with awarding La Guardia credit for this physical progress is that he was
just in time to cash in on the federal aids that were part of the New Deal.
These aids were not only extended generously for building public works
but also could be used for maintenance.

His fiscal failure in the long run is at least to be condoned by mitigating
circumstances. The underlying problem of New York was shared by other
American cities; all of them were in effect bankrupt by 1930 because the
municipality was not coextensive with the metropolis. Disaster had crept
upon them unaware, and there was by no means a wide acceptance of the
drastic cure that was indicated. La Guardia can be blamed for not having
grasped his opportunity, but not so much as he could have been blamed if
there had even been one example to follow. For another thing, much of
what needed to be done would have had to be authorized by state law.[1] He
could not have extended the city limits to include the suburbs which were
parasites on the city; nor could he have accomplished other reforms—alone.
But he might have furnished the same sort of leadership as had put through
the Charter of 1936. If he had I have no doubt he would have prevailed.
The trouble was that he seemed not to be convinced that the diagnosis was
correct. Anyway, he could not be roused. What was expected of him by the
city's older first citizens, he accomplished. He provided a reform administration on the traditional model, defended it, perpetuated it in a new charter,
and transformed New York from a notorious Tammany playground into a
place of pride and civic energy.

For still another thing, it can be argued that La Guardia went as far
in reform as he could and that if he had tried to do what I suggest he would
have failed; he might, moreover, have jeopardized more than he could have
gained. Rescuing New York from the moneylenders and reducing the pre-
dations of the real estate interests would have involved a struggle in which
all the conservatives, generally on his side as things were, would have united

---

1. In the case of New York, there was also the problem of New Jersey across the
Hudson River and even Connecticut a few miles to the north.

against him. This would have included the press, always so hot for reform until reform touches an influential interest.

La Guardia was entitled to say to me—as others had said—that his justification was that he won elections; and if I retorted that an election won was a victory only if it resulted in the gaining of some objective beyond an office for a politician, that was merely a matter of opinion. It is impossible to say for certain in his case that further objectives were attainable. It will always remain a matter of judgment.

# PHILADELPHIA: "GOOD GOVERNMENT" LEADS TO MORAL FRUSTRATION

## JAMES REICHLEY

REFORM, it has been said, is what we have in America in place of ideology. Political participation by those not professionally involved in politics is built around periodic attacks on the alleged corruption in government. Unfortunately, these attacks in most areas turn out to be few and far between, and the reform doctrine does not supply the kind of motivation that would keep the greater part of the population politically activated during the long dry spells between uprisings. What is the reason for this failure of "reform" to produce permanent interest in politics, and is there any possibility that it will in the future perform a function of social integration as well as eliminate the abuses at which it is primarily aimed? To answer these questions it will first be necessary to examine the nature of the reform idea.

Let us begin by turning back to the years immediately following the end of the Second World War when reform politics in Philadelphia was chiefly an exciting brew being passed from lip to lip among a little band of idealists in the city's gentleman's clubs and intellectual associations. A part of the nature of this mixture we have already suggested: Dislocated aristocrats were turning to politics as a means of winning back their own from the managerial class that was displacing them in practical life.

How was this strictly upper-class motivation, and the genuine social idealism that undoubtedly accompanied it, translated into a battle-cry that activated citizens of Philadelphia by the thousands to enlist in the army of reform? In the first place, of course, the reform spirit received its mass base by allying itself with the downtrodden city Democratic organization

Reprinted from *The Art of Government* (New York: The Fund for the Republic, 1959), pp. 107–114 and 122–124.

which had been waiting through almost half of the twentieth century for the logic of urban politics finally to sweep the local offices into the grasp of the party of the working man. But what was the aspect of the reform spirit that the Democratic politicians at last accepted, and how was it that this aspect was for a time not only acceptable but actually popular with the henchmen of the minority party organization? A clue to the answer to this question may be found in the story of the actual binding of the Democratic and reform causes.

Early in 1947, Michael Bradley, who was then chairman of the Democratic city committee and a leading proponent of alliance between his party and the reformers, gave consideration to four possible reform candidates for mayor: Walter Phillips, a leisured member of the upper class who had led the city planning crusade; Joseph S. Clark, a dabbler in Democratic politics over the years and anxious to be "rung in on things" since his return from the wars; Richardson Dilworth, a flamboyant war hero hovering on the outskirts of the city's old society; and Lewis Stevens, a starchy Philadelphia lawyer and leading lay figure in the Presbyterian Church of Pennsylvania. Phillips had gained attention through his association with city planning, Clark through advocacy of civil-service reform, Stevens through his religious activities, and Dilworth through his publicly expressed intention to "throw the crooks out of City Hall." With little hesitation, the Democratic city chairman chose Dilworth. Emotional moralizing over the alleged corruption of the opposition, it seems clear, was the element of the reform program that most appealed to the organization Democrats. Had they not for years been threatening to "throw the rascals out"?

Dilworth's campaign in 1947 and virtually every campaign he has waged since that time have been built around the image of himself as prosecutor of the "crooks" whom he has sought to represent as the leaders of the GOP. (A young lawyer, a typical "clean-cut" Republican member of the legal fraternity with no trace of underworld connections, tells of having asked Dilworth in the early Fifties a rather difficult but fair question at one of his street-corner rallies, to which the reformer replied in rasping tones, "Young man, may I ask what numbers bank you represent?") This strategy paid off at the polls, not so much in 1947 as Michael Bradley had hoped it might, but particularly in 1949 and 1951 after the newspapers had exposed the fact that there was indeed a good deal of corruption in the Republican administration of City Hall.

More recently, such an approach has been somewhat undermined by the fact that it has become Dilworth's own Democratic party that controls the city administration, but the reform leader, seeking to maintain his stance as champion of the only aspect of the reform movement that has seemed much to interest him, has pretty broadly suggested, particularly during the Blanc campaign, that even under Democratic rule the City Hall still has its share of crooks and that these would be likely to run riot were it not for the vigilant efforts of Richardson Dilworth. "I seem," he says, "to see the same faces in the corridors here that I saw eight years ago."

Unfortunately, the image of crook-catcher has been a little dimmed by the circumstances that Dilworth has in point of fact caught rather few crooks (the numbers racket, for instance, his special target, seems to thrive as much as ever throughout the city), and that his sometimes very courageous stands against the Democratic organization have usually been followed by back-sliding attempts to get back into the good graces of its leaders. The present mayor, it would seem, has been demoralizingly trapped between a desire to avoid Clark's outright defiance of the organization and a wish to be at the same time regarded in the public mind as the organization's re-forming nemesis.

The spirit of Clark and of Walter Phillips, which dominated the first reform administration elected in 1951, may be said, in the long run, to have channeled the reform impulse in Philadelphia more successfully than Dilworth's moral preachments against the rascals in City Hall.[1] This spirit, expressing the typical American mid-twentieth century philosophy of "good government," is less moral than institutional and economic. When Clark moved into the mayor's office in 1951, he directed, with the assistance of Phillips and the three governmental technicians who composed his cabinet, a thorough overhaul of the city's financial structure, its system of record, the operation of almost all its departments, and the entire decision-making process within the municipal hierarchy. At the same time, the new administration devoted serious attention to long-range problems like urban renewal and traffic control which had been almost completely neglected by its hand-to-mouth predecessors. Electronic machines appeared in City Hall to perform efficiently the tasks of recording that generations of ward-heelers had carried out with doubtful competence; trained economists brought fiscal sophistication to a budget that previously had been planned on the level of inky-ledgered arithmetic; employees hired under civil service replaced a large number of the party workers who formerly had given irregular service at their nominal jobs; great housing and commercial developments began to spring up in all parts of the city.

So complete were the changes made at this time that it is most unlikely that the return of any conceivable Democratic or Republican machine administration could alter many of the most important of them. It is probably true, as Lennox Moak, who served as first director of finance under Clark and now is director of the Pennsylvania Economy League in Philadelphia,

---

1. The religiously oriented spirit of the fourth proposed reform candidate for mayor in 1947, Lewis Stevens, is perhaps more difficult to find in any of the administrations that were later elected under the reform banner. The absence of any deep emotional content, such as might be produced by a religious basis for political action, may, I shall argue later, be the very thing that is wrong with the reform spirit. Stevens himself served as an excellent city councilman in the Clark administration, and was later appointed by Governor Leader, to the dismay of Bill Green, as State Secretary of Highways. On Green's insistence, he was passed over by Leader for a vacancy on the State Supreme Court in 1958. Green's, and as a result Leader's choice for this vacancy was the able Judge Curtis Bok.

says: "The reforms that will stick are the reforms that we made in the city's institutions. I cannot believe that any organization would wilfully put bad policies in place of good policies in areas where its patronage and so forth are not affected. The normal organization, once it gets into power, does things 'as they have always been done.' They will most probably in nine cases out of ten follow the precedents that we laid down for them." The city of Philadelphia will never return to the condition in which Joe Clark found it. With the single vital exception of civil service (ironically, Clark's special concern) the reforms that he and his collaborators made can almost certainly not be undone. And yet, in at least one respect, the Clark-Phillips school of institutional reform has been even less successful than the "throw-the-rascals-out" approach practiced by Richardson Dilworth.

"The problem that we have never solved is the problem of continuity," admitted Joe Clark in the summer of 1958. It is perfectly true that neither he nor Dilworth has constructed the kind of city-wide organization that could give any sort of permanence to the spirit as distinguished from the institutions of reform in city politics. Beyond a handful of activists in City Hall and the ADA, the reform movement appears to have lost all cohesiveness in the city; the Democratic organization, almost universally regarded as a "bunch of political bums," is universally rolling into power. This is due partly to certain biases within the spirit of reform. Before turning to these, however, it will be well to attempt to determine how much of the failure is due to the personalities of the two reform leaders themselves.

Despite their shared upper-class background and their common interest in reform, Richardson Dilworth and Joseph S. Clark are about as unlike as two men in public life can be. Dilworth is the warm, all-too-human, relatively simple extrovert in politics; Clark, in contrast, is reserved, reflective, some say cunning, complex, the thinker as politician. Dilworth seems to require heavy doses of admiration if not adulation from his sizable entourage; Clark, a loner by temperament, is sometimes accused of being difficult to work with. The current mayor, despite his retinue of supporters, runs what is in the last analysis a one-man show; all persons who deal with the city government are used to receiving phone calls from him in which pending problems are often settled in a few minutes of personal negotiation. The former mayor was a man of the staff who operated through his subordinates whenever he could; many of the people who now are consulted by Dilworth several times a month never had a personal conversation with Clark during his four years in office.

Dilworth rather resembles one of those heroes of F. Scott Fitzgerald, who came out of the Middle-Western gentry to be educated and make a name in the patrician East: Like them, he is charming, generous, unstable, not remarkably scrupulous, brave, ambitious, fond of high living, eager to make a splash, and fundamentally innocent. Dilworth, one feels, is forever playing out a role that he has only half understood, concentrating on the show while frequently growing bored with the substance. Like them, too, he seems to be motivated by an odd and not entirely ignoble idealism—the restless yearning to realize "the Platonic ideal of himself." It is harder to find a literary parallel for Clark. He is more tough-minded than the heroes of John Marquand whose background he shares, and he is more ambitious than the philosophic upstate squires created by James Cozzens (the Arthur Winner of Philadelphia is, in some ways, Walter Phillips). The truth is that he is the product of an upper class more deeply rooted in time than those which American novelists have usually got around to describing. To find his model one must probably turn to such European writers as Conrad, Stendhal, or Tolstoy; perhaps, even, it is in that crafty creator of a commonwealth, Shakespeare's King Henry IV, that one discerns his features most clearly.[2]

In attitudes toward government Dilworth seems at first the more conservative, but on further thought one realizes that he is merely the more conventional (T.R. riding forth for another loud and fairly ineffectual crack at the forces of political unrighteousness). Senator Clark, who is frequently accused of being a radical, may on the other hand be "the most conservative leader in American public life today," as a friend of his calls him, but, if so, it is the calculated conservatism of Disraeli rather than the visceral conservatism of Burke. The Senator has given ample evidence for his attachment to such non-radical concepts as class, authority, and tradition, but he appears to believe that these concepts can be preserved in the modern world only with the assent of the mass of ordinary human beings. He has thus become the aristocratic leader of the commons against the "oligarchs" who seek to diminish the formal government so that their wills may be informally absolute in their private baronies.

Were (or are) either or both of these two most fascinating individuals capable of building an organization that might carry on the good-government ideal after they themselves have passed out of public life or at least out of intimate connection with city politics? Certainly they would have had great difficulties—Dilworth perhaps because he is too much the prima donna anxious to win victories and big headlines rather than to attempt any fundamental restoration of civic life, Clark perhaps because the very ruthlessness and cold intelligence that have made him personally strong tend to alienate him from the camaraderie and fellow-feeling that form the indispensable mortar to any enduring political organization. All the same, both possess great natural talents—an unfeigned fondness for humanity in

---

2. A story which illustrates many of Clark's characteristics tells of a visit paid by a friend of his to the preparatory school in which the future statesman received his early education. The friend was shown a wall decorated with plaques carved by all of the school's graduates, and noted that on the plaque bearing the name of Joseph S. Clark was displayed a relief of the American flag. When this evidence of youthful interest in government was later mentioned to the Senator, Clark declared that he had aspired to the upper house of the federal legislature since he was a very small boy. Pausing, he then added: "The truth is, though, that I didn't really carve that plaque. I was never good with my hands, and, since I wanted the carving above my name to be well done, I hired another, more skilful boy to do it for me."

the case of Dilworth, a lucid understanding of human nature in the case of
Clark—which might well have suited them for the gigantic task of creating
a permanent reform movement in the city. That both have so signally failed
to do so (and with them the somewhat more earnest reformers like Phillips,
not to mention the Republican public-relations reformers like Longstreth and
Pomeroy) is, I think, partly due to the good-government philosophy itself
which all have in one way or another represented.

This philosophy, in both its moral and its economic forms, seems to be
oriented toward particular projects rather than toward any broad social
image. It promises to perform certain worthwhile tasks of government,
whether throwing the crooks out of City Hall or providing a more efficient
means of circulating downtown traffic, instead of seeking to understand and
to satisfy the fundamental needs of human beings. It takes the needs of
human beings as given, and sets out to eliminate obstacles to the relief of
these needs which it detects in the framework of society (like crooks) or
which have been created by society's own rapid expansion (like street congestion). These objectives, even the moral ones, seem finally to be reducible
to an economic view of the nature of man: Crooks are bad because they
steal the taxpayers' money; traffic congestion is bad because it is strangling
the economic life of the city; city planning is good because it provides an
orderly means for the development of metropolitan commerce (though with
city planning of the Bacon-Phillips kind, it must be admitted, a humanistic
note is often struck).

. . . The economic view, coupled with a prevailing individualism which
insists that government must limit itself to removing the obstacles to fulfillment of the economic needs of the population rather than undertake to fulfill
them itself, makes difficult if not impossible any sustained, large-scale political
effort dedicated to the objective of "reform." The declared purpose of
reform is the solution of this or that economic problem; when the problem
is solved or when it has turned into a bore, the whole reason for the effort
has collapsed. The possibility of "continuity" in the reform movement therefore becomes slim, and before very long it is "the same faces" of the organization politicians or ones very much like them that again begin to appear in
the halls of government.

. . . Most Americans do *not* actively participate in politics. The fact is that
most Americans, except for occasional bursts of reform spirit, have been
willing to permit their governments to be operated in a slovenly and irrational
fashion which they would not dream of tolerating in any field in which they
considered themselves to be personally concerned. The reason for this, I
suspect, is that the case for good government has as a rule been presented in
terms too simply economic: If elected, the reformer has generally seemed to
be saying, I will save you money and I will rationalize our government so
that our city will be a place in which you can make a good living. Well and

good, the voter has seemed to think, and has cast his ballot for a Dick Dilworth or a Joe Clark.

But if the motive for political participation is strictly an economic one, then it must take its place within the hierarchy of similar economic motives and concerns. Inevitably, the place that it enjoys there cannot be a very high one. It must rank behind the job which is the direct source of personal income; it must rank behind the nominally social activities that are really instruments for personal advancement; it must rank behind the numerous exercises for self-improvement which can be turned back into the direct economic struggle. Since man does not live by bread alone, it will also probably rank behind the explicitly non-economic activities of leisure time. Unable to gain a high priority among economic motives, it is removed by its economic taint from competition with the activities that are labeled "pleasure." If political activity is really primarily motivated by economic concerns, as many reform politicians have seemed to assume, there is little hope that the greater portion of the population can ever be drawn for long stretches of time into active politics. Luckily, this does not seem to be the case.

Let us look again at the sense of moral frustration that has overcome the reform movement in Philadelphia and that, we have suggested, is a common characteristic of reform campaigns in this country. At first sight the frustration seems somewhat unreasonable. Since the amount of corruption carried on under the Republicans was not really so very great, and since the amount of corruption being carried on now is very likely even less, and since the institutional changes that have been made have been of a worthwhile and permanent nature, the reformers seem to have little cause for the sense of moral dismay that they clearly feel. At the same time, however, we have noted that the reform movement in Philadelphia has suffered one real failure: It has failed to change in any fundamental way the practice of politics in the city.

Let us now suggest that the sense of frustration and the real failure in fact belong together: that the reformers and the voters are frustrated today not so much because a few crooks still loiter about in the corridors of City Hall but because they have failed in extending the opportunity for active political participation to the larger number of ordinary citizens. But why should these citizens feel frustrated over being denied the opportunity for political participation when, as we have argued, the economic motive for political activity is not a very intense one?

This returns us to the question of what the "boys" really mean when they say they "love politics." We have admitted that the quest for status is involved in this motivation, as no doubt it is with the urge that the ordinary citizen may feel toward the political realm. But we have also suggested that status hunger alone cannot explain the satisfaction the "boys" seem to gain from their work, just as it does not explain the clear emotional return experienced by a Joe Clark or a Richardson Dilworth or a Thacher Longstreth. Let us look more closely at the concept, "love politics." What, after all, is politics? Politics, we are told, is who gets what, when, and how. Viewed in one light, no doubt. But if that is politics, then what is economics? Is not economics also who gets what, when, and how? Are politics and economics then identical? Hardly, since there are clearly economic activities—like selling automobiles and buying cucumbers—that are not political activities. Is politics, then, a division within the general class of economics? One thinks not. The feeling of frustration associated with reform, for instance, seems to have little economic basis, and neither does the feeling of camaraderie that is so valued by the "boys." Is not politics more truly defined, all things considered, as the expression of the will of the individual within the society of his fellows, or, more completely, the participation of human beings in the activities of conserving, distributing, and improving the values that are created by a civilized community? In short, is not politics the "art of government"? And if this is true, is not the question of why human beings should "love politics" similar to the question of why men should love women? Is not the answer to both, that is, that it is the nature of the beast? Is it not true, then, that political activity is a normal manifestation of human nature, and the real question is: Why should there be men who do *not* love politics?

With this question in mind, let us return for another look at the Protestant group whose mores have set the dominant pattern in the United States, and whose general lack of political interest has been used as an argument in favor of the theory that politics, insofar as it is not economic, is a "status-conferring" function. Let us suggest now that the general lack of political activity among members of the Protestant middle class is due not so much to the fact that they may be in a secure status position as to the effect of any unduly individualistic philosophy which over-emphasizes the private will at the expense of the social context in which it seeks to operate.

# V

## THE TREND OF URBAN POLITICS

The most significant single fact for the future of urban politics in America is its changing class character. Until recently, our cities have been predominantly lower class. Today, they are in most cases predominantly middle class, and soon they will be overwhelmingly so. What has happened, according to Samuel Lubell, is that the sons and daughters, and the grandsons and granddaughters, of the immigrants (the "old underdog elements") have climbed into the middle class. These new elements of the middle class are different from the old middle class in several important respects. Having made their gains during a time of depression and war, they do not share the hostility of the older middle-class generation to Big Government. And whereas the old middle class was preoccupied with the task of creating a nationwide economy, Lubell thinks that the new middle class is ready for an "adventure in social unification." This "new frontier," he says, is the creation of the kind of nationwide social structure required by an industrial civilization. It is, therefore, an "urban frontier."

Lubell overlooks one striking feature of the situation: in spite of the differences in their history and outlook, the new middle classes have accepted the political ethic of the old. They have moved from what Jane Addams called a "personal" to a "social" morality. Most of those who were Catholic in theology before are so still, but they have become Yankee-Protestant in their political ethic. They are avid for ethnic recognition (Lubell points out that in this they differ from the old middle class), but they want a kind of recognition that is flattering by the new standards they have come to accept. To have a surname that marks one as a member of what Mayor Curley of Boston called "the newer races" is a political advantage in any large city, but only when it is accompanied by attributes—not only speech, dress, and manner, but also public virtues: honesty, impartiality, and regard for efficiency—that the public mind associates with the old Yankee-Protestant elite. The "new immigrants" indignantly reject those political ways—above all, the boss and the machine—that remind them of their pre-middle-class past. Thus, as Frank J. Sorauf explains, patronage, an indispensable element in the equilibrium of incentives of the machine, has practically disappeared in most cities. According to Sorauf a party that tries to clean house after an election is likely to encounter public indignation because the middle class respects the "public-spirited citizen" and not the "self-interested party worker," and because it will not excuse the presence of mediocrities in public service in the name of party loyalty. Edward C. Banfield shows how the one remaining powerful big city machine, that of Chicago, is beleaguered by middle-class elements in the outlying neighborhoods and suburbs. To get the necessary support from these elements, the machine must accept one reform after another, and so must eventually reform itself out of existence.

The new style of politics takes its character not only from the political ethic of the mass of voters, but more especially from the mentality of the elite. This elite, which is necessarily small, consists of those who run for office, select candidates, and manage and finance campaigns. About this mentality and its significance for urban politics, three political scientists, Robert C. Wood, Seyom Brown, and James Q. Wilson, tell us a good deal. Although the elites they describe are very differently situated—they are suburbanites in the case of Wood and Brown, and Manhattan cliffdwellers in the case of Wilson—it is nevertheless apparent that they share a single mentality. In other words, what is significant is not where they live (whether in the suburbs or the central city), but their class, age, and educational characteristics. Although these new-style political activists are likely to be hi-fi addicts and to wear toreador pants, these readings suggest that their outlook is not essentially different from that of earlier generations of reformers. They feel a lively concern (to use a characteristically Protestant word) for the welfare of the community and a corresponding obligation to participate in its affairs. They believe that disinterested and expert search for the interest of the community "as a whole" is far better than political struggle as a way of solving public problems. They believe, with Steffens and the Progressives, that the popular will, when it expresses itself without distortion by defective institutions or other "external" corrupting elements like the machine or, nowadays, TV or advertising, is always good, right, and wise, and that therefore the cure for the ills of democracy is more democracy. They think that a political party is tolerable only to the extent that it persuades on grounds of public interest, and they regard party discipline based on anything else—above all, on personal material incentives—as a form of corruption. And they conclude that for all practical purposes party is an evil, although perhaps a necessary one, and that the ideal should be nonpartisanship.

Carried to its logical conclusion, this ideal implies government without politics. An executive (whether called mayor, manager, or chairman) would run the government as if it were a business. Presumably he would decide matters strictly on the basis of technical criteria. He would be high-handed, of course, but he would "get things done" and the voters would have the satisfaction of knowing that things were being done honestly, impartially, and efficiently. For all practical purposes his tenure would be permanent—he would be re-elected or reappointed almost automatically—and he would play no part in the partisan politics of the state and nation. In the intervals between the going of one such executive and the coming of another, there would, of course, be flurries of what Robert L. Morlan calls "unorganized" politics. Interest groups and voluntary associations would move to the center of the stage, but the character of their performance would be influenced by that of their audience, which would, for the most part, be dedicated to the cause of "good government." And when another strong executive was found, "unorganized" politics would again dissolve into no politics.

# THE NEW MIDDLE CLASS

## SAMUEL LUBELL

THE ESSENTIAL DIFFERENCE between the Republican-rooted middle class and the newer Democratically inclined middle class is hardly one of conservatism versus liberalism, in the true meaning of these terms. What really separates these two middle classes is the factor of timing—of when each arrived at the state of middle-class blessedness. Because of the timing of their rise, the newer middle-class elements probably had tougher going during the depression and differ in occupational and business interests. Having achieved their gains in a period of expanding governmental authority, they are not as hostile to "Big Government" as the older middle-class elements. They also are apt to be of different ethnic or religious backgrounds.

The ethnic differences are not crucially important in themselves. What makes them so significant politically is that having come to this country in roughly the same period, the so-called "new" immigrants and their offspring shared common experiences in this country. All have been part of one of the epic population movements in history—of the upsurging out of the slums toward the middle class which has swept our major cities over the last fifty years and which still is going on.

Reprinted from *The Future of American Politics* by Samuel Lubell (New York: Harper & Brothers, 1952), pp. 60–67 and 75–78. Copyright 1951, 1952 by Samuel Lubell. Reprinted by permission of Harper & Brothers.

To map the growth of almost any of our larger cities since the turn of the century is to map this upward, outward push of the masses toward the greener suburbs, propelling the older residents before them. And the story of the Democratic party in the big cities is really the story of the social and political revolution which marched along with this exodus from the slums.

The exodus was not accomplished in a single, mass evacuation, but through successive moves, from one neighborhood to the next. Each new neighborhood represented a higher rung on the social and economic ladder. And as they climbed, the masses were transformed. By the time the heights of middle-class status had been scaled, the immigrant generation which had begun the trek had died off or had become grandparents, relegated to the role of baby sitters, and a new native-born generation had come into its own.

A similar clocklike progression through successive frontier zones marked our westward expansion. So alike, in fact, are the dynamics of the two movements that one is justified in asking: Did the frontier ever really pass from American life? True, the supply of free land was virtually gone by 1890. But did the frontier really die with the exhaustion of free lands? Or did it merely sink from sight temporarily, to reappear in a new form in our developing industrial civilization?

## The Old Tenement Trail

Possibly because it lacked the excitement of the Indian wars or because it still is so close to us, the saga of this twentieth-century odyssey of America's urban masses has gone unsung. Yet the parallels between the old western frontier and the new urban frontier are striking.

To Frederick Jackson Turner, who made American historians frontier-conscious, the ever-receding frontier was the zone of most rapid and effective Americanization. At the outer edge, "where civilization and savagery met," was where "men of all races were melted down and fused into a new race." Each new zone of frontier settlement was a "beginning all over again" which took Americans ever further away from dependence on Europe's economy and ways.

That holds equally true for the new frontier. For the urban masses each advance into a new neighborhood has also been a "beginning over again," which took them ever further from their European origins in the case of the immigrants, or, with Negroes, from the Plantation South. There has been much pooh-poohing of social climbing, without appreciation of the fact that it is a vital part of the Americanization process. The move to a "nicer" neighborhood would often be celebrated by a shortening or Anglicizing of names. Items of alien garb would be dropped; foreign accents would lighten. There would be more American food in the grocery stores, less orthodoxy in worship, more intermarriage with other ethnic elements and—as an ironical index of Americanization—more divorce.

The role of the railroads in opening up the Western lands has been duplicated first, by the subway and streetcars and, currently, by the automobile, in making ever newer housing accessible. The role of the pioneer woman was repeated in the immigrant mother who, with the sieve of drudgery, rescued the savings which enabled the family to climb to higher rental reaches. The immigrant mother was also the guardian of respectability on the urban frontier.

Like the Old West, the ever-changing urban frontier has been more "a form of society" than a geographical area. And as the story of America's social evolution could be read page by page in the successive frontier zones through which the pioneer pushed, so the march of the urban masses can be charted by tracing the neighborhoods through which these groups have climbed.

For example, when the late Arnold Bennett wrote his impressions of the United States in 1911, he closed his narrative with an account of a visit to New York's Lower East Side. The "astounding populousness" of the streets —some of which had more inhabitants per square foot than the most crowded areas of Bombay—roused the famous novelist to helpless indignation. On Rivington Street the "very architecture seemed to sweat humanity at every window and door." The thought of the "picturesque, feverish and appalling existences" endured by these "sickly-faced immortal creatures who lie closer than any wild animal would lie" stirred Bennett to protest to his American companions. They retorted, "Well, what are you going to do about it?"

The sequel to Bennett's visit can be read in any of several Old Tenement Trails which had their beginning in the dreary, cold-water flats of the East Side. The northward trail mounted first to Harlem or Yorkville, where hot water and steam heat were at least available, even if one had to bang the pipes before the janitor stoked the furnace. The next jump was out of Manhattan to the East Bronx, where trees stepped out of poems onto the streets; then to the West Bronx, crossing that Great Social Divide—the Grand Concourse—beyond which rolled true middle-class country. West of the Concourse, janitors were called superintendents; apartment houses had lift elevators and parquet floors, which needed no scrubbing. The migration then swept north paralleling the Concourse, the mink coats growing thicker as one mounted to Fordham Road and beyond.

Having run the length of both Manhattan and the Bronx, in recent years the Tenement Trail has swung abruptly eastward to the expensively filled-in marshes of Queens, which is currently the outermost fringe of New York's housing frontier. Here today will be found many of the "sickly-faced immortal creatures" whom Bennett saw. But how they have changed! Because they spent their youth in rootless tenements which knew no community life, they have been buying homes and have become doubly civic-minded in their eagerness to build a community in which their children might escape the deprivations of their own childhood.

From Rivington Street to Forest Hills in Queens is only a few miles. Historically, the spanning of that distance was a social revolution.

This same process of social exploration can be repeated with any of the former minority elements and in all of our larger cities. By going up and down the ladder of neighborhoods through which these different elements have climbed, one can see the progress they have made and the setbacks they have suffered—their clashes and reconciliations with other ethnic elements, and their assimilation into American society generally.

Do you wonder how the manners and habits of Negroes alter when they reach the middle class? In the North Bronx, around Gunhill Road, can be found a group of Negroes, mainly white collar and professional people, who have bought homes in recent years. As if feeling themselves on trial, they are as unlike the Harlem stereotype as imaginable in their habits. Their tastes in clothes and furnishings are sober. They pay cash at the neighborhood stores. At nearby Evander Childs High School their children rate tops scholastically. "Their drive to get an education is terrific," observes Dr. Hyman Alprin, Evander's principal. Oddly, every Negro child in the school takes Latin, as if seeking some mark of culture.

Or, one can follow the trek of the Irish in Boston, from the hilly streets of Charlestown out to Cambridge, on to Arlington and Newton; or of the Czechs in Chicago from South Lawndale, to Cicero and Berwyn. In Detroit the "uptown" upsurge has been eastward toward Grosse Point; in Milwaukee it has been northward along Lake Michigan and westward towards Granville.

If land hunger was the propelling force behind the agrarian frontier, the drive behind the urban frontier has been the hunger for social status. The changed nature of present-day political issues is largely a reflection of this contrast between the earlier agrarian frontier and its urban counterpart.

As the pioneers moved westward the obstacles they had to overcome were primarily physical and natural—breaking the sod in the semiarid plains, clearing the wilderness, driving railroad spikes across an untracked continent. Along the urban frontier the obstacles have been primarily man-made. The mountain barriers which have to be scaled are those of rents and restrictive covenants. Unemployment is the drought which could wither one's labors. The swiftly flowing rivers which have to be forded and bridged are those of class and social distinction, none the less treacherous because they are intangible.

The politics of westward expansion were bound to be sectional, since some parts of the country unavoidably lagged behind others and the newer settlements were often indebted, colonial offshoots of the older creditor areas. In contrast, the urban migration was bound to quicken class and social conflict, mirroring the uneven progress toward acceptance by different social groups.

In today's perspective, the Republican-dominated era can be said to have centered around one enormous historical fact: the spanning of the continent and the creation of a nation-wide economy. In the perspective of the future, we may look back upon today's Democratic era as an adventure in social unification, in the creation of the kind of nation-wide social structure which an industrialized civilization requires.

In any case, the reappearance of the frontier in a new urban form has been one of the most important political forces of our time. It explains the divisions between the old and new middle class. It generates the explosive force behind the civil rights issue. . . . It also has been transforming the big-city political machines, dooming the old-style political boss.

For the Democratic machines the spoils of office over the last twenty years have been fat indeed. Yet the reigns of the bosses have been growing progressively shorter. Fewer and fewer are dying with their patronage boots on. Usually this is credited to the fact that a beneficent federal government has replaced the political clubhouse in dispensing relief and other favors. Of equal, if not greater, significance has been the simultaneous coming-of-age of most of the old underdog elements.

As its large families have grown to voting age and as it has developed its own leadership, each minority group has been demanding an ever-increasing share of political recognition. Today, the plight of the Irish Democratic bosses, who managed most of the big-city machines, is not unlike that of the wearied rulers of the British Empire, who are everywhere on the defensive before the rising "nationality" elements they once ruled.

Tammany Hall, once as Irish as St. Patrick, fell to the Italo-Americans in 1947. A year earlier the Kelly-Nash dynasty in Chicago was superseded by Jacob Arvey, a Jew. In 1949, a coalition of dissident Irish, Italo-Americans and Polish-Americans terminated the thirty-two years, "I Am the Law" role of Frank Hague in Jersey City.

Currently, the most dramatic illustration of this trend is the rise of the Italo-Americans. In 1948 eight Italo-Americans were elected to Congress, twice as many as in any previous year. Two of these congressmen were from Newark, which in 1949 named an Italo-American mayor. Hoboken, Passaic and Paterson are among the other larger New Jersey cities which have elected Italo-American mayors since the war's end. Compared with 1936 more than twice as many Italian names are answering the legislative roll calls in Pennsylvania, New Jersey, New York, Connecticut, Rhode Island and Massachusetts—the six states with the heaviest Italo-American concentrations.

The intensifying Irish-Italian feud which has accompanied this rise wracks not only the Democratic party but also the Catholic Church whose hierarchy in this country is mainly Irish. It rocks gangland too. The struggle between James Pendergast and Charles Binaggio in Kansas City ended in violent murder. Of the gangsters cited by name in the Kefauver Crime Report, almost one half are clearly Italian.

That does not mean that Italians are peculiarly susceptible to criminal activity. The battle to control the nation's rackets now being pressed by Italo-American racketeers is part of the same "coming of age" process[1] which is

---

1. Both Frank Costello and Joe Adonis have attributed their interest in politics to the desire to gain greater recognition for Italo-Americans.

reflected in the growing frequency of Italian names on big league baseball and college football teams. Until 1929 not a single Italian name was listed on Walter Camp's annual all-star football team. Since then there has been hardly a year in which there wasn't at least one Italian name on the all-star list. . . .

## Jacob's Ladder

What is often described as "The March of the Masses" is usually thought of as a radical, even insurrectionary development. The very phrase murmurs suggestions of mob rule and political lynching. Yet, with the Italo-Americans we have seen that their political upthrust was sparked not by hard times but by boom times. Their leadership came not from the most oppressed and discontented, but from those with the strongest middle-class drive.

The same pattern holds for other minority elements as well. None were stirred to political uprising when their grievances were heaviest. It was as they emerged from the social cellar and got their first whiffs of the fresher, middle-class air that their political spirits quickened. The key to the political progress of any minority element in this country would seem to lie in just this success in developing its own middle class. Sheer numbers alone are not sufficient for political power—witness the ineffectiveness so far of the Mexican-Americans in the Southwest. To be effective, numbers must be supported by economic, educational and social progress.

The climbing masses can hardly be described as a conservative force. But are they as radical as they appear? Since their emergence stirs class conflict, it is easy to view their rise as confirming Karl Marx's dire prophecies of class warfare. Actually we are witnessing an almost complete refutation of the Marxian thesis. Our class struggle, if it can be called that, arises not from the impoverishment of the masses but from their progress. It is evidence not of the failure of the American dream but of its successes.

Despite all the talk of monopolistic control of American economic life and the supposed end of opportunities, even the most downtrodden elements have been able to climb. And if the urban masses are challenging the *status quo*, their challenge, essentially, is a demand for acceptance into our predominantly middle-class society.

The trends of our times seem to be strengthening this middle-class bias of American politics. Not so long ago political appointees were more often graduates of saloons and street gangs than of universities. Old-timers in the Bronx can remember an amusing pair of local Irish judges who not only knew no law but couldn't even read. One of these judges, after hearing a case, would take down a thick lawbook, pore over it learnedly and announce, "This is a fine point of law, I will reserve decision."

At lunchtime he would hotfoot it to a higher court, get coached on the law, return and announce his verdict.

The second judge, equally unlettered, kept making a spectacle of himself until he decided to imitate his colleague. After hearing one case, he reached up to the nearby shelf, took down a fat volume and thumbed through it. Making quite a show of learned deliberation, he announced, "An exceedingly fine point of law is involved. I think I'll reserve decision." The spectators burst into laughter. The book the judge had consulted so learnedly was the telephone directory.

Today college training or its equivalent is required for an increasing proportion of appointments. To register its political strength a minority group has to have its own lawyers or leaders with equivalent training. In turn, the broader the middle-class base developed by any upclimbing element, the more clamorous become its demands for political recognition.

Patronage is peculiarly important for minority groups, involving much more than the mere spoils of office. Each first appointment given a member of any underdog element is a boost in that element's struggle for social acceptance. It means that another barrier to their advance has been lifted, another shut door has swung open. Whenever Roosevelt nominated a Negro to a white collar post in the federal government, for example, he transmitted a vicarious thrill to every young Negro who thought instinctively. "Maybe there's a place up there for me or my child."

The opening of these new opportunities, in turn, stimulates the political consciousness of the group, encouraging its leaders to eye the next highest post on the patronage ladder.

In most northern cities, the Democrats have actually developed a ladder-like succession of posts, through which the political progress of various minority elements is recognized. Just as one can judge how far any minority has climbed economically from its position on the residential ladder, so one can measure its effective political power by its place on the patronage ladder.

The earliest stirrings of any group usually are appeased by an appointment as assistant district attorney, which entails little more than that some members of the group be educated as lawyers. A county judgeship, on the other hand, requires a candidate who has succeeded in a lower post, a large enough vote to withstand the competing claims of other minority blocs, and the economic backing to finance a campaign. Similarly, with elected posts, the solid vote of an ethnic element may win an aldermanic district or a seat in the legislature or even in Congress. But no minority group can be said to have arrived politically until its members can appeal beyond their own ethnic boundaries, to win a county-wide or city-wide election.

This system of succession obstructs as well as advances minority progress. By compelling each element to serve its apprenticeship in lower posts, the machine bosses have been able to slow and temper the rise of the underdog elements. Largely through this system of seniority and by playing off one ethnic element against the others the Irish have been able to cling to a much larger representation among officeholders than their voting strength would warrant.

The emphasis on hyphenated candidates, or what has come to be known as "League of Nations" politics, is often condemned as "un-American." Yet it is really an integral part of the Americanization process, serving as a means through which minority elements are assimilated into the structure of government. This was true during the Republican era, when the sons of the Norwegian, Swedish and German immigrants banded together to wrest greater recognition from the Yankee bosses who then controlled the Republican party. It holds equally true today.

Another fundamental difference between the Republican and Democratic parties is that they have been the vehicles for the political advancement of quite different ethnic elements. The Republicans, by political necessity, became sensitive to the aspirations of the "old" immigrant elements, who settled so largely on the farms. The Democrats, in turn, have been more alive to the aspirations of the "new" immigrant elements who crowded the teeming cities.

# THE SILENT REVOLUTION
# IN PATRONAGE

## FRANK J. SORAUF

WITH LITTLE FANFARE and only quiet celebration the movement to install merit systems in place of the older patronage is well on its way to full victory. The federal government has almost completely been conquered by one form or another of merit appointment, while the traditional political machines, long the major consumers of patronage, are everywhere else in hurried retreat. And the scholars and administrators who for so long fought in the vanguard of the movement now savor a triumph in practical affairs of the sort rarely vouchsafed to intellectuals.

The case against patronage, based largely on the need for administrative expertise and professionalism, is overwhelming. But only rarely have the opponents of patronage stopped to worry about the effects on the parties and political system of abolishing it.[1] Some scholars of political parties have

---

Reprinted from *Public Administration Review*, XX, No. 1 (Winter, 1960), pp. 28–34.

1. One would, however, have to mention three specialists in public administration who have recognized and addressed themselves to the conflicting needs of party and administration. See especially Harvey C. Mansfield's paper on "Political Parties, Patronage, and the Federal Government Service," in the American Assembly volume, *The Federal Government Service: Its Character, Prestige, and Problems* (Columbia University, 1954), pp. 81–112. Also relevant are Richard E. Neustadt's review, "On Patronage, Power, and Politics," 15 *Public Administration Review* 108–114 (Spring, 1955) and James R. Watson, "Is Patronage Obsolete?" 18 *Personnel Administration* 3–9 (July, 1955).

argued that patronage is important to the political process, but there has never been an attempt to compare the merit system's contribution to good administration with its supposed weakening of the party system in the total balance of effective government.

Such a comparison may not be necessary, however. Patronage is slowly dying out—more from its own political causes than from the campaigns of civil service reformers. However substantial the need of the parties for patronage fifty or even twenty years ago, the need is vastly less today. On the one hand, the organization, functions, and style of American politics, and the consequent need for patronage, have changed dramatically in the last generation; on the other hand, the nature and usefulness of patronage itself also have changed.[2]

## Uses of Patronage

Patronage is best thought of as an incentive system—a political currency with which to "purchase" political activity and political responses. The chief functions of patronage are:

### MAINTAINING AN ACTIVE PARTY ORGANIZATION

Experienced politicos maintain that the coin of patronage is necessary to reward the countless activities of an active party organization. The promise or actual holding of a political appointment, they report, is necessary to induce the canvassing of neighborhoods, mailing and telephoning, campaigning and electioneering, and other activities of the local party organization. Illustratively, many a city hall or county court rests vacant on election day as its denizens go out to man the party organization.

### PROMOTING INTRA-PARTY COHESION

In the hands of a skillful party leader, patronage may be an instrument of party cohesion, edging defecting partisans back into the discipline of the party hierarchy and welding the differing blocs within the party into a unified whole. In one sense President Eisenhower's historic agreement with Senator Taft in Morningside Heights represents an attempt to enlist the support of the Taft Republicans in 1952 by promising them consideration in the party's appointments.

---

2. Very few studies exist of the actual operation of patronage systems across the country. Among the few are: David H. Kurtzman, *Methods of Controlling Votes in Philadelphia* (published by author, 1935); Frank J. Sorauf, "State Patronage in a Rural County," 50 *American Political Science Review* 1046–1056 (December, 1956); and H. O. Waldby, *The Patronage System in Oklahoma* (The Transcript Co., 1950). In the absence of specific reports and data, one can only proceed uneasily on a mixture of political folklore, scattered scholarship, professional consensus, and personal judgment.

### ATTRACTING VOTERS AND SUPPORTERS.

The patronage appointment often may be used to convert the recipient (and a large portion of his family and friends) into life-long and devoted supporters of the appointing party. Gratitude for the job will win his support for the party, it is said, and a desire to retain the job by keeping the party in power will enforce it. In some urban areas of Pennsylvania, experienced party men calculate that a well-placed appointment should net the party between six and eight voters. The same reasoning, of course, lies behind the appointment of representatives of special blocs of voters, such as ethnic, national, or religious groups.

### FINANCING THE PARTY AND ITS CANDIDATES.

The cruder and more overt forms of this function of patronage have long been known to the fraternity as "macing" the payroll. In the heydey of patronage in American politics, something close to 5 per cent of the appointee's salary was thought a fair return to the party for its benefice. Patronage, always reward for past activity as well as inducement for the future, may also be used to reward a recent contribution to the party coffers.

### PROCURING FAVORABLE GOVERNMENT ACTION.

Less commonly acknowledged, perhaps for its dubious ethics and legality, is the use of patronage to secure favorable policy or administrative action for the party or its followers. At the local government level it may involve the fixing of a traffic ticket, preference for certain applicants for public assistance, the calculated oversight in a public health inspection, or the use of public equipment to remove snow from private rights-of-way. By exploiting the appointee's dependence on the party, the organization reaps the political advantages of a preferred access to public policy-making.

### CREATING PARTY DISCIPLINE IN POLICY-MAKING.

This last function of patronage redounds less to the advantage of political parties than to presidents and governors who use appointments to build support for their programs in legislatures. Franklin Roosevelt's wily use of the dwindling federal patronage, especially his delaying of appointments until after satisfactory congressional performance, scarcely needs more than mention. A number of governors still have at their disposal a vast array of political jobs to use in coordinating executive and legislative policy and in joining the separated powers of government.

But patronage may certainly be misused in ways that adversely affect the parties and political system. It may build up personal machines or followings that parallel and compete with the regular, formal party organization. Poorly administered, it may cause new resentments and hostilities, create more friction within the party than it eases. Also, patronage seldom can perform all of the six purposes at once since to use it for one purpose is to destroy its effectiveness for another. For example, appointments that solidify and activate local party organization may disturb centralized party unity at a higher level and impair party discipline within both party and legislature.[3]

Just how well patronage has performed the six functions for the parties over the years is a matter for considerable conjecture. Partisans usually claim patronage is the "life-blood" of American politics, and yet even among its most devoted and skillful users, many dissent and some are ambivalent. James Farley, for example, has boasted that he could build a major party without patronage, and yet he dissented from the recommendation of the second Hoover Commission that rural postal carriers be taken from the patronage lists.[4] The scholarly studies of patronage and general political folklore indicate that it is fairly effective in maintaining an active organization and, to a lesser extent, in attracting voters and supporters, but that its value in performing the other functions is highly questionable. Political appointees do contribute money to the party treasuries but hardly enough to run a party today. As for the promotion of party cohesion, the intra-party bickering and bitterness occasioned by the division of the spoils is, to this observer, truly staggering.

## Decline in Usefulness

Regardless of the effectiveness of patronage in the past, it is today undergoing rapid changes, most obviously in its steady shrinkage. One observer has estimated that the federal patronage available to the Eisenhower Administration has ". . . not exceeded a fraction of one per-cent of the total federal establishment."[5] A precise estimate of the number of jobs still under patronage in city, county, and state administrations throughout the country would be impossible to come by, but all hands agree it is declining.

There do remain states where merit systems have made few inroads into patronage and where large numbers of positions (about 50,000 in Pennsylvania, for example) remain at least technically available for distribution by the victorious. But even in these instances the parties are using a steadily decreasing percentage of the jobs for political purposes because patronage as a political currency has been devalued. Merit systems make their greatest inroads into patronage in the well-paid, specialized positions where the call for expertness and training is greatest. The parties are left the less-desirable, poorly-paid positions generally. With continued economic prosperity and high levels of employment the economic rewards of these jobs, hardly princely

---

3. I have questioned the political usefulness of patronage at greater length in "Patronage and Party," 3 *Midwest Journal of Political Science* 115–126 (May, 1959).

4. The claim is in James A. Farley, *Behind the Ballots* (Harcourt, Brace, and Co., 1938), p. 237, and the dissent in the Commission on Organization of the Executive Branch of the Government, *Report on Personnel and Civil Service* (U.S. Government Printing Office, 1955), p. 91.

5. Mansfield, *op. cit.* note 1 above, p. 94.

in most cases, are less appealing than formerly. While low pay and chronic job insecurity plague the patronage jobholder, private employment has become progressively more attractive with rising wage levels, union protections and securities, unemployment compensation, pension plans, and fringe benefits. Viewed by most Americans as a short-term, desperation job alternative, the patronage position has lost considerable value as a political incentive.

Patronage also is losing its respectability. Its ethic—the naked political *quid pro quo*—no longer seems to many a natural and reasonable ingredient of politics. Parties often find that the attempt to clean political house after an election produces public outrage and indignation. The mores of the middle-class and the image of civic virtue instilled by public education extol the unfettered, independent voter rather than the patronage-seeking party-liner. The public-spirited citizen rather than the self-interested party worker is celebrated. And the public no longer tolerates the presence of political mediocrities in public service in the name of party loyalty.

Even the job-seekers themselves no longer accept the political obligations of their appointments as readily as once they did. Briefly, patronage has fallen into public disfavor for appearing to approach an outright political payoff, with the result that its usefulness to the parties has diminished.

## Changes in Parties and Politics

The partial passing of the boss and the political machine has been perhaps the most obvious new development in party behavior. Depending heavily on the motive power of patronage, these machines long dominated big city politics and some county and state strongholds as well. They flourished especially in those urban centers inhabited by large groups of immigrants and minorities—groups not yet integrated into American life, often poor and insecure and bewildered by the traditions of American politics. The machine spoke to them in the simple terms of a job, of sympathy in city hall, and of food and fuel to soften the hardest times.

This is not to suggest that political machines have vanished or even that they will vanish within the next generation. But the machine, and the politics of the underprivileged on which it rests, is surely on the decline. Government and other private agencies have taken over the social welfare functions these organizations once provided. Furthermore, first and second generation groups, traditional recipients of the attentions of the machine, are disappearing, and their children and grandchildren now luxuriate in the prosperity and conformity of the suburbs, though in many cities their place will be taken for a time by immigrants from rural areas of the United States. In sum, rising levels of prosperity, higher educational levels, declining numbers of unassimilated groups, and greater concern by government for the unfortunate all point to a decline of the boss and machine and of the patronage they relied on.

Furthermore, party conflict since the 1930's has reflected social and economic appeals to a greater extent than in the preceding decades. Even though they do not yet approach the ideological fervor of European campaigns, American politics has become more involved with issues and less with the issueless politics of patronage, favor, and preferment. Campaigning, too, has shifted from the door-to-door canvass, local rallies, and controlled blocs of votes to the mass media and advertising agencies. Great, attractive candidates serve as the focus of these national campaigns. As a result the importance of the national party organization is increased—the center of party power shifting away from the local units just as clearly as the center of government power is shifting from the states and localities to the national government.

### THE NEW PARTY WORKER

What is emerging, then, is a system of political organization more compatible with the middle-class values of suburbia than those of the ethnic or racial neighborhood of the urban center. Rather than relying on the organized party hierarchy, it depends more and more on the volunteer and *ad hoc* political groups and personal followings. In some states, such as California and Wisconsin, party leaders are converting this fleeting volunteer activity into more permanent clubs and party organization,[6] but the manpower of these changing parties contrasts sharply with the ward or precinct committeeman of the older machines. The new political men are far more likely than their predecessors to be motivated by belief, by loyalty to an attractive candidate (e.g., the Citizens for Eisenhower movement), by a sense of civic duty, or by a more generalized social and sporting enthusiasm. They view their political activity more as avocation than vocation.

The parties also have found fresh resources in the organized power of the interest group. It recruits voters for the favored party or candidate and provides campaign and financial assistance as well. Many a candidate today prizes the contacts and communication channels of the local labor union or chamber of commerce more highly than he does the face-to-face campaign. Voters in many corners of the country can testify that candidates rarely knock on their doors any more. Business and labor are major sources of party funds; the contributions of payrollers no longer suffice. Even the "new style" political leader, in contrast with the classic model of the boss, usually has closer ties to interest groups in the community. He may even have been recruited from one.

For these educated, secure, and even prestiged workers and leaders of the new parties, a political appointment holds little fascination. One sophisticated and experienced politician has written that "Men and women are drawn into politics by a combination of motives; these include power, glory, zeal for contention or success, duty, hate, oblivion, hero worship,

---

6. The literature on the California political clubs is rather extensive, especially in the nonacademic journals, but the only general work on the volunteer movement in politics of which I am aware is Stephen A. Mitchell's *Elm Street Politics* (Oceana Publications, 1959).

curiosity, and enjoyment of the work."[7] Today's political worker may more and more find his reward in the satisfaction of a deeply-rooted psychological need, the identification with a purposeful organization or a magnetic leader, the ability to serve an economic or professional interest, the release from the tedium of daily routine, or the triumph of an ideal. His "pay-off," instead of a political job, may be endorsement for elective office, membership on a civic commission, access to new and influential elites, or a reception in the White House gardens.

## THE NEW PERSONNEL NEEDS OF THE PARTY

These shifts in organization, functions, and personnel of the parties have meant that the patronage that does remain is not the patronage that the parties might easily use. The parties cry for trained, educated, experienced men of ability and affairs, albeit fewer men than formerly. The vast majority of patronage positions are poorly paid and generally unappealing to the men and women of skills and achievement the parties would like to enlist. Very likely the man placed on a trash collection crew will lack the social and political experience to be useful in today's politics, and his meager pay offers the party scant opportunity for fund-raising. The middle-level job, potentially the most useful to the party in rewarding its more capable partisans, is rarely available for political appointment. These are the specialized, expert positions that are generally the first to be put under a merit system. When they do remain under patronage, their specialized qualifications are the hardest to fill from the rank and file of political job-seekers.

At the top, the party often has highly-placed positions available, at least in small number, to reward its leadership corps. Here, however, the party often fails to persuade its most capable men to give up, even temporarily, their positions in business and the professions for a political appointment. In turn, the party workers who would find the patronage position an attractive alternative to their private employment, lack the executive and administrative experience for the positions. Paul David and Ross Pollock write of these problems in the national government:

> For positions at the higher levels, the party organization has only rarely been successful in convincing the administration that its nominees were sufficiently qualified. The administration, on its part, has had to go out and hunt, cajole, and persuade in order to recruit the kind of talent it wanted. . . . The supply of persons with the requisite competence and availability is simply not large enough in either political party, and there is little evidence to suggest that the supply is on the increase.[8]

As its usefulness to them declines, patronage imposes hard and worrisome choices on the party hierarchies. Often the parties' appointments to the

---

7. Stimson Bullitt, *To Be a Politician* (Doubleday and Co., 1959), p. 42. The reader will, in fact, find all of chapter two a stimulating review of the incentives and motives of politics.

8. Paul T. David and Ross Pollock, *Executives for Government* (The Brookings Institution, 1957), pp. 25–27.

plenitude of unattractive patronage jobs go to the men and women with no particular record of service to the party and little promise for future service, or whose appointment will do little to integrate the party organization or build party cohesion. Their chief recommendation is their need for a job, and the party, functioning as employment bureau, hopes only for a little gratitude and possible support at the polls. The better paid, more enticing jobs are losing their incentive power for those partisans qualified to hold them, and the party finds itself haunted by the aggressive availability of unqualified job-hunters.

One is forced to conclude that the classic dependence of party on patronage is being undermined on both sides. Forced by the changing nature of American society and by new political problems and values, the parties are shifting to a new mode of operation that relies less than formerly on the incentives of patronage. Patronage, on the other hand, is declining in both quantity and quality, both in the number of jobs available and in their value to the party.

## Short-Term Adjustments

Since party changes were not simply adjustments to the gradual demise of patronage, a further reduction in the supply of patronage in those states where the supply remains large will hardly alter the long-run development of the party system. It may, however, accelerate change in party operations or produce short-term side effects.

In the first place, patronage has persisted chiefly at the local levels and remains the bulwark of local party organization, a faintly anachronistic bulwark, one might add, in an era of centralized party and government. It is in these state and local party organs, despite their declining vigor and importance, that one finds the most vocal proponents of patronage—even of the remaining federal patronage, much of which is channeled through them. This concentration of patronage in the localities fortifies the local party and permits it to resist discipline or centralization by organs higher in the party structure.[9] Thus fortified, these decentralized pockets of political power also fight party cohesion and responsibility in legislatures and, paradoxically, often nullify the value of executive patronage in achieving legislative discipline.

Inevitably, these local units, as they lose their vitality and their part in major policy-making, become primarily dealers in patronage, converting it from a political tool to a political goal. When patronage declines there, a major resistance to party centralization and to issue-centered campaigns and candidates will die with it.

Secondly, restrictions on patronage weaken the Democratic party more

9. The classic expression of this view is E. E. Schattschneider, *Party Government* (Rinehart and Co., 1942).

than the Republicans. Patronage appeals more predictably to lower economic strata, to unskilled and semiskilled workers, to urban dwellers, and to minority groups—all of the demographic groups which, studies show, support the Democratic party. Patronage as an incentive system comports with the economic needs, the understanding of the relationship between citizen and government, and the somewhat exploitative view of politics more common among lower social and economic groups than among the American middle class. Furthermore, the Democratic party also has greater problems in finding substitutes for it. The personal and financial support of the business community are not often at its disposal. The formation of a genteel party, dedicated to a philosophy of government and based on sociability and civic virtue, falls more easily to the Republicans.

Thirdly, since the appeals of patronage are largely economic, its political value and usefulness are apt to be greatest in the remaining pockets of unemployment and economic hardship, for it is there that private employment fails to provide opportunities superior to patronage positions. In these areas, and in the country as a whole if widespread unemployment returns, patronage might enjoy a brief renaissance as a political incentive.

Finally, patronage has been involved in legislative-executive rivalry. Presidents of the United States, harassed by congressional attempts to control patronage through clearance systems and "senatorial courtesy," have been more willing to surrender it than has the Congress. State governors, however, are not so willing to abandon one of the few weapons they have over unruly legislatures.[10] Since the loss of patronage will certainly affect legislative-executive relations in the states more sharply than in the national government, one is justified in supposing that its further loss will make the task of gubernatorial leadership just that much more difficult.

## In Conclusion

To expect anything but a further contraction of patronage would be naïve. 1. Patronage does not meet the needs of present-day party operations. Activities requiring a large number of party workers—canvassing, mass mailings, rallies—are being replaced by radio and television. Political costs are so high that assessments on public salaries are minuscule beside the party's cost. 2. Patronage no longer is the potent inducement to party activity it once was. Public attitudes are increasingly hostile to patronage and the political style it represents. Employment in the private economy also provides an increasingly attractive alternative to patronage positions. 3. As a result, the incentives once provided by patronage are being replaced in the political system. The persons who can contribute most to campaigns, in skill and

---

10. See Duane Lockhard, *New England State Politics* (Princeton University Press, 1959) for reports of the value of patronage to governors in New England. For instance, he describes patronage as "perhaps the most important of these gubernatorial weapons" in Massachusetts (p. 160).

funds, seek different payoffs—prestige, power, or personal satisfaction rather than jobs.

Even though the further decline of patronage will certainly not destroy or seriously hamper the parties, it will produce political shocks and pockets of discomfort. It will probably hurt Democrats more than Republicans, will be slower and more crucial in economically distressed areas, and will weaken the influence of governors on legislative action more than the President's influence on Congress.

American political parties have, after all, been getting along without patronage to various extents for some time now, and they have survived. Even many large metropolitan cities, whose patronage needs the scholars emphasize, have managed without it. The political party has its causes and justification deep in the American political process and not in the dispensation of political privileges. Patronage is necessary to a certain type of party operation, but others can be maintained without it. The old machines and local party organizations relied on patronage, but they were rooted in social and economic conditions that are disappearing. As they disappear, so will the parties and patronage they fostered.

Ultimately, the decline of patronage will, among a number of causes, speed the parties to further centralization, to the heightening of their ideological content, to a greater reliance on group participation in politics, to greater nationalization of the candidate image and party campaigning, and to the establishment of some modicum of party discipline.

There is something almost quaint in these days of big parties, big government, and advertising agency politics about a political institution that conjures up images of Boss Tweed, torchlight parades, and ward heelers. As the great day of patronage recedes into history, one is tempted to say that the advancing merit systems will not kill patronage before it withers and dies of its own infirmity and old age.

# THE DILEMMAS OF A METROPOLITAN MACHINE

## EDWARD C. BANFIELD

TO UNDERSTAND how the political heads evaluate their opportunities, i.e., how they decide the terms on which they will use influence or allow it to be used upon them, it is necessary to look at some salient facts of political geography.

Reprinted from *Political Influence* (Glencoe: The Free Press, 1961), pp. 244–253.

"Downstate" (all of Illinois outside of Cook County) is white, Protestant, Anglo-Saxon, rural, and normally Republican. It elects the governor (a Democrat has held the office in only 16 of the last 58 years), and it controls the General Assembly. Under a recent reapportionment, the Senate is safely downstate and Republican; a narrow majority of the House may be from Cook County, but some of the Cook County representatives are sure to be Republicans, and some downstate Democrats are almost sure to vote with the Republicans. Downstate hates and fears Chicago, which it regards as an alien land.

Chicago is heavily Democratic. The Democratic heartland is the slums and semi-slums of the inner city; here, in wards which are predominantly Negro, Italian, Polish, Lithuanian, or Irish, and (except for the Negroes) almost entirely Catholic, the machine gets the hard core of its support. The lower the average income and the less average education, the more reliably Democratic is the ward.

The vote is less Democratic as one moves outward from the center of the city. Some of the outlying wards are usually Republican. So are most of the "country towns" (that part of Cook County which lies outside Chicago); for the most part, the suburbanites of the "country towns" are white, Protestant, and middle-class. Their affinity is with downstate rather than the inner city.

The inner city wards are so populous and so heavily Democratic that they can usually offset the Republican vote of the outlying wards. In the future, the ascendancy of the inner city wards is likely to be even more complete. White, middle-class families are moving to the suburbs, and their places are being taken by Negroes and poor whites from the South. Since the newcomers are almost all Democrats, and since many of those who leave are either Republicans or upward mobile types likely to became Republican, the proportion of Democrats in the inner city is increasing.

One might expect, then, that a mayor of Chicago would make the maintenance of the Democratic machine his most important business. So long as he controls the machine and it controls primary elections in the inner wards, he is invincible. And, of course, the way to maintain the machine is to pass out "gravy" with a generous hand—to give jobs, favors, and opportunities for graft and bribery to those who can deliver votes in the primaries.

This is, in fact, the strategy followed by the bosses of the most powerful machine wards.

It is not, however, the strategy of the mayor. He is normally the chairman of the county Democratic committee and therefore the leading figure in the party in Illinois and one of its leading figures nationally. Consequently, it is not enough for him merely to maintain himself in office in Chicago. He must take a wider view. He must carry the county and, if possible, the state, and he must contribute all that he can to the success and prestige of the party nationally. When the interests of the party on the larger scene conflict with its interests in the inner city of Chicago, the interests of the party in the inner city must usually be sacrificed.

As the table shows, to win a county-wide election a heavy vote in the inner city wards is not enough. There must also be a fairly strong Democratic vote in the outlying wards and in the suburban "country towns." The voters in these places are not in the habit of doing what the precinct captains tell them to do; their incomes are generally high enough, and their positions in society secure enough, to make them indifferent to the petty favors and advantages the machine has to offer. Many of them even seem to have absorbed the idea that "independence," i.e., splitting the ticket, is a mark of middle-class sophistication. To get the vote it needs from these outlying areas, the Democratic party must appear not as a "machine" but as a "force for clean and progressive government." To do this it must offer "blue-ribbon" candidates, and it must give the city and county the kind of administration that will win the approval of the press and of "good government" forces generally. ("Good government" is some kind of a mixture—the proportions vary greatly from context to context—of the following principal ingredients: (*a*) "reform" of the old-fashioned kind, i.e., the suppression of vice, crime, and political corruption; (*b*) "efficiency" in the sense of doing what public administration "experts" recommend with respect to organization structure and "housekeeping" functions like budgeting and personnel management; (*c*) following "progressive" policies in the fields of housing, planning, race relations, and welfare; and (*d*) executing big projects—airports and exhibition halls, for example—to boost the size, business, and repute of the city.)

### Relative Importance in the Cook County Electorate of Inner City Wards of Chicago, Outlying Wards of Chicago, and "Country Towns"

| | POPULATION (IN THOUSANDS) | | PER CENT CHANGE | PER CENT CONTRIBUTED TO COUNTY DEMOCRATIC VOTE | |
|---|---|---|---|---|---|
| | 1950 | 1960* | | 1948 | 1956 |
| 18 Inner City Wards | 1,257 | 1,291 | 3 | 37 | 31 |
| Outlying Wards (Rest of Chicago) | 2,364 | 2,616 | 11 | 50 | 51 |
| "Country Towns" (Suburbs) | 888 | 1,532 | 73 | 13 | 18 |
| Total Cook County | 4,509 | 5,439 | 20 | 100 | 100 |

* Estimate

The preference of the outlying wards and "country towns" for good government has for a good many years been a force which the inner city machine has had to take into account. Its importance, moreover, is growing every year. In part, this is because the whole population—and especially that of the outlying wards and "country towns"—is becoming more discriminating in its voting behavior. In part, also, it is because the numerical strength of the outlying areas is growing while that of the inner city remains approximately the same.

In this situation, a rational county Democratic leader will be less attentive to the inner city wards, whose vote he can count on, than to the outlying areas, whose independence is a danger. His strategy in dealing with these outlying areas is clear: he must help his party live down its reputation as a "corrupt machine" and establish a new one as the honest and energetic servant of the people. The welfare of the suburbs must be his special concern; he must show the suburbanites that they have nothing to fear and much to hope for from the Democratic organization in the central city.

By the same token, a rational Republican leader will endeavor to keep alive the old image of the "boss-ridden" and "crooked" machine. He will do his best to frighten suburbanites and downstaters with stories of the growth and spread of the machine and of its designs on them.

These strategies are the ones the Democratic and Republican political heads do, in fact, follow. Mayor Daley, whose slogan is "good government is good politics and good politics is good government," has made it clear that he will not tolerate corruption in office and has kept a very tight rein on gambling, prostitution, and other organized crime. At the same time, he has inaugurated many reforms: he established an executive budget, introduced the performance-type budget, passed a performance zoning ordinance and housing code, extended the merit system, established a centralized purchasing system under a respected administrator, took control over contracts from the City Council, and transferred authority to issue zoning variation permits from the City Council to a Zoning Board of Appeals. His policy toward the suburbs has been sympathetic and generous: through James Downs, the highly respected businessman who is his consultant on housing and planning, he has offered them the assistance of the city-planning department and of such other technicians as might help with their transportation, water, drainage, and other problems. In his campaign for re-election in 1958, the Mayor presented himself as an efficient and non-partisan administrator. His principal piece of campaign literature did not so much as mention the Democratic party or the Democratic slate.

The Republicans have also followed a rational strategy. They have tried to paint the Mayor as a "boss" and the Democratic organization as a corrupt and rapacious "machine." In the 1958 election, for example, Daley was dubbed Dictator Dick, and the Republican organizations distributed buttons marked "S.O.S."—"Save Our Suburbs from the Morrison Hotel Gang" (the Morrison Hotel is Democratic headquarters in Chicago). Some buttons showed the Democratic machine as an octopus reaching out to grasp the unprotected suburbs.

These and other antagonisms put adoption of any plan of metropolitan area organization out of the question. Because of their strength in the outlying wards and in the suburbs the Republicans would have a good chance of controlling a metropolitan area government. But in order to avail themselves of the chance, they would have to relinquish their present control of most of the suburbs. For if the whole metropolitan area were, so to speak, put in the same pot, the Democrats might now and then win the whole pot, and even when they could not win it they could offer a troublesome and expensive contest. Therefore, although the bolder Republicans and the Republicans whose interests are mainly metropolitan favor proposals for putting one or more functions on an area-wide basis, the more timid ones and those whose interests are in particular "safe" suburbs are opposed to it. With the Democrats the situation is similar. Mayor Daley would probably be glad to take his chances with the electorate of the metropolitan area. But the leading ward committeemen of Chicago much prefer certain success in the central city to occasional success in the metropolitan area.

The central city-suburban cleavage is the fundamental fact of party politics in the metropolitan area. But the cleavage is not simply a party one. . . . Party differences reflect differences of interest and outlook that are deep-seated and pervasive.

It will be seen that the influence of the mayor depends largely upon his being "boss" of the party in the county and that this in turn depends upon his ability to maintain the inner city machine while attracting support from the "good government" forces in the outlying wards and suburbs. In short, the mayor must bring the machine and the independents into a working alliance.

To become the county boss, one need only have the backing of the principal ward bosses of the inner city. There are 80 members of the county committee, 50 from the central city and 30 from the "country towns," and their votes are weighed according to the number of Democratic votes cast in each district in the previous general election. The inner city wards are therefore in a decided majority. These are grouped into ethnic blocs each of which has its own boss: there is a bloc of Negro wards under the control of Congressman William L. Dawson, a bloc of Italian wards under an Italian leader, a bloc of Polish wards under a Polish leader, and certain mixed wards under Irish leaders. Four or five of the most powerful bloc leaders, together with the president of the County Board, can, by agreeing among themselves, choose the county chairman.

Left to themselves, the bloc bosses would doubtless prefer someone who would not trouble them with reform. They realize, however, that the voters in the outlying areas will not leave them to themselves and that, unless the machine's reputation is improved, it will be swept out of existence altogether. They accept, therefore—although, no doubt, as a necessary evil and probably without fully realizing the extent of the evil—the need of a leader who will make such reforms as will maintain the organization.

In choosing a leader, the bloc bosses look for someone whose identifications are with the inner city wards (he has to be a Catholic, of course, and one whom ward politicians will feel is "their kind"), whose "nationality" will not disturb the balance between the Italians and the Poles (this virtually means that he must be Irish), who knows the workings of the organization from long experience in it and who is felt to have "earned" his promotion, who has backers with money to put up for campaign expenses (for it will be assumed that the county chairman will have himself nominated for office), who is perfectly "clean" and has a creditable record of public service, and who has demonstrated sufficient vigor, force, and shrewdness to maintain the organization and lead it to victory at the polls.

Once he has taken charge of the machine, a new leader need pay very little attention to the ward bosses who selected him. If he can win elections, he is indispensable to them. Moreover, possession of office—of the county chairmanship and the mayoralty—gives him legal powers (patronage, slate-making, and control of city services, including police) which make the ward bosses dependent upon him. Without them to hold the ladder, he could not climb into his position. But once he is in it, they cannot compel him to throw something down to them.

He is likely, therefore, to prove a disappointment to them and a pleasant surprise to the friends of good government. The bloc bosses need him more than he needs them. They want "gravy" to pass out to their henchmen. But he is a county, state, and national leader, and as such his task is to limit or suppress the abuses upon which they fatten. To win the respect and confidence of the independent voters in the outlying wards and the suburbs, he must do the things that will hurt the bosses most.

The requirements of his role as a leader who must win the support of the independent voters are enough to account for his zeal to show himself honest and public-spirited. But it is likely that another circumstance will be working in the same direction. Ethnic pride may swell strongly in him and make him want to show the skeptics and the snobs that a man from the wrong side of the tracks can be as much a statesman as anyone from an "old family" or an Ivy League college.

The political head is not likely to take a lively interest in the content of policy or to be specially gifted in the development of ideas or in their exposition. If ideas and the content of policy interested him much, or if he were ideologically-minded, he would not have made his career in the machine, for the machine is entirely without interest in such matters. Similarly, he is not likely to be a vivid public personality, to be eloquent, or to have a flair for the direct manipulation of masses. The qualities that make a popular or charismatic leader would tend to prevent a man from rising within the organization. The kind of leader produced by it is likely to be, above all, an executive.

Any mayor of Chicago must "do big things" in order to be counted a success. It is not enough merely to administer honestly and efficiently the routine services of local government—street cleaning, garbage collection, and the like. An administration that did only these would be counted a failure, however well it did them. As a businessman member of the Chicago Plan Commission explained to an interviewer:

> The Mayor—no public official—is worth his salt if he isn't ambitious. That's true of you and everyone else. Now, what's a political person's stock in trade? It's government, of course. For a public official to just sit back and

see that the police enforce the laws is not dynamic enough. I don't know that he would reason it out this way, but you have to get something with a little sex in it to get votes. In the old days, there were ward-heelers with a fistful of dollar bills. But that, even in Chicago, is passé.

What makes a guy have a civic pride? A worker in a factory, a cab driver? He gets a sense of pride in taking part in an active community. The Mayor's smart enough to realize it. Today the tendency all over the country is for the public officials to take the lead more than they did a few years ago. . . .

Wanting to do "big things" and not caring very much which ones, the political head will be open to suggestions. (When Mayor Daley took office, he immediately wrote to three or four of the city's most prominent business-men asking them to list the things they thought needed doing.) He will be receptive, particularly, to proposals from people who are in a position to guarantee that successful action will win a "seal of approval" from some of the "good government" groups. He may be impressed by the intrinsic merit of a proposal—the performance budget, for example—but he will be even more impressed at the prospect of being well regarded by the highly respect-able people whose proposal it is. Taking suggestions from the right kind of people will help him get the support he needs in order to win the votes of independents in the outlying wards and suburbs.

For this reason, he will not create a strong staff of policy advisers or a strong planning agency. The preparation of policies and plans will be done mainly within those private organizations having some special stake in the matters involved and by the civic associations. Quite possibly, the political head might, if he wished, assemble a technical staff of first-rate ability and, working closely with it, produce a plan far superior to anything that might be done by the private organizations and the civic associations. But a plan made in this way would have one fatal defect: its makers could not supply the "seal of approval" which is, from the political head's standpoint, its chief reason for being. On the other hand, a plan made by the big business organ-izations, the civic associations and the newspapers, is sure to be acclaimed. From the political head's standpoint it is sure-fire, for the people who make it and the people who will pass judgment upon it are the same.

Under these circumstances, the city planning department will have two main functions: (*a*) to advise the mayor on the technical aspects of the various alternatives put before him by private groups, and (*b*) to assemble data justifying and supporting the privately-made proposals that the mayor decides to "merchandise," and to prepare maps, charts, perspective drawings, and brochures with which to "sell" the plans to the public. . . .

There are often fundamental differences of opinion among those whose approval the political head wants. Chicago is too big a place, and the interests in it too diverse, for agreement to occur very often. When there is disagree-ment within the "good government" forces, the rational strategy for the political head usually is to do nothing. Watchful waiting will offend no one, and to be negative when one does not have to be is . . . bad politics. The political head is therefore inclined to let a civic controversy develop in its own way without interference from him, in the expectation that "public opinion" (the opinion of "civic leaders" and the newspapers) will "crystallize." Controversies . . . serve the function of forming and preparing opinion; they are the process by which an initial diversity of views and interests is reduced to the point where a political head feels that the "community" is "behind" the project.

The political head, therefore, neither fights for a program of his own making nor endeavors to find a "solution" to the conflicts that are brought before him. Instead, he waits for the community to agree upon a project. When agreement is reached, or when the process of controversy has gone as far as it can, he ratifies the agreement and carries it into effect.

# THE NO-PARTY POLITICS
# OF SUBURBIA

## ROBERT C. WOOD

ESPECIALLY at the municipal level, suburban politics appear to differ, at least in degree, and probably in substance, from those of other American communities, both urban and rural. In the end, this difference has important implications for the state and national pattern.

One indication of this difference, which Harris has described, is the relative respectability and restraint of suburban politics at the local level— the yearning to shed the disreputable political habits of the big city. Another bit of evidence, which Whyte and Henderson have discovered on a sample basis, is the strong sense of community consciousness and civic responsibility that impels active participation in local affairs. Deeply concerned with the quality of schools, conscious of their new status, suburbanites are inclined to "care" about local affairs—zoning regulation, recreational plans, garbage collection, school curricula, street paving—in an especially intense way. As the logical converse of their apathy toward strong party affiliations, suburbanites approach the politics of the community on the basis of individual preferences; they are, more and more frequently, nonpartisan, sharply distinguishing their local public preferences from their views of national and state affairs.

Suburban nonpartisanship takes several forms. Sometimes, as in the

Reprinted from Robert C. Wood, *Suburbia, Its People and Their Politics* (Boston: Houghton Mifflin Company, 1959), pp. 153–158, by permission of and arrangement with Houghton Mifflin Company, the authorized publishers.

Washington environs, it is simply a way of interjecting another party on the local scene, an organization closely identified in attitude and outlook with a national party but separately organized to overcome the minority status of its big brother in the area. In these cases nonpartisan groups parallel the earlier efforts of municipal reformers in the large cities to overthrow an established—and in their eyes—unpalatable party machine. Sometimes, as is customary in New York and Connecticut suburbs, nonpartisanship takes the form of the inclusion of members of the minority party in local councils in a ratio that preserves the majority party's control but that the minority could never achieve on its own. Finally, and apparently most frequently, local politics have no association, open or covert, with the established parties at all. Public affairs are the province of essentially political organizations—civic clubs, social leagues, or improvement organizations—whose members are loosely tied together and whose announced goals are "what is best for the community." There are exceptions amid the variety of suburbs, of course; some remain staunchly and overwhelmingly partisan in outlook. But the general trend is in the other direction—nonpartisanship is legally recognized in 61 per cent of the suburban governments reporting in the *Municipal Yearbook,* and for those under 10,000 population, the percentage is probably even higher.

This emphasis on nonpartisanship is, of course, a familiar element in the local politics of many communities which are not suburban. As the authors of the Federalist Papers early noted and as V. O. Key has more presently pointed out, nonpartisanship reflects a highly integrated community life with a powerful capacity to induce conformity. "Party, as such, often has no meaning except as a combination to fight the opposition. It is rather an expression continued from generation to generation of the consensus of a more or less individual community or at least of a majority in such overwhelming command that it is unaware of any challenge to its position. The politics of the locality is a politics of personality and of administration rather than a politics of issues." In this broad sense, suburban nonpartisanship does resemble the politics of all localities, stressing the candidate and not the platform, and exhibiting a high degree of disorganization.

Yet there is a significant distinction between the no-party pattern common to suburbia and the one-party localism that Key identifies, just as there is a distinction between the structured homogeneity of a relatively isolated town, with its banker, lawyer, merchant, farmer, clerk, and workingman, and the more unified composition of an individual suburb. In traditional one-party politics, intramural competition among factions, interest groups, and cliques within the same organization is accepted as normal at the local level, disruptive as it may sometimes be for party leadership. This kind of factionalism, prevalent in one-party states and large cities, is not antagonistic to the idea of partisanship as such and does not preclude organized group action at higher levels. On the contrary, party regularity beyond primary or convention fights is expected and encouraged; the existence of the party structure, tightly or loosely organized, is taken as natural, and the politically minded work within it.

The no-party politics of so many suburban governments, however, often exhibits quite different characteristics. There is, first of all, an outright reaction against partisan activity, a refusal to recognize that there may be persistent cleavages in the electorate, and an ethical disapproval of permanent group collaboration as an appropriate means for settling public disputes. "No-partyism" eats away at the idea of partisanship by outlawing party influence to "outside" elections and by discouraging outright displays of party allegiance in the community as indicative of bad taste. The political animal is tamed; as the suburbanite approaches the ballot box in local elections, he is expected to strive for a consensus with his friends and neighbors, to seek "the right solution" as distinct from favoring one or another faction of his party.

One explanation for this rise in the number of independents is that this view of citizenship spills over into national and state campaigns. The "local political man" dampens proclivities of the party political man, restrains his condemnation of the Man in the White House or his suspicion of big business or his conviction that labor racketeers spell the downfall of the nation. Instead, the nonpartisan is more likely to believe that the good citizen seeks the best man and the right answer in every campaign, so that the almost inarticulate loyalties common in one-party localities are consciously rejected.

Thus, Edward Janosik, after an investigation of politics in 57 suburban counties around the 20 largest metropolitan areas, concluded: "Many suburbanites in the United States seem to take pleasure in cultivating a politically independent state of mind. Some counties normally designated as suburban have population densities as high, if not higher, than sections of the core city. Even so, the pattern of political favors and resultant political obligations characteristic of older urban areas has never been strongly established in suburban communities."

A second feature of nonpartisanship is the suburbanite's acceptance of an obligation for extensive civic participation on the part of the lay constituency. So far as general political activity is concerned, this proclivity shows up in the large proportion of eligible voters who actually get to the polls in national elections. Janosik estimates that for these elections the chances are nine to one that the eligible suburban voter will cast his ballot. On the local level civic interest may express itself in the citizens' inclination to undertake the supervision of the local bureaucracy directly, or in his suspicion of the role of the professional political leader. Here the image of resurrected grassroots democracy commits the citizen, theoretically at least, to a do-it-yourself brand of politics, in which as many issues as possible, simple and complex, require his personal sanction, and the acceptable elected official is the part-time amateur, taking his term in office just as he once led the community chest drive.

Finally, and most fundamentally, no-party politics implies some positive assumptions about political behavior that go beyond simple antagonism to partisanship. Inescapably, there is a belief that the individual can and should arrive at his political convictions untutored and unled; an expectation that in the formal process of election and decision-making a consensus will emerge through the process of right reason and by the higher call to the common good. Gone is the notion of partisan groups, leaders and followers, and in its place is the conscious or unconscious assumption that the citizen, on his own, knows best.

This set of convictions, of course, marks the basic distinction between one-party and no-party politics, for it establishes a standard for acceptable political behavior that antedates the party system. As a theory, nonpartisanship harks back to the traditional concept of local government, to Jefferson's high expectations for the rational capacity of the yeoman, and to that strand in American political reasoning that relies on unfettered individualism, and that manifests itself in the agitation for primaries, referendums and recalls. It is in these assumptions that the suburbanite is linked most directly with his small town ancestors, and not in a coincidence in political attitude, which the theory of conversion tried to establish between the two.

This resurrection of conscious nonpartisanship so evident in the suburban brand of politics—as distinct from big city and rural patterns—has some quite specific consequences in the modern world. The antagonism toward party, the obligation for extensive citizen participation, and the expectation that there is likely to be a single right answer to a political problem results in an unwavering commitment to political forms in which direct democracy can be applied. This commitment, in turn, leads to an important redefinition of the relationship between the citizen and the bureaucrat, and an equally important de-emphasis on the role of the politician. Most important, under the cloak of local nonpartisanship, specific patterns of small, informally organized cliques develop which interact against the doctrine of nonpartisanship itself.

# FUN CAN BE POLITICS

## SEYOM BROWN

ACCORDING to many prominent social diagnosticians, our great game of politics has become too much of a spectator sport. The nation would be healthier if there were less television-armchair quarterbacking and more

Reprinted from *Reporter*, November 12, 1959, with permission of the publisher and the author. Copyright 1959 by The Reporter Magazine Company.

participating. Fewer and fewer people even bother to attend political rallies, let alone hold forth in front of the cigar store.

Yet in California, during the past six years, in the very state where million-dollar election campaigns are conducted by giant public-relations firms, a large and active "grass-roots" movement has sprouted out of arid, treeless suburbia. Observers have been quick to label the growth of the California Democratic Council movement as just what doctors of political science ordered, invigorating to a party getting flabby from too much sitting on its New Deal-Fair Deal past. And the C.D.C. clubs, with their suburban do-it-yourself spirit, are given primary credit for the California Democratic renaissance of 1958 that gave the state its first Democratic governor since Culbert L. Olsen was succeeded by Earl Warren following the 1942 election. Whether all this amateur political activity (there are now about fifty thousand club members) is producing anything of quality is another question altogether and one that had better not be asked just now. But it is getting more and more people into politics, many of whom previously wore their apoliticism on their grey-flannel lapels. And this in itself is adjudged "healthy. "

Attempts are now being made in other states to build up grass-roots organizations on the West Coast model. Leaders of such movements, however, might do well to explore the roots as well as the grass of the California clubs. Possibly it is something peculiar to the California soil that gives them vitality.

## Moonlight Boat Rides . . .

Most important is the simple but often overlooked fact that the primary motive power behind the California Democratic clubs is social, not political. The new club member seems to join more to make new friends than to make public policy. In suburban California the new occupants of the housing developments have one thing in common: anonymity. They are less afraid of empty dinner pails than of empty evenings and weekends. Friends and relatives are often back East, and the city center is many miles away.

A happy situation exists for the organizational recruiter. The basis of the organization—whether it happens to be religious, political, or community service—is really not important. Who joins what type of group is for the most part dependent upon which organization gets to the new resident first.

Actually, there is much in common here with the operation of the old-type political machine. The urban boss was able to "deliver" on election day because he catered to the fundamental needs of the faithful throughout the year. If times were hard, the machine ran a kind of employment agency; when immigrants arrived they might be provided with temporary lodging; if someone got involved in a lawsuit and couldn't afford a lawyer, the boss might call upon a friend to take the case. The needs were different then, but the function of the machine was of the same order as that which the clubs are now providing to the middle-class "lonely crowd" in California. And then, as now, the political role was to a large extent a by-product.

This was dramatized for me at a Democratic club meeting I attended recently in a Los Angeles suburb. The first order of new business had to do with financing the campaign of a candidate for city council. The second item concerned plans for the next club outing. The time, energy, and enthusiasm of the members were devoted almost entirely to a hot debate over the second order of business. (A moonlight boat ride to Catalina eventually won approval.)

## ... and Faraway Places

The leisure-activity basis of the clubs has been obscured by another of their characteristics: the extent to which their politics is oriented toward ideology rather than toward power or interest groups. Most reports from California tend to dwell on this trait without analyzing its source. That source, again, is leisure.

Meeting in election-district councils, or at state-wide conventions when state offices are at stake, delegates from the local Democratic clubs hear and then pass upon prospective Democratic candidates in advance of the primary elections. So effective has the club movement shown itself in getting out the vote that few candidates will risk the effort and money of trying to win nomination in a primary election unless they can first get the clubs' approval. Aspiring Democratic politicians know that they don't stand a chance to realize their ambitions in California unless they give the right answers to certain "crucial" ideological questions. Thus, a prospective candidate for the state assembly from Azuza will be expected to demonstrate conviction on questions ranging from integration of the schools in Arkansas to hydrogen-bomb tests —even though during his tenure at Sacramento he will be unlikely to have the opportunity to vote on these matters.

One of the big Democratic guns in the state assembly recently confided to a gathering of political scientists that the way for a state legislator to be a success was to vote with the clubs on the Great Issues and with the powerful interest groups on mundane practical questions. After all, he explained, the large producers aren't really that excited one way or the other over the human-rights stuff, and the average club member never even heard of an oil severance tax.

Ask any state official or journalist covering Sacramento what he thinks is the Brown administration's greatest accomplishment for 1959, and he'll tell you it was the passage of the huge state water-development program. Ask the clubs, and the almost unanimous verdict will be the Fair Employment Practices Commission law.

The largest attendance at club "educational" (as distinct from "social") functions occurs when a Great Issue is to be discussed. Sewers, water power, or school construction will have their day, too, but a skillful program chairman knows that it is better to include them only as a prelude to some bigger event.

The point is that FEPC, wheat loans to India and loyalty oaths are ever so much more interesting to the club member. The accountant or engineer who belongs to his club in Palo Alto may in fact know something about local taxation problems, but talking about such matters is too much like what he does at the office. "Come on, let's get on with the show," is his typical attitude. "Who wants to talk shop?" There is seemingly an inverse ratio between the closeness of an issue and the interest of the club member.

This need for an issue to have entertainment value before the clubs will make it their own is probably the main reason why their ideological center of gravity is decidedly on the left side in the Democratic Party, certainly to the left of Stevenson, who nonetheless is still the clubs' hero. Their tendency is to deal with the remote issues, and then in terms of clear alternatives. The black gets blacker and the white gets whiter as the viewer's distance from the scene increases.

Thus, at their 1959 statewide convention club delegates were startled to hear keynote speaker Chester Bowles caution them against arriving at a hasty conclusion that the United States should recognize Communist China. Bowles's argument was that you don't just hand out recognition without exacting some pledge or accommodation in return. The Connecticut representative called for bold ideas but also for hardheaded ideas, and his speech, though enthusiastically applauded, reddened the faces of many present. In much that Bowles said was the implication that the California grass roots were possibly not devoting enough attention to some rather important homegrown weeds.

# EGGHEAD POLITICIANS IN MANHATTAN

## JAMES Q. WILSON

IN 1959 AND 1960, Tammany Hall was fighting for its life. The Executive Committee of the Democratic Party of New York County, formerly under the unchallenged domination of County Leader Carmine G. De Sapio, was subjected to the most vigorous and sustained attack since the days of the Seabury Investigation and the subsequent regime of Fiorello H. La Guardia. The position of Tammany boss De Sapio was threatened by a

Adapted from a longer work in preparation, by permission of the author.

group of self-styled "reformers" in Manhattan. Unlike reformers in the past, however, these men and women were not attacking the regular party organization in the general elections with Fusion or "good government" candidates, nor were they relying on legislative investigations, newspaper crusades, or grand jury indictments. Rather, they were challenging the regular organization in the primary elections, with control of the district and county leaderships at stake. The reformers were bent not on changing the system from the outside, but on capturing the system itself.

This new strategy of reform was no more than ten years old in New York City. By 1960, substantial gains had been registered. Since 1953, when the first "reform" club gained power (in the 9th Assembly District), eight Tammany district leaders had been defeated and replaced by reform leaders, together with their female co-leaders. The Executive Committee of the Democratic County Committee of New York County has 66 members (33 male and 33 female district leaders), who have a total of 16 votes distributed among them (one vote for each Assembly District, often split into halves or thirds to reflect the division of districts among leaders). The reformers numbered 16 of the 66 members and could cast $4\frac{1}{6}$ votes.[1] Several regular leaders were facing strong reform challenges within their districts, and it was not at all unlikely that by the spring of 1961, the reformers would win as many as 10 more seats, giving them an additional $1\frac{5}{6}$ votes and bringing their total to 6 votes—only a fraction more than two votes shy of a majority of the Executive Committee. At that point, they would be in a position either to dictate or strongly influence the choice of the next County Leader. And they had sworn that that man would not be Carmine De Sapio.

The political clubs that sustained these reform leaders were scattered throughout Manhattan and had a total of perhaps 4,500 paid members. In addition to these, other "insurgent" reform clubs had several hundred more members.[2] These people were an extraordinary new force in Manhattan

---

1. Cf. Wallace S. Sayre and Herbert Kaufman, *Governing New York City* (New York: Russell Sage Foundation, 1960), pp. 122–141, for a description of the formal structure of party machinery.

2. Some working definitions are in order. I shall speak of three kinds of Democratic clubs. "*Reform*" clubs are those whose district leaders are members of the "Reform Democratic Leadership Caucus" formed in August, 1960 (see *New York Times*, August 5, 1960). Most, but not all, of those leaders had previously been identified as reformers because of their association with the New York Committee for Democratic Voters and because they had abstained in the September, 1959, vote for County Leader and had signed the "reform manifesto" of February, 1959. "*Insurgent*" refers to those reform-oriented clubs that have not captured the leadership of their districts but have challenged the existing Tammany leaders. "*Tammany*" clubs are those that have not been associated with the reform movement and whose leaders voted for De Sapio in the September, 1959, election. Excluded from the definition of reform clubs are those in Harlem under the leadership of Rep. Adam Clayton Powell, Jr., even though they also abstained in the County Leader election. That conflict is unrelated to the reform issue. For a classic description of the political club, see Roy V. Peel, *The Political Clubs of New York City* (New York: G. P. Putnam's Sons, 1935). The reform clubs are consciously endeavoring to break with the pattern Professor Peel describes.

politics and, to a remarkable degree, they had a more or less common set of characteristics, beliefs, and goals. It is interesting to try to delineate the principal features of these reformers as a preliminary to understanding how and why they have been successful, the nature of their organization and leadership, the goals they seek, and the problems confronting them. It should be understood, however, that despite their many similarities, the reformers had important differences as well.

## Who Are the Reformers?

To a remarkable degree, the Manhattan political reformers are young, well-educated professional people including a large percentage of women. Almost all are under forty-five and most are under forty. In style of life, they appear to be distinctly middle and upper-middle class: in mood and outlook, they are products of the generation that came of age politically during and after the Korean War; along the spectrum of political beliefs, they fall almost entirely among the liberals of the left.

In 1960, 36 men and women were nominated for office in the Lexington Democratic Club, the oldest of the reform organizations. Of the 36, 26 were men and 10 women. Thirty-four had graduated from college, and of these, 19 had attended the desirable schools of the Ivy League. The majority (20) had completed law school and were practicing law in New York City (mostly with firms in and around Wall Street). Most of the rest were in "communications"—public relations, advertising, the theater, radio and television, and so on. Of the five who were in other business, most were associated with investment houses. In many cases, these young professionals were academically distinguished: there were 16 instances of school honors, including five Phi Beta Kappa members, two teaching fellows, and two law review editors. Although no precise determination of ethnic background is available, a rough estimate based on family names suggests that there were about 20 or 21 Jewish and 15 or 16 non-Jewish candidates for office. When another reform club, the Riverside Democrats, was organized in 1957, all eight of its officers were college graduates and seven had done graduate work in prestigious eastern universities such as Harvard, Yale, Columbia, and Princeton.[3]

Many reformers feel strongly the class distinctions that separate them from the old-line political leaders and their followers. The reformers are articulate, intelligent, well-educated, and well-mannered. Even in Greenwich Village, the men favor Ivy League suits and the women advanced styles. They share a compelling concern over public issues and take their political opinions from the weekly and monthly journals of liberal thought —the *Reporter, Commentary,* the *New Republic,* and the *Nation.* In con-

3. See Robert Lekachman, "How We Beat the Machine," *Commentary,* April, 1958, p. 292.

versation, they are earnest and questioning, offering or seeking generalizations to account for their situation and their prospects. Rarely does an interviewer encounter people so anxious to be interviewed, so willing to discuss
their lot, or so indiscreet in remarking on the shortcomings and vicissitudes
of their colleagues. They manipulate abstract notions easily. They are
greatly concerned for the opinion other intelligent people hold of them.
In all these ways and more they set themselves apart from the politicians of
the regular organization. The natural hostility of "outs" for "ins" is reinforced in their case by the conviction that the existing order of politicians is
a different breed of men, from a different background, with a wholly different
outlook on politics and life. And, of course, to a great extent they are
right. A typical expression of this felt difference is found in the remarks of
one reform leader:

> Our success is basically due, I think, to an aroused middle-class interest in
> politics. [We] realize for the first time, or at least for the first time in recent
> years, that politics affects [our] daily lives. Politics was formerly in the
> province of the upper classes who paid the bills and the lower classes who
> did the work. Now the middle classes, or at least the educated segment of
> them, are getting in on that. . . . There's a standing joke around that we're
> the first white Anglo-Saxon Protestants in Tammany in many, many years.
> There've been Negroes and Catholics and Jews for a long time, but a white
> Protestant showing up is a real revolution.

Not all reform clubs, however, are exclusively composed of Protestant
and Jewish middle-class young professionals. Some clubs are endeavoring,
amidst charges that they are "unrepresentative," to attract lower-income
Catholic, Negro, and Puerto Rican members. Other clubs, like the Riverside Democrats, inherited older political workers from pre-existing organizations. Perhaps 25 workers, many of them poorer Irish who live in West
Side tenements, entered the Riverside club. There is a fundamental dissimilarity between the young intellectuals and the older group. Because of
the polyglot character of the district, each group needs the other, but the
views of politics held by the two elements are far from identical. The young
reformer looks upon his older co-worker with doubts and uneasiness mixed
with a certain attraction for the "colorful" and curious manners of the latter.

Reform politics has, in great measure, become possible because the
class structure of Manhattan has undergone a fundamental change. It is
coming to consist of three groups: the wealthy, often older, residents of the
East Side, where new luxury apartments are rising at an incredible rate;
the lower-income Negroes and Puerto Ricans of Harlem and East Harlem;
and the highly educated young professionals, often married but frequently
with few or no children, for whom Manhattan has an irresistible fascination.
Gone or leaving is the conventional middle class, composed of people of
moderate or skimpy means, average education, a high proportion of children,
and no particular commitment to the presumed cultural and social ad-

vantages of life in Manhattan. These people have moved to Queens, the upper Bronx, New Jersey, and even farther.

Almost all politicians, reform and Tammany alike, agree that this change lies at the root of reform politics. A reform leader on the West Side speaks of the 5th and 7th Assembly Districts as about "the only area left in Manhattan in which young, professional people can find decent homes in rent-controlled apartments—people with education and little money, predominantly Jewish." Greenwich Village, which thirty years ago was perhaps one-half Italian, today is about one-third Italian. The new group is composed in part of bearded bohemians and social nomads, but more and more it consists of young middle-class families who regard the atmosphere of Village life as culturally and intellectually stimulating. The characteristics of the new group are graphically summarized by one observer:

> A growing number of the real residents hold down regular jobs (most often in what is now called "Communications" . . .), have husbands, wives, babies, and grocery carts. The main distinction in material possessions between them and the older Italian residents is that they have hi-fi instead of television sets. In the afternoon, they buy the *Post* instead of the *Journal-American,* and are likely to wear toreador pants or slacks instead of skirts and dresses when they wheel their babies into Washington Square Park. Many of them spent the protest years of their youth here, and when they closed that chapter with marriage, decided to stay on.[4]

In attracting this group into politics, the significance of the Presidential elections of 1952 and 1956 can scarcely be exaggerated. Adlai E. Stevenson was and is a figure of great emotional significance to the young reformers. To these people, who often were raised with the belief that politics is a dismal and mercenary process of choice between unpalatable politicians backed by corrupt bosses and party hacks, Stevenson seemed to embody sensitivity and intellect, liberalism and self-doubt in a way that was powerfully compelling. Said one reformer of his colleagues, "Stevenson is associated with a great event in their lives—their discovery of politics." It was the lure of a *national* campaign on behalf of a *national* figure that first brought most of the reformers into politics as part of the Volunteers for Stevenson in 1952 and 1956. The Lexington Democratic Club and the Stevensonian Democrats (an insurgent club on the lower East Side) received their real impetus from the campaign of 1952; the members of the Riverside, FDR-Woodrow Wilson, and other clubs were drawn into politics as a consequence of the 1956 campaign. One of the founders of the Lexington Democratic Club, and later executive director of the reform New York Committee for Democratic Voters, was state director of the Volunteers for Stevenson in 1952 and publicity director for a comparable organization in 1956. One West Side reform leader stated, "We would never have grown up without Adlai

---

4. Dan Wakefield, "Greenwich Village Challenges Tammany," *Commentary,* October, 1959, p. 308.

Stevenson. He, so far as I am concerned, is the spiritual and intellectual father of the reform movement."

The public and private remarks of reform leaders and followers are filled with reverential references to Stevenson. Indeed, in one club, a lengthy debate was held among members of the executive committee over whether Stevenson had become a "father figure" for the movement and whether this "canonization" of Stevenson was a good or bad thing.

## Goals of the Reformers

The process whereby this commitment to a national figure and this participation in a national campaign were transformed into a commitment to *local* goals and participation in a *local* political effort is of central importance in understanding the nature of the Manhattan reform movement. It was in this process of transformation that the goals and beliefs of the reformers were articulated and their appeal to the politically uncommitted was defined. In the course of the transformation, the reform movement came to attack Carmine De Sapio personally and as a symbol of a certain political order.

Carmine De Sapio and Tammany Hall, together with the Democratic political allies of De Sapio (such as State Chairman Michael Prendergast, Bronx leader Charles Buckley, and Brooklyn leader Joseph T. Sharkey), are attacked by the reformers because they are "reactionary," "undemocratic," "unrepresentative," and lack a "concern" for the community. Strangely enough, not more than four or five years ago Carmine De Sapio was being hailed by feature articles in *Harper's* and *Time* as a "new-style boss," an "enlightened political leader" with an interest in civic reforms.[5] In a sense, these plaudits were dated when they were written, for already Stevenson supporters in Manhattan were angry at what they regarded as the treachery of De Sapio in not giving full support to Stevenson. This was particularly true in 1956, when De Sapio had backed Governor Averell Harriman for the Presidential nomination against Stevenson, and after Stevenson was nominated, had appeared to "sit on his hands" in the fall campaign. Although regular organization leaders deny it, almost all reformers are thoroughly convinced that the Tammany workers failed to work for Stevenson and concentrated instead on the lesser offices of greater immediate importance to the machine (in terms of the patronage rewards). Reform opposition to Tammany coalesced out of the conviction that Tammany had betrayed Stevenson.

When the issue was joined, of course, the attack on De Sapio and Tammany Hall moved far beyond resentment at the alleged anti-Stevenson posture of the regular organization. A whole catalogue of Tammany evils

---

5. Cf. Robert Heilbroner, "Carmine De Sapio; The Smile on the Face of the Tiger," *Harper's*, July, 1954.

has been promulgated. The use of patronage, for example, is a prime target. "The regulars think only of pay-offs," according to one reformer. "They believe that only a pay-off, patronage or something, will keep people active in politics." Patronage is intrinsically wrong, the reformers think, and it is particularly wrong if it is used by the leader to enforce his will on the party workers and club members. Although the reformers differ among themselves over the extent to which political appointments should be eliminated, they all agree that sinecures are bad. Not only are the holders of such jobs parasites on the public payroll, but what is worse, they are parasites who must take orders. Control of their jobs gives the leader a "string" by which he can compel discipline and force workers to sacrifice their independent judgment.

The regular Tammany clubs are also charged with being "undemocratic." Specifically, the reformers allege that the clubs admit no new members and, indeed, discourage the participation of "outsiders," that they refuse to admit women on an equal basis, that they are subservient to the "bosses" in choosing candidates, that they are overly concerned with "ticket balancing" among major ethnic and religious groups, that they are not representative of districts in which they hold power, and that they take no interest in their communities. Given their undemocratic nature, it is contended, community-minded, liberal people cannot enter and reform them from within. Thus, it becomes necessary to overthrow the old clubs and replace them with democratic clubs.

Many reform clubs have sought to define reformism in a statement of principles or purposes. One of the earliest and best-known of these is the statement adopted by the Lexington Democratic Club, the eleven points of which can be summarized as three major demands: democratization of the party machinery, improvement in the caliber of party leaders and candidates, and emphasis on program and principle in attracting both party workers and voters. Of these, the first is clearly of greatest importance, both as a goal of the reformers and as a key to understanding their tactics and problems. The reformers are convinced that if the party is democratized, the other two goals will follow almost as a matter of course. Politics will then be in the hands of an educated, professional middle class that will fill all posts, even those at the bottom of the ticket, with qualified persons. Patronage will be restricted or—if the militants have their way—abolished altogether. No longer will there be a need for such "outmoded" practices as ticket-balancing.

Democratizing the party means making leaders responsible to members. To realize this goal, many specific reforms are envisaged. The party organization, particularly the district clubs, will be open to all enrolled Democrats, male and female, who pay modest dues and subscribe to a set of principles. A detailed constitution will define the procedures of the club and the authority of the leaders. All important matters will be decided by a vote of the membership, operating in accordance with strict parliamentary procedure. An elaborate structure of committees will be organized to handle club activ-

ities and to involve members in political life. Annual financial reports will
be issued. The operations of the club, including the deliberations of its
executive committee, will be public. Most important of all, the power of the
district leader will be reduced substantially. This democratization of political
machinery is not, of course, to be confined to the district club. The entire
party organization, from the state committee down, is to be made internally
democratic. This requires applying to the county committee, the county
executive committee, and the state judicial convention, and to the selection
of county leader, state committee chairman, and national committeeman the
same reforms as are applied to the district clubs and the selection of district
leader.

In the great majority of the reform clubs, intraparty democracy is not
only advocated but practiced. The meetings begin late and end very late,
often in the early hours of the morning. Everyone may speak, and virtually
everyone does. Roberts' *Rules of Order* is very much in evidence; indeed,
it is perhaps the only source of authority one can detect. Relatively little
deference is paid to elected officials or club leaders. Debates are lengthy and
conducted with passion and considerable parliamentary skill. Motions are
made, amended, and the amendments are amended in complex patterns.

Almost all of the clubs endeavor to diversify their incentives so that there
will be some reward in political activity for almost anybody who chooses
to join. The range of club work is staggering. The Lexington Democratic
Club, for example, had in 1960 thirty standing committees with a total of
sixty-one chairmen and vice-chairmen. The purposes of these committees
ranged from finance and campaigning to art, charter flights abroad, community affairs, housing violations and enforcement, national affairs, and
newspaper publication. The most important of these nonpolitical activities,
in the eyes of the reformers, are those related to community affairs. Even
allowing for a certain degree of exaggeration in describing the extent to
which reformers were the key agents in these activities, the list of the Lexington Democratic Club is impressive: stimulating building inspections north
of 97th Street; publishing a booklet for tenants explaining rent control and
eviction laws; initiating the organization of a group which secured a neighborhood conservation project for 97th and 98th Streets; advising tenants on
relocation; sponsoring an adult organization to provide services for problem
children in Public School 612; lobbying to continue the free performances
of Shakespeare in Central Park; administering over 1,000 polio shots in
1958; conducting public forums on local and national issues; arranging for
a bookmobile to provide library services; pressing for reopening of 97th
Street public library; passing resolutions supporting laws to end racial discrimination; and backing a $500 million school construction bond issue.[6]

When Lexington Club members were asked what club activity they liked
the most, more answers referred to forums and the discussion of large issues

6. From Lexington Democratic Club, "Community Affairs Fact Sheet," March,
1960 (mimeo).

than to any other activity. The club contributes amply to such interests. Scarcely a month passes in which a prominent speaker is not heard at the club. In two years (January, 1958, through January, 1960) there were twenty-eight such events, featuring Arthur M. Schlesinger, Jr., Mrs. Eleanor Roosevelt, William Zeckendorf, Senator Albert Gore, Senator Harrison Williams, Thomas K. Finletter, Edward Teller, and others. In this and in almost all other reform clubs, the attention paid to national and international affairs is striking. There are frequent discussions of these topics, with and without guest speakers, and all clubs pass resolutions on such matters as cloture in the United States Senate, the extension of the Reciprocal Trade Act, defense of the Chinese islands of Quemoy and Matsu, the Southern Negro student sit-in movement, and civil rights bills.

The importance of large questions, freighted with ideological significance, suggests a close parallel between the interests of Manhattan reformers and their counterparts elsewhere. Analyses of California Democratic Clubs, for example, stress the importance to the members of the "big issues" (such as civil rights, disarmament, and inflation) and lack of appeal of the more pedestrian, but locally more important, "little issues" (such as tax laws, mineral rights, and utility rates).[7] This analysis of California liberal clubs argues that the principal incentive for club participation is sociability and ideology; politics is "fun" as a leisure-time activity. That this is true in part for Manhattan reformers is clear. But an important distinction should be made. The Manhattan clubs are deeply involved in local contests against a strong political machine; California clubs arose in a political vacuum, never had to unseat an entrenched party organization in local contests, and from the first were free to concentrate on state-wide and national contests (and hence free to emphasize ideological questions to a much greater extent than the Manhattan clubs, which were compelled to concern themselves with questions of organizational reform).

Despite the differences between Manhattan clubs and those elsewhere in the nation, it remains true that there is a latent tension among the Manhattan reformers between the concern for local politics and the concern for national ideology. Many club members were attracted by the ideological orientation of the clubs rather than by the local goal of organizational reform, and the process of converting that interest, while successful with most active members, is far from complete. To the most militant leaders, reform politics is too *ad hoc*: it moves from campaign to campaign, busy with the exciting work of politicking, but heedless of the general aims and ultimate rationale of the movement. Said one West Side reform leader:

> Everybody works at the busy work of politics, and there's a great deal of it—planning rallies, where to have rallies, how to canvass, and so on. This is important but it's just busy work; it requires no real thought. The amount of time and money spent on this is truly fantastic. But nobody does the

7. Cf. Seyom Brown, "Fun Can Be Politics," *Reporter*, November 12, 1959, pp. 27–28, and rejoinders in letters-to-the-editor column of subsequent issues.

solitary work of [thinking things out]. They're all willing to talk in meetings and yell; indeed, this seems to be the principal source of satisfaction for them.

This leader and others like him (notably on the West Side) are anxious to develop a reform ideology that will set goals for reformism and provide it with a philosophic foundation. The questions to which a reform ideology would be addressed would include the proper attitude toward patronage, nominating procedures, and interclub relations. "The reform clubs are divided from each other," said another West Side leader. "I think the problem is that there is a lack of a real ideology to bind the clubs together." An East Side reform leader felt that the community services of the club should be conceived of as a "new kind of urban planning in which the citizen is brought much closer to his government." Said another, "I felt we needed a synthesis in this club between politics and . . . community service. . . . It ought to be a community neighborhood government." Asked why, he replied, "I wanted to justify this dabbling in politics to myself. I had to give it a value beyond narrow politics. That just wasn't sufficient for me, and I don't think it would be sufficient for other people. . . . We wanted to keep people involved with something more meaningful than politics."

Many leaders agree on the desirability of an articulated program, but few can agree on what such a program ought to contain. The strength of the reform movement has lain precisely in the fact that its "ideology" does not specify in any detail the concrete goals of the clubs. Reformism is basically a set of instrumental goals. The advantages of this are manifest. As long as democratizing the party and defeating Carmine De Sapio can be invested with sufficient moral fervor, there is little real need for agreement on more substantive ends. This is particularly true so long as the reformers are winning but have not as yet won the county leadership, the Borough Presidency, or the Mayoralty. Until then, reformers will not be called upon to make significant choices among competing alternatives. They will not be called upon to decide issues of public policy. They will not have to bear responsibility for their actions.

Avoidance of these substantive choices is advantageous for many reasons. One is that the choices are hard. It is easier to be a liberal in national than in local affairs. Indeed, in city politics it is often hard to know what liberalism is. Passing resolutions regarding national and international matters is much easier than passing resolutions on issues of public schooling, mass transportation, traffic control, housing, slum clearance, and local tax rates. One of the most oft-repeated observations of reformers in Manhattan refers to the change in their thinking caused by moving from the grand simplicities of national issues and national candidates (which in many cases lured them into reform politics in the first place) to the complexities of local issues and neighborhood problems. "You know," said one, "the more you learn about it, the harder it becomes. There just don't seem to be any black-and-white questions in city government. Everything is complicated."

# VI

## INFLUENCE AND LEADERSHIP

It is characteristic of the American political system that persons who have no office nevertheless participate actively in the conduct of affairs and sometimes exercise more influence than elected and appointed officials. In part, this is no doubt a consequence of the extreme decentralization of the system. Officials must collaborate with private interests in order to bring together the scattered pieces of power that are needed to get anything done. In part, too, it is a consequence of our conception of democracy, according to which everyone must be allowed, and indeed encouraged, to take an active part in the business of governing. The fact remains that by looking only at the activities of people who hold office, one can get an impression of the American political system so incomplete and distorted as to be downright wrong.

The first six readings in this Section are descriptive accounts of interests that figure largely in urban government. Floyd Hunter, a sociologist, asserts that in Regional City (Atlanta), decisions in community affairs are made by a few "power leaders" who are at the apex of a stable, hierarchical "power structure." These leaders, most of whom are heads of large corporations, pass directions on to second, third, and fourth rate personnel (the "under-structure" of power); public officials, it is interesting to note, are among the second and third rate personnel. The first two ratings are said to "set the line of policy"; the other two "hold the line." If an understructure man is presumptuous enough to question a decision made by the top leaders, he may lose his job or be otherwise punished. Robert A. Dahl, a political scientist, finds nothing like this in New Haven. There the Economic Notables, as he calls them, are only one among many groups "out of which individuals emerge" to exert influence; like other groups in the community (Negroes and schoolteachers, for example), the Economic Notables sometimes have their way and sometimes do not.

It may be asked why Hunter's findings differ so greatly from those of Dahl. One explanation may be that Hunter's research method, which involved asking people active in civic affairs to rate others according to their relative power, tended to produce the kind of answers that were expected, whereas Dahl's method, which was based mainly on observation of events rather than of opinions or attitudes, did not. Of course, it is also quite possible that there *is* a power elite in Regional City but none in the city studied by Dahl.

In most American cities, minority groups and organized labor have until recently exerted relatively little influence, and for that reason, perhaps, their civic roles have been little studied. James Q. Wilson describes two contrasting styles of Negro leadership—the militant and the moderate—and shows the characteristic affinities of each of these styles for certain ends and means. These pages are excerpted from a brilliant book on Negro civic leadership. Two political scientists, Kenneth E. Gray and David Greenstone, describe three levels of labor participation in local politics—intensive and general participation in a one-industry Northern city (Detroit), intensive participation by a single, relatively small union local in a mixed commercial-industrial border city (St. Louis), and withdrawal from politics in a vigorous, young commercial-industrial city of the South (Houston). So far as the editor knows, this is the only attempt that has been made to show how labor's political role varies with the general structure of city politics.

The press has always played an extraordinarily active and important role in local government in the United States. The reason, as de Tocqueville suggested, may be that the extreme decentralization of our political system gives the press great incentives to take and use power. Whether this influence is as important as it used to be is the question examined by Alvin J. Remmenga, a newspaperman.

The three remaining readings contribute to the theoretical understanding of influence relations and leadership. Robert K. Metron offers a useful pair of concepts in his discussion of the "local" and the "cosmopolitan." (The new-style reformers described in the last Section by Wood, Brown, and Wilson obviously belong to his cosmopolitan type, whereas the traditional machine politician just as obviously belongs to his local type.) Norton E. Long, a political scientist, presents a view very much at odds with Hunter's. The idea that there exists a "power elite" may be comforting, Long says, but observation in some communities (his article is based largely on interviews in Boston and Cleveland) shows little or no such informal organization. Instead, there is undirected cooperation of particular social structures, each seeking particular goals (for example, the newspaper, which seeks prestige, readership, and advertising) and, in so doing, meshing with the goals of others. He concludes that although this meshing makes possible cooperative action on projects, it is very far from constituting a structured government.

The final reading of the Section, by a sociologist, Peter H. Rossi, is a promising effort to construct a comprehensive and systematic theoretical model relating types of power structure to the larger political framework.

# THE POWER STRUCTURE OF REGIONAL CITY

FLOYD HUNTER

ONE OF THE FIRST INTERVIEWS had in Regional City was with James Treat of the Southern Yarn Company. He gave a great deal of information concerning power relations in the community. Among other things, he supplied a clue to certain existing clique relationships and considerable information about them which was later verified. Several times in his conversation he had used the term "crowds" in describing how certain men acted in relation to each other on community projects, and he was asked to explain the term. His reply ran in this vein:

"I simply mean that there are 'crowds' in Regional City—several of them—that pretty well make the big decisions. There is the crowd I belong to (the Homer Chemical crowd); then there is the First State Bank crowd—the Regional Gas Heat crowd—the Mercantile crowd—the Growers Bank crowd—and the like."

Mr. Treat was asked to give the names of some of the men who were active in each crowd, and he said:

"Sure! The biggest man in our crowd is Charles Homer. I belong to his crowd along with John Webster, Bert Tidwell, Ray Moster, Harold Jones, James Finer, Larry Stroup, and Harold Farmer. There are others, but they would be on the edges of this crowd. These would be the ones to be brought in on anything.

"In the State Bank crowd there would be Herman Schmidt, Harvey Aiken, Mark Parks, and Joseph Hardy. Schmidt used to be the biggest man in that crowd, but young Hardy is coming up fast over there.

"In the Regional Gas Heat crowd there is Fargo Dunham, Elsworth Mines, Gilbert Smith, and Percy Latham maybe. George Delbert might be said to belong to that crowd, but he is a pretty independent fellow. He moves around [from crowd to crowd] quite a bit.

Reprinted from *Community Power Structure, A Study of Decision Makers* (Chapel Hill: The University of North Carolina Press, 1953), pp. 77–81 and 108–112, by permission of the publisher.

"The Mercantile crowd is made up of Harry Parker, Jack Williams, Luke Street, Adam Graves, Cary Stokes, and Epworth Simpson.

"The Growers Bank crowd would be Ralph Spade, Arthur Tarbell, and Edward Stokes. They are kind of a weak outfit, but they come in on a lot of things. Spade is probably the most aggressive of the lot, but he's not too much at that!"

With this information given, Mr. Treat was asked to tell how these crowds would operate in relation to one another on a community-wide project, and he outlined the procedure very clearly. This type of action will be given in fuller detail in connection with the techniques of power wielding, but it may be said here that representatives from each crowd are drawn into any discussion relative to a major community decision. Each man mentioned as belonging to a crowd also belongs to a major business enterprise within the community—at least the clique leader does. His position within the bureaucratic structure of his business almost automatically makes him a community leader, if he wishes to become one. The test for admission to this circle of decision-makers is almost wholly a man's position in the business community in Regional City. The larger business enterprises represent pyramids of power in their own right, as work units within the community, and the leaders within these concerns gather around them some of the top personnel within their own organization. They then augment this nucleus of leadership by a coterie of selected friends from other establishments to form knots of interest called "crowds" by Mr. Treat. The outer edges of any crowd may pick up such men as Percy Latham, the dentist, who in turn picks up others in relation to any specific activity in which the crowd may be interested. The top men in any crowd tend to act together, and they depend upon men below them to serve as intermediaries in relation to the general community.

The crowds described by Mr. Treat were also mentioned by numerous other informants. These crowds did not, however, exhaust the possibilities of clique relations within the larger group of policy leaders. Twenty-one distinct groupings were picked up within the forty persons on the list, as the study proceeded, but the crowds mentioned by Treat seemed to be the most generally recognized groupings. Several of the top leaders within the crowds would "clear with each other" informally on many matters. The older men, as mentioned earlier, tended to get their heads together on most matters, as did the younger group, but such relationships were not completely stable. Each man at the top of a "crowd pyramid" depended upon those close to him in business to carry out decisions when made. An older man, for example, could not command another older man to do something, but within his own crowd there would be a hierarchy he could put to work. In most instances decision-making tended to be channeled through the older men at some point in the process of formulation, but many things may be done on the initiative of any combination of several powerful leaders in the crowds named. None of the leaders indicated that he could work alone on any big project, nor did any feel that there was any man in the community with such power. The individual power leader is dependent on others in Regional City in contrast to mill or mining company towns where one man or one family may dominate the community actions which take place.

Society prestige and deference to wealth are not among the primary criteria for admission to the upper ranks of the decision-makers according to the study of Regional City. The persons who were included in the listing of forty top leaders purely on the basis of their wealth or society connections did not, with three or four exceptions, make the top listing of persons who might be called upon to "put across a community project." As has been mentioned before, a distinction is made between persons of wealth and social prestige who engage in work and those who do not. The persons of wealth are perhaps important in the social structure of the community as symbolic persons. They may be followed in matters of fashion and in their general manner of living. Their money may be important in financing a given project, but they are not of themselves doers. They may only be called decisive in the sense that they can withhold or give money through others to change the course of action of any given project. Gloria Stevens spends large sums of money on Regional City projects, but the expenditures are made through her lawyer, Ray Moster. She does not interact with any of the top leaders whom we interviewed, other than Moster, so far as could be ascertained. Hetty Fairly, another woman of wealth, spends her charitable monies through a foundation handled by a lawyer not on the list of leaders. The lawyers may be vigilant in serving the interests of their clients in both instances, and a part of the vigilance exercised is in keeping abreast of possible tax incursions on the "frozen wealth" of the foundations. In this there may be some connection with power, but it is rather obscure in terms of the definition of power as being the ability of persons to move goods and services toward defined goals. If there is power in the charitable foundation structures, it resides in the lawyers who operate them, rather than in the donors who are largely inactive in the affairs of the foundations.

Political eminence cannot be said to be a sole criterion for entry into the policy echelons of Regional City's life, generally speaking. The two exceptions to this statement are embodied in Mayor Barner and County Treasurer Truman Worth. Both Barner and Worth were successful businessmen before becoming involved in local politics to the point of seeking public office. Their interests may be said to be primarily business in the strict sense of the word. Both have a popular following that has kept them in office, but their close associates are businessmen. Mayor Barner had only one picture in his office—that of Charles Homer, the biggest businessman in the community. Both Barner and Worth look to businessmen constantly for advice before they make a move on any project concerning the whole community. Furthermore, they do not ordinarily "move out front" on any project themselves, but rather follow the lead of men like Delbert, Graves, or any one of the other leaders of particular crowds. . . .

The channels of interaction are established in Regional City to conserve the time of the men of power. Even with the channels that are opened, there is still considerable burden of responsibility placed upon these men. In discussing this point with George Delbert, the question was asked, "With so few men in policy positions, isn't there a tendency to choke off many projects which may be of equal merit with those being given consideration?" He thought the question over for a moment and replied, "Yes, I suppose that may be true; but there's only so much time in a year, and we can only handle a certain number of things. Then there's not money enough to go around for everything that comes up. There is always anywhere from one to two million being raised in this community for one purpose or another. It takes time to get around to everything!"

The power leaders do get around with considerable facility in the area of economic activity. When a new corporation is started, as for example a new television company, or a multimillion dollar apartment building project recently established in the city, one or more of the leaders were observed to "find time" to be identified with such developments. Certainly, the top leaders would appear to have time for policy considerations of such economic projects, if one takes into account the reports in the business section of the local press. The day-to-day working arrangements of the corporations are put into the hands of trusted under-structure administrative personnel. The pattern of power implicit in the situation matches that of civic enterprises in formation and development.

"If two institutions," says Hughes, "draw upon the same people . . . they may compete in some measure, for people have but a limited amount of time and money to expend."[1] The leaders of Regional City tend to protect themselves from too many demands by channeling policy execution through an under-structure on matters of policy. This under-structure is not a rigid bureaucracy, as has been pointed out, but is a flexible system. It has elements of stability and tends to operate by levels. The men at each level are spoken of as first, second, third and fourth rate by the power leaders, who operate primarily in conjunction with individuals of the first two ratings. The types of personnel which may be found in each rating by a sample classification are as follows:

## Examples of Personnel from First to Fourth Rate in Regional City

FIRST RATE: Industrial, commercial, financial owners and top executives of large enterprises.

SECOND RATE: Operations officials, bank vice-presidents, public-relations men,

---

1. Everett C. Hughes, "Ecological Aspects of Institutions," *American Sociological Review,* I (April 1936), 186.

small businessmen (owners), top-ranking public officials, corporation attorneys, contractors.

THIRD RATE: Civic organization personnel, civic agency board personnel,
newspaper columnists, radio commentators, petty public officials, selected
organization executives.

FOURTH RATE: Professionals such as ministers, teachers, social workers, personnel directors, and such persons as small business managers, higher
paid accountants, and the like.

These ratings might be expanded. They are given simply to indicate
a suggested ranking of selected personnel who operate below the policy-
making leaders in Regional City. The first two ratings are personnel who
are said to "set the line of policy," while the latter two groups "hold the
line." The ratings are very real to the under-structure professional personnel.
One of these men said: "I know that the top boys get together on things.
This community is divided into tiers. You can't get the first-tier men to
work on anything originating in the second- and third-tier level. The top
ones may put their names on second- and third-tier projects, but you cannot
get them to work with you. They will not attend your meetings, but you
know they are attending their own meetings all the time." The top leaders
are conserving their time and energies for the primary role they play—policy-
determination. They are also interested in holding a balance of power in the
community.

In discussing the men in the lower group of the top leadership hierarchy,
one of the informants said: "When you see one of the little fellows move,
you know he is not moving on his own. Somebody is moving him, and it is
the bigger fellow who is moving him that you need to watch, if you want to
know what is going on.

"My father, who was a farmer, used to chop wood with me. He'd say,
'Son, when you see a chip in the woodpile move, look under the chip.
You probably will find something interesting under it.' I've always remem-
bered that. I've always looked to see what makes the 'chips' move."

The "little fellows" are continually moved to perform their proper tasks
by those above them. The roles defined for the under-structure of power
personnel are carefully defined in keeping with the larger interests. Their
movements are carefully stimulated and watched at all times to see that
their various functions are properly performed.

Stability of relationships is highly desirable in maintaining social control,
and keeping men "in their places" is a vital part of the structuring of community power. Andrew Carnegie expressed the idea of every man in his
place in this manner: "It is the business of the preacher to preach, of the
physician to practice, of the poet to write, the business of the college professor
to teach. . . ."[2] Each of these professions also has a role to play in the

2. *The Empire of Business* (New York: Doubleday, Page and Company, 1902),
p. 189.

community activities consistent with its economic or professional role. Such roles do not ordinarily include policy-making. If one of these under-structure men should be presumptuous enough to question policy decisions, he would be immediately considered insubordinate and "punished," first by a threat to his job security, followed possibly by expulsion from his job if his insubordination continued. To quote Homans:

> A social system is in a moving equilibrium and authority exists when the state of the elements that enter the system and the relations between them, including the behavior of the leader(s), is such that disobedience to the orders of the leader(s) will be followed by changes in the other elements tending to bring the system back to the state the leader(s) would have wished to reach if the disobedience had not occurred.[3]

There may be isolated dissatisfactions with policy decisions in Regional City, but mainly there is unanimity. The controversial is avoided, partly by the policy-making group's not allowing a proposal to get too far along if it meets stiff criticism at any point in decision-making. A careful watch is kept for what "will go" and for what "will not go." Luke Street says, "Most of the carping comes from people who are envious of some of the bigger crowds. When there is such envy, the crowds are talked about and criticized." Such criticism usually is not open. When criticism is open it is generally directed toward some of the under-structure men who are fronting for the larger interests. If criticism is directed toward the top leaders, the critic is liable to job dismissal in extreme cases or more subtle pressures in less flagrant cases. The omnipresent threat of power sanctions used against recalcitrant underlings is recognized by lower echelons of power, and they generally go along with most decisions, grumbling in private with close associates, if at all. Most of these third- or fourth-rate leaders rationalize their behavior—particularly when upper decisions are in conflict with their professional or private value systems.

# THE ECONOMIC NOTABLES
# OF NEW HAVEN

## ROBERT A. DAHL

THE HYPOTHESIS that an economic elite of bankers and businessmen dominates New Haven, dramatic and satisfying as it may be to many

Reprinted, somewhat revised, from *Democracy and Power in an American Community* (New Haven: Yale University Press, forthcoming 1961), by permission of the author.
3. *The Human Group* (New York: Harcourt, Brace and Company, 1950), p. 422.

people, is false. The temptation to fly from one falsehood to another at the
opposite extreme is unfortunately one of the commonplaces of human existence; and hence one might easily interpret the evidence as showing that the
Economic Notables[1] are virtually powerless: a conclusion surely as unwar-

> The president or chairman of the board of a corporation with property in New
>   Haven assessed in any of the five years 1953–1957 at a value placing it among
>   the fifty highest assessments in the city.
> Any individual or groups of individuals with property in the city assessed in the
>   years 1956–1957 at a value of $250,000 or more.
> President or chairman of the board of all banks and public utilities in the city.
> Any individual who was a director of three or more of the following:
>
> > A firm with assessed valuation of $250,000 or more.
> > A manufacturing firm with fifty or more employees.
> > A retailing firm with twenty-five or more employees.
> > Any bank.
> > All directors of New Haven banks.

ranted as the other. Nor does it get us much closer to the truth if we
simply offer the vacuous evasion that the truth lies somewhere between the
two extremes; for this is merely to reduce a social complexity to a loose
and misleading metaphor.

The most impressive evidence against the hypothesis that the Economic
Notables or their delegates completely dominate New Haven consists of a
detailed examination of eight major decisions on redevelopment, eight on
public education, and all nominations for elective office, but most importantly
for mayor, in both political parties for seven elections from 1945–1957. These
decisions have been reconstructed from records, newspaper files, and interviews with leading participants.

To reconstruct these decisions is to leave no doubt, I think, of the fact
that the Economic Notables, far from being a ruling group, are simply one
of the many groups out of which individuals sporadically emerge to influence
the policies and acts of city officials. Almost anything one might say about
the influence of the Economic Notables could be said with equal justice
about a half dozen other groups in the New Haven community. What
these other groups are and what can be said about *their* influence will develop as we proceed.

If the quantitative indications of the relative influence of the Economic
Notables belied the overwhelming testimony provided by the qualitative
inspection of these decisions, one might quite properly, I believe, reject the
quantitative rather than the qualitative interpretation of the evidence. But in
this case each kind of evidence supports the other.

Of the forty-eight Economic Notables participating officially in urban
redevelopment plus any additional ones who may have been participating
unofficially, only seven seem to have exerted any leadership. . . . Of these,
only one, a banker who was the first chairman of the Citizens Action

1. The group of Economic Notables, numbering some 238 persons, includes any
person in one of the following categories:

Commission, was among the top five; at least two and probably three others in the top five exerted considerably more influence over the actual course of decisions than he did. There were . . . no Economic Notables among the higher offices in public education; and none were turned up as covert leaders. Only one Economic Notable was a leader in either of the two political parties; and he was something of an anomaly. It will be worth our time to examine this case in some detail.

## Politician or Notable?

This unique individual was Mr. John Golden, a Democratic party leader for a generation and a man whom few people in New Haven, if they happened to know his name, would have considered as other than the boss of the Democratic Party.

Golden was, in some ways, a representative of an earlier era. As a political boss he was in the old tradition of urban politics. As a businessman he had this much in common with the entrepreneurs of the late nineteenth century: he had come a long way from modest beginnings.

He was born not far from New Haven in Old Saybrook, where his father was a station agent for the New Haven railroad. Of Irish Catholic stock, descended from a father and a grandfather who had both been Democrats, the boy quite naturally became a Democrat too. About the time of the First World War Golden went to work in the Greist Manufacturing Company and there he rose to the rank of superintendent. But he was evidently more interested in politics than in manufacturing; he became Democratic chairman in his ward in 1924 (a post he still held a quarter-century later) and in 1931 he ran for public office as Democratic candidate for Registrar of Voters. In the great depression-born surge to the Democrats, he won. But the newly elected mayor, who like Golden was an Irishman and a Democrat, offered him a city post as Director of Public Works; Golden thereupon resigned his job in the manufacturing plant and took the new one. Not wishing to be dependent on the modest income from his city job, he now started an insurance and bonding business; and as he rose in politics his business became highly lucrative. The connection was perhaps not accidental. In due course he was made a director of the General Industrial Bank, a small commercial bank that had been established by Jewish families in New Haven as a result of the systematic exclusion of Jews by other banks; it was probably the only bank in New Haven since Andrew Jackson's day that might be called a "Democratic" bank rather than a "Republican" one. It is by virtue of this directorship that Golden, under the generous conception of economic notability outlined earlier, falls into our present group. But he rightly belongs there, for he is reputed to be a well-to-do man by New Haven standards.

By the time the Democratic mayor under whom Golden served had been defeated in his last try for office in 1945, Golden was the real head of the Democratic organization. His rule was occasionally challenged; but the challengers were regularly defeated. It was Golden who saw possibilities in a young member of the Board of Aldermen, Richard Lee, who ultimately was elected mayor in 1953 with Golden's strong support. As Lee's prestige, confidence, and authority grew, Golden's own control over the organization waned. By the end of the decade it was no longer possible to say which of the two would win in a showdown over control of the organization. But neither man stood to gain by a contest, neither sought one, and except for a brief conflict over charter reform their coalition remained intact.

One could draw a pretty picture of the Economic Notables controlling Golden, and Golden in turn controlling the Democratic Party. But whatever else one might conclude about Golden's role in politics, it has been impossible to turn up any evidence to warrant the conclusion that he was an "agent" of the Notables. Like most successful politicians, particularly Democratic ones, he was not known to entertain a profound respect for the abilities or attainments of successful businessmen, and his style of life, outlook, and interests were those of the old-fashioned urban political leader rather than the man of business. For its part, the business community looked upon Golden with no little suspicion as an organization politician. (Because of their contacts with him on the Citizens Action Commission in recent years, some of the Economic Notables finally developed a grudging respect for his shrewdness and judgment.) Moreover most of the Economic Notables were Republicans who had supported Republican candidates and opposed the Democratic ones supported by Golden.

It might be thought that the Economic Notables had no need to "control" Golden since as a successful insurance executive and bank director his views on policy questions would surely coincide with theirs. There is not only a profound truth in this observation but also an important distortion. If one searches for a massive divergence in opinion between Golden and New Haven business leaders, one will not find it. But if one looks for massive divergencies between Golden and almost any other group in the community, one will not find that either. For like the United States, New Haven is usually governed by "consensus politics" rather than by "conflict politics." This is a matter we shall return to many times, but perhaps it is enough to say now that in the present period there are in New Haven no profound, persistent, invariant, and community-wide cleavages of a "fundamental" kind—e.g., of the kind that divide orthodox Communists and orthodox Catholics in Italy. If Golden's policies could be said to coincide substantially with those of the Economic Notables (in so far as the Notables even agree among themselves), they could be said to coincide in the same sense with the policies of union leaders, school teachers, and factory hands. In short, in New Haven, as in the United States generally, the search for political conflict is likely to turn up differences that will seem small measured by European standards or considered in the perspective of a revolutionary ideology (whether of the Left or Right), but which none-theless may be thought of by the participants as quite great.

From the moon, viewed with the naked eye, the Rocky Mountains would seem little different from the plains; but the closer one draws to the Rockies the greater the difference would become. So too in politics, differences shrink with distance. Many observers have viewed American local or even national politics as if they were standing on the moon looking at politics for signs of brutal class conflict and permanent cleavages. Finding only scattered and unsatisfactory evidence, they nonetheless take these as proof that the rich and wellborn have in devious and mysterious ways im-posed their policies on all the rest.

## The Economic Notables and Public Policies

Like many other groups in the community, from Negroes on Dixwell Avenue to teachers in the public schools, sometimes the Economic Notables have their way and sometimes they do not. As with other groups, the like-lihood of getting their way is a complex function of many factors: the relevance to political influence of the resources at their disposal; the extent to which they agree; their application, persistence, and skill; the amount and kinds of opposition they generate; the degree to which their objectives are viewed as consistent with the political aims of elected leaders; and the agreement of their aims with the fundamental political consensus of the community.

In many areas of public policy, the Economic Notables can hardly be said to have any direct influence at all, either because they do not agree or because they simply never enter the arena of policy. Their direct influence on public education and on political nominations, for example, is virtually nil.

Even on urban redevelopment, their record is a curious one. Few aspects of local policy could be more important to the Notables than efforts to "save" downtown New Haven. Yet the record reveals that the Economic Notables were able neither to agree on nor to put through a program of urban redevelopment, even under a Republican mayor who was as anxious as any mayor can be to please the Notables. When redevelopment came to New Haven the leadership for it came not from the Notables but from a Democratic mayor, whom most of them originally opposed and who as mayor had to wheedle, cajole, recruit, organize, plan, negotiate, bargain, threaten, reward, and maneuver endlessly to get the support and partici-pation needed from the Notables, the small businessmen, the developers (who came principally from outside New Haven), the federal authorities, and the electorate.

Normally, outside of redevelopment and concern over the diminishing prosperity of the city's heart, the main cutting edge of policy to the Economic Notables in their roles as businessmen and property owners is the tax on their property. The individual and particular interests of the Economic Notables can in this case, as in many others, conflict somewhat with their collective interests. Like anyone else a Notable can keep his taxes down by means of a relatively low tax rate, or a relatively low assessment, or both. Uniformly low taxes for the Notables require either that the general tax rate on real property must be reduced, or that the gains of the Notables from reduced assessments must be offset by relatively higher assessments for the other property owners. To an elected mayor—that is, to a politician uninterested in committing political suicide in order to win the gratitude and respect of his beneficiaries among the Notables—the possible advantages of favoritism to the Notables at the expense of other groups are minor compared with the possible costs; for the Notables cast a pitifully small fraction of the total vote at election time. And small property owners, who vastly outnumber the Notables, are no less sensitive to their assessments.

The greater numbers and equal sensitivity to taxes of small property owners help account for the fact that they are underassessed in New Haven as compared with large property owners or with owners of business and nonresidential property. In recent years small single-family dwellings have been assessed at somewhat less than 40 per cent of their market values (as indicated by sales prices for comparable dwellings), whereas large single-family dwellings have been assessed at nearly 60 per cent, and nonresidential properties at 60 to 80 per cent of their sales values. If, in short, there has been any shifting of the tax burden via assessments, it has been from the poor to the wealthy rather than the other way around. Hence if a Notable acting in his own personal or corporate interest succeeds in having his assessment reduced, the effect is mainly to pass the bill to another Notable.

Even this tactic is not always successful; for success varies, depending on how hard up the city administration is for money and how much of a *quid pro quo* it can foresee in campaign contributions. The political mores of the community and the dangers of public scandal forbid anything so crass and brutal as an explicit deal. But there are certain tacit understandings in the local political culture that sophisticated participants might hope to rely on. If a firm protests its assessment and threatens to appeal to the courts, the city attorneys may conclude that the reasonable course—particularly in view of genuine uncertainty as to whether the city's claims will hold up in court—is to reduce the assessment. Later, the firm's executives may contribute funds generously to the campaign of the incumbent administration. (Possibly they may then even recoup their contribution by awarding themselves a larger bonus out of gratitude for their labors on behalf of the corporation.)

An administration running close to the wind, however, may prefer a court fight to the loss in tax income from a settlement out of court; for in the case of a large firm a reduction sizable enough to make it worth while for the firm to engage in a court fight may also be big enough to throw the city's revenues out of whack. (In 1957, the ten largest owners of real estate in New Haven paid almost one-fifth of the total taxes levied by the city, and their taxes financed one-eighth of the city's total expenditures for that year.) Consequently, the city administration may prefer to contest the appeal. Thus the Lee administration, hard pressed for city funds and fearful of the political consequences of a tax increase, refused to settle with the National Folding Box Company on its 1954–1956 assessment, which was the fourth largest in the city. In court, the city lost the case—and $130,000 in taxes.

Moreover, the game of assessments can be played roughly by both sides. A city administration typically lives in dread of raising the tax rate. But a general increase in assessments, particularly on large firms, may do the trick instead. Under the Lee administration, current city expenditures rose by 45 per cent in five years with no increase in the tax rate; a policy of vigorous reassessment paid off in tax returns high enough to cover the increase in expenditures.

Because manipulating assessments is a game of beggar-thy-neighbor, the collective as distinct from the purely individual interests of the Economic Notables might seem to dictate a common strategy of keeping expenditures and taxes down. To a very great extent, however, this collective interest is highly abstract, for the impact of taxes and city outlays on the Notables varies with the extent to which their incomes are affected directly or indirectly by taxes and city services, their perspectives on policy questions and ideological matters, their loyalties and identifications, and other complex factors. To many corporations the local property taxes are such a small proportion of costs that corporate executives can scarcely be expected to give them more than marginal attention. Four of the twelve largest real property owners in New Haven are public utilities; because local property taxes are considered as costs in computing their rates, the taxes can be passed on to consumers. Mr. John Day Jackson, the nonagenarian owner and publisher of New Haven's two newspapers, one of the fifty largest property owners in the city, and a firm believer in the pure essence of Herbert Spencer, for many years carried on an unremitting campaign against every proposed expansion of governmental activity, local, state, or federal, on the grounds that it would cost money and raise taxes. Yet almost without exception the business and financial leaders we interviewed in New Haven looked upon Mr. Jackson's editorial policies with a mixture of amusement, disdain, and irritation; he was thought by them to be shortsighted, penny-pinching, and eccentric.

Despite all these qualifications, however, the main policy thrust of the Economic Notables is to oppose tax increases and hence expenditures for other than the minimal traditional city services. In this effort their two most effective weapons have probably been the mayor and the Board of

Finance. Since the members of the Board of Finance, aside from the mayor himself and one alderman, are appointed by the mayor, the influence of the Notables on the budget is sharply reduced if the mayor exerts strong leadership and has policies that differ from those of the Notables. Consequently, the policies of the Notables are most easily achieved when they have a strong mayor on their side or, under a weak mayor, if they have the support of the Board of Finance.

Historically, the relative number of businessmen of all kinds—the heads of large firms, small independents, and managers—on the two main legislative boards, the Board of Aldermen and the Board of Finance, has declined enormously since the high period of business eminence in the last half of the nineteenth century. But on the Board of Finance itself, businessmen have continued to play a predominant role; indeed, the heads of firms all but took over that Board in the twenties and even now comprise a large proportion of the Board's appointive members. The contrast with the position of the clerical and working class groups is striking. During the first half of the nineteenth century no one from these groups sat on either of the two boards; but at midcentury their numbers began to increase, and in the twentieth century they have averaged around 40 per cent of the membership of the two boards. This increase in clerical and working class participation, however, has taken place almost entirely on the Board of Aldermen; their relative numbers increased only slightly on the Board of Finance.

It seems reasonable to conclude that the steady pressure of the Notables against the expansion of public services and taxes has some effect. It is impossible to say, however, just what the magnitude of that effect has been. Had their demands for public economy been in opposition to the demands of a large proportion of the citizenry, the natural incentive of politicians to secure their own election would doubtless have resulted in policies designed to appeal to numbers rather than wealth.

But it would be wrong to suppose that Economic Notables and businessmen were in conflict with other significant groups over the policy of keeping taxes and expenditures low, or that they always succeeded. Their essential strategy was a familiar aspect of American politics: to gain services and benefits from government and, so far as possible, to displace the costs from themselves to others. In the context of American ideology and perspectives, contests over taxes and services were evidently seen less as grand conflicts among social classes over relative shares in the public pie than as struggles by individuals or small constellations of individuals: a family, a grocery store, a business firm, a neighborhood, or an ethnic or religious group. Even workers shared this view. In the depths of the Great Depression a sociologist interviewing workers in New Haven concluded that "no abstract ideal nor current issue matters very much to the politically minded wage earner. He cannot afford to be concerned over such matters, because he looks upon the political party as a source of help in time of need, to get a job, to get one of his boys out of a court scrape, to show him how to fill out forms."[2]

Thus the policies of the Economic Notables precipitated factional rather than class battles—if, indeed, they caused any conflict at all. For it must be remembered that throughout much of this century, Democratic and Republican mayors alike sought to outdo one another in their reputations for "economy." Until the New Deal, the national leaders of the Democratic Party, though less worshipful toward business than the general run of Republican spokesmen, were no less keen on economy and budget balancing. In Connecticut, even the Socialists were economy-minded; their "business-like" administration in Bridgeport drew the admiration and political support of conservative Republican businessmen. During the Depression the Democratic mayor of New Haven was a union official, the only person of nominally working-class status at the time of his election ever to hold the office of mayor in New Haven; yet his policy was one of such strict economy on public outlays that his defeat by a Republican in 1945 after fourteen years in office was widely attributed to general discontent with the shabby state of public services in New Haven, particularly with the semistarved condition of the public school system.

The fact was, then, that the Economic Notables operated within that vague political consensus, the prevailing system of beliefs, to which all the major groups in the community subscribed. Even the rather limited influence the Notables possessed over the level of taxes depended upon the extent to which their aims fitted within the dominant system of beliefs of the community. Within limits, they could influence the content of that belief-system; but they could not determine it wholly. As a belief system it contained elements of both rigidity and great flexibility; it had precise injunctions and vague mandates; and it was chock-full of inconsistencies. Skilled leaders, exploiting these various elements in the belief system (yet always imprisoned within its constraints), could manipulate the flow of local costs and benefits in different ways; some of these would be inconsistent with the dominant concern of the Economic Notables over low taxes.

Even a Republican mayor, elected in 1945 on a campaign to improve the public schools and city services in general after a long period of starvation, had to increase taxes; and his Democratic successor, as we have seen, had to raise assessments. Over the decade from 1947–1957, total city expenditures more than doubled, while income from taxes rose by more than 70 per cent as a result of increases both in the rate and in assessments. During this same period, the total assessments of the ten largest real property owners in New Haven rose by nearly 85 per cent.

Thus the influence of the Notables, though not feeble, is spotty and limited. To be sure, under certain circumstances they *could* exercise more influence in more areas of policy than they now do. But this is also true of every other significant group in New Haven.

2. John W. McConnell, *Evolution of Social Classes* (Washington, D.C.: American Council on Public Affairs, 1942), p. 156.

# STYLES OF NEGRO LEADERSHIP

## JAMES Q. WILSON

TWO POLITICAL STYLES emerge more or less clearly from a study of Negro civic leadership—the *militant* and the *moderate*. Negroes disagree both about ends and means, and the conflict over means typically takes the form of a dispute as to which political style is most appropriate for civil action. A description of these two styles can be obtained by assembling under these labels observations about the characteristic ways in which Negro leaders approach the world about them—how they see it, feel about it, describe it, and act toward it. No "pure" examples of such styles can, of course, be given, but so many close approximations exist among real leaders that it is useful to describe the artificially-polarized ideal types.[1]

The modes of thinking, speaking, and acting characteristic of these two styles can be described, for the sake of convenience, along a few simple axes: how the leader perceives and describes (1) the nature of the issues confronting him and the values he brings to bear on them; (2) the ends or goals he deems it appropriate to seek in the realm of civic action; (3) the means he employs in seeking these ends; and (4) the motives, goals, and attributes to the other actors, white and Negro, whom he sees in the world about him.

## The Militant Style

### ISSUES AND VALUES

The "militant" or "protest" style is often clearly revealed in the extent to which the leader sees the issues confronting the race and the community in simplified form. In those cases where information is shared on an approximately equal basis, the protester will see simplicities where the modern sees complexities. A vigorous NAACP officer, with experience as chairman of

---

Reprinted from *Negro Politics, The Search for Leadership* (Glencoe: The Free Press, 1960), pp. 214–221 and 230–239, by permission of the author.

1. These labels are used with the greatest misgivings. In order to avoid the tendency to read content into these words apart from the specific, substantive material for which they are mere rubrics, I was tempted to term these two styles simply "A" and "B." But that would be even more confusing to the reader than the names selected. It must be stressed, however, that these labels have no normative implications. Nor do they have any connection with the kinds of leaders mentioned by other authors writing on Negro leadership—for example, Myrdal's "protest" and "accommodation" leaders. Myrdal's typology and mine were devised for different purposes. Cf. Gunnar Myrdal, *An American Dilemma* (New York: Harper & Bros.), pp. 720ff.

its Housing Committee, brings the problem of residential segregation within the compass of a single paragraph:

> This whole housing problem could be solved in a few months. . . . All you have to do is find some decent white people and some decent Negroes who want to buy homes and get them together in a friendly way. . . . There won't be any trouble if they are properly brought in. . . . Then when the bullies start throwing the bombs, the community will be against them.

The consequences of an abrupt and radical change in the racial pattern of residence in the city are never considered to be serious by the great majority of these leaders. In almost every case, the questions raised by others regarding the impact of open occupancy on the movement of whites from the city to the suburbs, the possibilities of open violence, and the legal questions involved are regarded by the militant as a "smokescreen" purposely created by whites to confuse the issue and block action. And in the event some of these predicted consequences should come to pass, these leaders are prepared. The person quoted above continued:

> Why should the city be saved? I mean, if these people leave it, what difference does it make? . . . It only makes a difference to those who remain. They are happy out there, let them go. . . .

Not only do issues tend to be seen in simplified terms, but often many issues are brought together or agglomerated into a single general issue which should be considered and dealt with as a whole rather than in parts. Speaking of the problem of segregation in health facilities, one active voluntary association leader in a public address exemplified this tendency when he asked:

> What are the possible remedies? We can't tackle the problem piecemeal. We've got to hit all at once. It's no good to try to improve . . . these things.

A militant typically will present a maximum number of demands to a public agency for solution. This tendency to agglomerate issues rather than to deal with them singly is illustrated in the shift which occurred between the statement to the Chicago Board of Education in 1957 made by an NAACP militant leader and the statement made one year later by an NAACP leader who was a moderate. Where the former listed ten demands, covering all aspects of school board policy, the latter made only three recommendations which focussed on a single facet of school board policy— the work of its Human Relations Committee.

In describing the issues in civic affairs, the protester utilizes a vocabulary that invests his goals with moral principle. He tends to speak of these matters in terms of their ultimate rationale, rather than in relation to immediate needs, and justifies his demands with an appeal to an elaborate and highly general set of values and rights. A characteristic remark is one made by a vigorous lay civic leader who complains of the decline of this moral fervor in the work of professional staff members of voluntary associations:

> Now in human relations you have to "consider" the other fellow. It used to be a question of principle, of rights. . . . We didn't care what the other guy

thought. . . . We have the *right* to do this. Man, I believe, is a child of God, and God created everything he has on earth. The Constitution of the United States guarantees me these rights, and I don't have to ask the other citizen whether I can enjoy them. . . . There wouldn't be any point to it anyway, because they probably would object. . . .

The militant ascribes civic reputation to other leaders on the basis of both their civic posture and their rhetoric, and this rhetoric is most highly valued when it embodies a clearly moral attitude toward race issues:

> They wouldn't quarrel with him on the basis of right and principle. He was usually on the right side, and it was hard to argue with him. . . . They couldn't deny or oppose, on moral grounds, the fight for the complete liberation of the Negro people.

This high degree of commitment to goals of a general, morally rationalized character often leads the protester to adopt a flexible attitude toward means and the roles of voluntary associations working in the field. He possesses a firm image of those ends to which means and organizational roles should be adapted; the struggle for some should not be deflected or abandoned simply because it does not comport with the defined mission of the active organization. This is most clearly illustrated in the relative indifference of the protester to the distinctions which others make as to the proper function of the NAACP in contrast to the Urban League. He sees the Urban League's less militant role not as a strength but as a weakness, and a faint pallor of moral stigma clouds the fact that its maintenance needs require it to attract white business support through a more moderate approach.

The militant sees the world as it should be, and is therefore very conscious of its shortcomings and the obstacles to progress.[2] This attribute, which parallels in many ways what Karl Mannheim described as "utopian thinking" as well as some of the qualities Eric Hoffer found adhering to the "true believer," cuts across many of the other traits under discussion here. The tendencies, mentioned below, to see the opposition as not only powerful but also consciously co-ordinated into something akin to a conspiracy or at least a united front, the reliance on negative rather than positive inducements, the tendency to seek general, all-inclusive reforms rather than narrow, specific ones—these all may reflect an absorption in the extent to which the real world falls short of the desired world and the magnitude of the obstacles to progress.

At the same time, the protest leader is not an ideological isolate; in general, he shares the values of the white liberal or radical, with the exception that race is placed in a position of pre-eminence. Militants from

---

2. "Militancy" was defined by a militant leader in these terms: "Militancy means mass meetings, and having interracial ball games in tense areas to prove you have a right to be there, and going out into Trumbull Park, and talking to the Mayor with the gloves off. . . . We've always had the hards and the softs in the NAACP. . . . The softs don't want to rock the boat. They would rather play the game. . . . Try to bring about changes pleasantly."

the Negro community are characteristically found to be active members of a wide range of liberal causes and associations. One of the most militant NAACP leaders, twice a candidate for branch president, was also a vice-chairman of the Independent Voters of Illinois, the local affiliate of the liberal Americans for Democratic Action. In a more radical vein, a former staff member of the Urban League noted for his militancy was the chairman of the left-wing "Committee to End Mob Violence." He was not openly disturbed by the character of his associates in the organization.

> The Committee to End Mob Violence had an assortment of people in it, including the left-wing labor unions. . . . They [his opponents] painted me with a red brush because of that. The red scare was on then in full force. . . . I said that I didn't make any political distinctions as to who came into the Committee; I was interested in the community problem, not in people's politics.

ENDS

The Negro militant tends to seek what we have called "status" ends in distinction to "welfare" ends. His position is advanced; integration is the general goal, and the improvement of the welfare of the Negro is of secondary importance. Indeed, welfare measures are often seen as steps away from integration, for often—as in the case of the County Hospital branch or the extension of public housing in the Negro area—they reinforce the existing pattern of segregation and "take the pressure" off other areas of the city to admit Negroes on an equal basis. The protest leader will typically be found speaking and acting vigorously in favor of integrating schools through redistricting rather than merely seeking new or better schools in Negro areas; in favor of open occupancy legislation; in favor of checking the expansion of public housing in the Black Belt; and in favor of equal treatment of Negroes even at the expense of proportional representation in public agencies and affairs.

The militant is aware that these measures often do not touch the masses of Negroes as closely or as surely as do many welfare issues, but he is confident that the more subtle issues are the more important in the long run. Speaking of Negro reluctance to generate pressure on behalf of school redistricting, a former NAACP leader describes his problem:

> This is an intangible factor, a psychological factor. . . . How do you make the masses of people understand this? . . . It's easy for them to see the problem when their teachers get paid less, or they are on double shift, or less money is spent on Negro schools. . . . But when you have this feeling, that is harder to make them see—that education, if it is segregated, can do harm that nothing can undo. Modern psychological fact has proven that. . . . So we are trying to do this: make Negroes aware of the problem. . . . To meet this would take courage on the part of political leaders.

When a difficult choice must be made between welfare improvement now and integration gains later, the militant will press for the latter at the expense of the former and accept the cost in terms of immediate deprivations or even personal suffering. For him, results have a price. It is often a price which they, because of superior income or higher status or unique opportunities, would not have to pay personally, but this fact should not detract from the evident sincerity of their convictions.

A Negro leader in the cause of desegregating private hospital staffs in Chicago conceded that some Negro doctors felt they might lose Negro patients to white doctors if integration were a fact, but discounted the importance of their fears, adding that in any case "you have to be prepared to accept a temporary period of suffering if you are going to gain anything in the long run."

Another Negro leader, fighting the construction of a South Side branch to the County Hospital, urged in a public meeting that the Negro masses should be prepared to accept even a reduction in available medical care as a necessary cost of continued integration:

> I don't think it is brutal to say that there must be some suffering for a few for the good of the many. Look at Montgomery, Alabama. There people had to suffer in order to kill Jim Crow on their busses. If people hadn't walked to work and lost their jobs and given up their credit and lost their cars and their mortgages on their homes, they would be riding those Jim Crow busses today. But I doubt that we in Chicago could get people to put up such a fight in Chicago. Piecemeal solutions won't do.

Occasionally a Negro, in such a public meeting, will question whether the cost is not too high or whether in fact such a choice must be made. At an NAACP meeting, a speaker had urged, in impassioned tones, Negroes to carry the fight for a free housing market into the suburbs by buying in white areas and defending their purchases even if it involved "getting hurt." A Negro doctor rose to question the price the protest leader was asking them to pay.

> [*Doctor:*] We have enough laws. It's a question of enforcing them. It's all very well to talk about courage, but you can't expect a man to endanger his wife and children. That's not courage. You have to have police protection. . . .
>
> [*Speaker:*] Anyone who thinks more of life than of rights hasn't got any rights. Nobody is going to bother you if they know they are going to get hurt trying. You ought to be willing to die defending your home.[3]
>
> [*Doctor:*] That's not the question. What if I'm away at my office and come home and find my wife and children injured? That's not courage. It's not cowardice to say that you don't want that to happen. . . .

Almost without exception, the militant will select as the most important issue involving race relations, and therefore, of course, the most important issue generally, the question of housing and residential segregation. "Housing," a Negro labor leader remarked, "is the central problem. It not only

---

3. The speaker here, it should be noted, was displaying a *public* protest style. In private discussion, he showed no trace of this style. Interestingly enough, he himself had no intention of attempting to invade a white suburb; his home was located in the center of the Negro area, where, he said, he planned to remain.

affects people, but it also affects planning in the city. Real estate affects so many civic developments; nothing can happen, almost, that does not involve real estate." But more than its implications for city planning are the myriad other race relations problems that seem to arise out of housing. A young Negro doctor felt that not only was it desirable to collect a variety of race issues into a single package, but that in addition they could best be solved in this way:

> It all comes back to residential segregation. You can't get around it. They can segregate schools and hospitals by putting them in Negro areas, and then say, well, they are open to anybody, but of course only Negroes go there. . . . It shows up in education, where the school board is very flexible about adjusting school district lines to keep it all-Negro. . . . Residential segregation is the big problem that must be answered first. Residential segregation is the thing that creates the void, that destroys Negro-white communication. The people don't know the problems of the other group.

The belief that housing is *the* race issue is not of long standing. In the past, particularly before and during World War II, jobs and employment discrimination were the major pre-occupation of both whites and Negroes working in race relations areas. But when jobs became relatively plentiful, and access to jobs became somewhat easier—although by no means free— owing to the great demand for labor, particularly in the North, attention shifted to the problem of housing. But this shift has not, by any means, proceeded uniformly among Negro civic leaders. The primacy of housing as the race issue has been advocated by the professional staff of race relations associations and agencies, but it is principally among the militant leaders that the notion has found its quickest acceptance.

MEANS

In keeping with the tendency to agglomerate issues and to present a maximum number of demands, the protest leader seeks inclusive solutions of a public nature. In this respect, he has a greater confidence in politico-legal solutions (the passing of a law, the enforcement of a regulation or rule) and virtually no confidence in politicians (those who might pass or enforce the law). In most of the civic issues examined, the militant leader almost invariably called for the adoption of new legislation (an FEPC law, an open occupancy ordinance, a hospital integration ordinance) as the proper and definitive "solution" to the matter. . . .

## The Moderate Style

The political style which we have chosen to call, for want of a better term, "moderate" is much more in evidence in the Chicago Negro community than the militant style. Negroes in a position of prominence, or who are consulted about or participate in an issue, are typically those who exhibit aspects of the moderate or "bargainer" style.

ISSUES AND VALUES

The moderate perceives race and community issues as ones to which there are no easy solutions, if indeed there are solutions at all. He speaks much more frequently about how the other fellow will feel about a proposed solution:

> I try to put myself in the place of the property owners; for example, the people in those little red bungalows along East Garfield Boulevard. A [Negro] person gets turned down when he tries to buy [a home] there. Can you prove it was because of race or religion? I don't know, I don't know. . . . And if you can't prove it, you are creating trouble. . . . Chicago would erupt over a thing like this.

Very frequently, Negroes who share this style are lawyers and they often speak of the legal difficulties in the way of a solution to a problem in race relations. One lawyer, a former NAACP officer, was dubious of a proposed open occupancy ordinance governing sales and rentals in private housing:

> This is a constitutional problem. There is an equal protection problem here, and whether it is fair to classify this way I don't know. . . . The court might not see it. After all, the law is so amorphous on this point, and it looks like you are putting a premium on poverty.

The bargainer-lawyer's tendency to see complexities partly reflects the fact that most race issues revolve around questions of legislation and legal action in which lawyers are trained to see distinctions, difficulties, and the need for caution, but it also very likely reflects a general conservatism and pessimism about race progress through radical or compulsory means and a convenient rationale for not exerting oneself vigorously in behalf of such causes. Another moderate, also a lawyer and NAACP officer, could bring concern for the complexities of the problem to the point of opposition to the proposed measure—again, the open occupancy ordinance:

> I was opposed to the NAACP passing a motion to support open occupancy. . . . Not because I'm against the principle of it, you understand, but for procedural reasons. . . . I think we have all that we can do without getting involved in private housing. . . . It is ridiculous to go into private housing now. . . . You've got the enforcement problems. . . . How do you know when discrimination has been practiced? . . . Then, you know, you are telling people how they can dispose of their private property. There is a very serious constitutional question there for me.

But it is not only in the area of advanced integration goals where the bargainer sees problems. Even in the usually unifying case of race violence, some are hard put to find an easy solution:

> In a thing like that [the Calumet Park race violence] there are a lot of problems. . . . The prosecution . . . had very little to work with . . . no

witnesses. . . . Well, I sympathize with the lawyers and the judges in a case like that. I can't blame the courts . . . as some do just because there aren't more convictions.

Similarly, the moderates speak most often in terms of specific, concrete problems, rather than long-range, inclusive issues with many facets. The bargainer, unlike the militant, feels most comfortable in discussing an issue when it is limited in scope and when the solution proposed would be relatively simple and free from side effects.

The term "gradualism" has, in recent years, acquired an emotion-laden meaning among Negroes as a term—usually of opprobrium—used to denote an attitude toward integration. Without entering into the merits of that controversy, it is nonetheless true that Negro civic leaders can be distinguished by their differing attitudes toward time. Just as the moderate sees issues as complex and resists agglomerating them into omnibus problems, he also tends to place them in a longer time perspective than does the militant. A long, but illuminating, illustration of this occurs in the following remark, made by a prominent Negro concerning the progress of integration in employment. Time is seen, not only as a necessary perspective from which to view race issues, but also as an inevitable component of progress, a vaguely real agent of change:

> These problems all go back in time to the 1930's or even earlier. . . . It's a continuing proposition. You can't ever really tell why it happens. It just suddenly happens when the time is right, and then time marches on. The stage has to be set. These things work slowly. . . . Job integration is the product now of ideas sown twenty years ago and earlier. . . . Back in those days, we didn't even have the words, the concepts, to describe these things. . . . FEPC wasn't even a phrase. Integration didn't mean anything, except maybe in chemistry. . . . Human relations as a field of work wasn't even heard of. . . . Slowly the stage has been set through giving these words currency and talking and visiting. . . . But I don't know why [a certain firm] changed. I wouldn't want to pinpoint it.

Not only is time an inevitable element of change, it is also a desirable one:

> Yes, creeping integration, that's right. . . . But I think it is moving along quickly enough, quickly enough. Any faster and we would out-distance the readiness of the Negro to accept integration and measure up to it.

A reason for not acting is carried in all these remarks: problems are complex, and only time can sort out the complexities and prepare the solution. Active protest is not, to the bargainer, superfluous, but it does tend to be quixotic.

The moderate, unlike the militant, rarely asserts race. Rather, he responds to race; it is a background issue. One can interview such a person for over an hour without hearing race raised as an issue by the interviewee. This is quite often a conscious process. Negroes, in their business and professional dealings with whites, will often go out of their way to avoid raising the race issue, or indeed any controversial issue that would detract from other matters or destroy a relationship. One moderate remarked:

> I'm not ashamed of my position, but I will avoid talking about it if I can. But if I do talk about it, I won't retreat on it. . . . I don't think these men would respect me if I backtracked once the subject was raised.

Sometimes a Negro will profess that he was unaware of certain forms or areas of discrimination until it was brought forcefully to his attention. A Negro labor leader from a politically conservative union described a recent experience:

> I just came back from Peoria where I was at a convention where a surprising thing happened. Three motels cancelled our reservations on us when they found out that all but one man in our delegation was colored. . . . I had no idea of this.

As the Negro militant tends to share the general political value scale of the white liberal, with race elevated to a place of pre-eminence, so the Negro moderate tends to share the political value system of the white conservative, again with race displaced to a higher—but not always the highest—point. This rather simple fact accounts for a great deal. It means that one should not assume that because a Negro feels strongly about racial injustice, he will be inevitably liberal on other issues as well. Race can be kept independent of other values, such as one's attitude toward labor unions, free enterprise, communism, and so on. This independence can and often does lead to suspicion between militants and moderates. One Negro voluntary association staff member condemned Negro-led opposition to a civic proposal because the union which provided the leadership was "Commie from top to bottom." Another Negro was alarmed by the politics of those who volunteered themselves as his allies on an issue:

> You know, on a lot of these things I kept finding myself surrounded by Communists. . . . On that bill to outlaw segregation in public housing, they were all around me. . . . Boy, I stayed out of things after that. I don't want no part of those reds.

This fear of a Communist identification is quite real on the part of many Negroes, and has been commented upon extensively in a book by Wilson Record. Nor do business and professional Negroes always feel kindly toward labor unions, even those which work toward some race ends. A Negro doctor commented:

> I have never been convinced that labor organizations have a particular advantage. . . . They are an unstable foundation on which to do any constructive work. The present labor ethics seem to be to kick people around.

The moderate tends to see the world "as it is," and to accept the existing constraints on action without pressing for far-reaching or unprecedented charges. Moderates are usually recruited from business and the professions—men who are accustomed to working within the limits of the status quo. Even where—as is often the case—they have no personal stake in matters relating to race goals, they are nevertheless predisposed to move in customary ways and avoid the unusual, the disturbing, the Utopian.

In the same vein, a Negro moderate will typically have a relatively clear image of what constitute appropriate means to civic goals and of the proper roles of voluntary associations, and he will resist sacrificing or altering those means and roles in favor of some general goal. The bargainer is not as highly committed to specific ends as is the militant, and is correspondingly less willing to alter the mission of an organization to strike out at a target of opportunity not previously agreed upon as being within its purview. To do so would mean a sacrifice in other goals—such as friendly relations with supporters:

> The Urban League was taking over the functions of the NAACP and . . . it was abandoning its traditional function of an approach based on understanding and good will. It was moving in the direction of legal action and boycotting and introducing Negroes into white blocks. . . . This was irritating the people downtown, and I can understand why.

That view was stated even more forcefully by a prominent Negro lawyer who observed, after the League had been reorganized to remedy the problem spoken of above:

> Frankly, I think the Urban League has just about worked itself out of a job. It's getting into things it's not qualified to handle. All that policy and stuff. . . . It should leave it to the NAACP.

The Urban League itself, in a report on its Chicago organization, felt that the maintenance of the association should take precedence over the pursuit of attractive ends, even where that pursuit had brought it some popular acclaim:

> It should be repeated here that [although] these actions on the part of the Executive have had favorable and popular results, the . . . "right thing was done the wrong way."

The executive was criticized for "civil rights pursuits not in the Urban League purview" and admonished against "joint action with actionist groups" which "confuses the role of the organization in the community."

### ENDS

The moderate, in contrast to the militant, tends to seek welfare rather than status ends. This distinction cannot be driven too far, for *any* goal which has been firmly and publicly labelled as a "race" end is one which will elicit at least verbal agreement from almost all Negro civic leaders. But in those areas of civic life where the moderates contribute their own energies, they are far more often to be found on the side of immediate, tangible, specific, welfare-type goals. They are more likely to choose the welfare aspects of issues where such a choice is necessary, and they are the leaders responsible for those statements, cited previously, endorsing better schools, more public housing, a branch hospital, more Negro representation, and more private housing in preference to the more remote status ends. Some bargainers do seek status ends (although few protesters seek welfare ends at the expense of integration), but they tend to be exceptions. More typical is the Negro who remarked:

> As I see it, there is a *need*. . . . If I'm dying for lack of medical care, lying on a slab, I don't want to hear them arguing about integration. I want medical care now. Of course, the ideal would be integration in all hospitals, but if we can't have the ideal, I want to meet the need now.

The racial moderate will be most aroused by clear cases of abuse directed at Negroes that are the direct result of illegalities, maltreatment, or violence, and will support race efforts to counter them; he is less clearly aroused by cases that involve less apparent inequities that are the mediate result of patterns of segregation and discrimination. He will occasionally seek welfare ends even at the cost of postponing integration, provided always that such activity will not cause him to be publicly labelled as a betrayer of the race. More often, he will confine himself to expressing verbally his predisposition toward welfare ends: "There are many areas where we have to deal with the immediate problems today, now, and let integration wait until tomorrow."

In his response to a question asking him to name the single most important issue facing the Negro community, the moderate would often cite the problem of jobs and employment whereas the militant invariably cited housing and residential segregation. A moderate thinks

> . . . the job business is more important than housing. . . . If a Negro has the job and the money, then his housing will follow.

There are several possible explanations for this discrepancy between the moderate and the militant in their selection of ends. In part, the difference can be accounted for by a simple time lag in the spread of convictions from the racially *avant-garde* to the racially moderate. In some few cases, it might be the result of a stake in the ghetto. But in most cases this discrepancy appears to be the product of strongly-held convictions about self-improvement, about the value of progressing through one's own efforts and resources, and of a preoccupation with the economic axis along which the lives of ambitious businessmen are often oriented. Further, it may well reflect the fact that the money of some Negro leaders has enabled them to acquire in spite of restrictions what others seek through laws which will remove those restrictions. One very prominent Negro, who was a self-made man financially and who had acquired properties through clever use of his wealth stated this:

> I think that number one, you have to have more economic buying power for the Negro, in terms of jobs and education and money. . . . Jobs and education are probably first in order. I think that there's a way to move into any neighborhood if you have the money and the knowledge and a little imagination.

The Negro protest leader, or advocate of status ends, has not been able to persuade many moderates that the ability to acquire housing personally does not solve the problem created by the general pattern of a spreading all-Negro ghetto and, indeed, may aggravate it.

Where the militant was prepared to accept suffering as the price of mediate, even remote, intangible goals, the moderate will accept such deprivation only for proximate, tangible goals. Speaking of a Negro doctor's advocacy of blocking the proposed branch hospital even at the cost of some sacrifice, another Negro said:

> Yeah, but it won't be [X] that suffers. . . . He's not going to die for lack of medical care. . . . This is the same sort of question that was raised with the riders to the federal aid to education bills [the Powell Amendment]. Whether to have integrated schools as a goal and no federal aid, or federal aid without integration. I don't see how you could deny that . . . some schools, even segregated, were better than no schools at all.

On the other hand, when a Negro businessman's property values in a certain residential area were to be enhanced by a renewal program that would displace many Negro families from their homes in the area, he observed:

> You can't expect to change economic laws. . . . Somebody is always going to get hurt in these things, but that can't be avoided. . . . I think the good would overbalance the objections.

When challenged by militants that Negro business is in conflict with race ends, the moderate—himself usually a businessman—will deny this. Good business is good race relations. A Negro businessman said:

> I think that it's important to have demonstrations of the fact that the Negroes have the ability to succeed, and that this demonstration of success is a form of race relations.

He reflected for a moment on the problem, and after observing that he couldn't meet the demands on his time made by a voluntary association of which he was a board member, added:

> This is particularly important when I realize that the [organization] only wants me because I *am* a businessman with money. If I don't succeed in that, they have no use for me. . . . If I can build a successful business, this would gain respect for Negroes, and this in turn would help the [organization]. They could point to it.

MEANS

The moderate, in seeking means to deal with race problems such as residential segregation, displays less confidence in the efficacy of legislative solutions than does the militant. Although few will permit themselves to be understood as opposing such legislation as an open occupancy ordinance, they are far from enthusiastic about its merits:

I would rather that Chicago people would see their folly in what they are doing. . . . A law might help, but whether it will change things, I don't know. . . . I wish people would have a change of heart.

Such a person will concede privately that he has strong reservations about legislative solutions—"I think the industry could do it more quickly and easily . . . legislation [is not] the best way to handle it"—but in public discussion the same person can be placed by more militant Negroes in a position in which he feels obliged to endorse it:

[*Militant:*] I want to ask Mr. [X] whether he wouldn't agree that we still need an open occupancy law? You said laws wouldn't do the job, but . . . we must have an open occupancy law. . . .

[*Moderate:*] I support it. But the solution requires more. I mean the law will show the rank-and-file the problem. . . . But don't mistake me. I'll walk the picket line for an open occupancy law.

[*Militant:*] I want to make it clear that there is no one here who opposes the open occupancy law. There is no difference of opinion on that.

Although a moderate is reluctant to endorse the legislative solutions of the Negro protest leader, he is at the same time less critical of the Negro politician than is the militant. Where the protester presses for laws and distrusts law makers, the bargainer is skeptical of laws and less critical of those who enact them. In part, the begrudging respect for Negro politicians may reflect the view that, whatever else may be said of them, the successful Negro politician has achieved position and status, and achievement is a quality that can be admired in itself.

# ORGANIZED LABOR IN CITY POLITICS

## KENNETH E. GRAY AND DAVID GREENSTONE

LABOR'S PARTICIPATION in city politics varies from city to city, depending on the local strength and political motivation of labor and on the structure of city politics. Detroit, St. Louis, and Houston illustrate three levels of labor participation in local politics: intensive and general participation in a one-industry Northern city; intensive participation by a single, relatively small local participation in a mixed commercial-industrial border city; and withdrawal from politics in a young, vigorous, commercial-industrial city of the South.

Adapted by the authors from reports on city politics published by the Joint Center for Urban Studies of the Massachusetts Institute of Technology and Harvard University, 1960.

## Detroit and the UAW

After the passage of the reform nonpartisan charter of 1918 and before the rise of the labor movement, the strongest political interest group in Detroit was without question the business community. Exploiting an ideology of nineteenth-century liberalism and individualism, business was determined to keep Detroit an open-shop town. Unity and ease of communication among its leadership helped keep business politically strong. One industry, automobiles, dominated the city's economy, and a few companies dominated the industry.

Business control in politics was also facilitated by Detroit's nonpartisan system of government. The business community played a major role in securing the nonpartisan charter of 1918. In its origins and early history, nonpartisan government in Detroit was Protestant, high-status, eminently honest and efficient, and conservative. To a great extent these characteristics persist to this day.

With the unionization of the auto industry, labor emerged as a potential political power, but it was confronted by a hostile political system. Thus labor felt that it had to go into politics in a massive way, in search of total victory. While a series of political defeats in the 1940's changed some of labor's tactics and immediate objectives, it retains its original emphasis on mass political action.

In Detroit and Wayne County, the Wayne County AFL-CIO council, through its Committee on Political Education (COPE), functions as a political party. No labor party appears on the ballot, but the council drafts a platform, endorses candidates, and has in COPE the strongest precinct organization in the County. This organization largely accounts for labor's extraordinary success in Michigan. Under COPE's leadership the Democratic party in Wayne County wins about 70 per cent of the vote in partisan state and national elections. The proportion in Detroit proper is slightly higher.

Just as the automobile industry dominates the economy of the Detroit area, so the dominant union in the council and in COPE is the United Automobile Workers of America AFL-CIO (UAW). Before the merger of the AFL and the CIO, the UAW had about 82 per cent of the County CIO membership. Today it has only 55 to 58 per cent of the merged membership, but its influence is greater than this proportion would suggest. The key COPE official in each of Detroit's six congressional districts, the district coordinator, is a member of the UAW. The president of the AFL-CIO county council also belongs to the UAW.

The UAW has a militant attitude toward political action, which largely accounts both for its own dominance of Detroit labor and for labor's partisan success on the state level. This militancy stems from several sources. First, the union was organized and led for some time by radicals (including at one time the Reuthers), who fought violently among themselves but who agreed on the crucial importance of programmatic political action. Second, a bitter and violent struggle for recognition left the UAW with deep hostility toward management. This hostility was manifested in political action, particularly since the state's dominant Republican party was largely controlled by the big three automobile companies. Third, the union sought to ease a serious problem of ethnic and racial hostilities among its own members by emphasizing class solidarity of workers against management. This emphasis on the members' interest as a class strongly implied broad political goals rather than an exclusive concern with collective bargaining and benefits only for workers in the auto industry. Fourth, the automobile workers have a tradition of rank-and-file participation, which contributes to the intensity of their activity in COPE. The UAW was organized in the 1930's almost without professional help from established unions. Today it is the most democratic of the country's big unions. Political activity within the UAW has prepared many an auto worker for politics outside the union.

COPE's precinct work is extensive and meticulously organized. Each congressional district is divided into about thirty zones of five to ten precincts. COPE limits the number of zones in order to keep each district steering committee, made up of zone leaders, to a reasonable size. The steering committee meets four or five times a year to plan COPE activities and campaign strategy in the district. COPE tries to keep zones geographically compact and united by ethnic ties, socioeconomic status, or common neighborhood problems such as expressways or redevelopment. The steering committee screens candidates who run from its district for the state legislature and the national House of Representatives, but not candidates for local, state, or national office elected at large by the city or the state. Because the county leadership feels that the steering committees may overemphasize personal feelings, the AFL-CIO county council makes all final decisions on endorsements. It cares less than the district group whether a representative ignores his constituents if he has an excellent voting record. While the county group always takes the opinion of the precinct workers into account, it tries to weigh other factors. This arrangement for endorsements also ensures a considerable amount of influence for the union leadership in the county.

A major COPE objective is to provide effective workers for each precinct. To achieve this, according to one district leader, a year-round program of political education is carried on among union members. Classes in current events and civics are offered to convince the worker that gains won through collective bargaining alone may be eroded unless buttressed politically. In recruiting workers, COPE tries to get rank-and-file members rather than local officers, who are usually overworked. Members' wives are sometimes recruited. COPE has at least one or two workers in each precinct, amounting to 300 to 600 in a Congressional District. In some districts there are many more; the goal is one worker in every city block.

COPE workers are taught (1) how to get acquainted with the residents in their precinct and learn their political opinions; (2) how to spot cases of economic and social hardship and refer them to a private or public agency; and (3) how to evaluate the quality of city services in the area, such as street lighting and garbage collection. To some extent the activities of the COPE worker resemble those of the traditional ward politician, but unlike the machine politician, the COPE worker does not dispense material benefits nor does he act as a personal intermediary between the voter and the government. At election time the workers get voters to register, publicize COPE's position and answer questions about candidates and issues, man the polls, and bring voters to the polls. Since they do few personal favors, COPE workers must stress issues or the personalities of candidates in order to win their precincts. A county CIO official suggested that it is necessary to rely on issues rather than welfare favors in a city where factory pay averages over $5000 a year.

COPE is open to all liberal Democrats. Professional people, housewives and even a few real-estate dealers participate. Union members often choose better-educated, middle-class volunteers to represent them on steering committees or as Democratic party precinct delegates. Part of COPE's strength may be its willingness to use socially skilled liberals.

The Democratic party probably could not have carried Michigan repeatedly without labor support. For example, ten years ago there were 37 Republican precincts in the First Congressional District, but now every precinct there goes Democratic. Since the District still includes some relatively high-income residential areas in northern Detroit, it is doubtful that out-migration by the middle class alone accounts for the political shift. Even if COPE is not chiefly responsible for Michigan's Democratic majorities, it has at least amassed great power within the Democratic party. Since 1948, it has encouraged union members to run for precinct delegate in the party primary. Slightly under 40 per cent of the precinct delegates in Wayne County belong to COPE, and labor can rely on other liberal delegates for support. Under the unit rule for district delegations, labor and its allies thus dominate the state Democratic party conventions, although in the interests of party victory in November COPE has made compromises with Democrats outside the labor movement and the Detroit area. Although the Michigan delegation does not follow a unit rule, labor has had a majority of the Michigan delegation at the last three Democratic national conventions.

A major explanation for the success of Detroit's COPE in rivaling the power of the great patronage-based machines in other cities is that it has so successfully gone into the precincts—the central city slums—to win the allegiance of the electorate. COPE in Detroit, to be sure, is simply seeking to mobilize its natural allies, but probably no other urban labor movement in the United States has succeeded quite so well in mobilizing similar "natural allies." It seems plausible that this greater success is accounted for by the greater ideological commitment to political liberalism of the Detroit COPE. Detroit labor leaders repeatedly refer to labor's effort to "improve the lot of the people" and to "serve the needs of the people rather than seek power for itself." The ward politician succeeded because, in his desire for political power and its perquisites, he was willing to associate with socially under-privileged groups who often lived in urban slums. Similarly, the social welfare ideology of the UAW and COPE not only attracts labor precinct workers to politics but motivates them to go anywhere, even into the slums, to meet "the people." Thus, like the ward politician, the COPE precinct worker is able to organize a sizable vote.

At the same time, the intellectual content and rationale of COPE's political program appeals to certain middle class and professional groups which a traditional, patronage-oriented political organization would have great difficulty in attracting.

Despite its power, COPE has had relatively little success in local politics. It has never elected a mayor despite repeated attempts, and it has never won a secure majority on the Common Council. There are two major reasons for its difficulties. In the first place, COPE is neither a political party nor a good government group—it is a labor union, on its face a special interest. When COPE has tried to elect a mayor, it has been vulnerable to charges of "labor domination" and of being a limited (therefore, presumably selfish) interest trying to run the government of all the people. In the second place, nonpartisanship in local politics disrupts the complex of loyalties and issues that has led to Democratic victories in state and national elections. Many white union members, particularly the large group of Poles and the growing group of Southerners, are loyal Democrats who support the party's national social welfare programs. But they are also homeowners burdened with Detroit's heavy property tax. They are concerned about maintaining the economic level of their neighborhoods and keeping Negroes out. Because they are Democrats they might vote for liberal, pro-Negro candidates if city elections were partisan. But in nonpartisan elections they are free to desert the liberal alliance to support conservative, pro-white candidates like the late Mayor Albert Cobo without having to desert the Democratic party, for which they have great emotional loyalty.

In recent years labor has changed its strategy and met with some, though hardly complete, success at the local level. During the 1940's the CIO made at least three major attempts to elect a Mayor of Detroit (in 1943, 1945, and 1949). Each time, the contest was between a liberal and a conservative. The campaigns were fought, ostensibly at least, over such issues as "racial justice to the Negro," public housing, the role of private enterprise in urban re-development, the right of DSR (the publicly-owned mass transit system) employees to strike, high taxes and so on. In 1943 Mayor Edward J. Jeffries won against Frank Fitzgerald, the labor candidate, with 54 per cent of the vote; in 1945 he defeated Richard T. Frankensteen with 56 per cent of the vote; in 1949 City Treasurer Cobo defeated the popular president of the Common Council, George Edwards, with 60 per cent of the vote.

In the 1950's, labor refrained from involvement in mayoralty campaigns.

In 1953, while social issues reappeared (in contrast to the tepid 1951 campaign), the CIO failed to support a candidate. Cobo's opponent, James Lincoln, was never considered to have a serious chance. In 1957 there was no real contest for mayor at all. Council President Louis Miriani won support from every important group in the city, from business interests to elements of the CIO unions. Subsequently he proved to be friendly to labor, although not at all unfriendly to business. In addition to having a more acceptable mayor than Cobo, labor elected two new liberal councilmen—the council's first Negro and an international representative of the UAW. As a result it had a bloc of four firm liberals on the council (two were incumbents in 1957). Ordinarily this bloc was able to find a fifth vote from the other five councilmen to achieve a majority.

Two factors especially may have contributed to the change in labor tactics. First, it may well be that the structure of nonpartisan politics in Detroit has taught the labor movement to conform to the peculiar rules of the nonpartisan game. This has meant less aggressive behavior, less overt attempts by labor to control the government. It seems possible that repeated defeats have taught labor to select its candidates more carefully, making sure that they already have made a record in Detroit government and that they have a reputation for representing all interests in the city. When no such candidate is available labor seems to concentrate on supporting and influencing the best candidate it can find, like Miriani, and building up its strength on the Council.

Second, while the labor-backed liberal coalition has grown more cautious, it has also grown more powerful in Detroit city proper. The increase in its power may have mitigated the aggressiveness of its action. As middle- and upper-class whites have left the city and the percentage of Negroes has steadily risen, Detroit city government has visibly moved left.

## The St. Louis Teamsters and "Community Action"

St. Louis is a city of diversified industry; in 1952, no one class of industry had more than 8 per cent of the total number of persons employed in manufacturing. It is not growing: because its boundaries were fixed by the state constitution in 1876, it has not been able to envelop the population growth in its suburbs by annexation. Between 1950 and 1960, its population declined by 13.6 per cent to 740,424. Its rank by population among U.S. cities fell from eighth to tenth. While its total population dropped, its Negro population probably increased slightly, and its proportion of Negroes increased significantly. Local estimates of the Negro percentage of the population in 1959 varied between 25 and 35 per cent. Race conflict in St. Louis is moderate. In fact, if St. Louis has a single distinguishing characteristic, it is that all conflict is moderate. Moderation is a widely shared community value. Some say that this is because of the conservatism of the city's large number of Catholics (about 35 per cent) and persons of German origin. Labor, like other interest groups, feels that it should conform to the ethos of moderation.

The character and environment of the local political system help determine labor's local political allies, goals, and activities. Although St. Louis city officials are elected in a Democratic primary, the city government is largely nonpartisan because the primary is open, city elections are held in the spring of off-years, and there is virtually no local Republican party or organization to challenge the Democrats. Since 1949, all but four of the city's 28 wards have usually voted Democratic in all general elections. Local political conflict occurs between factions that are divided by organizational interests and issues. A local political scientist has described the factional split as an alliance between the "mayor's office group" (the three city officials elected at large—mayor, comptroller, and president of the board of aldermen) and the "civic progress" interests on the one hand, and the patronage-oriented ward machines, county officers, and state-controlled agencies on the other. Factional conflict is minimal, however, because both alliances need the other's help to maintain what to each has been a satisfactory organizational *status quo*. The mayor and his friends are strong in policy—through budget control—but lack patronage. Ward aldermen, committeemen, and county officers have independent, patronage-supported organizations, but they have no dependable city-wide organization or leadership. Lacking a city-wide machine, at-large elected officials are usually "newspaper candidates" supported by progressive downtown business interests.

In this moderately factionalized, Democratic one-party system, most of St. Louis labor—when it takes an interest in local politics—is usually allied with the patronage-oriented ward and county office group. In 1957, for example, the Teamsters, the CIO Industrial Council, the AFL Central Trades and Labor Union, and the Meatcutters Union Local 88 joined the ward organizations and county officers in opposing charter reform proposals that would have increased the mayor's power at the expense of the organization politicians. Recent city at-large elections have been contests between "blue ribbon," mayor's-group candidates and ward-county organization candidates. Most of St. Louis labor—notably the Teamsters and the Meatcutters—has supported the losing ward and county office alliance, but a few craft unions, the Machinists Union District Council for example, have supported the mayor's group. With the major exception of the Teamsters, however, most St. Louis unions have little time or interest for local affairs. They participate in local politics only to the extent of making formal endorsements and some campaign contributions. The AFL-CIO Labor Council, the UAW, and the Steelworkers are strong, but their leaders are almost wholly interested in union issues, narrowly defined, and hence direct their political action mostly to the national level where labor's stakes are high.

In contrast to the lack of interest in local affairs of most of St. Louis labor, one relatively small but militant union emerged as a powerful city-wide political organization in the late 1950's. Teamsters Local 688, Warehouse and Distribution Workers, had between 8,000 and 10,000 members, about 25 per cent of the total membership of Teamsters affiliates in the city. Because its members were distributed by residence throughout the city, Local 688 had unusual potential as a political organization. Under the aggressive leadership of two local officers who were also powerful national Teamsters leaders—Local 688 Secretary-Treasurer Harold Gibbons and Community Relations Director Sidney Zagri—the local became one of the most active and effective interest groups in city politics.

The vehicle for Local 688's political activity in the city is the "Community Action Stewards' Assembly," which union officials describe as "an attempt to use 'shop level' mechanics on the ward and township level." In each ward of the city, an attempt is made to have one community action steward elected for each twenty-five members of Local 688. "Community grievances" are reported to community stewards (these are not necessarily shop stewards) who investigate, confer with the ward alderman or take other action. Stewards' meetings, at which the Ward Alderman is present to discuss ward problems, are supposed to be held in each ward twice a year. Once a month assemblies of stewards are held at Teamsters headquarters to discuss city problems and to implement requests from ward meetings. In 1959, about a hundred of the 225 community stewards regularly attended these meetings. About fifty stewards formed the "hard core" of the assembly. Community Relations Director Zagri was in charge of the stewards' organization.

Stewards are said to be most active in the Twenty-fifth Ward (a newspaper ward, high-income and silk-stocking in some precincts). There are very few Teamsters living in Wards Six, Twenty-three and Twenty-eight, but members of the local are fairly equally distributed in the other twenty-two wards. Members of other Teamsters locals in the city and a Meatcutters local work with the stewards' assembly informally. Chief community stewards (elected by stewards in each ward) of the Teamsters ward organizations and the local's staff constitute a "Political Action Committee" (PAC).

Though it is primarily an instrument of political action and education on behalf of union members' interests, the stewards' group defines its interests broadly and at times secures benefits of a more general nature—as, for example, in demanding and obtaining the enforcement of the city's rat control ordinance. Union denials to the contrary, the stewards' group and the PAC are a serious challenge to the independent patronage machines in the wards. At least the ward politicians think so. Teamsters officials say that for the most part they stay out of ward campaigns and confine their endorsements of candidates and issues to city-wide, state and national elections. But the chairman of the city Democratic committee, who was also a ward committeeman, told an interviewer in 1959 that the Teamsters were "trying to take over" in his and other wards. "I don't tell them how to run the Teamsters," he complained, "and I don't see why they should tell me how I should run my ward."

Local 688 has used the stewards' assembly and other more conventional political tools to promote an extensive program at the local level. The Teamsters have recently criticized the *Post-Dispatch*, berated the Police Department for the actions of some of its officers, called for a graduated city income tax and opposed an increase in the earnings tax, recommended a metropolitan government based on the proposed functional "borough" plan, protested the cut-back in garbage collection, and threatened legal action if the city did not enforce the air pollution ordinance.

The Teamsters have won on some issues and lost on others. For six years after 1953, the Mayor and Local 688 carried on a running battle over the earnings tax. The Local's position was that taxes should be graduated; its attorneys opposed the legislative authorization for an earnings tax referendum in the State Supreme Court, but lost. Voters approved the earnings tax in 1959. In 1953 the Teamsters were largely responsible for petitions that forced a referendum on a proposal to establish a Board of Freeholders to study the metropolitan transportation problem. The voters rejected the proposal. In 1955 the Mayor, on grounds of economy, refused to order enforcement of the rat control ordinance in a blighted area that was scheduled for clearance and redevelopment. Public indignation rose as the PAC published reports that children were being attacked. Finally the union went to court for a writ of mandamus ordering enforcement of the law and won. The stewards and the PAC have pressured the city administration to enforce the air pollution ordinance more effectively, but they have had only limited success.

Aside from the skill and drive of its leadership and the residential distribution of its members, the Teamsters are influential because of their close relationship with the increasingly strong Negro community. Several of the top leaders of Negro organizations are also Teamsters officials. Negro organizations and the Teamsters' PAC nearly always agree on both goals and means in local politics. Moreover, since the Teamsters are sufficiently undemocratic in their internal organization, their leaders can usually subordinate internal racial antagonisms to external political goals. Though the Teamsters do not concern themselves with issues of civil rights, preferring instead such welfare issues as air pollution and garbage, moderate Negroes accept this approach, which is justified by the Teamsters on the grounds that it conforms to the moderate, conservative ethos of the city.

Some local observers in late 1959 thought that the Teamsters' influence in city politics was declining. For one thing, the Teamsters' effort to organize ward machines had failed in some wards. For another, a new militance among younger Negro leaders, manifested by their interest in civil rights, presaged a weakening of the tie between the Teamsters and the Negroes.

Also, the Teamsters were suffering from public suspicion stirred by U.S. Senate hearings on labor racketeering.

## Hands Off in Houston

Houston's distinguishing characteristics are its economic youth (as compared with the other great industrial and commercial cities of the United States), its economic and population boom, and its Southern, individualistic conservatism. Its local politics appear to be dominated by big business and its ally, the conservative press. But business control does not by itself explain the conservative character of Houston and Harris County government. Individual and conservative values predominate in the whole community. The conservative local government, therefore, is not so much business-controlled as genuinely representative.

Business interests are favored politically because there is no strong group to oppose them. Harris County has no political machine, just a handful of liberals, only weak labor unions, and a proportionately small (15 per cent of voters, 18 per cent of the population) Negro bloc, which is as often a liability as an asset to liberal or labor candidates. Harris County's Democratic Party is split into vigorous liberal and conservative factions, but the liberals and their Negro and labor allies concentrate on intraparty battles and state legislature elections. The liberal faction tries hard to stay out of city and county office elections. Its chief source of support, labor, cannot be a party to a liberal faction in city and county politics because individual unions have differing historical and personal allegiances and racial antagonisms that cross-cut the liberal-versus-conservative division in state and national politics. Furthermore, local government has too little to offer labor to warrant its risking participation in local politics. By staying out of most city and county political conflicts, the liberal faction saves itself for more important battles within the state and national Democratic party.

Organized labor's weak position in Houston can be compared to its status in Detroit twenty-five years ago. Harris County labor is handicapped by strong anti-labor feelings among citizens, internal dissensions, restrictive state laws (including a right-to-work law passed in 1947), antagonistic local and state officials, independent local unions, company unions, and union-breaking industries. But it is still the major source of the liberal Democratic faction's workers and voters. Of the county's approximately 165,000 skilled, semi-skilled and unskilled workers, about 75,000 are members of labor unions. Only two-thirds of these are members of locals that are affiliated with the newly merged AFL-CIO. Major unaffiliated groups include the generally conservative railroad brotherhoods, Teamsters, and building trades unions.

Houston labor's internal differences were apparent at the time of the AFL-CIO merger in Harris County in December 1959. Many locals exercised their option not to affiliate with the new central organization. And among the leaders of the combined organization, differences soon arose over policies and goals. CIO leaders, for example, did not wish the merged organization to continue publishing the newspaper formerly published by the local AFL. Also, officials of the AFL were less doctrinaire than those of the CIO about opposing public officials who were unfriendly to labor. AFL officials, for example, defended a city councilman who was a nonunion electrical contractor. They also disagreed with CIO criticism of a superintendent of schools who had long favored certain Houston craft unions.

Labor's goals are narrowly defined and self-serving. At the state capital it has sought to liberalize unemployment compensation, establish a state minimum wage, and discourage the use of *braceros* (Mexican laborers) by Texas employers. Locally, according to a senior Harris County AFL-CIO official, labor's major goals have not called for government action. Local labor can best serve its interests by promoting unionization of white collar and retail trades workers, by organizing more small businesses, and by building stronger Negro unions within the AFL-CIO. The largest Negro union in Harris County, a Teamsters local of about 5,000 members, is not affiliated with the AFL-CIO. Only a few locals, notably some building trades groups, are racially integrated.

Labor's internal divisions become visible when union action in local politics is proposed. "The closer politics is to the local level," an AFL-CIO Council official told an interviewer in 1960, "the more we stay out of it." This rule is followed, he said, chiefly because of the "friendship setup." He explained that "there are too many personal relationships—a kind of kinfolks system—in local politics." Because of these personal relationships and because not all labor leaders in Harris County are liberals, attempts to announce a labor position on local candidates and issues would only expose internal dissensions. Very few unions in Harris County endorse local candidates, although officials may sometimes announce at a meeting of a union local whether a candidate is "qualified." Also, endorsements in city elections are sometimes made by an independent union—most likely the Teamsters—which is "out to get" a candidate. Labor is much more interested in candidates for the state legislature than in city candidates. Union officials often meet with legislative candidates and ask them to declare a position on a list of issues. Local and state committees on political education make indorsements for state offices.

Conservatives and liberals alike agree that labor's votes and political workers are the backbone of the liberal Democratic faction in Harris County. Most union members vote liberal in state elections, about one-third of the liberal faction precinct chairmen are union members, and many union men and women do precinct work and serve as county and state convention delegates. Comparatively few union members hold public office, however. It is axiomatic that a good labor vote is essential to a liberal victory. Cooperation in 1958 among AFL-CIO unions, independent unions, Negroes, and liberal leaders produced a liberal victory (election of seven of eight legislature candidates). Conversely, many nonunion liberals blamed their 1960 primary defeat (in which all but one of the liberal incumbents were defeated) largely on labor's "failure to get out workers and a good vote."

Union officials and others seem to think that organized labor is reasonably well-treated by the Houston city administration. The incumbent mayor in 1960 always provided at least one "labor spot" on appointed commissions. When a major hearing on building codes was held in 1959, the mayor invited representatives of every building trades union to testify. Although the unions did not get everything they wanted in the building code, they had no serious objections to it. However, beyond this kind of consultation and representation, the city makes few concessions to labor unions. Mayors and councils before 1957 often granted contracts to nonunion employers or decided that union wage scales need not be paid on city-financed projects. No labor representatives held important administrative positions in the city government in 1960, although union officials said that this was because capable labor people found city salaries and jobs unattractive, not because the mayor refused to appoint them.

An exception to labor's general rule of reticence in local politics is the AFL-CIO Council's occasional assertion of a stand on some local issues that are not immediately subject to voter approval. It supported, for example, the city administration's proposal on water problems, federal funds for a school lunch program, and planning for urban renewal. On the other hand, it has avoided taking a stand on the volatile issue of zoning, even though it is not an issue that requires a referendum. Some local issues are so divisive that union leaders avoid them absolutely. Racial integration is one. "We don't ever permit a segregation question to come to a vote," a union official said.

# HAS THE PRESS LOST ITS INFLUENCE IN LOCAL AFFAIRS?

ALVIN J. REMMENGA

TO AN AUDIENCE of perhaps 100 million urban Americans, the press is the principal source of news about the municipal government under which they live. The nation's daily newspapers are, in effect, more than 58 million bulletin boards on which are posted what editors believe to be the newsworthy activities affecting the urban community and its residents.

Reprinted from *Nieman Reports*, October, 1959, by permission of the publisher.

Displayed on the newspaper pages, too, but perhaps not so evident to the casual reader, is the power to sway the opinions and actions of both the general public and municipal officials.

This influence, sometimes advocated in vigorous crusades but more frequently contained in the day-to-day presentation of news and ideas, may at times be difficult to recognize. It may not always be intended, but it does exist.

How important is this influence in the American community of today? Is it used in the common interest of the entire city, or is it more often an outlet for the personal attitudes and ideals of the reporter or editor? How often do newspapers, as a source of information and explanation, meet the challenges posed by new urban problems and modern social conditions? How is the newspaper received by those it attempts to influence or inform? What is the role of the newspaper in urban America, and how has it changed as a participant in the political processes of the city? Or has it changed at all?

A nationwide survey, conducted as part of this study, indicated that all but three of 309 municipal officials, journalists, political scientists and readers believed that daily newspapers were major influences in the affairs of local government. The survey also revealed:

Daily newspapers are no longer considered the commanding voice they once were in the urban community. Sixty-eight per cent of those questioned said newspaper influence on municipal affairs had declined since 1940.

Expansion of the radio and television industries is chiefly responsible for the decline of newspaper influence. Nearly nine out of ten officials and editors who thought the daily newspaper had declined as an urban influence blamed the decrease on radio and television.

Half the city officials, political scientists and readers believe newspapers would be more influential in municipal government if they were less sensational and more concerned about specific issues.

Daily newspapers deserve a scolding for the incompetence of their reporters of urban affairs. Fifty-seven per cent of the city officials and political scientists, most of them in cities where total daily newspaper circulation was less than 200,000, said municipal reporters were inexperienced, uninterested or uninformed on basic government procedures.

The importance of the daily newspaper to its readers is tied to the ability and desire on the part of the editors to inform through interesting, interpretive writing. Ninety per cent of those who believed newspaper influence had increased—most of them editors—said new concepts of reporting and news presentation were the responsible factors.

Another conclusion even more sharply delineated was that the role of the press in the urban community is not the same today as it was before World War II.

"A generation ago," recalled Scott Newhall, executive editor of the San Francisco (Calif.) *Chronicle,* "political pressure was exercised by direct orders from the editor to city hall. Today, news and editorial columns are used as a public voice and as the only means of pressure."

This changing role is part of a trend to more "community responsibility" on the part of the press, suggested Ernest W. Chard, managing editor of the Portland (Me.) *Press Herald-Express.*

"Consequently, newspapers can take credit less obviously for their influence," he noted. "They have fewer scalps at their belts but much stronger communities around them. They share their victories with the community."

But the methods of newspaper influence are not all that have changed in the past 20 years. Neither have the newspapers changed solely on their own initiative. Americans, themselves, are undergoing a sociological and technological revolution at a pace once thought impossible—a pace that could make the fantasy of Buck Rogers a reality within a decade.

The nation's population has grown by 40 million since 1940, with well over two-thirds of the 175 million Americans living in urban areas. Today, there are 39 million married couples in the United States, 37 per cent more than 20 years ago.

Perhaps the more significant ingredients of this 1959-style American revolt are the changing economic and educational standards.

Today, one out of every ten family heads is a college graduate. Public school enrollments have increased 25 per cent in two decades, and taxpayers are footing a public education bill five times the 1940 total. Keeping the wolf from the door, moreover, is not quite as difficult today as it once was. Half the nation's household heads have an annual income above $5,000. Five million of them earn more than $10,000 each year.

In essence, education and new desires are providing fresh horizons for urban Americans; higher incomes and adventuresome spirits with time to roam are bringing those horizons within reach.

"It means," said a Chicago editor, "that the average family of today is becoming more engrossed in a world clogged with social and business activities, a world where there is much less time or interest for the daily newspaper. The family even speaks in terms of television, jet airplanes and earth satellites—phrases that weren't heard in 1940."

Thus, the newspapers—while reaching many of the same readers they did 20 years ago—are meeting the public on different terms.

Before World War II, the urban populace depended primarily on newspapers with a daily circulation of 42 million and 51 million radio sets for the news of the community. Today, there are an additional 104 million radios and 50 million television sets that not only provide another news source, but also take huge chunks of reader time once claimed by the newspapers.

Neither have the newspapers been stagnant during this period, however. Daily circulation has climbed 16 million since 1940, and a survey by the

Newsprint Service Bureau showed the average daily newspaper in 39 cities had increased its size from 27 to 40 pages in 17 years.

Yet, newspapers today are faced with much stronger competition for the attention of the public, and not all the competition for an influential voice comes from other communication media.

"The importance of the role of newspapers," explained Charles B. Kopp, associate professor of journalism at the University of Georgia, "has been declining in proportion to the expansion of government, standardization and conservatism of newspapers and community life and the complacency and distractions of the masses."

What part do the daily newspapers play in municipal affairs?

William Randolph Hearst, Sr., who built a newspaper empire, in 1921 explained the role of newspapers with these words: "I rather think that the influence of the American press is on the whole declining . . . Newspapers do not form the opinion of the public; but if they are successful, they must express the opinion of the public."

Today, similar reasoning has led such editors as James E. Kuehn of the Rapid City (S.D.) *Journal* to question whether newspapers have the power to exert significant influence on their readers.

"While I like to think that they have, I believe there is a question as to whether the press could start or stop a trend," he declared. "The mere fact it reflects what is happening, through its news columns, does not necessarily permit the press to take credit for what results."

There are, however, countless instances in which newspapers claim credit—and perhaps rightly so—for suggesting, encouraging and aiding constructive developments in municipal government.

In Boston, a reorganization and modernization of the city's tax department was completed last year after a vigorous news and editorial campaign by the *Globe.*

In Great Falls, Mont., a water bond issue, with only mild editorial support from the *Tribune,* was defeated; a year later, the project received overwhelming approval after a series of newspaper editorials and explanatory articles.

In Charlotte, N.C., an attempt by the Teamsters Union to organize the city police force folded after the *Observer* campaigned against the drive.

In Nashville, the *Tennessean* hired its own accountant in 1956 to examine city tax assessments, and the newspaper successfully brought about a fairer system of tax increase notifications.

In Pittsburgh, extensive fire prevention measures were instituted last year in the school system after the *Sun-Telegraph* published a series of articles listing fire hazards in every one of the 112 public elementary schools in the city.

Campaigns against crime and corruption in municipal government have won Pulitzer Prize recognition for newspapers in Columbus, Ga.; Indianapolis; St. Paul, Minn.; St. Louis; Atlanta; Miami; Waterbury, Conn.; and other cities throughout the nation.

Even in New York City—where six of nine city officials questioned said newspaper crusades rarely constituted a direct influence on municipal actions —one administrative officer added: "I have been impressed by the really good job that newspapers can do in bringing to the attention of city officials things they don't know or things they don't want to have the public realize they know."

While these examples may indicate the presence of influence, they seldom serve as accurate measuring sticks of the power of the press. That must depend on the individual newspaper and the role in which it is accepted by those who read it.

To the city official, the newspaper may be both a good and an evil, depending on current press-city relations and on what appeared in the last edition. To the political scientist, the newspapers are likely to appear as an interest group or the voice of interest groups such as the downtown businessmen. To the reader, the newspaper may be an intellectual necessity or merely a source of sports scores and television schedules. The typical American editor may see himself as something of an embodiment of a community conscience.

A study conducted by Michigan State University in four communities indicated that the role of the press varied considerably from one city to the next even though many possible variables remained unchanged from city to city.

Despite these different viewpoints toward daily newspapers, the press is clearly a necessity to the processes of government in the urban American community. Every one of 51 adults interviewed in New York, Connecticut and New Jersey said that, for them, the local daily newspapers were the primary source of news about municipal affairs.

Surveys conducted during newspaper strikes last winter in New York City and Columbus, Ohio, also revealed that the wheels of municipal machinery turn slowly without newspaper publicity. Said Edward F. Cavanagh, Jr., fire commissioner of New York City: "Without the press, we could not equal our present public education accomplishments even if our department were increased to twice its present size."

The fact that the business of publishing newspapers is a business that must cater to its customers provides the impetus for the strongest complaint of municipal officials against the press. The newspapers, said half of the 80 city officials surveyed, are continually looking for controversy—something that will interest the reader.

"I think newspapers often are suckers for the fellow who yells loud about something just to see his name in print," complained a city manager in Maine.

A minority of municipal leaders, on the other hand, recognized a conflict of interest between local government and the press. Said Eugene Lambert, mayor of Duluth, Minn.: "Unfortunately, what a government official would like a newspaper to do and what a good newspaper must do to build readership are not always compatible."

Half the city officials and three of every five political scientists said newspapers pursue their own political goals by adding to or subtracting from the personalities of officials and municipal institutions.

The readers agreed that news reports frequently appeared to be slanted, but most gave the practice their approval. Sixty per cent of the 51 readers said that when a newspaper used its news columns to praise or reprimand an individual or institution, the criticism appeared to be deserved.

"I know Robert Moses (New York City's construction coordinator and park commissioner) isn't quite as infallible as the newspapers make him out to be," said a New York City attorney, "but he does have a tremendous knack for getting things done." Newspapers, noted a New York legislator, "do not by themselves make or break a public official, but few politicians can afford to ignore their influence."

One of the more discouraging trends of the press to the individuals surveyed was the declining number of daily newspapers. Today, the 1,750 dailies represent a decrease of 200 since the beginning of World War II. It has meant, said a third of those questioned, that many newspapers have lost a provocative appeal, both in the news columns and on the editorial pages.

"Newspapers today give more coverage, but they are less aggressive," said Floyd O. Flom, associate professor of political science at the University of Minnesota. "The monopoly status has taken away the incentive of competition for circulation."

Mayors in Rhode Island, Ohio and Wyoming agreed, and a Georgia newsman said: "Newspaper influence is declining because the trend to monopoly control in big newspapers means the single ownership is anxious not to offend either side in local government issues; the press in many city situations feels safer as part of the power structure of the community than as a critic of those in power."

Editors of newspapers in monopoly cities, however, dispute that reasoning.

An Iowa editor declared the combination of newspapers had ended "senseless competition," and Tom Pugh of the Peoria (Ill.) *Journal-Star*, said newspaper influence has increased "partly because of automatic unification of policy brought about by mergers, and partly because of increased attention to local governmental affairs."

"The greater attention to local government reporting," he added, "is due to a new social consciousness which can better operate under less competitive conditions which exist today."

While monopoly status has permitted many newspapers to expand their news coverage and to become—at least in theory—non-partisan reporters, Jay W. Jensen, head of the department of journalism at the University of

Illinois, believes that municipal officials have learned to use this new "un-critical, passive objectivity" for their own advantage.

"In short, the press is viewed by government more as a public relations channel than as something to be feared, assuaged or listened to," he declared.

One-fifth of the city officials and political scientists even complained that this passion for objectivity had filtered into newspaper editorials.

"The newspaper's editorial staff refuses to take a stand on many important government matters," charged a Sioux City, Ia., official; and a Missouri mayor said, "Very rarely is there an editorial on local issues, and if there is, you usually can't tell which side the editor is on."

A study during the first week of April of 12 daily newspapers from the nation's largest cities indicated that municipal officials might be entitled to more editorial attention. Of a total of 429 separate editorials, only 149—35% —were on local issues with most others on national or foreign subjects. This reflects, defended one editor, "a new public appetite for national and international news." Many urban readers might also agree that it reflects the ease of ignoring conditions at home and shouting about the neighbor's back yard.

Newspapers have also lost influence, said T. F. McDaniel, managing editor of the Emporia (Kan.) *Gazette,* because "the public is intrigued by newer media and they are a bit resentful that they have to cling to their newspapers" for news details and editorial opinions.

But what have radio and television done to the newspaper industry— and its influence—since World War II?

Many daily newspaper editors can point to increased circulation and agree with the reply of a Florida publisher that "it hasn't hurt us."

They would receive some support from Philip F. Griffin, chairman of the department of journalism at the University of California, who conceded that newspapers are probably less singularly effective in influencing attitudes than when they held a monopoly in the area of public informing.

Mr. Griffin added, however, that "it is possible that one means of persuasion reinforces another and that all of the instruments of public information have gained in persuasional strength."

Most of the individuals surveyed, however, thought differently. Of 210 who believed the influence of newspapers had decreased in recent years, 87 per cent cited the expansion of the electronic media as one of the principal causes. Urban Americans, they agreed, are not only spending more time with the radio and television set for entertainment purposes, but more local news is being supplied by those media.

There were clear indications, however, that the public tends to take local television news in the same manner that it takes commercials—away from the set.

The 51 readers surveyed estimated they spent an average of 17.4 minutes with the daily newspaper but a daily average of two hours and 52 minutes with the television set. Yet, less than half the readers said they regularly watched a local newscast on television, and all reported that most of what they knew about their local government was learned from the newspapers.

While television has undoubtedly assumed an influential role as a pictorial and entertainment medium in urban life concluded John L. Taylor, vice president of the Boston *Globe,* "the value of facts and figures in black and white, interestingly presented, has a lingering effect on the reader. He can refer to what he still can hold in his hand."

Even more alarming to many press and government observers than the threat of TV addiction is the spread of a new urban disease—public complacency about local government.

"The American people," charged M. L. MacSpadden, mayor of Juneau, Alaska, "have let government get away from them."

"Why not?" retorted a grocer in Newark, N.J. "The little man doesn't have much of a chance against the big businessmen and the politicians that run the city."

Many critics are quick to shift the blame for this feeling of despair and indifference on the communication media. After all, the press is the traditional guardian of the public's right to know—and that role carries not only the responsibility to inform, but also to interest. But government officials must share part of the blame, Neil Plummer, director of the school of journalism at the University of Kentucky, pointed out.

"Government, at all levels, is fast losing the concept of responsibility to the people," he said. "The vested interests of government resent efforts of the press to get access to information, and the steady criticism of the press by political leadership is taking its toll in public confidence in the press."

But how influential are the newspapers to a municipal official? Are they of real significance? Or are they something to be collected along with the pile of complaints and suggestions in a drawer in the city clerk's office?

The survey of 80 municipal officials indicated that newspapers have a greater direct influence in local government than many editors might believe.

Only one mayor dismissed the newspapers as an inconsequential influence, and 11 other city officials conceded the press was an influence in the community but not directly on them. Of the others, 18 said they considered or sounded out the views of newspapers or municipal reporters on all major issues, 28 said they did on most major issues and 22 said they considered the views of the press at infrequent intervals.

A Louisiana mayor explained, however, that the strength of newspapers as an influence is more democratic today than it was 20 years ago—but not as apparent.

"If an editor hopes to achieve success in a fair proportion of his causes, he must have some public support," the official said. "That is why I often follow the advice of civic groups even though the newspapers may have advocated their proposal earlier. When the people come to me, I know the newspaper's proposal carries some weight."

The relative importance of newspapers also varies according to the size of the city and the type of political institution that exists. For example, said Dr. Charles R. Adrian, director of the Continuing Education Service at Michigan State University, "the political machine in Chicago undoubtedly makes the press less important than in a city with weak political organization such as Detroit."

Newspaper influence, in addition, depends on how closely municipal officials must rely on the individual voter for support at the polls. Three of every five city managers, who were not themselves elected officials, and most mayors in cities of more than a quarter million population, said newspapers were not a major direct influence in city government. On the other hand, elected officials of smaller cities indicated they paid much closer attention to the newspapers and what they said.

Yet, the majority of government leaders believed that newspapers produced more influence through distortions, omissions, condensations and coloration of the news than through direct editorial demands and suggestions. Fifty-four officials said most newspaper influence was expressed in this manner in the news columns, 20 said editorials were more influential and six said the influence of editorials and news columns was equal.

To the readers, a newspaper editorial still appears to be the primary source of press influence, but this is frequently an illusion.

Half the readers surveyed said they read at least one newspaper editorial with some frequency, and nearly all of these felt they were influenced by newspaper editorials. Yet, they admitted that—if they already had an opinion on the subject—their point of view generally coincided with that of the newspaper and an editorial rarely changed their mind.

The reader survey in New York City indicated, however, that the limited-circulation weekly newspaper can often claim a stronger influence in matters of municipal government than the large downtown dailies.

Collectively, these specialized papers have a wide audience and a discernible impact. The reason is that these community publications are usually aimed at a definite clientele in a suburb or neighborhood area of a core city, members of a particular ethnic group, a labor union, Negroes, Catholics or Jews. Since they emphasize the interests of these special groups, they are able to call specific candidates or issues to the attention of their readers and discuss them in terms of his interests.

In New York City, 16 of 18 persons who read both a large daily newspaper and either the *Greenwich Village Voice*, the *West Side News* or a labor newspaper, said they received most of the news of city government from the large daily but generally made up their minds on specific issues that affected them after reading the community or labor press.

The daily newspaper that reports a subject in a simple, thorough and objective manner, however, can exercise immeasurable influence both in the news and editorial columns.

"Thorough news coverage of government, plus editorials that take a stand, cannot help but carry influence," said Donald C. Urry, editorial page editor of the Phoenix (Ariz.) *Gazette.* An Oklahoma journalism professor added: "If the newspaper does not carry weight with its readers, the fault is in the superficial, once-over-lightly approach by the paper."

The problem—from a newspaper point of view—is internal, he said. Large metropolitan newspapers have the means to do this type of reporting, and the "small city dailies must provide time and adequate compensation for a skilled reporter who can also be a continuing student of municipal and county government."

F. J. Price, director of the school of journalism at Louisiana State University, put the problem in these words: "Serious as is the problem of access to information at higher levels of government and at some lower levels, it is my feeling that a lack of reportorial industry on the part of many papers is much more serious."

"When a new reporter comes to city hall," said a mayor of a Midwestern city of 150,000 population, "he has no idea at all how the city operates. After he spends a year or two learning, he goes to something bigger and better. I feel like I'm in charge of a journalism school instead of a city."

Half the mayors and city managers surveyed believed that reporters should have better preparation or more interest in their work. Ten said reporters were sufficiently experienced but not interested in city government, and 28 said reporters were sufficiently interested but without adequate experience.

Charged the mayor of one of the largest cities in upstate New York: "Reporters have inadequate experience and background, and they are prejudiced in their reporting."

"With more drive by reporters," added a Tacoma, Wash., official, "a much better job could be done to keep the reading public informed."

Two-thirds of the 44 college instructors questioned said municipal government reporters were sufficiently interested but not adequately experienced for responsible city hall coverage. Six said reporters were experienced but not interested and eight said reporters had both sufficient interest and experience.

A political scientist at the University of Montana said reporters too often show "a tendency to wait for the news to come to them rather than to look for it," and a University of Vermont instructor said the reporter's instructions from his desk encouraged "inaccuracies and rather bland exaggerations."

What can newspapers do to improve the quality of municipal reporting?

One frequent suggestion was that editors ought to scrutinize their policies on hiring and assigning reporters. Karl A. Bosworth, associate professor of government at the University of Connecticut, suggested that newspapers "pick as municipal reporters people well trained in political science, probably to the Master of Arts level."

Another suggestion was that the academic training of a reporter should not stop when he gets to city hall. A North Dakota city manager said that all government reporters should be sent to "refresher courses such as those given by Northwestern University to orient them or re-orient them in municipal government." Mayors in California, Alabama, Delaware, Colorado and Idaho made the same proposal.

Despite the many complaints of city officials against the newspapers and those of the press against government, however, many on both sides agreed that newspapers will become of more importance to both municipal officials and the taxpayers as the growing pains sharpen in urban areas.

Newspapers, said Elmer E. White, secretary of the Michigan Press Association, "are awakening to the challenge. They are spending more time and taking a deeper interest in local government so that they can do a better job of interpreting."

The Houston (Tex.) *Post,* for example, was cited by one mayor for its practice of assigning a competent reporter to a single public issue and permitting him time to devote to research, study and writing on that issue.

In Cincinnati, Brady Black, executive editor of the *Enquirer,* noted that "we do many more stories in depth than we formerly did and have a specialist reporting on such problems as expressways, slum clearance and transportation."

Last year, the *Enquirer* sponsored a public service program—Job of the City—to which it brought experts on municipal problems from throughout the country to meet with community leaders from the Cincinnati metropolitan area. The only objective, said Mr. Black, was to awaken public interest in municipal problems and to inform.

"The successful crusade of today," said an Indiana journalism professor, "rests on careful study and analysis, an attempt to enlist interested groups and a support of group action by adequate exposition and argument."

It means that daily newspapers no longer possess the singular influence they once did in municipal government. Their power today is dependent on the actions of their readers, and the strength of the power must depend on the ability of the newspapers to interest and inform the public.

# TYPES OF INFLUENTIALS:
# THE LOCAL AND THE COSMOPOLITAN

ROBERT K. MERTON

THE TERMS "LOCAL" AND "COSMOPOLITAN"[1] do not refer, of course, to the regions in which interpersonal influence is exercised. Both types of influentials are effective almost exclusively within the local community. Rovere has few residents who command a following outside that community.

The chief criterion for distinguishing the two is found in their *orientation* toward Rovere. The localite largely confines his interests to this community. Rovere is essentially his world. Devoting little thought or energy to the Great Society, he is preoccupied with local problems, to the virtual exclusion of the national and international scene. He is, strictly speaking, parochial.

Contrariwise with the cosmopolitan type. He has some interest in Rovere and must of course maintain a minimum of relations within the community since he, too, exerts influence there. But he is also oriented significantly to the world outside Rovere, and regards himself as an integral part of that world. He resides in Rovere but lives in the Great Society. If the local type is parochial, the cosmopolitan is ecumenical.

Of the thirty influentials interviewed at length, fourteen were independently assessed by three analysts[2] as "cosmopolitan" on the basis of

---

Reprinted from Paul F. Lazarsfeld and Frank N. Stanton, eds., *Communications Research 1948–1949* (New York: Harper & Brothers, 1949), pp. 189–202.

1. Upon identification of the two types of influentials, these terms were adopted from Carle C. Zimmerman, who uses them as translations of Toennies' well-known distinction between *Gemeinschaft* (localistic) and *Gesellschaft* (cosmopolitan). The sociologically informed reader will recognize essentially the same distinction, though with different terminologies, in the writings of Simmel, Cooley, Weber, Durkheim, among many others. Although these terms have commonly been used to refer to types of social organization and of social relationships, they are here applied to empirical materials on types of influential persons. Cf. Ferdinand Toennies, *Fundamental Concepts of Sociology* (New York, 1940), a translation by C. P. Loomis of his classic book, *Gemeinschaft und Gesellschaft,* and more importantly, a later article bearing the same title. See also Carle C. Zimmerman, *The Changing Community,* (New York and London: Harper & Brothers, 1938), especially pp. 80 ff. For a compact summary of similar concepts in the sociological literature, see Leopold von Wiese and Howard Becker, *Systematic Sociology* (New York: John Wiley & Sons, 1932), especially pp. 223–226n.

2. This complete coincidence of assessments is scarcely to be expected in a larger sample. But the cosmopolitan and local syndromes were so clearly defined for this handful of cases, that there was little doubt concerning the "diagnoses." A full-fledged investigation would evolve more formal criteria, along the lines implied in the following discussion, and would, accordingly, evolve an intermediate type which approaches neither the local nor the cosmopolitan pole.

case-materials exhibiting their orientation toward the Rovere community, and sixteen, as "local."

These orientations found characteristic expression in a variety of contexts. For example, influentials were launched upon a statement of their outlook by the quasi-projective question: "Do you worry much about the news?" (This was the autumn of 1943, when "the news" was, for most, equivalent to news about the war.) The responses, typically quite lengthy, readily lent themselves to classification in terms of the chief foci of interest of the influentials. One set of comments was focused on problems of a national and international order. They expressed concern with the difficulties which would attend the emergence of a stable postwar world; they talked at length about the problems of building an international organization to secure the peace; and the like. The second set of comments referred to the war news almost wholly in terms of what it implied for interviewees personally or for their associates in Rovere. They seized upon a question about "the news" as an occasion for reviewing the immediate flow of problems which the war had introduced into the town.

Classifying influentials into these two categories, we find that twelve of the fourteen[3] cosmopolitans typically replied within the framework of international and national problems, whereas only four of the sixteen locals spoke in this vein. Each type of influential singled out distinctively different elements from the flow of events. A vaguely formulated question enabled each to project their basic orientations into their replies.

All other differences between the local and cosmopolitan influentials seem to stem from their difference in basic orientation. . . .[4] From the group-profiles we see graphically the tendency of local influentials to be devoted to localism: they are more likely to have lived in Rovere for a long period, are profoundly interested in meeting many townspeople, do not wish to move from the town, are more likely to be interested in local politics, *etc.* Such items, which suggest great disparity between the two types of influentials, are our main concern in the following sections. There we will find that the difference in basic orientation is bound up with a variety of other differences: (1) in the structures of social relations in which each type is implicated; (2) in the roads they have traveled to their present positions in the influence-structure; (3) in the utilization of their present status for the exercise of interpersonal influence; and (4) in their communications behavior.

---

3. It should be repeated that the figures cited at this point, as throughout the study, should not be taken as representative of a parent population. They are cited only to illustrate the heuristic purpose they served in suggesting clues to the operation of diverse patterns of interpersonal influence. As is so often the fact with quantitative summaries of case-studies, these figures do not confirm interpretations but merely suggest interpretations. The tentative interpretations in turn provide a point of departure for designing quantitative studies based upon adequate samples.

4. Nothing is said here of the objective *determinants* of these differences in orientation. To ascertain these determinants is an additional and distinctly important task, not essayed in the present study.

## Structures of Social Relations

ROOTS IN ROVERE

Local and cosmopolitan influentials differ rather markedly in their attachment to Rovere. The local influentials are great local patriots and the thought of leaving Rovere seems seldom to come to mind. As one of them gropingly expressed it:

> Rovere is the greatest town in the world. It has something that is nowhere else in the world, though I can't quite say what it is.

When asked directly if they had "ever thought of leaving Rovere," thirteen of the sixteen local influentials replied emphatically that they would never consider it, and the other three expressed a strong preference to remain, although they believed they would leave under certain conditions. None felt that they would be equally satisfied with life in any other community. Not so with the cosmopolitans. Only three of these claim to be wedded to Rovere for life. Four express their present willingness to live elsewhere, and the remaining seven would be willing to leave under certain conditions. Cosmopolitans' responses such as these do not turn up at all among the locals:

> I've been on the verge of leaving for other jobs several times.

> I am only waiting for my son to take over my practice, before I go out to California.

These basic differences in attitude toward Rovere are linked with the different runs of experience of local and cosmopolitan influentials. The cosmopolitans have been more mobile. The locals were typically born in Rovere or in its immediate vicinity. Whereas 14 of the locals have lived in Rovere for over twenty-five years, this is true for fewer than half of the cosmopolitans. The cosmopolitans are typically recent arrivals who have lived in a succession of communities in different parts of the country.

Nor does this appear to be a result of differences in the age-composition of the local and cosmopolitan groups. The cosmopolitans are more likely to be younger than the local influentials. But for those over forty-five, the cosmopolitans seem to be comparative newcomers and the locals Rovere-born-and-bred.

From the case-materials, we can infer the bases of the marked attachment to Rovere characteristic of the local influentials. In the process of making their mark, these influentials have become thoroughly *adapted to the community* and dubious of the possibility of doing as well elsewhere. From the vantage point of his seventy years, a local judge reports his sense of full incorporation in the community:

> I wouldn't think of leaving Rovere. The people here are very good, very responsive. They like me and I'm grateful to God for the feeling that the people in Rovere trust me and look up to me as their guide and leader.

Thus, the strong sense of identification with Rovere among local influentials is linked with their typically local origins and career patterns in this community. Economically and sentimentally, they are deeply rooted in Rovere.

So far as attachment to Rovere is concerned, the cosmopolitans differ from the locals in virtually every respect. Not only are they relative newcomers; they do not feel themselves rooted in the town. Having characteristically lived elsewhere, they feel that Rovere, "a pleasant enough town," is only one of many. They are also aware, through actual experience, that they can advance their careers in other communities. They do not, consequently, look upon Rovere as comprising the outermost limits of a secure and satisfactory existence. Their wider range of experience has modified their orientation toward their present community.

## Sociability: Networks of Personal Relations

In the course of the interview, influentials were given an occasion to voice their attitudes toward "knowing many people" in the community. Attitudes differed sharply between the two types. Thirteen of the sixteen local influentials in contrast to four of the fourteen cosmopolitans expressed marked interest in establishing frequent contacts with many people.

This difference becomes more instructive when examined in qualitative terms. The local influential is typically concerned with knowing *as many* people as possible. He is a "quantitativist" in the sphere of social contacts. Numbers count. In the words of an influential police officer (who thus echoes the sentiments of another "local," the Mayor):

> I have lots of friends in Rovere, if I do say so myself. I like to know everybody. If I stand on a corner, I can speak to 500 people in two hours. Knowing people helps when a promotion comes up, for instance. Everybody mentions you for the job. Influential people who know you talk to other people. Jack Flye [the Mayor] said to me one day, "Bill," he said, "you have more friends in town than I do. I wish I had all the friends you have that you don't even know of." It made me feel good . . .

This typical attitude fits into what we know of the local type of influential. What is more, it suggests that the career-function of personal contacts and personal relations is recognized by the local influentials themselves. Nor is this concern with personal contact merely a consequence of the occupations of local influentials. Businessmen, professionals, and local government officials among them all join in the same paeans on the desirability of many and varied contacts. A bank president recapitulates the same story in terms of his experience and outlook:

> I have always been glad to meet people . . . It really started when I became a teller. The teller is the most important position in a bank as far as meeting people goes. As teller, you must meet everyone. You learn to know everybody by his first name. You don't have the same opportunity again to meet

people. Right now we have a teller who is very capable but two or three people have come to me complaining about him. He is unfriendly with them. I told him, you're got to have a kind word for everyone. It's a personal and a business matter.

This keynote brings out the decisive interest of local influentials in all manner of personal contacts which enable them to establish themselves when they need political, business, or other support. Influentials in this group act on the explicit assumption that they can be locally prominent and influential by lining up enough people who know them and are hence willing to help them as well as be helped by them.

The cosmopolitan influentials, on the other hand, have notably little interest in meeting *as many* people as possible.[5] They are more selective in their choice of friends and acquaintances. They typically stress the importance of confining themselves to friends with whom "they can really talk," with whom they can "exchange ideas." If the local influentials are quantitativists, the cosmopolitans are "qualitativists" in this regard. It is not *how many* people they know but the *kind of people* they know that counts.[6]

The contrast with the prevailing attitudes of local influentials is brought out in these remarks by cosmopolitan influentials:

> I don't care to know people unless there is something to the person. I am not interested in quantity. I like to know about other people; it broadens your own education. I enjoy meeting people with knowledge and standing. Masses of humanity I don't go into. I like to meet people of equal mentality, learning and experience.

Just as with the local influentials, so here the basic attitude cuts across occupational and educational lines. Professional men among the cosmopolitans, for example, do not emphasize the importance of a wide and extensive acquaintanceship, if one is to build up a practice. In contrast to a "local" attorney who speaks of the "advantage to me to know as many people as possible," a "cosmopolitan" attorney waxes poetic and exclusive all in one, saying:

> I have never gone out and sought people. I have no pleasure in just going around and calling. As Polonius advised Laertes,
>
>> "Those friends thou hast, and their adoption tried,
>> Grapple them to thy soul with hoops of steel,
>> But do not dull the palm with entertainment
>> Of each new-hatch'd unfledged comrade . . ."

5. This was interestingly confirmed in the following fashion. Our informants were confronted with a random list of names of Rovere residents and were asked to identify each. Local influentials recognized more names than any other group of informants, and cosmopolitans, in turn, knew more persons than the non-influential informants.

6. In this pilot study, we have confined ourselves to the expression of attitudes toward personal contacts and relations. A detailed inquiry would examine the quantum and quality of *actual* personal relations characteristic of the local and cosmopolitan influentials.

In a later section of this study, we shall see that these diverse orientations of locals and cosmopolitans toward personal relations can be interpreted as a function of their distinctive modes of achieving influence. At the moment, it is sufficient to note that locals seek to enter into manifold networks of personal relations, whereas the cosmopolitans, *on the same status level,* explicitly limit the range of these relations.

## PARTICIPATION IN VOLUNTARY ORGANIZATIONS

In considering the "sociability" of locals and cosmopolitans, we examined their attitudes toward informal, personal relationships. But what of their roles in the more formal agencies for social contact: the voluntary organizations?

As might be anticipated, both types of influentials are affiliated with more organizations than rank-and-file members of the population. Cosmopolitan influentials belong to an average of eight organizations per individual, and the local influentials, to an average of six. There is the possibility that cosmopolitans make greater use of organizational channels to influence than of personal contacts, whereas locals, on the whole, operate contrariwise.

But as with sociability, so with organizations: the more instructive facts are qualitative rather than quantitative. It is not so much that the cosmopolitans belong to *more* organizations than the locals. Should a rigorous inquiry bear out this impression, it would still not locate the strategic organizational differences between the two. It is, rather, that they belong to different types of organizations. And once again, these differences reinforce what we have learned about the two kinds of influentials.

The local influentials evidently crowd into those organizations which are largely designed for "making contacts," for establishing personal ties. Thus, they are found largely in the secret societies (Masons), fraternal organizations (Elks), and local service clubs—the Rotary, Lions, and the Kiwanis, the most powerful organization of this type in Rovere. Their participation appears to be less a matter of furthering the nominal objectives of these organizations than of using them as *contact centers.* In the forthright words of one local influential, a businessman:

> I get to know people through the service clubs; Kiwanis, Rotary, Lions. I now belong only to the Kiwanis. Kiwanis is different from any other service club. You have to be asked to join. They pick you out first, check you first. Quite a few influential people are there and I get to meet them at lunch every week.

The cosmopolitans, on the other hand, tend to belong to those organizations in which they can exercise their special skills and knowledge. They are found in professional societies and in hobby groups. At the time of the inquiry, in 1943, they were more often involved in Civilian Defense organizations where again they were presumably more concerned with furthering the objectives of the organization than with establishing personal ties.

Much the same contrast appears in the array of public offices held by the two types of influentials. Seven of each type hold some public office, although the locals have an average somewhat under one office per official. The primary difference is in the *type* of office held. The locals tend to hold political posts—street commissioner, mayor, township board, etc.—ordinarily obtained through political and personal relationships. The cosmopolitans, on the other hand, more often appear in public positions which involve not merely political operations but the utilization of special skills and knowledge (*e.g.,* Board of Health, Housing Committee, Board of Education).

From all this we can set out the hypothesis that participation in voluntary associations has somewhat different functions for cosmopolitan and local influentials. Cosmopolitans are concerned with associations primarily because of the activities of these organizations. They are means for extending or exhibiting their skills and knowledge. Locals are interested in associations not for their activities, but because these provide a means for extending personal relationships. The basic orientations of locals and cosmopolitan influentials are thus diversely expressed in organizational behavior as in other respects.

## Avenues to Interpersonal Influence

The foregoing differences in attachment to Rovere, sociability, and organizational behavior help direct us to the different avenues to influence traveled by the locals and the cosmopolitans. And in mapping these avenues we shall fill in the background needed to interpret the differences in communications behavior characteristic of the two types of influentials.

The locals have largely grown up in and with the town. For the most part, they have gone to school there, leaving only temporarily for their college and professional studies. They held their first jobs in Rovere and earned their first dollars from Rovere people. When they came to work out their career-pattern, Rovere was obviously the place in which to do so. It was the only town with which they were thoroughly familiar, in which they knew the ins and outs of politics, business, and social life. It was the only community which they knew and, equally important, which knew them. Here they had developed numerous personal relationships.

And this leads to the decisive attribute of the local influentials' path to success: far more than with the cosmopolitans, *their influence rests on an elaborate network of personal relationships.* In a formula which at once simplifies and highlights the essential fact, we can say: *the influence of local influentials rests not so much on what they know but on whom they know.*

Thus, the concern of the local influential with personal relations is in part the product and in part the instrument of his particular type of influence. The "local boy who makes good," it seems, is likely to make it through good personal relations. Since he is involved in personal relations long before he has entered seriously upon his career it is the path of less resistance for him to continue to rely upon these relations as far as possible in his later career.

With the cosmopolitan influential, all this changes. Typically a new-comer to the community, he does not and cannot utilize personal ties as his chief claim to attention. He usually comes into the town fully equipped with the prestige and skills associated with his business or profession and his "worldly" experience. He begins his climb in the prestige-structure at a relatively high level. It is the prestige of his previous achievements and previously acquired skills which make him eligible for a place in the local influence-structure. Personal relations are much more the product than the instrumentality of his influence.

These differences in the location of career-patterns have some interesting consequences for the problems confronting the two types of influentials. First of all, there is some evidence, though far from conclusive, that the rise of the locals to influentiality is slow compared with that of the cosmopolitans. Dr. A, a minister, cosmopolitan, and reader of newsmagazines, remarked upon the ease with which he had made his mark locally:

> The advantage of being a minister is that *you don't have to* prove yourself. You are immediately accepted and received in all homes, including the best ones. [italics inserted]

However sanguine this observation may be, it reflects the essential point that the newcomer who has "arrived" in the outside world, sooner takes his place among those with some measure of influence in the local community. In contrast, the local influentials *do* "have to prove" themselves. Thus, the local bank president who required some forty years to rise from his job as messenger boy, speaks feelingly of the slow, long road on which "I worked my way up."

The age-composition of the local and cosmopolitan influentials is also a straw in the wind with regard to the rate of rise to influence. All but two of the sixteen locals are over forty-five years of age, whereas fewer than two-thirds of the cosmopolitans are in this older age group.

Not only may the rate of ascent to influence be slower for the local than for the cosmopolitan, but the ascent involves some special difficulties centered about the local's personal relations. It appears that these relations may hinder as well as help the local boy to "make good." He must overcome the obstacle of being intimately known to the community when he was "just a kid." He must somehow enable others to recognize his consistent change in status. Most importantly, people to whom he was once subordinate must be brought to the point of now recognizing him as, in some sense, superordinate. Recognition of this problem is not new. Kipling follows Matthew 13 in observing that "prophets have honour all over the Earth, except in the village where they were born." The problem of ascent in the influence-structure for the home-town individual may be precisely located in sociological terms: change of status within a group, particularly if it is fairly rapid, calls for the revamp-ing of attitudes toward and the remaking of relations with the mobile individual. The pre-existent structure of personal relations for a time thus restrains the ascent of the local influential. Only when he has broken through these established conceptions of him, will others accept the reversal of roles entailed in the rise of the local man to influence. A Rovere attorney, numbered among the local influentials, describes the pattern concisely:

> When I first opened up, people knew me so well in town that they treated me as if I still were a kid. It was hard to overcome. But after I took interest in various public and civic affairs, and became chairman of the Democratic organization and ran for the State legislature—knowing full well I wouldn't be elected—they started to take me seriously.

The cosmopolitan does not face the necessity for breaking down local preconceptions of himself before it is possible to have his status as an influential "taken seriously." As we have seen, his credentials are found in the prestige and authority of his attainments elsewhere. He thus manifests less interest in a wide range of personal contacts for two reasons. First, his influence stems from prestige rather than from reciprocities with others in the community. Secondly, the problem of disengaging himself from obsolete images of him as "a boy" does not exist for him, and consequently does not focus his attention upon personal relations as it does for the local influential.

The separate roads to influence traveled by the locals and cosmopolitans thus help account for their diverging orientations toward the local community, with all that these orientations entail.

## Social Status in Action: Interpersonal Influence

At this point, it may occur to the reader that the distinction between the local and cosmopolitan influentials is merely a reflection of differences in education or occupation. This does not appear to be the case.

It is true that the cosmopolitans among our interviewees have received more formal education than the locals. All but one of the cosmopolitans as compared with half of the locals are at least graduates of high school. It is also true that half of the locals are in "big business," as gauged by Rovere standards, whereas only two of the fourteen cosmopolitans fall in this group; and furthermore, that half of the cosmopolitan influentials are professional people as compared with fewer than a third of the locals.

But these differences in occupational or educational status do not appear to determine the diverse types of influentials. When we compare the behavior and orientations of professionals among the locals and cosmopolitans, their characteristic differences persist, even though they have the same types of occupation and have received the same type of education. Educational and occupational differences may *contribute* to the differences between the two types of influentials but they are not the *source* of these differences. Even as a professional, the local influential is more of a businessman and politician in his behavior and outlook than is the cosmopolitan. He utilizes personal relationships as an avenue to influence conspicuously more than does his cosmopolitan counterpart. In short, *it is the pattern of utilizing social status and not the formal contours of the status itself which is decisive.*[7]

While occupational status may be a major support for the cosmopolitan's rise to influence, it is merely an adjunct for the local. Whereas all five of the local professionals actively pursue local politics, the cosmopolitan professionals practically ignore organized political activity in Rovere. (Their offices tend to be honorary appointments.) Far from occupation serving to explain the differences between them, it appears that the same occupation has a different role in interpersonal influence according to whether it is pursued by a local or a cosmopolitan. This bears out our earlier impression that "objective attributes" (education, occupation, etc.) do not suffice as indices of people exercising interpersonal influence.

The influential businessman, who among our small number of interviewees is found almost exclusively among the locals, typically utilizes his personal relations to enhance his influence. It is altogether likely that a larger sample would include businessmen who are cosmopolitan influentials and whose behavior differs significantly in this respect. Thus, Mr. H., regarded as exerting great influence in Rovere, illustrates the cosmopolitan big-business type. He arrived in Rovere as a top executive in a local manufacturing plant. He has established few personal ties. But he is sought out for advice precisely because he has "been around" and has the aura of a man familiar with the outside world of affairs. His influence rests upon an imputed expertness rather than upon sympathetic understanding of others.

This adds another dimension to the distinction between the two types of influential. It appears that the cosmopolitan influential has a following because *he knows;* the local influential, because *he understands.* The one is sought for his specialized skills and experience; the other, for his intimate appreciation of intangible but affectively significant details. The two patterns are reflected in prevalent conceptions of the difference between "the extremely competent but impersonal medical specialist" and the "old family doctor." Or again, it is not unlike the difference between the "impersonal social welfare worker" and the "friendly precinct captain." It is not merely that the local political captain provides food-baskets and jobs, legal and extra-legal advice, that he sets to rights minor scrapes with the law, helps the bright poor boy to a political scholarship in a local college, looks after the bereaved—that he helps in a whole series of crises when a fellow needs a friend, and above all, a friend who "knows the score" and can do something about it. It is not merely that he provides aid which gives him interpersonal influence. It is *the manner in which the aid is provided.* After all, specialized agencies do exist for dispensing this assistance. Welfare agencies, settlement

---

7. The importance of actively seeking influence is evident from an analysis of "the upward mobile type," set forth in the monograph upon which this report is based. See also Granville Hicks, *Small Town* (New York: The Macmillan Co., 1946), p. 154, who describes a local influential in these terms: "He is a typical politician, a born manipulator, a man who worships influence, *works hard to acquire it,* and does his best to convince other people that he has it." (Italics supplied)

houses, legal aid clinics, hospital clinics, public relief departments—these and many other organizations are available. But in contrast to the professional techniques of the welfare worker which often represent in the mind of the recipient the cold, bureaucratic dispensation of limited aid following upon detailed investigation are the unprofessional techniques of the precinct captain who asks no questions, exacts no compliance with legal rules of eligibility and does not "snoop" into private affairs. The precinct captain is a prototype of the "local" influential.

Interpersonal influence stemming from specialized expertness typically involves some social distance between the advice-giver and the advice-seeker, whereas influence stemming from sympathetic understanding typically entails close personal relations. The first is the pattern of the cosmopolitan influential; the second, of the local influential. Thus, the operation of these patterns of influence gives a clue to the distinctive orientations of the two types of influential.

# THE LOCAL COMMUNITY AS AN ECOLOGY OF GAMES

## NORTON E. LONG

THE LOCAL COMMUNITY whether viewed as a polity, an economy, or a society presents itself as an order in which expectations are met and functions performed. In some cases, as in a new, company-planned mining town, the order is the willed product of centralized control, but for the most part the order is the product of a history rather than the imposed effect of any central nervous system of the community. For historic reasons we readily conceive the massive task of feeding New York to be achieved through the unplanned, historically developed co-operation of thousands of actors largely unconscious of their collaboration to this individually unsought end. The efficiency of this system is attested to by the extraordinary difficulties of the War Production Board and Service of Supply in accomplishing similar logistical objectives through an explicit system of orders and directives. Insofar as conscious rationality plays a role, it is a function of the parts rather than the whole. Particular structures working for their own ends within the whole

Reprinted from *American Journal of Sociology*, 64, No. 3 (November, 1958), 251–261, by permission of The University of Chicago Press.

This paper is largely based on a year of field study in the Boston Metropolitan area made possible by grants from the Stern Family Foundation and the Social Science Research Council. The opinions and conclusion expressed are those of the author alone.

may provide their members with goals, strategies, and roles that support rational action. The results of the interaction of the rational strivings after particular ends are in part collectively functional if unplanned. All this is the well-worn doctrine of Adam Smith, though one need accept no more of the doctrine of beneficence than that an unplanned economy can function.

While such a view is accepted for the economy, it is generally rejected for the polity. Without a sovereign, Leviathan is generally supposed to disintegrate and fall apart. Even if Locke's more hopeful view of the natural- ness of the social order is taken, the polity seems more of a contrived artifact than the economy. Furthermore, there is both the hangover of Austinian sovereignty and the Greek view of ethical primacy to make political institu- tions seem different in kind and ultimately inclusive in purpose and for this reason to give them an over-all social directive end. To see political institu- tions as the same kind of thing as other institutions in society rather than as different, superior, and inclusive (both in the sense of being sovereign and ethically more significant) is a form of relativistic pluralism that is difficult to entertain. At the local level, however, it is easier to look at the municipal government, its departments, and the agencies of state and national govern- ment as so many institutions, resembling banks, newspapers, trade unions, chambers of commerce, churches, etc., occupying a territorial field and inter- acting with one another. This interaction can be conceptualized as a system without reducing the interacting institutions and individuals to membership in any single comprehensive group. It is psychologically tempting to envision the local territorial system as a group with a governing "they." This is certainly an existential possibility and one to be investigated. However, fre- quently, it seems likely, systems are confused with groups, and our primitive need to explain thunder with a theology or a demonology results in the hypostatizing of an angelic or demonic hierarchy. The executive committee of the bourgeoisie and the power elite make the world more comfortable for modern social scientists as the Olympians did for the ancients. At least the latter-day hypothesis, being terrestrial, is in principle researchable, though in practice its metaphysical statement may render it equally immune to mundane inquiry.

Observation of certain local communities makes it appear that inclusive over-all organization for many general purposes is weak or non-existent. Much of what occurs seems to just happen with accidental trends becoming cumulative over time and producing results intended by nobody. A great deal of the communities' activities consist of undirected co-operation of partic- ular social structures, each seeking particular goals and, in doing so, meshing with others. While much of this might be explained in Adam Smith's terms, much of it could not be explained with a rational, atomistic model of calculat- ing individuals. For certain purposes the individual is a useful way of look- ing at people; for many others the role-playing member of a particular group is more helpful. Here we deal with the essence of predictability in social affairs. If we know the game being played is baseball and that X is a third baseman, by knowing his position and the game being played we can tell more about X's activities on the field than we could if we examined X as a psychologist or a psychiatrist. If such were not the case, X would belong in the mental ward rather than in a ball park. The behavior of X is not some disembodied rationality but, rather, behavior within an organized group activity that has goals, norms, strategies, and roles that give the very field and ground for rationality. Baseball structures the situation.

It is the contention of this paper that the structured group activities that coexist in a particular territorial system can be looked at as games. These games provide the players with a set of goals that give them a sense of success or failure. They provide them determinate roles and calculable strategies and tactics. In addition, they provide the players with an elite and general public that is in varying degrees able to tell the score. There is a good deal of evidence to be found in common parlance that many participants in contemporary group structures regard their occupations as at least analogous to games. And, at least in the American culture, and not only since Eisenhower, the conception of being on a "team" has been fairly widespread.

Unfortunately, the effectiveness of the term "game" for the purposes of this paper is vitiated by, first, the general sense that games are trivial occupations and, second, by the pre-emption of the term for the application of a calculus of probability to choice or decision in a determinate game situation. Far from regarding games as trivial, the writer's position would be that man is both a game-playing and a game-creating animal, that his capacity to create and play games and take them deadly seriously is of the essence, and that it is through games or activities analogous to game-playing that he achieves a satisfactory sense of significance and a meaningful role.

While the calculability of the game situation is important, of equal or greater importance is the capacity of the game to provide a sense of purpose and a role. The organizations of society and polity produce satisfactions with both their products and their processes. The two are not unrelated, but, while the production of the product may in the larger sense enable players and onlookers to keep score, the satisfaction in the process is the satisfaction of playing the game and the sense in which any activity can be grasped as a game.

Looked at this way, in the territorial system there is a political game, a banking game, a contracting game, a newspaper game, a civic organization game, an ecclesiastical game, and many others. Within each game there is a well-established set of goals whose achievement indicates success or failure for the participants, a set of socialized roles making participant behavior highly predictable, a set of strategies and tactics handed down through experience and occasionally subject to improvement and change, an elite public whose approbation is appreciated, and, finally, a general public which has some appreciation for the standing of the players. Within the game the players can be rational in the varying degrees that the structure permits. At the very least, they know how to behave, and they know the score.

Individuals may play in a number of games, but, for the most part, their major preoccupation is with one, and their sense of major achievement is through success in one. Transfer from one game to another is, of course, possible, and the simultaneous playing of roles in two or more games is an important manner of linking separate games.

Sharing a common territorial field and collaborating for different and particular ends in the achievement of over-all social functions, the players in one game make use of the players in another and are, in turn, made use of by them. Thus the banker makes use of the newspaperman, the politician, the contractor, the ecclesiastic, the labor leader, the civic leader—all to further his success in the banking game—but, reciprocally, he is used to further the others' success in the newspaper, political, contracting, ecclesiastical, labor, and civic games. Each is a piece in the chess game of the other, sometimes a willing piece, but, to the extent that the games are different, with a different end in view.

Thus a particular highway grid may be the result of a bureaucratic department of public works game in which are combined, though separate, a professional highway engineer game with its purposes and critical elite onlookers; a departmental bureaucracy; a set of contending politicians seeking to use the highways for political capital, patronage, and the like; a banking game concerned with bonds, taxes, and the effect of the highways on real estate; newspapermen interested in headlines, scoops, and the effect of highways on the papers' circulation; contractors eager to make money by building roads; ecclesiastics concerned with the effect of highways on their parishes and on the fortunes of the contractors who support their churchly ambitions; labor leaders interested in union contracts and their status as community influentials with a right to be consulted; and civic leaders who must justify the contributions of their bureaus of municipal research or chambers of commerce to the social activity. Each game is in play in the complicated pulling and hauling of siting and constructing the highway grid. A wide variety of purposes is subserved by the activity, and no single over-all directive authority controls it. However, the interrelation of the groups in constructing a highway has been developed over time, and there are general expectations as to the interaction. There are also generalized expectations as to how politicians, contractors, newspapermen, bankers, and the like will utilize the highway situation in playing their particular games. In fact, the knowledge that a banker will play like a banker and a newspaperman like a newspaperman is an important part of what makes the situation calculable and permits the players to estimate its possibilities for their own action in their particular game.

While it might seem that the engineers of the department of public works were the appropriate protagonists for the highway grid, as a general activity it presents opportunities and threats to a wide range of other players who see in the situation consequences and possibilities undreamed of by the engineers. Some general public expectation of the limits of the conduct of the players and of a desirable outcome does provide bounds to the scramble. This public expectation is, of course, made active through the interested solicitation of newspapers, politicians, civic leaders, and others who see in it material for accomplishing their particular purposes and whose structured roles in fact require the mobilization of broad publics. In a sense the group struggle that Arthur Bentley described in his *Process of Government* is a drama that local publics have been taught to view with a not uncritical taste. The instruction of this taste has been the vocation and business of some of the contending parties. The existence of some kind of over-all public puts general restraints on gamesmanship beyond the norms of the particular games. However, for the players these are to all intents as much a part of the "facts of life" of the game as the sun and the wind.

It is perhaps the existence of some kind of a general public, however rudimentary, that most clearly differentiates the local territorial system from a natural ecology. The five-acre woodlot in which the owls and the field mice, the oaks and the acorns, and other flora and fauna have evolved a balanced system has no public opinion, however rudimentary. The co-operation is an unconscious affair. For much of what goes on in the local territorial system co-operation is equally unconscious and perhaps, but for the occasional social scientist, unnoticed. This unconscious co-operation, however, like that of the five-acre woodlot, produces results. The ecology of games in the local territorial system accomplishes unplanned but largely functional results. The games and their players mesh in their particular pursuits to bring about over-all results; the territorial system is fed and ordered. Its inhabitants are rational within limited areas and, pursuing the ends of these areas, accomplish socially functional ends.

While the historical development of largely unconscious co-operation between the special games in the territorial system gets certain routine, over-all functions performed, the problem of novelty and breakdown must be dealt with. Here it would seem that, as in the natural ecology, random adjustment and piecemeal innovation are the normal methods of response. The need or cramp in the system presents itself to the players of the games as an opportunity for them to exploit or a menace to be overcome. Thus a transportation crisis in, say, the threatened abandonment of commuter trains by a railroad will bring forth the players of a wide range of games who will see in the situation opportunity for gain or loss in the outcome. While over-all considerations will appear in the discussion, the frame of reference and the interpretation of the event will be largely determined by the game the interested parties are principally involved in. Thus a telephone executive who is president of the local chamber of commerce will be playing a civic association, general business game with concern for the principal dues-payers of the chamber but with a constant awareness of how his handling of this crisis will advance him in his particular league. The politicians, who might be expected to be protagonists of the general interest, may indeed be so, but the sphere of their activity and the glasses through which they see the problem will be determined in great part by the way they see the issue affecting their political game. The generality of this game is to a great extent that of the politician's calculus of votes and interests important to his and his side's success. To be sure, some of what Walter Lippmann has called "the public philosophy" affects both politicians and other game-players. This indicates the existence of roles and norms of a larger, vaguer game with a relevant audience that has some sense of cricket. This potentially mobilizable audience is not utterly without importance, but it provides no sure or adequate basis for support in the particular game that the politician or anyone else is playing. Instead of a set of norms to structure enduring role-playing, this audience provides a cross-pressure for momentary aberrancy from gamesmanship or constitutes just another hazard to be calculated in one's play.

In many cases the territorial system is impressive in the degree of intensity of its particular games, its banks, its newspapers, its downtown stores, its manufacturing companies, its contractors, its churches, its politicians, and its other differentiated, structured, goal-oriented activities. Games go on within the territory, occasionally extending beyond it, though centered in it. But, while the particular games show clarity of goals and intensity, few, if any, treat the territory as their proper object. The protagonists of things in particular are well organized and know what they are about; the protagonists of things in general are few, vague, and weak. Immense staff work will go into the development of a Lincoln Square project, but the twenty-two counties of metropolitan New York have few spokesmen for their over-all common interest and not enough staff to give these spokesmen more substance than that required for a "do-gooding" newspaper editorial. The Port of New York Authority exhibits a disciplined self-interest and a vigorous drive along the lines of its developed historic role. However, the attitude of the Port Authority toward the general problems of the metropolitan area is scarcely different than that of any private corporation. It confines its corporate good citizenship to the contribution of funds for surveys and studies and avoids acceptance of broader responsibility. In fact, spokesmen for the Port vigorously reject the need for any superior level of structured representation of metropolitan interests. The common interest, if such there be, is to be realized through institutional interactions rather than through the self-conscious rationality of a determinate group charged with its formulation and attainment. Apart from the newspaper editorial, the occasional politician, and a few civic leaders the general business of the metropolitan area is scarcely anybody's business, and, except for a few, those who concern themselves with the general problems are pursuing hobbies and causes rather than their own business.

The lack of over-all institutions in the territorial system and the weakness of those that exist insure that co-ordination is largely ecological rather than a matter of conscious rational contriving. In the metropolitan area in most cases there are no over-all economic or social institutions. People are playing particular games, and their playgrounds are less or more than the metropolitan area. But even in a city where the municipal corporation provides an apparent over-all government, the appearance is deceptive. The politicians who hold the offices do not regard themselves as governors of the municipal territory but largely as mediators or players in a particular game that makes use of the other inhabitants. Their roles, as they conceive them, do not approach those of the directors of a TVA developing a territory. The ideology of local government is a highly limited affair in which the office-holders respond to demands and mediate conflicts. They play politics, and politics is vastly different from government if the latter is conceived as the rational, responsible ordering of the community. In part, this is due to the general belief that little government is necessary or that government is a congery of services only different from others because it is paid for by taxes and provided for by civil servants. In part, the separation of economics from politics eviscerates the formal theory of government of most of the substance of social action. Intervention in the really important economic order is by way of piecemeal exception and in deviation from the supposed norm of the separation of politics and economics. This ideal of separation has blocked the development of a theory of significant government action and reduced the politician to the role of registerer of pressure rather than responsible governor of a local political economy. The politics of the community becomes a different affair from its government, and its government is so structured as to provide the effective actors in it neither a sense of general responsibility nor the roles calling for such behavior.

The community vaguely senses that there ought to be a government. This is evidenced in the nomination by newspapers and others of particular individuals as members of a top leadership, a "they" who are periodically called upon to solve community problems and meet community crises. Significantly, the "they" usually are made up of people holding private, not public, office. The pluralism of the society has separated political, ecclesiastical, economic, and social hierarchies from one another so that the ancient union of lords spiritual and temporal is disrupted. In consequence, there is a marked distinction between the status of the holders of political office and the status of the "they" of the newspapers and the power elite of a C. Wright Mills or a Floyd Hunter. The politicians have the formal governmental office that might give them responsible governing roles. However, their lack of status makes it both absurd and presumptuous that they should take themselves so seriously. Who are they to act as lords of creation? Public expectation neither empowers nor demands that they should assume any such confident pose as top community leaders. The latter position is reserved for a rather varying group (in some communities well defined and clear-cut, in others vague and amorphous) of holders for the most part of positions of private power, economic, social, and ecclesiastical. This group, regarded as the top leadership of the community, and analogous to the top management of a corporation, provides both a sense that there are gods in the heavens whose will, if they exercise it, will take care of the community's problems and a set of demons whose misrule accounts for the evil in the world. The "they" fill an office left vacant by the dethronement of absolutism and aristocracy. Unlike the politicians in that "they" are only partially visible and of untested powers, the top leadership provides a convenient rationale for explaining what goes on or does not go on in the community. It is comforting to think that the executive committee of the bourgoisie is exploiting the community or that the beneficent social and economic leaders are wearying themselves and their digestions with civic luncheons in order to bring parking to a congested city.

Usually the question is raised as to whether *de facto* there is a set of informal power-holders running things. A related question is whether community folklore holds that there is, that there should be, and what these informal power-holders should do. Certainly, most newspapermen and other professional "inside dopesters" hold that there is a "they." In fact, these people operate largely as court chroniclers of the doings of the "they." The "they," because they are "they," are newsworthy and fit into a ready-made theory of social causation that is vulgarized widely. However, the same newspaperman who could knowingly open his "bird book" and give you a run-down on the local "Who's Who" would probably with equal and blasphemous candor tell you that "they" were not doing a thing about the city and that "they" were greatly to be blamed for sitting around talking instead of getting things done. Thus, as with most primitive tribes, the idols are both worshiped and beaten, at least verbally. Public and reporters alike are relieved to believe both that there is a "they" to make civic life explicable and also to be held responsible for what occurs. This belief in part creates the role of top leadership and demands that it somehow be filled. It seems likely that there is a social-psychological table of organization of a community that must be filled in order to remove anxieties. Gordon Childe has remarked that man seems to need as much to adjust to an unseen, socially created spiritual environment as to the matter-of-fact world of the senses.

The community needs to believe that there are spiritual fathers, bad or good, who can deal with the dark: in the Middle Ages the peasants combated a plague of locusts by a high Mass and a procession of the clergy who damned the grasshoppers with bell, book, and candle. The Hopi Indians do a rain dance to overcome a drought. The harassed citizens of the American city mobilize their influentials at a civic luncheon to perform the equivalent and exorcise slums, smog, or unemployment. We smile at the medievals and the Hopi, but our own practices may be equally magical. It is interesting to ask under what circumstances one resorts to DDT and irrigation and why. To some extent it is clear that the ancient and modern practice of civic magic ritual is functional—functional in the same sense as the medicinal placebo. Much of human illness is benign; if the sufferer will bide his time, it will pass. Much of civic ills also cure themselves if only people can be kept from tearing each other apart in the stress of their anxieties. The locusts and the drought will pass. They almost always have.

While ritual activities are tranquilizing anxieties, the process of experimentation and adaptation in the social ecology goes on. The piecemeal responses of the players and the games to the challenges presented by crises provide the social counterpart to the process of evolution and natural selection. However, unlike the random mutation of the animal kingdom, much of the behavior of the players responding within the perspectives of their games is self-conscious and rational, given their ends in view. It is from the over-all perspective of the unintended contribution of their actions to the forming of a new or the restoration of the old ecological balance of the social system that their actions appear almost as random and lacking in purposive plan as the adaptive behavior of the natural ecology.

Within the general area of unplanned, unconscious social process technological areas emerge that are so structured as to promote rational, goal-oriented behavior and meaningful experience rather than mere happenstance. In these areas group activity may result in cumulative knowledge and self-corrective behavior. Thus problem-solving in the field of public health and sanitation may be at a stage far removed from the older dependence on piecemeal adjustment and random functional innovation. In this sense there are areas in which society, as Julian Huxley suggests in his *The Meaning of Evolution,* has gone beyond evolution. However, these are as yet isolated areas in a world still swayed by magic and, for the most part, carried forward by the logic of unplanned, undirected historical process.

It is not surprising that the members of the "top leadership" of the territorial system should seem to be largely confined to ritual and ceremonial roles. "Top leadership" is usually conceived in terms of status position rather than specifiable roles in social action. The role of a top leader is ill defined and to a large degree unstructured. It is in most cases a secondary role derived from a primary role as corporation executive, wealthy man, powerful ecclesiastic, holder of high social position, and the like. The top-leadership role is derivative from the other and is in most cases a result rather than a cause of status. The primary job is bank president, or president of Standard Oil; as such, one is naturally picked, nominated, and recognized as a member of the top leadership. One seldom forgets that one's primary role, obligation, and source of rational conduct is in terms of one's business. In fact, while one is on the whole pleased at the recognition that membership in the top leadership implies—much as one's wife would be pleased to be included among the ten best-dressed women—he is somewhat concerned about just what the role requires in the expenditure of time and funds. Furthermore, one has a suspicion that he may not know how to dance and could make a fool of himself before known elite and unknown, more general publics. All things considered, however, it is probably a good thing for the business, the contacts are important, and the recognition will be helpful back home, in both senses. In any event, if one's committee service or whatever concrete activity "top leadership" implies proves wearing or unsatisfactory, or if it interferes with business, one can always withdraw.

A fair gauge of the significance of top-leadership roles is the time put into them by the players and the institutionalized support represented by staff. Again and again the interviewer is told that the president of such-and-such an organization is doing a terrific job and literally knocking himself out for such-and-such a program. On investigation a "terrific job" turns out to be a few telephone calls and, possibly, three luncheons a month. The standard of "terrific job" obviously varies widely from what would be required in the business role.

In the matter of staffing, while the corporation, the church, and the government are often equipped in depth, the top-leadership job of port promotion may have little more than a secretary and an agile newspaperman equipped to ghost-write speeches for the boss. While there are cases where people in top-leadership positions make use of staff from their own businesses and from the legal mill with which they do business, this seems largely confined to those top-leadership undertakings that have a direct connection with their business. In general, top-leadership roles seem to involve minor investments of time, staff, and money by territorial elites. The absence of staff and the emphasis on publicity limit the capacity of top leadership for sustained rational action.

Where top leaderships have become well staffed, the process seems as much or more the result of external pressures than of its own volition. Of all the functions of top leadership, that of welfare is best staffed. Much of this is the result of the pressure of the professional social worker to organize a concentration of economic and social power sufficient to permit him to do a job. It is true, of course, that the price of organizing top leadership and making it manageable by the social workers facilitated a reverse control of themselves—a control of whose galling nature Hunter gives evidence. An amusing sidelight on the organization of the "executive committee of the bourgeoisie" is the case of the Cleveland Fifty Club. This club, supposedly, is made up of the fifty most important men in Cleveland. Most middling and even upper executives long for the prestige recognition that membership confers. Reputedly, the Fifty Club was organized by Brooks Emery, while he was director of the Cleveland Council on World Affairs, to facilitate the taxation of business to support that organization. The lead time required to get the august members of the Fifty Club together and their incohesiveness have severely limited its possibilities as a power elite. Members who have tried to turn it to such a purpose report fairly consistent failure.

The example of the Cleveland Fifty Club, while somewhat extreme, points to the need on the part of certain activities in the territorial system for a top leadership under whose auspices they can function. A wide variety of civic undertakings need to organize top prestige support both to finance and to legitimate their activities. The staff man of a bureau of municipal research or the Red Feather Agency cannot proceed on his own; he must have the legitimatizing sponsorship of top influentials. His task may be self-assigned, his perception of the problem and its solution may be his own, but he cannot gain acceptance without mobilizing the influentials. For the success of his game he must assist in creating the game of top leadership. The staff man in the civic field is the typical protagonist of things in general—a kind of entrepreneur of ideas. He fulfils the same role in his area as the stock promoter of the twenties or the Zeckendorfs of urban redevelopment. Lacking both status and a confining organizational basis, he has a socially valuable mobility between the specialized games and hierarchies in the territorial system. His success in the negotiation of a port authority not only provides a plus for his taxpayers federation or his world trade council but may provide a secure and lucrative job for himself.

Civic staff men, ranging from chamber of commerce personnel to college professors and newspapermen, are in varying degrees interchangeable and provide an important network of communication. The staff men in the civic agencies play similar roles to the Cohens and Corcorans in Washington. In each case a set of telephone numbers provides special information and an effective lower-echelon interaction. Consensus among interested professionals at the lower level can result in action programs from below that are bucked up to the prestige level of legitimitization. As the Cohens and Corcorans played perhaps the most general and inclusive game in the Washington bureaucracy, so their counterparts in the local territorial system are engaged in the most general action game in their area. Just as the Cohens and Corcorans had to mobilize an effective concentration of top brass to move a program into the action stage, so their counterparts have to mobilize concentrations of power sufficient for their purposes on the local scene.

In this connection it is interesting to note that foundation grants are being used to hire displaced New Deal bureaucrats and college professors in an attempt to organize the influentials of metropolitan areas into self-conscious governing groups. Professional chamber of commerce executives, immobilized by their orthodox ideology, are aghast to see their members study under the planners and heretics from the dogmas of free-enterprise fundamentalism. The attempt to transform the metropolitan appearance of disorder into a tidy territory is a built-in predisposition for the self-constituted staff of the embryonic top metropolitan management. The major disorder that has to be overcome before all others is the lack of order and organization among the "power elite." As in the case of the social workers, there is a thrust from below to organize a "power elite" as a necessary instrument to accomplish the purposes of civic staff men. This is in many ways nothing but a part of the general groping after a territorial government capable of dealing with a range of problems that the existing feudal disintegration of power cannot. The nomination of a top leadership by newspapers and public and the attempt to create such a leadership in fact by civic technicians are due to a recognition that there is a need for a leadership with the status, capacity, and role to attend to the general problems of the territory and give substance to a public philosophy. This involves major changes in the script of the top leadership game and the self-image of its participants. In fact, the insecurity and the situational limitations of their positions in corporations or other institutions that provide the primary roles for top leaders make it difficult to give more substance to what has been a secondary role. Many members of present top leaderships are genuinely reluctant, fearful, and even morally shocked at their positions' becoming that of a recognized territorial government. While there is a general supposition that power is almost instinctively craved, there seems considerable evidence that at least in many of our territorial cultures responsibility is not. Machiavellian *virtu* is an even scarcer commodity among the merchant princes of the present than among their Renaissance predecessors. In addition, the educational systems of school and business do not provide top leaders with the inspiration or the know-how to do more than raise funds and man committees. Politics is frequently regarded with the same disgust as military service by the ancient educated Chinese.

It is possible to translate a check pretty directly into effective power in a chamber of commerce or a welfare agency. However, to translate economic power into more general social or political power, there must be an organized purchasable structure. Where such structures exist, they may be controlled or, as in the case of *condottieri*, gangsters, and politicians, their hire may be uncertain, and the hired force retains its independence. Where businessmen are unwilling or unable to organize their own political machines, they must pay those who do. Sometimes the paymaster rules; at other times he bargains with equals or superiors.

A major protagonist of things in general in the territorial system is the newspaper. Along with the welfare worker, museum director, civic technician, etc., the newspaper has an interest in terms of its broad reading public in agitating general issues and projects. As the chronicler of the great, both in its general news columns and in its special features devoted to society and business, it provides an organizing medium for elites in the territory and provides them with most of their information about things in general and not a little of inside tidbits about how individual elite members are doing. In a sense, the newspaper is the prime mover in setting the territorial agenda. It has a great part in determining what most people will be talking about, what most people will think the facts are, and what most people will regard as the way problems are to be dealt with. While the conventions of how a newspaper is to be run, and the compelling force of some events limit the complete freedom of a paper to select what events and what people its public will attend to, it has great leeway. However, the newspaper is a business and a specialized game even when its reporters are idealists and its publisher rejoices in the title "Mr. Cleveland." The paper does not accept the responsibility of a governing role in its territory. It is a power but only a partially responsible one. The span of attention of its audience and the conventions of what constitute a story give it a crusading role at most for particular projects. Nonetheless, to a large extent it sets the civic agenda.

The story is told of the mayor of a large eastern metropolis who, having visited the three capital cities of his constituents—Rome, Dublin, and Tel

Aviv—had proceeded home via Paris and Le Havre. Since his staff had neglected to meet the boat before the press, he was badgered by reporters to say what he had learned on his trip. The unfortunate mayor could not say that he had been on a junket for a good time. Luckily, he remembered that in Paris they had been having an antinoise campaign. Off the hook at last, he told the press that he thought this campaign was a good thing. This gave the newsmen something to write about. The mayor hoped this was the end of it. But a major paper felt in need of a crusade to sponsor and began to harass the mayor about the start of the local antinoise campaign. Other newspapers took up the cry, and the mayor told his staff they were for it— there had to be an antinoise campaign. In short order, businessmen's committees, psychiatrists, and college professors were mobilized to press forward on a broad front the suppression of needless noise. In vindication of administrative rationality it appeared that an antinoise campaign was on a staff list of possibilities for the mayor's agenda but had been discarded by him as politically unfeasible.

The civic technicians and the newspapers have somewhat the same relationship as congressional committee staff and the press. Many members of congressional committee staffs complain bitterly that their professional consciences are seared by the insistent pressure to seek publicity. But they contend that their committee sponsors are only impressed with research that is newsworthy. Congressional committee members point out that committees that do not get publicity are likely to go out of business or funds. The civic agency head all too frequently communicates most effectively with his board through his success in getting newspaper publicity. Many a civic ghost-writer has found his top leader converted to the cause by reading the ghosted speech he delivered at the civic luncheon reported with photographs and editorials in the press. This is even the case where the story appears in the top leader's own paper. The need of the reporters for news and of the civic technicians for publicity brings the participants of these two games together. As in the case of the congressional committee, there is a tendency to equate accomplishment with publicity. For top influentials on civic boards the news clips are an important way of keeping score. This symbiotic relation of newsmen and civic staff helps explain the heavy emphasis on ritual luncheons, committees, and news releases. The nature of the newspapers' concern with a story about people and the working of marvels and miracles puts a heavy pressure for the kind of story that the press likes to carry. It is not surprising that civic staff men should begin to equate accomplishment with their score measured in newspaper victories or that they should succumb to the temptation to impress their sponsors with publicity, salting it to their taste by flattering newspaper tributes to the sponsors themselves. Despite the built-in incapacity of newspapers to exercise a serious governing responsibility in their territories, they are for the most part the only institutions with a long-term general territorial interest. In default of a territorial political party or other institution that accepts responsibility for the formulation of a general civic agenda the newspaper is the one game that by virtue of its public and its conventions partly fills the vacuum.

A final game that does in a significant way integrate all the games in the territorial system is the social game. Success in each of the games can in varying degrees be cashed in for social acceptance. The custodians of the symbols of top social standing provide goals that in a sense give all the individual games some common denominator of achievement. While the holders of top social prestige do not necessarily hold either top political or economic power, they do provide meaningful goals for the rest. One of the most serious criticisms of a Yankee aristocracy made by a Catholic bishop was that, in losing faith in their own social values, they were undermining the faith in the whole system of final clubs. It would be a cruel joke if, just as the hard-working upwardly mobile had worked their way to entrance, the progeny of the founders lost interest. The decay of the Union League Club in *By Love Possessed* is a tragedy for more than its members. A common game shared even by the excluded spectators gave a purpose that was functional in its time and must be replaced—hopefully, by a better one. A major motivation for seeking membership in and playing the top-leadership game is the value of the status it confers as a counter in the social game.

Neither the civic leadership game nor the social game makes the territorial ecology over into a structured government. They do, however, provide important ways of linking the individual games and make possible cooperative action on projects. Finally, the social game, in Ruth Benedict's sense, in a general way patterns the culture of the territorial ecology and gives all the players a set of vaguely shared aspirations and common goals.


# POWER AND COMMUNITY STRUCTURE

## PETER H. ROSSI


THIS PAPER DEALS WITH some structural characteristics of local communities which are relevant to their power structure and decision making processes. The ideas presented constitute a theory both in the sense of a conceptual scheme and in the sense of a set of propositions, albeit only loosely interrelated. The theory has its origins both in the growing body of

Reprinted from *Midwest Journal of Political Science,* IV, No. 4 (November, 1960), 390–400, by permission of the author and of Wayne State University Press.

A revised version of a paper delivered at the 1959 Annual Meeting of the American Sociological Association, Chicago, Illinois, September, 1959. Preparation of this paper and some of the author's research cited were supported by a grant from the Social Science Research Council, hereby gratefully acknowledged.

literature on the power structures of local communities and in the field experiences of the author.

The immediate impetus to the construction of this theory was a growing dissatisfaction with the non-cumulative character of the field to which it purports to apply. Case study after case study of communities has appeared within the past few years, each contributing its part to a body of knowledge best characterized by the statement, "It is different here than elsewhere."[1] The author often inserts a particular comparison somewhere into his paper: Hunter's Regional City, Schulze's Cibola, Rossi's Mediana, and so forth. Each author owns his own town, defending it from the erroneous and somewhat heretical conceptualizations of others much the way a feudal lord defends the integrity of the local patron saint against the false counterclaims of nearby realms.

One firm generalization emerges from the literature: the power structure of local communities and the decision making processes to be found therein show a significant range of variation. This range can be only partly dependent on the differences in research technology employed by each researcher, for the same researchers have found different patterns in different communities. No firm generalizations emerge, however, concerning the sources of these variations.

There are two main reasons for the failure of generalizations of this sort

---

1. An early bibiographic review was published by the author as "Community Decision Making" in *The Administrative Science Quarterly*, I (March, 1957), 415–43. An incomplete list of more recent studies follows:

Warner Bloomberg, *The Structure of Power in Stackton* (Unpublished Ph.D dissertation, University of Chicago, 1960). James S. Coleman, *Community Conflict* (Glencoe, Illinois: Free Press, 1957). William H. Form, "Organized Labor's Place in the Community Power Structure," *Industrial and Labor Relations Review*, XII (July, 1959), 526–39. William H. Form and William V. D'Antonio, "Integration and Cleavage Among Community Influentials in Two Border Cities," *American Sociological Review*, XXIV (December, 1959), 804–14. Orrin E. Klapp and Vincent L. Padgett, "Power Structure and Decision Making a Mexican Border City," *American Journal of Sociology*, LXV (January, 1960), 400–406. Delbert C. Miller, "Decision Making Cliques in Community Power Structure," *American Journal of Sociology*, LXIV (November, 1958), 299–310. Delbert C. Miller, "Industry and Community Power Structures," *American Sociological Review*, XXIII (February, 1958), 9–15. Roland J. Pellegrin and Charles H. Coates, "Absentee Owned Corporations and Community Power Structure," *American Journal of Sociology*, LXI (March, 1956), 413–19. Nelson W. Polsby, "Three Problems in the Analysis of Community Power," *American Sociological Review*, XXIV (December, 1959), 796–803. Nelson W. Polsby, "The Sociology of Community Power: A Reassessment," *Social Forces*, XXXVII (March, 1959), 232–36. Edwin H. Rhyne, "Political Parties and Decision Making in Three Southern Counties," *American Political Science Review*, LII (December, 1958), 1091–1107. Peter H. Rossi, "Industry and Community," National Opinion Research Center, Report No. 64, October, 1957 (mimeo.). Peter H. Rossi and Phillips Cutright, "The Political Organization of an Industrial Community," in Morris Janowitz and Heinz Eulau (eds.), *Community Political Systems* (Glencoe, Illinois: Free Press, 1960, forthcoming). Peter H. Rossi and Robert A. Dentler, *The Politics of Urban Renewal* (Glencoe, Illinois: Free Press, 1960, forthcoming). Robert O. Schulze, "The Role of Economic Dominants in Community Power Structure," *American Sociological Review*, XXIII (February, 1958), 3–9. Arthur J. Vidich and Joe Bensman, *Small Town in Mass Society* (Princeton, New Jersey: Princeton University Press, 1959).

to emerge. First, with few exceptions, comparative studies are rare. Most studies are concerned with establishing a pattern within one particular community, setting it off at best against one other community. Studies in which a large number of communities are systematically contrasted with comparable communities are the sources from which desired generalizations will emerge. The empirical relationships between power structures and other community social structures will provide the data.

The second main reason lies in the inadequacy of social theory. Despite the many community studies which have been undertaken since the classic Booth study of London, we are still lacking a conceptual scheme specifying with some degree of clarity what are the important elements in community structure. Indeed, the operational form that Hunter gave to the conception of community power structure will probably remain as his greatest contribution.[2] Before Hunter only the Lynds[3] paid attention to this feature of social structure, and this interest of the Lynds did not start a tradition because they were unable to communicate the techniques by which they singled out the "X" family as the dominant center in Middletown. After Hunter laid out his quasi-sociometry, community studies experienced a revival, all centered around some modification of his device.

Of course without a conceptual scheme, comparative studies are difficult to plan and to achieve. What should the researcher and his team look for? He now knows that to define the powerful he can employ some modification of Hunter's balloting. The census and other published sources provide additional ways of classifying communities, but these provide at best only indirect indicators of social organization, and the researcher must still have a rationale for choosing among the possible indicators. Researchers are therefore forced to collect their own data. To do so obviously requires some *a priori* conceptions as to what is important. The vicious circle is closed: comparative community studies are one of the important sources of ideas concerning the structural concomitants of variations in power and decision making, but properly to conduct such studies requires some framework for the collection of such data.[4]

## Gaps in the Conception of Community Structures

To characterize communities we need some sort of framework which can guide observations, alerting the researcher to the crucial elements in the structure of the community. What form should such a conceptual scheme take? Should we construct some grand scheme which would be the all

2. Floyd A. Hunter, *Community Power Structure* (Chapel Hill, North Carolina: University of North Carolina Press, 1952).

3. Robert S. and Helen M. Lynd, *Middletown in Transition* (New York: Harcourt Brace and Company, 1937).

4. An important exception to this characterization is the studies undertaken at Michigan State University by C. P. Loomis, W. Form and others.

around best way of characterizing communities or should we work piecemeal, building one scheme for one problem and another scheme for another? It is my conviction that the latter path will prove most fruitful: namely, the construction of schemes which are specific to the particular substantive problem at hand. Thus the best way of characterizing communities for the purpose of understanding fluoridation controversies in principle may be different from the best way for understanding some other community process.

Even if one were to grant the soundness of this notion of specific theories for specific purposes, there still remains a considerable problem in the construction of such theories. Although we have made much progress through the work of the human ecologists in classifying cities according to their economic functions and their relations to their environments, we have done little with the internal social organization of communities. In this last respect, perhaps the best known structural characteristic of communities is along stratification lines. A large enough body of research and thinking has gone into the definition of stratification both on the purely nominal level and on the operational level for the researcher to have a fairly clear idea of how to use this term, how to measure stratification systems, and how to locate the positions within such systems of particular individuals or groups. Similar amounts of thinking and effort have not been expended on invention of an appropriate methodology for studying other kinds of organized relationships among the members of a community. Although on the abstract level sociometric devices might seem useful tools in the study of large communities, on the empirical level they prove impractical.

The gap in the conception of community structure is most serious in the area of social organization. This paper is intended to fill in part of this conceptual hiatus by constructing a scheme for classifying the political structures of local communities. The scheme purports to be useful specifically for understanding variations in power structures. Hopefully it may also turn out to be of some utility in the study of closely related community characteristics.


## A Conceptual Scheme for the Political Structure of
## Local Communities

The purpose of the scheme to be described here is to account for the variations in power structures to be found among American local communities. It may also prove of some utility in other areas, for example, community conflicts. The general thesis underlying the scheme is a simple one: the pattern taken by the power structure of a community is a function of the kind of political life to be found therein. My reasons for postulating this relationship are also simple and somewhat obvious: the political institutions of a community are the ultimate locus of the decisions that are binding on the total community. Hence much of the power exercised is focused on the government institutions of the local community.

For our present purposes, it is useful to regard the political life of a community as occurring at two different levels, interrelated but to some degree independent. On the one hand, there is a set of governmental institutions manned by officials and employees with defined functions and spheres of authority and competence. On the other hand, there is the electorate, the body of citizens with voting rights, organized to some degree into political parties. We expect that phenomena appearing on each of these levels independently influence the forms taken by community power structures.

On the institutional level, there are several characteristics of local government that are of some consequence. First, communities vary according to the degree to which the roles of officials are *professionalized*. In many communities, mayors and city councilmen and often other officials are employed in their official capacities only part time and lack the opportunity to become fully engrossed in these roles. At the other extreme, some communities employ professionally trained officials—city managers, school superintendents, etc.—who are full time employees expecting to remain in their occupation— although not in any particular post—for long periods of time. In communities where local officials exercise their functions on a part time basis and where the qualifications for incumbency are not exacting, the incumbents are less likely to segregate their official roles from their other roles and hence extra-official considerations are more likely to play roles of some importance in their decisions. Thus the informal cabal which ran Springdale, as described by Vidich and Bensman,[5] hardly distinguish between their roles as city fathers and their roles as businessmen and professionals. At the other extreme are the professional politicians who run Chicago, whose independence is curbed very little.

A second important structural characteristic of local government refers to the rules by which officials are selected. Two aspects of electoral rules are significant. Electoral rules can either retard or facilitate the development of enduring political alignments in the community, and the latter are important determinants of the forms of decision making. In this respect, the crucial differences lie between communities which have non-partisan and communities which have partisan elections. Non-partisan electoral rules discourage the development of enduring political alignments by reducing the advantages to candidates of appearing on slates, whereas partisan elections facilitate cooperation among candidates and the drawing of clear lines between opposing slates of candidates. It should be noted in this connection that primaries are in effect non-partisan elections in communities which are predominantly Democratic or Republican.[6]

---

5. Vidich and Bensman, *op. cit.*

6. Non-partisan elections operate to the benefit of the highly organized political minority. Hence, usually, non-partisan elections operate to the benefit of the white collar groups in industrial communities and to the benefit of the Democratic Party in middle class suburbs.

Another structural characteristic which tends to reduce the importance of political organizations is the rule concerning the number of officials elected by popular vote. Short ballots on which only a few candidates compete for the major offices tend to reduce organizational importance by lowering the benefits to candidates of cooperation with each other.

These structural characteristics of the governmental institutions of the local community underlie the ability of these institutions to develop an independence of their own and also indicate the extent to which conflicts within the community are manifested in the political realm or in some other fashion.

Moving now to the level of the electorate and its organization, there are two important dimensions to be considered. First, we must consider the political homogeneity of the electorate, roughly defined as the extent to which the community is divided equally or unequally among the contending political factions of the community. The more unequally the community is divided, the less likely are open political struggles to be the major expressions of clashes of interest and the more likely is decision making to be a prerogative of a "cozy few."

Borrowing from Gerhard Lenski, a second characteristic of the electorate might be called "political crystallization": the extent to which the lines of political cleavage within the community coincide with major social structural differentiations. In this connection the crucial modes of social structural differentiation are along class and status lines. The more political lines coincide with class and status lines, the more likely are community clashes to take a political form. These are important lines of differentiation within communities because they are likely to endure over time.[7] Political differences which coincide with class and status differences are for these reasons likely to be reinforced by the double factors of differential association and connection with important interests.

If we now consider the entire set of community characteristics distinguished here, we see that they may be conceived of as indicators of two more abstract attributes of communities: first, the institutional indicators express the degree of segregation of political institutions from other community institutions; second, the indicators relating to the electorate reflect the extent to which partisan politics is a crucial arena for the important decision making within the community.

It is important to note that these characteristics of communities can be easily translated into operational forms. The city charter can tell us how officials are elected and whether their jobs are full or part time. Election statistics and survey research can tell us the degree of political homogeneity and political crystallization.

---

7. On a large space scale—i.e., for regions and nations—regional differences would also play important roles, but since the micro-regional differences in the American city tend to be wiped out quickly by residential mobility, they play only a minor role within communities.

Two broad hypotheses can be formulated at this point. (1) The more segregated are political roles from other roles played by incumbent officials, the more independent the governmental structure of a community from other institutional structures. (2) The more heterogeneous the electorate and the greater the degree of political crystallization, the more important the governmental institutions as loci for important decision making.

## Implications for Community Power Structures

The studies of community power structures have universally found the upper levels of the occupational hierarchy to occupy prominent power positions. In no city—even heavily working class Stackton—have proprietors, managers, and professional men played insignificant parts. Often enough some members of these groups do not play as prominent a part as others, even though they are as wealthy and as important in the economic life of the city, but in all cities members of these groups were to be found in some kind of inner circle.

The disagreement among researchers concerns two important matters. First, there is disagreement over the pattern of power, with some researchers preferring the monolith as their model and others preferring polyliths or more complicated forms. Second, there is disagreement over the roles played by public officials and voluntary associations. Hardly anything could be written about Chicago, Stackton, or Philadelphia without reference to the mayor's office and other top level public officials. In contrast, in Regional City and some of the towns studied by C. P. Loomis and his research workers, public officials and often labor leaders appear as minor and insignificant personages. It should be noted that these two kinds of disagreements among researchers are related. A monolithic model for a power structure generally goes along with a very subordinate role for voluntary associations and public officials. Thus, in Hunter's Regional City public officials are explicitly viewed as the handmaidens of the elite group, and labor leaders are scarcely worth mentioning.

A polylithic power structure tends to mean a number of small monoliths each centering around a particular sort of activity. Thus in industrial Stackton, the civic associations and community service organizations were the preserves of the business community, whereas local government was safe in the hands of professional politicians resting on the mass base of the Democratic Party and its heavy support from among ethnic groups of relatively recent arrival from abroad. Indeed, respondents rarely reported that any one individual was powerful in all spheres of community life.

To some degree the disagreements among researchers on the forms taken by the power structures in communities and the place to be accorded public officials and associational leaders are functions of the different research techniques employed. Some approaches preclude the finding of polylithic power structures. However, in much larger part, the differences among researchers are functions of "reality," representing major ways in which communities *in fact* differ. My general thesis is that these differences are functions of the differences among communities in their political structures.

If we look carefully at the studies of community power structure we may discern the following types:

(1) *Pyramidal.* Lines of power tend to have their ultimate source in one man or a very small number of men. Decision making tends to be highly centralized, with lower echelons mainly carrying out major policy decisions made by the small group at the apex.

Examples: Middletown, Regional City

(2) *Caucus rule.* Lines of power tend to end in a relatively large group of men who make decisions through consensus. Decision making tends to be a matter of manufacturing consent among the "cozy few" who make up the caucus. Typical power structure in the small town or dormitory suburb.

Examples: Springdale, Mediana

(3) *Polylith.* Separate power structures definable for major spheres of community activity. Typically, local government in the hands of professional politicians backed by the solidary strength of voluntary associations, with the community service organizations in the hands of the business and professional subcommunity.

(4) *Amorphous.* No discernible enduring pattern of power. Logical residual category. No examples.

Note that the first two types of power structures are very similar, differing only in the number of decision makers who share power among themselves. The major differentiation is between the first two types wherein lines of power tend to converge and the last two types wherein lines of power tend to diverge.

The divergence of power lines has its source in the existence of the possibility for occupational groups other than business and professional to occupy positions of importance within major community institutions. This occurs typically when there is political crystallization in a community which is heterogeneous class wise or status wise. When the lower status or class levels have a political party representing them which has a chance to get into office, there is the possibility that public office can become one of the important sources of power.

The conditions under which the political parties have a vigorous life are defined by the structural features described earlier. Under partisan electoral laws, when officials are professionalized, when either the majority of the electorate favor the underdog party or when the parties are balanced in strength, then the political institutions and public officials assume a position of importance within the power structure of the community.

Another way of putting this thesis is to say that the leaders of the dominant economic institutions ordinarily wield power, but they are forced to take others into account when popular democratic rules allow the lower levels of the community an opportunity to place their representatives in public office. The elements of the community political structure we have distinguished here are those which facilitate the development of governmental independence from the business and professional community.

The general hypothesis may now be stated more precisely, as follows: *in communities with partisan electoral procedures, whose officials are full time functionaries, where party lines tend to coincide with class and status lines and where the party favored by the lower class and status groups has some good chance of getting elected to office, community power structures tend to be polylithic rather than monolithic:* Since these characteristics of community political structures are to some unknown degree independent of one another, different combinations of such characteristics can appear empirically. The patterns in such communities cannot be deduced from this hypothesis since we do not specify the weights to be assigned to each characteristic.

There are further expectations implied in the general hypothesis. Some examples follow:

(1) Homogeneous middle class communities, for example, dormitory suburbs and the like, will tend to have monolithic power structures, since the class basis for countervailing political power does not exist.

(2) In communities where the lower class party has a clear majority there will be moves on the part of the business and professional community to introduce structural changes in city government to undermine this majority, as for example, nonpartisan elections, short ballot, and the like.

(3) In polylithic communities, city government and private community organizations try to limit the sphere of each other's operations by moving more and more functions into their own spheres of authority.

(4) In communities with monolithic power structures, conflicts tend to take on the character of mass revolts in which small incidents are magnified out of proportion because there are no regularized means for the expression of conflict.[8]

(5) Historically, the development of voluntary civic associations may be interpreted as a reaction to the loss of local political power by high status groups. Since these community organizations were not governed by the mass vote of the lower class groups, high status groups could keep control over them.

---

8. See Coleman, *op. cit.*

Additional similar propositions may be generated from the basic hypothesis set forth in this paper. Although I believe that such propositions will be upheld in general by empirical data, I am also sure that considerable modifications will be made in them.

## Conclusions

To sum up, I have presented in this paper a conceptual scheme which provides a way of classifying the political structures of local communities. I have also tried to spell out how these political features may modify the power structures to be found in such communities. The utility of the scheme obviously requires for testing empirical data generated by comparative community studies. Though I have no doubt that the hypotheses presented here will at best suffer considerable modification when confronted with such data, I hope they will serve the purpose of providing some impetus for comparative community studies.

# VII

## PROBLEMS OF MANAGEMENT

The mayor of today's large city occupies a position his predecessors would in some ways have envied. At last most legislatures have ceased to be meddlesome, and the cities in general have a degree of home rule that is adequate for most of their purposes. The authority of the mayor has been vastly strengthened. There are still many independent and quasi-independent offices and bodies, but these are fewer than before. In the city government proper the mayor is now very strong indeed: he appoints department heads, who are accountable directly to him, he makes up the budget, which the council does little more than approve; and he has the advantage of a large, competent, professional staff. The voters—most of them—want and expect government that is honest, impartial, and efficient, and the mayor knows that he will generally be applauded if he resists unreasonable demands from special interests and condemned if he does not.

These very improvements in the mayor's situation have created their own characteristic difficulties, however. For one thing, committed to good government and with no patronage or other "gravy" to dispense, the present-day mayor cannot exercise power as informally as the old-fashioned boss could. What he cannot do by an exercise of formal authority or by salesmanship, he cannot do at all. Thus, despite gains in his formal authority, his net influence position may in some matters be weaker than before. Moreover, since the mayor is supposed to be impartial and even nonpartisan (this is often expected of him even when he is elected on a partisan basis), he cannot let narrowly political criteria guide him in making policy decisions. The interest of the community "as a whole," which his good government supporters tell him should replace "politics," turns out, however, to have no concrete meaning in important and controversial matters. Thus, although he is not permitted to rely on political criteria, he cannot find others that are adequate.

The consequence of all this is that he is likely to manage the routine business of the city fairly well but to lack force and vision in dealing with the city's largest and longest-run problems. This accounts, perhaps, for the widespread concern about the organization and functioning of "top management" in the city government. This concern is especially evident with respect to two problems: (1) how to organize the executive branch so that the mayor can maintain control over it and make it an effective instrument for carrying out a comprehensive program of action on matters of fundamental importance, and (2) how to use the technical knowledge of planners and other professionals to frame a comprehensive program that represents the interest of the community "as a whole." It is with these two general problems that most of the readings in this Section deal.

The article by Seymour Freedgood, a *Fortune* writer, is particularly valuable because it gives a general review of current trends and problems in big city management from the perspective of these underlying political changes. The big city, Freedgood says, is better managed (he is evidently referring to routine matters) than many corporations. The real problem today is not to secure honesty and efficiency—these may generally be taken for granted now—but to put the mayor in a position where he can and will exercise leadership. In accomplishing this, "good government" may be something of a handicap: the mayor may be hemmed in by experts, bureaucrats, and technical procedures. In general, big city mayors are doing fairly well with particular improvements—an expressway here or a renewal project there—but they are not thinking deeply enough about larger, longer-run problems. Planning is usually "an exercise in futility" because the mayor does not give it the necessary leadership.

The next two readings look closely at the questions of how "top management" should be organized. Charles R. Adrian describes three patterns. The council-manager system has never been tried in a large city, perhaps because it is not well suited to provide political leadership. The management cabinet plan, a second pattern, may be either a formal body or an informal group of advisers, especially personal staff members, who stand in close relation to the mayor; this pattern is in operation in New York, Philadelphia, and several other cities. The chief administrative officer system is the third pattern. This postwar development is in some ways a compromise between the council-manager and the strong-mayor plans; Adrian thinks it is likely to spread to middle-sized cities. In the future, he concludes, the problem for the large cities will be to find mayors who are willing to delegate administrative tasks to professional assistants.

The third reading of this Section takes us behind the scenes for a discussion of these matters by a big city mayor and some practicing politicians. One day in 1954 Mayor (now United States Senator) Joseph S. Clark, Jr., the reform leader of Philadelphia, sat down with the Chicago Home Rule Commission, a body of politicians and civic leaders appointed to recommend changes in the structure of the city government, to explain how he had organized his very energetic and successful administration. Clark, it will be seen, made use of a combination of devices: a cabinet, a chief administrative officer (although called managing director and given charge only of the line departments), a housing coordinator, and a strengthened planning body. Obviously he was trying hard to create an executive establishment that could deal effectively with the larger and longer-run problems of the city.

But having a well conceived and competent organization and getting a big job done are two very different things. Rexford G. Tugwell observes that the really big undertakings—vast urban renewal projects, for example— are remarkably resistant to even the largest-scale organization. The specific for this standstill phenomenon is the Moses Effect. This is the unique combination of qualities, skills, and talents that have made Robert Moses of New York a governmental institution *sui generis*. In this article, Tugwell, an old associate of Moses', explains how the Moses Effect works and why it succeeds where other large-scale organization fails. It is worth noting that he thinks the Moses Effect is probably incompatible with comprehensive planning.

The next two readings discuss the uses and limitations of planning. William H. Brown, Jr., an economist, and Charles E. Gilbert, a political scientist, tell how Philadelphia, one of the most advanced cities in planning matters, programs its capital expenditures. Political and other institutional obstacles to planning exist in Philadelphia, of course, but they are relatively unimportant. The real difficulty, Brown and Gilbert say, is intellectual, which is to say that it lies in the nature of the planning process itself. The professional planner has no intellectual procedure for establishing a set of formal criteria such as is implied by the cherished notion of the master plan. About the best that the planning agency can do, therefore, is to provide information and to encourage and make more meaningful popular consultation by supplying perspectives on benefits and costs.

In the next reading Martin Meyerson, a city planner, tries to redefine the planning function and to suggest how the planner's desire to deal comprehensively with matters can be harmonized with the politician's desire to find practical solutions for pressing problems. What is needed, he believes, is a type of planning that will give the politicians an enlarged view of the context in which they are acting and yet not be beyond the intellectual and other resources of the planners. He amplifies this "middle-range" conception of planning in terms of five more or less separate functions, one of which is not altogether unlike the traditional view of comprehensive planning.

The last two readings deal with problems of a different kind and at a lower level of hierarchy. Charles G. Sauers, Sr., for thirty years general superintendent of the Cook County (Illinois) Forest Preserve District, one of the country's notable park systems despite its nearness to a notorious political machine, gives his fellow administrators some practical tips on how to get along with politicians without losing one's professional integrity. The other reading is concerned with the lowest level of hierarchy, and specifically with the cop on the beat. It is of interest not only for what it says about recruitment, training and discipline in one of the biggest and best-run departments of our largest and perhaps best-run city (an appalling story, many will think), but also for the nature of the report itself. It was prepared by the Institute of Public Administration and is a good example of the kind of professional study on which the administration of large cities often depends.

# NEW STRENGTH IN CITY HALL

### SEYMOUR FREEDGOOD

AT THE TROUBLED CORE of the big city stands City Hall, a block-square, granite citadel heavily encrusted with myth. It was a half-century ago that Lincoln Steffens described the "shame of the cities"—the bosses, the boodlers, the job sellers, and the hopeless inefficiency of the city's housekeeping. The image persists. Most people are aware that the machines have fallen on parlous times—but they're not sure that what's left is much better. The dramatic corruption may have gone but the belief that the big city's government is a mess remains. When people look for models of municipal efficiency, it is outward, to the hinterland, that they are apt to turn; here, where "grass roots" are more visible, are the slumless smaller cities and the towns with city managers, and it is to them that most of the accolades for municipal success are directed.

The emphasis is misplaced. Where the problems are the toughest—in the big, crowded, noisy city—government has vitally transformed itself. Today the big city must rank as one of the most skillfully managed of American organizations—indeed, considering the problems it has to face, it is better managed than many U.S. corporations.

The suburbanization of the countryside has plunged America's big cities —specifically the twenty-three cities with population of 500,000 and over— into a time of crisis. Hemmed in by their hostile, booming suburbs, worried about the flight of their middle class, and hard pressed to maintain essential services for their own populations, they need, if they are to hold their own, let alone grow, top-notch leadership.

They have it. Since the 1930's, and at an accelerating rate after the

Reprinted from the November 1957 issue of *Fortune Magazine* by Special Permission; © 1957 Time Inc. The material appears also in *The Exploding Metropolis* (New York: Doubleday and Company, 1958).

second world war, the electorate in city after city has put into office as competent, hard-driving, and skillful a chief executive as ever sat in the high-backed chair behind the broad mahogany desk. At the same time they have strengthened the power of the office.

This has not been a victory for "good government." To most people, good government is primarily honest and efficient administration, and they believe that the sure way for the city to get it is to tighten civil service, eliminate patronage, and accept all the other artifacts of "scientific" government, including the council-city-manager plan. But today's big-city mayor is not a good-government man, at least in these terms, and if he ever was, he got over it a long time ago. He is a tough-minded, soft-spoken politician who often outrages good-government people, or, as the politicians have called them, the Goo-Goos.

One of the biggest threats to his leadership, indeed, is too much "good government." The big problem at City Hall is no longer honesty, or even simple efficiency. The fight for these virtues is a continuous one, of course, and Lucifer is always lurking in the hall, but most big-city governments have become reasonably honest and efficient. Today, the big problem is not good housekeeping: it is whether the mayor can provide the aggressive leadership and the positive programs without which no big city has a prayer. What is to get priority? Industrial redevelopment? More housing? (And for whom?) There is only so much money, and if hard policy decisions are not made, the city's energies will be diffused in programs "broad" but not bold.

The mayor is hemmed in. As he strives to exercise policy leadership, his power is challenged on all sides. In his own house the staff experts and the civil-service bureaucrats threaten to nibble him to death in their efforts to increase their own authority. Then there are the public "authorities." Some are single-purpose authorities—like the city housing authorities, and the sewer districts; some, like the Port of New York Authority, handle a whole range of functions. They are eminently useful institutions, but however efficient they may be, they are virtually laws unto themselves and they have severely limited the mayor's ability to rule in his own house and, more important, his ability to plan for long-range development.

The power struggle also goes on between the mayor and the state legislature, which has a controlling voice in the city's fiscal affairs, but whose membership is apportioned in favor of the rural areas. It is the rare mayor who need not make frequent trips to the state capital for additional funds, and the legislature is usually unsympathetic. Colorado's, for example, gives Denver a niggardly $2,300,000 a year in state aid for a school system of 90,000 children; right next to it, semi-rural Jefferson County, with 18,000 pupils, gets $2,400,000.

There is the continuing struggle between the mayor and the suburbs, whose people, the big city firmly believes, are welshing on their obligations to the city. The mayor must win the cooperation of his suburban counterparts if he is to do anything at all about the city's most pressing problems—

e.g., the traffic mess—and the going is grim. No one is against "saving our cities," but in this seemingly antiseptic cause there are fierce conflicts of interests and the power struggle is getting more intense.

## What Citizens Want: More

There has been a change in City Hall because there has been a change in the city itself. For the better part of a century, the core of big-city life was its immigrants—waves and waves of them, many illiterate, few English-speaking, all poor. Their grinding misery kept the machine in power at the hall. The machine fed on the immigrants, but it also helped them—with jobs, with welfare services and personal favors, with Christmas baskets and dippers of coal—and the immigrants, in turn, were generous with their votes. The 1924 Immigration Act put an end to this cycle. Reduced immigration gave the city time to absorb the earlier newcomers, reduce the language barriers, educate them and their children, and raise many of them into the middle class. This, along with federal social security and unemployment insurance, reduced the dependence of the big-city masses on the political machines. After World War II came the huge influx of southern Negroes and Puerto Ricans, but by this time the machine was beyond a real comeback.

A half-century's work by the National Municipal League, the Institute of Public Administration, and other government research groups was a big factor. They fought and in many places won the hard fight for the short ballot, which eliminates "blind" voting, and for better city charters, better budgeting, and more efficient management methods.

Better-qualified people came into government. During the unemployment of the 1930's governments could recruit talent they couldn't before. Most of the bright young men went off to Washington, but many of them went into city government too. Some now man its top administrative posts, and they have done much to raise civil-service standards.

Most important, the public began asking for more. It now demands as a natural right better-administered services—police and fire protection, water, sewerage, and all the rest—and it judges its public officials on how well they are able to satisfy this demand. It also demands services—psychiatric clinics, youth boards, air-pollution control—it never had before. City government, as a result, has been transformed into an enormous service machine, infinitely complicated to run.

## The Management Men

To many an aspirant who wouldn't have thought of city politics a generation ago, the mayoralty is now eminently worth his mettle. This has been particularly true in cities where long-standing sloth and corruption had created the possibility of a dramatic reversal; in these places an able and ambitious man might well conclude that his opportunities for spectacular, visible achievement outran those of a governor or senator. But the new mayors are more than opportunists. They come from widely different social and economic backgrounds, and they differ as widely in temperament, but all share a sense of mission: while it also happens to be good politics, they feel deeply that they should make their decisions in terms of the community-wide interest rather than the interest of any one group.

The profile of today's big-city mayor—with one difference—is quite similar to that of the chief executive of a large corporation. Typically, the mayor is a college graduate, usually with a legal or business background, and is now in his late fifties. He puts in hard, grinding hours at his desk, sometimes six or seven days a week, and his wife suffers as much as his golf game. The difference is in salary: he usually makes $20,000 to $25,000. There is also a chauffeur-driven limousine and, in some cities, an expense allowance, ranging from $2,000 (Milwaukee) to $55,000 (Chicago).

"Public relations" take a big chunk of his time. He is aggressively press-conscious, holds frequent news conferences, often appears on TV-radio with his "Report to the People"; and from his office flows a flood of releases on civic improvements. About five nights a week there are civic receptions, banquets, policy meetings, and visits with neighborhood civic groups. In between he may serve as a labor negotiator, or a member of the Civil Defense Board.

The mayor is also seeing a lot more of the city's business leaders, whose interest in urban renewal is growing steadily. Despite the fact that His Honor is likely to be a Democrat, he gets along very well with the businessmen, though he is apt to feel that they have a lot to learn about political decision-making. A City Hall man recently summed up the feelings of his fellows: "These businessmen like everything to be nice and orderly—and nonpolitical. They're getting hot now on metropolitan planning. They think it's not political! Throw them into shifting situations where there are a lot of conflicts and no firm leadership and they're completely buffaloed. It's painful to watch them trying to operate. But once there's a firm program lined up and they've bought it, they're very effective."

Above all the mayor is a politician. True, he may have risen to office on the back of a reform movement. But he is not, as happened too often in the past, a "non-political" civic leader who rallies the do-gooders, drives the rascals out of City Hall, serves for an undistinguished term or two, and then withdraws—or gets driven out—leaving the city to another cycle of corruption. Instead, he fits the qualifications of the mayors whom Lincoln Steffens called on the public to elect: "politicians working for the reform of the city with the methods of politics." His main interest is in government, not abstract virtue, and he knows that the art of government is politics.

DeLesseps Morrison of New Orleans is a notable example of a political leader who leaped into office on a reform ticket, then used the methods of politics to put his programs across. In the years since insurgents elected Mayor Morrison over opposition from the long-entrenched regulars who had run the town wide open, he has done more than demonstrate that hard-working and efficient management can change the face of a city. Morrison has consolidated the gains—in large part by his ability to turn the loose organization that first supported him into a thoroughly professional political organization, which regularly helps elect friendly councilmen. The Morrison organization, not surprisingly, is anathema to the old Democratic machine.

In Philadelphia, Richardson Dilworth and his predecessor, Mayor (now Senator) Joseph Clark, have followed the Morrison pattern up to a point. In 1952 Philadelphia civic groups wrested control of City Hall from a corrupt and contented Republican machine, and the Clark and Dilworth administrations have given the city vigorous and honest government ever since. Mayor Dilworth, in office since 1956, is making considerable headway with his programs; unlike Morrison, however, he has not yet chosen to organize his followers into a political organization that can regularly get out the vote on election day. The old-line Democrats and Republicans, as a result, have been increasingly successful in electing their own men to the council.

The new mayor, of course, does not need a dragon to fight. Indeed, some of today's best mayors are in cities that have enjoyed reasonably honest government for quite some time. Detroit's late aggressive Mayor Albert Cobo was one of these. He believed that government should be run like a business: during his eight years in office he overhauled the city's government, department by department, replacing the old, wasteful ways of doing things with machines and management systems that would do credit to any corporation.

St. Louis, Cincinnati, and Milwaukee, all with long traditions of honest government, have a remarkable trio of mayors: each wears a distinctively scholarly air, and is a pretty good politician to boot. St. Louis, once an ailing city, has found one of the ablest leaders in its history in an engineering professor, Raymond Tucker. Enthusiastically backed by the city's business leaders and the St. Louis press, Mayor Tucker has persuaded the voters to approve new taxes and public-improvement bond issues with which he has pulled the city out of the red and away from the blight. Milwaukee, a well-governed city since 1910, now has professional, mild-mannered Frank P. Zeidler as its mayor. He too has stimulated a conservative, frugal citizenry into approving needed physical improvements. Cincinnati, under council-city-manager government since 1926, has Charles Taft, a top mayor who has given the city's urban-renewal and highway programs a powerful boost.

## Bridging the Gap

The mayors of Pittsburgh and Chicago bridge the gap between the traditional machine-boss mayor and today's management-man mayor. Pittsburgh's David Lawrence and Chicago's Richard Daley are both powerful Democratic organization leaders as well as strong mayors: each has given his city increasingly good government—and a big push forward in meeting its problems—while at the same time maintaining his organization in viable if declining power. Of the two, Daley has been the bigger surprise. When he was elected many people believed he would sell City Hall to Cicero without a qualm. Instead, Daley went along to a remarkable extent in putting into effect reform legislation that tightened and improved the structure of Chicago's city government. Chicago, Senator Paul Douglas once observed, is a city with a Queen Anne front and a Mary Ann rear. That may still be the case with its government: it undoubtedly has much to do before its rear is as respectable as its front. But Daley, a man who has been known to do odd things with the queen's English, seems determined to close the gap. "We will go on," he once announced at a town-and-gown dinner of the city and the University of Chicago, "to a new high platitude of success."

## The Strong Mayor

In his drive for more power, the big-city mayor is in direct conflict with a strong trend in municipal government. This is the council-city-manager plan, which is the fastest spreading form of government among cities of 25,000 to 100,000. To many do-gooders, it is the ideal form of government for the American city, big or small. Basically, it is government by a board of directors: an elected committee decides on city policies, and the hired manager and his experts carry them out.

The system has been most successful in smaller cities—e.g., Watertown, New York (population, 35,000), whose inhabitants are for the most part homogeneous and native born, where ethnic and economic tensions are low, and where the future holds no big threats. Cities like Watertown may thrive under such government; most big cities cannot.

Their electorates seem to sense this. When asked to vote on a new city charter, they have usually settled on one providing for a strong mayor rather than committee leadership. As a result, the trend to the strong chief executive, long evident in the federal government and the urban state capitals, is now running high in the cities. Of the twenty-three largest, fourteen have adopted some kind of "strong-mayor" charter, five still vest most power in the council, and four use the council-manager plan.

Philadelphia, which is symbolic of so much of the best and worst that can happen to a city, has indicated why the major cities are choosing the strong-mayor-council rather than the council-city-manager form of government. In 1949, civic dissatisfaction with the machine was picking up so much steam that Mayor Bernard Samuel consented to the appointment of a fifteen-man bipartisan commission to draft a charter for the better government of the city. After months of study, the commissioners arrived at these alternatives:

## NEW YORK

Under the 1938 charter, drafted by a commission appointed by Mayor La Guardia, New York's mayors were given strong statutory powers, and the city council, then called the board of aldermen—and sometimes the Boodle Board or the Forty Thieves—was cut in both size and authority. The charter gave the mayor two prime tools of the strong chief executive: the right (1) to hire and fire his key department heads and (2) to make his operating budget, which the council may cut but not increase. He may also veto council ordinances, and a two-thirds vote is needed to override him. But the mayor's fiscal powers were shackled from another direction: the city's "upper house," the board of estimate, may do almost as it pleases with his budget and the mayor has no veto there.

## CINCINNATI

In 1924, civic reformers, now called the Charter party, swept out the corrupt administration of Boss Rud K. Hynica and adopted a package of related reforms—the city-manager plan with a nine-man council elected at large on a nonpartisan ballot by proportional representation. Under the plan, the council elects the mayor, who, with the council's approval, appoints the city manager and the city's boards and commissions. The manager, in turn, picks his department heads and is responsible for administration.

The Philadelphia commissioners, at least half sold on the beauties of the council-manager plan, decided to visit Cincinnati to take a firsthand look at a successful city-manager city. They spent a day in the city, and consulted closely with Charles Taft and other Cincinnati officials. Finally, the Philadelphians asked Taft if he would recommend the manager plan for a city of two million people—i.e., as large as Philadelphia. "No," he said flatly.

"When the Lord himself said he didn't want those ten commandments spread elsewhere," an ex-commissioner observes, "that was the death knell."

One reason the manager plan has worked admirably in Cincinnati is that the Charter party—which first sponsored the system—is a fairly well-organized political party, and it has been helped considerably at the polls by proportional representation. The Charterites, a fusion of independent Republicans and Democrats, have been able to beat off the regular Republican machine at election time and thus maintain a majority—or at least a strong minority—on the council. (The city, although technically nonpartisan in municipal elections, has local political parties, and the voters generally know who the parties' candidates are.)

In other cities, however, the council-manager form of government revealed a significant flaw: it failed to produce political leadership on which responsibility for the city government could be pinned. The very large cities, with all their complex needs and challenges, require an elected chief executive to serve as the center of political leadership and responsibility, and to provide policy guidance and planning.

The new Philadelphia charter, overwhelmingly approved in 1951, incorporated the elements of New York's "strong mayor" plan with the significant omission of the board of estimate and with some very important additions. Most notably, the mayor's office was strengthened by permitting him to appoint a managing director, who, with the mayor's approval, appoints most of the city's department heads and is responsible to the mayor for overall administration. The idea was to relieve the chief executive of routine administrative chores, and thus give him more time for the important job of hammering out policy.

## Built-in Bureaucrats

Presumably, the professionalization of his staff is a great help to the mayor in his efforts to provide leadership for the city. Increasingly, his appointed department heads are top specialists in their fields. The public-health commissioner, in vivid contrast even to twenty years ago, is a Doctor of Public Health, or at least an M.D. The public-works and sanitary commissioners are graduate engineers. Almost always, the men serving as division and bureau chiefs under the executive staff are career civil-service officers. The trend to professionalism is at high tide in Dallas, San Antonio, Cincinnati, and Kansas City—all manager cities. But it is also far advanced in the very big cities, where the need for expertise is great. Mayor Wagner's first city administrator (New York's version of the general-manager idea) was Luther Gulick, perhaps the country's foremost specialist in municipal affairs. In Chicago, reformers were incredulous when Richard Daley announced on taking office: "I'm going to listen to the professors." He has done so, and he has also hired some of them. His city controller and guard of its moneybags, for example, is Carl Chatters, onetime executive director of the Municipal Finance Officers Association, and a distinguished public servant.

Almost everywhere, in fact, only one big soft spot seems to remain—the police department. There are some exceptions. One is Cincinnati. Another is Milwaukee: its police department is one of the few in the country where organized crime has never acquired a foothold, and the city's policemen, long free from political taint, are professional from the top down. But in most big cities the gambling fix is still a problem, and corruption appears to be endemic—in spite of many top-notch police commissioners.

On the whole, however, the mayor—and the city—has profited from this administration by specialists. To many a big-city government, hard pressed to find money to maintain essential services, much less to provide new ones, the presence of a band of top professionals at City Hall has probably meant the difference between success and failure in operating the big service machine.

## Curbing the Specialists

But this aspect of "good government" has its drawbacks too. "The next big concern for the big city electorates," says Columbia University political scientist Wallace Sayre, "is how to curb the bureaucrats, how to keep the experts under control, how to keep them from making all the decisions."

The mayor can hire and fire his appointed experts. Controlling the civil servants beneath them, however, is something else again. In Newark, Mayor Leo Carlin was recently confronted with a typical case of a bureaucracy trying to extend its control over a city government. Carlin, under his city's "strong mayor" charter, adopted in 1954, has the right to hire and fire his aides with the council's consent. The New Jersey Civil Service Commission, which gives the examinations for and acts as the guardian of all "classified" city employees, challenged the mayor's right in the case of his deputy: it attempted to bring the deputy mayor's job under civil service, claiming the post was within its jurisdiction under the wording of the state law. The city rejected the claim, and the commission seems to have backed down. If the civil service is able to extend its authority to city officials as well as employees, many people feel, it will be able to hamper, if not control, city government and policy making in the same way that the French civil service controls much of the government of France.

## Too "Tight" a System?

The municipal civil-service system, ordinarily, is administered by a semi-independent commission whose members are appointed for fixed terms. Once in office, they have wide latitude in running their show. In addition to setting up and conducting the examinations, they see to it that employees are dismissed only for "cause," usually after trial by the commission. The system, as a result, is fairly "tight" in most big cities—i.e., the vast majority of city employees are hired through civil-service channels and enjoy full job security. But tightness, whatever merit it once had in discouraging politically motivated hirings and firings, can make for considerable inefficiency. The entrenched bureaucrats, protected by tenure, tend to develop a clique feeling among themselves, and the clique is opposed to all change—except in the direction of greater rigidity.

The mayor may try to solve this problem by exerting greater executive control over the civil-service commission, and by raising wage scales to attract higher-caliber civil servants. Each course is difficult, the first perhaps more than the second. The commissions were originally set up as semi-autonomous agencies to "take them out of politics." The do-gooders feared—with great justification a half-century ago, with much less justification now—that if the commission was made directly responsible to the chief executive, he might use his influence over the commissioners to get patronage jobs for his followers, and the fear persists. For the mayor intent on providing aggressive, efficient government, the net effect is to put him at a competitive disadvantage in hiring new, better-qualified people, and at an institutional disadvantage if he wishes to clear some of the tenured deadwood out of the hall.

## "Outside of Politics"

As the mayor struggles to enlarge his freedom of action in dealing with his own bureaucracy, his ability to exercise policy and planning leadership for the city is being challenged by a growing external bureaucracy. The challenger is the public corporation or "authority," a legal device created by the state with power to raise money, hire specialists, and administer a bothersome facility, whatever it is, from managing the port to providing water. Today the authority is the fastest-growing division of local government in the U.S., but its increasing use has alarmed many political scientists.

Robert Moses, no mean authority himself (he holds ten jobs in New York City and State, among them the chairmanship of two authorities), disclosed the great attraction of the authoritarian device, and the major argument against it, in a recent issue of the New York Sunday *Times*. "The nearest thing to business in government is the public authority, which is business with private capital under public auspices, established only when both private enterprise and routine government have failed to meet an urgent need, and this device is often attacked because it is too independent of daily pressures, too unreachable by the boys and therefore essentially undemocratic."

The authority, indeed, has many attractions, not the least of which is its right to incur debt outside the limits imposed on the city by the state. It has performed notable service, especially by its ability to handle bistate problems, as in the case of the Port of New York Authority, and area-wide problems, as in the case of the Metropolitan Water District of Southern California. But the device also has major disadvantages. All too often, the new authority is created to do something more than evade a debt limit or handle an area-wide function. Under pressure from the interested specialists —the sewer and water engineers, the transit experts—it is created to remove an undertaking from "politics," and hence from democratic controls. The result, as Moses indicated, is "independent" government, which may or may not be beneficent government. But in neither case will it be self-government.

The New York Port Authority is a classic example of the independent authority at work. Its officers, appointed for six-year terms by the Governors of New York and New Jersey, are far removed from public or political pressures, on either the state or local level. In part as a result, the N.Y.P.A. is perhaps the most efficiently run public-works agency in the world. It has performed unequaled services for the bistate port area: it has built tunnels and bridges, and it has taken over the airports. But the N.Y.P.A., its critics charge, does not make its decisions to build another tunnel, or to expand an airport instead of investing in mass-transit facilities, in terms of the whole public, or of the interest of the whole area, including the needs of New York City. It makes its decisions in terms of its own, more limited public— i.e., the auto driver who keeps it going with his tolls, and the bond market. The N.Y.P.A., set up to handle a bistate problem, and, like many another authority, ostensibly "nonpolitical," has developed a politics of its own, a politics of specialists who may or may not be responsive to the public interest.

## Dividing the House

His Honor may have no choice in the matter. Until a more democratic way of managing interstate or area-wide functions is invented, he must live with what he has. But the mayor has another charge against him, and for this one he alone is accountable. He has encouraged the rash of authorities and independent boards that have emerged—not in the area of city-suburb or interstate relations but within the framework of the city government itself—and their growth has put him in an exceedingly odd spot. These are the municipal authorities—the housing, airports, and redevelopment authorities, the special transit, sewer, parking, recreational and park districts, and all the rest.

For even the strongest mayor, the temptation to create a municipal authority to build and manage the airport or the city's parking lots—and thus relieve his own departments of new burdens—can be most compelling. The municipal authority, too, allows the city to get around its debt limit. Like its interjurisdictional sisters, the municipal authority usually has "tax" powers of its own: it pays for its revenue bonds by exacting a user's fee, rather than by calling on the city treasury for tax money. The authority has other advantages, and the mayor who is sold on the device—like Pittsburgh's David Lawrence—is particularly warm about one of them. In naming members to the boards, he is likely to choose the city's leading citizens, and he usually does so on a nonpartisan basis. Thus, as he enjoys pointing out, investors are more willing to buy bonds to finance the city's comeback. As for the charge that the authority, in effect, is a separate government divorced from the formal government, the mayor replies: "I do the appointing."

## Too Much Authority

The mayor may do the appointing; it is much more difficult for him, however, to reverse the process. Except in cases of dishonesty, he may not be able to get rid of a board member who is bucking his policies. As in the case of the older, semi-independent civil-service commissions, the over-all result is still another core of bureaucrats within the city government—but fairly well insulated from it, and as often as not indifferent or hostile to the chief executive and his plans for the city. A strong mayor, of course, will be able to bring about some coordination between the authorities—both area-wide and municipal—and the city government. But their very existence severely limits his policy-making role, for no one body—and certainly not the mayor's office—is responsible for over-all planning. The public authority, as municipal specialist William A. Robson has pointed out, may solve the particular problem that has been assigned to it, and sometimes solve it very well, "but only at the cost of weakening the general structure of local government in the great city and its environs, whereas the real need is to strengthen it."

## Child of the State

The big test of the mayor as policy leader is whether he can provide the city with vigorous programs of development and expansion—if possible, within an organized plan. The problem is awesome, and much of it boils down to money—money for capital development, and money to meet the rising costs of city services, including services to suburbanites who don't want to pay for them. The city's own tax revenues are rarely enough to pay for all its needs, and to raise taxes much higher would simply drive more people to the suburbs. For a solution of his money problem, the mayor must rely on governments other than his own. He must look to the encircling suburban governments, and to the state legislature. When he looks, he may be excused for blanching.

The arena in which the big-city mayor wages this fiscal struggle is the state legislature, and the struggle can be rough. The city, as a municipal corporation, is the child of the state, and the state legislature or constitution usually limits its power to levy taxes or borrow money. City dwellers, more-over, pay a wide variety of state taxes, but the big city, as likely as not, gets a disproportionate share of the return. Pennsylvania, for example, pays every nonsectarian hospital $8 a day for care of indigent patients—except Phila-delphia's city-owned General Hospital. The revenue loss to the city is almost $2,500,000 a year.

## Low on the Totem Pole

Chicago's Daley has summed up the consistent lament of most big-city mayors: "I think there's too much local money going to the state capitals and Washington. It's ridiculous for us to be sending them money and asking for it back. I don't think the cities should have to go hat in hand when they need money for improvements. We're going to have to clarify the role of the locality in relation to state and national governments. The cities and metropolitan areas are the important areas of the country today, but they're still on the low part of the totem pole."

Chicago isn't starving for money: its maximum property-tax rate is not set by law, and Daley recently won an additional privilege—although at a price. He got a bill through the state legislature giving him a ½ per cent sales tax, which the state collects and returns to the city, minus 6 per cent for its bother. A number of other cities, among them New York, Los Angeles, and New Orleans, are in fairly good financial shape, in part because they have been authorized by the state to levy special taxes in addition to the basic property tax. They and others—among them Pittsburgh and Dallas— have also been helped by their building booms, expanding the property-tax base. But some of the rest are in trouble, and the trouble can be bad. Boston, perhaps, is in the worst shape of all. It has had a legacy of inefficient government; both its population and its property-tax base are shrinking, and the state government, itself strapped for funds, won't help the city with its problems.

## Wanted: Supercities?

The mayor's big problem with the suburban and state governments arises from his need to plan ahead for the physical development of the city. But here he is besieged with troubles. No big city, for example, has yet approached its transportation problem in such a way as to come out with an integrated plan of street systems, parking, mass surface transportation, and railroads. The failure is not the result of simple negligence. The city itself is not the master of its transportation fate. Such problems are area-wide, not city-wide, and their solution, if there is to be a solution, will require co-operation between the city government and all the other governments in the metropolitan area—those of the satellite towns and cities—and the co-operation of the state and federal governments as well.

One solution to the metropolitan problem that is being talked about a lot is the creation of a supergovernment; it would absorb all the duties and functions of the local governments in the metropolitan areas, and would reign as a single unit over the new supercity. But such a supergovernment, in most cases, is a political impossibility: for one thing, the big cities, by and large, are Democratic and the suburbs are Republican, and neither is willing to relinquish its sovereignty to a new layer of government where these differences are likely to be intensified or, what may be worse, blurred. And even if supergovernment were feasible, there is doubt that it would be desirable. Government so big would be remote from the particular needs of the localities. And bigness and remoteness, in turn, would accelerate the trend to rule by specialists.

Many big cities have sought to solve their suburban problem by wide-scale annexations, but some of them have come to realize that the cost of providing services for the newly annexed suburbs outweighed the anticipated tax return and other advantages of consolidation, including the over-all planning advantage, and the movement seems to have subsided. The suburbs, moreover, have fought back in many places by incorporating themselves as municipalities to prevent annexation. In 1956 only two large cities, Houston and Dallas, sought and obtained the authority to annex large surrounding areas.

Since neither supergovernment nor annexation seems feasible, the big cities are considering other ways to coexist with their booming suburbs. The Metropolitan Toronto plan is a significant approach. Under it, a federated government was established for Toronto and twelve surrounding municipalities to provide area-wide services for all of them, leaving the local governments their control over local services. There are similar approaches in the U.S.—notably in Dade County, Florida, which includes Miami and twenty-five smaller communities. Dade County recently accepted a plan strengthening the county government, and giving it powers to provide for such county-wide needs and services as sanitation, arterial highways, water supply, and comprehensive planning. Many students of municipal government, most notably the University of California's Victor Jones, maintain that no attempt at metropolitan government can work well unless, as in Miami, it is based on the "federal" principle—that is, a system that will render unto the central authorities only those matters that cannot be dealt with locally.

## The Federated Region

Seattle's Metro Plan, for which Mayor Gordon Clinton has helped win legislative sanction, is another example. Metro will allow Seattle and some 175 towns, special districts, and other units in the Lake Washington area to work as a single unit in sewage and garbage disposal, water supply, mass transportation, parks, and planning.

Even without a formal arrangement cities can do a great deal. Dallas, for example, works closely with its outlying communities on specific issues—water supply, zoning—and Mayor Thornton has helped set up the Dallas County League of Municipalities, which includes all the incorporated towns in the area, to act as a frame for working out mutual problems on an area-wide basis.

Notably against all these devices is Milwaukee's government, which sells water to the suburbs. "This city," snaps Mayor Zeidler, "consults with suburban governments, but we do not believe they have a reason for existing." Zeidler, who loathes the suburbs and takes every opportunity to say so, wants no functional federation with their governments. He believes that if they want to use Milwaukee's costly water-distribution system they should consolidate with the city in all things. Milwaukee, however, is an exception: most cities have lost their appetite for the suburbs.

## Tactics vs. Strategy

In dealing with the how-to problems of government, the mayor is making considerable progress. At another task, however, he is failing. In his preoccupation with means, he is in danger of neglecting ends. He is not doing a good job of planning the city's future. When he is asked for his ideas on what the city should be like in twenty years, he is apt to reel off a long list of particular improvements—a new expressway here, a new superblock of housing there. Sometimes he will point to a spanking marble-and-glass civic center built in the downtown business district to increase property values and to act as "a center of decision making."

But the projects, however worthy, are too often unconnected: the mayor doesn't really seem to have a general plan for the city's development. His pragmatism, of course, is not to be scorned, and a static, all-embracing master plan would never really work. But while any plan must be revised time and again, without a continuing effort to look ahead—far ahead—many basic policy questions will be left unasked. Everybody, for example, enthuses about redevelopment. But redevelopment for *whom?* Is it to be redevelopment for the middle-income groups? Or should the city woo first the upper-income groups? If so, is the accepted super-block design the way to do it?

Poked off in a corner of most city halls are a couple of rooms housing the city planning commission. The unit is topped by a board of prominent citizens and it has a staff: a full-time director, professional planners, architects, engineers, draftsmen. They prepare, with more or less foresight, the capital budget. They may also be at work on a general plan for the physical development of the city. As defined by the 1954 Housing Act, which requires that a city have in hand some kind of broad community plan as a condition for receiving federal urban-renewal funds, the general plan should include and consolidate the city's renewal projects with its zoning and land-use plans, and its thoroughfare and public-improvements programs. Most large cities are now preparing or claim to have completed such over-all plans. But with a few exceptions—notably Detroit and Cincinnati—few major cities are using their plans as genuine guides for decision making.

Expert as professional planners may be, planning is ultimately a line rather than a staff function. To be effective, it requires the mayor's active support and coordination. It is here more than anywhere else that he is required to serve as a center of leadership and responsibility: if he is unwilling to mesh planning and execution, no one else can. In too many cities the mayor has abdicated this responsibility, and when he has, planning becomes an exercise in futility. Even in cities where planning and management are meshed, there remain many obstacles to effective planning. In New

York, for example, where Mayor Wagner has made planning a genuine arm of the administration, he and his planning commissioners still have to sweat to establish some connection between the city's projects, the authorities' projects, and what often seem to be the personal projects of Mr. Moses.

On the other end of the scale is Houston, the only major city still without a zoning ordinance, where Mayor Oscar Holcombe recently turned down a suggestion that he adopt capital budgeting over five-year periods, as do most other big cities. Mayor Holcombe frowns on budgeting—which is the area in which plans are transformed into policy decisions and programs—beyond the term of the administration that is in power at the time. Pittsburgh's Lawrence, who contenances both planning and fragmentation, may have been speaking for the middle ground when he said recently: "My effort must go not into architectural and planning critiques, but into the limited, tedious, persevering work of making things happen."

The mayors, indeed, have made things happen—and this is prerequisite. But it is not enough. Long-range strategy for *what* is to happen is as badly needed. If the city is to reassert itself as a vital center in American life and, not so incidentally, if it is to help the federal and state governments prevent the rest of the country from turning into a suburban mess—the mayors must take the lead. The omens are promising.

# RECENT CONCEPTS IN LARGE CITY ADMINISTRATION

## CHARLES R. ADRIAN

THERE ARE a variety of historical reasons for the slowness with which concepts for the government of our largest cities have developed. Until recent years, most of these cities were dominated by political machines little interested in governmental structure and even less interested in professional administration. The reformers of the efficiency and economy movement, when they were inspired to action, spent most of their time in the essentially negative activity of fighting the machines. Even when they concerned themselves with positive activity, their almost religious devotion to the council-manager plan kept them from examining concepts. The administrative reform air became charged with emotion, and skepticism concerning any part of the council-manager plan was regarded as heresy that could not be tolerated or discussed on its merits.

The efficiency and economy movement contributed much to the modern

Published for the first time in this book, by permission of the author.

management of America's small and moderate-sized cities. But it was of little help to our largest cities, perhaps chiefly because the reformers' two basic assumptions—that politics and politicians are evil and untrustworthy, and that city government is almost entirely a matter of applying the principles of efficient business management—could not be reconciled with the political realities of the large city.

Thus we find that there was little administrative reorganization of large cities between the beginning of the century and the advent of World War II. Some changes took place, to be sure. The very great pressure of demands for complex and technical services in itself produced some modernization of the municipal civil service. Some large cities that matured after the heyday of machine politics—notably Detroit and Los Angeles—developed structures that were integrated to a considerable degree, with administrations that were honest (by middle-class standards) most of the time, and with political atmospheres that allowed reformers an opportunity to operate to some degree. Two large cities—Cincinnati and Kansas City—and ten cities of over one-quarter of a million people have adopted the manager plan.

But it was not until after World War II that attention came to be sharply focused on the large city administrative structure. To some extent, this organizational soul-searching has come about because of the decline of the boss and machine, a change that decades of bombardment by reformers have helped bring about but which is largely the result of a basic change in the social environment, which had formerly supported this institution.[1] In part, also, it is probably a reaction to the pressing problems of the core city, which have resulted from the move to the suburbs,[2] and to the increasing technical complexity of governmental services.

In looking at this postwar trend toward the formulation of a set of concepts for the management of large cities, we might consider three areas of activity: council-manager government, the management cabinet, and the chief administrative officer (CAO).

## Council-Manager Government in Large Cities

From the second decade of this century to the present, reformers have urged the adoption of the council-manager plan regardless of the size of a city. They have urged—with little empirical basis for their assertions—that size is an irrelevant, or at best insignificant, factor in determining the type of structure to be used.

Habitual iconoclasts, on the other hand, have sought to make light of

---

1. For background, see any number of sources, including my *Governing Urban America* (2nd. ed., 1961), Chaps. 3, 6, and 8.
2. *Ibid.*, Chap. 2; and Robert C. Wood, *Suburbia* (1959).

the semideified manager plan and have insisted that it cannot work in large cities for a variety of reasons, but especially because it does not provide for political leadership in complex situations. Effective government, those on middle ground note, has been achieved in two large cities that have tried the council-manager plan: in Cincinnati from the beginning and in Kansas City after the ousting of the Pendergast machine. They point out that nineteen of the twenty-two California cities with populations of between 50,000 and 500,000 use some version of the manager plan. But only San Antonio of our larger cities has adopted and retained the plan since the years of the Great Depression.

Why have the large cities not turned toward the council-manager form? Does a failure to make adequate provision for political leadership and policy development render it unsuitable? Has the tendency of persons in large cities to look to the mayor rather than the council for leadership in problem solving been a principal factor in the avoidance of the manager plan in such cities? Just why does the public perceive this role of the mayor differently in large cities as against medium-sized cities? Or does it? Do political leaders fear the plan as much as is often claimed? If so, how can their views be reconciled with those of Thomas Pendergast, who could have junked the plan in Kansas City but did not? These questions, and others, lend themselves to empirical research and need testing.

There are other questions involving matters of fact that can be partially answered through the conventional techniques of historical research. Why have study commissions in large cities so often failed to recommend the council-manager plan even when many reform-oriented persons are members? Why, for example, did the study commission appointed by Governor Thomas E. Dewey and the General Assembly recommend the CAO plan rather than the manager plan for the city of New York even before it began public hearings? The reports of study commissions are consistently inadequate in describing the conceptual schemes of commission members who reject the manager plan.

Some clues as to why the manager plan has been rejected exist, but these merely suggest the need for further study. In 1931, Lent D. Upson recommended the creation of an administrative assistantship to the mayor of Detroit, rather than adoption of the manager plan, because he felt that Detroit's government was at "too high a level" of competence to justify a drastic shift to another plan.[3] Is this a plausible reason in other cities, too—or at any rate, a more important practical consideration than some of the others often mentioned?

In 1926, a committee sponsored by the San Francisco Bureau of Governmental Research considered a manager plan for their city, and at the same time the *San Francisco News* advocated the plan. But a large majority of the 1930 charter revision commission membership opposed the manager plan

---

3. Cited in *American City*, 44 (June, 1931), 93.

and rejected it by a decisive vote.[4] Why? Was the size of the city a principal factor in this rejection? In Los Angeles, the CAO plan was thought to be "an improvement over the ordinary city manager proposal—tailored to fit the practical requirements of our great city."[5] What impracticalities did these commission members think they saw in the manager plan? Mayor Fletcher Bowron said he thought a manager plan would never work in Los Angeles because of the "size and complexity" of the city. Did he have reasons for thinking so?

In Philadelphia, the Home Rule Charter Commission felt that the manager plan would not be suitable for local needs because of "the size of the city, its nature, its traditions, its election laws and the patterns of its political life."[6] Yet laws can be amended, and traditions are violated and patterns of political life are modified whenever any city adopts the manager plan.

What is it about large cities that convinces members of study and charter commissions that the manager plan "cannot work" in a large city? The existence of many cultural subgroups with consensus on few matters of consequence, the hostility of political chieftains, the fact that greater public attention is focused on the mayor, and the fact that there is greater inertia working against radical structural changes—all these may well be important factors in preventing the adoption of the manager plan in large cities. But we need to know if these are the real factors, or if there are others, and we would like to know the degree to which each is important.

## The Management Cabinet

There is a popular illusion in the United States that the President settles the most vital issues of national policy in meetings with the cabinet and that members of that body are necessarily the principal administrators and top policy advisers in the government. In reality, the cabinet may be highly unimportant, as was the case under Franklin D. Roosevelt, or relatively near the popular image, as was true under Dwight D. Eisenhower. Some of its members are top political advisers, others definitely are not. The fact of the matter is that the President's top political advisers often are not department heads at all, but members of his personal staff. Of particular importance are the assistant to the President and the press secretary. This is significant and is relative to an understanding of recent municipal developments.

The President's cabinet grew out of British practices and developed in the days before the chief executive had a clearly defined personal staff. The

---

4. John C. Bollens, *Appointed Executive Local Government* (1952), p. 12.
5. *Ibid.*, p. 46.
6. *American City*, 66 (April, 1951), 118.

attempt to make department heads perform functions more effectively handled by staff personnel has long limited the value of a cabinet whose officers are chosen for reasons independent of their ability to serve as close and confidential advisers to the chief executive.

Although remnants of the old pattern of a cabinet made up of line organization members are still to be found, the trend today is toward the informal operation of an advisory cabinet made up of persons close to the chief executive and consisting largely of his personal staff. The full blossoming of a professional staff for the mayor is in itself a new development and its rise may help account for acceptance of the CAO idea.

We see the beginnings of a management cabinet for large cities in Philadelphia (under the charter) and in New York (by action of Mayor Robert F. Wagner, Jr.). In Philadelphia, cabinet members are directly selected by the mayor (though council approval is required). The body consists of the Managing Director (CAO), the Director of Finance, the City Solicitor and the City Representative (a new post for handling ceremonial functions and the all-important area of public relations). These are the mayor's top aides, excepting for his personal staff.

In New York, a similar cabinet was established in 1954. The group includes the Deputy Mayor, the City Administrator (CAO), the Director of the Budget, the Director of Planning, the Director of Personnel, the chief legal officer of the city and the mayor's principal personal staff members, including his public relations officer.

Some semblance of a management cabinet probably already exists in quite a number of large cities on a very informal basis. It is likely that such a group, gathering at the call of the chief executive, could be most effective as an informal organization whose membership is determined by the desires of the chief executive, and which is not limited by restrictive requirements established in a charter. Its principal function would logically be found in the threshing out of problems connected with policy development and with political strategy. These were the functions attributed to the traditional cabinet. Large city governments need such a group to allow for frank discussions which permit the ironing out of "bugs" in proposed policy and strategy in governmental situations where complex problems exist.

The New York cabinet has not been especially successful. Members responsible for overhead agencies (such as planning and budgeting) have tended to protect their independence and themselves from criticism by withholding matters from discussion, and there have been other difficulties. To be most effective, an advisory group (perhaps called a cabinet in deference to American tradition) should probably not include persons who have to defend the perimeters of personal empires. The New York and Philadelphia experiments may thus eventually prove to be as unsatisfactory as a cabinet of department heads. Personal staff members seem to be the best sources of advice for the large city chief executive.

## The Emerging Post of Chief Administrative Officer

### BACKGROUND

The establishment of a top personal aide to the mayor who serves as the CAO is a postwar development. Whether it represents a new form of city government is an unimportant question. Clearly, it is a special outgrowth of the mayor-council plan. By examining the literature prepared in various cities that have adopted the plan, we find that the CAO's post seems to have been established largely for two reasons: (1) As a compromise between the manager plan and government by a strong mayor; and (2) as a means of providing for professional administration without eliminating the mayor as the symbolic head and chief policy maker of the city.

In the years before World War II, there was little discussion of a post such as CAO. Reformers were generally so bent on ending "politics" in city government—and therefore on removing the powers of the elective mayor—that they failed to recognize that a political chief executive, responsible to the voters, is capable of choosing able underlings. (Reformers have long labored under the strange illusion that a politician's friends and acquaintances and persons recommended to him for appointment are necessarily incompetent, if not downright dishonest.)

We find, for example, no mention of a professional administrator as a possible top executive aide in A. C. Hanford's review of municipal problems in the mid-twenties.[7] Of course, this may partly be the result of the fact that the strong mayor plan, though it dates from the 1880's, was not fully accepted, despite the approval of reformers, until fairly recently. As late as 1929, Chester C. Maxey saw in the choice of a strong mayor "a municipal Mussolini to run the whole works."[8] Persons with such a viewpoint were unlikely to look with favor upon plans designed to strengthen the mayor by adding a professional administrator to superintend the principal departments and thus complement the "dictator's" powers.

During the Great Depression, when municipalities were in serious financial difficulties, E. S. Griffith, musing over the question of improved structural forms, noted that "it is still possible that in the future the American city will continue to evolve new types. None are in sight now."[9]

Actually, two hints of a new type had appeared by then, though one could excuse even the sharpest observer for not having seen them. In fact, their existence was scarcely noticeable for the next decade and a half. The CAO plan first took form in a suggestion from Lent D. Upson and in a provision of a new city charter for San Francisco.

In Detroit, Upson suggested that the office of administrative assistant to

---

7. A. C. Hanford, *Problems in Municipal Government* (1926).
8. C. C. Maxey, *Urban Democracy* (1929), p. 118.
9. E. S. Griffith, *Current Municipal Problems* (1933), p. 185.

the mayor be created.[10] His view was that such a person could handle much administrative detail, that an incoming mayor would have an experienced person upon whom to rely, that programs would have continuity of administration and that the mayor would be freed for policy development and promotion.

The influence of the efficiency and economy movement was strong in Upson's thinking. His idea emphasized the value of experienced personnel, continuity in office, and independence from "political influence." He suggested that the assistant, rather than serving at the pleasure of the mayor, should be appointed by the mayor in accord with minimum qualifications described in the charter and from a list of the three or four highest names on a roster established by the civil service commission after examination. The assistant would be dismissable after a hearing on preferred charges. Upson even saw this system being extended to other top administrative officers, so that periodic dismissals and resignations could be curtailed—a reflection of the reformer's belief that the goal was to establish government on a "businesslike" basis.

The CAO provision in the San Francisco charter of 1931 grew out of agitation for the manager plan.[11] A movement for the manager plan had begun in 1926 with support from the Bureau of Governmental Research and the *San Francisco News*. The research subcommittee of the 1930 charter revision commission was generally favorable to the manager plan. Some members of the commission, on the other hand, made statements sharply favoring the strong mayor plan. Finally, "the hearings indicated the necessity for a compromise between a strong mayor and a manager form." As a result, the post of CAO (as it was called) was created, but powers were assigned in a piecemeal fashion, with each proposed function being subject to a vote of the charter commission members.

Thus, the first position of CAO was established in a typically American pattern of expediency and compromise. In accord with the reformer's distrust of politicians, the CAO was made appointive by the mayor, but could be removed only by recall or by hearing followed by two-thirds vote of the board of supervisors.

The San Francisco CAO was given authority over a number of departments, but he has never been given the full powers that his title implies. He is powerless so far as overhead (staff) functions are concerned.

Criticism of the proposed plan in San Francisco ran along the usual lines to be found when the manager plan is proposed. Opponents said it provided for a "dictator" and Jacksonian sensibilities were shocked when it was found that the CAO need not be a resident of the city when hired.[12] On the

---

10. *American City*, 44 (June, 1931), 93.
11. Bollens, *op. cit.*, pp. 12–13; J. M. Selig, "The San Francisco Idea," *National Municipal Review*, 46 (June, 1957), 290–295.
12. Bollens, *op. cit.*, p. 45.

other hand, one contemporary proponent viewed the CAO provision as "one of the outstanding features of the charter,"[13] and another thought that "this will make for improved coordination and more efficient business administration."[14] A political scientist, noting that something new had arrived on the scene, commented that "the 'chief administrator' is not a manager in the usual understanding of the term. He is entirely restricted in his powers by the mayor."[15]

Local reformers in other cities did not rush to take up the new mechanical gadget for better government, and no John M. Patterson came along with cash and a propaganda machine to support it. In fact, seventeen years were to pass before the next municipal CAO came into being. (In 1941, however, a St. Louis study recommended consideration of the desirability of an administrative assistant to the mayor. Such an official, it was thought, would "keep the mayor informed on the operations of the city government, and would follow up on the carrying out of his instructions to officials."[16])

In 1948, Charles P. Farnsley, mayor of Louisville, appointed a "consultant" at a salary of $15,000—higher than that of any city officer.[17] Farnsley was an advocate of reform and of administrative efficiency. (He had majored in political science in college.) His idea proved attractive; the new post was later adopted by ordinance and it was retained by Farnsley's successor.

Even the Louisville adoption was not decisive, however, and it was not until 1951 that a trend toward the use of the CAO plan could be said to have become established. In that year, Philadelphia and Los Angeles adopted versions of the plan, the former much stronger than the latter. They were followed the next year by New Orleans and Hoboken. In 1953, New York, Boston, and Newark were added. A 1954 staff report by the Chicago Charter Revision Commission recommended the adoption of the CAO plan, but Mayor Richard J. Daley refused to give his support. Others have adopted the CAO plan since.

THE FUNCTIONS OF THE CHIEF ADMINISTRATIVE OFFICER

There has been a great deal of controversy over the question of what powers the CAO ought or ought not have—whether he is to perform essentially staff or line functions and whether or not he is "practically a city

---

13. William H. Nanry, "San Francisco Adopts a New Charter," *National Municipal Review*, 20 (May, 1931), 259–263.

14. *American City*, 44 (April, 1931), 5.

15. E. A. Cottrell, "Three California Charters," *National Municipal Review*, 20 (April, 1931), 242.

16. Mayor's Advisory Committee on City Survey and Audit, *The Government of the City of St. Louis* (1941), pp. 16–17.

17. George Kent, "Mayor Charlie Cuts Corners," *National Municipal Review*, 38 (October, 1949), 433–436.

manager."[18] There has also been considerable variation in the amount of study given the plan before adoption.

In Los Angeles, the CAO plan was considered superior to the manager plan because it was tailored to fit the "particular requirements" of the city.[19] The charter amendment was submitted with little advance study (the major department heads had urged the plan two years earlier). Newspapers strongly supported this move toward "efficiency." Opponents—some labor and civic groups, and the League of Women Voters—felt that further study was needed. Others thought there would be conflict between departmental boards and the CAO; still others wanted the manager plan.

In Philadelphia the Home Rule Charter Commission did an especially careful job of checking into the plans adopted or being studied in other cities, and it held public hearings. The reform-minded *Philadelphia Inquirer,* thinking of decades of machine mayors, could not believe that a strong chief executive would allow the managing director (CAO) much actual power.[20]

The Hoboken Charter Commission chose one of the options under the Faulkner Act which provided for the CAO. Under this plan, "the business manager would be somewhat akin to a city manager," but the manager plan itself was avoided lest an antireform group secure a majority on the council and appoint an "unqualified" manager.[21] For some reason, it was assumed that such a group would not be able to dominate the mayor and CAO.

The philosophy of the efficiency and economy movement was most strongly reflected in Boston, where the administrative services department was established as a staff agency under a board, principally as a means of increasing "administrative efficiency." The board, under the chairmanship of the director of administrative services, consists of the personnel officer, the purchasing agent, the auditor, the treasurer, the budget officer, and the assessor. The directorship is only a feeble first step toward a chief administrative officer, however. The narrow scope of the office is indicated in the first annual report, which said that "our experience in this new field of government management . . . has given us the incentive to lay the groundwork for an organizational setup that we trust in the future will be a pattern to be followed by other large cities throughout the country for efficiency and businesslike methods in the daily operation of city government."[22] The department reported that it had busied itself with such things as the establishment of a performance budget, a survey of typewriter use by line

18. For detailed comparisons among various CAO plans, powers assigned, and methods of appointment and removal, see W. S. Sayre, "The General Manager Idea for Large Cities," *Public Administration Review,* 14 (Autumn, 1954), 253–258.

19. Bollens, *op. cit.,* p. 46.

20. *National Municipal Review,* 40 (March, 1951), 150.

21. *New York Times,* July 15, 1952.

22. City of Boston, *Annual Report of the Administrative Services Department* (1954), p. 14.

departments, the renumbering of offices in the city hall, and a survey of the use of city telephones for private calls.

## THE NEW YORK TESTING GROUND

Since the San Francisco charter and Upson era, the general trend has been toward the creation of a CAO responsible only to the mayor and serving at his pleasure. In New York, however, where Tammany is not yet a ghost, reformers have expressed skepticism concerning the current theory that administrative expertise and mayoralty politics can be bedpartners—at least they do not see municipal bliss as a result.

The City Manager Study Committee of the Citizens Union wanted to have the CAO appointed after selection by the mayor, a public hearing, and approval by the Board of Estimate. Removal would be similarly cumbersome. The Committee thought that independence for the CAO would "make the position more attractive to a high-grade man."[23] (Later, when the post of city administrator was created with responsibility to the mayor, Luther Gulick, than whom no higher grade could be found, was the first appointee to the post.)

There has been considerable conflict over what role the CAO should play in New York. This has been reflected in editorials, statements by the mayor, and interagency feuds. An editorial in the *National Municipal Review* expressed the hope that New York would be the first city where the CAO would be given management tools—especially over personnel and finance.[24] But it has developed that it was precisely lack of control over these agencies that at first threatened to relegate the city administrator to the role of advisor on management efficiency. This, despite the fact that the Mayor's Committee thought the CAO "would be virtually a general manager for the city" who would assist the mayor "in the general coordination of all departmental activities."[25]

The complex administrative structure proposed by Mayor Wagner when he took office in 1954 made necessary a general briefing session for department heads on who was to report to whom.[26] After the meeting was over, many department heads complained that they still did not know whether they reported to the Mayor through the Deputy Mayor or through the City Administrator. There was evidence that the Mayor was a bit confused, too. He gamely tried to explain the role of the new CAO, saying that he would be an important advisor on "managerial matters" and would be neither a city manager nor a narrow coordinator. Rather, the CAO would be "executive vice president in charge of operations," acting as general manager in dealing with the administrative agencies.

---

23. *National Municipal Review*, 42 (March, 1953), 134.
24. *Ibid.*, 43 (January, 1954), 4.
25. Mayor's Committee on Management Survey, *Modern Management for the City of New York* (1953), I, 31. On postwar management trends in the nation's largest city, see Wallace S. Sayre and Herbert Kaufman, *Governing New York City* (1960).
26. *New York Times*, January 6, 1954.

The question of whether a position of any real consequence had been created was quickly raised in connection with an open dispute that arose shortly after the Wagner administration got under way.[27] The adversaries were the City Administrator and the Budget Director.

The new arrangement provided for the Budget Director to report directly to the Mayor. It also happened that proposals for administrative improvements by the CAO had to be referred to the Budget Bureau's division of analysis, which then investigated them and made recommendations to the Budget Director, whose recommendations to the Board of Estimate were normally decisive. This phenomenon had the practical result of placing the CAO, for many purposes, under the Budget Director.

In the struggle that ensued, most reformers sided with the CAO. (In his first annual report the City Administrator claimed that "management savings" accomplished by his agency had trimmed $25 million from the city budget.[28]) Wagner tried to steer a middle course which, for some time, seemed to indicate a lack of understanding of the fundamental problem involved. In April, the proposed budget left the Budget Director with his powers unchanged, but two months later the Board of Estimate, on the Mayor's motion, transferred the controversial division of analysis to the City Administrator.

The New York experiment thus survived a vital early test. If it had failed at this juncture, the whole pattern of development might have changed sharply. If the City Administrator had become merely an individual heading a small office that recommended management economies to the Budget Bureau, the healthy development of the CAO plan might have been dealt a very serious blow.

But such was not the case. By 1960, according to Wallace S. Sayre and Herbert Kaufman, the CAO and his office staff had become "the most fully realized assets of the Mayor's office . . . the Mayor's most active problem-solvers, especially in matters requiring interdepartmental agreements or departmental reorganizations." The office of Managing Director, in Philadelphia, had "contributed both to strong, productive political leadership in the office of mayor and to high-quality professional administration in most departments of Philadelphia's city government."[29]

THE COMING PATTERN

The future prospects for a further spread of the plan look favorable. Middle-sized cities are beginning to provide for a CAO in reference to a manager when reforms are attempted. St. Cloud, Minnesota, did so in a new charter in 1954, followed by Duluth and Lansing in 1956 and by other

27. See *New York Times*, April 4, April 14, May 19, and June 14, 1955.
28. Cited in *ibid.*, May 19, 1954.
29. Sayre and Kaufman, *op. cit.*, pp. 665–666; J. C. Phillips, *Municipal Government and Administration in America*, (1960), p. 327.

cities since then. In Duluth, the CAO was given sweeping powers over all line departments except the city attorney, while in Lansing the post was conceived of principally as an assistant to the mayor.

It seems likely that we can expect a further spread of the plan into middle-sized cities, if for no other reason than that the adoption of a CAO charter provision is a much less radical break with the past and is therefore politically more feasible than the adoption of the manager plan.

## Conclusions

It may be, as Wallace Sayre has said, that the CAO plan reflects "the judgment in the larger cities that the council manager plan represents an unnecessary surrender of the value of leadership and accountability found in the instrument of the elected chief executive."[30] It may be, on the other hand, that the plan represents the only practicable administrative modification available to large cities where, for some reason or reasons, new charters and radical reforms encounter greater inertia or overt resistance than is the case in smaller cities. The factors accounting for the current pattern require more empirical study before they can be stated with conviction.

The officer I have called the CAO has a great variety of powers. In some cities, especially in Philadelphia, in New Orleans, and in New Jersey cities of over 250,000 under the CAO option, he has many of the line and staff powers of a manager. In other cities, such as San Francisco, he presides principally over some line functions; in still others, he is viewed mostly as a staff aide to, or agent of, the mayor; and in Boston, he is interested chiefly in the economies of management reorganization. This narrower concept of the CAO, which is in the tradition of the efficiency and economy movement, hardly establishes a city government organization that maximizes the use of the skills of a first-rate professional administrator.

In each case, regardless of the powers given the CAO, we have seen a movement away from the idea of a professional administrator independent of the mayor and toward the idea of a competent top leadership in the executive office responsible to the mayor, who in turn is accountable to the voters for administration as well as for policy. The desire of the mayor to make a good record for himself rather than the older reform notion of some mechanical device is counted on to keep the officer in line.

The degree to which the CAO plan will operate successfully probably depends as much on the personality of the chief executive involved as upon anything else. The problem today is no longer that of finding "honest" public officials. For the most part, we have them. Nor is the problem any longer one of securing the adoption of the manager plan, for the CAO plan seems to make this sharp change of course unnecessary in large cities. (In smaller

---

30. Sayre, "The General Manager Idea," p. 253.

cities, where the mayor is a part-time official and much less in the spotlight, the relationship of mayor to professional administrator is not the same and the CAO plan may be less appropriate.) The problem is no longer one of trying to find a mayor with unusual administrative ability. The problem today for large cities is rather one of finding a mayor who is willing to delegate responsibility for administrative detail to a CAO and of finding a CAO who can secure the confidence of the mayor.

It is too early to predict with confidence that the CAO plan will become a permanent instrument for municipal government. It is certainly possible that too much depends upon the personality of the mayor and upon his willingness to delegate appropriate authority. It is also possible that not enough power will be assigned to the CAO to permit full use of his capabilities. It is possible that department heads cannot be persuaded to report to the CAO rather than to the mayor, or that the mayor will not deal with department heads through the CAO. But if such dangers as these do not prove to be insurmountable barriers, it may be that the long-standing problem of finding an appropriate form of government for our largest cities has been resolved.


# AN INFORMAL TALK
# WITH A BIG CITY MAYOR

## THE CHICAGO HOME RULE COMMISSION INTERVIEWS JOSEPH S. CLARK, JR., MAYOR OF PHILADELPHIA


MAYOR CLARK: . . . I have a cabinet, consisting of originally four and now six, and sometimes seven people. Ostensibly the most important one is the so-called managing director, who has under him ten line departments. That is to say, police; fire; streets; water; health; recreation; welfare; public property; licenses and inspection; and records.

He is the principal administrator for those ten departments; and it's a rare day when I see any of those commissioners. We have quarterly meetings of commissioners, and on occasion one will come in with the managing director about a particular problem. I get weekly reports from them on what they are doing. But the managing director is in line control of those ten departments.

Reprinted from *Modernizing a City Government* (Chicago: The University of Chicago Press, 1954), pp. 351–360, 368, 370–371.

He has, however, nothing to do with finance. The finance director has charge of budgeting and accounting, municipal-bond issues, and city finance. He also supervises the collector of revenue, who is our collector of taxes, and the procurement commissioner, through whom all purchasing is done.

There is, in addition, a city representative and director of commerce, which is a weird combination. I think that is one of the mistakes we made. The city representative is in charge of public relations, and he is also supposed to be the chief ceremonial representative of the city. I am able, as a result, to cut most, but not all, of the ceremonials—greeting the Elks and all that sort of thing.

ALDERMAN BECKER: Cut the ribbons—

MAYOR CLARK: He cuts the ribbons, if they're not too important ribbons.

CHAIRMAN LYON: Politically important?

MAYOR CLARK: Yes, politically—that's right. And he is, also, however, as I said, in charge of public relations, which is very different—and he's also director of commerce, which is completely different. As director of commerce, he's in charge of the promotion of the Port of Philadelphia, in charge of its operation, and also a member of the Delaware River Port Authority. He is in charge of the operation of our airport; and he also has control of our convention hall and our commercial museum, which is devoted to the promotion of commerce.

So he has a weird series of assignments, for which it would be very difficult for anybody but a genius to combine the qualifications necessary to do that job. I would certainly advise you not to do that if you have a charter here, although each of these functions is very important. And the fellow who does it is a first-class fellow and does it very well. He is obviously, however, better at some than others.

The three men I mentioned—the managing director, the finance director, and the city representative—sit on the city planning commission, which is also appointed by the mayor and consists of nine individuals, of whom these are three, the others being nonpaid, outstanding civic leaders.

They have a pretty good budget, and the executive director is a pretty high-powered fellow; and they have the responsibility of submitting to the mayor for submission by him to council every fall a so-called "capital budget and capital program," which deals with the public improvement program in the city, the capital budget being for the ensuing year and the capital program being a six-year program of public improvements, of which the capital budget for the coming year is the first step.

Then there is the city solicitor, whose duties are obvious, but have been terribly important in these two years because of the large number of legal questions arising from implementing a new charter, which, frankly, was badly overwritten. I would certainly not advise you to write one 99 pages long. Try to write one like the Constitution of the United States, because the problems of interpretation and the red tape which results in trying to lay down the detailed procedures to keep people from stealing and all that sort of thing are really in this modern day and age a great deterrent to that type of prompt action which I feel is so necessary in municipal affairs, as, indeed, it is in business or in running a labor union or whatever else you have.

I created, although it is not in the charter, a deputy to the mayor, whom I put in charge of relationships with the council and of all political matters, and I would strongly urge you to do that. It has been absolutely invaluable. It is an essential part of American government at all levels, I think. We just can't ignore those practical political problems, and I think it is wrong to try to do so. The deputy to the mayor is a former Democratic ward-leader and is an extremely competent and able fellow who has been absolutely invaluable to me.

Another thing which would be of interest to you is the personnel setup. In their desire to counteract the complete lack of anything approaching a merit system at any level, the charter commission took drastic action. In Philadelphia for years we had, ostensibly, under the 1919 charter, civil service in the city offices, but it had become a very bad joke—for two reasons. First, because of the complete control of city government by one political party for so long a period of time. I have no doubt that if we Democrats had been in control for as long, it would have been just as bad our way; but we weren't; and also, because the city council had starved the civil service commission by not giving it enough money to give it adequate personnel to conduct the merit system and put the thing on the level.

In their desire to overcome that, the charter commission set up a civil service commission of three, who were to be appointed by the mayor from a list of nine names submitted to him by a group of leading citizens, which included the president of Penn; the president of Temple; the president of the Bureau of Municipal Research; the head of the Chamber of Commerce; the heads of the CIO and A F of L, and one or two others whom I don't remember at the moment, the thought being that the nine nominees to the mayor would be individuals completely removed from politics; from those nine I select three commissioners who would serve two, four, six years, to give them terms which would overlap part of the mayor.

They had the job of appointing a personnel director; and he had complete charge of all matters of personnel administration and policies and procedures; and there's been a good deal of chatter as to whether that was a good thing or not.

The job of personnel director in a government with a spoils system tradition is a very difficult one, because he obviously was going to be the bad boy in the eyes of the politicians of both parties. He has certainly turned out to be such.

And, on the other hand, being completely independent of the mayor may be a good thing. I know over in New York they've concluded it is not; that the mayor should be responsible for personnel just as he is for operations and finance.

But you can't hold him completely responsible if that is the case. Certainly my managing director and my director of finance, whenever I chide them briefly for perhaps not being right on the ball the way they should be, they say, "How can we do anything with that clown over there in personnel, who is holding us up and won't give us people?"

And he replies by saying they don't ask him at the right time.

I, of course, have attempted to and have not been able to mediate it except on a friendly basis.

ALDERMAN BECKER: How long is their appointment for?

MAYOR CLARK: The civil service commission—one for two; one for four; one for six years. They overlap the mayor, as such.

There are two other points that I would comment on briefly.

MR. FARR: Are those the six now who are—those six people who are on your cabinet? Would those be the six—the managing director, the finance director, the director of commerce, the city solicitor, the deputy mayor, and the personnel director?

MAYOR CLARK: The personnel director is brought into cabinet meetings when personnel problems are involved—with some hesitation, because I felt it was not really intended by the charter that he should be a member of the mayor's cabinet. It was a sort of separation of powers and checks and balances; but we found ourselves in such a snarl that everybody agreed, including me, that it would be wise to bring him in; and we occasionally bring in the chairman of the civil service commission when something of considerable importance of a personnel nature needs to be discussed in the cabinet.

The other thing that has come up in the last two years has been that one of the overwhelmingly vital problems that we have to deal with is this whole business of urban blight, the relationship of public and private housing —the whole question of shelter. And I succeeded in persuading the city council last fall to appropriate some money for a housing co-ordinator, who would attempt to bring together the manifold and hitherto completely unco-ordinated activities in the housing field.

I was encouraged to do that by the reports which came from Chicago, about your attempts out here to create a housing department; and if we were to do it again, I would, without any question, recommend the creation of a housing department. And I think I would put him directly under the mayor, because, as you see, under this system, the mayor doesn't have too many to supervise, and the managing director does; he has ten, which I think is too many for any one man.

I think personally the matter of curing blight and the whole housing situation is so terribly important for the future that that man should be at the cabinet level; and I have brought him into the cabinet.

MR. FARR: How does that relate to the plan commission?

MAYOR CLARK: It's interesting. What he has to do is co-ordinate the activities from a long-range planning point of view—the planning of the

Philadelphia Housing Authority, which is the body which deals with the federal government on low-cost housing, low-cost rental housing; the Philadelphia Redevelopment Authority, which is dealing with both state and federal projects; the Department of Licenses and Inspections, which is under the managing director but has the whole enforcement problem and the home-building industry, in addition to neighborhood groups who are interested in rehabilitation and shoring up neighborhoods so they won't disintegrate.

He has a perfectly fiendish job. He's been at it only two months. It is fascinating to see; he's a very capable fellow—how he has been able to bring the situation together, with just the powers of the co-ordinator; and we're all enthusiastic about it.

MR. FARR: They report to him?

MAYOR CLARK: They report to him. And it's a heaven-sent relief to me. I can kick it downstream to him and sit in only on the vital matters as they come up. As a matter of fact, he's down testifying today before the House of Representatives on the federal program for housing, where I can't be because of this.

CHAIRMAN LYON: This is much more important.

MAYOR CLARK: I thought so.

One other little gimmick we have which I'll mention, and that is the mayor's Office of Information and Complaints.

I recommended to the charter commission, while it was sitting, that we should have a department of investigation, like the one they have over in New York, but that didn't go down. They didn't want to do it. Instead, they created a small agency in the mayor's office, called the Information and Complaint Agency, and that has been a huge public relations success. Last year they handled 250,000 inquiries or complaints. I'm glad to say most of them were inquiries, although there were a substantial number of complaints.

That gives the average citizen an opportunity to come to one place in the city hall, and they tell him right away where to get a marriage license; what he has to do to get a permit for a house; and generally it's resulted in a much happier relationship between the citizens and government, because in the old days they would wander around forever and a day, not knowing where to go or how to get things done.

It's been interesting to me to get from that source a check on the efficiency of the various departments. You know most of the complaints are going to be directed against the police and street departments and the collector of revenue. But with proper discount of that sort of thing, you can still get a pretty good idea of where the weak spots are in your organization from screening the complaints which come in. If they're reiterated time after time, it looks as though there is something wrong.

The only other thing that I would like to mention is that we have found in two years that the man or men who wrote the charter were quite naturally and quite properly thinking in terms of a municipal government as it came to them, largely on a prewar basis. . . . This may sound stuffy and highhat, but I found that in municipal government, as in almost any other field of life, there is an enormous amount of cultural lag. People were coping with a problem, and usually thinking in terms of an experience two, three, four, five, or ten years ago. We have, therefore, had to improvise in order to meet what to me are the three critical problems which our city is confronted with. One is housing, which I've spoken of. The other is traffic and transportation, which I think is a headache in every city in the world everywhere, and there is literally nothing in our framework of government to cope with that.

We have a traffic manager, who is the head of a department in the bureau of streets. We temporized for a while with citizen committees, and finally we got an agency called the Urban Traffic and Transportation Board, with a decent appropriation; and that is made up of a rather large-sized citizens' group, twenty-one in this instance—the presidents of the railroads; the president of the traction company; the head of the trucking industry; the topflight fellow in the teamsters' union, and so on down the line. They have gotten, just the other day, an executive director to whom they are paying $18,000 a year for the purpose of getting a long-range plan for the solution of getting people in, through, and around the city.

Now theoretically that, of course, should have gone to the planning commission; but the planning commission, having six of its nine members as citizens serving part time without pay, were so swamped with the problem of the public improvement program, the capital budget, and the need to pass—which I think is foolish—on every zoning change and every street opening, it just didn't seem feasible to give them this additional load.

If you're going to frame a new charter here, I should think you would want to give very serious consideration to how you're going to handle that traffic problem as a matter of governmental setup, as well as the shelter and blight problem.

The third great problem which confronts us, and I think you, to some extent—I don't know how much—is this problem of metropolitan government —what you're going to do with the suburbs, the outlying areas, taxwise, sewerwise, housingwise, civil defensewise, and an infinite number of other ways. And I would think you would give some thought to having some kind of a niche in your city government which would enable you to have somebody other than the mayor who would be in a position to deal, probably on a co-operative basis, with other communities with that whole problem of suburban government. . . .

I should have mentioned a provision which I think has been very valuable, which requires the council to appropriate to the civil service commission for the activities of the personnel director not less than one-half of 1 per cent of the personnel items in the budget each year, thus making it impossible for the personnel department to be starved into submission.

Under our Pennsylvania law it is possible to mandamus to enforce that provision. . . .

CHAIRMAN LYON: Thank you, Mayor Clark, for all of us.

I am sure there are questions.

ALDERMAN CULLERTON: Mr. Mayor, the director of finance—is he directly under the mayor's office?

MAYOR CLARK: Yes, he is. He, too, is selected by this panel system. That is to say, the charter sets up the president of the Philadelphia Clearinghouse Association; the president of the Philadelphia Association of Certified Public Accountants; and the dean of the Wharton School at the University of Pennsylvania, and says they shall select and submit to the mayor three names from whom he must select his finance director.

In case the mayor doesn't like those three names, he can throw them back; and they have to keep putting them up until he finds someone satisfactory.

Being the first mayor under the new charter, it seemed to me we would have gotten off to a bad start if we began by doing that.

The original finance director has just returned to the Bureau of Municipal Research, a civic agency from which he came, and I have just appointed a new one.

I was faced with a particular dilemma because the panel consisted of three Republicans. Of course, as you know, I'm a Democrat; and while they're very decent and high-grade fellows, they didn't have the same "bleeding-heart" attitude toward getting somebody who was really friendly to the administration as I did.

We have what I consider a prejudice in Philadelphia, and I don't know whether you have it here, or not—but we haven't grown up to it yet. I think it is concurred in by every single member in city council, against what we call "carpetbaggers." They just don't like anybody who doesn't live in the city of Philadelphia, and say you find somebody to take that job that lives in Philadelphia, whether he can read or write or not. It's an insult to the intelligence of the citizens to suggest that any job in the world can't be filled by a local resident. They are perfectly willing to admit that everybody who plays on the Phillies and the Athletics should come from outside Philadelphia, but not when it comes to this situation. I have kind of ignored it, and I have brought in a number of people from out of town; and they are now known as "carpetbaggers." Anybody who comes into Philadelphia is a carpetbagger. So, to help me out, this panel gave me two carpetbaggers, and a former Republican city controller.

ALDERMAN CULLERTON: For how long a term?

MAYOR CLARK: Well, under Pennsylvania law the power to appoint includes the power to dismiss, so the staggered term of the civil service commission, which we talked about a little while ago, is legally ineffective because the appointing power can fire at any time.

So far as the finance director is concerned and the managing director and all the rest of these people, they serve at the pleasure of the mayor and can be fired at any time, except that the managing dirctor, if he thinks he's been fired for an insufficient reason, can appeal to the civil service commission. If the civil service commission sustains him, he has to be paid for the full balance of his term, whether he goes out and gets another job or not.

Finally, on Sunday, I took the top carpetbagger on the list, and I have my fingers crossed. And he said he wouldn't go to work unless the salary was raised from $15,000 to $18,000. I tipped off some of the leaders of the city council that this was the choice, and they said they'd rather have the carpet-bagger because he was a Democrat. So, I think I'm all right. [*Note:* Council raised the salary of the finance director to $18,000 on April 12, 1954.]

MR. McFETRIDGE: What right does this charter give you in the matter of raising revenue, particularly the revenue on real estate; the right to license?

MAYOR CLARK: The city council has complete power over that. You can mandamus the council to levy the taxes necessary to balance the budget, but they have both the appropriating and tax-levying power.

The procedure is for the finance director to prepare for the mayor, during the course of the summer, after consultation with the department heads, the operating budget and for the city planning commission to prepare the capital budget. Then they're screened during the month of September by me, and I get estimates of revenue from the finance director, too. We try to bring the two in balance.

With respect to the capital budget, we have to think in terms of the constitutional debt limitation and the extent to which we want to burden current revenue with the carrying charges on the bonds necessary to keep the capital outlay and how much we want to pay out of current revenue.

.   .   .

ALDERMAN BECKER: Would you say your managing director is something in the nature of a city manager?

MAYOR CLARK: Well, you see, he does not have vast areas which a city manager controls. He doesn't have finance. He doesn't have law. And he doesn't have commerce. He doesn't have public relations. And he doesn't have personnel. He is not allowed to engage in political activity, so his relations with the city council are strictly on a governmental basis.

ALDERMAN BECKER: Well, except for that would you call him a city manager, in a sense?

MAYOR CLARK: No, I don't think so. I think he is *sui generis*. He has ten line departments.

ALDERMAN BECKER: You lean a good deal on him?

MAYOR CLARK: Yes, but not any more than on the finance director; and in these two hectic years on the solicitor and the deputy mayor, on the political business.

ALDERMAN BECKER: With that kind of setup with the finance director—I have no preconceived ideas, and I want to get it on the basis of your experience—would you feel, after your experience there, that a so-called "deputy mayor" or "city manager" would be of help to you in performing your functions?

MAYOR CLARK: Well, I think they're very different. I think a deputy mayor and a city manager would be very different people.

ALDERMAN BECKER: Let's call him a city manager.

MAYOR CLARK: Except that now I'm not objective, and I'm afraid I'm egotistical—I like to run the show myself.

. . .

ALDERMAN BECKER: Do you have any agency in municipal government to constantly appraise the efficiency of operations and economy of operations other than through your finance director and budget director?

MAYOR CLARK: That is the principal one. It was intended that the Office of Information and Complaints should do that, because it is permitted to make any investigations which the mayor asks it to do of the efficiency of the operation of any of the other departments. I believe that is what the department does in New York. I personally felt that we should have it, and still do. For budget reasons I haven't attempted to build that up, so it would have the type of personnel to do it. The managing director has a number of administrative analysts in his office, who are engaged in a constant screening of that.

ALDERMAN BECKER: Who has that—the managing director?

MAYOR CLARK: Yes. That was a row, because the finance director wanted them in his office.

. . .

MR. FARR: Who does the controller work under?

MAYOR CLARK: The controller is elected; and it's been my unhappy lot to have a Republican controller ever since I've been in. The initial Republican controller was a swell guy, and we got along fine. He was tough. You couldn't get away with anything.

The present city controller has been in office two months. He was elected on a platform of "throw the rascals out," and I was the principal rascal.

MR. FARR: Does he have pre-audit authority?

MAYOR CLARK: Well, he has; in my judgment, that is a mistake, too; I don't think he should. I was controller before I was mayor, so I know a little about it, even though I'm a lawyer. I think he should be confined to post-audit, but he isn't. He is a double-check.

The principal draftsman of the charter was a very able and an extremely capable lawyer, who had been a Republican attorney-general of Pennsylvania and had a strong belief in the theory that everybody in government is a crook; and he felt that we needed not only the finance director to pass on all requisitions, whether for personnel, purchases, or anything else; and that he should have an elaborate system of books, where you could go in and check him—but also, the controller had to approve it before it went on through. And this controller has started putting monkey wrenches in that particular wheel.

. . . However, to answer your question—we have a lump-sum budget, and that's a godsend to the executive branch. We go in and justify before the council all of our appropriations in four or five categories; I can't remember them all.

One of them is personal services; another is contractual services; a third is material and supplies; and there are one or two minor ones that I can't remember. They tell us what they want the money for. They ask questions. They give us a lump-sum appropriation, and we don't have to spend it the way we say we're going to.

We are bound by rudimentary elements of good faith, and we wouldn't think of spending it in a way we haven't justified before council without talking it over with them.

This may be a little interesting example. We have a rather temperamental and imaginative director of recreation, and after the budget was passed he concluded that it would be a wonderful thing to have an ice-skating rink out on Rayburn Place, which is right next to the City Hall.

He got a promoter from whom he got a contract, saying he would furnish ice for 30 days; and they had a little Muzak piped in; and built it up, for $6,000, for 30 days, to make the ice. Well, there wasn't a darned thing in the budget. He didn't think about it until after the budget had been passed. We went around to the boys in the city council and said, "I think it's a good pitch." He let the contract. The city controller has said that is an illegal expenditure, and he quoted a couple of provisions of the city charter which led him to believe that. He said it's an immoral and improper thing to do, because you didn't tell the council about it.

We, in effect, said, "Nuts to him."

He's held up the requisition; but, curiously enough, his lawyer is the city solicitor, and the city solicitor is my appointee, so the city solicitor is rendering an opinion telling him the holding-up of that requisition is illegal, and he has to pass it. I don't say that that's necessarily good government.


# THE MOSES EFFECT

### REXFORD G. TUGWELL


IN 1960, when Robert Moses resigned as Commissioner of Parks (and from a few other positions), there was in the City of New York that shocked awareness that comes when people are rudely reminded that all of

---

This article was written especially for this volume.

us are mortal. By then it seemed impossible to think of New York parks without thinking of Moses. It was as though Brooklyn Bridge had tumbled down or the Hudson River had dried up; it was a calamity of nature. It was announced simultaneously, it should be said, that he was to be put in charge of planning and developing a World's Fair to be held in 1964. But he had never before felt it necessary to give up anything to do something else; he had simply done whatever it was suggested that he do in addition to all his other jobs.

Suddenly it was realized that he was now seventy-two years old and that he had been Commissioner of Parks for twenty-six years. By the time the World's Fair had run for two years (as that of 1938 had) and one or two more had been spent in demobilization, he would be getting on toward eighty. Could it be that he was feeling the weight of his years and getting ready to abandon the public service?

There was considerable relief when it got around that time had not really been responsible. A close watch disclosed no apparent slackening of his energies. And his burdens seemed to be carried with the same insouciance New Yorkers were used to. It was explained that his resignations were more in the nature of a strategic regrouping. He would still be around, as available and as formidable as ever. Sighs of relief infused public comment. His detractors subsided in disappointment.

But the scare led to a certain questioning of what would happen when the day did come, even though it might still be relatively distant, when indeed he would be gone from all the familiar offices. There were admiring reappraisal of his contributions and wonder that one man could have done so much. And it is probably quite true to say that, even if his career had ended then—in 1960—he would have held a greater number and variety of public offices than any individual in American history. These were of course only his formal activities. But it was not the amazing list to be found in *Who's Who* that constituted the real account of his achievement. These formal positions were only tags attached to his services to city and state. Quite often, as everyone knew, he had done things without any title, perhaps without any authorization. And in other instances rearrangements were made or new names invented so that he could work more handily. New Commissions and Authorities sprouted perennially in his vicinity, to last as long as was convenient and then to be superseded by others.

It was realized that there had been a common character in all these activities. They were different; yet in significant ways they were alike. They were all public; they were all developmental; they all added to the civic estate; they would all belong to the people; and most of them, or at least many of them, would not have come into existence if Moses had not created the circumstances for their beginning and maneuvered them into being. The Moses effect was to apply the needed energy at the right time and to embody a conception in structure, clearing away all obstruction and leaving a functioning new facility.

## II

Moses' Park Commissionership dated back to 1934 when La Guardia had appointed him. But this was not the beginning of his public service. He had become a city investigator in 1913 even before he had finished his graduate work at Columbia. But it was in 1921 that the pattern afterward so familiar began to show itself. In that year, after being for two years Chief of Staff of a New York State Reconstruction Commission, he became secretary of a coalition committee for the municipal campaign of that year. He was half in and half out of politics, working here and there at any job he found interesting. There were even those who considered that he was promising material for political candidacy; he himself was among these, and it required some sharp lessons to convince him that this was not his métier. He learned finally from the defeat of 1934, when he had the temerity to run on the Republican ticket against Herbert Lehman. In the preceding year he had, with better judgment, declined a coalition nomination for Mayor; he could now see that this decision had been a better one. He was destined to be the administrator par excellence, a sort of super civil servant. Whatever the blandishments, he thereafter kept to this role.

Under Democratic, Republican, and Fusion Mayors (the "under" being a formal but not an actual description of status), and under various Governors, he thereafter went on to be the constructor of any building operation that needed to be carried out. Tunnels, bridges, housing complexes, highways (of various ranks), recreation facilities, forestry works, hospitals, schools, zoos and aquariums, water control and power dams and their adjuncts—it was all the same to him. If they were to be built, he took on the jobs and rammed them through. But he was always more than just a builder; he was often an originator and he was a gifted administrator. Moreover, all the jobs he undertook were carried out with an appreciation of their marginalia, the neighboring country, that was unique. Superhighways cleared slums, and parks appeared along them; housing developments involved recreation facilities; power works were an excuse for the extension of forests. The vast development along the St. Lawrence and at Niagara mothered highways, parks, and recreation facilities that transformed and glorified huge acreages of the state. It was always this way.

It will be recognized that this sort of thing is not at all easy to do. There are always penny pinchers who want to narrow the scope of projects they cannot prevent entirely; and there are always those who want to exploit the proximity of any public work to properties they may own. That Moses always got his way about the extension of the public estate is one of the virtues that so endeared him to all those who would be spoken of as good citizens. These are people who mean well but who are usually timid and ineffective. Moses became their hammer, occasionally their dynamite, and continuously the guardian of their wealth.

For a man who trod on so many feet, who ruthlessly brushed aside objectors—sometimes even those with valid points—he came out in the long run with a surprising number of friends. There was hardly a gathering in New York where it was safe to say anything derogatory about Moses. He was firmly fixed in people's minds as the author of their progress.

Let me illustrate with a typical instance. One evening in 1939 I was sitting at a dinner given in honor of the Planning Commissioners, of whom I was one. Next to me was a distinguished architect, rather old, and perhaps a little out of touch with current events. He had been discoursing to me about Moses' virtues, which I was not at all disposed to deny; but when he made the chief matter for praise the recently completed East River Drive, I had to protest. This was a project Moses had for some reason not approved. It had been carried out by Stanley Isaacs, then President of the Borough of Manhattan, against continuous opposition from Moses.

I simply said that my distinguished friend had chosen a bad illustration. He must recognize that it was Isaacs who deserved the credit in this instance. The old gentleman drew himself up, turned to look me in the face, and said with all the sternness that he could command: "It is perfectly amazing to me the lengths Moses' detractors will go to keep his achievements from being recognized."

I subsided. I recognized that I was up against a symbol. It was George Washington and the cherry tree all over again. If it weren't so, it ought to be; and to question it was to damage values worth more than veracity in history.

### III

The condition for which the Moses effect is a specific is the check, amounting to a standstill, that well-meaning efforts to get going and keep going often encounter when large-scale organization is involved.

Take, for instance, urban redevelopment. Efforts to rehabilitate city cores have been in process now for several decades. There has been an elaborate deployment of civic forces, a flood of propaganda, libraries of theorizing, immense efforts at fact-gathering, and an expenditure of large sums. And the situation has grown alarmingly worse year by year. This is not because nothing had been done. A few impressive projects have been completed. But in sum they have never amounted to more than a fraction of the worsening that took place concurrently.

If good will, earnest activity, and willingness to argue could have got ahead of the degeneration, we should by now be emerging into an era of municipal wonders. But they have not sufficed. While hands have been wrung and warnings issued, the slums have grown, the traffic problem has become more nightmarish, the inner areas of the cities have rotted, and suburbia has sprawled over the surrounding countryside, escaping any kind of responsibility for the heart region.

What the Moses effect is in situations of this sort can be seen in the instances of success. Whenever bureaucratic ganglia have been broken up and reshaped, wherever blocking interests have been circumvented, wherever there has been ruthless efficiency in administration, wherever the necessary funds have been found at the time they could be of most use—wherever all these problems have converged, the Moses effect has been present. In the best instances, that remarkable patriotism that is latent in every old city has been mobilized and the community has found a new pride in regeneration.

The most significant observation to be made about the Moses effect in action is that it is an increasing, a multiplying force; there is a gathering and discharge of energy which becomes a tide of change. It is a tide to match and meet the sinister degenerative changes that beat on the city from amorphous and extraneous sources—real estate speculation, developers, the increase or decrease of manufacture and commerce and the alteration of its nature, the incoming and outgoing of population, and the emergence of new habits and facilities that displace old ones (such as those that follow from increased productivity—automobiles in vast numbers, for instance). A Moses rides the tides when he can, deflects them where possible, and when necessary builds dams against them. But he is a restless force operating constantly to make out of what is happening what he wants to happen.

A Moses is everywhere at once. He never refuses a job. And he takes on the whole of it. If a tunnel or a bridge is indicated, or the rebuilding of a neighborhood, or new facilities for commerce, for recreation or for the arts, he starts from the beginning. He first mobilizes all the available support. He next overwhelms potential objections with concise, well-illustrated literature, with speeches, interviews, and so on, and then assumes that anyone who is still recalcitrant is either an idiot or self-serving. And almost before anyone realizes that a commitment has been made, he is hard at work getting the funds. He prefers that they be given him; but he often has to get them the hard way. If public sources fail—if he cannot persuade federal, state or city governments to come across—he goes straight to Wall Street.

The favor a Moses enjoys among investment bankers is a source of deep suspicion among those who are conditioned to believe that bankers never invest except when a profit is probable; and profit from a public enterprise is hardly its first purpose. This suspicion Moses does not attempt to allay. His projects are, he thinks, desirable; if they cannot be financed in any other way than by persuading investors to put up the funds, then that way must be taken. He makes his requests specific, separable, and answerable to such a demand that payment will not be grudged. Because Moses subdues the suspicious and rides over their prostrate forms, the bankers, who do not usually enjoy such championship, are delighted to cooperate. And when it is seen how complete the engineering evidence is, they have no hesitation in following the financial plan he prefers. This is to discharge the indebtedness regularly, out of income, over a period of years, at the end of which title passes to the public.

This is not invariable. It may be expedient to integrate funds from many sources, both public and private, in getting a complex project done. Insurance companies may be interested in housing, for instance, and associations or individuals in art or museum projects. But what Moses has always placed the strongest reliance on is the unimpeachable nature of the investment he requests. To maintain a reputation for the planning of solvent enterprises he has for decades maintained a relationship—in one or another way—with architects and engineers who in time have become almost indistinguishable from his own individuality. They save him many arguments; they keep him out of trouble; they enable him to move into and through his various operations with bewildering speed.

All this works together. The first thing Moses does when the time is right to start something is to get it clearly in focus for everyone likely to be concerned. This means that while he has been doing his own casting about he has had studies made—often elaborate and costly ones—as to the feasibility of the project, its best structure and method, and its permanent value. When he goes to his bankers and begins to ask for authorization from the appropriate public bodies, he is ready with the kind of publicity that it seems churlish to oppose.

The Moses pamphlet is really formidable. A file of them shows such similarity that clearly a most effective model has been evolved and has been followed faithfully. It can be understood at a sharp glance. Pictorial charts and superb photographs are accompanied by descriptive sentences that are little more than captions. Predictions are unequivocal; concise references are made to time and to costs. And usually they run in series. As the work progresses, its various stages are followed. One can see the project take shape and become operational on the schedule that was originally laid out.

The impact of this reporting is tremendous. It creates confidence, it builds pride. As a result, when another project is proposed, the original doubts are bound to be less than they would otherwise have been. In New York, anything Moses wants to do is presumed to be worth doing. The faint voices of objectors are carried away on the wind of his propaganda.

## IV

It will be said—indeed it is said—that there can be too much even of such a good thing. This is true. The deduction to be made from the beneficence of the Moses effect is that it may run wild. It may become something that is not examined and cannot be criticized. The effect is one of uncontrolled force. It involves ingenuity and aggressive pursuit of adopted objectives; but it does not accept the sincerity of any opposition, loyal or other. It becomes irresponsible, encroaches on other areas than its own, eats up income that ought to be shared out, monopolizes attention, and shuns coordination with others' work.

The Moses effect is not a substitute for the thoughtful consideration of structure and of function generally; it will not result in the recasting of governmental relations—federal, state, and city. The impatience and intolerance associated with it are likely to smother considerations that in the long run are vital. The Moses kind find it difficult to accept the framework and the continuing contribution of the professional planner. Nothing, in fact, creates such a fury in the Moses enclave as the suggestion that there is a master plan to which conformance is important. There is a terrible kind of vigilance against potential limitation. I have never been able to make up my mind whether the antagonism here is an integral part of the Moses effect or whether it may be possible to tame the effect to the uses of civilized organic growth. We are, in our generation, apt to regard the characteristics of the original Moses as an irrefragable whole. But this is not necessarily true. And anyway the original is only the most remarkable model of something known before his time and even among his contemporaries. Ranch foremen known as "ramrodders" are of the authentic breed. General Somervell was an even more gaudy example of the effect operating on a grand scale. Has anyone who saw it happen ever been able to forget the way the Pentagon materialized out of nothing? And there have been others. But Robert Moses himself has gone on so long, and carried through so many enterprises, that he is generally accepted as *the* example.

At the same time that he has been exhibiting the methods by which programs can actually be realized, there has been developing in our civilization an organizational inertia that tends to prevent decisive action. The plans and hopes so widely conceived for our society everywhere are often brought to a virtual standstill. The Moses effect prevents this from happening by subduing friction, pointing up objectives and applying irrepressible energy. It is no doubt as necessary in the crises of our organizational affairs—both public and private—as have been the great social inventions of the past, such as scientific management, the use of the budget, or personnel testing. But it could be far more beneficial if exerted within a plan.

The Moses effect certainly has a relationship with one of the most puzzling areas of social theory. Inventions and discoveries ought to have had far more results in bulk than they have had; these effects ought to be more than linear; they ought to spread as constellations of influence wherever suitable conditions exist. If the results that ought to have been expected had occurred, change would have gone on at many times the rate experienced in reality. In fact, inventions are sometimes smothered, they come to a dead end in one application, or they lie dormant, available but unused. The growth in national productivity has been slowed down, at least temporarily, to a third or a quarter of the rate experienced in some other economies. It could well have been several times what, for more than a decade, it has been.

It is apparent that inertia has tended to become stronger as social organization has become more sophisticated. The contending forces within organizations use their energies in contending rather than in increasing output. This subject does not have to be pursued very far to discover the inertial block.

It lies in the rigidity of organizations as they achieve maturity. Once a scheme of job descriptions has been completed and individuals have been assigned to duties, there is automatically set up a defense against modification; and there is relaxation within the protective cover of classification. In the modern organization individuals move within a strictly defined order. Their promotions are from one to another in an understood way—usually seniority; and they are defended by an association (the union, perhaps) devoted to the status quo. Any threat of disturbance is met with a furious onslaught by their officials, lobbyists, and propagandists.

For these, and for other, reasons, social invention has become an unwelcome element, a potential danger to an order constantly trying to find balance and inertia. Invention tends to be smothered and denatured whenever it appears. It is possible to conceive of devices for dissolving this systemic constipation. Planning is, in fact, a way of institutionalizing change instead of inertia. It thus makes use of the tendency toward stasis to make certain that it will not occur.

But planning is not a substitute for the Moses effect; it is rather a container for it. The Moses effect explodes in the midst of tight restrictions and procedures, breaking up defenses, putting objectors rather than innovators in the wrong. All this can happen within the over-all concept of the organism and need not disturb its march toward whatever destiny it has. It is the virtue of the effect that it causes a general facing forward, a coagulation of interests about an objective to be joined in by all. It reduces the role of individual or group aims and substitutes more general or public ones. It is this glorification or inspiration that is sometimes transformed into a splendid movement.

But the effect is a phenomenon social analysts find refractory. It has to do with personality, character, leadership, dedication, ambition, vanity, identification with objectives, and plain obstinacy. It might be possible to work out a specification sheet that would describe the Moses make-up; if this could be done, a search could be made for individuals with potentially similar qualities. This would not be easy, for much of the effect is the result of unexpected—I almost said unpredictable—inspirations, sudden enthusiasms, or even infuriated resentments. What Moses has done in these transports has usually been disconcerting and often devastating. And this shows how complex an analysis would be required to uncover others, for it must be recalled that his opponents have often been skilled and determined too and have not neglected to do their best in sizing up the monster they were attempting to subdue. They have almost failed and fallen before his blandishments or his onslaughts.

If what this country needs is a Moses for each of its social organisms, a deliberate search for them will not be easy. But they are not arising in sufficient number. The suppressing mechanisms are too efficient. They did not stop the rugged original; but they bend and break his would-be successors.

## V

An examination of the Robert Moses history would probably yield many clues to the method by which more of his kind could be found. But even if they were discovered, they would be no more than potentials: a set of circumstances would have to be arranged, or would have to happen spontaneously, which would allow the Moses effect to operate.

The identification of individuals with the apparent qualifications might not be too difficult, for there are plenty of intelligent young people in every generation who go to good educational institutions (Moses went to Yale), who develop an enthusiasm for administrative careers with a bias toward the general interest, and who prepare themselves by doing graduate study, though not necessarily, as Moses did, at Oxford and Columbia, although Oxford did bring him into admiring contact with the British Civil Service, then at its most inspiring period. Many such young people also find sponsors, sometimes ones as helpful as Al Smith was in the case of Moses. But out of the hundreds of this annual crop, most are absorbed in the practice of professions or in jobs where they get ahead individually but make only minor impressions because they lack the force that is the identifying mark of the true Moses.

It may be some defect of character, assurance, ambition, ability, capacity for indignation, or ingenuity that softens them. It may be that they are simply unable to absorb punishment and go on functioning. They are, at any rate, resigned to subordination. But what is more likely to have happened is that they have had so long and so effective a training in tolerance, good manners, discretion, the overlooking of injustices and minor corruptions, and so on, that they never built up a really good head of steam. They may get ahead in corporate or in government service, become moderate successes, enjoy good incomes, have reputations for rectitude and neighborliness. But they do not become a Moses unless they explode and shatter the complacency and order all about them, creating an unholy mess, but also making it necessary to clean it up and start over.

A Moses has to be an indignant fellow, intolerant of inefficiency and abuses, aggressively righteous, incorruptible and unforgiving, impervious to criticism, vain to the point of belligerently identifying himself with his adopted objectives, and willing to attack anyone or any group brash enough to oppose him. He must also have a talent for attracting attention and he must possess the ability, in seeming contradiction to the other qualities he has, of organizing support in such volume that he can ride, like a surf rider, the waves that sweep toward the completion he has visualized.

The circumstances in which a young person with these characteristics can reach a strategic situation are obviously unusual; and an older generation that will allow it, much less encourage it, is even more unusual. Moses found Al Smith and his colleagues at the right time. Their position and their sophistication were such that he could make a start. Al, in his own way, was an indignant fellow too, although his wrath was very selectively discharged. He knew better than to engage in too many fights at once and he had an exquisite sense of the risks he ran. Moses learned a good deal in a rough school.

The simile of the battle is almost inevitable. Battles, however, should be engaged in only when they can be won. For this to be certain, the preparation has to be long and meticulous. Also, when the issue is joined the first attack must be so massive as to be overwhelming. When Moses came to have autonomy he used these lessons with great skill. His fury in early engagements was useful in preventing later ones from developing. His potential opponents were intimidated: he was known to have a low boiling point and a talent for invective. These were deterrents that saved him many a struggle.

But it would be a mistake to picture the original of the Moses effect as having clawed, screamed, and wrestled his way to the top. It was not that way at all. He was a Phi Beta Kappa to begin with, that is to say an intellectual; and he had acute perceptions. He was as curious as a cat and quite unable to keep quiet about what he discovered. That he had these abilities was fortunate. They enabled him to investigate and report, to suggest and to demonstrate. For a Moses to develop, they would always have to be welcomed by those who have the power to accept or reject. And this is a narrow condition. Persons in power are apt to be protective and fearful that investigation will open chasms of doubt in their vicinity.

It was not until he reached autonomous positions—or ones that were relatively so, such as cabinet positions under an elected chief—that there began that continuous and increasing clatter and sparking afterward recognized as the Moses effect. What this amounted to, in the long run, as authority was accumulated, was the institutionalization, in an unorthodox mode, of dynamic change. It had, unfortunately, no relation to anything except what had made Moses indignant or had struck his imagination. It might not be at all the most important thing to be done, to use resources for, to be given priority. But it seemed so, lit as it was by the flame of the Moses exposition. And, if it was not the most useful, it was still admirable, and so could be counted as a gain. Only his wistful competitors for funds had reservations—they and the planners who had larger views of city and the state and would rather have seen priority given to some more basic improvements.

## VI

The worst that may have to be admitted is that the dangers of the Moses effect may be inherent in its virtues. Perhaps it could not function in the containing ambient of a master plan. This is the possible dilemma. To harness the force, to direct it toward the most necessary objectives, may be to smother it. A Moses may be denied the incentive essential to his behavior. The explosions may never come off.

On the other hand, if the effect does function uncontrolled, the danger of vanity, arrogance, bullheadedness, is a real one. Moses happened to be Park Commissioner, so New York got more parks, and ones more elaborately equipped, than could be maintained if other services were not to be skimped —not more parks than were desirable ideally, but more than were relatively feasible. But Moses had support, so much that he could stamp down doubters; and press, pulpit, and all good citizens were behind him. Cautious caveats by competing commissioners and by general planners were met by such effective abuse that their authors retired with such dignity as they could salvage.

This was equally true of other favorite enterprises. They got done. They were pridefully exhibited. But New York—and this seemed surprising to those who had been fed on the Moses legend—was still less than a civic model. Perhaps if Moses had been in charge of everything it might have been better. Eventually, of course, he *was* put in charge of all development activities. This was, however, late in his career when he had become a behemoth no politician would think of crossing. It would, we must imagine, always come late in such a career. It can be counted as part of the Moses effect that its full force will usually be exerted in special sectors and rarely on matters important to the whole organism.

It would be impossible to list the goods, services, facilities, amenities, New York State and New York City would not have if Moses had not existed. But it is not really necessary to make such an appraisal. Everyone— even those whose dislike amounts to obsession—acknowledges that they are everywhere. This is an argument it is impossible to confute. It is also an unanswerable argument for other Moseses in other situations. It points to the need for finding out how to select them, how to get the most out of them—and how to reconcile their activities with more sophisticated social strategy.

# CAPITAL PROGRAMMING IN PHILADELPHIA

## WILLIAM H. BROWN, JR., AND CHARLES E. GILBERT

MUCH, THOUGH SURELY NOT ALL, of city planning today is directly related to capital programming. This is especially so in *large* cities for at least three major reasons: basic physical plant and utilities are often run down or obsolescent for a complex of historical reasons; many routine programs are "capital-intensive" and are becoming more so under the impact of new technology and professional standards; and urban renewal has entailed an increasingly entrepreneurial approach to land-use planning. Capital programming itself is a process of separate budgetary decision on capital items, however defined.[1] The rationale for the separate decision process values "planning" highly and emphasizes *fiscal* planning of outlaying that is loan-financed and *physical* planning of projects distinguished by "lumpiness" and/or longevity. It follows from these considerations that the planning and programming of physical improvements cannot be sharply separated from the remainder of municipal policy. City planning as applied to capital programming has to do not only with land use but with most functional programs and with fiscal policy.

While some long-range municipal planning will probably take place in the line departments, the focal point of planning is likely to be the review and assembly of the over-all capital program, at which point fiscal, programmatic and land-use planning all come into play even if the principal competence and concern of the planning agency is in land-use planning. The planning agency can be conceived as performing any or all of the four roles of *research, integration, allocation,* and provisions of the *long view.* While conceptually distinguishable, these roles tend to merge in the practice of capital program review. Thus planning research tends to support a longer view of policy and facilities through the anticipation of trends and the gradual adumbration or articulation of goals, perhaps in a master plan. Integration of projects for the effective fulfillment of program goals and the avoidance of land-use conflicts or premature project obsolescence tends to slide into inter-agency capital budgetary allocations as priorities are attached to project requests.

Students of municipal affairs have differed as to the proper role or balance of roles of the planning agency in capital programming. Some have argued that over-all efficiency of the city's programs and physical plant will best be served if the planning agency in effect confines itself to research and integration; others have maintained that these same ends require more-or-less authoritative capital budgetary allocations by the planner based upon more-or-less definitive determinations of city goals.[2] Much, though not all, of the literature of city planning has been tending to expansiveness about the role of the planner and the comprehensive plan in capital programming and in

---

Reprinted from *American Political Science Review,* October, 1960, pp. 659–668, by permission of the publisher and of the authors.

1. An excellent treatment, with references to the not voluminous literature, is Jesse Burkhead, *Government Budgeting* (New York, 1956), ch. 8.

2. For the first view, see Allison Dunham, "A Legal and Economic Basis for City Planning," *Columbia Law Review,* Vol. 58 (1958), pp. 650–671. For a thoroughgoing statement of the second view, see Rexford G. Tugwell, "Implementing the Public Interest," *Public Administration Review,* Vol. 1 (1940), pp. 32–49.

municipal policy generally.[3] Yet the recent literature of public administration
has increasingly emphasized constraints and limitations upon "rationality"
and thus, by implication, upon long-range and comprehensive planning.[4]
The arguments most relevant here have been those of economists who for a
combination of institutional and intellectual reasons have been skeptical of
the "efficiency" implied in the "classical" or "neo-classical" organization theory
and in central and comprehensive decisions, and who have questioned
whether administration—especially in a pluralistic political context—can
possibly or profitably operate in a logical and long-range optimizing fashion.[5]

Capital programming should provide a good test of these conflicting views
of the intellectual and institutional role of planning in city administration
(though our treatment is largely confined to its institutional role). Both
recommended and ultimate decisions and eventual accomplishments are
clear, more-or-less quantified, and recorded. Agencies of planning, administration, and politics are involved at various points in the decision process
and so is the entire spectrum of municipal policy in its physical, fiscal, and
functional aspects.

The Philadelphia experience should provide an especially critical test for
reasons that can only be briefly listed here. Capital programming in that
city has attained a reasonable maturity: the process of decision and of ultimate
appropriation and execution was mandated in the Home Rule Charter of
1951 and has since been conscientiously implemented by two "reform"
administrations. Some say that capital programming is now further developed
in Philadelphia than in any other American jurisdiction.[6]

The *political setting* of capital programming is one in which public expectations (as manifest in citizen organizations and the press) appear to

---

3. See, *e.g.,* Harvey S. Perloff, "Education of City Planners: Past, Present and Future," *Journal of the American Institute of Planners,* Vol. 22 (1956), pp. 186–217;
and the rejoinder by James M. Lee, "The Role of the Planner in the Present," *ibid.,*
Vol. 24 (1958), pp. 151–157. See also Henry Fagin, "Organizing and Carrying Out
Planning Activities within Urban Government," *ibid.,* Vol. 25 (1959), pp. 109–114,
which appeared after completion of our study and while this article was in a draft.

4. Though "rationality" is among the slipperiest of terms, we use it here to imply
clear-cut and central decisions about goals (usually based upon research into alternatives
and consequences) and the more-or-less rigorous "suboptimization" of such decisions at
lower administrative levels. The term embodies meanings often given to "coordination"
and "efficiency," and emphasizes long-range perspectives. On "efficiency," see Herbert
Simon, *Administrative Behavior,* 2d ed. (New York, 1957), ch. 9.

5. See C. E. Lindblom, "Policy Analysis," *American Economic Review,* Vol. 48
(1958), pp. 298–312, "Tinbergen on Policy-making," *Journal of Political Economy,*
Vol. 66 (1958), pp. 531–538, and "The Science of 'Muddling Through,'" *Public
Administration Review,* Vol. 19 (1959), pp. 79–88; and Roland N. McKean, *Efficiency
in Government through Systems Analysis* (New York, 1957), Part II.

6. We are not aware of any written statement to this effect, but several students of
municipal government have expressed this view to us. For treatments of the Philadelphia
experience, see Aaron Levine, "Philadelphia Story: A New Look," *New York Times
Magazine,* July 14, 1957, p. 8 ff.; and Edmund N. Bacon, "Capital Programming and
Public Policy," *Journal of the American Institute of Planners,* Vol. 22 (1956), pp. 35–
38. The authors are executive directors of, respectively, the Citizens' Council on City
Planning and the Philadelphia City Planning Commission.

support "planning" and "rationality" in City decisions. There is active and organized citizen support for city planning and public improvements, extending from what is loosely termed the "grass roots" to what can equally loosely be termed the "power structure." While providing support for the process of capital programming, however, the various citizen groups differ over the substance and extent of improvements.[7] The city's "organization" politics offers few obstacles to long-range planning, in our observation, and might on balance be classified as a stabilizing factor.[8]

The *governmental setting* seems equally appropriate to a test of planning. Philadelphia is decidedly a strong-mayor city. The small (17-member) Council is partially elected at large and its role in budgeting and personnel policy is sharply limited by the charter. The mayor is served at the top level by a Managing Director who heads the principal line departments, a Commerce Director in charge of major transportation *termini* and promotional and commercial facilities, and a Finance Director under whom most financial functions are centralized. These three officials are *ex officio* members of the quasi-independent Planning Commission. The small number of departments and the Planning Commission are highly professionalized. Urban renewal and transportation policy alone cut athwart the remainder of the administration, and these functions are served by coordinators in the mayor's office.[9] In summary, government in Philadelphia generally conforms to the conventional canons of "sound" city organization. A more favorable setting for long-range planning in a still highly pluralistic society would seem hard to find.

Our study of capital programming in Philadelphia began with an examination of its "stability"—that is, of the extent to which projects and allocations in the later years of six-year programs actually move forward on their original schedule to budgeting and execution. Taken in this sense stability should provide a good (though not literally sufficient) index of the effectiveness of long-range planning. Our unequivocal finding was that the

---

7. The principal city-wide groups concerned with capital programming are: The Citizens' Council on City Planning; the Philadelphia Housing Association; the Health and Welfare Council; the Chamber of Commerce; the Bureau of Municipal Research-Pennsylvania Economy League; and the Greater Philadelphia Movement (and its auxiliary, the Citizens' Budget Committee). Some idea of the concerns of these groups can be gained from their titles. The last-named (GPM) is a prestigeful and primarily businessmen's organization which has conceived and strongly supported a number of policy and capital improvements; its subsidiary (CBC) is primarily a fiscal watchdog agency. The leading interests of the other organizations broadly include: tax-consciousness, government organizations and reform, welfare and social service, urban renewal and housing, industrial promotion and renewal, and citizen involvement in planning. Some of these agencies reach into the neighborhoods directly or through affiliates.

8. For a recent study see James Reichley, *The Art of Government: Reform and Organization Politics in Philadelphia* (New York, The Fund for the Republic, 1959).

9. See Lenox L. Moak, "Background and Principal Features of the Philadelphia Charter," Appendix 1-A of Leverett S. Lyon, ed., *Modernizing a City Government* (Chicago, 1954); and Joseph S. Clark, Jr., "Experience with Philadelphia's New Charter," *ibid.*, Appendix 1-B.

process was characterized by a marked lack of stability as here defined, even allowing for the vicissitudes of intergovernmental grants, "forced" deferred maintenance, and acts of God.[10] This led us to an analysis of the main institutional processes bearing upon stability and instability. The characteristic roles of public agencies (though not, by and large, of private parties) are discussed in the remainder of this paper.

## II

Since 1952 capital programming decisions in Philadelphia have tended to gravitate from the Planning Commission to the administrative line. While the literature of public administration would suggest such a development, expectations surrounding capital programming in Philadelphia appear to point rather to a definitive (though penultimate) allocative (as well as integrative) role for the Planning Commission.[11] Though its intent was somewhat obscured by the *ex officio* device, the charter evidently envisaged such a role for the Planning Commission, and the Commission evidently performed a more decisive role in adjudicating among agencies and allocating funds in the early years than it has more recently.

Capital budget and program requests usually originate with the departments and are revised and assembled in the capital program and budget by the Planning Commission. The recommendations of the Commission go to the Mayor for review and eventual transmittal to Council, which must adopt a capital budget as an actual appropriation for the year ahead and a capital program as a six-year guide. Neither budget nor program can be amended without requesting the advice of the Planning Commission. Not all of the capital program receives the same treatment in the initial and reviewing stages. Some items—they are usually "lumpy" and exigent—are matters of top administrative policy and receive their impetus or their

---

10. Space precludes extensive documentation of the point here, though we have made a number of measurements in terms of funds and projects. Many changes are made between the second year of any capital program and the year following when it becomes a capital budget; and changes measured from the more remote years of capital programs are even more numerous and sizeable even though the most remote years are "filled up" to the $25 million ceiling on annual tax-supported city funds. In the 1959 capital budget no department's appropriation differed (up or down) by less than 13% from the previous year's schedule; 6 departments showed changes of more than 30% and one department of more than 100%. Eleven departments are included, and the net dollar changes tend to hide a number of project changes. *Most* projects and appropriations, moreover, are amended during the executory period of capital budgets.

11. For a representative statement in the literature of public administration, see Herbert A. Simon, Donald W. Smithburg, and Victor A. Thompson, *Public Administration* (New York, 1950), ch. 20, esp. pp. 442–447. The prevailing Philadelphia view is expressed in the following editorial comment on an issue between City Council and Planning Commission: ". . . the Planning Commission is only doing its job when it reshuffles priorities. Its purpose is to consider the City as a whole, and to balance desirable capital spending ideas against each other, and against the amount of money which may be spent. Without over-all planning, the Commission would have no function. City building would then descend to pork-barrel tactics. . . ." *The Evening Bulletin* (Philadelphia) 27 October 1958.

argument from the Mayor and his cabinet. The remainder of the program is finally settled at the level of the staff principals and deputies in the Planning Commission, the Managing Director's office, the Finance Director's office, and the office of the Director of Commerce. For the most part these decisions result from a collective, constant, cooperative, and consultative process which, however, is not without administrative bargaining at departmental and cabinet levels. In this process it now appears that the point of most influence is the Managing Director's office.

The principal factors in line predominance appear to be the following:

(1) The importance of being on the spot and active in day-to-day operations is considerable; policies (or projects) tend to emerge from on-going operations or immediate necessities.

(2) There has been an improvement in long-range planning in the departments stimulated, in fact, by the role of the Planning Commission in programming the demand for better project justifications. Progress has varied among departments because of substantive difficulties and factors of leadership and bargaining power. Such plans as there are fall into three main types: (a) efforts at broad definitions of public responsibilities in certain fields (*e.g.*, medical care for the needy) which have been produced by broadly representative committees; (b) essays at standards for services and facilities (*e.g.*, recreation space standards) embodying in varying degree existing professional standards; and (c) attempts simply to schedule facilities, modernizations or improvements, generally but not always on the basis of some data on age or cost (*e.g.*, the replacement of water mains). Actually, few detailed, written departmental plans are in existence.

(3) The Managing Director is formally charged with coordination of most departments. The City's Managing Directors have been able and vigorous, and have believed that the principal responsibility for all aspects of forward planning save over-all physical planning should rest with the departments rather than with the Planning Commission.

(4) The Managing Director's office has kept a rather tight grip on the departments through central staff work in reviewing their operating and capital budgets. It has instituted an initial screening of departmental capital project requests both at their inception and on an over-all basis before their submission to the Planning Commission. The rigor of this preliminary screening has varied among departments but has increased in recent years. It has reflected the Managing Director's view of a reasonable capital allocation among agencies and his judgment of projects' chances of survival later in the reviewing process. The Planning Commission, for its part, has often cut departments financially, leaving to them the decisions as to which projects are to be eliminated or deferred (save for those projects that raise problems of integration with one another or with the Commission's developing land-use projections and policies). Not infrequently the Managing Director intervenes at this stage also.

(5) Recently the administrative screening process has been extended and formalized by creation of a cabinet subcommittee charged with reviewing the "big" projects of large displacement that are the troublemakers in capital programming.[12] Naturally, this means scanning the capital program as a whole to see what projects can be deferred or displaced. The subcommittee does not finally decide these points; it reports to the Cabinet which then decides and communicates its decision to the Planning Commission. While the Commission staff may not follow the policy of the Cabinet, it will know that the *ex officio* Commission members will be following that line in Planning Commission meetings.

(6) The *ex officio* device has all along given substantial weight to the administration members of the Commission, but it has left to the Commission a function of arbitrating or adjudicating those cases in which the *ex officio* members were unable to reach prior agreement. Such cases were not infrequent in the past, but the cabinet subcommittee appears to have reduced their number.

(7) The ability of the Planning Commission to cope with its *ex officio* members has depended upon the information and interest of the Commissioners respecting the capital program. While these appear to have been considerable in the early years, there is much testimony to the effect that they have declined. Chairmen excepted, many Commissioners have attended hearings and meetings on the capital program less frequently in recent years and have tended to concentrate on a few pet projects. The role of the Commission's staff *vis à vis* the Commission appears to have grown, and it may be that some commission "marasmus" has set in where capital programming is concerned.[13]

(8) Two staff divisions of the Planning Commission are involved in capital program review and assembly; these are the Projects Division and the Comprehensive Planning Division. The latter has entered the picture only in recent years, reviewing departmental requests for conformance with the City's projected comprehensive plan. This review has not had much influence to date—despite the imminence of the comprehensive plan—because that plan has been tentative and has provided broad standards, projections and goals rather than concrete criteria for fund and project allocations.[14] The

---

12. Members of the subcommittee are the Managing Director, Finance Director, Director of Commerce, and Development Coordinator.

13. These observations apply only to the Commission's work in capital programming. Some informants have argued that, as the outline and specific requests of capital programs have matured and become familiar, less detailed Commission consideration is necessary to control of the program. This argument would not, however, appear to affect our conclusions about the Commission's role in relation to its *ex officio* members and its staff, and several informants who are very close to the Commission agree with our conclusions.

14. This conclusion rests upon testimony of some staff members of the Division and of other divisions, and upon our own comparisons of the recommendations of the Comprehensive Planning Division with the Planning Commission's final capital program document.

Projects Division is formally in charge of assembling the capital budget and program and, on the testimony of those most closely involved, the decisions result from informed judgment rather than explicit criteria. The leading members of the Division are long-time City servants (not trained planners) who know intimately the departments and attendant political pressures. They consciously and continuously supplement desk and drawing board decisions with the gleanings of sidewalk and corridor conversations. They have been prone to recognize that the range of choice for the Commission is limited by continuing programs, administrative and Councilmanic attitudes, top-level policies and popular demands for some projects working their way forward in the program. Their decisions thus rest substantially upon (a) their knowledge of the projects' etiology in the departments and their assessment of departmental planning and appraisal of "need," and (b) the "law of anticipated reactions" with reference to administration and Council. Integrative and long-term considerations are far from being ignored but the Projects Division lacks explicit criteria. The nature and sources of its information and the personal background of its members probably cause it to act to some extent as a buffer between administrators and planners.[15]

The Commission's role remains a significant one. Its vigorous Chairmen have prevailed in numerous policy decisions; generally they have been consulted in such decisions. Its prestige has given weight to its occasional protests over projects or scheduling. It has been conceded a genuine role of an integrative sort in the prevention of future diseconomies through conflicting projects or land uses or (from the City-wide view) inefficient scheduling. Increasingly the administration has been attending to some of these aspects itself, thus restraining the integrative role of the Planning Commission from becoming one of thoroughgoing allocation, but the Commission will clearly continue to play a role in identifying and shaping long-range goals and in integrating the scheduling of projects over the shorter run.

## III

Philadelphia's capital budgets and programs are, in the first instance, shaped by processes of planning and administration designed to maximize integration and the long view, and the City Charter seeks to maximize administrative initiative *vis à vis* Council. Capital programs are bulky and complex and the annual capital budgets carry more than a hundred line items, thus complicating Council's role in long-range planning. In general, it is clear that the administration has the initiative, but Council is none-

---

15. Though perhaps peculiar to Philadelphia, it may be worth noting that there are differences in orientation toward capital programming within the Planning Commission relating to function and background. Thus, the projects Division relies upon administrative contacts and "informed judgment"; the Comprehensive Planning Division is interested in more abstract and categorical analysis; the executive director relies a good deal upon personal identification with the city and upon esthetic and fluid rather than categorical and abstract approaches; and the Commissioners' approaches appear to be quite individual.

theless active in capital programming—largely through shifts in scheduling of projects rather than through their initiation, or the broad review of policies. Its effect is felt in three main ways, which may be briefly reviewed.

(1) Council tends to exert pressure for regional parity in the distribution of projects, for four apparent reasons. One is the structure of Council, in which ten of the seventeen Councilmen are elected from districts.[16] Councilmen agree that district and at-large members have characteristically different orientations to capital programming.[17] A second distributive tendency probably lies in the legislative process of decision, which is said to lend itself more to trading and logrolling than does hierarchical organization. Philadelphia's Council, dominated by one party, takes its capital program decisions in the closed caucus of that party, and the decision is reportedly characterized by a good deal of trading in which the party leadership is careful to see that everyone gets something to show his district, though no one gets all he wants. A third factor doubtless tending toward regional parity, and accentuating Council's concern for this value in comparison with the administration's, is the fact that most Councilmen are members of the dominant Democratic "organization," while the Mayor is not and is frequently at odds with it. A frequent generalization about big-city political organization runs to the effect that, while it is capable of achieving some centralization and overview, its most basic virtues are sectional responsiveness and flexibility.[18] The following news item is illustrative:

> Democratic Ward leaders in the Northeast will ask that $250,000 which was stricken from the capital program for acquisition of land for recreation purposes be restored, it was announced today.
> The leaders met Monday with City Council leaders to discuss with them the needs of the Northeast area. . . .
> This item was knocked from the program by the City Planning Commission (Councilman) McDevitt said. "All of the Northeast Democratic leaders are pledged to have this item reinstated. The Councilmen who met with us indicated agreement with this and have agreed to have this item added to the 1959–64 Capital Program."[19]

Finally, government and city-wide citizen organizations in Philadelphia have actively encouraged and created citizen organizations in the neighborhoods. The political party is far from being the only method of voicing or creating local demands. Administrative agencies, as well as district Councilmen, work

---

16. The Charter provides that each district shall contain aproximately 10% of the population by the decennial census, and the districts are, in fact, fairly equal in population. The total voting population of the city is about 1 million, so the districts are quite populous.

17. One Democratic Councilman-at-large, who lives in a district now represented by a Republican, told us that he is under constant pressure from his party leadership to "represent" that district, and that he takes great care to avoid being labeled as the Councilman from that district in order to preserve his independence and breadth of view.

18. For a recent discussion, see Martin Meyerson and Edward Banfield, *Politics, Planning and the Public Interest* (Glencoe, Ill., 1955), chs. 3, 9–11.

19. *The Evening Bulletin* (Philadelphia) 12 November 1958, p. 24.

closely with the neighborhood groups, which are alert to capital program decisions and mark the progress of relevant items in the printed Capital Program. Thus, the news account just quoted had its origin in a review of the Planning Commission's capital program recommendations by the Philadelphia Health and Welfare Council, which notified its Northeast Area Committee, which put "heat" on the Democratic organization and on a Councilman who was already faced with a difficult primary fight.

City informants agree that Council is more solicitous of regional parity than either the administration or Planning Commission; but, to the extent that the other parties endeavor to anticipate Council, the tendency toward parity spreads beyond Council. Council's regional distributive bent shows up chiefly in annual scheduling decisions. While the administration is likely to attempt a measure of geographical distributions in the six-year program as a whole, Council tends to make this an annual goal.[20]

(2) Council exhibits a marked tendency toward financial conservatism. It has strongly supported the existing $25 million ceiling on tax-supported City funds in capital budgets and has usually cut the budget somewhat below this figure, accomplishing still further reductions during the execution of the budget. The relative tight-fistedness of Council challenges explanation, since city councils might be expected to approximate more closely than other governmental bodies the model of Anthony Downs, in which governments spend up to the point at which the financing of projects outweighs in adverse votes the votes gained from the projects themselves; and because the chief pressures upon councils might be expected to be spending rather than retrenching pressures.[21]

We think there are two explanations of Council's fiscal conservatism, and that both are about equally important. One relates to the representative structure of Council and the distribution of organized attitudes and interests in the city. The small Council, partially elected at-large, with a strong leadership based in an entrenched party organization, appears to respond to the several city-wide citizen organizations that serve as fiscal watchdogs.[22] Significantly, the fiscal conservatism of Council is centered in its leadership rather than in the rank-and-file, and serves as something of a counterweight to the pressures for regional distribution discussed above. A second explana-

---

20. Space precludes a detailed discussion; but examination of Council's decisions, and a comparison of them with those of the Planning Commission and administration, bears out the thesis put forward here.

21. Anthony Downs, *An Economic Theory of Democracy* (New York, 1957). Downs' simplified theoretical model does not include separated governmental powers, however; and it appears to deal mainly with operating expenditures, or, at least, reasonably divisible expenditures.

22. *Cf.* the discussion in Leverett Lyon, *op. cit.*, ch. 4. There Gilbert Y. Steiner, discussing the advantages of election at-large *versus* election by districts, suggests that the "city-wide" interests that are alleged to prevail over "local" interests in councils elected at-large are chiefly interests in tax reduction, whereas the "local" interests tend to favor projects. Three citizen organizations in Philadelphia are primarily based upon tax and fiscal concerns; Council's leading fiscal monitor is elected at-large.

tion relates Council's fiscal conservatism to its governmental, rather than its political, role. On this view, Council's economizing tactics can be seen as an aspect of legislative-administrative rivalry, as a reaction to the administrative budgetary initiatives provided in the strong-mayor Charter, as a means of publicly demonstrating some form of budgetary participation and control, and—in the absence of more formal criteria for investment decisions—of forcing detailed project justifications from departments and administration.

(3) Council's orientation to capital programming tends to be immediate and concrete rather than long-run and abstract. It is more interested in capital budgets than in the program as a whole, and displays little interest at all in the remote years of capital programs. Its principal point of assertion is in the scheduling of projects rather than in over-all allocations or the initiation of projects, though a few projects are conceived or introduced by Councilmen and scheduling changes in capital budgets of course produce changes in programs. Councilmen argue that *they* are the "experts" on scheduling since they know what the people want at the moment.

Such abstract investment criteria as professional standards for service levels and facilities, or land use prescriptions, do not weigh heavily with Council, but it is difficult to show that the legislative body consistently favors certain types of projects at the expense of others. It is commonly said that Council prefers "visible" projects (*e.g.*, health centers over storm sewers), by which is really meant "politically popular," and *most* projects command popularity in *some* quarters. It is clear that recreation centers, health centers, and fire stations have been especially popular in Council and that libraries have had an indifferent reception; but there are two qualifications on any order of preferences. One is that projects of all types have been deferred in Council to make room for exigent items at administrative urging (recreation centers lend themselves to this treatment because they are numerous and individually inexpensive); the other is that Councilmanic attitudes (particularly among the leadership) seem to be undergoing some change. More receptivity to "economic base" projects at some cost to "welfare" projects is in evidence today than was the case three or four years ago—a change that may reflect recent progress and a widely acknowledged "catching up" in some welfare fields, together with the fiscal conservatism of Council's leadership and of other influential groups. But the political appeal of "welfare" projects remains strong, as election campaigns indicate.

Two general comments are in order respecting Council's participation in capital programming. One is that there are conflicting tendencies and orientations within Council itself—*e.g.*, between regional or neighborhood parity and fiscal conservatism—and that these tendencies marginally distinguish the leadership from the rank-and-file with respect to political pressures and tactics. The other comment is that, despite the complexity of capital programming and the administrative initiative it entails, Council's activity in scheduling indicates a continuing legislative role in relating "planning" to popular tastes and utilities. Capital programs, unlike operating budgets, closely approach the "alternative budget" conception in giving Council a cafeteria of projects to choose among. Given the official promises in printed capital programs, popular interest in the projects, and organized reactions and importunities, Council is likely to amend the judgments of professionals and planners by applying its own political conclusions respecting the people's wants.[23] It should be added, however, that amendments by Council account directly for only a small proportion of the "instability" noted above in Philadelphia's capital programming; *most* deviations from the capital program result from decisions in the administration and Planning Commission, and from delays and amendments during execution of the capital budget.

## IV

Generally speaking, the time horizons of the planners outrun those of the administrators; administrators take a somewhat longer view than the mayor's; and the time horizons of Council are the shortest of all. For many planners, of course, such a statement simply amounts to an implicit definition of "planning," "administration," and "politics."[24] The use of the comprehensive plan as a guide to capital budgeting, or the emphasis upon spending today for site acquisition rather than on immediate improvements, are both commonplace evidences of the planner's concern with the long-run.

Administrators might be expected to be less firmly committed to the future, more committed to flexibility in decision and action. The administrator is skeptical about the ability of anyone to predict accurately the circumstances under which he will be operating in two or three years, let alone six or twenty. His attitude may reflect in part the importance he attaches to administrative detail as a determinant of decision and action; in part it may be a reflex bow to the political environment. In any event, some of Philadelphia's top overhead administrators evince some feeling that even six-year capital programming tends to hamper administrative initiatives and action, and that a better procedure might be one in which departmental plans were only roughly blocked out in capital programs for, say, a three-year period, thus reserving funds but reserving, too, the right to change course when necessary and to determine details at a later date. Although long-range planning in the departments has increased in recent years, such plans fall far short of definite commitments in most cases and leave ample room for adjustment. Administrators are inclined to defend flexibility in capital budget execution—a process that has to date been quite unpredictable.

---

23 On the "alternative budget" proposal see Verne B. Lewis, "Toward a Theory of Budgeting," *Public Administration Review*, Vol. 12 (1952), p. 42 ff.

24. For a classical statement in the planning literature that planning means (1) applying the factor of adjustment and coordination among competing ideas, specialties and pressures, (2) supplying the long-range view and counteracting the pressures of the moment, and (3) research and data-gathering free from the pressures of the moment, see Alfred Bettman, *City and Regional Planning Papers* (Cambridge, 1946), ch. 5.

Though it is now general practice to schedule funds for project planning and site acquisition for the first year of the project, with the larger construction funds following later, capital budgets are still amended freely in the executory period. This period (the capital budget "fiscal year") consists of eighteen months, but several top administrators have argued for its extension.

The mayor actively intervenes in capital programming only in the case of major policy decisions and implications. Informants in the City government generally agree that neither of Philadelphia's mayors since 1952 has had a capital program, though each has pressed certain pet projects, programs or general but imprecisely defined emphases respecting the direction of city development. Both mayors have characteristically reserved major capital policy decisions until as late as possible; though both have on occasion attempted to take leadership for certain projects and, on a few occasions, have retreated in the face of opposition. To the extent that firm investment decisions were made for the long-run the mayor's freedom to respond to or manipulate the pressures on his office would probably be reduced and his political risks would probably be enhanced. Generally, then, and with some exceptions, it would *a priori* seem to be to the mayor's advantage to postpone decisions; the exceptions relate to the testing of public reactions or the heading off of developing opposition. In Philadelphia a large proportion of the major policy items (which tend to be "lumpy" items) enter the capital budget late in the game and have often not appeared at all in the capital program.

The short time horizon of Council has already been discussed. The mayor, due to his city-wide constituency and his administrative protection, is probably not as exposed as Council to a broad range of immediate pressures. While the hypothesis of a kind of hierarchy of perspectives of the sort discussed here is widely current, its illustration in this instance may be worthwhile because of its implications for long-range planning and central decision. Much of the "instability" of capital program decisions probably results from the differing time horizons of participants in the decisions, and these differences in perspective seem embedded in institutional activities, interests, and pressures.

## V

Until quite recently there has been little interest in or employment of explicit or formal criteria in departmental programming or central review and allocation.[25] One key official in the process aptly describes it as "more like peeling an apple than slicing a pie." Sophisticated economic analyses or professional standards are difficult to develop and apply because of measurement problems and frequently arbitrary assumptions, and a few City

---

25. There have been continuing overhead efforts to sharpen project cost estimates relative to both capital and operating budgets, but these efforts are of a different order from formal criteria for decision, though they might facilitate their use.

officials have hoped that the long-awaited comprehensive plan (which is mandated by the City Charter) would provide scheduling criteria. Others probably hope it will never arrive, distrusting its inflexibility; still others doubt that the plan will greatly change or govern capital programming. But there are other reasons for reliance upon "informed judgment" besides these.

One is a complex of administrative factors. Philadelphia, like many cities, emerged from the years of depression and World War II with its physical plant run down to the point where a number of underdeveloped area" analogies applied, and it lacked a vigorous administration until 1952. When thorough-going capital programming began under the Charter of 1951, large allocations went for deferred maintenance and were simply "forced."[26] While substantial "forced" allocations are probably a thing of the past, each capital budget contains a number of lines of "continuing programs" or recurring expenditures—some of them simply deferred maintenance.[27] The fact that roughly one quarter of the tax-supported segment of capital budgets consists in such programs and that nearly one-half is comprised of projects only secondarily related to land-use planning probably tends to reinforce administrative initiatives, judgment and flexibility in capital programming and to narrow the area of explicit decision open to planners in the field of their principal and traditional expertise.[28] Intergovernmental aids in selected fields appear to narrow reviewing discretion somewhat further and to lend leverage to particular departments. Thus, the Planning Commission's Projects Division finds that, within the $25 million tax-supported limit, there is annually only $10 to $13 million to manipulate, once allowance has been made for administrative "givens" and political pressures (sometimes building on the prescriptive prior appearance of projects in capital programs). Finally, the emphasis of the Clark and Dilworth administrations upon energizing and professionalizing the departments has probably encouraged "flexibility" and "informed judgment" at the expense of formal standards and criteria in departmental programming.

A complex of political factors has seemingly served as a second discourage-

---

26. A striking example occurred as late as 1955 when, as a result of State and City inspections, some 24 bridges were declared unsafe, facing the administration with a choice between closing down important parts of the City's circulation system or repairing the bridges immediately at a large sacrifice to the rest of the capital program. The second alternative was chosen and the current capital budget and capital program were drastically revised to accommodate the deferred maintenance. Ultimately, some of the bridges were simply posted with weight limits and remain to be repaired.

27. For example, such programs for the Streets Department total about $3.5 million annually within the $25 million limit, and have deviated by more than $25,000 from that total in no year save 1955 (on which see the previous note). The programs are: grading and new paving; street openings; street lighting; unallocated engineering services; traffic signals; road construction and paving in Fairmount Park; construction of traffic islands.

28. For an argument, on this basis, for narrowing the content of capital programs in New York City to primarily land-use-related items, see Frederick C. Mosher, "Fiscal Planning and Budgeting in New York City," in *Report* of the New York State-New York City Fiscal Relations Committee (New York, 1956), pp. 65–84 at pp. 80–81.

ment to the adoption of formal criteria. The 1951 election overturned an administration of many years' incumbency and was fought by the victors with emphasis on specific reforms as well as general City redemption. It could be argued from the tenor of the campaign and the drama of the victory that the new administration had a mandate for large-scale development that would support its leadership and judgment on issues upon which campaign promises or emphases provided no guidance. On the assumption that the City was badly run down and "behind," it could further be argued that political demands should not be discounted nor administrative responsiveness discouraged; that expressed demands reflected real needs and that large (if intangible) returns would accrue to projects that commanded political support. We are not aware that such arguments received explicit statement during the Clark administration (1952–1956); we simply suggest that they provide a rationale for the fact that the use of informal political and professional judgments was generally accepted without debate in the early period of capital programming.

## VI

Nonetheless, as the City catches up to what are by publics and professionals considered more satisfactory levels of service, and as the comprehensive plan approaches completion (it is expected in 1960), the pressures for more complete and sophisticated project justifications are likely to mount.[29] Such pressures will probably be resisted by those departments that are politically and administratively in a good bargaining position (e.g., the Streets Department), but political necessity as well as professional pride may foster more long-range planning in other departments. Such plans have now appeared in a very few departments; but, for the most part, they constitute adumbrations of department responsibilities rather than the articulation of standards from which the programming of facilities might in turn be derived.

This experience in part reflects intellectual as well as institutional difficulties in the formulation of formal criteria for capital programming. Without taking the space to argue the point here, it may be said that: derivation of service "standards" from broad statements of "responsibilities" or goals is often a logically loose enterprise; that most existing professional standards, on the contrary, imply goals without making them explicit, lack inter-agency comparability, and often tend only to rationalize pressure group claims; that insofar as city planners' comprehensive plans simply embody such standards elsewhere than in land-use fields they are unlikely to afford a basis for capital program allocations; and that techniques of economic analysis (such as benefit-cost or rate-of-return) are limited today to a few fields. At the same time, comprehensive plans, while affording a basis for the *integration* of

---

29. The comprehensive plan did appear in 1960. It is too early to assess its effect on capital programs, but it may be noted that its statements as to goals and levels of service tend to be broad ones.

projects, are unlikely to afford a basis for firm *allocations* unless they embody a more specific articulation of goals than the political agencies or the publics of Philadelphia have yet provided or seem likely to provide, on the findings presented above.

Thus the institutional and intellectual constraints upon long-range planning appear mutually reinforcing and in the political and administrative pluralism of the metropolis there is probably a more-or-less irreducible minimum of both. Philadelphia, we think, is close to the institutional minimum, and the intellectual problems of planning and "suboptimization" remain to be solved. Our findings on the lack of "stability" in capital programming and its institutional bases, together with the intellectual difficulties with comprehensive planning as a basis for central capital allocations, lead us to conclude that the comprehensive plan is as likely to follow from the process and substance of capital programming as *vice versa*. If this is so, attention should then be centered upon the *process* of capital programming for the procedural desiderata that it may serve.

Four principal conclusions can be derived from the foregoing. (1) Political and administrative forces, working together, induce instability (*i.e.*, limit long-range planning) as well as stability. There are conflicting tendencies, but the institutional constraints upon long-range planning are real. (2) On this interpretation, the probable role of the planning agency in capital programming is basically one of *research* and project *integration*; though to some extent research may gravitate toward the definition of goals, and integration may approach allocation through temporal scheduling decisions and deferrals. (3) To some extent the constraints upon long-range planning result from a perhaps inevitable diffusion of responsibility in the process; yet the machinery described above is probably as centralized as that of any American municipal government.[30] It seems doubtful that a reorganization of planning would have much effect upon stability, though it might adversely affect other desiderata.[31] (4) Several other ends are served by the process. Administrative initiative, energy, and competence are encouraged. It provides a "rational" context for popular consultation through the pre-provision of alternatives and of temporal and regional perspectives on benefits and costs. It encourages the contributions of city planning in the land-use fields of its traditional competence and provides a broader field for planning research. These are important accomplishments by which Philadelphia has been well served and, in the light of them, the tentative nature of long-range planning may be unimportant. Expectations of stable or predictable long-range planning are likely to be disappointed; they are also likely to conflict with other ends.

30. Compare the discussion of the effectiveness of "comprehensive" planning and its relation to governmental organization in Myerson and Banfield, *op. cit.*, pp. 273–275.

31. On the organization of planning see, *e.g.*, Robert A. Walker, *The Planning Function in Urban Government*, 2d ed. (Chicago, 1951); Henry C. Fagin, *op. cit.*; and Fagin and C. McKim Norton, "Physical and Fiscal Planning," in New York State-New York City Fiscal Relations Committee, *Report* (New York, 1956), pp. 85–94. The last is most expressly aimed at capital programming.

# HOW TO BRING PLANNING
# AND POLICY TOGETHER

## MARTIN MEYERSON

WHEN DE TOCQUEVILLE visited here well over a hundred years ago, he commented that whenever two Americans got together, they formed an organization. In recent years, it has become fashionable for European observers to laugh about our tendency to elaborate on organization—now, these observers say, whenever two Americans doing the same sort of work get together, they form a profession.

## *Professionalization*

The social scientists have also focussed on this tendency to professionalize. They have analyzed certain general procedures followed by all emerging professional groups. Their analyses amount to a recital of the natural history of professionalization. First, persons of imagination and vision, and a profound dissatisfaction with the world as they see it, outline the scope of new problems and propose new approaches to these problems. These are persons trained in other disciplines, often diverse disciplines; they are people of broad interests and an ability to dramatize problems and inspire others. Whatever literature is produced is polemic, general, devoted to portrayal of problems, and clamors for the attention of a citizenry already perplexed and vexed by other matters.

As more and more recognition is given to the importance of the newly discovered problems, limited funds are made available for exploring or solving these problems. More people are attracted as lay enthusiasts or as practitioners in the field; organizations are set up; conferences are held. Schools are established to give specialized training; the course of instruction grows longer and longer. A unique vocabulary is developed; nonprofessionals cannot talk it. A literature geared to specific problems emerges; nonprofessionals find it complex and dull. Soon people begin to think in terms of "careers" as well as in terms of solving problems. Salaries, job classifications, personnel qualifications, specialization within the field become important. Attempts are made to broaden functions and responsibilities, to grow bigger and bigger, to be imperialistic in scope and numbers. More and more efforts are made to make the activity expert, technical, scientific—and beyond the

Reprinted from *Journal of the American Institute of Planners*, Spring, 1956, where it appeared under the title "Building the Middle-Range Bridge for Comprehensive Planning," by permission of the publisher and the author.

ken of nonprofessionals. This culminates in licensing or registration to keep out pretenders. By this time, the profession has "institutionalized"; its members acquire the power of reproduction—that is, it is the present professionals not the market situation who determine what standards must be met by new entrants.

Despite the gibes of some European observers and despite the implied gibes of the social scientists, I think our American tendency to professionalize on the whole is a good one. By being self-conscious about our work activities we do try to develop our methods and body of knowledge and to improve our competence. The danger lies in the stage when we become too rigid, when we are no longer capable of absorbing new ideas or going in new directions, or willing to discuss our problems with people in other fields. However, planning is too new an activity to be that institutionalized. We are in the expansionist, imperialistic stage, and who am I to go counter to the natural history of our emerging profession?

Therefore, I want to speak today as an imperialist for city planning. I want to speak today about expansion—about increasing our numbers, multiplying our budgets, strengthening our effectiveness, expanding our functions, and, of course, raising our salaries.

## Expanding Functions

I shall focus on expanded city planning functions and responsibilities which if not performed by planning agencies may very well be performed by other agencies of local government. However, I believe planning agencies are not only best equipped to perform these functions, but their own effectiveness will be enormously increased by doing so.

However, we might well ask if increasing our scope of operations will not be done by sacrificing preparation of long-range plans. Do not the administration of zoning and subdivision control already rob us of time and energy to devote to long-range planning? Of course they do. Yet they are also ways in which planning is translated effectively into daily changes of urban development.

For background to some of the additional functions I want to discuss, let me wear two hats. One is my hat at ACTION—the American Council to Improve Our Neighborhoods. The other is my hat as city planning professor. Wearing ACTION's hat, my responsibilities during the past year and more have required me to travel to many parts of the country, and to talk with many of the people who made the key decisions which shape our cities and towns. These are the mayors, the city managers, the heads of operating municipal departments, the homebuilders, the merchants and industrialists, the civic leaders. Their decisions are the decisions that set the stage for the decisions of the everyday citizen—his choices on where he lives, his kind of work, the activities he and his family will have an opportunity to participate in. And I was struck by the fact that the mayor and the merchant, the head of the renewal agency and the homebuilders are at a loss to find the specific framework to provide them with the kinds of guidance they need to make rational decisions.

As I talked with these people, it was very encouraging to me to find the respect in which they hold the city planner and to recognize it as a tribute to the responsible growth of our profession. However, their respect is rarely derived from an awareness of the importance of long-range comprehensive planning. Rather their respect is based on the project-planning accomplishments of the city planner and related officials. They speak their admiration for the highway extensions, the new zoning districts, the design of a group of public buildings, the development of a park preserve or a new terminal improvement. Partly, of course, it is because so much of our attention has necessarily gone to project-planning that little effort has been left for long-range comprehensive planning, and thus little opportunity for it to be understood, let alone for it to be vigorously supported.

Yet the framework required by the people who make some of the key decisions for both private and public community development is not provided by project-planning. Nor is the urgency of these decisions met by the kind of long-range comprehensive planning we usually do. I have concluded that a middle ground is needed. An intermediate set of planning functions must be performed on a sustained, on-going basis to provide the framework for the homebuilder who must decide how many units he should, as well as can, build next year; for the government official who must decide whether the signs of unemployment in the locality require special public action; for the appointed commissioner who has no sense of whether a particular policy which his agency might follow and obtain bonds to execute will fit in with other current city policies; for the industrialist who wants to know what specific land use changes will be made in an area within the next few years before he commits his corporation's resources; for the redevelopment agency which has no knowledge as to what the effects of previous slum-clearance projects have been and the lessons that can be learned from them.

Now changing my hat, as a professor of city planning, one of my major concerns is that we train students for the responsible posts they will hold not only this year but ten years from now. An apprenticeship might be a far superior way to a university curriculum if our main object were to prepare people for specific present jobs. What kind of a job will the planner be expected to do ten years from now? I have been trying to get some sense of this and thus of needed educational programs. I am of course talking primarily about city planning, although I believe what I am saying applies to resources planning and other kinds of planning as well. I also recognize that most city planners in the future may not work for what we regard as city planning agencies. This does not mean that they should not be trained as city planners.

Now, wearing both my hats at the same time, I wonder very much whether the impressions I have got for the need and importance of a middle-ground planning activity may not be a clue to some of the crucial functions of the profession in the years ahead, and thus a clue to planning education in the years ahead as well. The additional functions I propose are suggested not to detract from long-range planning but to make it more meaningful.

I propose that we consider whether the following middle-ground community planning functions are appropriate to our province:

1. *A Central Intelligence Function* to facilitate market operations for housing, commerce, industry and other community activities through the regular issuance of market analyses

2. *A Pulse-Taking Function* to alert the community through quarterly or other periodic reports to danger signs in blight formation, in economic changes, population movements and other shifts

3. *A Policy Clarification Function* to help frame and regularly revise development objectives of local government

4. *A Detailed Development Plan Function* to phase specific private and public programs as part of a comprehensive course of action covering not more than 10 years

5. *A Feed-Back Review Function* to analyze through careful research the consequences of programs and projects activities as a guide to future action

These are interrelated functions. The intelligence, pulse-taking and review functions roughly parallel the types of measures we are learning to utilize nationally, for example through the Council of Economic Advisers, to encourage equilibrium and new growth in employment and investment. On the community level, we would not want to restrict ourselves to just economic concerns. But nationally we have developed during the last twenty years a type of sensitivity to changes in the economy which permit adjustments when the economy gets markedly out of balance. We have developed a whole series of statistics and indices such as building starts, prices of hogs, consumer credit, a type of periodic information which we never had before. Then, if there are maladjustments in the economy revealed through periodic checks, we may adjust the mortgage rate, place governmental orders in areas where there is unemployment and try to take other measures to bring about equilibrium.

The five functions I want to discuss envisage a similar role for the city planning agency—a role which brings planning and policy closer together. They are functions which city planning agencies to some extent fulfill already. However, they are not part of the routine view of appropriate city planning activity.

What do these five functions mean for municipal planning?

1. *The Central Intelligence Function:* The planning agency as the local G2 to aid the operations of the market.

The market place—the mechanism which brings together producer and consumer, supply and demand—is the primary method under democratic capitalism by which land and other resources are allocated to those activities by which people live, work, play and raise their families.

Market decisions are more important than governmental ones in giving substance to the design and structure of our urban communities. In our cities, for example, we see that people who desire housing accommodations are more and more choosing to live in the suburbs. These represent individual choices to satisfy individual values and fit individual circumstances. But these individual choices add up to a major shift in urban patterns—not only in housing, but in shopping and many other facilities as well. The changes in urban patterns due to market selection are so decisive and have such widespread and interlocking consequences that they almost appear as though someone had directed them. (Perhaps this is the invisible hand of the market to which Adam Smith refers.)

However, the local businessman, the industrialist and the consumer rarely have the kind of accurate information to make rational decisions. Currently, builders, investors, business and industrial firms have such vast unknown factors with which to deal that the risks involved either operate as brakes on activity or inflate the costs of production or financing. The consumer has to act on conjecture rather than real knowledge of choices open to him.

The city planning agency in most communities is the local unit of government best equipped to provide a market analysis function. Data would have to be obtained and analyzed continuously. Regular market reports would be issued by the planning agency. Depending on the urgency of the market decisions, some of the reports could be issued monthly, some quarterly, some semiannually, some annually. There could be special reports on the new home building market, on investment in plant, on consumer income and spending, on land and building costs. The planning agency is an appropriate one for this function, not only because it has a nucleus of people dealing with these community characteristics but also because this kind of regular and constant market analysis is crucial to the achievement of present functions of planning and some of the other ones I am discussing today.

Detailed market analysis for the city, for the metropolitan area and for subregions in this area would enable both the producer and the consumer to make more intelligent choices in respect to the location, investment, building and land utilization for industry, commerce, housing and other main facilities and activities. The political philosophy of the country rests on the market as the key means to allocate resources. If the city planning agency regularly checks and interprets the local market situation as I suggest here, it can lubricate the process of urban development and achieve many of the main objectives of city planning by facilitating intelligent individual actions.

2. *The Pulse-Taking Function:* The planning agency as the watchdog for community danger signs.

It is true that most community development decisions are made through market mechanisms rather than through governmental planning mechanisms.

However, one of the reasons why planning has become an accepted governmental activity is that the market has frequently exhibited such frictions and even malfunctioning that desired community ends have not been achieved. For example, a main impetus to planning came from the fact that the market was not allocating land uses in such a way as to preserve residential values during the useful life of the property. Planning was expected, through land use and other controls, to compensate for the problems—the failures—of the market.

However, planning has too often been in the position of correcting mistakes after they have happened rather than in the position of detecting and removing trouble spots before they lead to major mistakes. I therefore recommend that the planning agency submit a quarterly or other periodic report to the local chief executive alerting the community danger signs. Which neighborhoods are showing blight factors at an increased pace? Are certain transit routes losing most of their passengers? Are there signs that certain industries are about to either come in or leave the area? The planning agency should thus perpetually scan the community for indications of maladjustment. Failures of firms, increased congestion, incipient changes in land use, new demands for services might thus be detected before they gather a momentum almost impossible to stop.

To be effective the planning agency's pulse-taking report must not only alert the community to trouble spots, but must also point to remedial action. Inevitably this means a policy focus.

3. *The Policy Clarification Function:* The planning agency as an aid in framing and regularly revising development objectives of local government.

I have just suggested that the planning agency be alerted to detect any trends potentially harmful to the community. This implies that policies would be devised to halt undesirable changes and promote desired ones in the community, and that the planning agency would take some initiative in indicating the most suitable policy measures. Specific inducements to encourage private actions as well as direct public measures would be needed.

Much of the determination of community policy will evolve through the political process. In a pluralistic society such as ours, there are many conflicting values and there is, as a result, competition among goals. The competition will be expressed and settled largely through politics.

The planning agency, however, can analyze alternative policies. It can help determine what benefits can be achieved as against what costs will be incurred by different specific policies.

Politicians could be given detailed information on the advantages and disadvantages of alternative courses of action to achieve desired goals. Planners should be prepared to say to politicians—if you wish to do such and such, then such and such consequences are likely to result. The planning agency would not be usurping the task of political decision-making but it would be making clear what the implications of alternative policy decisions are, so that more meaningful policy choices can be made. The planning agency, furthermore, can serve as the instrument for making known the policy choices once they are made. The planning agency, by suggesting revisions to policymakers on the basis of changed condition, can encourage periodic presentations of community development policy. Probably a coherent development policy statement should be consciously revealed each year through the mass media of communication.

4. *The Detailed Development Plan Function:* The planning agency as the preparer of a short-range comprehensive plan spelling out specific actions to be taken.

The gap between the developmental policies of government discussed above and a long-range master plan for the future community can be bridged by the preparation of short-run plans, of five to 10 years in time span. The development plan would link measures to deal with current problems with long-range proposals to attain community goals.

For many politicians and businessmen the master plan is too generalized and too remote to seem real. For planners, on the other hand, ameliorative measures which attack symptoms rather than basic problems are too piece-meal, too hastily considered to seem worthwhile. I suggest the short-run development plan as that compromise between immediate problems and future expectations which will permit coherent policy effectuation. This type of plan preparation will require detailed, timed and localized programming of governmental policies for private as well as for public actions. Detailed cost estimates of private as well as public development, and specific administrative and legal measures to carry out the programs will have to be worked out.

Long-range comprehensive plans commonly reveal a desired state of affairs. They rarely specify the detailed courses of action needed to achieve that desired state. By their long-range nature they cannot do so. The development plan, in contrast, will indicate the specific changes in land use pro-grammed for each year, the rate of new growth, the public facilities to be built, the structures to be removed, the private investment required, the extent and sources of public funds to be raised, the tax and other local incentives to encourage private behavior requisite to the plan. The development plan—which incidentally in a more limited form is required by law in England—would have to be acted upon each year and made an official act for the subsequent year, much as a capital budget is put into law. Revised yearly it would become the central guide to land use control, to public budgeting and to appropriate private actions to achieve directed community improvement.

5. *The Feed-Back Review Function:* The planning agency as analyzer of the consequences of program and project activities in order to guide future action.

Currently, we in planning agencies have no systematic means of analyzing the effect of planning measures or programs of action. It is astonishing, for example, that we have never analyzed the effects of zoning. We have never studied what the effects of this interference in the land market have been on the monopoly position of different kinds of businesses, on the costs of land, on the encouragement or discouragement of certain types of development.

I suggest that we maintain a constant feed-back of information on the intended and the unintended consequences of programs that are adopted locally. For example, if a new area is developed in the central business district with new office buildings, shopping facilities, and cultural activities, we ought to assess the unintended effects as well as the intended ones of just what happens to the older, existing sections of the central business district and to the surrounding area. Does the new development serve as catalyst and stimulator of further improvements or does it drain off activities from the remainder of the district? These kinds of questions must be asked and answered so that we can learn from our experiences and can adjust our future programming and planning.

The more such a review function is performed, the more readily it can be performed. As a body of review knowledge is built up on the parking effects of highways, on the use made of playgrounds, on whether public housing and redevelopment projects achieve their objectives, on the impacts of off-street loading ordinances, the more simply can new measures be gauged.

## Implications of These Functions for Planning Agencies

This may sound like a formidable range of new or at least much enlarged functions. Whether such proposals are practical depends on the situation in particular cities.

I have made a plea that we consider adding certain functions intermediate between ad hoc decisions on a subdivision plat, for example, and long-range comprehensive planning. The capital budget and program in current city planning practice comes closest to this intermediate position. Of course I believe that the functions I have suggested are ones that would be of great benefit to local government and to community development. However, the functions I mentioned could be lodged in various existing or possible municipal agencies. Assuming these functions have merit, I am convinced that the planning agency should be the appropriate niche for them. This is for us in the A.I.P. to decide, or it may be decided for us. We will not have a great deal of time in which to decide. Two cities, a large one and a moderate-sized one, both known in recent years for their good government, are establishing posts called "development coordinator." Should this responsibility not have been delegated to or assumed by city planning? It is too early to say that this is prophetic of a trend. It is not too early, however, to say that planners have the opportunity to take on the development coordination function, to extend their range from the generalized plan on the one hand and the day-to-day demands on the other to the intermediate type of sustained on-going planning activities I have suggested.

But a planning agency capable of achieving some of the functions I have suggested today will require far greater specialization than we have ever had in municipal planning. It is true also that more planners will be required by specialized agencies in transportation, housing and other fields. They will be required especially in such agencies if the functions I suggest above develop. However, the specialization will be required mostly by the planning agencies themselves to prepare detailed development plans, perpetual inventories of market characteristics and the other tasks demanded. It will require personnel with joint specialization, or more properly, people who are specialists in a particular field and generalists in planning. Joint designer-planners, statistician-planners, highway expert-planners, real property lawyer-planners, utility engineer-planners and other dually trained personnel will be necessary. Incentives will have to be provided to enable people willingly to acquire such dual background—in other words, we will have to pay them as well as offer intellectual satisfactions and the satisfactions which come from socially useful work.

But if we do extend our planning functions—and even if we merely try to fulfill our present tasks as we see them—we need a level of budget for local planning of a kind we have never seen before. The planner currently is responsible for advising on expenditures running into hundreds of millions of dollars and on programs intimately affecting the lives of thousands, or in some cases, millions, of people. Decisions of such far-reaching consequences should not be financed through substandard salaries, blighted budgets and penny-pinched research. It is true that planning costs our local communities in the United States between 7½ and 10 million dollars annually. But this is insignificant when a single mile of an expressway in a single city may cost twice that much. It is unnecessary for me to point out that the total annual expenditure on city planning in the United States is less than the cost of a single public building or a fraction of the budget of my own and other academic institutions or that some of the efficiencies which can be derived from city planning in even a single city could pay for the entire cost of city planning in the country.

I do not know how much the additional functions I have suggested would cost. Costs would vary, of course, with the thoroughness of performing each function and with the size of the community. (I have completely side-stepped the issue of whether the planning agency should also attempt to administer or to oversee the short-range development plans, and if so, to what degree.) However, such planning will clearly be very costly.

My own basic premise is that good staff is essential to the performance of planning functions and good staff is expensive staff. I agree completely with the statement in the Schuster report of Great Britain that "more than ever before the planning authorities need to recruit people with first-class intellectual qualities and first-class educational attainments. Everything else that we have to say is secondary in importance to this."

It is to the credit of planning that we have been able to attract people so far through the challenge of the field rather than the remuneration offered them. However, we must recognize that just as our universities and colleges cannot well exist from the subsidy of low salaries, so planning and other governmental activities cannot sustain high quality work through the subsidy of underpaid labor. Beardsley Ruml recently advocated paying professors as much as $30,000 a year. We should hardly be expected to feel that the top jobs in planning should pay less than that.

I prefaced my comments with a thumbnail sketch of the natural history of all professions. Each attempts to get for itself a bigger share of the pie of responsibility, of status, of resources and of income. Just within this last week a colleague, a neighbor, and a third person whom I did not know, made the following claims in the press: The race relations expert said discrimination was America's Number One problem. The criminologist said the rising wave of juvenile crime was America's Number One problem. The third person—the psychiatric administrator—said mental health was America's Number One problem.

But these claims are not true. Naturally, you and I as city planners are convinced the Number One problem of America is the development of America's cities, their housing, their transportation and all the other elements that make them viable.

In conclusion, as an imperialist for the profession I have computed that about one-half of one per cent of municipal expenditures in the United States could result in an expenditure for planning of almost ten times what it is now. Such an expenditure I feel sure would clearly enable us to do our day-to-day jobs, to do long-range planning, and to add major substance to our work through the on-going middle-range type of comprehensive planning I have described. Since Chicago 50 years ago, we have urged others to make no little plans. Let's make no little plans for the development of our own profession in terms of resources, in terms of public support, in terms of education, and in terms of laying claim to emerging new functions.

# HOW TO DEAL WITH POLITICIANS

## CHARLES GOODWIN SAUERS, SR.

POLITICS ARE part and parcel of all public business. The degree of involvement varies but it is always present. It is present because it belongs

Reprinted from *Parks and Recreation*, April, 1959, where it appeared under the title "Parks and Politics," by permission of the publishers.

there—it is an essential factor of democratic government. Our greatest presidents have been our most able and professional politicians. So it is with governors, presidents of elected boards, mayors, aldermen, commissioners and trustees. A park district completely divorced from politics is likewise divorced from realities. The chances are that in such case there are no politics in the usual sense but there is substituted the personal whims, desires and indigent relatives of board members—which is worse.

Drury in California, Donoghue in Chicago, Moses in New York and Wirth in Washington operate in a political milieu. They are surrounded by highly professional politicians. They know them, understand them, realize their problems and work with them—successfully.

The park administrator or employee who decries politics and politicians is spitting into the wind and hinders rather than improves his work. The politician, the elected official, is the center upon which the pressures of groups, orginizations and individuals impinge. These pressures are many in type and purpose (good and bad)—jobs, special developments, purchases, land acquisition problems, special privileges and so on ad infinitum. He is a politician, therefore his stock in trade is VOTES. His is a difficult vocation because votes mean people and people mean problems in all shapes and complexities. There is the never-ceasing demand for favors or donations from organizations (charitable, churches, health, veterans, business and the like). The butcher, the baker, the candlestick maker want to sell their wares. Then there are job demands. "My wife's cousin, he is not too bright, but give him some kind of a job and get my wife out o' my hair"; or "You know my uncle voted for you, he is not too strong and he's a lush, but give him a chance"; or "I need this guy around the ward office nights so can't you set him up where he don't have to report every morning." You name them and the politician has them on his hands or rather his doorstep. In the practice of his profession, the politician transmits the pressure to the park administrator, directly and through the park board he has had a hand in appointing or electing and through various other channels.

The park administrator usually arrives at his position through direct appointment by an elected official, an elected board or a board appointed by an elected official or by civil service. He needs to establish with his superior or superiors and their official staff that he is honorable, without personal axes to grind, has ability sufficient to his position and is completely sincere and enthused in what he is doing. Further, that he has the courage to fight for his beliefs. These qualities are essential to the confidence and respect he must receive from politicians for the discharge of his responsibilities. In fact, by Webster's definition the park superintendent is himself a politician.

Where he is confronted by an aggressive demand for jobs, the park superintendent will seek to establish the necessity for technically qualified appointees in engineering, landscape architecture, horticulture, naturalists, accounting, mechanical and the like. Then comes the majority of his staff— laborers, janitors, police, foremen, supervisors. One policy he may adopt is

that he will try anybody in these non-technical jobs provided the period of pro-
bation is short and the appointee will be separated if he does not qualify or
indicate qualities sufficient to warrant his in-service training.

At this point there comes into play one of our greatest resources. This is
the attraction of almost everyone to the out-of-doors, their pride in doing
work that they can see, for instance—a clean picnic grove; a well-mowed
meadow; a beach free of debris; a newly repaired and painted toilet; a fine
stand of trees and shrubs; a happy individual, family or crowd enjoying the
results of his work. Often the man who has been engaged in uninteresting
jobs and is an indifferent employee becomes pleased with his work and himself in the out-of-doors. His improved health is often a delight to him. This
will surprise him and more so his political sponsor. He becomes an asset
rather than a liability to the park organization, his sponsor and most important to himself.

The politician is a most practical person and will press hard for jobs,
favors and privileges which he transforms into votes. The park superintendent must be practical and aggressive in return. He must state his case
with forthrightness and have the facts to justify his stand. "The fellow you
sent me only shows up three days a week—please replace him"; or "He
reports late, skips out early and wants an hour and a half for lunch—send
me another"; or "He is a good workman but shows up drunk and useless—
we will pay him only for the days he is able to work well"; or "He is not
physically well but is willing—we will try him another month to see if his
health improves"; and so on.

If the judgment is fair the politician will know it. His respect will be won
and he is very apt to be fair in return.

Other than jobs the requests are many and various. No matter how small,
if the request is proper and feasible it should be done with dispatch and
courtesy. Sometimes the smallest or most trivial matter is of genuine importance to the practicing politician. Although small, it may mean to him the
return of a favor, the fulfilling of a promise or saving of face. Where the
request is improper, contrary to rules and policy or impractical, the superintendent may save the situation for the politician by asking permission to
contact the source of the request in person so he may call upon, telephone
or write directly to him. He thus interposes himself as a buffer for the politician and is in position to state his position and justification for refusal which
is accepted gracefully ninety-five percent of the time.

Procrastination and evasion are of little avail in the matter of refusals.
Cleverness is never effective in public business.

The professional park man will abstain from party politics, KEEP HIS
MOUTH SHUT on politics and have no party label. If he achieved his position
through political activities then he must either take the chances of his party
or strive to achieve a professional and technical status aside from party
politics. His interests and ambitions are in his WORK and this he must demonstrate to the political pros. Moreover, if he is in direct disagreement with

elected officials superior to him or has complaints on personnel, his case should be stated in face to face conference but *not in writing*. Professional politicians regard such written statements as attempts by the writer to protect himself at the expense of the politician.

We have a saying in the District about operating parks and park districts. Any damn fool can give it away and another damn fool may say no to all proposals. Neither will last long.

Politics is a recognized, essential and difficult profession. Politics is the motivating force of democracy. Parks are created by politics—first in the legislature where every legislator is a politician, then in state governments by governors, who are politicians, then by mayors who are politicians, or by boards who are elected and are, perforce, politicians. All park budgets are politically controlled, by legislatures as to tax rates and by lesser bodies as to quality and quantity.

Politicians must be understood and the profession respected. There are some bum ones just as there are bum doctors, physicists, teachers and businessmen. They all respect honesty, forthrightness, courage and ability.

Publicity may become a bone of contention and cause for difficult relationships between administration and elected officials. Publicity is genuinely essential to the elected official because it may be translated into votes. Publicity is not necessary to the administrator. We believe that the administrator should at all times strive to see that publicity, i.e. public credit, should go to the elected official or board. Such a policy serves to further prove the sincerity of the administrator. Furthermore, if the publicity is difficult or derogatory, the administrator should shoulder his share or all the blame as a buffer to the politician. That's one of the things he is hired for—trouble.

# A SURVEY OF NEW YORK'S FINEST

## THE INSTITUTE OF PUBLIC ADMINISTRATION

AMONG ALL of the great cities of this nation and the world, New York's police defenses stand at or near the top in three respects. Numerical strength of its manpower is currently close to 20,000 men. Cost of operation and maintenance, including salaries, pensions, physical plant, equipment, and supplies, stands at a level far above the nearest competitors. Problems of

Reprinted from *Modern Management for the City of New York,* Report of the Mayor's Committee on Management Survey, undated, II, 820–826. Digest from "The New York Police Survey," by the Institute of Public Administration, July, 1952.

law enforcement, while by no means unmatched elsewhere for complexity, are on so large a scale as to lift New York into a class by itself.

Because New York's police establishment is so large, its problems are often held to be unique. This leads naturally to the further conclusion that the usual tests of performance do not apply and that the policies, structure, and experience of other forces both large and small have no bearing upon the methods that must be employed here. However, while large centers and smaller places alike have special situations that require special treatment, they also have so many characteristics in common that police methods originating on the Pacific Coast are easily adapted to the Atlantic Seaboard, and experiments undertaken by small towns may hold significance and value for substantial portions of great cities.

## Personnel Controls

Since the basic unit of all policing is the policeman, we began our survey with an inquiry into the manner of his selection, promotion, training, and discipline. By far the largest single element in the situation is the Municipal Civil Service Commission. It establishes many of the qualifications for police recruits, examines prospective patrolmen, and exercises a preponderant influence at all promotional stages up to and including the rank of captain. Its successes or failures in performing these vital functions therefore are controlling factors in the police service.

In its handling of police selection and promotion, the Commission displays some grave weaknesses. They may be summarized as follows:

(1) It does not assure that the best qualified applicants will be declared eligible for original appointment or for promotion.

(2) It is preoccupied with the interests of the job seeker at the expense of the interests of the Police Department.

(3) It is excessively slow in processing police recruits.

Local residence requirements under the restrictive terms of the Lyons Law deprive the City of available resources when, in times like the present, young and capable manpower is hard to find.

The minimum age of 20 years is widely suspect because immaturity can be a menace when clothed with police authority. But if police are actively to seek able and ambitious youths with any large degree of success, they must compete with the military arms and with the opportunities offered by industry, commerce, and governmental service at the time when these young prospects become available for regular career employment. In most cases, that is not at the police minimum of 20 years, not at the police average of 26 years, but at 18 or 19 years. To pass up this opportunity for first choice is to wait for the misfits and the rejects to come looking for a job at a much later date.

POLICE CADETS

Youths of quite extraordinary qualities leave promising careers of many kinds to join our police forces. But not enough of them are impelled by such urgent preferences. If more men of high intelligence and sanguine temperament really are to fill the blue ranks, they must be sought at high school age, and employed for some time at police tasks not requiring law enforcement authority; they must be schooled, guided, transferred, and rigorously screened by special supervisors until they can finally be offered as preferred candidates for appointment as probationary patrolmen.

No anxiety need arise about the opportunities available for such on-the-job selection and training. In the precinct stations are 626 police assignments as clerks, attendants, stenographers, patrol wagon drivers, and switchboard operators. Headquarters has several hundred more of the same or similar categories.

The pay of police cadets can be established in accord with age, experience, and duties performed, with substantial payroll economies and with pension funds fortified by longer years of service without reducing the age at retirement. But cost is a secondary consideration where the future of the force is concerned.

RECRUITMENT AND PROMOTION

Character investigations, like physical qualifications, are a joint responsibility of the Civil Service Commission and the police force, with the Commission holding the final decision in such matters. It therefore must shoulder most of the blame for official complacency in clearing men with criminal records and disabling physical defects. Undue reliance is placed upon form letter inquiries. Unfavorable replies are not followed up. Criminal records of a wide variety, paternity proceedings, and other objectionable features are waived by the Commission in three-fourths of the cases in which they arise.

Written examinations for patrolmen are little concerned with native intelligence, aptitude for police work, or ability to learn. They emphasize the three R's, local geography and civics, and the rudiments of law enforcement. Why the latter should be included is difficult to understand, since prior experience is not required and all newly appointed police must attend from 8 to 10 weeks of instruction at the Police Academy. An unfavorable result of the information type of questions on patrolmen's examinations is to force aspiring candidates to enroll in one of the privately conducted cram schools for Civil Service applicants. Urgently recommended on the basis of successful operation in other forces are test batteries for general intelligence, observation, memory selection, and arithmetical reasoning. Despite a widely held belief to the contrary, such tests are not barred by New York State's Constitution or statutes; in fact they are extensively employed with success by the State Civil Service Commission itself.

Medical examinations are conducted under the auspices of the Civil

Service Commission on a mass production basis. Average time devoted to each candidate is only 45 seconds, with laboratory tests postponed until just prior to final certification. Police surgeons frequently reject men accepted by the Civil Service Commission; but the Commission, not the Police Department, says the final word on eligibility. The records show acceptance of men impaired by foot injuries, flat feet, over-weight by as much as 70 pounds, leg wounds, missing fingers or injured hands, defective hearing, and mental disorders. By negligence and by connivance, both the present and the future value of each complement of recruits is heavily discounted at the outset.

Physical tests are highly specialized and exacting and are scored on a competitive basis. Without reflecting upon the value of strength and agility in police work, the tests now applied invite so much specialized preparation by the candidates as partially to defeat their purpose. If placed on a qualifying rather than a competitive basis, much of the undesirable overemphasis would disappear.

The Civil Service Commission makes convulsive efforts to examine great numbers of police recruits in a single elaborately staged operation. Owing in part to sheer weight of numbers and in part to complacent, time-consuming attitudes by processing agencies, the various physical, character and mental tests require from 14 to 18 months for completion by the examining units. The whole process could be expedited if police recruiting were conducted on a continuous basis, with highly selective tests applied at the very outset.

Continuous recruiting will make panels of qualified aspirants constantly available for final competitive examination on short notice. Police cadres can then be filled from the top of the current eligible list, and both the necessity and the temptation to draw upon the lower portions of stale lists will be avoided.

An alternative approach that has much to commend it would consist of annual examinations held on fixed dates, with mechanical grading of tests and quick certification of lists, thereby reaching the current crop of promising candidates while they are still actively seeking a police appointment. A part of the present delay stems from the large number of aspirants who cannot be processed quickly, but this in turn is directly traceable to the fact that examinations are held at intervals of about four years, which causes a congestion of aspirants.

A useful method of narrowing the field and speeding selection will be to require graduation from high school, or an equivalent education. This simple rule would bar at the outset those who lack an aptitude for learning the varied subject matters of the policeman's art, while preserving the availability of the young men and women who leave high school from economic necessity.

Promotional examinations lay considerable stress upon police subjects, and properly so. The Police Academy operates refresher courses at which attendance is voluntary. The program could have great value and significance. But not enough effort has gone into organizing the subject matter to the end that it may have enduring value for police who enroll. Too often the lecture hour is devoted to a quiz based upon earlier promotional examinations. Patrol-men, sergeants, and lieutenants are separately scheduled but are likely to be brought together into joint session for common instruction. A great many aspirants for promotion choose to attend the special courses offered by one of the private cram schools. These may provide a desirable competition for the Police Academy's efforts to offer promotional instruction. However, the Police Academy should be the source of police doctrine and the inspiration of professional attitudes.

Gross inadequacies in recruitment are not matters of great concern to the Civil Service Commission because it does not stand or fall according to the quality of the police it selects and promotes. That hazard is assumed solely by the Police Commissioner and his chief aides, who are boxed in by the provisions of the Civil Service law. But selection of the right man for the job in hand should not be conducted at arm's length as is now the case with the Civil Service Commission. So unless the Police Commissioner is given power to establish and apply practical standards for the selection of police, there can be no large expectation of a steadily mounting competence in the ranks, upon which the largest advances in law enforcement must depend. Conferral of these essential powers can be accomplished without contravening the provisions of the State Constitution and without impairing the essential principles of the merit system.

Promotional procedures for police, like the original selection of patrol-men, should rest with the Police Commissioner. Positive rather than negative approaches, active rather than passive policies, can mark a better ordered system of recruitment and advancement.

To the Municipal Civil Service Commission should be reserved the role of testing and approving the procedures that are adopted by and for the Police Department, with plenary power to suspend the application of standards that do not attain acceptable levels.

The most successful efforts toward building law enforcement bodies of exceptional quality have involved freeing the police administrator from some or all of the unfavorable traditions of Civil Service control. This has been demonstrated in local, state and Federal police alike. It also characterizes all of the forces, large and small, of England and Wales, Ireland and Scotland, including the widely heralded and much admired Metropolitan Police of London. Eire's Civil Guard, the Royal Canadian Mounted Police, famed in the legends of the Northwest, and some of the other leading forces of Canada. One and all they rest upon the same firm foundation of a personnel control that is the abiding responsibility and concern of the chief police administrator.

The new merit system should be extended within the police force. It should reach to the rank of inspector, as well as to patrolmen, sergeants, lieutenants, and captains, as is now the case. The underlying purpose in giving the Commissioner his present authority to select higher officers from among the whole body of police captains is sound in principle; but in this

City its intent is largely thwarted by the fact that 278 officers holding the permanent rank of captain are distributed among more than 100 separate and distinct commands. They do not and cannot all come under the appraising eye of the Commissioner. Hence his executive powers in freely selecting inspectors and deputy inspectors, as well as higher functionaries, are necessarily delegated to those who have a wider acquaintance among the eligibles, thereby setting up numerous patterns of favoritism and bargaining and intrigue that start in the precinct stations, traverse many extraneous fields, and reach clear up to police headquarters.

Thus the Commissioner's essential control will not be diminished—on the contrary, it will be substantially increased—if the new merit system, operating under the administrative audit of the Civil Service Commission, is extended up to and through the rank of inspector. Beyond that point may stand a mere handful of higher officers—about 25 at the present time—which can be made and unmade at will from a general cadre of some 60 or 70 inspectors of permanent rank.

## THE POLICE ACADEMY

Hand in hand with an improved merit system should go a complete renovation of the Police Academy.

New York's first police training school dates back a half century or more. For years following its inception it was one of the best of its kind. The original curriculum for recruits has expanded in many ways. Thirteen schools now comprise the Academy, with a wide variety of specialized and refresher courses for nearly all police arms, services, and ranks. Much of this represents healthy growth and a desirable extension of the sphere of in-service training. However, when viewed from the qualitative angle, some grave defects become apparent, summarized in the oft-repeated judgment of graduates that attendance at the recruit school represents "just a waste of time." This is a shocking commentary by policemen of mature years, several of whom have gone on to receive some of the highest ranks and honors that the Police Department can bestow.

The judgment may be unfair. It may reflect the training program at its worst, without offsetting credits. Nevertheless, it serves to underscore the fact that no matter how much the academy has expanded, and no matter what its achievements in specific fields, a large part of its early momentum is gone. Today it stands in need of a thorough overhaul and a vigorous push towards new and higher goals. The manpower involved both as instructors and trainees is impressive to say the least. It represents an investment that should be carefully conserved, with an unremitting emphasis upon the quality of the instruction and hence of the product.

## PROBATION AND DISCIPLINE

Although the Police Department largely neglects the probationary period as an essential stage in the process of selection, considerable difficulty would be encountered in doing full justice to many borderline cases within the present narrow confines of the six months' probationary period. Extension to not less than 18 months will prove necessary to the development of a thoroughgoing procedure. This can be accomplished by simple change in the Civil Service rule. . . .

In 1928 the charges on which policemen were accorded a departmental trial totaled well over 5,000 in number. The intervening years witnessed an almost uninterrupted decline in such rough indexes of disciplinary action, with the level dropping to only some 600 charges by 1950. Court convictions of police show a slow decline over the years, but dismissals from the service have gone down by 90 percent.

Following are the summary results of the administrative trials of 584 individuals, for the 20 years from 1931 to 1950 inclusive. They represent all of the major cases heard throughout the period, plus others who had lengthy disciplinary records:

|                                              | Percent |
|----------------------------------------------|---------|
| Charges dismissed                            | 11      |
| Reprimand administered                       | 31      |
| Fined one day's pay or less                  | 37      |
| Fined two or three days' pay                 | 12      |
| Fined five days' pay                         | 5       |
| Fined 10 to 30 days' pay                     | 1       |
| Discharged, resigned or dropped              | 2       |
| Pending, or filed without action             | 1       |

The relatively small number of individuals involved might be viewed as offering striking evidence that the police force has had few offenders against good discipline in its ranks, but several factors are at work that operate to hold their number to modest levels.

(1) The penalties imposed are generally so light as to discourage police commanders from bringing formal charges against their men. Many disciplinary breaches are handled within each police command without recourse to the trial procedure, and without any record.

(2) Some police offenders are disposed of by informal means, particularly by transfer to other duty, and on rare occasions by forced retirement.

(3) Very few charges are brought against sergeants and almost none against lieutenants or officers of higher rank, unless and until criminal proceedings are initiated against them by other public agencies.

(4) The same striking absence of charges is to be noted with respect to extortion or other venal offenses. Here again is disturbing evidence of a policy to dispose of such irregularities without drawing public attention to them.

The extraordinary fact is that individual members of the force may be charged repeatedly with absences from duty, improper patrol, an occasional lapse into intoxication while on duty, assaults on citizens, and unlawful use

of firearms, without suffering more than a reprimand or the forfeiture of
one to five days' pay. Some offenders who have been found guilty scores of
times are still members of the force. Some were promoted despite their bad
records.

ILLNESS AND INJURY

Illness among members of the uniformed forces each year costs approximately $3.5 million in lost time. For the year 1950–1951, an average of
14.7 days was chargeable to illness and injury. This rate is approximately
twice as high as prevails in most private industry and it also appears excessive
when compared with recent rates for other police forces. Some of the increases are directly traceable to more generous statutory provisions for sick
leave. While the more liberal sick-leave provisions are commendable, they
require tight controls if abuses are to be avoided.

High illness rates represent undetected malingering and poor supervision.
A major part of this problem stems from faulty distribution of police surgeons,
inadequate supervision of their work, and failure to establish standards to
which surgeons must adhere.

Because of the uneven distribution of police surgeons, most police find
themselves residing at points that are inconveniently remote from the district
surgeon's office, in fact as far removed as the City's geographical spread permits. No surgeons whatever have offices in Queens and Staten Island. The 23
district surgeons need not be increased in number, since the present ratio of
surgeons to men is entirely adequate. But redistribution is urgently needed.
Surgeons' offices should be located in each of the Boroughs, with the ratio of
surgeons per Borough bearing a direct relation to the number of police to be
served therein. And police surgeons should be required to hold regular office
hours. District health centers of the Department of Health, and in some
instances the City hospitals, may be able to provide part-time facilities for
them.

To avoid future concentration of district surgeons in Boroughs having few
police residents, the Civil Service Commission can specify Borough lists for
new applicants, with an established quota of surgeons for each Borough,
based upon an actual census of police residents. A review of pertinent
judicial decisions indicates that such an arrangement will be sustained by
the courts.

Evidence of uncontrolled malingering is so common as to demand a far
more rigorous treatment than has been accorded thus far. Police surgeons
must understand that they are disciplinary officers as well as healers.

# VIII

## SOME QUESTIONS OF POLICY

This last section deals with the process of policy formation and with the concrete content of policy in several fields of particular interest. The readings have been chosen for what they tell about the matrix out of which policy emerges (especially the "givens" that constrain policy-makers, the interests and groups that shape policy, the nature of the interaction among these interests and groups, and the terms on which differences of interest are adjusted or balanced) and about the major alternatives that are open to decision-makers—not only politicians and administrators, but also ordinary citizens.

In his discussion of the urban transportation problem, Wilfred Owen emphasizes its organizational aspects. There exist so many agencies and jurisdictions, he says, that coordinated management of a metropolitan transportation system is out of the question. But an even more fundamental difficulty arises from disorganization of another kind—haphazard development of urban communities, which has brought about patterns of mobility that are inherently unmanageable. The congestion of transportation facilities at rush hours could be reduced by staggering working hours in the cities, but even then the situation would remain unsatisfactory unless the metropolitan population were dispersed according to a proper regional plan. Owen's treatment of the policy problem suffers from his failure to take its political dimensions into account. He writes as if improved transportation were the only aim of policy. Actually, the public, although disliking congestion, apparently dislikes even more those measures (regional planning, for example) that are necessary to cure it. Thus the policy problem is a good deal more complicated than it is here made to appear.

Policy questions in public school affairs, according to Thomas H. Eliot, a political scientist, mainly concern five matters: curriculum, facilities, the units and organization of government, personnel, and finances. Professionals and laymen are both active in the discussion of all of these matters. The professionals (especially organized teachers, representatives of teachers' colleges, and school administrators) have decided views and a marked distrust of lay "interference." But by long-standing tradition the policy-making function is in the hands of locally elected lay boards. The dynamic element in the policy-formation process, therefore, is largely the interaction, especially conflict, between professional and lay points of view.

The public library, according to Oliver Garceau, a political scientist, has no natural enemies and no natural allies either. The apathy with which it is regarded has its advantages for the librarian as policymaker. He (or, very likely, she) can usually perform the delicate operation of book selection, and thus of censorship, without interference. But apathy must be overcome to some extent if the library is to get support from reluctant taxpayers. Accordingly, the library offers a great many special services—to the old, the young, immigrants, labor union members, church members, and so on—in order to mobilize group affiliations that will support it politically.

The case study by A. Theodore Brown, an historian, of the development of the Community Service Division of the Kansas City Welfare Department gives a vivid picture of the political and other realities that lay behind decisions in welfare matters in one city. This account is particularly interesting for what it shows of the way a "good government" administration may combine the ideology of "liberalism" with the technique of the machine to maintain itself in office despite the distaste of many voters for government that is honest, impartial, and efficient. This effort was not finally successful in Kansas City, however. On March 31, 1959, the voters turned the reform government out after nineteen years in office. City Manager Cookingham and his chief assistants, including Richardson, resigned almost immediately.

In the final reading, a fictional case study by Edward C. Banfield, we follow a newspaper reporter who is gathering information for a story on urban renewal, a story intended to help his readers decide what to do about blighted housing in their city. The policy problem becomes more and more difficult as the reporter talks to a lady crusader, a redevelopment project official, a planner, the mayor, and an economist. Finally, with a great many complications spread out before us, we are asked what recommendations we would make. This piece was written for use by adult discussion groups. Students who have done their homework should be provoked to lively discussion by the concluding question: If *you* were in this reporter's place, what recommendations would you make?

# MANAGING THE TRANSPORTATION SYSTEM

WILFRED OWEN

A MAJOR STEP toward planning and financing a satisfactory urban transportation system will be to establish the necessary governmental organization. Urban transportation must be removed from the administrative vacuum that has kept it from playing a full role in the development of better cities. Urban communities that divide the transportation problem into small parts cannot expect to get whole answers.

The need for organizing all available transportation facilities and for financing and operating them as a system is becoming increasingly apparent as we review the methods of supplying transport services today. . . . The division of responsibility among political jurisdictions and among different agencies and departments within a single unit of government is the most obvious defect of current policy. The fact that roads and streets are provided by a number of jurisdictions in the metropolitan area is a frequent source of planning and financing difficulties, especially in the many instances where two or more states are involved. The large daily influx of commuters from outlying areas to the central city pose additional problems of supporting needed facilities on an equitable basis. Public transportation operations are often circumscribed by local government boundaries that impose economic burdens on both the carriers and the public. In many cases, political units have been made obsolete by the very transportation services they are attempting to furnish.

The administrative separation of different methods of transportation imposes a serious obstacle to effective community mobility. Decisions with respect to transit, for example, may have a controlling influence on the volume of automobile use, while pricing decisions governing parking may have a significant impact on transit patronage or highway requirements. The need for planning and financing all facilities with these interrelations in mind is apparent, but this is not possible with transportation responsibilities divided among separate agencies and jurisdictions.

The state highway departments have in many cases become an anachronism in the urban area. They are responsible for some of the most important travel routes in cities, and yet their limited jurisdiction precludes a broad approach to the needs of the city from the standpoint either of transportation or community planning. Urban highway work under the state is rapidly increasing in importance, but it is generally governed by the concept that

Reprinted from *The Metropolitan Transportation Problem* (Washington, D.C.: The Brookings Institution, 1956), pp. 258–266, by permission of the publisher.

city streets are merely connecting links in a state-wide system. It is little wonder that the city, confronted by the highly complex problem of accomplishing a total circulatory system properly related to over-all community goals, has often found limited relief in state highway construction projects.

Transit is also the victim of partial remedies. The transit patron is not interested merely in the bus he rides but in the ride itself—which means the highway as well as the bus. Public transportion depends on both. As the transit company is not responsible for roads or their use—but only for the vehicle and its operation—the chances of getting good transit service are poor. Transportation policy needs to be aimed not simply at supplying the various elements of movement, but at improving standards of mobility.

A number of approaches toward integrating urban transportation functions have been noted. . . . No one of them has gone far enough to achieve, in any comprehensive way, the provision of good passenger service in the urban area. In the case of public transportation, the transit system has not been made part of a total transportation system, nor has any city solved the management and financial problems that the quest for reasonable standards of public transportation service introduce. It must be concluded that the attempt to overcome urban transportation problems with privately owned transit facilities is unrealistic. The provision of tolerable standards of service in the peak hours calls for much more equipment than can be profitably provided. At the same time, it is clear that neither public ownership of transit nor the transit authority has succeeded in providing satisfactory standards of service or financial strength. Deficits persist, and patronage continues downward on private and public lines alike. Only if transit were to be made part of a total transportation system, under unified policy direction or unified management, would the possibilities of more effective operations be realized.

It is equally clear that metropolitan areas are not organized to carry out an effective attack on their highway problems. Obviously, there must be greater local autonomy with respect to the location, design, and use of highways in urban areas to permit a closer relation between highway construction and urban development. To the extent that state highway departments continue to perform road construction work in cities, they must be better equipped to deal with the specialized problems encountered in urbanized areas. The establishment of strong urban divisions in state and federal highway bureaus is becoming increasingly necessary. Administrative machinery to achieve a co-ordinated transportation-community planning approach at the local level is also imperative if urban areas are to adapt to the automotive age.

The transportation difficulties of metropolitan areas, then, are not likely to be overcome by anything short of a complete alteration of administrative machinery. The need is for a physical plan and for investment and operating decisions designed to accomplish the plan. The solution might be a "port authority," a "transportation district commission," or some form of metropolitan government. Some of the organizational experiments tried to date indicate what can be done. Facilities might be publicly owned and operated, publicly owned and privately operated, or privately owned and operated on a management contract basis. The essential requirement is that plans and policies should be uniform for the entire geographical area as well as for all relevant transportation facilities and services. This means uniform policies and integrated plans for major expressways and highways, related parking and terminal facilities, transit and railroad commuter services, taxi operations, and traffic engineering and control. It also means integrating the transportation function with metropolitan planning.

## The Community Plan

The problem of achieving satisfactory standards of mobility for urban communities is only partly a transportation problem. The difficulties of urban mobility stem from more deep-seated causes, principally the concentration and haphazard development of urban communities. . . . There is need to do more than organize, plan, and finance additional transport capacity. It will be necessary to exert a positive control over the demand for transportation as well.

Two approaches have been indicated that can level the peaks of travel that are placing an impossible burden on the transportation system. One, designed to furnish immediate relief, is a community-wide program of staggered hours for working, shopping, and school. A spreading of the urban traffic load might prove highly advantageous to the city, the worker, and the economy as a whole. The cost of peak-hour highway and public transit capacity and the economic losses from traffic delays and personal annoyance are heavy. Actually, it may be costing more to accommodate the peak than it would cost if the length of the work day were reduced to promote the staggering of arrivals and departures.

The peak, in addition to being spread over more time, should be spread over more space. Cities can never solve their transportation problems if they continue to crowd too many people and too much economic activity into too little space. Congestion in the rush hours is inevitable as long as we insist on living in the suburbs, working downtown, and starting off at the same time to get to the same place. In these circumstances no transportation magic can make the journey to work a joy ride. We will have to avoid unmanageable transportation demand through the dispersal of population and economic activity, the preservation of open spaces, and the planning of land use densities and arrangements.

Both population limits and geographical limits will have to be imposed on urban development if the metropolis is to avoid strangling in its own prosperity. There is increasing evidence of the need for directing more urban growth into new towns and existing smaller towns. This would seem preferable to the overcrowding that modern transportation now makes unnecessary, or to the endless sprawl that modern transport has made possible. But there is the further need for redeveloping existing urban centers to assure a generous balancing of developed land with open space, and for planning new suburban growth to assure the preservation of surrounding low-density land. Otherwise a solid build-up will ultimately deny easy access to the open country, and communities may become so unwieldy that the task of providing transportation and other community needs may destroy the advantages of urban living.

Redevelopment of existing urban communities and plans for new urbanization can help overcome peak-hour congestion by enabling people to live and work in the same areas, either close-in or on the periphery. Traffic can in this way be reduced by the elimination of unnecessary travel, a dispersal of the total volume of movement, and a reversal of peak-hour flows. Approaching the demand side of the problem offers a real hope of halting the endless race between traffic growth and the capacity of the transportation system. The fact that major development of the urban area has already taken place frequently discourages efforts that seem too late. Yet renewal of the city is constantly taking place, and comprehensive planning is giving cities a second chance.

The seeds of better community planning that are finding fertile ground in the decay of downtown, however, need to be transplanted to the fringes. Events that have left large areas of the central city in economic ruin are being reenacted in the suburbs. Planless growth is adding to the transportation problems of the metropolitan area faster than the central city can hope to overcome its past mistakes through redevelopment. Whether in the city or in the suburbs, the isolation of urban planning from transportation planning has proved impractical. Both problems are compounded by the attempted separation. Satisfactory transportation is impossible without comprehensive planning that exploits to the fullest the relations between good transportation and good communities.

The federal government has promoted metropolitan area planning through recent housing legislation requiring urban renewal projects to be related to a comprehensive urban plan. Planning of transportation facilities has also been furthered through transportation surveys jointly supported by federal, state, and local governments, with federal funds supplied through federal-aid highway legislation. A total approach is obviously desirable, and more effective federal encouragement of metropolitan area planning is badly needed. An indication of the need is the accelerated program of urban highway development sponsored by the national government. This program could have highly damaging effects in urban areas unless it is carried out as part of an area-wide community development plan. Federal approval of projects should be made contingent on their relation to over-all transportation objectives and to comprehensive community planning.

An effective solution to the urban transportation problem, then, should meet three tests. First, it should be functionally comprehensive by including all forms of transportation applicable to the problem. Second, it should be comprehensive geographically by including not only the city but the metropolitan area and all the affected region. Third, it should be comprehensive from a planning standpoint by assuring that transportation is used to promote community goals, and that community plans make satisfactory transportation possible.

This latter test is the most important. The basic need is to achieve satisfactory conditions of living. In the cities that made American industry the most prosperous in the world, slums and blight are an anomaly that needs to be attacked with all the resources at hand. Transportation development that merely helps to move us more expeditiously through areas of urban decay misses the mark.

The transportation industries, operating under archaic public policies, have failed to contribute their full potential to the building of better communities. Yet an attack on transportation inadequacies, broadly viewed, is not something apart from an attack on the inadequacies of the city. Transportation facilities that now provide the escape from undesirable urban conditions can help to overcome these conditions. Decisions governing transportation can exert an overriding influence on future patterns of urban development. Transportation facilities can blight the area through which they pass, or they can restore it. They can further the development of park and recreation lands and other objectives of the city, or they can simply carry traffic. And in doing so, they can support pleasant neighborhoods and prosperous communities, or they can nullify efforts to attain a higher standard of urban living.

In American communities most of the housing and commercial developments now taking place make little sense in relation to the ways that people move today or will be moving in the future. At one extreme, we are preserving the old congested way of urban living as if the technological innovations in transportation and communications—and the threat of modern warfare— did not exist. At the other extreme, we are reacting against high densities by substituting endless sprawl, with no effort to control growth, preserve open spaces, or apply our new-found mobility to the enhancement of urban life.

In a nation that is both motorized and urbanized, there will have to be a closer relation between transportation and urban development. We will have to use transportation resources to achieve better communities and community planning techniques to achieve better transportation. The combination could launch a revolutionary attack on urban congestion that is long overdue.

# PUBLIC SCHOOL POLITICS

## THOMAS H. ELIOT

MOUNTING CONCERN over the aims and achievements of American public schools emphasizes the need for continuing analysis of how the schools are run and who runs them. The general theory is simple enough: schools are objects of local control, the people of a local school district exercise that control through an elected school board, and the board appoints a superintendent to act as the chief executive of the district. There are variations from this pattern—in some places school boards are appointed rather than elected, in others the school system is formally a part of the city government, and in a few districts other officials, such as a business manager or building superintendent, share the top executive authority—but it is by far the most common arrangement among the nation's approximately 50,000 school districts.

## I

The formal structure is based on state constitutions and statutes, and the latter have tended to confirm the historical development of education in the nineteenth century, especially in one respect: the district system of organization.[1] The desirability of *local* control of the public schools is an article of faith among most trained educators and many other Americans, including President Eisenhower.[2] Laymen assume that local control means control by the people of the district, usually through elected representatives. Professional educators, however, are less clear about this. Their books and journals are rife with intimations that the people and even the school board members should keep their hands off the schools.[3] Even James B. Conant's "report," after echoing the typical recommendation that school boards should confine

---

Reprinted from *American Political Science Review*, 53, No. 4 (December, 1959), 1032–1051, where it appeared under the title "Toward an Understanding of Public School Politics."

1. Adolph E. Meyer, *An Educational History of the American People* (New York McGraw-Hill Book Co., 1957), esp. pp. 39, 116, and ch. 9.

2. When President of Columbia University, Mr. Eisenhower, in a letter to Representative Ralph Gwinn, pictured general federal aid for education as "another vehicle by which the believers in paternalism, if not outright socialism, will gain still additional power for the central government." *Congressional Record*, Vol. 95, Pt. 14, p. A3690, June 14, 1949.

3. *E.g.,* "We should never wish to remove the teacher altogether from social control, for the school is, after all, a social institution serving the needs of the community. But we should hope in the years to come to erect new agencies of control which would oversee the work of the educational profession at a little greater distance than is now the case." Van Cleve Morris, "Grass Rootsism and the Public Schools," *School and Society*, Vol. 85, No. 2114, June 22, 1957.

themselves to "policy" as distinguished from "administration," says that they should refrain from interfering with curricular development.[4] But where is educational "policy" made, if not in the development of the curriculum? Doubtless Conant's remark was an inadvertent slip, for his book as a whole deals primarily with the curriculum and is addressed to "interested citizens," a category which surely includes more than educators; but many educators are insistent in urging, in effect, that the schools are the special province of the professionals, the voters being a necessary evil who must be reckoned with because they provide the money. In this view, the school board's primary functions, aside from directing the district's business affairs, are to hire and support a competent professional as superintendent, defend the schools against public criticism, and persuade the people to open their pocketbooks.[5]

This seems like turning representative government upside down. It also reflects a somewhat specialized concept of democratic theory, not unlike that expounded by Walter Lippmann—namely, that the experts should initiate policy and carry it out, with the people's representatives properly confined to the negative function of checking any gross abuse of power.[6] Lippmann was referring primarily to foreign policy, and could argue plausibly that the control of foreign policy—Locke's "federative power"—was a matter for special treatment in an otherwise self-governing society.[7] It seems questionable whether the considerations favoring executive (or expert) direction of foreign policy are equally applicable to the control of school districts. Nevertheless, there are observable reasons for the desire to limit the role of the school boards and the people who elect them. The chief one is the professionalization of public school education.[8]

---

4. James B. Conant, *The American High School Today* (New York, 1959), p. 43.

5. Consider the recommendations of W. W. Theisen, *The City Superintendent and the Board of Education* (New York, 1917) which, on the assumption that they represent agreement among "authorities in the field of school administration . . . [and] have stood the test of time," are endorsed and quoted in the competent manual for school board members prepared by Professor Reeder of Ohio State University: a school board member, to perform his "proper duties," should "Represent needs of the schools before city authorities or the legislature . . . [and] before the public. . . . Serve as laymen (even after retiring from the board) to champion school needs and to further public support of the schools," Ward G. Reeder, *School Boards and Superintendents* (New York, 1954), pp. 20–21. The chief organization of superintendents, addressing board members, did lay more stress on the board's supervisory and critical role, in *School Boards in Action* (Washington, D.C.: American Association of School Administrators, 1946).

6. Walter Lippmann, *Essays in the Public Philosophy* (Boston, 1955).

7. *Cf.* Woodrow Wilson, *Congressional Government*, 15th ed. (Boston, 1900), pp. xi–xiii.

8. The application of the professional concept to public school teaching faces one peculiar difficulty: "Teachers are recognized as a profession. . . . But unlike other professions, the entire control of education lies outside the profession." "Ten Criticisms of Public Education," *Research Bulletin*, Vol. XXXV, No. 4 (Washington, D.C.: National Education Association, December, 1957), p. 135. For relevant discussion of the necessary elements of any profession see Edgar B. Wesley, *NEA: The First Hundred Years* (New York, 1957) 349–350, and Hyman G. Rickover, *Education and Freedom* (New York, 1959) 61–81.

The professionals consist of three groups. Numerically the largest, and politically today the least significant, are the school teachers.[9] A hundred years ago, school teaching, in contrast to university teaching, law, medicine, and the ministry, was a vocation rather than a profession. A prime purpose of the National Education Association, originated in 1857, was to raise it to a professional status. By a kind of bootstrap operation, this was largely achieved, though it took eighty years to do it. The early normal schools, essentially vocational training institutes, were supplemented by colleges and graduate schools of education; and states were moved to pass certification laws prescribing educational qualifications for teachers.[10] The second professional group is composed of the pedagogues' pedagogues—the faculties of teachers colleges and university departments of education. Their professional status was ready-made, but as the justification of their existence depended largely on the professionalization of school teaching itself, they naturally took a leading part in that process. They also were foremost in creating the third group, the professional school administrators.[11] School administration, as a profession, is a latecomer, but in terms of understanding the politics of the public schools it is perhaps the most important of all. School administration is a decidedly hierarchical and disciplined business and the top administrator, the local school superintendent, holds the key position in each school district. Indeed, there seems to be professional agreement that the most significant duty of the people's representatives on the local school board is the selection of the superintendent.[12]

The thoroughly defensible assumption that school teaching and school administration are the specialized tasks of persons with professional training and status leads inevitably to a professional distrust of lay interference.[13] This distrust has been accentuated by the frequency with which lay demands have conflicted with the convictions of the educators, seeming to them to be destructive of the very purposes of education.[14] Even well meant lay sugges-

9. Embattled teachers have, of course, on occasion been politically effective at the local level, as in the Boston school committee election of 1957; at the state level, their impact on the legislature may be considerable, as in California, but tends to depend on the vigor of organizations which in most states are guided by other segments of the profession.

10. Wesley, *op. cit.*

11. "So great is the importance of the [superintendent's] office, and so elaborate its exactions, that special training for it is almost indispensable—a fact which, luckily, has long since been grasped by every first rate teachers college in the land." Meyer, *op. cit.*, p. 105.

12. "Probably the most important responsibility resting upon a modern board of education is that of keeping a competent superintendent in charge of the community's schools." *School Boards in Action, op. cit.*, p. 11.

13. "Because teaching, supervision, and administration have been specialized professions, the modern board of education cannot waste its time and jeopardize educational results by trying to do the work of technically trained educators." *Ibid.*

14. See Robert M. Hutchins, "Are Our Teachers Afraid to Teach?," *A.A.U.P. Bulletin,* Vol. 40 (Summer, 1954), pp. 202–208. For an example of vigorous lay incursions into the selection of textbooks (presumably a professional function) see *Third Report: Un-American Activities in California* (Sacramento: California State Printing Office 1947), pp. 353–354.

tions that more emphasis should be placed on the "three r's" have caused flutterings of alarm, for too often such criticisms have been the softening-up forerunners of assaults on the freedom of the teachers and so on the whole professional concept.[15] Such assaults have caused one writer to describe the politics of public education as "ideological politics," otherwise a comparative rarity on the American scene.[16]

But are we permitted to speak of the "politics" of education? To many educators the word seems abhorrent: not even the admonitions of George S. Counts[17] can overcome their aversion to it. Again, this is understandable. Whole school systems have been blighted by the intrusion of certain aspects of politics, especially the use of patronage in appointments and contracts in apparent disregard of the need to give children the best possible education.[18] Yet because school districts are governmental units and the voters have ultimate responsibility, school board members and school superintendents are engaged in political activity whether they like it or not. The standard professional terminology for this—a semantic triumph—is "community relations"; a successful superintendent, particularly, must be skilled in community relations. Why not say frankly that he must be a good politician?[19]

Surely it is high time to stop being frightened by a word. Politics includes the making of governmental decisions, and the effort or struggle to gain or keep the power to make those decisions. Public schools are part of government. They are political entities. They are a fit subject for study by political scientists.

Yet neither educators nor political scientists have frequently engaged in the examination of public education from this angle. Educators have shied away not only from the word "politics" but from political scientists as well. (The terminology of social scientists who deal with "power structures" and "communications" they find more acceptable.) Their suspicion of political science stems in part from the writings of some public administration professors who have occasionally urged that school systems, being part of local government, should be merged with multi-purpose local units—namely cities and towns—thus losing their "independent" status,[20] and at the state

15. Robert A. Skaife, "Know the Enemy," *Connecticut Teacher* (December, 1951), pp. 68–71, reprinted in C. W. Scott and C. M. Hill, *Public Education Under Criticism* (New York, 1954), pp. 233–239.

16. Robert C. Wood, *Suburbia* (Boston, 1958).

17. "The profession should seek power and then try to use that power fully and wisely and in the interests of the great masses of the people." George S. Counts, *Dare the Schools Build a New Social Order?* (New York, 1932), p. 29.

18. See, *e.g.*, Vincent Ostrom, "School Board Politics in Los Angeles," unpublished thesis, University of California, Los Angeles, 1948.

19. A refreshingly frank statement by a superintendent of his political role can be found in Nicholas Moseley, "Politics and School Administration," in C. M. Hill, *ed.*, *Educational Progress and School Administration* (New Haven, 1936) pp. 61–76.

20. See, *e.g.*, Ernest A. Engelbert, "Educational Administration and Responsible Government," *School and Society*, Vol. 75, No. 1035, Jan. 19, 1952. Independence of the municipal government is a professional article of faith. "The organizational control and tax levying structure for education should be separate from other units of local

level, that a department of education, like other departments, should be headed by an appointee of the governor rather than a quasi-independent board. These proposals are in direct conflict with the passionate convictions of professional educators,[21] and so have given political science a bad name in the teaching profession.

As for the political scientists, the running of the public schools—except for national defense the most extensive and expensive governmental activity in this country—has seldom seemed worth more than a chapter or two in a text on state and local government. There are honorable exceptions, but they are very few indeed.[22] The taboo has worked both ways, almost as if by tacit agreement: if politics has been anathema to educators, the governing of the public schools has seemed inconsequential to political scientists.

The taboo should be exorcised, for the future of public education, at every level of government, is not only a political issue but an increasingly crucial one. It requires analysis not only in terms of political institutions (almost the only point of contact, and friction, between educators and political scientists in the past) but in terms of voting behavior, ideological predispositions, the clash of interests, decision-making, and the impact of individuals and organizations on nation-wide trends in educational policy. Of these only the first two have been examined at all extensively (and then usually by social scientists whose primary concern is not politics) and even those have not been the source of any noticeable amount of published material.[23] If all the significant political factors are revealed, the people can more rationally and effectively control the governmental process. Such, at least, must be the faith of the political scientist who, devoted to the search for truth, believes that "what can be" is no less the truth than "what is."

## II

The most significant subjects for decision by whoever runs the public schools concern the curriculum, the facilities, the units and organization of

---

government." *Guides to the Improvement of State School Finance Programs* (Washington, D.C.: National Education Association, April, 1958), p. 14. The justification for such independence is stated in terms of the complexity of educational issues (requiring the "undivided attention" of board members), the need for continuity of policy, and the undesirability of mixing educational issues with other public issues. Arvid J. Burke, *Financing Public Schools in the United States*, rev. ed. (New York, 1957).

21. The writer well remembers an occasion when, as director of a state "little Hoover" commission, he asked why the state department of education should be organized differently from any other department. The inquiry, advanced innocently enough, threw the commissioner of education into a purple and highly articulate rage.

22. *E.g.*, John A. Vieg, *The Government of Education in Metropolitan Chicago* (Chicago, 1939); Robert L. Morlan, *Intergovernmental Relations in Education* (Minneapolis, 1950); Nelson B. Henry and Jerome G. Kerwin, *Schools and City Government* (Chicago, 1938). See also Carl F. Stover, "Local Government and the Schools: The Debate over Independence," Ph.D. thesis, Stanford University, 1955.

23. Some of the unpublished scholarly material seems to deserve a wider audience. Perhaps the ice has been broken by the publication of Neal Gross's misnamed but interesting study of superintendent-board relationships, *Who Runs Our Schools?* (New York, 1958).

government, and personnel; and partly shaping them all is the omnipresent issue of finance.

Since World War II a war of words over the *curriculum* has been waged at white heat.[24] Because their professionalism seems to lack full public acceptance and because any attack may make it harder to raise the money needed for good schooling, educators tend to object vehemently to most lay criticism. The laity, of course, embraces most of us, including school board members and university professors (of everything but Education), so the inference might seem to be that no one but a professional educator has any business criticizing the methods or ideas of professional educators. This was a typical answer to the vigorous attack on the curriculum mounted by Arthur E. Bestor, professor of history at the University of Illinois.[25] However, by stepping carefully even an outsider may win a hearing. Constructive suggestions so phrased as to avoid sensitive toes, especially if preceded by well-publicized and protracted study, are treated with respect: witness the generally deferential reception of the report of James B. Conant, who is just as much a "layman" as Bestor. Any citizen who wants to influence the conduct of the schools might be well advised to follow Conant's example. And the person seeking to portray the political process in relation to education must also resist the temptation to be drawn into the controversy over "progressive education," "life adjustment," whether Johnny can read and if not why not, and the curriculum generally.[26] His task is not to say what should be in the curriculum, but how, by whom, and through whose influence that decision is or might be made.

It is hard to read professional pronouncements on this subject without concluding that in professional eyes, the curriculum is essentially the school superintendent's business. To be sure, a committee of the American Association of School Administrators, in a report addressed to school board members, did say that the school board had "general responsibility" for the curriculum. The emphasis, however, seemed to be on the word "general," as was indicated by the committee's statement that "Curriculum planning and development is a highly technical task which requires special training. . . . Board members

---

24. The best-publicized attack on the curriculum, aside from those of "super-patriotic" groups, include the books of Arthur E. Bestor, especially *The Restoration of Learning* (New York, 1955); Mortimer Smith's artistically written *And Madly Teach* (Chicago, 1949); John Keats, *Schools Without Scholars* (Boston, 1958); and the recent call to arms by Vice Admiral Rickover, *Education and Freedom, op. cit.* The educators' defense and counterattack have been confined almost wholly to articles in professional journals: a number of them can be found in Scott and Hill, *op. cit.*

25. "After all, as a scholar, the Illinois professor should realize that education (or Education) is a field of inquiry vast enough to consume a person's full time." William T. Brickman, "Critical Analyses of American Education," *School and Society*, Vol. 80, No. 2045 (Oct. 30, 1954), pp. 135–136.

26. The temptation to plunge into the fray is aggravated when a dean of a state school of education makes a provocative statement like this: "The most important objective of public education . . . is the development in each student of attitudes of courtesy, respect, and helpfulness toward others." M. R. Trabue, "The Fundamental Purpose in Public Education," *School and Society*, Vol. 66, No. 1718 (Nov. 29, 1947), p. 416.

do not have and cannot be expected to have the technical competence to pass on the work of expert teachers in this field. . . . Nor can the board pass upon specific textbooks."[27] Conant likewise assumes that "the school board will leave the development of the curriculum to the administrative officers and the teaching staff but will be kept informed of all developments."[28] Even this, however, leaves some doubt about the school board's role, or lack of it. Is curriculum "development" something different from educational "policy," and if so, what is the line that separates them?

A school board member, impressively instructed to stick to policy and allow others to develop the curriculum, might well ask this question. But he might also ask why, if the curriculum is of great importance in educating children, he and his colleagues on the board should not take the responsibility for developing it? They are the people's representatives, elected to run the schools. Professional educators may say that they should not run the schools, but the law says that they must. (The law, of course, was made by some more laymen, called legislators.) Of course a strong argument can be made that usually the curriculum stands a better chance of improvement if it is "developed" by knowledgeable experts. But one may also suggest that experts can occasionally be wrong. Even Conant tacitly admits this, in his assumption that the school board will be "kept informed" and, also, that its members will "reserve (and exercise) the right" to question the superintendent and high school principal. One can imagine school board members, reading this, who will snort: "Reserve the right? We have no right to *refrain* from questioning our employees; we're to govern the school district and not to have some one else do it. There has been too much delegation of authority by elected officials lately. The people elected *us* to run things and we're going to run them."

---

27. *School Boards in Action, op. cit.,* p. 178. For a less guarded professional viewpoint, consider the implications of an "opinion survey" of a sample of teachers from eighteen scattered states. Asked who they thought should make various kinds of decisions, they were in substantial agreement on the curriculum-making process, as follows: "Determination of the objectives for the total instructional program of the school: principal, groups of teachers, and superintendent." Chiranji Lal Sharma, "Practices in Decision-Making as Related to Satisfaction in Teaching," unpublished dissertation, University of Chicago (1955), quoted in The Midwest Administration Center's *Administrator's Notebook,* Vol. III, No. 8 (University of Chicago, 1955). See also E. M. Tuttle, *School Board Leadership in America* (Danville, Ill.: Interstate Printers and Publishers, 1958), pp. 31, 40, wherein the first secretary of the National School Boards Association, Inc., says that the board's "policies on the educational program should set forth clearly the goals which the community is seeking" and that the board should "interpret, defend and support constructive educational programs when the need arises." Mr. Tuttle does, however, also imply that some more direct board participation is desirable, including meeting with the superintendent and "professional educators and consultants" to consider "new ideas and concepts of instruction and curriculum planning" (p. 66). A teachers college professor expresses his assumption that in fact, the curriculum is largely shaped by what the professionals believe to be local lay opinion: he believes that this inchoate lay influence is highly unfortunate. Myron Lieberman, "Let Educators Run Our Schools," *The Nation,* March 7, 1959, pp. 206–209.

28. Conant, *op. cit.,* p. 43.

Although recent controversies give the impression that the professionals have made the curriculum "progressive" (whatever that may mean) and want the school boards to keep hands off, there are indications that in many districts the shoe is on the other foot. Through conviction, or perhaps through ignorance and indifference, school boards have often adhered to curricula which the superintendents consider sadly out of date. Neal Gross quotes as typical of a sizeable minority view among Massachusetts superintendents the following complaints: "The selectmen and the town finance committee take the attitude, 'What was good enough for me ought to be good enough for them (the children).' And so do some of my school committee members. How can you run a modern educational program with . . . a classical curriculum when 80% of the kids don't go on to college?"[29] And again: "My committee is primarily interested in keeping costs down. They don't want to discuss or even consider the need to revise the curriculum."[30] The burden is on those who want change: if the Bestors feel frustrated by the insistence on professional domination of curriculum-making, the professionals feel blocked by lay conservatism or apathy.

The question of whether board or superintendent should dominate is important, but nowhere near as significant as what the curriculum contains. The question is reminiscent of the excitement about balancing the Federal budget before World War II. Many people in the 1930s were convinced that to save the country expenditures must be drastically cut—which meant, of course, the reduction or elimination of the relief programs that gave work and wages to millions of otherwise unemployed men and women. Came the war in Europe, and by 1940 many of these same economizers, fervently pro-British and anti-Hitler, enthusiastically favored vast increases in Federal expenditures for defense and aid to Britain. Whether the budget should be balanced was less crucial than what the money was spent for. In the same way, while a certain form of board-superintendent division of authority may, like budget-balancing, seem generally sound, the real question is what kind of school it produces. The basic problem, therefore, is not one of "school administration"; it is the political issue of what is to be taught or read in our schools. We may wish to leave this decision to the experts; we may wish to make it ourselves. This issue is decided chiefly at the local level, and to a lesser extent in the state capitols by legislatures and state education departments. For the last forty years it has also been affected by national legislation granting federal aid for vocational education.

The decisions concerning *facilities*—chiefly school buildings—are made very largely in the districts, with a comparatively high degree of popular participation. The people get engaged in school-building politics more than in any other phase of public school politics, for two reasons. First, a building program requires a major capital outlay, and in nearly all states the bond

---

29. Gross, *op. cit.*, p. 10.
30. *Ibid.*, p. 13.

issues which such capital outlays necessitate are by law subject to popular approval. Second, buildings being tangible and the distance a child must walk or ride to school being measurable, most people feel more qualified to have opinions about the need, nature and location of the schoolhouse than about what goes on inside it.[31]

Closely allied with the location and adequacy of buildings is the issue of *district organization*. Like the former, it is profoundly affected by finance: the Conant report, for instance, calls for reorganization of districts to eliminate small high schools because a really good small high school is, Conant believes, prohibitively expensive.[32] On the other hand, the problems of location cause Alvin Eurich of the Fund for the Advancement of Education to criticize this recommendation: in sparsely populated areas, a large high school would be too far from many children's homes.[33] The decisions on district size are sometimes made directly by state legislatures, or by state departments of education, but more often by the voters in the districts affected. The local voters' capacity to consolidate districts, is, however, profoundly affected by the kind of statutes enacted by the legislature.[34] The internal organization of a district—its system of government, whether its board shall be elected or appointed, its budgetary connection with the municipality—is ordinarily decided at the state level, though some states permit a certain amount of local option.[35]

*Personnel* decisions include one which, in most districts, is made directly by the people—the election of school board members. Here is politics at its plainest, despite the non-partisan ballot that prevails in the majority of such elections, yet few efforts have been made to analyze the nature of school board campaigns and patterns of voting behavior therein.[36] The educators and such useful publicists for education as the National Citizens Council for Better Schools rightly emphasize the importance of choosing "good" school boards, but their hortatory efforts are seldom buttressed by information as to

31. Even in a small district, popular ignorance concerning the school system may be abysmal. See Leo A. Haak, "The General Public and the Public Schools," in the Midwest Administration Center's *Administrator's Notebook*, Vol. IV, No. 8 (University of Chicago, May 1957).

32. Conant, *op. cit.*, p. 37.

33. *New York Times*, Feb., 1959. Evidently, the question depends in part on how much the district is willing to pay for bus service.

34. See Harlan Beem, "School District Reorganization in Illinois," *State Government*, July, 1951, pp. 178–181, and also *Path of Progress for Metropolitan St. Louis* (St. Louis: Metropolitan St. Louis Survey, 1957).

35. *E.g.*, in New Jersey a city constitutes a "chapter six" district, with an appointed board, unless in a popular referendum it votes to become a "chapter seven" district with an elected board and popular budget control.

36. Studies, unpublished, have been made in "Bay City," Mass., by a group including J. Leiper Freeman, and are in process in St. Louis under the direction of Robert H. Salisbury and the writer. See also Ostrom, *op. cit.*, and William B. Milius, "The Riverview Gardens Superintendent," unpublished thesis, Washington University, St. Louis, 1956.

what factors actually decide school board elections. The next significant personnel decision is the selection of a superintendent by the school board. He is often the key figure (as the professionals wish him to be) on the local educational scene.[37] Indeed, his selection or retention sometimes is the central issue in school board elections; the voters thus occasionally affect the choice directly, and their potential ability to do so influences board action.[38] Also for local decision is the matter of appointment, retention, and promotion of the teachers. Here direct, official popular intervention via the ballot box is rare indeed, although it has happened,[39] and although occasionally a school board election has revolved around the retention of a school principal or teacher rather than a superintendent.[40] In the main the decisions, formally made by the board, are based on the superintendent's recommendations. Chiefly on the superintendent, therefore, beat the informal pressures for appointment, transfer, or removal of a teacher, often in an emotional context arising naturally out of the complex psychology of the teacher-parent relationship.

While these personnel decisions are made locally, in most districts they are constrained by state legislation, particularly laws prescribing minimum qualifications of superintendents, principals, and teachers, and governing the conditions of promotion and discharge. At the state capitols, more than anywhere else, the educators have fought and largely won their fight for professional status.[41] Tenure laws are, in the main, protections against "politics," but a tenure system may enhance status as well as security. More important, as a recognition of professionalism, are the certification statutes. To be sure, state occupational licensing laws hardly confer professional status, in the traditional sense, on every occupation licensed, such as those of elevator operator or hairdresser. In the case of teachers, however, they have been

---

37. "The selection of the superintendent of schools is the most important single decision the board of education makes." *Choosing the Superintendent of Schools* (Washington, D.C.: American Association of School Administrators, 1941). *Cf.* Charles E. Reeves, *School Boards: Their Status, Functions, and Activities* (New York, 1954), p. 234. For illustrations of the superintendent's significance in the community, see Richard Conrad, "The Administrative Role: a Sociological Study of Leadership in the Public School System," unpublished dissertation, Stanford University, 1951; and Edmund G. Gleazer, Jr., "The Identification of Certain Alignments of Social Power Impinging on Decision-Making of School Committee and Superintendent in a New England Community," unpublished dissertation, Harvard University, 1953.

38. In Riverview Gardens, Mo., in 1955 a discharged superintendent successfully campaigned for the election of his friends to the school board and was reinstated. See Milius, *op. cit.*

39. In preparation, under the direction of the writer, is a study of a referendum in 1957 in which the voters of Cambridge, Mass., nullified the school board's promotion of seventeen members of the instructional staff.

40. See, *e.g.*, *Monroe, Michigan: Report of an Investigation* (Washington, D.C.: National Education Association, 1958); *cf. North College Hill, Ohio: Report of an Investigation* (Washington, D.C.: National Education Association, 1947).

41. Progress up to twelve years ago (which has continued since) is summarized in *The Forty-Eight School Systems* (Chicago: Council of State Governments, 1948).

accompanied—indeed, have often been preceded—by state provisions for substantial formal training. This gives an additional justification for the claim of professionalism, especially as certification requirements, which obviously influence teachers' college programs, may also be to some extent geared to the courses offered by the teachers' colleges. The establishment of teachers' colleges, furthermore, has created an institutional pressure center which some critics claim has a dominant effect on state and local curriculum decisions and on the selection of superintendents.[42]

Schools cannot be built, equipped, or staffed without money. The problems of *financing* are inherent in virtually all the issues just discussed. Indeed, they are so omnipresent and so grim that if we were required to give one general explanation of the behavior of professional educators, we might frame it in terms of a ceaseless search for funds. Here may well be the basic reason why educators react so emotionally to criticism: any adverse criticism may make it harder to raise money. When school board members are instructed to go out and "support the schools" in the community, it is not because the superintendents and teachers are thin-skinned or prefer praise to criticism. It is because schools, good or bad, cost money, which must be provided by vote of the people or of their elected representatives on the school board, in the city or county government, and in the state legislature.[43] At each level, the issue of school finance is a focal point of several obvious and broad conflicts of interest. The desire for low taxes clashes with the wish for good schools, in a struggle which is waged not only in the community by organized groups but within the mind of the thoughtful householder. A conflict between the owners of real property, on the one hand, and retailers and consumers on the other becomes increasingly important as proposals are made to shift the growing burden from the real property tax to the sales tax. The interests of those who live in wealthy districts with low taxes and good schools clash with the need to provide good schooling in less fortunate districts, through consolidation or equalization formulae. The local taxpayer wants relief which can be provided by state or federal aid, yet fears such aid because it might open the door to state or federal control: he who pays the piper calls the tune. The professionals are apparently less fearful of dictation from distant seats of power,[44] perhaps because what they really distrust is dictation from any lay source, including the local citizenry: the people should pay for the schools but the professional educators should run them.

Financial decisions traditionally have centered in the districts. Studies have consistently shown that citizens who are interested in the substance of education and have some knowledge of what the schools are doing tend to

---

42. See, *e.g.*, Lynd, *op. cit.*; Bestor, *op. cit.*; and Henry J. Fuller, "The Emperor's New Clothes, or Prius Dementat," *The Scientific Monthly*, January, 1951, pp. 32–41.

43. An excellent comprehensive study of school finances is Arvid J. Burke, *Financing Public Schools in the United States*, rev. ed. (New York, 1957).

44. For many years the National Education Association has led the fight for federal aid.

support the educators' demands for money more than do the less informed voters: hence the great emphasis, in the training of the superintendents, on public relations and "communications."[45] But the ways in which decisions are made are fixed by state laws, and often profoundly affect the decisions themselves. Thus in one state a school board may finally approve a budget which increases the property tax rate; in another the tax increase must be approved by the voters; in a third, the budget itself is the subject of a popular referendum. Bond issues may be voted by simple majorities in some states but require a two-thirds approval in others. The states, then, play a vital role in the local settlement of financial issues. They also are playing a more direct part, for state funds provide now an estimated 39.7 per cent of all money spent for public schools.[46] What new part, if any, the federal government will play remains a matter of conjecture. Today about 3.5 per cent of all school funds spent by school districts comes from federal sources.

## III

The fading away of the drive for federal aid to education in the last decade has been a most curious political phenomenon. In 1948 and 1949, with the powerful backing of Senator Taft, a massive federal aid bill passed the Senate by large majorities, 58 to 22 and 58 to 15. The movement foundered in the House Committee on Education and Labor, but even there a large majority of the members appeared to approve the principle. This majority, however, split on the question of whether, as the Senate bill provided, states receiving aid should be allowed to use it (within the limits of the First Amendment) to assist pupils in private and parochial schools in such matters as bus transportation, or whether the federal statute should strictly limit the use of the federal grants to public schools and public school pupils. A small minority of the committee were against federal aid in principle. They held the balance of power. By voting first with the anti-parochial school faction and then with the "state discretion" group, they kept the committee from reporting any bill.

The next years saw the problems of school finance become ever more pressing. Public opinion polls consistently showed overwhelming popular

---

45. See, *e.g.*, T. J. Jensen, *"The Importance of Public Opinion,"* in The Midwest Administration Center's *Administrator's Notebook,* Vol. 1, No. 7 (University of Chicago, February 1953); H. V. Webb, *Community Power Structure Related to School Administration* (Laramie, Wyo., Curriculum and Research Center, University of Wyoming, 1956); Chilton R. Bush and Paul J. Deutschmann, "The Inter-Relationships of Attitudes Toward Schools and Voting Behavior in a School Board Election," dittoed report to the Pacific Southwest Project of the Cooperative Program in Educational Administration (Stanford University, 1955); *cf.* John M. Foskett, "The Differential Discussion of School Affairs," *Phi Delta Kappan,* April, 1956, pp. 311–315.

46. *Estimate of School Statistics, 1958–1959* (Washington, D.C.: National Education Association, 1958), p. 15; in southern states the percentage runs much higher, up to 75 or more.

support for federal aid.[47] Yet in Congress, after Senator Hill's abortive attempt to tie federal aid to the tidelands oil bill in 1953, the drive for general financial support petered out; and the Eisenhower administration's modest proposals for federal grants for school building failed.

It may be reasonably predicted that general federal aid is still far off. If the parochial-school question was an insuperable obstacle ten years ago, the segregated-school issue seems like a much higher hurdle now and for some years to come. On the other side of the ledger, however, is the increasing insistence that public school education is a matter of national concern, profoundly affecting the long-run safety of the country.[48] Furthermore, in many ways existing federal statutes do inject the national government into the picture, with administrative authority scattered among literally dozens of agencies. The time is ripe for searching inquiry of several kinds. A "public administration" type of study is needed, to discover the extent of overlapping and conflicts of purpose in existing programs[49] and, perhaps, to produce a reorganization which might result in more effective leadership (without enforceable controls) toward national goals. And two kinds of comparative investigations are indicated: one to measure the extent of federal control over local policy in those existing programs which provide states and districts with federal funds, and one to analyze the pressures for uniformity which result from formal centralized control in other free democratic societies such as Great Britain. We may learn something about the possibilities, or lack of them, of retaining wide areas of local discretion even when local districts are dependent on federal funds. Must he who pays the piper always call the tune?

Today, in theory at least, the piper is paid and the tune is called by the citizens of each school district. School district government and politics would, therefore, seem to be the natural center for most research in the field of public control of public education. A considerable amount of such research has been undertaken and is now in process. Research projects range from case studies of elections and referenda, to power structure analyses, to attitude surveys—some try to combine all three.[50] Internal relationships be-

---

47. *Life's* poll in 1950 showed 65.4 per cent favorable to federal aid. The Gallup polls in 1956 and 1957 produced majorities of 67 per cent and 76 per cent respectively, for federal aid for school buildings; in 1957 Elmo Roper and Associates reported 73 per cent favoring federal aid, including 43 per cent who would extend it beyond aid for construction. See *Public Opinion Polls in American Education* (Washington, D.C.: National Education Association, May, 1958), pp. 17–20.

48. Rickover, *op. cit.*, and Fred M. Hechinger, *The Big Red Schoolhouse* (New York, 1959).

49. *Cf.* Hollis P. Allen, *The Federal Government and Education* (New York, 1950).

50. *E.g.*, Ostrom, *op. cit.*, Milius, *op. cit.*, and Bush and Deutschmann, *op cit.*; also Vincent Ostrom and Robert E. Agger, "The Comparative Study of Politics in Local Communities," an appendix to the *Fifth Annual Report, Northwest Regional Project* (Eugene, Ore.: University of Oregon, 1956); Harry M. Scoble, Jr., "Yankeetown," unpublished dissertation, Yale University, 1956; and current research into budget referenda in New Jersey by Alan Rosenthal.

tween superintendents and school boards have been analyzed.[51] Numerous reports have described controversies which rocked or wrecked particular school systems.[52] A substantial amount of the material, published and unpublished, seems to be inspired by a desire to educate school superintendents in the political facts of life, despite the customary avoidance of such forthright terminology. Some more popular accounts appear intended to stimulate citizens to defend the professionals in their direction of the schools. The constructive scholarly efforts to explain the voters' rejection of bond issues in districts where new school buildings are obviously needed may help the professional leaders get bond issues adopted.[53]

Much of this reasearch may be highly productive. The great difficulty about it, of course, lies in the safety of any generalizations that might be drawn from it. There are too many school districts, no two of them exactly alike. Some surprise was expressed at Conant's pronouncement that "there is no such thing as a typical American high school [and that] it is impossible to draw a blueprint of an ideal school,"[54] but nobody remembering his scientific background and eminence should have been surprised. The differences among thousands of communities and the schools which serve them impose limitations on the scope of valid recommendations just as they limit the possibilities of valid generalizations. It may well be true, as both experience and occasional research indicate, that by and large, the better-educated elements of a community tend most to agree with and uphold the professionals' conception of a good school, and that the more the superintendent and school board can stimulate public interest in the schools, the more likely will be popular support for bond issues and tangible improvements. Even this generalization, however, is strictly limited: the tendency of well-educated people to "back the schools" can be reversed by countervailing influences, especially the pressure of high taxes, and the public's involvement may produce results adverse to the superintendent's education program unless he or the board inspires and directs it. Popular interest is a two-edged sword, as the experiences of

---

51. *E.g.,* Gross, *op. cit.*; H. L. Condit, "Some Activities and Opinions of Missouri Boards of Education," unpublished dissertation, University of Missouri (1952); Richard E. Whalen, "Effectiveness of Elected and Appointed School Board Members," unpublished dissertation, University of Indiana (1953); Richard E. Barnhart, "The Critical Requirements for School Board Membership," unpublished dissertation, University of Indiana (1952).

52. *E.g.,* the brief accounts of controversies in Port Washington, N.Y., Pasadena, Calif., Denver, Colo., and Eugene, Ore., in the *Saturday Review of Literature,* Sept. 8, 1951; David Hulburd, *This Happened in Pasadena* (New York, 1951); Robert Shaplen, "Scarsdale's Battle of the Books," *Commentary,* December, 1950; Joseph F. Maloney, "*The Lonesome Train" in Levittown* (University, Ala.: published for the Inter-University Case Program by the University of Alabama Press, 1958); and the numerous "reports of investigations" published by the National Education Association's National Commission for the Defense of Democracy Through Education.

53. The U.S. Office of Education is currently supporting a sizable research project focussing on bond issue referenda, under the direction of Wilbur Schramm and William R. Odell of Stanford University.

54. Conant, *op. cit.,* p. 96.

Pasadena, Houston, and other places remind us. Much may depend on whether the hand that holds the sword is guided by the professionals or the laymen.

Analysis of the social composition and political behavior of local school districts must, then, take a long time and cover a great deal of territory before the findings can be presented with any sense of certainty that they are applicable or even useful as predictive devices beyond the boundary of the particular district where the research was undertaken. There are, however, some readily available bases for comparison among districts with structural or legal differences which may affect the outcome of voting on school issues. For instance, what is the effect on building expansion when a bond issue can be approved only by a two-thirds popular vote instead of a simple majority? Do the voters show more or less concern, and vote more or less favorably, in districts where the full school budget is submitted to them for approval than in districts where they pass only on the tax increase which reflects an increased budget? To what extent has the consolidation movement prospered in states whose statutes permit a merger of district by area-wide majorities or encourage it by special financial aid, as compared with states where separate majorities in each merging district are required and no financial inducements are offered? These kinds of statistical questions can be answered while the more deep-delving sociological and behavioral studies proceed.

These questions, furthermore, point directly toward one focal point for research where findings of general applicability could perhaps have fairly immediate practical effect. All of them relate to state statutes. Public education is a state function, and the school districts are creatures of the states. In recent years, the state share of financing the public schools has risen to the point where nearly two-fifths of all the money spent for the schools comes from state funds. As we have seen, the pressure for professional status and security has largely centered on the state legislatures. So, occasionally, has pressure from lay organizations interested in particular kinds of curricular requirements.[55] In many instances, judging by the statutory results, these lay pressures have been similar from state to state. The legislators, as well as the local districts, are also affected by the recommendations of the state departments of education; the latter, inevitably, tend to become additional focal points of professional and lay pressures. There are fifty states; but general propositions are likelier to be valid for fifty units than for fifty thousand. Few studies have been undertaken of the politics of education at the state

55. T. F. Armstrong, Jr., "The Public Educational Programs of Selected Lay Organizations in Pennsylvania," unpublished dissertation, Temple University (1947); C. A. Sommer, "The Attitudes of Organized Farm Groups Toward Education in Michigan," unpublished dissertation, University of Michigan (1953); George A. Male, "The Michigan Education Association as a Pressure Group," unpublished dissertation, University of Michigan (1950); William Gellerman, *The American Legion as Educator* (New York: Teachers College, Columbia University, 1938).

level. The significance of the subject is, however, illustrated by the findings of one research group, to the effect that on paper, at least, the amount of state control over local policies and administration in a dozen mid-western states does not appear to be related to the amount of financial aid furnished by the state.[56]

## IV

Although political power is centered in groups and individuals, its effectiveness and use are shaped by institutions. The institutional pattern of public education may seem firmly fixed, firmly enough, certainly, so that any proposal, to have a chance of success, must appear to conform to it. The pattern, of course, is one of local control through the democratic process. Yet, as we have seen, questions can and should be raised as to the actual extent and nature of local democratic control. If the image is inconsistent with the reality, we should know it, and change one or the other.

The basic public objective is to have American school children taught what they should be taught by able and dedicated teachers.[57] As to what they should be taught, the broad conflict seems to be chiefly between most of the professional educators and some articulate laymen. General public knowledge about school curricula is hardly less than general public interest in the subject—both are small. But the launching of the first sputnik did stir the people—including educators—more than had the books of Lynd and Bestor, Keats and Smith. A typical professional response was to start teaching algebra in the eighth grade—as an "answer to the Russians" and, more realistically, as a defensive move against possible public criticism.[58] The question remained as to what affirmative role, if any, the layman should play in curriculum development.

The pressures for changes in the curriculum seem to have come from three sources. First is the professional viewpoint itself, shaped largely in teacher-training institutions and often reflecting or adapting the ideas of individuals of almost prophetic stature, such as John Dewey. Second is the need for money causing modifications of the program designed to anticipate public demand—a minimum obeisance to the sovereign people. Third is the activity of organized lay groups. At the local level, the "citizens' committee" usually lacks any real power base and hence is stalemated by the disciplined ranks of the professionals if it tries to engage in curricular reform.[59] Other

---

56. J. G. Fowlkes and George E. Watson, *State Finance and Local Planning* (Chicago: Midwest Administration Center, University of Chicago, 1957).

57. See "Revised Teaching Aims Urged," *New York Times*, Feb. 8, 1959.

58. About half the nation's secondary schools were occupied with curricular revision in science and mathematics in the months following the launching. *Research Bulletin*, Vol. 36, No. 3 (Washington, D.C.: National Education Association, October, 1958), p. 67.

59. Citizens' committees had an exuberant growth in the 1950s. Studies of their operations in two states indicated that they served as sources of ideas and suggestions,

lay groups, however, such as industrial associations, unions, and patriotic organizations often seek to influence the content of the curriculum; if they have electoral strength in the community, they may be hard to resist. At the state level they may have an easier time, for the legislators are not professional educators. In the legislature, the educators' professional associations constitute pressure groups competing with the lay organizations, in the familiar fashion of American politics. Perhaps the very fact that the legislature constitutes a battleground which educators cannot dominate is a basic reason for the professional insistence on local control. By making local control a virtual article of faith to which all good Americans, including state legislators, should subscribe, the educators have gained an advantage at every capitol. They can always argue politely and persuasively that regardless of the possible merit of any legislative proposal to require the teaching of particular subjects, discretion must be left to each school district. Compulsory uniformity would be a departure from the American way.

As for the quality of the teachers, it may be true, as Bestor and others have implied, that the kind of training prescribed as a prerequisite to entry into the profession discourages able men and women from becoming school teachers. It is a reasonable hypothesis, too, that the vested interests of the teacher-training institutions impose overwhelming obstacles to any radical reform, for the laymen who would like to substitute subject-matter scholarship for courses in pedagogy have two or maybe three strikes against them before they begin. They lack political power, they lack the experts' status, and they can find no short and simple answer to the question: "As teaching is a profession, why shouldn't prospective teachers be taught how to teach?" If the reform of teacher-training must precede the recruitment of an adequate number of new and highly competent teachers, it must be sparked by the profession itself[60]—or so, at least, the political realities seem to suggest.

The profession by itself cannot, however, gain the other objective which must be reached if first-class teaching is to be the rule: it cannot raise the money needed to hire and retain excellent teachers. Good salaries, by themselves, do not produce good teachers, as Eurich has emphasized, but bad salaries certainly are a factor in driving able teachers into more remunerative

---

were frequently considered by superintendents as a good public relations device, almost always regarded the superintendent with favor, and were usually dominated by him in the selection of committee projects. Charles F. Lehmann, "A Study of the Interpersonal Role Perceptions of School Administrators, Board of Education Members, and Members of Lay Citizen Committees in Michigan Public Schools," unpublished dissertation, University of Michigan, 1956; and Herbert W. Schooling, "The Use of Lay Citizens Advisory Committee in Selected Missouri Public Schools," unpublished dissertation, University of Missouri, 1954, both summarized by Roderick F. McPhee in the Midwest Administration Center's *Administrator's Notebook*, Vol. 5, No. 7 (University of Chicago, May, 1957).

60. The possibility of such a development is suggested by the Gallup poll's finding in April, 1958, that of 1100 school principals, 72 per cent advocated changes in the training of teachers.

pursuits and in keeping potentially fine prospects out of the schools.[61] Here, and also in the matter of school buildings, the educators have taken the lead and have sought to stimulate organized lay support. Their professionalism does not greatly enhance their persuasiveness, for salary scales and class-rooms are not occult mysteries. In fighting for financial support, therefore, their influence must stem less from their specialized knowledge than from their dedicated concern or their political power.

As a working hypothesis concerning the political system of public edu-cation, the following summary might be useful in facilitating analysis and putting the emphasis on the significant spots: As to what should be taught, generally the professionals are dominant, and this may be altogether neces-sary and proper. Their financial dependence on public approval makes them somewhat responsive to reasonable public demands, tactfully presented, al-though their very professionalism forces them to resist proposals of which they disapprove and causes them to react adversely to most lay criticism. Pro-fessional influence is usually preponderant in local districts where the school superintendent is, or can be, the leader of the school system. It is much weaker in the state legislatures, but even there it is aided by the tradition of local diversity and the easy access afforded by the presence of professionals in official state positions—the heads of teachers colleges and state depart-ments of education. As to who should teach, the profession has generally sought state protection against pressures for local personal and partisan patronage. This protection, as a by-product, has solidified the position of the teachers college where most prospective teachers must be trained and which increasingly influences boards of education in the selection of superintend-ents.[62] As for the acquisition of sufficient funds to build and run adequate schools, the decision-making authority rests partly in the school boards, partly in the local electorates, and partly in the state legislatures. To these lay groups the profession comes as supplicant, its demands competing with other demands (for highways, hospitals, etc.) and meeting the inevitable resistance of the taxpayer. If there are to be good schools, the competition must be largely won and the resistance broken down. To achieve these ends at the local level, the professionals seek to stimulate public interest in education, at the risk of lay interference with the schools. Their achievement at the

---

61. In 1957–58 the average salary of a classroom teacher was $4520. In thirty-five states most teachers were paid less than $4500. "The imbalance between teacher-supply and demand continues. In the fall of 1957 the demand stood at an estimated 227,500. . . . To meet this demand the colleges produced the preceding year slightly less than 100,000, 30 per cent of whom would probably not take teaching jobs." *Research Bulletin*, Vol. 36, No. 1 (Washington, D.C.: National Education Association, February, 1958), pp. 5, 10.

62. A fairly sizable sampling in thirteen states indicated that in about two-thirds of the districts the superintendents had been recommended by colleges and universities. John E. Baker, "The Selection of Superintendents of Schools by Boards of Education," unpublished dissertation, University of Chicago, 1952, quoted in the Midwest Adminis-tration Center's *Administrator's Notebook*, Vol. IV, No. 6 (University of Chicago, Feb-ruary 1956). A retired professor of education told the present writer that he alone had recommended and placed at least a thousand superintendents.

state level depends more on the effctiveness of the professionals operating as pressure groups, with lay support which is less likely to involve lay dictation in curricular and personnel matters. At the federal level they have not yet been achieved. Unsuccessful drives for federal financial aid have been sparked by the largest professional pressure group and have been balked by a combination of three factors: the peripheral but highly charged issues of religion and race, the pocketbook interests of taxpayers in relatively wealthy states, and the traditional fear of central dictation. Perhaps only the passage of time can overcome the first of these obstacles, though acute public awareness of a national need for better schools might be enough. Such awareness is obviously needed to overcome the second. The third is not likely to be overcome without a more thorough, comprehensive analysis of its validity or unsoundness than has yet been forthcoming.[63]

The fact that the professionals, who have the greatest power stake in local control, are the people least afraid of federal aid[64] may be an indication of the needlessness of any fear of federal control. But it may also indicate something more basic. Is it conceivable that national financial aid and its concurrent possibility of national standards is acceptable to a national professional organization because that organization itself believes in or recognizes the existence of national standards? Perhaps we have been tending for a long time toward a greater degree of national educational uniformity than the old theory of local discretionary control implies. The professionalization of the school superintendency surely pushes us in that direction. The superintendent, like a city manager, moves from district to district. His methods may alter to conform to the local mores, but his basic educational philosophy remains the same. And, by all appearances, one modern superintendent's educational philosophy is likely to be much like another's, for more and more of them qualify for the position through studies at teachers colleges of largely similar outlook. The profession is certainly not intellectually monolithic, as the debates and disagreements in journals and conventions show; but it may well be growing more unified in its devotion to agreed-upon professional standards and goals.

If this is so, what is the future for the "diversity" which justifies unimpaired local control? If local control in the most fundamental matters—curriculum and teaching—is largely in professional hands, are there even now fewer significant differences between districts than was formerly the case? Granted that state requirements differ, that local interests may differentiate

---

63. A thoughtful argument for federal aid and leadership is presented by Dawson Hales, *Federal Control of Public Education* (New York: Teachers College, Columbia University, 1954).

64. A poll in 1948 in Indiana, for example, reported 70 per cent of the professional educators questioned as favoring general federal aid to all states, in contrast to 43 per cent of the "community leaders" and 39 per cent of the "rank and file" laity. Conversely, any federal aid was opposed, as a matter of principle, by 25 per cent and 32 per cent of the two lay groups, respectively, but by only 9 per cent of the educators. Paul C. Fawley, "The Measurement of Attitudes Toward the Basic Administrative Organization of Public Education in Indiana," unpublished dissertation, University of Indiana, 1949.

programs in rural districts from those in urban districts, and that the curricula and teaching in particular schools or districts take account of the varying backgrounds and objectives of the student population; still, the classifications are broad. In thousands of districts the educational needs are similar. Conant may disclaim any intention to provide a blueprint, but his recommendations are not intended as the basis for a single district's experimentation: they are aimed at innumerable American high schools. And, significantly, the professional reaction to the Conant report has included little, if any, objection to the basic curricular uniformity which it implies. Perhaps, then, at least within broad urban-rural or socio-economic categories, local diversity is or will soon be significant only with respect to those matters where professional domination is weakest: school buildings (including site selection), transportation of pupils, and finance. Decisions as to the last, assuming any real public desire for improved schooling, will continue gradually to move out of local hands and into the state legislatures. Certainly the extent and nature of inter-district diversity in basic educational processes need prompt analysis. If, indeed, they are minimal, then the lay proponents of complete local control must be prepared to defend their position in terms of their convenience and their pocketbooks rather than their concern for educational content.

This kind of inquiry seems best suited for specialists in education, checked by "lay" scholars from other disciplines who are free from any charge of bias. The latter might or might not include political scientists. Many of the other questions raised in this paper, dealing directly with governmental and political processes, more immediately challenge students of government and politics. They point to the need for research in the following areas:

(1) At the local level, (a) structural analysis, in terms of familiar public administration concepts, the forms of school district organization being relatively few in number and providing a manageable field of comparative study; (b) behavioral analysis, especially of the impact of professional and lay leadership and group pressures on the decision-making process—such analysis can provide helpful insights even though, as the writer believes, school districts are too numerous and too disparate for safe generalization in this field; and (c) the voters' responses in bond issue or consolidation referenda, under various but comparable conditions imposed by state law.

(2) At the state level, studies of (a) the organization and financial administration of the state's educational activities; and (b) the pressures on the legislatures and their response to those pressures. The view indicated in this paper is that state action, especially in the legislatures, is now significant and will soon have a crucial impact on educational development, and that useful findings can result from a comparative study of state influence, management or control.

(3) At the federal level, as suggested heretofore, the history of school legislation since World War II needs searching analysis, down to and including the National Defense Education Act of 1958, which may point a way

around the impediments to earlier federal aid bills but which raises anew the question of federal control.

Three other fields of study are also relevant to political science. One involves comparison with countries having unitary governments, central fiscal control, and many local school districts where curricular innovation may or may not be possible.[65] Another, which should not be limited to the segregation issue, concerns the impact of the judiciary on the school systems: the questions here involve both federal and state courts, the conditions, values, or pressures which affect their decisions, and the ways in which the schools and their government have been influenced by those decisions.[66] Finally, the speculative political scientist may find fruitful a field heretofore ploughed chiefly by professional educators: namely, the relationship of the school curriculum (and the interests and training of the teachers) to the values of American political society. Here the political philosophers, perhaps bemused by the mysteries of "education" or thwarted by the old taboos, have been silent. The leadership was taken by articulate professional educators who propounded social and political goals for the schools, and sometimes by lay pressure groups which stressed conformity to prevailing economic norms and the instillation of national and local patriotism.

In all such studies, the realization that public policy in education is the product of discernible professional-lay interaction (sometimes conflict) at different governmental levels, may serve as a unifying conception. The conception itself needs to be tested by acute political analysis. If it is valid, it can lead to the identification of the real sources of power and the main roadblocks to progress, however defined—and so to new concepts of organization and more productive leadership, professional or lay or both.


# THE PUBLIC LIBRARY IN THE POLITICAL PROCESS

## OLIVER GARCEAU


ALL [OF THE LIBRARY'S] ACTIVITIES—group relationships, service to clubs, business and industrial departments, school affiliation, and liaisons with

Reprinted from *The Public Library in the Political Process* (New York: Columbia University Press, 1949), pp. 130–141.

65. See Edmund J. King, *Other Schools and Ours* (New York, 1958).

66. Works related to this area include Clark Spurling, *Education and the Supreme Court* (Urbana, Ill.: The University of Illinois Press, 1955); and J. B. George, *The Influence of Court Decisions in Shaping School Policies in Mississippi* (Nashville, Tenn.: George Peabody College for Teachers, 1932).

government agencies—would seem to add up to a widespread community influence resulting in considerable political power. But actually normal library influence amounts to little more than a surface chop running against the ground swell of public apathy. The opposition the library must face is not an active, directed campaign against it, but the general public unwillingness to tax itself for a service of which it makes limited use. Such organized opposition as there is, finds expression in taxpayers' associations, usually dominated by the large property owners, such as real estate interests; in an indirect way they can hold the fate of the library in their hands. They are not hostile to the library as such, but to taxes, and more especially to taxes, and directly to expenditures, that are not backed by a vigorous, organized vocal group.

Libraries usually depend upon the property tax. They must attempt to gain by diplomacy what they have not the political power to gain by attack. Here library board affiliation with large property holders has sometimes softened the opposition. In one city library, where the state votes the property tax, the state legislature tends to vote any increase the city taxpayers' association is willing to impose on its members. The chairman of the library board, an influential businessman, had a prominent role in getting his friends to accept a tax rate increase this year. In some communities the Chamber of Commerce is approached as a taxpayers' association and placated as much as possible prior to tax hearings. In several cases we have found that the public library could successfully parry the thrusts of real estate lobbies by choosing a library trustee of high economic standing who was a large taxpayer of the community yet a warm supporter of library service. In one small town in a rural county the local manager of a very large absentee-owned corporation was able to play this role to perfection; for as observed by the librarian, it was not he, but the corporation, that paid the taxes, and he and his family enjoyed the books. But to match this case there are many in which the carefully chosen businessmen trustees have in practice thought in terms of taxes rather than in terms of public services rendered.

In one respect, and only one respect, public indifference is an advantage to the library: when people ignore what is on the bookshelves, they are not acutely concerned over book selection. Yet, historically there is inevitably tension and censorship of a kind established in every society that has put much faith in reading; witness the Puritans in this country. The business department of one library, hoping to be of service, approached the Small Business Men's Association with a description of its usefulness. After much prodding, the association sent an envoy to the library to reconnoitre. He came back to report that he had uncovered a Communist outpost, bristling with radical, New Deal books, a threat to the American way of life. It was a small blast, and the library came through it unscathed, but it left the business librarian rather shaken about the value of stirring up the attention of his potential clientele, and he was completely confused about where to turn next. It is odd examples such as this, found occasionally in the sample, that indicate a deep-grained distrust of reading accompanying the apparent approval of it. This must be taken into account, as well as the open censorship attempted by church and patriotic groups.

Most librarians do, in fact, exercise constant vigilance in book selection. The censorship of library holdings does not often become a public issue, largely because it is an intramural activity. As a member himself of the white collar middle class that uses his library, the librarian has a green thumb for cultivating those books that will be popular and an equal knack for weeding out what will be considered dangerous. Most libraries effect a compromise between the extremes of removing entirely from the library books subject to criticism and on the other hand boldly displaying books which they believe are unjustly challenged. They do this by removing the questionable book from the open shelves, sometimes from the card catalogue, but retaining it on a private shelf in the librarian's office, to be handed out to the hardy customer who inquires for it, provided he is beyond the tender years of adolescence. Many librarians in our sample are ruthless in their own censorship, often unconsciously so, because they feel certain that they act as the library public would have them act. Book selection becomes inevitably a question of political judgment; it is not just a technical problem. In this most librarians, in following their own predispositions, are better politicians than they may realize.

One of the first research methods attempted in this study of the matrix of political forces within which the public library must operate was directed precisely at the issues of censorship. It was thought that, at the very least, book selection and censorship policies would give valuable leads to the interest groups in the community who were actively concerned, negatively and positively, with public library service. It soon became apparent, however, that while librarians were in general extremely insistent upon the stereotypes of democratic freedom of expression and diversity of opinion, they were inclined to count with close attention the political costs of asserting these democratic rights in their own institutions. There were very few cases of public criticism of library holdings and still fewer in which organized groups had gone on record with regard to books. It also became apparent that the reason lay in the caution of the librarian rather than in the tolerance of the community.

It is further important to note that librarians have reconciled democratic ideals with political practice by a general practice of minimizing to themselves the extent to which the issue arises and also by stressing that they are interpreting, as they properly must, the mandate of policy established by the library board. At least three librarians interviewed had so far suppressed the issue in their own conscious thinking that they could, with every evidence of honesty, assert that there was absolutely no censorship of any kind in their libraries, only for us to find that in fact the staff were following careful guide lines in book selection and, more important, had large bookcases full of books under lock and key that had been subject to public criticism. At the other extreme were those so constantly aware of the pressure of organized groups that they lived under very great emotional strain. One librarian had transferred the idea of limiting the overfrank book on sex to the much less relevant field of social reform, and would circulate "radical" books only to those who appeared substantially uninterested in radical change or who could be counted on to oppose "dangerous thoughts." A very few librarians interviewed regarded the issue with serious dread not untinged with hysteria and in these cases there were circumstances that related their attitudes to particular situations on the board of trustees rather than to overt pressures from the community.

The research was unsuccessful, therefore, in its original objective of illuminating the group politics of library government by means of censorship issues. Politically significant uniformities did develop, however. The three great issues everywhere were sex, religion, and politico-economic change, the order of priority varying with the community, but moving up or down in intensity more or less together. Only the very largest libraries seriously attempted to resist all pressure and to select books on their merits alone. All libraries have inevitably political decisions to make in controlling the circulation of books subject to criticism. The psychological convenience of never facing squarely the conflict of abstract ideals and local reality has left under lock and key books whose sting has passed, of which the most commonly noted were *All Quiet on the Western Front* and *Grapes of Wrath*. The degree to which forgetfulness was encouraged to heal the irritations of past "mistakes" was strikingly revealed by the inability of librarians and staffs to recall what books were under lock and key, the inability to recall who in the community had ever objected to these books, and the genuine surprise with which librarians discovered what books had been sequestered. Undoubtedly many libraries need periodically to purge the purged and restore the shocking to the shelves of modern classics.

The politics of book selection is, therefore, a real enough part of library politics. But it is essentially a negative part, and confused by a good deal of rationalist idealism in conflict with practice. Yet there have been cases of courageous positive action. In the South our sample noted libraries prominently displaying a very full selection of social studies on race relations, books highly critical in their premises toward the prevailing social relations of Southern communities. There have been libraries that deliberately undertook through promotional devices to counteract prejudice and violent outbreaks of group conflict in their local communities. Evidence is not available to measure the political results in the long run of such library experiments with constructive education. It may be supposed that on the whole colleges and universities have strengthened their position, despite many temporary setbacks, through a firm policy of resisting the more narrow types of censorship. The libraries have on the whole stood out strongly for intellectual freedom as a principle, but in the group politics of their localities they have played safe with the safe groups.

## The Strategy of Group Relationships

Although the library has no natural enemies, it suffers concurrently from the fact that it has no natural political allies. In a political system where governmental action follows the main stream of pressure from producer groups, as it does in the United States, the library, serving a minority of individual consumers, floats along helplessly. In this it is not different from many institutions representing consumers. Consumer groups as a usual thing benefit only incidentally and individually as rival producer groups struggle for political power. They are not organized economically, impelled emotionally, or united politically in such a way as to form a group that can join battle with the producers. Consumers must play balance-of-power politics, making temporary alliances with whatever forces are most favorable to their interests. Because producer groups are the great political rivals in our political system, the new alliance developing between libraries and big business research carries much significance. Here the library may have found an ally that can bring it real support. The dangers of such an alliance to a public institution, traditionally neutral in politics and non-discriminating in its service, are too obvious to need description. Without some such alliances, however, the temperature of library politics and the nature of its support are likely to be low.

What the library does, the service it renders, does not build a persuasive political platform. This comes about, not from any failure on the part of the library, but because the character of its influence is imponderable; it cannot be made clear and incontrovertible. Its value to the community can only be measured by its effect upon the minds of individuals and the growth of their personalities. It is an article that can be sold on the political market only by the eloquence with which it can explain the inexplicable.

In order to get some tangible evidence to satisfy the public and their own consciences, librarians have developed certain standard statistical measures. They chart how many books are taken out; whether juvenile or adult; representing what category of reading. They tabulate the number of reference questions asked and answered and how many speeches to how many groups containing how many people. They compare the statistics month by month, year by year, and decade by decade. How much of this is needed to set administrative policy is not here to the point. As a device for showing the public what the library does, which is our present concern, these statistics are basically unreliable. Circulation figures cannot show how the library is influencing the minds of the public. Furthermore, the statistics are not always comparable; they can be increased by stocking cheap fiction and comic books; by lessening the borrowing period; by dissatisfied users who take out a lot of books, no one of which ever proves satisfactory; by the quick readers, the nervous types who must open and close a book a night; and by students who want to crib term papers from obscure sources. Reference figures are increased, often much against the librarian's wishes, by quiz programs, parlor games, and prize contests. These figures cannot take into account what happens to the reader for whom one book may have opened a new realm of experience, another for whom literary resources have opened up the possibility of an intellectual life. Yet in a profound sense this is what the library does; and it is out of an obscure belief in this serious contribution to an unmeasured number of people that the public gives support.

The evidence from library statistical studies has little political force. The old rationalist dream that all the people thirst for knowledge and, given the means, will educate themselves has been shattered by the facts now laid bare. In Berelson's *The Library's Public,* which analyzes existing studies of library use for the Public Library Inquiry, the character and size of the public library's actual clientele is made clear: few people read books; still fewer read much; and still fewer read for enlightenment. It has become evident that the major part of library service is given to a small portion of the population. The Likert survey, *The Public Library and the People,* also prepared for the Inquiry, indicates that of the 18 percent of the population who visited the library in the past year, "the 10 percent of the population who made the most visits account for 71 percent of all the visits that were made."[1] These figures are substantially corroborated by other surveys.[2] This is not a new discovery, but it has now been made so dramatic and convincing that the librarian can no longer defend his institution on the basis of active use of self-education facilities by the masses that are exposed to radio, newspapers, movies, and popular magazines. From a political point of view, however, it is significant that the public, although it may not use the library, believes it an important institution for others to use.[3] Three quarters of the population want it there, although many of them may never enter it. For what it is worth, this sort of left-handed approval is a library asset.

It is not, however, an asset upon which a library can build much of a constructive program. For that, our study indicates that the librarians are sound in their attempts to mobilize community support by library participation in group activities. By this method the temperature of library politics can be raised to the fusion point. One case history will have to suffice as an illustration of how this has been done. The Denver library serves a population of 322,412 persons. The librarian has shown great capacity for dynamic leadership, tying his library to a system that includes the library of the municipal university, a library school, a regional bibliographical center, and the Adult Education Council. He and his library provide the executive leadership in this system. He has become a man of importance in the city, serving,

---

1. Survey Research Center, "The Public Library and the People," Ann Arbor, Michigan, University of Michigan, 1949, p. 3, mimeographed.

2. See Bernard Berelson *The Library's Public,* New York, Columbia University Press, 1949, pp. 10, 99–101.

3. *Ibid.,* pp. 85, 87.

beyond his immediate interests, upon the executive committee of an opera association and as a director of the symphony society and a fine arts center. He is almost invariably called upon by the city to serve on committees connected with educational problems. His staff has followed his lead and affiliated with a much longer and more improbable list of clubs, committees, councils, centers, associations, commissions, leagues, campaigns, conferences, and fraternities.

These widespread personal affiliations are joined to a matured system of contacts with groups through library service, flexible and realistic in organization so that each staff member can perform the duties for which she is best fitted. To bring these contacts to a focus there is a co-ordinator of adult special services, who is also the person giving continuity to the work of the Adult Education Council, the offices of which are in the library. Her basic function is to co-ordinate all phases of library service and every department of library organization to serve the individual needs of community groups, which number more than two thousand in her card file. Under her is a field representative, who acts as the sales agent to groups, goes to their meetings, explains what the library can do, and reports back the needs to be filled by the various departments. Other members of the staff, quite regardless of their official title, have established contacts with groups in whose civic activity they have a personal interest and knowledge. This is the superstructure upon the usual framework of extension services. One of the more valuable features of it is the Adult Education Council, which is part of the library in fact and in the public mind. The key technique has been the freeing from intramural routines of about a half dozen staff members of unusual capacity for working in the field with people and groups.

When in 1947 the municipal institutions of Denver waged a campaign for building funds and it was finally agreed that each institution should use its own tactics, the library within five or six weeks mobilized a political following that voted in the bond issue for a new central building. This was done by having daily staff rallies to assign everyone to do leg work or make speeches. Mailing lists of key group leaders and library users were prepared. Publicity was written showing how the new building could better serve each large group and was sent separately to the Parent-Teachers Association, labor unions, clubs, and branch neighborhood organizations. Releases were given to the press, and one-minute radio spots were arranged through a regional radio council. The co-ordinator made forty speeches in five weeks, and the field representatives visited every AFL and CIO local in the city. The Adult Education Council suggested sixty volunteer speakers, who gave four hundred and fifty addresses. All of this carried the bond issue against a drift that defeated most of the other civic improvements.

When in the same year a proposed rewriting of the city charter threatened to modify the institutional relationships, particularly of the library board, the library spearheaded an attack against the charter by circularizing all library users, plus the huge mailing list prepared for the bond issue. In its circular the library was careful to give both sides of the case by including an official statement on the charter and the library by the president of the Charter Convention, who naturally favored what the library was opposing. A citizens' committee opposed to the charter was organized late in the campaign and undertook an intensive radio attack. The charter was defeated in almost every precinct. Although its defeat cannot be attributed solely to the merits of the library case, it is agreed that the library initiated the opposition which finally proved so effective. In both of these campaigns the basis of the library's political support was its group affiliations. It is clear that these can be so used as to mean real political power.

This one example does not prove the general political worth of group services. The figures and examples obtained by our survey are too fragmentary, and statistical norms for the measurement of library support are too unreliable, to attempt a correlation between wide community activities by the library and the strength of its public support. But it must be said in passing, and only for its suggestive worth, that the one library of the survey that is admittedly embarrassed by its riches from public taxation has as extensive a program of group services as the ingenuity of man can dream of. From these examples, and others less striking, but yet unequivocal, we may safely observe that services to groups are political weapons to be recognized by an institution so poorly armed as the library. It should be emphasized, however, that such a conclusion concerns the library as a political institution in a political situation. This is not to argue that group affiliations are necessarily the soundest approach to the educational objectives of the public library. Other considerations may limit the development of the use of such political ties.

## The Library Faith in Practical Politics

In political campaigns carried on by the library, the main armament is still supplied by the eighteenth-century rationalists. The traditional character of this pattern of values is not necessarily a handicap. The new realities, in all but a revolutionary or disintegrating society, are explained in the words, the ideas, the values, and the relationships of the past. The disparity between formal statement and current practice is not necessarily ruinous to an interest or to an idea. But the configuration of competing forces and the climate of opinion are in constant change. The particular interest, committed to a traditional body of thought, must exercise sustained political skill in reintegrating its own social myths in the total pattern of ideas. This is a never-ending imperative of political growth or even survival in our dynamic society.

# THE POLITICS AND ADMINISTRATION
# OF WELFARE

## A. THEODORE BROWN

It is conceived that the Department should be regarded as the human side side of the city's administration, dealing with the masses of people, both of the socially maladjusted and those in need of help, and we are trying to show the people of Kansas City that an efficient and honest government also has a heart.

—Director of Welfare, *Monthly Report to the City Manager*, August 2, 1940.

The Kansas City Welfare Department has discovered something: that if a decent, efficient municipal government is to stay in office, it must offer something more than decency and efficiency. It must practice the art of being as helpful, as warm, as personal as any ward heeler from Tammany Hall.

—*Survey Midmonthly*, February, 1948.

A PROFESSOR TOOK OVER the Kansas City Welfare Department in 1940 and brought it back into prominence as an agency of government. Dr. Hayes A. Richardson was thirty-eight years old when he took office. A native Virginian, he received his A.B. at Randolph-Macon College and his Ph.D. in economics at Johns Hopkins. He was professor of economics and director of the evening college at the University of Kansas City when he entered the reform administration.

Dr. Richardson is an idealist in politics. He believes ardently in the "nonpartisan" philosophy of municipal government and in the reform group that called him to office. A tireless publicist, he is in constant demand as a speaker on the council-manager form of government and its problems.

Richardson entered his new job with two leading ideas: that the activities and interests of the Department of Welfare ought to be extended and elaborated in the public interest; and that the Department ought to promote the free and full participation of Kansas City's citizens in the affairs of their city government. The Department, therefore, was to have a wide spectrum of activity. To the deprived, it was to be a friend; to those more fortunate, it was to symbolize the reform of city government.

In his first budget request, Richardson remarked:

At this time, I believe it would be most impolitic to set a standard in the Department of Welfare of monetary savings in any place other than where good business practices and good administration may effect reductions in cost. It

Adapted from *The Politics of Reform: Kansas City's Municipal Government, 1925–50* (Kansas City: Community Studies Inc., 1958), by permission of the publisher and author.

is necessary that it be shown to Kansas City that an efficient and honest administration can do more for the masses of people than the opposite type of government can do.

The aim of the casework section, for instance, he noted elsewhere, was "to bring it as close to the people as is possible." Public welfare must "attempt to supply every one with those things necessary to make him a normal and well-balanced individual." This ambition for his department characterized nearly everything Richardson did. Frequently, too, the stated goals of departmental policy were so broad that they seemed to permit well-nigh unlimited expansion of its operations. According to this outlook, it would be difficult to say, with confidence, at what point public welfare ends.

In many ways the reform Welfare Department's most interesting new contribution to Kansas City's municipal affairs was the Community Service Division. The direct cause of its creation was the increasing incidence of juvenile delinquency during World War II. It is extremely likely, however, that the Division, or something closely resembling it, would have been called into being even without this precipitating cause. No other aspect of the Welfare Department represents so well the philosophy and goals of its Director. To him, and to those who favor its activities, the Community Service Division appears as a device to secure citizen participation in municipal government. Others have thought of it as the reform government's precinct organization.

During World War II the city government received complaints from the Army about the frequency with which soldiers contracted venereal diseases from women and girls congregating around various dancing establishments. Since the regulation of commercial recreation is a responsibility of the Welfare Department, these complaints came to Richardson's attention. Many of the girls involved were not prostitutes, and the whole matter seemed to be a "youth problem." After a discussion with an army officer, Richardson suggested to City Manager Cookingham

> that you have a meeting with representatives of the Police Department, of the City Counselor's office, the Health Department, Major Mitchell, the Provost Marshal, and our department. Should you desire it, I shall be glad to call this meeting at your convenience. I do think that you should sit in on it. Please let me know where you would like to have it called—either in your office or elsewhere, on the eleventh floor.

At around the same time, the Office of Civilian Defense in Washington held a Community Planning Institute. Richardson was invited to attend. The invitation said,

> This Institute should serve two purposes: (1) Formulate basic principles in program making that can be useful not only to our field staff, but to defense councils in our more important urban areas, and (2) give a selected number of our best staff people an opportunity for study of practical community planning problems.

Meanwhile, the Kansas City *Star* had carried an article headlined "The Youth Problem," which called attention dramatically to the statistical rise in Kansas City's juvenile delinquency rate. The directors of the Kansas City Social Hygiene Society, who were also concerned with the question, met with Richardson, Chief of Police Anderson, and Superintendent of Schools Harold C. Hunt. Since the problem involved members of the armed forces, the Education Section of the local Office of Civilian Defense, of which Dr. Hunt was chairman, was given the job of outlining a program of action.

Dr. Hunt's section—with Anderson and Richardson present by invitation—decided to investigate the possibilities of a campaign of public education. Cooperation from City Hall and from the Council of Social Agencies was to be solicited. So far, the initiative of the Welfare Department was not prominent; but the circle of interested groups widened with each meeting. The war, with its obviously disturbing effects upon young people, furnished an opportunity to mobilize public opinion and to get groups within the city to cooperate in launching a new venture.

Richardson agreed to organize a fact-finding committee and to assist in planning the educational campaign. This committee was composed of several people in the field of social work and welfare; also present were Dr. Ernest Manheim, University of Kansas City sociologist, and members of Richardson's Welfare Department staff. At its second meeting, the committee heard a report from Dr. Manheim on his survey of delinquency in Kansas City in the year ending September, 1942. He showed correlations between delinquency and density of population, with home ownership (negatively), and for several variables. The most significant part of the report, however, bore upon a delinquency-control program as a *long-range* objective—by implication, not one limited to wartime—for the city government, one requiring a co-ordinating agency of some kind, which apparently was not yet in existence:

> A great many agencies, including the Parent Teacher Association, should cooperate and there should be some one to co-ordinate their activities. Unless someone does this, their people will arrange lectures and baseball games but in the long run they will not bring about any change.

In the course of his discussion, Manheim gave "delinquency" a definition broad enough to cover a good many things beyond the pale of wartime stresses on the young people: "Delinquency may be said to be behavior which antagonizes the immediate community."

The committee heard this theme repeated when Dr. Richardson reported on an investigating trip he had made in the East, with Councilman Frank Backstrom and Mrs. J. W. Stephenson, of the Welfare Department staff. The trip was made under Civil Defense auspices, and was made to study the child-care centers that war work had rendered necessary in several urban locales. Kansas City, according to Richardson, was no worse off, as far as a feasible and coherent program for dealing with this problem was concerned, than were other American cities. All were groping. No simple approach had proved adequate.

> The obligation reverts back to the community as a community problem. When we study delinquency we study only one phase of the whole problem also. We have need of some sort of clearing body to get us an over-all picture.

The committee agreed that a city-wide youth council be organized. It was to be a fact-finding body, and was to cooperate with public and private community agencies. It was to have a connection with civilian defense. Backstrom, in fact, suggested that it be organized *either* by civilian defense *or* by the Welfare Department. Responsibility for its initiation was placed on Dr. Richardson.

On the next day, Richardson wrote to Mayor Gage, requesting that he call together representatives from all existing organizations that were in any way concerned, in order to form a youth council. The problem, Richardson wrote, was not only one of people under seventeen—the legal "juvenile" age limit—but of young people in general. As the existing organizations did not work very well together, he said, a new one was called for. Mayor Gage answered,

> I believe that Civilian Defense should take a more prominent part in the organization than is indicated by your letter. Furthermore, I think the Council should be tied in very closely to the war activities in order that the whole program may have the benefit of the patriotic spirit to support the war enterprise.

The meeting was held in City Hall on June 2, 1943. Richardson was chairman and the proceedings were opened by Cookingham, with about sixty community leaders present: ministers, representatives from social groups, labor organizations, and business associations. Mrs. Elizabeth Lingenfelter, of the Psychiatric Center; Dr. Sylvia Allen, of the Child Guidance Clinic; James Young, of the Missouri State Board of Labor; and Les Warren, of the Division of Public Recreation; in all, a wide range of well-informed viewpoints was represented. Background information on delinquency was offered by Richardson. The major speech of the day was again given by Dr. Manheim. He cautioned the audience that the public should not be made panicky—no campaign should be launched until a definite policy objective had been defined. The problem, said Manheim, was one of community organization: the enterprise must be a cooperative one, with all existing interested agencies taking part. He suggested that the programs planned might center around each school district. This, it might be noted, is substantially what emerged as Community Service Division— with the addition of part- and full-time community workers employed by the Welfare Department to help organize the districts into community neighborhood councils and to assist the councils thereafter in programming their activities.

By July, Richardson was ready with a plan, which he had discussed with several agencies outside the city government and to which they had agreed. The City Council had informally requested him to draw up such a plan on June 21. As he now sketched it for the City Manager,

> the problem is not primarily that of juveniles, but rather a youth problem. It goes beyond the legal age of juveniles into the middle twenties and thirties. It is not a problem to be handled by just one organization, group, or institution in the city, but is a problem that will require complete community cooperation. This means the cooperation of churches, schools, police, the juvenile court, the various private character-building agencies, and of the public agencies in order to provide the necessary cooperation.

The plan called for a representative of the Department in each school district, charged with the "collecting of information about the young people in his district." This information would be presented to a council in the district, to be made up of people from various interested organizations. Plans for dealing with the problems uncovered, both local and city-wide, could be drawn up on the basis of the shared information.

Three weeks later Richardson submitted a tentative budget, requesting $19,000 for the remaining nine months of the fiscal year. It is fairly clear that, almost from the beginning, some people expected Community Service Division to extend its operations after the war years beyond the borders of specific youth problems. "Incidentally," Dr. Richardson noted for the City Manager,

> we have had unusually favorable comments on our plan. By directing all community resources towards our youth problem, I believe we will be able to do an outstanding job in meeting other problems. . . . In addition I believe that the City government may be recognized throughout the various communities of the city for its interest in all the human problems. At the same time we will be doing a much more effective job on what may become an overwhelming problem with a very small amount of money by mobilizing all community resources to help.

The new organization extended its scope from the relatively restricted field of juvenile delinquency to the broad area of general community planning. The process was gradual. Enough has been said to show that even at the outset different notions of its ultimate purposes were held by different people. When one attacks any major social problem, one is led logically to community planning. This, it would seem, was the way this new venture grew.

Most of the early activities of the Community Service Division centered around youth problems. A Central Coordinating Council was set up, including the Superintendent of Schools, the Chief of Police, the Director of Health, the Catholic Bishop, the Secretary of the Council of Churches, the Director of the Council of Social Agencies, a juvenile court judge, the president of the city council of the P.T.A., a representative of the Urban League, and the Welfare Director. Youth councils, made up of interested people in the neighborhoods, operated in school districts. One of these said its purpose was

> to promote community understanding; strengthen collective responsibility and self-government . . . ; encourage the use of those conventional standards which regulate social habits; and plan for the future improvement of the area as regards its youth.

Setting up the Central Coordinating Council generated considerable friction. Some agencies showed "a reluctance to let the Welfare Department plan and operate a program which so vitally affected all of them. They spoke of the departure from ordinary procedure, which would be to call these executives together in the beginning to plan the program, rather than to ask them at the end to approve it."

An organization meeting for one of the youth councils indicated, too, that "there seemed no spontaneous action to form a council or to organize in any fashion." This is noted to indicate that although social workers favored this kind of community organization, there was no widespread demand among the public-at-large for a program such as the Welfare Department was planning. The Department took the initiative and guided the program through despite opposition and apathy.

In addition to the youth councils, community councils were organized in the school districts (with smaller subgroups, called neighborhood councils) whose objectives were not confined solely to the solution of young people's difficulties. In each community council, there was a full- or part-time employee of the Welfare Department called the "community worker." These were generally women with college training and a background of work with groups of one kind or another. Some had taught school or classes in adult education projects. All had participated vigorously in clubs and social life generally: P.T.A., International Sunshine Guild, Camp Fire Girls, Red Cross, churches, musical groups, sororities, and the like. "I have appeared," one wrote in an autobiographical statement for the Community Service Division, "at numerous churches on programs, teas, funerals, weddings, etc., which enabled [me to make] many contacts, and [gave me] an opportunity of being well-known throughout the city." "It seems," said another, "that I have always been interested in community enterprises." "To help people help themselves," said still another, "is a job with no end—and this is just the way I want to look at this job of mine—one which will go on forever!"

The wide scope of the Division was manifest fairly soon after it was established. Richardson wrote in December, 1944, that its purpose was "to activate the citizen and his neighborhood," particularly with respect to the problems of young people:

> The ultimate purpose of these coordinating councils is to strengthen collective responsibility and self-government in Kansas City. This can best succeed within the framework of the neighborhood, where people face a variety of

problems together, and where community understanding and joint responsibility can be accomplished more perfectly than on a city-wide scale. Democracy must begin in the neighborhood where young people grow up and where the school and the churches are located. This imperative explains the program and purpose of the coordinating councils in Kansas City.

Clearly, the concentration on wartime needs had vanished from the picture. A year and a half later (June, 1946), in an article by Richardson in the *National Municipal Review* entitled, "The Children Get a Chance," the focus on youth and children had almost vanished too:

> In meeting the needs of a large city we too seldom recognize the fact that cities are divided into many communities, that no one group of people understands all phases of community life even if they are interested in the problems of the whole city; that where a nonpolitical, nonpartisan government exists there is too little opportunity for people to express their desires and plans and hopes so that they will be recognized. Until the organization of community councils there was no machinery through which those who were interested in over-all living in a community could voice their plans.

From neighborhood problems—such as better street-lighting, area cleanups, building playgrounds—the activities of the councils further ramified to consideration of the wider policies of the city government itself.

Gaining public support for increased taxation, or dealing with public sentiment for lower taxes, is one of the most delicate tasks of an elected government. The councils were particularly useful in this in 1952–1953.

Members of the City Council—with the Chairman of its Finance Committee playing a prominent role—addressed gatherings sponsored by the local councils. There was a real financial problem facing the city: physical expansion brought need for more services; inflation cut the value of its existing sources of revenue; and the disastrous Missouri River flood of 1951 entailed a great deal of extraordinary expense. The city administration set itself to get the voters to make financially painful decisions, or at least to share responsibility in making them. As an official put it to the Association's Budget and Finance Committee, "Do the people want to cut down services? Which ones? Help us in this way. Do you see a way of new sources of revenue?"

The Budget and Finance Committee recommended that the local councils lay aside every possible item of business in order to discuss the tax situation, preferably with a competent speaker on hand.

Four hundred sixty-one people attended fourteen local meetings. All the local councils indicated that more of this type of meeting was desired. A number of cuts in services were suggested at the meetings; on the other hand, some citizens wanted new and better services. Higher taxes were discussed, as well as new ones. None of the suggested service cuts received a majority in the discussions, but it is not clear that an actual vote was taken in each case. Twelve of the fourteen meetings favored an earnings tax, but objections to this source of revenue were also made.

The Budget and Finance Committee concluded, with more definiteness than the character of the meetings seems to have warranted, that the public did not want any municipal services curtailed and that it favored an increase in taxes—or, as the Committee report put it, "an increase in present sources of revenue that are of a general nature and impose the burden . . . on the greatest number of taxpayers."

A vast number of specific questions were discussed at local meetings of this kind. Not all of these questions—not even most of them—involved matters of wide-ranging city policy. Neighborhood law enforcement, aid for flood refugees, and special assessments for neighborhood improvements, for example, made up a great part of the Community Service program.

An example of how such a local question was dealt with may be found in the efforts of the "Roseland" (a fictitious name) neighborhood to get satisfactory water service. "Roseland" is a Negro community, somewhat isolated from the surrounding area because it is on a hill. Its citizens are far from wealthy, and its streets to this day are not as well paved as those elsewhere.

In 1943 and 1944, after race riots had broken out in Detroit and elsewhere, Kansas City, in common with many other cities, became especially concerned about race relations. Richardson sent City Manager Cookingham some of his reflections on the subject:

> Our Community Service Division has been used often to meet racial tensions. . . . After all, most racial problems must be settled with little publicity without directly recognizing the existence of the problem, but attempting to bring about an understanding, which, in turn, will bring support to the various groups against heated actions.

> The need of having a group of outstanding citizens that can be called in quickly in an emergency is most important. It is possibly next most important to keep down feeling through recognizing irritants before the irritants are recognized by those who might attempt to take action.

The case of Roseland illustrates how the Division was used to improve race relations. Roseland had great difficulty with its water supply and sewage disposal systems. It installed an improved sewage disposal system, to be paid for by special assessment, but the water supply remained inadequate, and this of course reduced the efficiency of the sewage disposal system. The terrain was rough and rocky, making installation of mains and sewers very expensive. Most of the land, moreover, was owned by an out-of-town resident who bought water from the city and supplied it to the residents through a system of her own.

The neighborhood council went to the city government for assistance. The result was not encouraging. Water Chief Hatcher explained that to extend the mains would be very expensive. The owner of the private water system, some Roseland people thought, was behind this discouraging view of the situation. Feeling began to mount. A community worker reported to the Division:

Rev. ———— attempted to increase the group into demanding action from the city. He said "Mr. Hatcher could tell us anything that sounded nice, but he had no intention of doing anything toward installing water mains. We were just wasting time." He intimated very clearly that the city had no intention of doing anything as long as [the landowner] wished to continue collecting money for her private line. . . . In all he sorta belittled the efforts and suggestions of the president and worker.

It was the unusual handling of a tense situation by Rev. Robinson that finally brought forth a vote to let the president follow through as he had started. There is no question, however, but what Rev. ————'s persuasive words had weight and may still cause confusion and lack of confidence on the part of the people in the president's leadership.

When one woman refused to pay the water bill, Mrs. [landowner] questioned her as to who told her not to pay. The answer was "the city." Then Mrs. ———— stated, "I'd sure like to know who is waking you people up out there."

Many residents of Roseland thought that the special assessment they paid for the sewage improvement was to include city water service as well. A small part of the area had been connected to a city main after a flood disaster, and no charge had been levied for this extension of the main. This created heightened expectations in the rest of the area for similar service.

Without specifically requesting free installation of mains for the Roseland people, Richardson forcefully described the existing situation for the City Manager:

The residents of the [Roseland] area, as you know, are a very worthy group of Negro citizens. For many years they have visualized owning their own homes. A large number of these homes are owned by a woman who is a non-resident . . . and have been sold to [Roseland] citizens in a manner that often they find that, instead of owning the property, it may be found either in Land Trust or in someone else's name.

They have been looking forward to having running water in their homes and have been planning considerable improvements. They are threatening, as an emergency, to cut the water line provided by Mrs. ————. This, of course, would be unfortunate and Mrs. McAllister . . . is attempting to stop it. I have talked with Mr. Hatcher . . . and he states that their present plan requires that the number of houses justify the expenditure, which does not exist in the [Roseland] area.

There is no area in Kansas City available for development of new Negro residences. It has been contemplated that this would be a good area but without water future development cannot take place. . . . Incidentally, this area has a very fine group of people who have generally been in favor of a city government that was interested in the citizens; at one time one of the few areas of its sort in the city. I am not mentioning this because special favor should be given it. . . . I know they would appreciate now, some suggestion from you as to how they can proceed.

The community, represented by their council's president, the Rev. Robinson, now went directly to Cookingham, pointing out that the average cost of the sewer extension had been $240 per family and that a significant number of the residents were on relief. Cookingham assigned his assistant, Ray Wilson, to tour the area with Hatcher, of the Water Department, and to discuss with the residents how much they could afford to pay. The city ultimately agreed to install the water mains.

The neighborhood council in this case served as an effective mechanism for transmitting an urgent request from a limited public of citizens to the whole city government. It also served to keep discontent within manageable bounds while the lengthy and difficult operations required to solve this particular problem were carried through to a successful conclusion.

It is not at all easy to say precisely where "machine organization" leaves off and "citizen participation" begins. The idea behind Community Service is plastic enough, or ambiguous enough, to include a good deal of both.

The political value of the neighborhood and community councils is well understood at City Hall. Manager Cookingham has always been interested in them. When the new division was less than a year old, he called Richardson's attention to the interest of Roy Roberts, the influential publisher of the Kansas City *Star*. Requesting a copy of local council schedules for the *Star*, Cookingham told his Welfare Director, "I think it would be a good idea to get some publicity on these meetings, because in my opinion, they are worthy of all the publicity they can get."

In his reports, Dr. Richardson has frequently mentioned the favorable opinion that the councils were able to mobilize toward the administration. In a newly annexed area, where there was considerable ill-feeling toward the city, a local council, he wrote, has the means of convincing "the majority of skeptics that they are receiving benefits heretofore not enjoyed." In another case, a protesting council averted the creation of a city dump in its area. "This," he said, "advanced the city administration's stock a good many points and the gain in good will is immeasurable."

Viewed in another light, Community Service provides a channel for distributing information from the administration to the voter. It supplies interested citizens with copies of proposed ordinances and other material on city government and policy. It is also a listening post for the city administration:

> Extensive visiting was done of the families displaced by the Southwest Trafficway. Very few families have moved or found places to move. There does not seem to be any ill will against the city administration, just a feeling of desperation as to where they can move.

Viewed in still another light, Community Service is a way of encouraging the people of the city to help themselves through neighborhood action. "I would emphasize that what we are trying to do is to get the community to do things for *itself*," Richardson wrote to all community workers early in Community Service's history. "The city will act only in a residual capacity." On another occasion he wrote that "the members of the council should be encouraged to work out their own problems. The less they are 'talked at' the better off they will be."

Whatever its complexities, this much is clear: the city administration, through its Welfare Department, has gone in search of good will. Director Richardson has emphasized the public-relations aspect of his department's work; many of his most important efforts have been predicated upon a diligent quest for clients. In this way, the traditional understanding of the term "welfare" in government administration, as something closely associated with relief, has undergone a remarkable expansion. It has come to mean, in Kansas City, an attempt to involve as many people as possible with the problems of city administration.

# THE CASE OF THE BLIGHTED CITY

## EDWARD C. BANFIELD

I WAS JUST PUTTING MY COAT ON when the managing editor called me into his office and handed me a cigar.

"Sit down," he said. "I have a special assignment for you. You're going to help the *Sentinel* and its readers decide a very important question. This town's been getting shabbier and shabbier and some people want us to launch a big campaign to fix it up. Tear down the slums. Bring in grass and trees. Put up modern apartments. 'Fight blight!' is the slogan. The trouble is, we don't know enough about it. There's lots of talk about 'urban renewal' and so on. Those are just words to me. We haven't got the facts. We want to know what we're doing before we commit ourselves. That's where you come in. I want you to get us the facts and tell us what they mean. Take what time you need and go wherever you want. Bring back a story that'll help us make up our minds."

That was all. The rest was up to me.

I took an overnight train to the state capital. That was the logical place to start. They had done more about their slums than any other city in the state. Besides, that happens to be the home of a very dignified and determined lady—Mrs. Belknap is her name—who has been a leading crusader in housing matters for the last twenty years, ever since she gave up being a social worker. She was very anxious to help, and she had the whole story right at her fingertips.

"I'm glad the *Sentinel* is finally taking this matter seriously. I've been

Reprinted from a pamphlet of the same title, by permission of the American Foundation for Continuing Education, 19 South La Salle Street, Chicago, Illinois. This case study was perpared as part of a series entitled Case-Stories in American Politics.

trying for years to get them to take a progressive stand in housing and planning matters," she told me. "Everybody knows that slums are one of the main causes of crime, divorce, disease—tuberculosis, especially—and poverty. I pointed that out to your editors years ago. I told them that if they'd just put a map of the city showing the distribution of crime over a map showing the distribution of slums and blighted areas, they'd see a very striking connection. Most of the juvenile delinquents would turn out to be in the areas of bad housing. So would TB cases. So would insanity.

"Just from an economic standpoint it would pay you to get rid of your slums, regardless of the cost. Why, the savings from a reduction in crime alone would be fantastic, simply fantastic. Think what it costs to maintain all the prisons and jails! But that's just the money costs. The costs of slums in human values are far greater. Imagine what it must be like to have to spend one's life in those horrible, depressing flats where so many thousands of people are condemned to live. It makes one physically ill just to see those places, they're so ugly. I don't see how you people can stand the sight of them. That's what I told your editors, but it didn't do any good. They wrote a very bad editorial."

I didn't remember any editorial referring to her and I asked her what it said.

"It was one of these very patronizing, know-it-all things," she replied. "The *Sentinel* had no doubt that there was more crime and disease in the slums than anywhere else. But how were they to tell whether this was cause or effect? Maybe criminals go to live in the slums even if they're reared somewhere else. And maybe tuberculosis is most common in the slums not because housing is crowded and unsanitary but because the poorest people live there. If I had any evidence of a scientific kind showing that bad housing caused anything at all they'd be glad to see it. It was that kind of thing. Very unconstructive."

"Were you able to send the editors any scientific studies of these things?"

"No. It's almost impossible to prove what effects are caused by housing as such and what effects are caused by the surrounding conditions in which bad housing always exists. That's the irritating thing about the argument they made. Everybody knows that these connections exist, even though they can't be proved scientifically. Talk to people who have some practical knowledge of these things—social workers or criminal lawyers, for example. You'll find their opinion is practically unanimous."

I told Mrs. Belknap that what I wanted right now was a quick rundown on the main features of the public programs for urban renewal. What, for example, did the words "urban renewal" mean exactly? And how does a city get urban renewal under way? What does it cost? Who pays for it? That sort of thing.

The place for me to start, she told me, is with the United States Housing Act of 1949. In that act Congress declared that,

. . . the general welfare and security of the Nation and the health and living standards of its people require housing production and related community development sufficient to remedy the serious housing shortage, the elimination of substandard and other inadequate housing through the clearance of slums and blighted areas, and the realization as soon as feasible of the goal of a decent home and suitable living environment for every American family, thus contributing to the development and redevelopment of communities and to the advancement of the growth, wealth, and security of the Nation.

The 1949 Act recognized, Mrs. Belknap told me, that there are very serious obstacles in the way of slum clearance by private enterprise. The worst of these obstacles is the prohibitively high cost of slum properties. They are very much overvalued because of speculation, the misuse of property, and high population densities. The result is that to buy them in order to tear them down and rebuild according to proper standards would cost so much that the new housing would have to sell for perhaps twice as much as other housing of the same quality. In other words, the price of the slum land is way out of line with the value of the same land in a proper use.

Congress dealt with this difficulty by providing for the "write-down" at public expense from the too-high market value to the "use value." For example, it might be impossible to buy a particular slum property for less than say $9 a square foot. Then it would cost some more—say $1 a foot—to tear down the old buildings and to plan a pleasant and convenient new neighborhood. If cleared land cost $10 a foot before any construction took place, the new buildings would be so expensive that practically no one could afford to live in them, and so they would never be built. In a case like this, the Housing Act enables the public to pay enough of the $10 for the builder so he can build new housing at a price ordinary people can afford. For instance, the public may sell the $10-a-square-foot cleared land to a builder for only $1.50 a square foot. At that price he has an incentive to build houses for ordinary people. The difference—$8.50 a square foot—is the subsidy the public pays.

A second serious obstacle in the way of private slum clearance is the difficulty of assembling land. In order to make a real and lasting improvement it is necessary to clear and redevelop a fairly big tract. This is often impossible for a private enterprise because there are always some owners who don't want to sell their properties or who refuse to sell them at reasonable prices. The Housing Act requires that every state that wants to cooperate under the terms of the Act set up an agency—in this state we call ours the Clearance Corporation—which will use public powers to acquire land, by condemnation if necessary, for resale to the private developer.

This is what is called "urban redevelopment." As Mrs. Belknap explained it to me, here is the way it works:

A local government designates a particular site for a redevelopment project and approves a plan for its development, financing, and so forth.

At the same time the local government undertakes a "positive program" for the modernization and enforcement of zoning laws, building codes, and other regulations to improve housing and prevent the spread of slums.

The local plan is carefully scrutinized by the regional office of the Federal Housing and Home Finance Agency. HHFA has to make sure that it meets certain standards provided by Federal regulation. For example, the project must make suitable provision for housing people who will be displaced by the slum clearance and it may not discriminate against minorities.

When the plan is approved, the Clearance Corporation gets an advance appropriation from the Federal government to acquire and clear the land. It then offers the land for sale to private redevelopers who agree to work within the plan established by the Clearance Corporation and approved by HHFA. Very often the land is sold by competitive bid.

The difference between the amount paid by the redevelopers and the cost of acquiring the land and planning the project is the "project cost." Two-thirds of this cost is paid by the Federal government and one-third is paid by the local governments—usually the state, county, or city.

In the Housing Act of 1949 Congress authorized the expenditure of a billion dollars for slum clearance over a five-year period. The war in Korea interfered with this somewhat, and in 1953 an advisory committee appointed by President Eisenhower found that if slum clearance was not speeded up it would take two hundred years to finish the job. The committee came to the conclusion that redevelopment projects were not enough; the slums were growing faster than they could be redeveloped. What was needed, the committee decided, was a way of preventing the growth of new slums: to stop the "blight" of old neighborhoods and make them "healthy" again.

In the end they recommended three approaches which, taken together, constitute the "renewal process": one, by the strict enforcement of housing and building codes to prevent the spread of blight; two, by improving local services and facilities—schools and parks, for example—to rehabilitate areas worth saving; and three, by clearance and redevelopment to get rid of areas not worth saving. These recommendations were incorporated into the Housing Act of 1954, which established the Urban Renewal Administration.

"As for appropriations and expenditures," she said, "it's hard to give a clear picture because the money actually being spent and the money only intended to be spent if plans go through are sort of mixed in together in the figures. Hundreds of communities have even more hundreds of renewal plans in different stages of completion. If all the money set aside were actually spent, it would amount to two billion dollars or so. Then, too, there is always talk in Congress of providing a few billion more. Some proposals go as high as six billion dollars to be spent by the Federal government alone, not counting what the local governments would add."

These figures impressed me. I said to Mrs. Belknap that it seemed to me that the country is now pretty well along the way toward solving the slum problem.

"Not at all," she said. "We have hardly begun. Most of these projects are in the planning stage, and I'm afraid that a good many of them will never get beyond the planning stage, for one reason or another. So far, about 20 per cent of the projects begun have been abandoned, mostly because the communities that start them can't seem to find a way to finance them even with the Federal help. And about a quarter of the total Federal capital grants will go to only four big cities—New York, Chicago, Washington, and Philadelphia. So you see, the picture isn't quite as rosy as it may seem at first glance."

Mrs. Belknap told me that I could see a good example of a rehabilitation project right there on the west side of town.

"You can see a redevelopment project, too," she told me. "But it looks more like the ruins of a bombed city than anything else right now. We've got the old buildings torn down, but for various reasons we haven't got the new buildings up in their place. So there's really nothing to look at. The rehabilitation project, on the other hand, is something wonderful you simply must see."

I thanked Mrs. Belknap for her help and went over to the Clearance Corporation office. One of their men was willing to take me on a guided tour of the rehabilitation project Mrs. Belknap had told me about and I gladly accepted. We got in his car and drove to the other side of the business section. He stopped in front of a little white frame house. "Here we are," he said.

I peered around in all directions. It was just another street as far as I could see. The houses were quite ordinary, all more or less like one another. At the end of the street some kids were playing in a vacant lot. Some of the houses had a little garden space in front and most of them had television aerials. A woman was sweeping off the front steps of her house.

"They look all right to me," I said. "What's the matter with them?"

The Clearance Corporation man reached around into the back of the car and brought out a set of photographs mounted on cardboard. He handed them to me.

"The same street *before* rehabilitation," he said.

I was astonished. The pictures showed a street of shacks. But when I looked closely I could see that they were the same houses. The difference was that they had been painted, porches had been repaired and screened, fences had been built. One place had been torn down altogether; that was what made the vacant lot.

"There's plenty of difference inside too," the Clearance man told me. "Most of those houses didn't have inside toilets, believe it or not. Now they've all got 'em. Most of them didn't have hot running water. Now they've all got it. Most of them didn't have adequate windows. Now they've got 'em. None of them had any screens. Now they've all got 'em."

"How was it done?" I asked.

"It was simple," he said. "So simple I don't know why it didn't happen years ago. The Chamber of Commerce was embarrassed about these places.

They made the city look bad. So about three years ago some of the leading men in the Chamber went to the Mayor to point out the sad state of housing in these neighborhoods and to tell him that we were getting a reputation for being backward. The Mayor appointed a committee of two dozen leading citizens representing every facet of community life. The committee got some assistance from the University, and it came back to the Mayor and City Council with a draft of a comprehensive ordinance setting up all kinds of minimum standards for housing. The ordinance provided that every room must have adequate windows, that every dwelling be adequately weather-proofed and heated, that sleeping rooms have a minimum number of square feet, and so on.

"The City Council passed the ordinance and set up a special agency to enforce it. Of course, there was lots of screaming at first. These houses here, for example, are mostly owned by one or two landlords. When they heard they were going to have to practically rebuild these places they made an awful fuss. But the Mayor and his Committee finally made them see the light, and I know for a fact that now that they've improved their properties they're very glad of it. It's turned out to be a paying proposition for them."

"Were they subsidized by the Federal government?"

"No, this project has very little subsidy in it from any source. There were a few places—like the one that was at the end of the street where that vacant lot is now—that were too dilapidated to be repaired. Those were condemned and torn down. Here and there a little land has been bought for redevelopment, and that'll involve some write-down when it's sold to a private re-developer. But in the main this has all been private enterprise."

"You say that the landlords are finding that it pays to fix these places up. What were the rents before and what are they now?"

It turned out that the average rent went up about $40 a month.

"How do the tenants like it?"

"They think it's fine," the Clearance man said. "You can go right down the street here and ask at every door. You won't find a single one who isn't happy about what's happened here. They're very proud of their neighborhood."

"Like it better than before?"

"Oh well, they didn't live here before. These are different people living here now."

"What happened to the people who used to live here?"

"They moved. They couldn't afford the higher rents. They're all gone."

"Where?"

"I don't know. Your guess is as good as mine. We didn't keep any records of that."

The Clearance man dropped me off at the Planning Commission. Mrs. Belknap had phoned to make an appointment for me with the city planner, a man named Kipner, and as soon as I'd taken my coat off and shaken his hand I asked him what had happened to the people who had formerly lived in the rehabilitation area.

He gave me a wry smile.

"They've gone off to make some slums somewhere else, I'm afraid. Some of them have moved into other slums where, for political reasons, the minimum housing code hasn't been enforced. Those slums were already terribly overcrowded, but now they're much worse. But they have to live somewhere, so you end up by moving the slum from one place to another. Of course, that's all some people were interested in doing anyhow—"

"What do you mean by that?" I asked.

"It's simple. Slum dwellers are mostly Negroes these days. If you want to get the Negroes out, a rehabilitation project is one way to do it. I don't mean that all the people who favored that project had that in mind, but some of them did."

"You mean the people who lived there before were colored? The ones I saw there today were all white."

"Sure," Kipner said. "They were low-income Negroes. As far as I've been able to find out, many of them actually had to leave town because they couldn't find housing they could afford. I suppose some of them headed in your direction. Maybe that's why the *Sentinel* is getting worried. And other Negroes who would like to come into town from the South don't come because there's less and less room for them. By making less housing Negroes can afford they hope to have fewer Negroes. For people who have been looking for a way to reduce the Negro population, enforcing the housing code seems to be the answer. Nobody can accuse them of bias. They're not against Negroes; they're against slums and greedy slum landlords. Understand?"

"Slum clearance may be a good thing even if some people support it for the wrong reasons," I said.

"I agree," Kipner said, "but it's no answer to the fundamental problem."

"What fundamental problem?" I asked.

"It isn't popular to say this," Kipner went on, "and I don't want to be quoted on it. But the fact is the real problem is not buildings, it's people. There are some people whose living standards are so low that they'd change any place into a slum. They're almost like animals, some of them. They'd just as soon live in filth as not. Some of them have never known anything else and wouldn't like anything else. Some of them are not very intelligent, maybe not much more than morons, but not so bad that they have to be put in institutions. Others have normal intelligence, but never had any opportunities to learn anything. You can't blame them. It isn't their fault. But there it is just the same. Improving old houses or building new ones isn't going to solve their problem. Oh, it might in a generation or two, I suppose. But that's a long time to wait and it's terribly expensive meanwhile. Why, they can turn a new building into a slum almost as fast as you can build it. If you really want to rehabilitate a neighborhood, you've got to get those types out of there, or change them. That's the problem."

"What's the answer?" I asked.

"I don't know," he said. "I've thought about it a lot, but I'll have to admit I don't know. As a planner, I'm used to looking at every situation as a whole. The city is an organism like the human body. A symptom that shows itself in one place may be caused in quite a different place. We have to try to understand the system as a whole, and often we find that in order to change one part of the system we have to change the whole of it. As, for example, you might have to change the whole way of living of a human being in order to cure a particular illness in one part of him.

"If you look at it this way, housing programs are not very good ways of getting at the problems the slums represent. It might be better to invest the same amount of money in some kind of program to train people to live properly in the city. Train them to keep their garbage cans covered, for example, and to screen their windows. Train them to be a bit more enterprising and to take some pride in things, if that's possible. It's wonderful what people with the right attitude can do with a few gallons of paint, a few boards, a hammer and some nails. I don't know. I'm just speculating. But this is one of those cases where a poultice on the place that hurts won't cure anything. What's needed is, so to speak, a fundamental change in diet.

"On the other hand, urban renewal is a wonderful tool for planning. The best yet, I'd say. Having the funds and authority to change the residential use of some parts of the city gives us a leverage we can use to bring some order out of the chaos—to put into effect a pattern of land use that makes sense. So, while the housing programs don't accomplish what they're supposed to accomplish, they do accomplish—or at least they can accomplish —something else. And since I'm a planner, I happen to be more interested in that something else."

"Tell me about the 'something else,'" I said.

Kipner stared out the window at the city below.

"It isn't easy to explain these things," he began. "I think of the city as a complicated machine. It ought to be a well-designed machine. Every part ought to be designed and put together so that the machine will do its work with as little effort and as little waste as possible. And the machine ought to be beautiful, the way anything truly functional is beautiful."

"And you don't find the city efficient?"

"Of course not. It's ridiculously inefficient. Take the journey to work, for example. Thousands of people drive from the east side of the city to the west side and back again every working day. At the same time other thousands are driving from the west to the east and back again. Sweating and swearing and paying taxes to build all those new highways. Why not have those who work on the west side live there too? And the same with those who work on the east side? Why not have them live there? Or, at least, why not support a modern and efficient mass transit system? It's absurd for all those cars to be choking the highways every day, especially as most of them carry no one but the driver. Take the parks. They are mostly on the outskirts of town, as far as possible from the people who need them most—I mean the people in the high-density areas downtown. Take schools. We're still building schools where kids have to cross busy highways to get to them."

"I don't see how that sort of thing can always be helped," I said. "Suppose a man *likes* living on one side of the town and *likes* his job, which happens to be on the other side—"

"Most people don't like it," Kipner said. "Take my word for it, planners have figured out quite a few ways to solve such problems and to give people what they *really* want. I'll have to admit that the solutions are mostly on paper. We don't get much chance to put them into practice, and the reason can be summed up in just one word: politics. Somebody always has something to gain by putting things like schools and parks in the wrong places and somebody always has something to lose by putting them in the right places. And these somebodies always have the ear of the Mayor and the City Council. When it comes to supporting a rational plan, nobody is interested except Mrs. Belknap and a few old reliables like her. It's very discouraging."

"And how does urban renewal improve the situation?"

"Well, it gives us something to work with. When we design a new neighborhood we can see to it that the parks are in the right places and that there are no highways cutting the school off from the homes. We may even be able to locate the project so as to improve the circulation in the city—cut down the journey to work and eliminate cross-hauling. Looked at solely from the standpoint of housing, a project may not make a great deal of sense. But, personally, I am convinced that even then its value from a general planning standpoint may more than justify it. And if it weren't for politics we could do a lot more with urban renewal."

"You're against politics?"

"No, of course I'm not. I believe in democracy, and you can't have democracy without politics. But I think where planning is concerned, politics has to be kept within bounds. If planning projects are taken out of politics, decisions can be made rationally, not on partisan grounds or to satisfy special interests. Planning is technical; it isn't the sort of thing that should be decided by majority vote."

Kipner got to his feet.

"I'm sorry," he said. "I'm due on the other side of town in just exactly fifteen minutes. I'll have to go."

I went to my hotel, typed up my notes, read the local papers, had a good dinner, hung around the bar for a while talking about politics, then went to bed. I'd arranged for an early appointment with the Mayor next morning and I wanted to be in good shape for that.

The Mayor turned out to be a little roly-poly fellow, very jolly and red-faced, and a real pro. He made a big show of telling his secretary that this was an important conference and he wasn't to be disturbed. Then he gave

me a cigar and lit one himself. I told him that I wanted him to talk off the
record and that if later I wanted to use any quotes I'd ask his permission.
What I wanted most, I said, was background.

"O.K.," the Mayor said. "Here's the picture. This town's been getting
seedier and seedier for years, just like most other towns. The people who pay
taxes have been moving out to the suburbs by the thousands. It's been easier
for them to get FHA loans for houses out there and the state and Federal
government have been building 'em fancy expressways to drive back and
forth on. I don't blame 'em. I wouldn't mind having a little more room myself. But let's not kid ourselves. With them gone, who's going to pay the
taxes? We have to keep on providing the same old city services, you know—
police, fire, schools and all the rest.

"Well, that's a different problem. What I was getting at is that the
people who are moving into the city to take the places of those who leave
are pretty backward types for the most part. Pretty backward. This is off
the record now. Most of them are Negroes who've never lived in a city
before and don't know how. If they got garbage, they dump it out the
window into the street. They forget there aren't any pigs down there like
there was at home. Naturally, there are rats, but those people don't care—
most of them don't, that is. Once in a while you find one who looks at these
things just like you and me but he doesn't generally stay in the slums long.
Somehow he gets out. If it gets cold enough and they don't have anything to
burn, they're likely to tear off a door and break it up.

"Don't get me wrong now. There are white people that's just as bad.
Lots of them. When I was a kid I used to live in one of those neighborhoods.
It was Irish then and people in the other parts of town used to say we lived
like pigs. I guess some of us did. Anyway, I remember there used to be signs
up, 'No Irish Need Apply.' Then the Irish moved out and the Italians
moved in. I wouldn't be surprised if some Irishmen said some uncomplimen-
tary things about the Italians. Now it's the Negroes. Who'll it be next?

"Well, to get back to the point. Naturally the housing in those places
has been getting worse and worse all this time. There's at least a square
mile of it that ought to be torn down and rebuilt from scratch. If we could
rebuild that, we might be able to bring back some of those people who've
left to go to the suburbs. I don't see why we can't offer all the advantages
of suburban living right in the center of the city—and more, too. It's just
a matter of planning it right. Getting those people back would help a lot. It
would keep the big department stores from pulling out. That would give
investors confidence. Property values would stop dropping, and one thing
would lead to another. I believe it would touch off a real revival for the
town.

"Well, my idea was to have one of the biggest redevelopment projects
in the country. Tear down that whole slum and rebuild it."

The Mayor inspected the end of his cigar very carefully. I waited for
him to go on, but he said nothing.

"But that's not what you ended up by doing," I said finally. "I've been told that the redevelopment project is east of the slums in what used to be mainly a warehouse district. And I've seen the rehabilitation project. That's part of what used to be the slum, but not all of it, as I understand."

"I was waiting for that," the Mayor said. "Only I didn't expect you to be so polite. I expected you to say, 'Why did you waste good money repairing houses that should be torn down anyway, especially as repairing them wouldn't bring back the taxpayers from the suburbs? And why did you tear down perfectly good warehouses in the name of slum clearance?'"

"I admit that's what I was thinking," I said. "I just didn't want to get thrown out of your office."

"Well, we might as well talk frankly," the Mayor said. "The reason I didn't do it the way it ought to be done was that I just couldn't. The people wouldn't stand for it. I would have been out on my ear if I had tried to tear down that slum. I would have been right square in the middle of the worst row you ever saw.

"In the first place, there were the people who lived in the slums. I soon found out that a lot of them didn't want to move . . . not even if we provided them public housing at low rents. Some of them didn't want to move because they had some kind of a racket that couldn't exist outside of the slum—prostitutes, gamblers, dope peddlers, and so on—and of course their customers, too. And, believe it or not, some people just like living in a slum. Or, put it this way: they'd rather live in a slum than in a public housing project."

"You were afraid that if you tore down the slums and gave the slum dwellers better housing they would get even with you by voting you out of office? Is that what you mean?"

"No. It wasn't them I was afraid of. They'd vote for me in those precincts anyway. Those are organization precincts. As long as I've got jobs to pass out, I don't have to worry about them. No, what stopped me was a few people who own a lot of slum properties and are getting rich on them. Some of the most respectable people in town, both white and Negro. Some churches too. I could see they were going to fight hard for those big profits.

"And there were the white neighborhoods on the edge of town; they were another thing. Those are the only places where there's any vacant land. The rest of the town's all built up. So that's where the public housing would have to go—the housing for the people from the slums that would be torn down. Relocation housing, it's called. Well, those neighborhoods don't want public housing because it would bring Negroes into sections where there aren't any Negroes. Those people out there on the edge of town aren't exactly social register characters themselves, but they think they've got high-class neighborhoods—and by their standards they have. Some of them spent all their lives scrimping and saving enough to move out of the neighborhoods their people came to from the Old Country. Now they hate to see their new neighborhoods go downhill. Having public housing projects nearby—whether there's Negroes in them or not—is bad for property values. And their homes are all those people have. They're the ones who could have beat me at the polls. The organization isn't very strong out there."

"Maybe you should have made your fight and taken your licking," I said.

The Mayor stuck out his jaw. "Personally, I don't look at it that way," he said. "I don't have any respect for a politician with such high principles that he can't get re-elected. In this game you got to do what it takes to win. Either that or let somebody else play in your place. If you've got such a sensitive conscience that you can never make any compromises, you're too good for politics. You owe it to your party to step aside for someone else. After all, the party wants to win, not just make your conscience feel good.

"I admit, though, I did fool a little with the idea of fighting the thing. But I had the feeling that I might start something I couldn't stop. This race business has me scared. I didn't want to get the white people on the edge of town stirred up against the Negroes. They're troublesome enough as it is now. But there might have been real riots if I had pushed too hard. I just didn't know whether it would be a good thing to do or not.

"Finally the decision was made for me. The Federal government ran out of money for public housing. Congress cut it down for some reason. Without relocation housing it was out of the question to tear those slums down. We had to do something though. Mrs. Belknap and all that crowd were after us and the Chamber of Commerce felt that it looked bad for the city not to have any kind of a housing program."

The Mayor leaned back and brushed the cigar ashes off his trousers.

"Then it would be fair to say that you favored the rehabilitation project because it had the advantage of not requiring the relocation of Negroes? And the big advantage of the warehouse site was that practically nobody lived there, so it wouldn't require any relocation either? Right?"

"That's the truth," the Mayor said, "but don't put it that way. Or if you do, don't connect me with it. And anyway, you've got to admit that there's something to be said for what we've done. The rehabilitation project really has improved a lot of houses. Let's not forget that."

"What do the Negro leaders think of all this?"

"That's a funny one. It really is. There are two important Negro organizations here. I had the presidents of both of them in for a talk while I was mulling over the slum clearance idea. One of them was sitting there where you are; the other was over there. I put it to them. You know what happened?"

"What?"

"They agreed on just one thing—they didn't like my slum clearance idea. On everything else they disagreed. When you come right down to it, there's no such thing as Negro opinion, any more than there's white opinion."

"What was their objection to slum clearance?"

"They kept trying to tell me my plan was anti-Negro. Negroes, they said—and of course this is right—have been having a hard time getting their hands on some housing. Now I was trying to take it away from them. In a way that's true, you know. It's a fact that whites would have moved back into that section once it was redeveloped. We would have *some* Negroes there. In fact, I told these two guys I would personally guarantee to find houses for them. But it's true I wouldn't have had many Negroes there. I couldn't. If you get more than a certain number in a project like that, the whites will start moving out and pretty soon it will tip over and be all Negro. But even if the project was to be *all* Negro they would have been right. There just wouldn't be as many people living there after redevelopment as before. After all, that's the point of having a project like that—to reduce congestion and overcrowding. I told them I am the best friend the Negro ever had in this town, which is true, but I could see I wasn't getting anywhere."

"What did they have to suggest, anything?" I asked.

"That's the funny thing. One of them wanted a lot more public housing. Housing is the Negro's chief problem, he kept saying, and the only way to solve it is to build it, not tear it down. Build a lot of housing that Negroes can afford to rent. That means public housing.

"The other fellow said he was absolutely opposed to public housing and would fight it every inch of the way. Public housing, he said, is bound to be segregated whether anybody intends it to be or not. There aren't enough whites in the low-income group to go very far and most of them won't live in a project with Negroes if they can help it. Not only that, but the better class of Negroes doesn't want to live among the worst class—that's the way he put it himself—of Negroes or whites. So, he said, the projects are likely to be places that nobody will be proud of—and all the worse for being sponsored by the city. Frankly, I think he's right. And if you take into account the interest of the white property owner, that settles it as far as I'm concerned."

"This second fellow," I said. "He was against slum clearance and he was against public housing. What was he *for?*"

The Mayor wrinkled up his face and rolled his eyes from side to side.

"He's not a very practical fellow," he said. "I've never been able to figure him out or make any kind of a deal with him. A fanatic, you might say."

"Well, what did he say?"

"He said, 'Just treat the Negro as you would anybody else and there won't be any housing problem for Negroes. Give the Negro the same job opportunities that whites have—same pay, chance to work up from the bottom, and so on. Give him the same opportunity to buy or rent that whites have. Let him buy or rent on the same terms as whites in any part of town. Just treat him as if he were white. That's all. If you do that, he'll have just as good housing as the whites and maybe better.' Simple, isn't it?"

"It sure is."

"Yeah, one other thing I remember now. He said any housing program for Negroes is an insult to them."

"Well, in a way that seems right," I said. "It does imply that the Negro can't be treated, or oughtn't to be treated, like a white."

"That's what I was telling you. This man is very idealistic and very impractical. It takes all kinds to make a world, doesn't it?"

"To change the subject," I said. "How about the redevelopment project you started over there in the warehouse district? What's happening on that? The land is all cleared. Now what?"

The Mayor made another face.

"That was easy," he said, "and I got a lot of credit for it in the press and with the civic organizations. The big department stores were glad to have those warehouses down because they were afraid Negroes might move into that district and because they want to see the area developed for white customers. The department stores are the big advertisers, so the newspapers were for it. It took us about two years of full-time work to fill in all the forms for the Federal government. What a mess of red tape! But we finally got it approved, and now we've got everything cleared. There's just one thing holding us up now. We can't seem to find anybody who's interested in investing his money in the project. Without a private redeveloper, we're stuck. It'll take quite a few millions There's nobody in town with that kind of money. I sent a committee of businessmen to talk to the biggest real-estate developers, but they didn't get any satisfaction."

"What do you think the trouble is?"

"I haven't really been able to find out. Some people think they're scared because the project has to be bi-racial—that's required by the Federal regulations, you know. They don't give a damn about race one way or another themselves, of course. After all, they're businessmen and besides they don't live here. But they think if it's bi-racial it may not make money. At least that's what some people think is their reason. I do know this: the trouble is not with the project itself or with us. Cities all over the country are having trouble getting money for redevelopment. You just about have to give the land and improvements to the private investor to get him interested, and even then you don't always succeed. Maybe the reason is that the investors can get a bigger return on their money somewhere else.

"Anyway, it's a lousy situation from my standpoint. I had all the bugles blowing while I tore those warehouses down. Now I have to figure out how to put something up in their place."

The interview was over. The Mayor stood up and held out his hand.

"Let me give you one piece of advice," he said as we shook hands.

He grinned. "Never run for office."

I had lunch at a restaurant where newspapermen hang out. One of them told me I ought not to leave town without seeing an economist named Allen at the University. Allen had testified against the warehouse redevelopment project at a public hearing, and although his testimony wasn't considered newsworthy by any of the city desks the reporters thought he would give me a slant I wouldn't get elsewhere. "He's a real sour apple," one of them said. "You'll come away thinking there aren't anywhere near slums enough in this country."

After lunch I went around to the University and found Professor Allen in a cubbyhole office which he shared with a great number of books. He looked like a sour apple.

"Sit down," he said after I had introduced myself. "Have they told you how they justify paying $12 a square foot for the warehouse district, then turning around and giving it away, or almost giving it away, if they can find anyone to take it? Has that been explained? If it has, I wish you'd explain it to me."

I said I had been told that the land was over-priced and that it had been necessary for a public agency to subsidize a "write-down" to get the land to its "use value."

The Professor snorted.

" 'Over-priced' !" he said. " 'Use value' ! I hope they told you what those fancy words mean."

"Why, yes, as a matter of fact they did," I said. "They said that land is over-priced if no one can afford to buy it and use it for decent housing. 'Proper use value' is the price at which it would be used for adequate housing. Is there anything the matter with that?"

"There's everything the matter with it," Professor Allen said. "Suppose I said to you that the big red apples in the corner grocery store are over-priced because I can't afford to make cider with them. Suppose I said a public agency ought to buy them from the grocery and re-sell them to me for practically nothing to bring them down to their use value. What would you say to that?"

"I don't think the two cases are comparable," I said. "Cider is a less important use of apples than is eating them out of hand or making pies with them. But housing is a more important use than warehouses."

The Professor leaned back and put his glasses on to look at me more closely.

"All that statement means is that you prefer other uses of apples to cider. Suppose the demand for cider was so active and the price so high that apples for eating became outrageously expensive. Would you conclude from that that cider apples represent a 'proper' or an 'improper' use?"

I was getting a bit confused but I decided to stick it out to see what the Professor was driving at.

"I would say," I told him, "that if there is competition between cider drinkers and apple eaters for a particular supply of apples, and if the drinkers are willing to pay more for the apples than the eaters, it means that the people with the more intense demand will be made happier by turning the apples into cider."

"Good," the Professor said. "And that being the case, would you favor a subsidy to bring the price of apples down to what the eaters choose to call their 'use' value, meaning, of course, their 'eating' value?"

"No," I said, "I wouldn't. On a matter like that, market demand should rule."

"Right again," the Professor said. "That's exactly the point."

"But," I went on, "houses aren't apples."

"What's the difference? If people will pay $12 a square foot to use the property for warehouses and only $2 after the land is cleared, isn't there a presumption that the land and buildings ought to be kept for warehousing? The fact that a warehouse district looks dilapidated doesn't mean that it isn't useful or valuable. It just doesn't happen to be the kind of business that needs to put up a front for the public. But the fact that warehousemen are willing to pay $12 a foot for the land is significant. It means that it's a good location for them, that a less good location would mean a higher cost of doing business and higher prices to the users of warehouses, which is pretty nearly everybody, directly or indirectly."

"But what if by putting a housing project in there the city could raise the value of downtown real estate, the big department stores and all that? Wouldn't that justify tearing down the warehouses?"

"It would on two conditions," Professor Allen said. "One is that property values elsewhere would have to increase enough to offset the amount of the subsidy. For example, if it could be shown that a project involving a subsidy of say $1 million increased surrounding property value by $3 million, we could say that the net 'profit' to the society was $2 million. So far as I know, no one has taken the trouble to measure carefully the increases in property values that are said to occur when such projects are built. I may be prejudiced, but my guess is that they seldom amount to more than a tenth of the subsidy. But as I say, that's just a guess. Somebody ought to study the matter carefully before we go much further."

"What's the other condition?" I asked.

"The other is that the subsidy for the project should be taken out of taxes levied against the increase in the surrounding property values. Why should you and I, to say nothing of all the other people from Maine to California, pay taxes for the sake of increasing the value of those department store properties? I don't know about you, but I can think of things I'd rather do with my money."

We looked at each other. I couldn't see what was wrong with the Professor's argument, but I felt in my bones that the problem wasn't quite as simple as all that.

"You'd be willing to let the downtown district deteriorate," I said.

"Why, of course, I would," he replied. "If it doesn't pay the downtown property owners to make the investments that are necessary to prevent it from deteriorating, then let it go. I wouldn't substitute my judgment and my money for their judgment and their money."

"But won't it eventually be terribly costly for the whole public if we let the central cities deteriorate prematurely? All those great stores and office buildings will have to be rebuilt somewhere else. It seems terribly wasteful to let a great city go to pot when you could prevent it by a small investment of public money."

"It wouldn't be a small investment," the Professor said. "It would be a very large one. At least a billion a year. Besides, there's very little chance, in my opinion, that such projects will have any very profound effect on the future of the city. But apart from that, there's really no reason to talk about 'premature' deterioration. In our economy all kinds of things become obsolete very fast. Sometimes a manufacturer discards an entire plant and all the equipment in it only five or ten years after building it. He does so because it will pay him to use a new process. We call that progress, and it is progress. We don't shed tears about the old plant. Instead we congratulate ourselves that we have something still newer and better. Why shouldn't we take the same attitude towards our cities? How much are we willing to pay for the sake of slowing down progress?"

"You're getting away from the housing question, Professor," I said. "How about a situation where the spread of a slum forces down property values in a residential neighborhood. Doesn't that represent a real loss?"

"The fact is," he said, "property values often go up, not down, as the slum moves closer. There's a very good reason why. The land is going to be used much more intensively than before. That makes it more valuable. The argument that we need these housing programs at public expense to keep property *up* is as phoney as it can be. We're holding property values *down* with such projects, in most cases."

I thought that one over. It seemed crazy to me. If the spread of slums *increases* property values, then from an economic standpoint we ought to encourage their spread. We ought to have a Slum Creation Administration instead of an Urban Renewal Administration. I put this absurd conclusion to the Professor just to see what he would say.

"Quite right," he said. "Quite right."

For the first time the sour apple smiled. At least I thought he smiled.

"Let's get back to the human side of this problem," I said. "Think of all the people condemned by poverty to live in the slums. Isn't giving them a decent environment just as much a public responsibility as is building bridges and fighting wars?"

"Certainly not," the Professor replied. "In the first place, most slum dwellers aren't 'condemned' by poverty to live in the slums. By race prejudice, maybe, but not by poverty. Most slum dwellers have incomes large enough to rent or buy decent housing. They happen to prefer to spend their money for other things. They buy fancy cars, or TV sets, or they go to the races. I don't object to their making these choices. Why shouldn't they? But I don't like being taxed to give them housing after they have chosen to spend their money for something else."

"How about the Negroes who can't get good housing because of prejudice? Don't you think public housing ought to be provided for them?"

"No. I think the only fair thing is to give minorities full access to the housing market. That can be done by law. In fact, it is being done in New York."

"Surely you admit that *some* people absolutely can't afford decent housing. How about them?"

"I wouldn't give them public housing. I'd give them cash grants instead. Then they could spend their money as they thought best, just as you and I do."

"But they might not spend it for housing. They might buy cars and TV sets and go on living in the slums. The slums might be as big as ever after millions had been paid out in grants."

"Very likely. But I say if that's what people want, that's what they should have. Why should the rest of us tell a poor man that he should have a coat of paint on his house instead of a TV set? If you think his level of living is too low, give him some money. But don't tell him how to spend it. Respect his preferences."

I wondered what Mrs. Belknap would say to that. The way to cure the slum dweller's preference for cars and TV sets would be to give him the experience, just once, of living in decent housing. Most slum dwellers, she would probably say, don't know what decent housing is. A radical change in their housing would make a radical change in their preferences. Kipner would say they have to be educated first, but that once they have been educated, they'll know how to make the most of good housing. Well-designed structures without, well-behaved people within, in a well-planned city. It occurred to me that Professor Allen was the only one of them who wasn't trying to change people and things into something they weren't.

Housing is different from other things, Mrs. Belknap would argue. You can't leave it to market demand. You have to have decent housing to make a decent society, but you don't have to have new cars or big-screen TV sets to make a decent society. Publicly subsidizing housing, she would probably say, is the most practical way of seeing to it that people spend what they should for housing.

I wanted to try these arguments out on Professor Allen, but I could see that he wanted to get back to his books. I thanked him and left.

On the train going home I tried to collect my thoughts. I was supposed to help the *Sentinel* and its readers make a decision. "Get the facts. . . . Bring back a story that'll help us make up our minds," the managing editor had said.

The trouble was I couldn't make up my own mind on the basis of the facts I had. There were too many angles.

My interviews with Kipner, the city planner, and with Professor Allen had raised the question whether urban renewal programs could be justified even theoretically. Maybe Kipner was right in saying that the real trouble is not buildings, but people, and that you have to find some way of changing the whole way of living and outlook of the people who live in slums. But wouldn't changing their housing change them? And maybe the Professor was right in arguing that it was uneconomic to use land for housing when people were willing to pay more for it in other uses. But should "the market" control everything?

Then it occurred to me that if you threw out all these theoretical objections to renewal, there would still be practical objections of very great weight. Even if you made the big assumption that the principle was good, you could say the practice was so bad that the whole idea should be dropped. The Mayor had said that he had found it politically impossible to carry out the kind of renewal program the theory implied. Was it really impossible? Well, the facts were that his city was clearing warehouses, not slums, and it had forced people to repair slum buildings that were hardly worth repairing just because that way they had no responsibility to find any other place for the Negroes. Was it an accident that things worked out this way? Could it have turned out any other way? It seemed clear from what Mrs. Belknap had told me that the situation was not very different in most other cities.

At that point the train stopped and switched and I looked out the window at some of the slum shanties on the outskirts of town not far from the *Sentinel* office. I was close enough to see into some of the houses through the open doors. There were two double beds in one room. The window was out, there was no screen, and I could imagine ten million flies. A woman stood in the window holding a skinny baby and staring at the train. We have a blighted city all right, I reflected. But is urban renewal the way to fix it? Is it fair to the taxpayer? And considering the political realities, will it work? I wondered about these questions for a while. Then some others came into my mind. Was it fair to let children grow up in such shanties as the one before me? What kind of neighbors and citizens would such children make? For that matter, would *not having* urban renewal work?

These were questions I would have to answer when I sat down at my typewriter in the *Sentinel* office the next morning.

> If *you* were in this reporter's place, what
> recommendations would you make?

# GLOSSARY

ANNEXATION (*see* METROPOLITAN ORGANIZATION)

AUSTRALIAN BALLOT (*see* BALLOT)

BALLOT

A ballot is a list of candidates for office, on which the voter makes his choices, either by marking a piece of paper or by pulling the levers of a voting machine. In the early years of the United States, officials were generally elected by a voice vote, a show of hands, or by the deposit of small objects such as beads in urns. This system was gradually replaced by the use of printed ballots, which were prepared and distributed to voters by individual candidates or political parties. Secrecy was virtually impossible, for party ballots were readily distinguishable by their color, size, or symbols. Intimidation, bribery, and fraud were relatively easy. These abuses occurred particularly in cities, where the vote of large immigrant groups could easily be manipulated by party leaders.

The Australian ballot was designed to end these abuses. Originated in Australia in 1858 and introduced in the United States in 1888, the Australian ballot was printed at government expense, distributed at polling places by officials of the government, and marked in secret by voters. Candidates of both parties were listed on it. All states use it today, although Georgia makes its use optional with the counties.

The Australian ballot reduced fraud but did not eliminate it. Though preparation and distribution of the ballots was placed under public control, the "public" officials who administer elections have usually been the choices of political parties, for which electoral jobs constitute a form of petty patronage. Party organizations that obtain control of election machinery can find ways of manipulating the vote, even a secret vote. Spoilage of ballots is one possible technique. Deliberately inaccurate reporting of returns is another.

The length of the ballot has been an issue in municipal politics. Voters are often asked to decide on a long list of candidates and propositions, especially under the weak mayor form. Critics of the long ("bedsheet") ballot have claimed that if voters made fewer choices, their choices would be better informed. Specifically, short-ballot advocates have argued (1) that only policy-making officials should be elected, and (2) that few offices should be filled at any one time.

Partly as a by-product of the short-ballot movement, which flourished in the early 1900's, many city councils were reduced in size, and city elections were timed not to coincide with national and state elections.

## Borough

A borough is a type of municipal corporation larger than a village but smaller than a city. Only four states—Connecticut, New Jersey, Pennsylvania, and Minnesota—include boroughs.

## Boss

A boss is the leader of a political machine. From the Civil War until the Second World War, the boss system flourished in most large and many small United States cities. In its classic form, boss rule concentrated control over city government in a hierarchical organization of professional politicians—the machine—which placed its candidates in public office, filled city departments with its appointees, and controlled the actions of the mayor, the council, and municipal courts and departments, including the police department.

Bosses were criticized for exercising power not legally theirs and for being corrupt and indifferent to the public interest. But even if these criticisms were justified (as in many cases they undoubtedly were), they do not adequately describe the distinguishing characteristics of the machine. The boss system was also significant as (1) a vehicle for the centralization of power in city government, (2) a means of providing social services to lower-class, mostly immigrant groups, and (3) an organization for the material maintenance of its members. (*See the introduction and readings in Section III.*)

## Budget

A city budget is an annual statement of planned revenues and expenditures. In most cities it is prepared by a finance department under supervision of the mayor or city manager. In some it is prepared by an independently elected controller. In a few it is prepared by a committee of the council.

Early in this century, before widespread adoption of the strong mayor form of government, the budget was generally prepared by the city council or by an independent board of estimate. But as strong municipal executives developed, they acquired additional powers of budget control. The role of the council is now typically confined to holding public hearings on the budget, perhaps amending it, and adopting it through an appropriation ordinance. The extent of the council's power to amend the budget varies from city to city; some charters permit the council to reduce items in the mayor's budget but not to increase them or add new items. (*See also* Finance, City.)

## Caucus

A caucus is an informal meeting at which candidates for public or party office are nominated. In the early history of the United States, caucuses were the most common nominating procedure. With the growth of urban populations, however, the caucus gave way to the convention, a more formal gathering better suited to making nominations for large, populous jurisdictions. By the end of the nineteenth century, party candidates for city office were generally nominated in city-wide conventions, and those for state office in state-wide conventions. Delegates to the city conventions were chosen in meetings at the precinct or ward level. Sometimes called caucuses, these meetings were also termed primaries. All party members were entitled to attend, but in practice the meetings were controlled by party leaders—the "machine."

During the early 1900's the convention system of nomination was replaced by a system of "direct" primaries, under which party members could vote directly on contestants for nomination rather than indirectly through convention delegates. But although the direct primary is now predominant in the United States, not all candidates for city office are nominated in party primaries. In nonpartisan cities, candidates obtain nomination by filing petitions signed by some specified number of voters. Ordinarily a nonpartisan primary is held, to pick two candidates for each office to oppose each other in the general election. But party committees continue to exist at the ward and district levels in many cities, and, even where elections are formally nonpartisan, these may "caucus" to endorse candidates or pick convention delegates in those states that still hold party conventions as well as direct primaries.

CHARTER, CITY

The charter of a city is its fundamental law, given by the state. The charter fixes the form of city government, defines the city's powers and the area of its jurisdiction, and describes the manner in which its powers may be exercised. Often the charter is not a single document, but includes all constitutional provisions, legislative acts, and judicial opinions that affect the structure and powers of the city.

CITY

"A comprehensive definition of a city," William B. Munro wrote in 1930, "must indicate that it is a social, political, legal and economic unit all rolled into one. It is a concentrated body of population possessing some significant social characteristics, chartered as a municipal corporation, having its own system of local government, carrying on multifarious economic enterprises and pursuing an elaborate program of social adjustment and amelioration." (*Encyclopaedia of the Social Sciences*)

CITY MANAGER (*see* FORMS OF CITY GOVERNMENT)

CIVIL SERVICE (*see* MERIT SYSTEM)

COMMISSION PLAN (*see* FORMS OF CITY GOVERNMENT)

CONSOLIDATION, CITY AND COUNTY (*see* METROPOLITAN ORGANIZATION)

CORPORATION, MUNICIPAL

In law the city is a municipal corporation created by the state for the purpose of local government. Like any other corporation, public or private, it is invested with an artificial personality, may own property, make contracts, sue and be sued, and normally exists in perpetuity. But unlike a private corporation, the municipal corporation may exercise only such powers as are authorized under state law, and it may act only for a public purpose. Furthermore, its powers may be altered or revoked at will by the state legislature within limits imposed by state constitutions. The village and borough are also municipal corporations.

(*See also* CHARTER, CITY, *and* DILLON'S RULE.)

## COUNCIL, CITY

The council is the legislative organ of city government. Generally, it possesses all powers granted to the city that are not specifically vested elsewhere. This means that the council enacts municipal codes (ordinances) on crime, sanitation, traffic and streets, building and housing standards, zoning, taxation and appropriations, regulation of public utilities, organization of city departments, and other matters of local concern. The council also has some administrative duties, which vary greatly depending on the form of government. Under the council-manager form the council has sole responsibility for supervising administration, which is in the hands of the manager; under the weak-mayor form, the council has extensive responsibility for the performance of administration; under the strong-mayor form, its interest in administration is largely confined to occasional inquiry into the functioning of city departments.

In the early years of the United States the council was the most important organ of municipal government, but its power and prestige have steadily declined and it is now greatly overshadowed in cities where there is a strong mayor. The council has also decreased in size. Many councils were bicameral throughout much of the nineteenth century; today, all but a very few are unicameral. They range in size from three to Chicago's fifty, but the most common size is nine, even in cities with a population of over 500,000.

Accompanying the decrease of the council's size has been a trend toward election at-large rather than on the basis of wards. In 1958 a sizable majority of cities under 500,000 elected councilmen at large on a nonpartisan ballot.

The small at-large council, a favorite of reformers, is said to serve better the interests of the whole city, to attract better-quality candidates, and to be immune to pressures of a ward-based machine. Critics point out that it discriminates against minorities, increases the cost of councilmanic campaigns (thereby restricting candidates to high-status groups), lengthens the ballot, and increases the influence of wealthy city-wide pressure groups such as retail merchants and newspapers. The usual term of office under either the ward-based or at-large council system is two or four years.

The office of councilman rarely constitutes a full-time job, except in the largest cities, and the pay is low. Frequency of meetings varies greatly with the size of the city, ranging from perhaps once a month in small cities to once a day in large cities with full-time councilmen. Much council work is performed through committees, the chairmen of which are sometimes significantly influential.

(*See also* FORMS OF CITY GOVERNMENT.)

## COUNTY

The county, like the city, is a creature of the state, deriving its powers from the state constitution or a grant of the state legislature. But while cities exist primarily for purposes of local government, counties function primarily as agents of the state. There are county governments in every state except Rhode Island, though in Lousiana the unit comparable to a county is called a "parish."

## COURTS, MUNICIPAL

The administration of justice is primarily a state function, but state legislatures have authorized the establishment of municipal courts with limited jurisdiction.

In practice, the function of local courts is to relieve state courts of the burden of many minor cases, both civil and criminal. In large cities there are often many courts—for example, recorders courts, small claims courts, traffic courts (which handle a large volume of cases), domestic relations courts, and juvenile courts. Judges are either appointed or popularly elected. The salaries of most municipal judges are so low and their jurisdiction so limited and routine that competent men often are not interested in serving. Municipal benches have frequently provided patronage for party organizations. The quality of municipal justice is generally considered to be low.

### DEPARTMENTAL ORGANIZATION, OF CITY

The functions of city government are commonly administered by departments, which typically include, police, fire, health and welfare, parks and recreation, public works, buildings, elections, libraries, personnel, and planning. Departments that perform direct public services, such as police and fire, are usually called "line" agencies, while those that advise and service the city government, such as finance or personnel, are called "staff" agencies.

In the early days of municipal government, when the council was the dominant city agency, administrative functions were performed by council committees. Following the Civil War, the use of bipartisan or nonpartisan boards and commissions became widespread, reflecting a reformist desire to take government "out of politics." City departments are still often supervised by boards and commissions, especially in the case of transportation, libraries, planning, parks, and welfare. But the trend is toward placing each department under one man, an appointee of the mayor or, in the case of council-manager governments, the manager. This concentrates authority over city administration and maximizes the opportunity for coordination of functions. Under the weak-mayor form, major department heads are popularly elected.

### DILLON'S RULE

This is a rule, widely accepted by courts, that the powers of a municipal corporation shall be narrowly construed. As set forth in John F. Dillon's *Commentaries on the Law of Municipal Corporations* (1911), the rule states:

> It is a general and undisputed proposition of law that a municipal corporation possesses and can exercise the following powers, and no others: First, those granted in express words; second, those necessarily or fairly implied in or incident to the powers expressly granted; third, those essential to the declared objects and purposes of the corporation—not simply convenient, but indispensable. Any fair, reasonable, substantial doubt concerning the existence of the power is resolved by the courts against the corporation, and the power is denied.

### DISTRICT

Electoral units within cities include not only wards and precincts but also state legislative districts, which sometimes constitute an element in party organization. Large cities also usually encompass one or more congressional districts, which also provide a basis for party organization.

### ELECTORATE (*see* VOTER, QUALIFICATIONS OF)

### ELECTIONS, MUNICIPAL

Some municipal elections coincide with state and national elections, whereas others occur in "off-years"—that is, when there are no major national or state contests. When local elections occur apart from state or national elections, voter turnout is often extremely low. When they occur together with state or national elections, turnout is higher but the number of votes cast for municipal offices is lower than those cast for state or national offices.

The low turnout in municipal elections probably has made it easier for a party organization—the "machine"—to manage the outcome. Party organizations have found it easy to control the outcome of municipal primaries, in which (apart from some one-party states) participation is even lower than in general elections.

All elections—national, state and local—are administered by local officials, usually a bipartisan board or commission of the city or county or a city or county clerk of elections. Subject to state law, the board or clerk issue regulations for the conduct of elections and is responsible for selection of polling places; selection, instruction and supervision of precinct officials to conduct the election; preparation and distribution of booths, ballots, voting machines and other supplies; identification of voters; and tabulation of ballots. In practice, precinct election officials are chosen by party organizations (usually by the precinct captain), though in theory they are named by the central election agency.

The number and kind of choices put to the municipal voter vary greatly from city to city and state to state. He may be called to vote on many candidates (in the case of a weak-mayor form) or few (in the case of a strong-mayor or council-manager form). If he lives in a city with a council elected at large he will have to vote for more candidates than if he lives in a city that elects councilmen as ward representatives. But even under an at-large system, he is not likely to have to vote on a whole council at once, since councilmanic terms are usually staggered. In a few cities that use proportional representation, he may have to indicate a ranked preference for council candidates. He may be asked to vote on bond issues for major construction projects, although in some cities, for example Detroit, he may not be allowed to vote on these questions if he does not own property. If he lives in a home-rule city, he may be asked to approve amendments to the city charter. Or he may be asked to approve a tax increase. A great variety of questions are submitted in referenda.

## FEDERAL SYSTEM

A federal system divides sovereignty between a central authority and regional authorities—in the case of the United States, between the national government and the fifty state governments. This arrangement is prescribed in the United States Constitution. Municipal corporations and other local governments are often popularly considered a third element in the federal system, but strictly speaking they are subdivisions of the states. Local government is not mentioned in the Constitution.

## FEDERATION, METROPOLITAN (*see* METROPOLITAN ORGANIZATION)

## FINANCE, CITY

The major source of city revenue has long been the tax on real property—land and buildings. In 1958 property taxes, including also some taxes on personal property such as automobiles and home appliances, accounted for three-fourths of city tax revenue. Taxes on sales, gross receipts, and payrolls accounted for most of the rest. All municipal taxes together accounted for nearly two-thirds of general revenue. Other major revenue sources were: (1) federal and state grants-in-aid and taxes shared by the states, and (2) fees collected for water, electric power, gas, transportation, licenses, and other services.

The major problem in administering the property tax is assessment, the process of determining property values. This is ordinarily the job of a city assessor, who is often an elected official and therefore sometimes vulnerable to pressures from property-owners seeking low valuations. Even impartial assessors are not necessarily good assessors, however, since the job requires a high degree of technical competence and judgment. And even for the competent, the job of keeping assessments current is sometimes nearly impossible.

Assessment abuses and inequities are varied and widespread. Undervaluation is quite common. One result of this is to limit the borrowing and tax capacities of the city, since these capacities are often fixed by state legislatures at some percentage of assessed valuation. On the other hand, some cities also have artificially inflated assessments. Some steps have been taken in recent years to end assessment abuses. Especially in large cities there is a trend toward appointment of assessors and creation of trained assessment staffs. In some places, county and state equalization boards have been set up to standardize assessment practices.

Though much criticized, the real property tax is likely to remain the mainstay of city revenues, since there are few other tax sources that have not been preempted by federal and state governments.

The lack of adequate tax revenue and a need for capital projects have led cities to increase their borrowing through issuance of municipal bonds. These are of three types: general-obligation, revenue, and mortgage. General obligation bonds are supported by the full faith and credit of the municipality. Payments on interest and principal are met out of tax revenues, and are protected by a statutory requirement that the annual tax levy must be sufficient to cover the debt service. Municipalities that have reached their statutory debt limit, however, cannot issue general obligation bonds. Revenue bonds are used to finance revenue-producing properties, such as toll bridges, tunnels, or gas and water supply systems, the returns from which are pledged to debt service. Municipalities agree to set rates high enough to meet debt payments. Mortgage bonds are often used for the purchase or construction of utilities, and they offer as security a mortgage on the utility. Because they bear a higher rate of interest than general obligation or revenue bonds, mortgage bonds are less widely used. In general, municipalities meet current operating expenses out of revenue and borrow for permanent improvements. The issuance of bonds is frequently submitted to the electorate in referenda, but in many cases councils possess the authority to issue them without voter approval.

FORMS OF CITY GOVERNMENT

Four forms of city government are usually distinguished:

1. The *weak mayor-council* form, reflecting the American practice of separation of functions, assigns legislative powers to a council and executive powers to a mayor. However, the mayor has limited power to supervise administration. Administrative officers and department heads, such as the city attorney, city engineer, assessor, and controller, are either popularly elected or appointed by the council. The mayor may recommend legislation, preside over the council, and even exercise a veto, but he does not prepare the budget or possess full authority to administer ordinances. The weak-mayor system was the first to develop in the United States and remains in widespread use, particularly in small cities.

2. The *strong mayor-council* form vests broader administrative powers in the mayor. He appoints and removes department heads and prepares and administers the budget. Since he receives much publicity, he often overshadows the council altogether.

In practice the distinction between weak and strong mayors is often hard to make. Gradations of mayoral authority are so subtle that they resist arbitrary classification. The trend is toward stronger mayors. According to the 1960 *Municipal Yearbook*, 1,238 cities used mayor-council forms. The *Yearbook* did not classify these as strong-mayor or weak-mayor.

3. The *council-manager* form vests in a small council (five to nine members, commonly elected at large on a nonpartisan ballot) the authority to legislate for the city and to hire, supervise and dismiss a full-time professional manager, who is charged with city administration. Ultimate responsibility for both legislative and executive functions is concentrated in the council. The council chooses a mayor from its own members, but he has only ceremonial functions. Promoted by reformers, this form was introduced in 1908 and spread rapidly. According to the *Municipal Yearbook* of 1960, it was used by 931 cities. Only one of these cities, however, (Cincinnati) had a population of more than 500,000. On the other hand, 48 per cent of cities in the 25,000-to-100,000 population range used it.

4. The *commissioner* form vests executive and legislative powers in elected commissioners (usually five), each of whom serves as head of a city department. Together they form a policy-making body. Like the council-manager plan, the commission plan was promoted by reformers, but it has not enjoyed comparable popularity. Introduced in Galveston, Texas, in 1900, it spread rapidly and by World War I was used in at least 500 cities. However, the number had dropped to 309 by 1960 and is still declining.

## GERRYMANDER

This term refers to the practice of fixing legislative district boundaries in such a way as to gain partisan advantage. This may be accomplished in at least two ways. The dominant party in the legislature may create a peculiarly shaped district in which its voters will constitute a majority. Or it may attempt to concentrate the voters of the opposite party in as few districts as possible. Gerrymandering is done mostly by the state legislatures, which fix congressional as well as state legislative districts. Although it has usually benefited rural Republicans at the expense of urban Democrats, it also occurs within cities, where councils sometimes draw wards so as to minimize the voting strength of Negroes or other ethnic groups.

The word was derived in 1812 from the name of Governor Elbridge Gerry of Massachusetts, who allowed the state to be apportioned into fantastic shapes.

## "GOOD GOVERNMENT" (*see the introduction to Section IV*)

## GOVERNMENTAL AND PROPRIETARY FUNCTIONS

These terms describe the legal status of city functions. "Governmental" functions are those done involuntarily as an agent of the state, in pursuance of such state purposes as protection of public health and safety. Fire and police protection are examples of governmental functions. "Proprietary" functions are those performed as a convenience to the municipal community—for example, public transportation. The distinction is significant because, as a general rule, a municipality is not liable for torts resulting from the performance of its governmental functions. The city cannot be sued, for example, by a pedestrian who suffers injury from a police cruiser pursuing a speeding car. But a pedestrian injured by a city transit bus may sue the city. In practice, distinctions between the two categories are hard to draw, and legislatures and courts have drawn them in different ways in different states.

## HOME RULE

Home rule is the power of municipalities to conduct their affairs without interference from the state.

Ever since the late nineteenth century, reformers have argued for home rule. As a result, more than half of the states have adopted home-rule constitutions or statutes, which grant their cities powers "relating to municipal affairs" or "[the city's] own government." Interpretation of these powers is left to courts, which have construed them narrowly. Acts of the state legislature normally take precedence over the charter provisions or ordinances of home-rule cities. As a result, a large majority of cities remain subject to extensive state control with respect to matters in which the state has a substantial interest such as law enforcement, welfare, education, utilities, and finance.

## INITIATIVE, REFERENDUM, AND RECALL

These are three procedures for providing popular access to political power. Initiative is the proposal of legislation by the electorate. A referendum is the submission of a proposal of the legislature to the electorate for approval. Recall is the removal of public officials before expiration of their terms.

Initiative and recall begin with circulation of a petition. An initiative petition proposes language changing the city's charter or ordinances. If it receives the required number of signatures (usually 5 to 10 per cent of the vote cast at the preceding election), the proposal is considered by the council, which in some cases may adopt it outright. If the council does not adopt it, the measure is placed on the ballot at a special or general election. Usually recall petitions must bear a higher percentage of voter signatures than initiative petitions. If the prescribed number of signatures is secured, a recall election must be held. Voters may be asked simply whether they wish the officer to be removed, or they may be given an opportunity to vote on other candidates for the office.

Referenda, too, may originate with petitions, but often city councils are required by law to submit certain proposals—especially bond issues—for popular approval. Sometimes city councils may voluntarily seek popular advice in "straw votes." Such referenda require no action by the city government; they merely give evidence of popular opinion. San Francisco and Houston both use this procedure. Referenda are far more frequent than the initiative and recall, which are used very little.

These procedures have been most widely used in states and municipalities west of the Mississippi, where the Progressive movement was strongest. All three procedures have been criticized on the grounds that they lengthen the ballot, place excessive demands on the capacities of the electorate, and subject government officials to harassment by organized interest groups.

## LEGAL STATUS OF CITIES (*see* CORPORATION, MUNICIPAL)

## MACHINE, POLITICAL (*see* PARTY, POLITICAL)

## MANAGER, CITY (*see* FORMS OF CITY GOVERNMENT)

## MAYOR (*see* FORMS OF CITY GOVERNMENT)

## MERIT SYSTEM

Under a merit system government employees are selected on the basis of technical or professional competence, usually as determined by an examination. They are protected from removal for political reasons.

The first municipal merit systems were introduced in the 1880's at the same time as the merit system in the federal government. But the merit principle did not become widely accepted in municipalities until the 1930's when it was stimulated by the federal government, which frequently required state and local governments to adopt merit systems as a condition of grants-in-aid. Merit systems spread fastest among large cities.

While they have contributed to the decline of the machine, merit systems have not eliminated patronage altogether. In many cities some important positions, such as department heads or the mayor's staff, are exempt. Temporary jobs, particularly in the administration of elections, also provide patronage. One way of circumventing merit system regulations has been to classify a large number of jobs "provisional."

Civil service systems were at first administered by bipartisan commissions independent of the city administration. There is a trend, however, toward creation of a personnel department under a director who is responsible to the mayor or manager. This form of personnel administration, like the merit system itself, is most commonly found in council-manager governments.

## Metropolitan Area

This term refers to the aggregate of a large central city and its surrounding communities—smaller cities, villages, and townships. In 1960 the U.S. Census Bureau reported data for units called "standard metropolitan statistical areas." According to a publication of the Census Bureau, these areas:

> are integrated economic and social units with a large volume of daily travel and communication between the central city (50,000 or more population) and outlying parts of the area. Each area (except in New England) consists of one or more whole counties. An area may contain not only highly industrialized counties but also adjoining counties which, though primarily residential in character, contribute significantly to the industrial counties' labor force.

As of 1960 there were 212 SMSA's containing 111,802,884 persons, 62.9 per cent of the population of the United States.

## Metropolitan Organization

No city has boundaries coinciding with the limits of the metropolitan area. There are no metropolitan governments; in every metropolitan area there are several governments (cities, villages, school districts, special districts, counties), each serving some part of the whole metropolitan area.

Major complaints against this division of authority in metropolitan areas are: (1) that functions that must be conducted on an area-wide basis, such as planning and transportation, are neglected; (2) that it is wasteful; (3) that it is inequitable because the quality of services varies throughout the metropolitan area; and (4) that it places a disproportionate burden of taxation and services on the central city. The suburbs, critics point out, have drawn high-income residents, retail and wholesale services, and industry from the central city, thereby reducing its tax base; at the same time, suburban residents use city services—transportation, hospitals, libraries, parks, and so forth—without paying city taxes.

Proposals for metropolitan integration have taken several forms:

*Annexation of Adjacent Territory by City Governments.* Several hundred annexations take place each year, but most are small. Legislatures in most states—Virginia, Texas, California, and Missouri are exceptions—have placed almost insuperable barriers in the way of annexation. There is in most places no practical prospect that metropolitan integration can be achieved by this method.

*Consolidation of Counties and Cities.* New Orleans, Boston, Philadelphia, and New York resulted from the consolidation of cities and counties. There have been no successful mergers in recent years excpt for Baton Rouge, Louisiana, which was consolidated with East Baton Rouge Parish in 1947. A variant of the consolidation scheme calls for transferring some municipal functions to county governments.

Under a charter adopted in 1957, Dade County, Florida, which includes Miami, performs many functions of local government under the administration of a manager. Los Angeles County also provides some municipal-type services. An obvious shortcoming of this plan is that counties themselves are not necessarily contiguous with the metropolitan area. Furthermore, like annexation, county-city consolidation has failed to win support from state legislatures.

*Federation of Local Governments.* Under this plan, which has had no successful application in the United States, there would be two levels of government in the metropolitan area, one area-wide to perform services appropriate to area administration, the other local to handle functions of more narrow concern.

*Voluntary Cooperation among Governmental Units.* Agreements, formal or informal, between city and county governments or between city and suburban governments are an increasingly common means of metropolitan integration. Cities and counties often cooperate, for example, in the administration of hospitals, maintenance of a city-county building, traffic control, or other functions that they have in common. Central cities may make contracts with suburban governments or directly with suburban residents for the provision of water and gas or the disposal of sewage, garbage and rubbish. Some cooperation on fire and police protection is also fairly common. Though such agreements are politically more feasible than other forms of integration, they are not generally considered adequate to solve the problem.

The chief reason for the failure of proposals for metropolitan integration is that the suburbs and the central cities are divided by class, race, and party. Apart from these cleavages, there are also inevitable conflicts of interest between cities and suburbs with respect to transportation, taxes, and other problems of local government. These differences between central city and suburb are reflected in the state legislature, which in almost every case must approve proposals for metropolitan integration.

## MUNICIPALITY

This term is synonymous with "municipal corporation." Cities, villages, and boroughs are municipalities. As of 1957 there were 17,183 municipalities in the United States.

## NONPARTISAN SYSTEM OF ELECTIONS

According to the formal definition, a nonpartisan system of elections exists where candidates are not identified by party affiliation on the ballot. More realistically, a nonpartisan system is one in which candidates receive no support from either the Republican or the Democratic party. Purely local parties may exist in such a case.

The nonpartisan ballot was introduced early in the twentieth century by "good-government" reformers, who hoped to divorce municipal government from state and national politics. According to the *Municipal Yearbook* of 1960, it is used by 61 per cent of cities over 5,000 population. Sixty-five per cent of the 17 cities of over 500,000 population use it.

The nonpartisan ballot has weakened party organizations, though strong parties manage to exist in a few cities where it is used. It gives an advantage to candidates who receive much publicity, who have names that appeal to large ethnic groups, or who are incumbent office-holders.

## ORDINANCE

An ordinance is a rule or regulation issued by a municipal corporation. It must be made under authority granted in the corporation's charter and in conformity with state and national laws. Its application is limited to the area over which the corporation has jurisdiction. Technically, an ordinance is not a "law," since laws can be enacted only by sovereign bodies.

## PARTY, POLITICAL

Political parties are groups that nominate and support candidates for public office. In theory, they compete for the control of the machinery of government by placing alternative programs and candidates before the electorate. Party organizations have often controlled municipal nominations and elections, but they have rarely been concerned with programs of governmental action.

Party organization in cities was strongest in the era of the machine, between the Civil War and World War II. An outstanding characteristic of the machine was the preoccupation of its members with personal gain and their indifference to political principle. One consequence of the pragmatic character of machines was that they did not compete against each other. Where more than one machine existed in the same city, they often cooperated in protecting each other from destruction by reformers.

In comparison to the machine era, municipal parties are now weakly organized. In many places party organizations continue to function, conducting campaign activity, handling federal, state, and city patronage, and putting forth candidates for public office. But nowhere, except possibly in Chicago, does this organization control municipal government as it once did. The amount of patronage available is often slim; blocs of "deliverable" votes are rare; and many municipal candidates are independent of party organization. The party organization is likely to be a loose congeries of factions and minor personal followings rather than a unified group consisting of a leader and loyal subordinates as in the days of the boss. To the extent that party organizations exist in large cities, they are likely to be Democratic, since a large majority of big-city voters favors the Democratic party in state and national elections.

## PATRONAGE (see SPOILS SYSTEM)

## PLANNING

According to one of the standard works on city planning, Robert A. Walker's *The Planning Function in Urban Government* (1941), "The local planning process is an aspect of the process of local government. It is government looking to the future, determining desirable objectives and seeking the best and most economical means for achieving them." Walker also says:

> The over-all planning agency is designed to assist officials in formulating a public policy which treats the problems of the community as a closely knit whole. . . . The several operating departments can and should plan for their respective spheres of activity. The contribution of the planning agency is not found in a duplication of this work but rather in supplying the element of "comprehensiveness" and hence integration, to planning the future development of the city. This calls for a systematic program of assembling information about the city (research), discovering what it means (analysis), and indicating what action it seems to call for (planning and specific recommendations).
> . . . the theoretical goal of a planning agency's work [is] the preparation of a plan for the future of an area—a plan which portrays the development conceived to make that area the best possible for human habitation.

According to the 1960 *Municipal Yearbook,* 914 of 1,002 cities with a population over 10,000 had official planning agencies. Only 303 of these had a full-time planning director.

PRECINCT

A precinct is a unit for the casting and counting of votes in elections and for police administration in a city. Precincts typically contain several hundred residents. Ten to thirty precincts usually constitute a ward. The party leader in the precinct is the "precinct captain."

PRESSURE GROUPS

These are organizations that attempt to influence the actions of government. They are active at all levels of government—local, state, and national. At the local level such organizations usually include: chambers of commerce, retail trade boards, real estate boards, and taxpayers' associations, which represent the interests of business; neighborhood improvement associations, which represent homeowners; citizens leagues, municipal research bureaus, and the League of Women Voters, which promote "good government"; AFL-CIO locals and units of COPE, labor's Committee on Political Education; municipal employee unions; and chapters of the National Association for the Advancement of Colored People and the Urban League, which represent Negroes.

Pressure groups seek to influence the actions of city government in various ways. Their representatives may speak at sessions of the city council or meet with the mayor and his administrative subordinates. They often use propaganda— posters, pamphlets, newspaper releases, and radio and TV appearances. Some exercise influence through campaign contributions or campaign activity in support of candidates or propositions. Municipal employees may exercise influence through strikes.

Groups with an interest in local affairs often concentrate much of their activity on the state level, where many decisions affecting local government are made.

PRIMARY ELECTIONS

These are elections in which candidates for office are nominated. Most are "closed" primaries, in which a voter may participate only in balloting for nominees of the party to which he belongs. An "open" primary allows the voter to participate without regard to his party affiliation.

Primary elections are usually held even in cities that use a nonpartisan electoral system. All candidates appear on the primary ballot, having qualified by obtaining petition signatures and/or paying a fee. The two candidates receiving the highest vote for an office compete in the final election. In some cases a candidate who receives a majority in the primary is declared elected.

PROPERTY TAX (*see* FINANCE, CITY)

PROPORTIONAL REPRESENTATION

This is an election system under which voters indicate their preferences among the candidates in a ranked order—1, 2, 3, etc. These votes are weighted in determining the outcome. The purpose of proportional representation (PR) is to provide representation for elements of the electorate exactly in proportion to their numerical strength.

In the United States, PR was used first in Ashtabula, Ohio, in 1915. Since then it has been adopted by 24 other cities, but few have retained it. The experience of New York, Cincinnati, and other cities suggests that PR succeeds in providing minority representation, but arouses opposition from the disadvantaged majority. It is little used today.

Proprietary Functions (*see* Governmental and Proprietary Functions)

Recall (*see* Initiative, Referendum, and Recall)

Referendum (*see* Initiative, Referendum, and Recall)

Registration

Registration is the procedure whereby a list of qualified voters is compiled for use at elections. Such a system is required in urban areas in order to prevent fraud. Registration laws were adopted therefore in response to growth of the cities in the late nineteenth century.

Registration may be periodic or permanent. Under a periodic system the voter is required to register at regular intervals and is dropped from the rolls if he fails to register. Under a permanent system the voter registers only once, and remains on the rolls unless he moves or dies. About three-fourths of the states provide for permanent registration.

Representation of Cities in Legislatures

Historically, cities have not been represented in state legislatures in proportion to their population. This situation encouraged state action that was disadvantageous to urban areas. The recent decline of population in the central cities means that underrepresentation of these areas has been alleviated or ended.

Short Ballot (*see* Ballot)

School Districts

In all but four states, according to the *Municipal Yearbook* of 1960, school districts constitute a unit of local government independent of other units (counties, cities, villages, towns). In those four states, schools are administered by the state or by general-purpose local governments. Some states use both systems.

Special Districts

These are units of local government that perform one or a few specific functions, in contrast to municipalities, which are general-purpose governments. According to the *Municipal Yearbook* of 1960, there were 14,405 special districts in the United States in 1957, nearly half of them for fire protection, soil conservation, or drainage. Other special districts provided irrigation and water conservation, highways, sanitation, hospitals, libraries, and many other services.

Special districts often overlap other units of local government, and thus provide a partial solution to the problem of metropolitan organization. They are also a way to avoid placing additional service burdens on other local governments, many of which have reached statutory debt and taxing limits. Finally, special districts have been promoted as a device for taking some activities "out of politics." Usually they are directed by boards appointed by state or local officials. They are relatively immune to popular pressures.

The powers of special districts are fixed by state laws and vary greatly. In general these governments possess some corporate powers such as perpetual succession, the right to sue and be sued, to make contracts, and to acquire and dispose of property. Some have the power to tax and borrow. Most are limited to one function, but the best known, such as the Port of New York Authority and the Metropolitan District Commission of Massachusetts, perform many services. The number of special districts has increased substantially since World War II.

SPECIAL LEGISLATION

Acts that apply to specific cities are called "special legislation." Between the Civil War and 1900 many state legislatures regulated the affairs of individual cities in detail. Virtually usurping the functions of city councils, they passed laws governing police departments, utility franchises, street paving, and even construction of municipal buildings. The home rule movement was a response to this practice. (*see* HOME RULE.)

Many states have adopted constitutional prohibitions against special legislation, but it continues to be used, especially in New England and the South. Legislatures sometimes circumvent the prohibition with acts that apply to certain categories of cities. For example, a legislature may pass a law applying to "all cities of over 500,000 population" when there is only one such city in the state.

SPOILS SYSTEM

This term refers to the practice of placing party workers in public jobs. The spoils system prevailed at all levels of government throughout much of the nineteenth century. In the cities, the promise of public employment—perhaps a municipal judgeship or a desk job at city hall—constituted the major incentive for machine workers at the precinct and ward level. Their ability in turn to dispense petty jobs to precinct residents was a means of building a following among the electorate. Jobs (usually called "patronage") were allotted through the machine hierarchy. Not only did patronage provide an incentive for machine workers, but it also helped finance campaigns. Men who owed their jobs to the organization were commonly expected to contribute a share of their salary to it at election time. The spoils system has been largely replaced in most cities by a comprehensive merit system.

STAFF SERVICES

Staff services assist the mayor with city administration. The principal staff services are planning, personnel, legal advice, and finance.

STATE CONTROL OVER CITIES (*see* CORPORATION, MUNICIPAL, *and* REPRESENTATION OF CITIES IN LEGISLATURES)

TAXES (*see* FINANCE, CITY)

TOWN

In a few states the "town" constitutes one class of municipality, like the city, village, and borough, but more generally it is an unincorporated unit of local government. In New England states the town is irregular in size and shape and often includes one or two villages as well as some rural area. New England town governments are authorized to perform certain functions of local government such as police, fire, welfare, streets, and water supply. Throughout the Midwest there are "townships," which are subdivisions of county government. Located in predominantly rural areas, they are regular in size and shape, usually five or six miles square. As of 1957 there were 17,198 towns or townships in the United States, roughly equivalent to the number of municipalities.

URBAN AREA

In 1960 the Census Bureau defined urban areas as: (1) places of 2,500 inhabitants or more that are incorporated as cities, boroughs, villages, and towns (except towns in New England, New York, and Wisconsin); (2) the densely settled urban fringe, whether incorporated or unincorporated, around cities of 50,000 or more; (3) towns in New England and townships in New Jersey and Pennsylvania which contain no incorporated municipalities as subdivisions and have either 25,000 inhabitants or more or a population of 2,500 to 25,000 and a density of 1,500 persons or more per square mile; (4) counties in states other than the New England states, New Jersey, and Pennsylvania that have no incorporated municipalities within their boundaries and have a density of 1,500 persons or more per square mile; and (5) unincorporated places of 2,500 inhabitants or more. All other territory is classified as rural.

## URBAN RENEWAL

Urban renewal is the process of restoring city slums. Renewal may be accomplished by redevelopment—the replacement of old buildings—or by rehabilitation of such buildings. Major governmental programs for urban renewal began with the Housing Act of 1949, which authorized federal grants to finance two-thirds of the net cost of acquiring, clearing, and preparing slum land for new construction. Housing Acts in 1954 and 1956 broadened the 1949 Act and placed new emphasis on rehabilitation and conservation as alternatives to redevelopment. Almost all of the states have authorized participation in the urban renewal program and have provided for financing the local share of the costs. The objective of urban renewal, according to the Housing Act of 1949, is "the realization as soon as feasible of the goal of a decent home and suitable living environment for every American family, thus contributing to the development and redevelopment of communities and to the advancement of the growth, wealth, and security of the Nation . . . and to an economy of maximum employment, production, and purchasing power."

## VILLAGE

The village is a common type of municipality, usually (though not invariably) smaller than the city.

## VOTER, QUALIFICATIONS OF

Almost everywhere, anyone who qualifies as a voter under state laws is entitled to vote in municipal elections. The usual requirements are U.S. citizenship, a minimum age (eighteen in Georgia, twenty-one in all other states), a minimum period of residence in the electoral jurisdiction, and registration (though not all rural residents are required to register). In a few states, only property owners are permitted to vote on bond issues.

## WARD

A ward is an electoral subdivision of a municipality, larger than a precinct and smaller than state legislative districts (though wards and districts are sometimes coterminous). Except where councilmen are elected at large, wards are the units from which councilmen are elected.

## ZONING

Zoning is the control of land use and the size of buildings and lots. Virtually all large cities have adopted zoning ordinances, which divide the city into areas for commercial, industrial, and residential use. If a property owner wishes to deviate from the prescribed use, he must obtain approval of the city council.

*Note:* Books and articles from which materials have been reprinted are not included in this listing.

## BIBLIOGRAPHICAL

*The American Political Science Review,* a quarterly journal, contains a current list of publications in the field of state and local government.

Daland, R. T. "Political Science and the Study of Urbanism," *American Political Science Review,* LI (June 1957), 491–509. An essay describing the literature of urban politics.

Government Affairs Foundation, Inc., *Metropolitan Communities: A Bibliography.* Chicago: Public Administration Service, 1956. A comprehensive annotated list of publications on the government and politics of metropolitan communities. A supplement issued in 1960 brings the list through 1957.

Graves, W. Brooke (comp.). *Intergovernmental Relations in the United States: A Selected Bibliography on Interlevel and Interjurisdictional Relations.* Commission on Intergovernmental Relations, mimeo., June 1955. An extensive compilation of publications on intergovernmental relations. There is a section on metropolitan regionalism.

## SERIALS AND PERIODICALS

City Politics Reports. A series of mimeographed reports on the politics of major central cities, issued beginning in 1959 by the Joint Center for Urban Studies, Cambridge, Mass. The reports bring together basic background data on the structure of government in the city, party organization, voting behavior, influence structure, and the content of certain key issues (e.g., race, urban renewal, metropolitan organization, etc.). Reports are organized to facilitate comparisons between cities.

*Journal of the American Institute of Planners.* A quarterly publication with many articles on urban planning and redevelopment.

*Municipal Yearbook.* A publication of the International City Managers' Association which summarizes municipal activities each year and provides basic statistical data on U.S. cities. A source of bibliography.

*National Civic Review.* Monthly publication of The National Municipal League. Until 1959 it was entitled *The National Municipal Review.*

*Public Administration Review.* A quarterly journal of the American Society for Public Administration. Contains frequent articles on municipal administration.

*Public Management.* Monthly journal of the International City Managers' Association.

# BOOKS

Banfield, Edward C. *Political Influence.* Glencoe: The Free Press, 1961. A theoretical analysis that draws on case studies of political decisions in Chicago.

Bean, Walton. *Boss Ruef's San Francisco.* Berkeley: University of California Press, 1952. An account of a well-known boss.

Bollens, John C. *Appointed Executive Local Government: The California Experience.* Los Angeles: Haynes Foundation, 1952. Discusses executive management in California cities.

Childs, Richard S. *Civic Victories: The Story of an Unfinished Revolution.* New York: Harper & Brothers, 1952. The history of municipal reform by one of its foremost leaders.

Curley, James M. *I'd Do It Again.* Englewood Cliffs, N.J.: Prentice-Hall, 1957. The autobiography of one of the last and most popular of the big city bosses.

Dillon, John F. *Commentaries on the Law of Municipal Corporations.* 5 vols. 5th ed., Boston: Little, Brown, 1911. A standard source on municipal law.

Duncan, Otis D., and others. *Metropolis and Region.* Baltimore: Johns Hopkins University Press, for Resources for the Future, 1960. An analysis of the economics of metropolitan regions, with emphasis on the relation between economics and geography.

——, and A. J. Reiss, Jr. *Social Characteristics of Urban and Rural Communities, 1950.* New York: John Wiley & Sons, 1956. Elaboration and interpretation of data from the 1950 census.

Forthal, Sonya. *Cogwheels of Democracy: A Study of the Precinct Captain.* New York: William-Frederick Press, 1946. A brief description, derived from interviews in Chicago, of the machine's hardest workers.

Grodzins, Morton. *Local Governments in the American Federal System.* Rand-McNally, 1961. A descriptive and analytical account of the way in which the functions of governments are shared by local bodies.

Handlin, Oscar. *The Newcomers* (see New York Metropolitan Regional Study, below; 1959). Discusses changes in the status of Negroes and Puerto Ricans in the New York metropolitan region.

Hawley, Amos H. *The Changing Shape of Metropolitan America: Deconcentration since 1920.* Glencoe: The Free Press, 1956. A report on patterns of population change in U.S. metropolitan areas.

Helfgott, Roy B., Eric Gustafson, and James M. Hund. *Made in New York* (see

New York Metropolitan Regional Study, below; 1959). Examines the impact of three key manufacturing industries on the economy of New York City.

Hofstadter, Richard. *The Age of Reform.* New York: Vintage Books, 1960. An interpretation of reform in the United States, 1890 to 1940.

Hoover, Edgar M., and Raymond Vernon. *Anatomy of a Metropolis (see* New York Metropolitan Regional Study, below; 1959). Discusses the changing distribution of people and jobs within the New York metropolitan region.

Janowitz, Morris. *The Community Press in an Urban Setting.* Glencoe: The Free Press, 1952. Describes the political and other functions of community newspapers in Chicago.

Jones, Victor. *Metropolitan Government.* Chicago: University of Chicago Press, 1942. An analysis of metropolitan problems. Includes a discussion of the political interests involved in metropolitan integration.

Kurtzman, D. H. *Methods of Controlling Votes in Philadelphia.* Privately printed, 1935. A detailed study, based on field investigation, of the techniques for influencing votes in a major city.

Lee, Eugene C. *The Politics of Nonpartisanship: A Study of California City Elections.* Berkeley: University of California Press, 1960. Although based largely upon data gathered in six California cities, this is the most comprehensive account of the subject in print. Good bibliography.

Lichtenberg, Robert M. *One-Tenth of a Nation (see* New York Metropolitan Regional Study, below; 1960). Discusses the growth potential of the New York metropolitan region.

McBain, Howard L. *The Law and Practice of Municipal Home Rule.* New York: Columbia University Press, 1916. Though dated, this and the following volume, by McGoldrick, remain the standard works on home rule.

McGoldrick, J. D. *Law and Practice of Municipal Home Rule, 1916–1930.* New York: Columbia University Press, 1933. A sequel to an earlier volume, by McBain, listed above.

McKean, Dayton D. *The Boss: The Hague Machine in Action.* Boston: Houghton Mifflin, 1940. A thorough study by a political scientist of one of the last machines.

McQuillin, Eugene. *The Law of Municipal Corporations.* 3rd ed.; Chicago: Callaghan and Co., 1949. A leading commentary on municipal law.

Mosher, Frederick C., and others. *City Manager Government in Seven Cities.* Chicago: Public Administration Service, 1940. A collection of case studies on the development, politics, and administration of the city manager plan.

Myers, Gustavus. *History of Tammany Hall.* New York: Boni and Liveright, 1917. The basic source of information on Tammany.

New York Metropolitan Regional Study. Cambridge, Mass.: Regional Planning Association and Harvard University Press, 1959–1960. A series of reports on the economics and demography of the New York metropolitan region, prepared for the Regional Planning Commission by the Graduate School of Public Administration at Harvard. For specific works in the series see separate listing under authors. (The authors are: Hoover, Edgar M., and Raymond Vernon; Helfgott, Roy B., and James M. Hund; Handlin, Oscar; Segal, Martin; Robbins, Sidney M., and Nestor E. Terleckyj; Wood, Robert C.; Lichtenberg, Robert M.; and Vernon, Raymond.)

Ostrogorski, M. *Democracy and the Party System,* New York: Macmillan, 1910. An analysis of the machine by a contemporary European observer.

Peel, Roy V. *The Political Clubs of New York City.* New York: G. P. Putnam's Sons, 1935. An outstanding study of urban political activity.

Perloff, Harvey S., (ed.). *Planning and the Urban Community.* University of Pittsburgh Press, 1961. A collection of short essays representing the orthodoxy of the city planning movement on a dozen matters. Suitable for beginning students.

President's Commission on National Goals. *Goals for Americans.* Englewood Cliffs, N.J.: Prentice-Hall, for the American Assembly, 1960. This report contains a section entitled "Framework for an Urban Society" and one on "The Federal System"; both of them are relevant to urban politics.

Ridley, Clarence E., and Orin F. Nolting. *The City Manager Profession.* Chicago: University of Chicago Press, 1934. Two city managers describe briefly the development and functions of the manager.

Robbins, Sidney M., and Nestor E. Terleckyj. *Money Metropolis* (see New York Metropolitan Regional Study, above; 1960). A locational study of financial activities in the New York region.

Salter, J. T. *Boss Rule: Portraits in City Politics.* New York: McGraw-Hill, 1935. A study of ward politicians, chiefly in Philadelphia.

Schlesinger, Arthur M. *The Rise of the City.* New York: Macmillan, 1933. A study of U.S. history from 1878 to 1898, years of rapid urbanization.

Segal, Martin. *Wages in the Metropolis* (see New York Metropolitan Regional Study, above; 1960). Discusses the impact of wages and labor skills on the location and development of industries in New York City.

Segoe, Ladislas. *Local Planning Administration.* 3rd ed.; Chicago: International City Managers' Association, 1959. A handbook designed for planning officials.

Steffens, Lincoln. *Shame of the Cities.* New York: Sagamore Press, Inc., 1957. First published in 1904, this is a collection of articles on corruption in seven major cities.

Stewart, Frank M. *A Half Century of Municipal Reform: The History of the Municipal League.* Berkeley: University of California Press, 1950. A sympathetic account of the League.

Stone, Harold A., D. K. Price, and Kathryn H. Stone. *City Manager Government in Nine Cities.* Chicago: Public Administration Service, 1940. Case studies on the city manager plan.

Straetz, Ralph A. *PR Politics in Cincinnati.* New York: New York University Press, 1958. An analysis of politics in Cincinnati during the 32-year period of proportional representation (1926–1957).

U.S. Department of Commerce, Bureau of the Census. *Governments in the United States in 1957.* Washington, D.C.: 1957. Basic data on all governmental units in the U.S.

Vernon, Raymond. *Metropolis 1985* (1960). This key volume in the New York Metropolitan Regional Study offers a synthesis and interpretation of the other seven specialized volumes in the series.

Vidich, Arthur J., and Joseph Bensman. *Small Town in Mass Society.* Princeton, N.J.: Princeton University Press, 1958. This study of a small community in upper New York State includes detailed treatment of local politics.

Walker, Robert. *The Planning Function in Urban Government.* Chicago: University of Chicago Press, 1950. Describes the functions of city planning agencies.

Warner, W. Lloyd. *The Living and the Dead: A Study of the Symbolic Life of Americans.* New Haven: Yale University Press, 1959. Describes the symbolic significance of a colorful mayor of "Yankee City," the pseudonym for a New England community.

————, and Associates. *Democracy in Jonesville.* New York: Harper & Brothers, 1949. A study by a social anthropologist of an American community.

Wood, Robert C. *1400 Governments* (see New York Metropolitan Regional Study, above; 1961). Analyzes the functioning of local and regional units of government in the New York metropolitan area, and their relationship to the area's economic system.

Woodbury, Coleman (ed.). *The Future of Cities and Urban Redevelopment.* Chicago: The University of Chicago Press, 1953. A collection of essays on urban redevelopment.

Zink, Harold. *City Bosses in the United States.* Durham, N.C.: Duke University Press, 1930. Analyses of the biographies of twenty bosses.

# ARTICLES AND PAMPHLETS

Adrian, Charles R. "A Typology for Nonpartisan Elections," *Western Political Quarterly,* XII (June, 1959), 449–458. Nonpartisan elections are classified in four categories, differentiated by the degree of party support for candidates.

Anderson, William. "The Units of Government in the United States." Chicago: Public Administration Service, 1949. An analysis based on census data and private research. Enumerates and describes units of government in this country.

*Annals* of the American Academy of Political and Social Science, Vol. 314 (November, 1957). A collection of essays on metropolitan problems.

Baker, Gordon E. "Rural versus Urban Power." Garden City, N.Y.: Doubleday. Short Studies in Political Science No. 20, 1955. A Study of urban underrepresentation in state legislatures.

Banfield, Edward C. "The Case of the Handcuffed Sheriff." Chicago: American Foundation for Political Education, Case Story No. 2, 1957. A discussion pamphlet raising some pros and cons of patronage.

Bebout, John E. "Management for Large Cities," *Public Administration Review,* XV (Summer, 1955), 188–195. An argument for adoption of the council-manager plan in large cities by the then assistant director of the National Municipal League.

Bosworth, Karl A. "The Manager Is a Politician," *Public Administration Review,* XVIII (Summer, 1958), 216–222. A discussion of the various roles of the city manager. The author concludes that the city manager, whatever role he may choose, is and always has been involved in politics.

Brazer, Harvey E. "City Expenditures in the United States." New York: National Bureau of Economic Research, Occasional Paper 66, 1959. An analysis of variations in expenditures among cities and the causes for these variations.

Commission on Intergovernmental Relations. "Advisory Committee Report on Local Government." Washington, D.C.: U.S. Government Printing Office, 1955. One of a series of reports by the Kestnbaum Commission (so called for its chairman), which was established by the federal government in 1953. The committee summarized its findings in a report to the President in 1955.

Council of State Governments. *The States and the Metropolitan Problem.* Chicago: 1956. A report to the Governors' Conference on techniques of metropolitan integration.

*Daedalus,* Vol. 90 (Winter, 1961). "The Future Metropolis." Twelve essays by specialists in metropolitan affairs.

Harder, Melvin A. "Nonpartisan Election: A Political Illusion" (Case Studies in Practical Politics.) New York: Henry Holt, 1958. An account of the Wichita municipal election of 1957.

*Harvard Law Review,* 73 (January, 1960), 526–582. "The Urban County: A Study of New Approaches to Local Government in Metropolitan Areas." A legal discussion of proposals for metropolitan integration.

Jones, Victor, and Herbert Kaufman. "The Mystery of Power," *Public Administration Review,* XIV (Summer, 1954), 205–212. A critical review of Floyd Hunter's *Community Power Structure.*

Mott, Rodney L. "Home Rule for America's Cities." Chicago: American Municipal Association, Urban Action Series Publication 101, 1949. A study of the operation of home rule. Useful as a recent supplement to the book by McGoldrick.

Nolting, Orin F. "City Manager of Tomorrow," *Public Management,* XL (October, 1958), 234–237. A prediction of new responsibilities for the city manager by the executive director of the International City Managers' Association.

Patton, Clifford W. "The Battle for Municipal Reform: Mobilization and Attack, 1875–1900." Washington, D.C.: American Council on Public Affairs, 1940. A brief account of the municipal reform movement.

Polsby, Nelson W. "Power in Middletown: Fact and Value in Community Research," *Canadian Journal of Economics and Political Science,* XXVI (November, 1960), 592–603. A criticism of the literature on community power structures.

Sayre, Wallace S. "The General Manager Idea for Large Cities," *Public Administration Review,* XIV (Autumn, 1954), 253–258. A discussion of the idea that management of large cities can best be handled by a general manager responsible to the mayor.

Williams, Oliver P., and Charles R. Adrian. "The Insulation of Local Politics under the Nonpartisan Ballot," *American Political Science Review,* LIII (December, 1959), 1052–1063. An analysis of relationships between partisan and nonpartisan voting patterns in four Michigan cities.

Wilson, James Q. "Two Negro Politicians: An Interpretation," *Midwest Journal of Political Science,* IV (November, 1960), 346–369. The contrasting behavior of Congressmen Adam Clayton Powell and William L. Dawson is related to the contrasting maintenance needs of their local organizations.